GREEK AND ROMAN NAVAL WARFARE

A Study of Strategy, Tactics, and Ship Design
from Salamis (480 B.C.) to Actium (31 B.C.)

GREEK AND ROMAN NAVAL WARFARE

A Study of Strategy, Tactics, and Ship Design from
Salamis (480 B.C.) to Actium (31 B.C.)

By

WILLIAM LEDYARD RODGERS

Vice Admiral, U. S. Navy (Retired)

NAVAL INSTITUTE PRESS
ANNAPOLIS, MARYLAND

Printed in the United States of America

CONTENTS

CHAPTER   PAGE

PREFACE xi

INTRODUCTION xiii

I   OBJECTIVES OF NAVAL WARFARE 3

II   GRECO-PERSIAN WAR—MARATHON 11

     Appendix   Types of rowing ships 29

III   GRECO-PERSIAN WARS—SALAMIS AND MYCALE 54

     Appendix 1   Aeschylus' account of Salamis 106

     Appendix 2   The forces employed 108

IV   PELOPONNESIAN WAR 117

V   DIONYSIUS—SICILY AND CARTHAGE 196

VI   THE PENTERE AND ITS OARS 206

VII   EXERCISES AND STRATAGEMS OF THE GREEK FLEETS . . . 213

VIII   ALEXANDER'S NAVAL CAMPAIGNS 218

IX   NAVAL WARS OF ALEXANDER'S SUCCESSORS 227

     Appendix 1   The great ships of Demetrius and

            Ptolemy 254

     Appendix 2   Cost of wars at end of fourth century B.C. 262

X   FIRST PUNIC WAR 266

     Appendix   Roman Quinqueremes 306

XI   SECOND PUNIC WAR 308

XII   WAR OF RHODES AND PERGAMUM AGAINST MACEDON . . 377

XIII   WAR OF ROME AND ANTIOCHUS 387

XIV   NAVAL WARFARE IN THE FIRST CENTURY B.C. 424

XV   NAVAL WARS OF CAESAR, 49-45 B.C. 432

XVI   CAMPAIGN OF PHILIPPI, 42 B.C. 486

XVII   SICILIAN WAR, 38-36 B.C. 496

     Appendix   Agrippa's ships 514

XVIII   CAMPAIGN OF ACTIUM 31 B.C. 517

INDEX 541

ILLUSTRATIONS

	PAGE
Medieval method of rowing	35
Pentekonter, Early, according to Serre	37
Pentekonter, Early, its oars and benches, according to Serre	40
Pentekonter, Early, cross section, according to Serre	40
Relief from Acropolis .... *faces*	43
Triere, Model of, by Busley .... *faces*	45
Triere, Model of, by Serre .... *faces*	45
Triere, early part of fifth century B.C., reconstruction	46
Triere, Peloponnesian War, cross section, reconstruction	47
Triere, Early, reconstruction	47
Triere, Model of, by Serre, cross section .... *faces*	47
Triere, Peloponnesian War, reconstruction by Busley	48
Rowing frame, Medieval	49
Triere, Stern of, at Rhodes .... *faces*	49
Stone ship of Aesculapius on the island in the Tiber .... *faces*	49
Dispatch boat of third century B.C., reconstruction	50
Pedestal of Victory of Samothrace .... *faces*	50
Themistocles .... *faces*	83
Battle of Machaon and Phormio near Patras, sketch	130
Catastroma, Development of	210
Pentere of Dionysius, reconstruction	211
Demetrius, and the prow of his ship, from a coin .... *faces*	241
Octere, reconstruction	255
Sixteener (16-er), reconstruction	257
Tesserakonter (40-er), reconstruction	259
Tablet commemorating Caius Duilius, Consul in 260 B.C. ..... *faces*	277
Mt. Ecnomus, Battle of—sketches	281-89
Quinquereme, Roman, time of First Punic War, reconstruction	307
Pompey and Caesar .... *faces*	459
Octavianus Caesar and Marcus Vipsanius Agrippa .... *faces*	506
One of Agrippa's lighter ships at Actium .... *faces*	514
Bireme, time of Augustus, reconstruction	515
Marcus Antonius and Cleopatra of Egypt .... *faces*	534

MAPS

			PAGE
Map	1	Persian Empire	12
	2	Aegean Sea .... *faces*	14
	3	Battle of Marathon	18
	4	Campaigns of Thermopylae and Salamis	56
	5	Battles at Thermopylae and Artemisium	65
	6	Saronic Gulf	79
	7	Battle of Salamis	89
	8	Entrance to Gulf of Corinth	131
	9	Siege of Pylos	138
	10	Lower Italy .... *faces*	144
	11	Syracuse	151
	12	Region about the Hellespont	178
	13	Battle of Arginussae	186
	14	Siege of Motya: Battle of Drepanum	198
	15	Asia Minor	220
	16	Siege of Tyre	223
	17	Egypt	244
	18	Siege of Rhodes	247
	19	Western Mediterranean .... *faces*	266
	20	Punic Wars, and Caesar's African Campaign	290
	21	Northern Italy .... *faces*	322
	22	Cartagena	354
	23	Roman Wars in Africa and the Aegean ...... *faces*	364
	24	West Coast of Asia Minor	378
	25	Caesar's Campaign against the Veneti	427
	26	Oricum	453
	27	Alexandria	467
	28	Actium	524

PUBLISHER'S PREFACE

This book, and its companion, NAVAL WARFARE UNDER OARS, was originally published in the late 1930's, when naval warfare still centered on big guns and the battle line, much as it had for centuries past. The technological era that came with World War II vastly complicated the art of war with sophisticated weapons, complex communications, and electronic search, detection and guidance systems which have taken much of the control of battle away from the admiral on his bridge and turned it over to a computer in the combat information center. Accordingly, the big guns and the battle line have become history.

But though the weapons and tactics have changes, the basic reason for the existence of any naval force is as it was when the Venetians and Spaniards engaged their enemies centuries ago—to control what happens at sea. The principles of strategy which the ancients developed still remain valid, and a thorough understanding of them as they are presented in this text might well tip the balance in favor of the better informed of two otherwise equal opponents.

Admiral Rodgers spent many years in preparing this work, a classic in the history of naval warfare. Long out of print, it has been reissued in keeping with the U.S. Naval Institute's editorial policy of making such material readily available for professional naval officers.

PREFACE

This book had its origin many years ago at the Naval War College when I listened to a lecturer on the Battle of Salamis, with whose views on naval tactics I did not agree. Later, I delivered some lectures on joint Army and Navy operations at the Naval War College and at the Army School of the Line at Fort Leavenworth and served for several years at the Army and the Naval War Colleges. After retirement, this background of professional work led me to continue the studies I had begun many years before.

It seemed that the naval history of each campaign should be preceded by some examination of the political and economic situation of the two belligerents leading to the war and establishing its military objectives. Therefore each chapter has been made to stand by itself in this respect and there has been some repetition, I hope not too much, on this account.

Together with the strategic and tactical account of the wars there is an examination of what kinds of men-of-war nations had at various times in order to act as they are alleged to have done. This part is chiefly carried on in a series of appendices to successive chapters. The literary records as to ancient ships are supplemented by many archaeological remains: vase-paintings, wall paintings, mosaics, and sculptures; but, in spite of all these data, students disagree greatly as to what a triere (for example) was really like. As the practice of shipbuilding in the Mediterranean embodied a continuous tradition, we may with advantage draw inferences from the construction of medieval and later rowing ships of which we have full accounts, and apply these to earlier ships. No one can be sure of precise conclusions, yet for the reconstructions which I have attempted here it may be said that the behavior of such ships on the sea would be such as we are told was that of ancient ships.

Ancient money values are given in gold dollars of 25.8 grains 9/10 fine.

I hope to be able to continue this volume by another giving an account of navies and types of ships until the Battle of Lepanto whose date marked the practical close of the period of rowing ships of war.

Judge John Bassett Moore was good enough to write a kind and flattering introduction and Captain D. W. Knox, U. S. Navy (Retired), gave many suggestions and much good advice. Captain William McEntee, (C.C.) U. S. Navy, in charge of the ship-model tank at the Washington Navy Yard, gave me valuable data on the speed and horsepower of galley-formed ships. The drawings and battle plans were made with much skill by Mr. R. N. Jones, of the Bureau of Construction and Repair, Navy Department, and the maps by Mr. F. G. Perkins, of the naval Hydrographic Office. My sister, Mrs. Robert Giles, has read and corrected my manuscript repeatedly and to all I have named I offer my best thanks for their assistance and interest.

WILLIAM LEDYARD RODGERS

INTRODUCTION

In essaying, as a civilian, to write an introduction to a history of the art of naval warfare so comprehensive in its scope and so minute in its learning as the present work, I cannot help feeling that some explanation is due. I might assign various reasons, but it may suffice to mention only two: In the first place, the author's name is linked in my mind with a long and distinguished naval tradition; in the second place, my associations with him, both official and personal, incline me to comply with his requests.

Having thus particularly justified my instant venture, I confess that I am also influenced by a more general interest in the subject of the present work. As a lifelong student and frequent administrator of international affairs, I have been much thrown with military and naval men, and especially with the latter; and the better I have come to know them, the more have I learned to appreciate the spirit of unselfish loyalty that underlies their devotion to their profession and their pride in it. Though they neither declare war nor create the occasions for it, these functions being vested in the civil government, yet, when a rupture occurs, on them falls the burden of conducting the national defense; and it is not for them to question the wisdom, or the justice, or the propriety of the measures by which the crisis was precipitated. This being so, they are naturally in favor of preparedness; and especially must this be their attitude in times when great military powers profess to be committed to the enforcement of "world peace" by the united suppression of alleged "aggressors," whether by starvation or by implemental wounds and death. Although the full demonstration of the actual potentialities of such a scheme of peace has, after a preliminary test, lately been abandoned in order to avert a general war, the uncertainties and perils that must attend the attempt to apply it, and the extent to which it may draw upon military resources, may easily be shown without extended argument.

Passing over, with bare mention, the initial difficulty that no definition has been or ever will be framed by which the true "aggressors" in armed conflicts can offhand be certainly identified, we are confronted with the palpable and overshadowing reality that, while all great nations and many lesser ones have been charged with wars of aggression, they are not accustomed themselves to think of their conduct in that light, but are, on the contrary, disposed to commend it on grounds of national dignity and security, and perhaps also of "humanity." Not infrequently they have found occasion to justify conquest as a benefit to the conquered and a contribution to civilization. It is a notorious fact that, under Article 22 of the Covenant of the League of Nations, which declares that "the well-being and development" of "peoples not yet able to stand by themselves under the strenuous conditions of the modern world . . . form a sacred trust of civilization," members of the League have, in the exercise of the mandates granted to them over their allotted conquests, employed armed forces on a very appreciable scale. Nor is such a condition of things in its nature evanescent, as native peoples may find the yoke of their primitive state less exacting than that of a higher civilization.

Taking history as a whole, the vital part which sea power has played in it has been recognized from the earliest times to the present. As an example of such recognition the letter of Cicero to Atticus, written in the year 49 B.C., is often cited. But Cicero invoked the testimony of Themistocles, who, nearly four hundred years before, declared "that whoso can hold the sea has command of the situation" (*qui mare teneat, eum necesse rerum potiri*). Two thousand years later this opinion, held in common by ancient Greece and ancient Rome, was re-echoed by Lord Bacon, who declared it to be "certain, that he that commands the sea is at great liberty and may take as much and as little of the war as he will"; while Bacon's famous contemporary, Sir Walter Raleigh, yet more sententiously expressed the same thought in the maxim: "Whosoever commands the sea, commands the trade of the world; whosoever commands the trade of the world, commands the riches of the world and consequently the world itself."

Were these two great Englishmen now in a position to claim for themselves a prophetic rôle, they no doubt would assign as a convincing proof the existence of the British Empire in its present extent and strength. They would point to the colonial expansion that took place in the century that followed them. They might claim that the ultimate result of the Napoleonic wars was assured by the naval victories that culminated at Trafalgar. They might also maintain that, although the merits of British naval strategy at Jutland may ever be a subject of debate, there can be no doubt that the retirement of the German fleet on that occasion and its subsequent failure to reappear assured the eventual triumph of Great Britain and her allies.

I am wont to remark that history is the record of mass psychologies. This results from the inevitable tendency of the human mind to be preoccupied with present things, and especially with new things. Today, there is a popular tendency to be absorbed in the spectacular and fascinating activities of aircraft. We see cities razed, land forces harassed and crippled, and naval forces destroyed from the sky, with a facility that seems to assume that aircraft will not themselves be subject to attack. No doubt the use of aircraft will continue to expand for purposes of war as well as of peace. But, in the face of what has taken place during the past twenty years, we can hardly deny that land and sea forces have tended to increase. Navies continue to command the sea; and we are justified in believing that, in spite of the encouragement given to the supposition that war may be avoided by peoples suddenly shutting themselves up, suppressing their trade, and staying at home, naval power will play in the future a part no less important than that which it has played in the past.

On the technical phases of the present work I will not venture to comment at length. They are, I believe, unrivaled in previously recorded naval history; and they bespeak a prolonged, extensive, and painstaking research beyond all praise. Many of the earlier weapons and methods have indeed, at least in name and ostensible form, fallen into disuse, and have been superseded by later inventions. It is often remarked that we now live in the machine age, and, with the development of the physical sciences, novel devices will continue to be invented. But, in spite of the employment of different physical processes, the course of history remains essentially the same, because the human beings by whom it is determined continue, in spite of a somewhat popular supposition to the contrary, to be characterized by the same traits that they exhibited when their activities were first observed. In his celebrated work on the principles of war[1] that great master of the history as well as of the conduct of war, Marshal Foch, profoundly says: "In spite of all, the fundamental truths which govern this art remain immutable, just as the principles of mechanics always govern architecture, whether the construction is of wood, of stone, of iron, or of cement." Although weapons change, their relative effect not only on material things but also on the mind must continue to be a question of fundamental importance in the study of the problems of peace and of war.

JOHN BASSETT MOORE

---

[1] Foch, *Des Principes de la Guerre*, Paris, 1918, Preface, IX.

GREEK AND ROMAN
NAVAL WARFARE

CHAPTER I

OBJECTIVES OF NAVAL WARFARE

BEFORE going to the discussion of naval strategy and tactics, it is necessary to examine the objectives of naval warfare which are inherent to it without regard to the nature of the ships employed or the period of history. This examination may be somewhat tedious to readers who are already well acquainted with the subject, but is necessary for those not familiar with the broad principles of warfare.

Naval warfare, or war on the sea, is, of course, prehistoric in its origin and at first it was no more than a seizure of booty from traders trafficking upon the seas. It was unorganized and predatory.

The organization of maritime warfare on a scientific basis cannot well be traced much beyond the beginning of the fifth century B.C. At an earlier date the Cretans and Egyptians possessed sea power and the *Iliad* tells us of the battle for the ships before Troy. But in this battle the ships were already pulled upon the beach, where they were valuable as prizes, but were neither weapons nor carriers. However, the appearance of these Greek ships at Troy suggests the whole objective of naval warfare through the centuries, for probably the expedition was undertaken to control trade.

The sea is barren but is a route for traffic. Until the past century, the sea was by far the best route for long-haul traffic, and the merchant trader spread civilization with his ships, but needed protection from violence.

The origin of navies is to be looked for in the necessity for national protection of commerce to the advantage of the state and its citizens, both in peace and in war.

In the specialization of industries which has gone on for so many centuries, that of arms is one of the most essential.

When every man personally had to protect himself and his industry, much waste of effort was entailed. Governments exist to provide national good order as their first objective, and the safety of trade is an essential to developing civilization. In ancient times and until the last century, piracy was almost universal. Everywhere an unarmed ship was liable to attack and

3

pillagè. The present safety of commerce is due far more to quick communications and ease of pursuit of pirates than to any change in the morals of mankind. In ancient times, the colonies sent out by all Greek centers of trade were very largely undertaken to provide bases for the protection of their own trade and also, be it said, as bases for attacking their rivals' shipping.

The siege of Troy was doubtless undertaken for the control of the line of sea communications through the Dardanelles between the Black Sea and the Mediterranean, for the destruction of Troy did away with hostile control at the entrance of the Hellespont and probably provided a Greek outpost for the greater security of Greek trade.

In the great battle, when Hector reached the line of beached ships and drove Ajax from his stand on deck, laying fire under the keel of the helpless ship, he threatened the Greek sea power with ruin; for with the burning of the ships, the Greek army would be without means of either supply or retreat and destruction would be inevitable.

But although the importance of sea power is recognized in the *Iliad*, we have no knowledge of the stage of naval tactics at this time. We can see little of any organization into fleets or squadrons except that each local leader held his ships in a body, as he held his men after they had landed.

The shipping was primarily for transport of men and freight. Fighting at sea was incidental and may be assumed as having no well-observed rule or form of tactical procedure. Hostile craft came together and the decks furnished platforms for struggles in which the contestants engaged much as they did on shore, except that the sea was always underfoot, ready to drown a stumbler.

By the time of the Greco-Persian Wars, naval organization was further advanced. Many of the Grecian city states were dependent on their manufactures and commerce for their food supply, as their farm lands were not equal to their nourishment. Indeed, all the shores of the Levant were the homes of shipping and commerce. When rival city states found cause for dispute, it was natural and easy for them to organize their pirate adventurers into navies and seek national objectives. But even when naval organization had gone further and there were permanent fleets and squadrons guarding trade, these were not always above seizing an opportunity to capture a ship of a rival city.

Tactical Objectives of Warfare

When a nation sets out to fight another, it intends that as victor it will impose its will on the opponent. There are two ways of reaching this objective. One is the direct attack upon the life of the adversary by bloodshed, and the other is the indirect attack upon his life by destroying his property and cutting off his means of livelihood. A man will fight as readily to retain his property and subsist his family as he will for his life itself. Further, although the attack upon property may sometimes be temporarily parried by some form of retreat with the property, yet eventually the continued effort against property must end either by battle or by submission, when the loser yields without fighting and makes his bargain in order to retain some part of his property in danger.

Particularity of Naval Warfare

In general it may be said that maritime warfare has for its final objective the seizure of property rather than mastery of persons. (Although, of course, persons are by no means exempt in naval war.) Therefore, in its nature maritime war is secondary to that on land. Mankind lives on the land and draws its supplies from the land. The objective of land warfare is to occupy territory and take tribute from the inhabitants by various economic devices. It is a war against persons to compel their service. In early times, slavery was the crude and general form of tribute. Now, the forms of tribute are more complex; such as the reparation payments of Germany and the French occupation of the Ruhr in 1923. But however the loser in war may be required to render service to the victor, the operations and consequences of war are primary upon the land.

As for the sea, it is not habitable nor productive; it is a cheap and convenient highway and means of communication. All war upon the sea, therefore, has for its ultimate objective the control of sea-borne commerce, in which transportation may be either for civil or military purposes. Such attack upon property is an indirect way of striking at the national life of the enemy. The battle of fleets is not profitable unless victory alters the conditions of traffic in favor of the victor, for in war the normal production of supplies within the theater of war and the territory of the combatants is reduced and the seat of war and the contestants engaged there must be supplied by products drawn from afar. Thus a navy's strategic rôle in major warfare is limited to the secondary one of facilitating supplies to one's own people and denying them to the enemy. In the above definition of naval warfare as an effort directed upon supplies moving across sea, we must not forget that it includes the attack and defense of military expeditions over-seas. An army and its munitions embarked on transports is not an effective army, but merely material for making one after disembarkation. And so it is true to say that the objective of naval warfare is material and property; and fleet battle is an effort to clear the way for the victory to control civil and military commerce.

There is one more general point to be brought out as to naval warfare which distinguishes it from land warfare. On land, the main attack in battle is directly upon the life of the enemy. Combatants have always sought to protect themselves by fortifications and, consequently, means of breaking down the defenses have always been necessary; yet, when this has been accomplished, it has still been requisite to attack the personnel. The encounter of man against man is the decisive thing in land warfare; but in war afloat the sea is always ready to drown the fighters, and so the attack on ship material may be as fatal as the direct attack upon life. Thus tactical choice may always be made whether to attack the persons of the enemy, or the ship structures which support them above the sea. As ships and weapons vary, one course or another is forced upon the admirals as best suits their material, for tactics must be such as will best develop the strong features of the available material of each side in ships and weapons. Fortunate is he whose ships and armament are such that he is strong in two ways, so that he has a choice of conduct, in that his enemy while preparing against one form of attack lays himself open to another. Today, for instance, such is the advantage of torpedo armament of battleships. Although their main weapon is the heavy gun, even if not used, the dread of torpedoes limits the enemy's maneuvers. For if the threat of torpedoes is disregarded, they will be used, and the enemy must pay the penalty of his disregard. (The British fleet at Jutland turned away from the enemy and lost him, fearing torpedoes.)

Returning to the means of attack on the person and on the ship structure, through all the ages we have had hand weapons for attacking persons, which are more or less known to us today, if not as present-day weapons, then as out-of-door childish amusements: namely, short arms—swords, axes, and spears for wounding, and clubs and maces for bruising. Second, there were small missile weapons—slings, javelins, and archery—in ancient times, and small-arms now. The shield was a means of active defense and helmets and body armor of passive defense. In the third class are air-borne poisons, anciently quicklime and stinkpots, and now modern gases. As for the attack on ship structure, the ship herself was used to drive her ram into the enemy, and there were dolphins (falling weights),[1] flamepots, and flamethrowers, fire ships and mechanical artillery for the ancients and explosive artillery, mines, torpedoes, and aerial bombs in recent times. It is perhaps open to debate whether the chief purpose of the present-day heavy artillery is to attack persons or structures, but the manner of applying deck and side armor to ships convinces me, at least, that the primary purpose of armor is to protect structure and that heavy projectiles are employed to break up and sink the ship, although incidentally they may cause great loss of life before the ship goes down.

In the interplay between attack on the person and attack on the structure, and in the development of instruments and methods to facilitate the attack and defense of each as the general progress of the arts and sciences warrants, we find the basis of the origin of naval tactics. Tactics is the art of applying the available forces of destruction to the best advantage in battle to overcome the oppositional will of the enemy, while resisting his counter effort by taking every practicable step for the preservation of life and structure. In any tactical effort, a commander's line of effort is partly indicated to him by the nature of the ships and weapons held respectively by him and by his enemy, and partly it depends on his own imagination and initiative. In the subsequent pages, describing successive campaigns, particular attention will be paid to the part played by the weapons each leader accepted as the gift of his country, according to the stage of its civilization and industry.

GENERAL CONSIDERATIONS

The size and speed of rowing ships

Before taking up the subject of tactics, we must form some idea of the ships and weapons available. We may arrive at a conclusion as to the

---

[1] It was early the practice to use great pikes to pierce the enemy's side when alongside. Homer describes Ajax defending his ship (pulled up on the shore as was the custom) against Hector with a ship's pike over 30 feet long.

approximate size of early ships. The time of the *Iliad* was late in the second millennium B.C. (traditional date 1194 B.C.). Jason's Expedition for the Golden Fleece was a generation earlier. Jason's *Argo* was a ship rowed by 50 heroes of whom Hercules was one. The largest ships mentioned in the *Iliad* had 120 men on board; other ships mentioned had 50 rowers. We may assume with reasonable probability that the *Argo* and the ships mentioned in the *Iliad* were the largest warships of their time. At the present day, large men-of-war carry launches 50 feet long, in which it is possible and customary to embark nearly 200 men with a little water and provisions when abandoning ship in an emergency. Such boats then displace nearly 30 tons. On these same craft, it is quite feasible to man 26 oars with 50 rowers (the bow oars with one man each). The British Navy still holds pulling races with ships' boats having 2 and 3 men per oar. We may postpone discussing whether the heroes of the *Argo* each pulled his own oar or whether there were two men to each oar, as in navy heavy boat racing today.

But we may assume that the Greek ships of the time of the siege of Troy, and for several centuries afterwards, used for war and piracy were of about 20 to 30 tons load displacement with a cargo of 10 to 15 tons in crew, freight, stores, and equipment.

This conclusion is not in rejection of the evidence that there were sailing ships of 200 tons displacement or more in existence before 1000 B.C., although such large craft could not have been common, for the traffic of the time was on a small scale.

Such sailing ships were probably not unlike those of 2,000 years later, round and moderately deep. If of 200 tons displacement, they would have been about 60 feet long, 22.5 feet wide, and 8.5 feet draft. Such proportions were not unusual in the middle ages. (Columbus' *Santa Maria* was 71'x25.5'x8.8' and about 240 tons displacement.)

Probably, however, the majority of sailing ships carrying most of the trade then were less than 50 feet long, and under 100 tons displacement, carrying cargoes not exceeding half their displacement. We know that later, at Rome, apparently to keep Senators out of big business, they were forbidden to own ships carrying more than 300 *amphoræ*, i.e., 2,200 gallons of wine; the wine in jars would weigh 11 tons and the ship would displace 25 to 30 tons (dimensions, say, 35'x12'x4').

Our knowledge of naval history and tactics only acquires some definiteness from the time of Herodotus' writing about the middle of the fifth century B.C.

We must therefore begin our study of naval tactics, and of its development through the general progress of the arts and sciences, after the close of the sixth century B.C., with the Greco-Persian Wars, and assume ships such as those mentioned above were then usual.

Previous to this time, the pentekonter, or ship with 50 rowers, was the principal form of "long ship" or man-of-war, driven primarily by oars, although not without a mast and sail.

The triere, or ship with three banks of rowers, had been invented a century or more previously, but did not immediately become predominant. About this time (500 B.C.) it superseded the pentekonter as the principal type of ship in the national fleets of Persia and of Greece. In our study of ancient naval tactics, it is our first affair to picture to ourselves what these ships must have been like in order to behave as we are told that they did.

At the beginning of the time which we are discussing, about 500 B.C., standard battleships were comparatively small, perhaps 70 to 80 feet long, with a displacement of scarcely 50 tons. The rowers were exposed to the enemy and took part in the fight after collision. In the course of the next century the size of the standard ship increased considerably. The rowers were protected by a deck over them. The draft was small so the ships could be readily drawn on the beach. They were not good sea boats and could not venture far from land as they needed immediate shelter if bad weather threatened. All through the period of rowing men-of-war, the maximum racing speed was about 7 knots or a little more. In three watches, the rowers could make 60 to 70 miles a day in a calm. The subject is more fully discussed in the appendix to next chapter.

The Ram and Its Tactics

The ram was sometimes at the water line, but frequently well below it. As the ships were light, with planking not over 2.5 inches thick, and much of it was thinner, a very moderate speed would suffice to penetrate the hull, but apparently it was not the practice to attempt a headlong attack with the ram, for when once committed to the attack, a slight error in judgment or a change of course of the adversary might make the difference between giving and receiving a fatal injury. Consequently, the two opposing adversaries maneuvered for position with caution while the archers and slingers and javelin men used their weapons and, later, as the ships came together, the spearmen and swordsmen also became occupied. A weapon much used was the dolphin, a heavy weight slung at the yardarm and dropped upon the enemy to bilge him. A weight of 100 or 200 pounds dropping 30 feet would be very likely to start a plank in the bottom.

Battle Maneuvers

As for the ram, there were two main maneuvers with it known as the *diekplous* and the *periplous*. The first was a passage through the hostile line and the second was a turn around his flank (in military language an "envelopment"), so as to attack him in the rear, or at least before he could turn himself to meet the attack bows on. The *periplous* required superior numbers or great superiority in maneuvering in order to place ships on both sides of the hostile line, or on a part of it. In the *diekplous* (the charge through), the effort was to injure oars or gain some advantage in the exchange of missiles and, having established some superiority in this way, the captain made a quick turn about, called *anastrophe*, in order to ram before the enemy could complete his own turn about.

To use the ram effectively, great maneuvering power was necessary. This was obtained by the double rudders which could be used like a whaleboat's steering oar to turn the ship, when at rest. Moreover, by placing the tholepins halfway between the thwarts, the whole rowing crew could step over their oars with great ease and row with full effect in the opposite direction, sitting on the thwart astern of their oars. This could not readily have been done with one man on each oar in three ranks. But in spite of all the talk of the ram, it does not seem to have been the chief weapon except in the hands of Phormio in the Peloponnesian War.

To protect the oars from the passage of the enemy in the *diekplous*, the catheads were very long and heavy and heavily strutted from astern. It is clear that unless the enemy came close in passing, the oars, if depressed, or trailed, would be within the line of the cathead, and if the enemy came close to pass by without ramming, the catheads themselves would sweep his sides and break up the rowing organization.

CHAPTER II

GRECO-PERSIAN WAR

FLEET TACTICS

AFTER this preliminary review of ships and their speeds, we may take up the great campaigns of the Greco-Persian Wars in the early part of the fifth century B.C.

This was the beginning of more or less reliable accounts of strategy and tactics, although it is apparent as we read these accounts that there had been study and tradition of tactics long before. We must commence the study of naval tactics with that of land tactics, and for this reason I take up the campaign of Marathon as an introduction. It is only since the advent of steel armor necessitating very heavy artillery for ships that the battle maneuvering of ships has lost all semblance to that of armies. We no longer attempt to decide the victory by hand-to-hand fighting. The reason is a simple one. Until the invention of ship armor and very heavy artillery, the attack on personnel was, on the whole, more effective than the attack on ship structure. As long as weapons had only human strength with which to strike, and even in the early days of artillery, weapons were more effective when directed against men than against ships. Now men sink with their ships; similarly with the ships themselves. As long as they were driven by rowers, there were many advantages in bringing about a situation in which the rowers could drop their oars and share in the fight. It is true that for a short period during the fifth century B.C. the Athenian skill in ship handling was such that their fleets depended more on the ram than on personal struggle, but this was a very brief period in the history of naval warfare. In general, fleets wished to approach each other for a hand-to-hand struggle, and at the same time they wished to protect their oars on which their mobility depended. This protection to oars was offered by the line formation in which each ship had a friend on each side and threatened the enemy with its own ram. The consequence was when the fleets drew together and began action, they were immobilized, and the battle was fought out where the fleets first came in contact. Individual ships, withal, maneuvered about

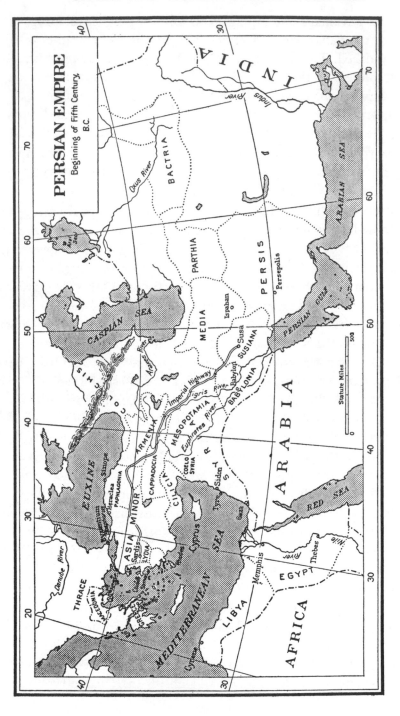

PERSIAN EMPIRE

Beginning of Fifth Century, B.C.

MAP I.

each other for advantage in bringing about collision; and enveloping movements about the flanks were effective owing to the concentration of force thus accomplished. The fighting men were armed and equipped after the fashion of soldiers of their own countries and the crews of every pair of opposing ships sought to get positions of advantage for the style of hand-to-hand fighting suited to their own national infantry. Accordingly, in beginning the study of naval tactics with the events of the Persian Wars, as a preliminary we shall discuss military tactics as exemplified in the opening campaign of Marathon in 490 B.C., in which the Persian fleet performed transport service only and the Greeks made no use of naval forces. This is done because military tactics were more advanced than naval tactics and formed a basis for the latter.

Relations between Greece and Persia

The great war between the Greeks and Persians in 480 and 479 B.C. had its origin a generation or more earlier, after Darius had reunited the Persian Empire established by Cyrus. The center of the Persian might lay in Persia and Media between the Caspian Sea and the Persian Gulf. Since the middle of the sixth century B.C., Cyrus and his son, Cambyses, had extended their power towards India on the east, and to the west they had conquered Syria, Egypt, and Asia Minor. In the latter region were included the Greek settlements which fringed its coasts and were particularly strong along its western shores bordering on the Aegean Sea.

After Darius had established himself in mastery of the Empire, he extended its eastern limits as far as the Indus River and about 512 B.C. he crossed the Bosphorus and invaded Thrace. He seems to have gone as far north as the mouth of the Danube, but his movement in this direction does not seem to have been successful. Nevertheless, he held all the southern part of Thrace, although his hold on the warlike inhabitants was not secure. On the whole, the Persian prestige was not raised by the expedition.

It is not entirely clear to modern historians what was the inducement for Darius to wish to extend his domains into Europe. It seems probable, however, that the free Thracians in Europe were in sympathy with their blood kindred in northwestern Asia Minor, as the Greeks of Europe were in sympathy with those living on the eastern side of the Aegean. It is well known that the political subjugation of part of a district inhabited by a

single race does not make for a quiet border. It might well seem to Darius
that it was necessary for him to rule in the Balkan peninsula for the sake of
preserving peace in western Asia Minor.

A few years after the somewhat insecure Thracian conquest, difficulties
between Athens and Sparta caused the former to turn to the Persian Governor of Lydia bordering on the Aegean Sea and to ask his aid. It is unnecessary to trace the relations between Athens and Persia. The result was
that Athens became convinced that it must be prepared for open enmity
with Persia; but hostilities were postponed by the outbreak in 499 B.C. of
an Ionian revolt among the Greek colonies along the eastern shores of the
Aegean, which had not long been subject to the Persians. In the first year
of the insurrection, the Athenians and Eretrians aided in it, but then withdrew, although for a time the Ionians held their own. The revolt was not
finally ended until 494 when the King's fleet destroyed that of the Ionians
in the Battle of Lade, a position on the west coast of Asia Minor, about 30
miles south of Ephesus. The advance of the coast line upon the sea has now
made the scene of the fight an inland position.

The Persian fleet proceeded to gather the fruits of its victory by reducing the island states of the Aegean Sea. Macedonia and Thrace had taken
advantage of the revolt to throw off Persian rule, but had not taken part in
hostilities, so the fleet next went to the farther shores of the Propontis
which it subdued.

In 492 the King was once more ready to push into Europe. Large
Persian re-enforcements were sent west from Susa, the Persian capital, and
Mardonius, the son-in-law of King Darius, took command of all the forces
ashore and afloat. He was successful in establishing his authority in Macedonia and southern Thrace; but, after this conquest, the fleet was greatly
damaged by a gale it met in passing the promontory of Mount Athos and
further advance was prevented. Nevertheless, the King by no means renounced his purpose of punishing Athens and Eretria for their aid to the
Ionian revolt, while on the other hand these cities had abundant warning.

Persian Plan of Campaign against Athens in 490 b.c.

The experience gained in overcoming the Ionian insurrection combined
with the further difficulties met by Mardonius seems to have caused the
King to decide that the difficulty of moving a combined fleet and army

MAP 2.
AEGEAN SEA

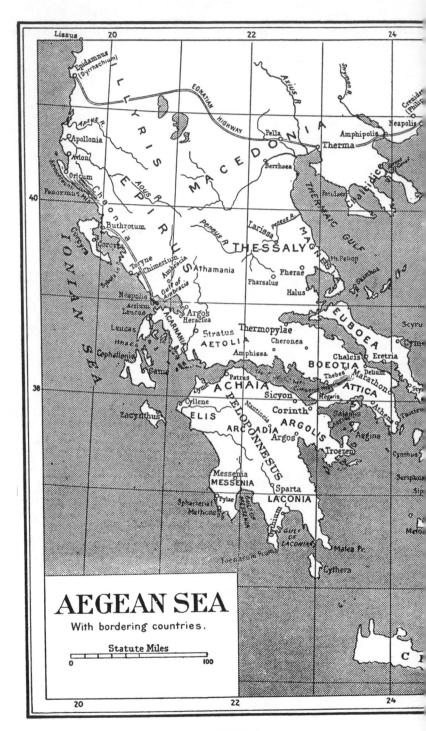

AEGEAN SEA

With bordering countries.

Statute Miles

0   100

MAP 2.

through and beyond Macedonia for the conquest of Greece was such that, while he would not renounce his purpose, he would change his method of accomplishment.

He determined that the obstacles to co-operation between army and navy on the long coast route from the Hellespont to Greece made a movement advisable by the short sea route directly across the Aegean from Samos to Euboea (Negropont) by the chain of islands. That line of travel forbade a great expedition, as the ships of those days were unequal to the transportation of the whole military strength of the great Empire, and successive trips would be needed. It was the practice for rowing men-of-war to carry very few supplies on board in order to be light and speedy on the day of battle. They were therefore under the necessity of renewing stores at brief intervals. In particular, there was little drinking water carried, and to the last days of rowing ships they were constantly hindered in the execution of their plans by the need of breaking off to renew their water.

Consequently, Darius decided to limit his objectives. He announced that he proceeded against the Athenians and Eretrians only, who had aided at the outbreak of the Ionian revolt. But it is probable that beyond the acknowledged purpose, the King wished to seize a secure base in the Attic peninsula whence he might afterwards advance to conquer all Greece.

The Persian fleet and army assembled in the summer of 490 in Cilicia on the south coast of Asia Minor, under the command of Datis, a Mede, who replaced Mardonius on account of the latter's ill-success in 492. Herodotus does not tell us the number of men in the force, but says there were 600 trieres which carried the infantry in addition to their crews and there were horse transports. As has been previously mentioned, these early trieres were smaller than those of a generation or two later. Estimating their normal crews at 120 men (see appendix to this chapter), we may assume that the carriage of army stores would reduce the men on board to 100 men each. Allowing 50 rowers, 10 mariners and officers, and 10 soldiers as the reduced crew of each, we have left room for not exceeding 30 soldiers as passengers.

When Herodotus says that the trieres numbered 600, his statement may mean that the horse transports were altered from trieres and were included in the 600. In ancient statistics of this sort, it is better to accept minimum figures. Let us suppose that 300 trieres were fitted to carry horses at the usual rate of 1 horse as the equivalent of 5 men. Then each horse ship would take 5 horses with their riders. The ships' crews would then come to 6,000 officers and mariners, 30,000 rowers, and 6,000 ship soldiers (*epibatæ*). To these we add as passengers 1,500 cavalry, 7,500 infantry, and 1,500 noncombatants, a total of 52,500 men with a combatant landing force, including the ships' soldiers, of 15,000 men as a maximum. (Some modern commentators put the Persian host present at the battle as low as 4,000.) This calculation merely serves to show that even on Herodotus' statement the expedition was not a very large one.

The Persian Army

As for the organization of the Persian army, the Empire was divided into some 20 satrapies in each of which a state or group of states was allowed a considerable measure of local self-government, under the control of an imperial satrap, who was civil ruler and levied a provincial tax, payable to the King. Local security and order were imposed by a royal garrison in each satrapy, composed mainly of Medes and Persians, under a commander appointed by the King, directly responsible to him and independent of the satrap. When a great war made it necessary, provincial levies were made in addition to the regular army.

The Persian army took over much of its organization and armament from that of the Assyrian Empire which it overcame. There was cavalry, at first mounted archers and later lancers, but always skirmishers rather than shock troops. The infantry were divided into light and heavy archers, the latter having helmet and armor, and frequently an attendant with a shield. There were also slingers who wore armor and took their places with the infantry of the line. I quote from Spaulding's *Ancient Warfare*:

> The Assyrian tactics, as indicated above, depended upon fire power, open order, and free maneuver. The Medes, naturally a race of mounted archers, grafted the Assyrian infantry system upon their own, and adopted their wicker shields and short spears. Being horsemen, they continued to emphasize the cavalry, and being mountaineers, they neglected the chariot. The Persians copied the Medes; their native institutions being presumably very similar. They made the bow their principal weapon, and their infantry armament and equipment were not well adapted to the phalanx and shock tactics. The spear was short; the shield small and rounded, or else copied from the Assyrian type and used primarily to cover an archer while firing. * * *

No great changes had taken place between Cyrus and Darius. A comparison of accounts of both earlier and later dates would indicate a steady increase in weight of cavalry armor, a gradual substitution of the javelin for the bow in the mounted service, and an increase in the use of slingers. But these modifications did not affect the essential character of the army. It still made cavalry its principal arm and fire (meaning missile discharge) its principal mode of action. The heavy infantry formed the center of the line; having come to bowshot, it halted and opened fire from behind its wicker shields. The slingers and light infantry undoubtedly acted as skirmishers, retiring behind the line when they were "squeezed out," and possibly using overhead fire, although the opportunity for this must have been very scant, for the heavy troops themselves were formed with considerable depth. The infantry made no effort to close with the enemy; the fire must have been in the nature of a holding attack. The decisive charge was given by the cavalry on the wings.

The Greek Soldier

Unlike the Persian, the Greek relied on shock tactics rather than on missiles.

The Greek military system was based on universal military service. * * * Organization and tactics were based on heavy infantry and shock. * * * The typical Greek warrior was the *hoplite* or armored pikeman. As auxiliary arms there were cavalry, and light infantry including archers, slingers, and *peltasts* or javelin men, protected chiefly by the small shield which gave them their name. The universal formation was the phalanx,—a heavy line of armored pikemen. * * * Eight ranks was a very common depth. * * * Of course, only the front ranks could engage, the others replaced losses and kept up the forward pressure. * * * The fire power of the phalanx was zero. Its auxiliaries remedied this defect only in part, for if used in front as skirmishers, they had to be drawn off to the flanks some time before contact, and their weapons being of short range, overhead fire could not be very effective. The charge of the phalanx, however, was almost irresistible, its defense almost unbreakable. In either case, its weakness was the flank, for its maneuvering ability was very small, and it was difficult to change front or refuse a flank. * * *

Here was where it most needed its auxiliary arms. But these auxiliaries dared not attack decisively, even in flank; they might annoy the (hostile) phalanx, check the momentum of its charge, or weaken its defense; but only another phalanx could break it.

Although the decisive battles, both by sea and land, were fought in the second Persian expedition under Xerxes, yet the first in Darius' reign with

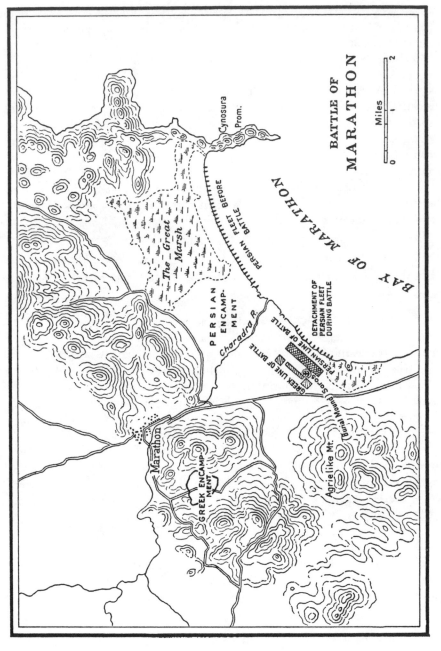

BATTLE OF
MARATHON

Miles

0   1   2

Cynosura Prom.

PERSIAN FLEET BEFORE BATTLE

The Great Marsh

BAY OF MARATHON

PERSIAN ENCAMPMENT

Charadra R.

DETACHMENT OF PERSIAN FLEET DURING BATTLE

PERSIAN LINE OF BATTLE

GREEK LINE OF BATTLE

Soros

Marathon

GREEK ENCAMPMENT

Agrielike Mt.

Burial Mound

MAP 3.

Datis as commander was most important to both sides in giving them knowledge of each other's strength, armament, and practices.

Campaign of Marathon

This account of the campaign of Marathon follows generally as to times and geography, the comments of Grundy on Herodotus as given in his work *Great Persian War*. The fleet, with the army on board, left Cilicia in the summer, probably in the latter part of July, 490 B.C., and proceeded to Samos in Ionia.

From Samos the fleet steered west southwest to Naxos which had resisted the Persians in 499. This time the Persians had a partial success, but most of the inhabitants escaped to the hills. After burning the city, the expedition moved through the islands towards Eretria, collecting troops and hostages from each. (There could not have been many additional men embarked, for lack of room.) Eretria, the first objective of the expedition, is in the island of Euboea on the Strait of Euripus which separates Euboea from Attica. The city had heard of the coming expedition and sent to Athens for help. Athens could spare little aid, but did what she could. On arrival at Eretria the Persians met resistance and for 6 days they were withstood until treachery gave them possession. They pillaged the city and enslaved the inhabitants.

After a short delay the Persians crossed the water to Marathon, a point on the Attic coast about 25 miles from Eretria and 26 miles by road and 60 miles by sea from Athens. Hippias, an exiled Athenian tyrant and renegade, had advised this place for disembarkation, as it was suitable ground for a cavalry camp. The site of the landing was a beach rather over 5 miles long, running northeast and southwest, protected from the northeast by the rocky promontory of Cynosura or Kynossema, extending out as a breakwater for more than a mile. A plain reaches inland from the beach for a distance varying from 1.5 to 2 miles. A large marsh fills most of the northeast part of the plain and a smaller marsh terminates it on the southwest, and the bed of the torrent Charadra cuts across the middle of the plain. Behind are rocky hills. The total area of the plain is about 10 square miles, but of this the marsh cuts off one-half and the torrent bed forms an obstacle running through the other half. Two roads lead to Athens. The more direct one running back into the hills, leaves the plain by two branches which soon join and lead to Athens over a difficult path impracticable to cavalry, which was the most valued arm of the Persians. The other road leaves the plain along the line of the beach and later turns inland to Athens. This was a very good route for cavalry.

The reason for landing at Marathon as given by Herodotus is not very convincing; for the Athenian plain itself and the neighboring one on the Bay of Eleusis were better for cavalry than that of Marathon, although more exposed to counter attack during disembarkation, on account of the proximity of the city. The political situation in Athens gives an adequate explanation of the landing at Marathon. The party divisions were very high in the city. Hippias, who was with the Persians, had his party in Athens and they were expected to aid in giving possession to the enemy. Herodotus tells of a helio-message by a flashing shield within the city, which was believed to have guided the Persian movement, although no one could be discovered with whom to connect it. The Aristocratic party in Athens, headed by Miltiades, was anti-Persian; the Democratic party was willing to have Hippias restored to the control of the city by the help of the Persians. The probable object of the Persians in landing at Marathon was not to seek a battle there, but to draw the Athenian garrison away from Athens. At Marathon the Persians could afford to wait while treachery should have time to work, and if the garrison should come to Marathon, there would be more opportunity for the conspiracy to grow in the city. Then, either with or without a battle at Marathon, a part of the Persian force might embark with the fleet and proceed with the fleet to Athens (about 60 sea miles) while the remainder of the Persians at Marathon could contain the Athenian field army there.

In readiness for the campaign, the Athenians had an understanding with the Spartans who were to come to the aid of the former when summoned. Accordingly, on the news of the fall of Eretria, the Athenians sent a runner to the Spartans to call them out. He is said to have finished the trip of 140 miles on the second day, which was the ninth day of the third (lunar) month (about September 2). He returned immediately with the announcement that the Spartans would come, but that religion required them to wait until after the full moon. They started on the fifteenth and arrived at Athens on the seventeenth (of the third month).

Herodotus does not tell us on what day the Athenians heard of the

Persian landing at Marathon, but a comparison of other dates makes it appear to have been about the tenth of the month. The Athenian field force then departed to meet the enemy, under Callimachus, the polemarch (commander in chief), and ten generals, each commanding one of the ten tribal regiments which made up the army. Of these leaders, Miltiades was the most prominent politically and the council of war and the polemarch seem to have deferred very much to his views as to the conduct of the campaign. It is probable that his ascendency in the decisions affecting the actions of the army was largely due to the powers of the army council whose majority was led by Miltiades. It may be that when Callimachus and the council had decided on the general plan, they left Miltiades with a free hand to carry it out, or Miltiades may have been the author of the plan which the council adopted.

Herodotus does not give the size of the Greek army which went to Marathon, but later classical authors estimate it at from 9,000 to 10,000 Athenians and 1,000 allied Plataeans. Grundy points out that as the Athenian numbers at Plataea in 479 B.C. were 8,000 heavy-armed and as many light-armed troops, and that many citizens were serving at the same time in the fleet at Mycale, we should think that 10,000 at Marathon is an under-estimate, although not a large one. In spite of the large party in the city hostile to the government, Grundy believes that no considerable garrison was left in the city. On the other hand, if we start with an estimate of the Persian forces based on 600 ships carrying 1,500 cavalry and 13,500 infantry, of which 6,000 properly belonged to the ships' crews, and suppose that half of the ship soldiers were landed at Marathon, we have only 10,000 infantry available for the battle and we know that the Greeks were less, so we may suppose their numbers to have been only 7,000 to 8,000, leaving a considerable garrison in the city.

When the Athenians marched out over the upper road on the tenth, they were under the impression that they would meet the Persians on the way. However, the Persians had not moved since landing on the spot, and the Athenians camped in the hills, about a mile from where the road forks as it goes down to the plain. This was a strong position, as the Persians could not effectively attack in the hills, and were they to march by the beach road on Athens or begin embarkation to move there by sea, they could be attacked at a disadvantage. Here the enemies lay for several days, the Persians encamped on the plain with their ships anchored close to the beach, probably with their sterns aground for easy communication. The Greeks held their strong position in the hills. There must have been some communication between the Persians and their partisans in the city, so that they learned that the Spartans were to start out on the fifteenth after the full moon. As time passed and the expected uprising in the city did not take place, it must have become apparent to the Persians that they would have to take decisive action before the arrival of the Spartans, or the campaign would fail. In consequence, it seems probable, although Herodotus' account is not informative, that the Persians embarked a part of the army, including all the cavalry, to move directly on the city, while the other half remained in position to hold the Athenian army away from the city.

It is probable that the Persian camp was northeast of the torrent bed, between it and the marsh, with the ships nearer Cynosura. The position gave room enough for both infantry and horses and the nearer the ships were to Cynosura the better shelter they had from the usual north and northeast winds. Moreover, there was only a narrow stretch of beach between the marsh and the sea, so that it was possible for a very small force at the end of the beach to cover the embarkation of the entire expedition. If the ships had their sterns resting on the beach as previously suggested, the embarkation could be very readily carried out, even in the presence of the enemy. Although the Persian camp was on the northern side of the Charadra torrent bed, it was from the southwestern end of the plain that the best road led to Athens. Therefore, the part of the Persian army which was to contain the Greeks moved to a position on the right bank of the Charadra in order to be able to take the road itself and at the same time close it to the enemy. This decision of the Persians seems to have taken effect on the sixteenth of the month (September 9).

Upon the arrival at Marathon, the Athenian generals held a council of war, as a result of which Callimachus, strongly urged by Miltiades, decided in favor of battle; but there was no need for haste. The longer the Persians remained inactive, the better chance there was that the Spartans would arrive before the battle. The conduct of the battle was left by consent of the council to Miltiades. He was the leader of his party and a distinguished ruler and soldier, and Callimachus was willing to be guided by him, although in the battle he did not relinquish the position of honor on the right flank which was his as commander in chief and occupying which he lost his life in the pursuit of the enemy. The center of the field of battle is no doubt indicated by the great mound (*soros*) heaped up over the graves of those who lost their lives in the fight. It is a mile and a quarter south of the Charadra and half a mile from the shore, and about the same distance from the Little Marsh.

As the Persian fleet with the cavalry and right wing on shipboard stood off for Athens, the remaining left wing drew up nearly parallel to the beach and offered battle between the road and the beach with the necessary detachment of ships against the beach in the rear ready to take the soldiers off when their object had been accomplished. As was said, the usual Persian tactics was to stand and open a missile fire with their main body, while the flanking cavalry enveloped the enemy and attacked his rear. On this occasion there was no cavalry, for that had started for Athens on shipboard; but the idea of envelopment was an essential part of the missile fight for which the Persians were armed. We must give their intelligence service credit for having ascertained the number opposed to them, and, consequently, it would have been prudent for Datis, the Persian commander, to have retained enough with him to form a line longer than that which he might expect the Greeks to occupy in confronting them. Probably he did so. But this superiority in length of the battle line would not be excessive, for his available strength was not overwhelming, and he had to take Athens and possibly meet the Spartans before completing the work. On the side of the Greeks, their strength was in the frontal charge and the close spear-fight, and their weak point was in the flank, where a serious attack was disastrous.

If we take the grave mound as being near the center of the battle ground, and note the remark of Pausanias in his geography that part of the Persian army was driven into one of the marshes, it then seems probable that the Persian line faced northwest with the left resting near or even across the beach road to Athens, with the marsh nearly in its rear, and the right wing extending nearly parallel to the beach. Its length did not exceed a mile, and was probably less. It was Miltiades' solution of the problem of preventing Persian envelopment to which our European civilization is indebted for victory, and which gave him enduring fame. The council and Callimachus consented to his spreading the somewhat scanty Greek numbers over the entire frontage of the enemy so as to deprive him of the opportunity of envelopment except by weakening his main front. The light-armed Greeks no doubt were stationed so as to give what protection they could to the flanks of the phalanx.

But the mere extension of the Greek line was not the principal feature of Miltiades' plan. Not only did he make the phalanx cover the whole Persian front, but he still further reduced the number of ranks in the center in order to increase them in the two wings. This strengthening of the flanks at the expense of the center gave the Greeks the best chance of success where it would be most profitable to obtain it, and where the enemy was accustomed to make his victorious effort.

The sight of the Persians embarking half their army while the other wing formed to close the beach road was clearly the opportunity for which Miltiades was waiting. The Greek army descended from its hill camp and formed opposite, and about a mile away from, the Persians who, as Herodotus says, were surprised to see so small a body venture to attack without either archers or cavalry. It is not necessary to believe that this means that there were no light-armed Greeks at all, merely that the Persians were not looking to have a close fight thrust upon them. Herodotus says that the Greeks having formed their line, then advanced on the Persians at a run; but it is impossible that heavily armed men could have run a mile and had strength remaining for a fight with unwearied foes. All through the history of warfare, both ashore and afloat, every prudent commander husbands the strength of his men to bring them fresh to the great exertions and exhausting emotions of battle. What is probable is that the attacking Greeks advanced slowly until they approached archer's range. There, just outside of range (say 200 yards)[1] they waited to rest and restore alignment, and when ready and the sacrifices were reported as favorable, they moved at speed through the fire zone and attacked with the spear in close formation.

The battle is described as long and obstinate. The weak Greek center was not strong enough to overcome the opposing archers, who were Persians by race and the best troops and who were armed also with short swords for in-fighting. On the contrary, the Persian center was able to break through the thin hostile line and pursue it towards the

---

[1] In the Middle Ages, extreme range extended over 100 yards farther, but was weak and random. To judge from contemporary sculpture, the Persian bows were weak.

hills. But the heavy Athenian wings, secure from envelopment, were successful and having broken their opponents they suffered them to go at will and, keeping well in hand, the two victorious wings, both turned on the Persian center. In this new situation the Greeks must have been nearer to the beach than the enemy, if, indeed, they did not actually interpose. In this second phase of the action, it became completely favorable to the Athenians. They destroyed the Persian center also and pursued it to the beach and laid hold of the ships to which the fugitives were escaping. They called for fire to destroy them,[2] and succeeded in capturing seven. When we think of the physical difficulty in wading out to take possession of ships manned by seamen and rowers who had not been engaged and were waiting only to rescue their comrades, it is evident that the defeat of the Persians must have been overwhelming to permit of as many as seven prizes. The Greek effort at the water's edge must have been the supreme one, for here fell the commander in chief as well as another of the ten generals, besides many others of note.

The Persians at Athens

The escaping ships with the defeated army went to Aegileia Island (see Map 6), about 8 miles away from Marathon, where they had confined their Eretrian captives and, having embarked them and the booty, followed the other division around Cape Sunium to the Bay of Phalerum off Athens. While the battle was in progress, the first division of the Persian force was on its way to the anchorage off Athens. It is not likely that it could have made the passage in less than 30 hours. The speed of such a great number of ships, laden with troops and spoil, must have been less than usual, not more than 2 knots. Thus it was that the victorious Greeks, not delaying for rejoicings, hastened back to Athens (only 26 miles away) and were able to camp outside the city on the hills above the port before the enemy had arrived. At Marathon they had camped on the ground of a temple to Hercules, so here they chose the precincts of another temple to the same deity who had brought them good fortune the day before.

The Spartans started from home at the full moon and made the march

---

[2] The Greeks called for fire, but we are not told they got it. The expression reminds us of the difficulty of procuring fire in the poorer regions of the United States until as recently as 60 years ago, when people whose hearth fire had gone out would go half a mile to get it from a neighbor rather than try to make it for themselves.

to Athens, of 140 miles, in 3 marching days.[3] They arrived before they were expected, on the seventeenth and only a few hours after the Athenian army returned. No doubt their presence still further discouraged the Persians, who made a brief stay at Phalerum for a junction with the second division of the fleet bringing the Eretrian captives, after which all departed for Asia.

Review of Campaign

The Athenian tradition magnified this great victory, and Creasy, in his *Fifteen Decisive Battles of the World,* includes it in his series. Such a place it scarcely deserves, for his defeat merely provoked the Great King to put forth the utmost might of Persia to overcome this petty people whence encouragement had come to his revolted subjects in 499 and who had now defeated and driven off his punitive expedition. He was resolved on an ethnic frontier like so many other great rulers, and for such as Europe has recently striven without success. But Darius did not live long enough to complete his preparations and left the accomplishment of the task to his son and successor, Xerxes. The decisive battles came ten years later in the sea battle of Salamis and still a year later on shore at Plataea, when European superiority in battle over Asiatics was established in that part of the world, the region of the Aegean, till the Turks came 1,500 years later.

In reviewing the campaign, whose tactics set the precedent for the conduct of later maritime effort, we must first note the supreme strategic and tactical skill shown by Miltiades. Although not the commander in chief, his hegemonic control over the Council of tribal leaders was such that he did with the army as he pleased. No doubt when the Athenians hastened from Athens towards the landing place of the enemy, they expected or thought it probable that the encounter would take place in the hills. But as they marched, successive runners must have told them that the enemy was inactive, on the beach. When the Athenians arrived and recognized that they held the entrance to the hills and were nearer to Athens by that route than the enemy was by the beach road, Miltiades

---

[3] Comparable in speed with the 25-hour march of 50 miles of the British Light Division in heavy marching order to join the army for the Battle of Talavera in 1809, but three times as far.

had the strategic insight to perceive that he could choose the place and time of battle. For him, delay was advantageous, for the Spartans were coming, although late. He therefore did nothing till the Persians should show their hand, confident that then he could fight them to advantage either in the hills, if they made a frontal attack on his camp, or as they embarked, if they took ship; or if they took the beach road he could forestall them before Athens.

As for the tactical features, Miltiades so managed it that there was no opportunity for the Persians to use the maneuver for which they were armed and trained, namely, the enveloping archers' fight. In their charge the heavy-armed Greeks were under fire scarcely more than a minute and a half, and in that time a good bowman could get off no more than seven or eight arrows.[4] The total losses of the Greeks were 192 killed against 6,400 Persians, and the severest fighting was in the close action when attempting to seize the ships. It is plain that the admirable thing above all was Miltiades' decision to attack the army of the great Empire and abide by the result. We can now see that the victory had to go to the spear and the panoply but it was to Miltiades' credit that he was the first of European Greeks to venture and win and show the way to many others.

This chapter has described the land fight at Marathon for two reasons, first because naval warfare in early times was largely an affair of landing and raiding for booty, as in this case; and, secondly, because the tactics of land fighting developed before their principles were applied in fleet battles. The tactics of Marathon became the norm of naval battle for the next generation, after which tactical novelties found a basis in improved ships handled by skillful seamen who were also thorough drill masters. Marathon taught the Greeks that successful land battle against Asiatics would be through the spear fight against missiles and the refusal of envelopment. We shall see the development of this idea in naval warfare as we go on.

The Victory at Marathon Was Inconclusive

The captives Datis brought back from Eretria were well treated by Darius who settled them on lands he gave them near Susa, his capital.

---

[4] In the middle ages 6 bowshots a minute was excellent practice.

But the capture of Eretria was a small accomplishment for the Great King. In spite of the final suppression of the Ionian revolt after years of effort, the campaign of Marathon must have greatly shaken Persian prestige, for the King's authority was based on his Medes and Persians by race who held in subjection a great number of unrelated and unsympathetic tribes and nations. The royal garrisons everywhere imposed peace and order under which labor and industry were remunerative to all the vast population of workers. If the King's armies failed for long to grant his subjects peace, his Empire would pass away like those of his predecessors, the Assyrians and the Babylonians.

A new attempt against Greece was therefore indispensable, and the King had been shown that he could establish a foothold in European Greece only by a force large enough to meet a formidable combination among the Greek states. This would require much time, for the organization of the Empire was such that it was a prolonged affair to call out the tribal levies to supplement the standing army of Persians by race. Not only the men but the munitions required time to provide, as we saw for ourselves in the recent great war. Besides, Darius was now growing old and it is very probable that his personal weakness was felt in the outlying provinces. However this may be, in 486 Egypt revolted and the next year the old King died. It was not until 484 that his successor, Xerxes, recovered Egypt, and was able to prepare for an European campaign.

PRINCIPAL AUTHORITIES CONSULTED FOR THIS CHAPTER

ANCIENT

Herodotus.
Aeschylus: *The Persians*.
Thucydides.

MODERN COMMENTATORS

Beloch, J.: *Bevölkerung der Griechische-Römischen Welt*.
Bury, J. B.: *History of Greece*.
Delbrueck, H.: *Geschichte der Kriegskunst*.
Grundy, G. B.: *The Great Persian War*.
Hauvette, A.: *Hérodote, Historien des Guerres Médiques*.
Kromayer-Veith: *Schlachten Atlas*
                Antike Schlachtfelder, Perser Krieg.
Macan, R. W.: *Herodotus*.
Munro, J. A. R.: *Cambridge Ancient History*, vol. 4.

APPENDIX TO CHAPTER II

TYPES OF ROWING SHIPS

Many learned writers of recent times, in dealing with the maritime affairs of the Greeks, make it plain that they consider little but the text of the classic writers. Even where they do consider the engineering and nautical difficulties raised by the text of the ancient writers, they abide by the written word. They analyze the phraseology and consider possible errors in copying, but few sufficiently reflect that these ships were practical constructions of a gifted race and must have been eminently successful in use. As an example, the article in the *Encyclopedia Britannica* on "ships" (edition 1911) says that it is wholly inadmissible to think that the ancients ever had any other arrangement than one man to one oar. The writer then goes on to talk of short oars of 12 to 14 feet and long oars of 53 feet. His statements show the absurdity of attempting to deal with a mechanical question on the basis of knowledge of the Greek language. Every mechanical engineer and every practical seaman knows that one man swinging an oar 53 feet long, weighing 450 to 500 pounds, could not get efficient work out of it. Going beyond the apparent meaning of the classical text, we have the right and the duty to examine whether such meaning is compatible with engineering and nautical efficiency, and, if not, I, for one, believe that the text lacks complete authority and must be glossed or construed into harmony with practical efficiency, or else totally rejected as erroneous and misleading. A bad design now must have been a bad design 2,500 years ago.

Among the various writers on the ship construction of the ancients, and particularly on the much-vexed subject of propulsion by oars, I shall be greatly guided by the authority of Rear Admiral Paul Serre, of the French Navy, whose classical studies in nautical matters were guided by his practical accomplishments as a seaman.

He stated in the introduction to his work, *Marines de Guerre de l'Antiquité et du Moyen Age,* that whereas his predecessors worked analytically, his method would be synthetic; he would work towards the past from things known and admitted by seamen and naval architects of today. The seasons and the climates, the ports and the high seas of the eastern Mediterranean, and the manual strength and dexterity of men are not now materially different from what they were at the beginning of history. He assumes that any ship which we may imagine to have been in use then must have been seaworthy, handy, swift, and strong, and if a reconstruction does not demonstrably possess these qualities, it must be cast aside.

Following Admiral Serre's suggestion and practice and working backward synthetically from known data, we must start with the long ships of the Middle Ages whose dimensions, costs, operation, and administration are well known to us from contemporary records. Shipbuilding was continuous through all the centuries and we cannot doubt the records and data of successful ships were handed down from father to son in families of successful shipwrights. The mechanical problems of every age were solved in accordance with the principles of mechanics which never changed.

I start, therefore, with the assumption that what we know of the long ships of the medieval times, the last of which went to Egypt with Bonaparte, in 1798, must be used to control our ideas of their prototypes of 500 B.C.

THE OAR AS MOTIVE POWER

Everything turns about the oar as the motive power, and the size of the oar depends on the size, weight, and number of the men who are to use it.

We all know how the oar is used. A man of average weight uses an oar 10 to 14 feet long. About one-third, or a little less (sometimes 27 per cent) of the length is inboard of the tholepin. A 12-foot ash oar weighs about 12 pounds.

For two men to sit on one thwart, each handling one 12-foot oar on his own side of the boat, the width of the boat between the tholepins should not be less than 6 feet. The distance which each sitting rower must have to swing his oar without hitting his neighbors in front and behind him is 3 feet; that is, there should be 3 feet between successive tholepins and successive thwarts for best efficiency. It is known that for the Greeks this distance was standard,

It is also a constructional fact that a ratio of ten beams to the length of a ship is the utmost that can be permitted if the ship is not to become too slender; and even this was inadvisable in the days of wooden ships. The French and Italian galleys seldom had as high a ratio as 8 to 1, although this figure was sometimes reached. The remains of the Greek dockyards at the Piraeus indicate the same proportions.

If we consider the other dimensions of a craft of 6-foot beam, we may admit that she may be as long as 48 feet without becoming structurally too weak.

Experience has shown that the draft of seagoing craft should not exceed one-half the beam, nor is it usually less than one-fourth when deep loaded. One-fifth the beam is found in recent Mediterranean small craft (see *Souvenirs de Marine,* by Vice Admiral Paris). One-third is an ordinary ratio of draft to beam. Such a craft 48'x6'x2' with a block coefficient of 0.55[1] would displace about 9 tons.

It will be seen later on that 7 knots (8.07 statute miles per hour) was a high speed.

For this craft (adding for keel) we have wetted surface equal to 340 sq. ft. For a speed of 7 knots the frictional resistance is 114 lbs., and residual 75 lbs., giving a total resistance of 189 lbs. and an effective horsepower of 4.0.[2]

If we increase the length of our boat to 60 feet while retaining the same cross section, the length available for rowers will increase somewhat faster than the resistance, so the longer boat would be a trifle faster, but weaker and less seaworthy.

We must not forget that in these long ships built to prey on com-

---

[1] *Block coefficient* is the ratio of the ship's immersed volume to that of the containing parallelepipedon, i.e., V/LBH where V = volume of immersed ship's body, L = length, B = beam, and H = draft of water.

[2] The *effective horsepower* is calculated by Taylor's formula (see *Encyclopedia Britannica*—"Ship-building," 11th Edition).

The fluid resistance to the movement of the ship is made up of two parts, known as the frictional and the residual resistances. The first reference is proportional to the wetted surface (submerged surface) of the hull, and for 7 knots is about $\frac{1}{3}$ lb. per sq. ft. It varies as $S^{1.83}$ where S is speed.

The wetted surface is calculated by the formula, W.S. = $L \times H \times 1.7 + V/H$, where L = length, H = draft, V = displacement in cu. ft., and W.S. is in sq. ft.

The second, or residual resistance is calculated roughly by the formula $R_r = bD^{\frac{2}{3}}V^4/L$, where R_r is the resistance in pounds, D is the displacement in tons, V is the speed in knots, and b is a variable coefficient, being as much as 0.45 or more for broad cargo ships and only 0.35 for fine-lined ships.

merce, although the chief requisite was speed, yet other qualities were very essential and could not be unduly sacrificed.

In the simple system of oars, where every man sat on his own thwart and manned his own oar, his labor was most efficient. The number of men that could be employed in rowing was proportional to the length of side available for oars. Yet the whole length of side could not be used. At the bows room was needed for handling anchors, besides which the ship forward becomes too narrow for the oars. At the stern, the helmsman needed room, the passengers and soldiers also needed space.

So in our hypothetical boat of 48 feet in length, we might put 12 oars on a side, occupying 36 feet in length.

We know that U. S. Navy light racing cutters of 31 feet in length, with fixed seats, can do 7.0 knots in a 3-mile race, and trials in the model tank show that at this speed the crew of twelve men must develop 2.05 effective horsepower, or $\frac{1}{6}$ effective horsepower per man. As these men are selected for weight, strength, and skill, we may assume that a man of average weight, not too well fed, can develop $\frac{1}{7}$ e.hp. in a simple system of oars.

This assumption as to the mechanical efficiency of the average man at his own 10- to 14-foot oar will be the basis of all future consideration of systems of rowing, both ancient and medieval.

Then if one man is good enough for $\frac{1}{7}$ hp. the hypothetical fast boat of 48 feet mentioned above, with 12 oars on a side, could scarcely make 7 knots, for she would develop only 3.5 e.hp., whereas 4.0 is needed for 7 knots.

By stripping her light to 5.5 tons, carrying little more than the rowers and their oars, it might be possible to drive her at $7\frac{2}{3}$ knots, over a 3-mile course.

We must now pass to a physiological point which may be learned from any good handbook that a man working for 8 hours a day can only develop about one-fourth the horsepower he is capable of putting forth for a spurt of say 20 minutes. Hence we perceive that a man working on his own oar for a watch of 4 hours can develop little more than 3.5 per cent of a horsepower, and the corresponding power for the 48-foot boat would be less than 1 hp., giving scarcely 4.5 knots. A longer exertion than 20 minutes at full power would result in complete exhaustion, and, indeed, the seamen of 300 years ago, writing of their experiences (in much heavier ships with more rowers), say that a speed of 4.5 knots could not be maintained for more than an hour, after which it fell off rapidly.

The 48-foot boat described above, although the speediest possible for a simple system of installment of oars, would not be a serviceable type; for she would be somewhat crowded by her rowers alone, and fit only for smooth waters. The Greeks found larger craft were desirable for service and the engineering problem of the ancients, which modern students must solve anew, was to find an arrangement of oars practicable in larger craft which will give the highest speed and yet not be irreconcilable with the majority of ancient evidence. Withal, an acceptable solution must offer in a high degree the qualities of seaworthiness and habitability which we know *a priori* ancient craft must have had.

It is first necessary to state the engineering rule. For ships of similar proportions, the displacement of the ship increases as the cube of the linear dimensions, yet for equal moderate speeds, necessary power increases only as the square of the linear dimensions.

In the present day, the weight of machinery and consequent power which it is possible to put in the ship is directly proportional to her displacement or to the cube of the linear dimensions.

As the power necessary to drive the big ship at any speed increases in a less ratio than the displacement, it is clear that big ships nowadays are capable of higher speeds than smaller ones. But when oars were the means of propulsion, it was the length of side along which the men were placed to row which limited the development of power. As we have seen, the simple system of oars reached its greatest speed in a 48-foot boat of 9 tons or less, and this craft was too small to be generally serviceable with the number of men required to row her at fast speed.

The engineering problem being to increase the number of rowers per running foot of side, we know that medieval seamen had two ways of accomplishing it. One way, the earlier, was to incline the rowers' thwarts from the transverse direction so that they tended somewhat aft from outboard. Three rowers each with his own oar (of differing lengths) were seated on the same inclined thwart. The tholepins were about 8 inches apart in each group and the thwarts were spaced about 4 feet apart.

This gave a density of rowers of one man to each 16 inches of side, instead of one to 36 inches, as in the simple system. This way of rowing was known as "zenzile" (see p. 35).

This compound system called for longer oars (the inboard rower on each thwart who pulled the after oar of his group had an oar 36 feet long.[3] The outboard man had one several feet shorter). Of course, these great oars were not as handy as smaller ones, the stroke was slow and the individual rowers were not quite so efficient, but the number of men per running foot of side was greater and that was the crucial point.

But as the medieval ships increased in size, it became necessary further to increase the density of rowers if speed was not to be sacrificed, and another rower on the same thwart would need a still longer oar, which was impracticable for one man to handle. The solution adopted about the middle of the sixteenth century was a single oar to each thwart with four men on every oar; and later, a 42-foot oar, with five men ("scaloccio" system). Still later, in the great galleasses of the seventeenth century, nine and ten men, facing each other in double ranks, manned each oar. Thus several men working on one great oar divided among them the waste work of swinging it and could provide more power in the same length of side than by short oars with one man to each. And this was true even though the efficiency of the men on the great oar was less.

These great oars required a spacing of 55 inches between tholepins and were 53 to 58 feet long. The backs of the crew of each oar were in contact with the backs of the adjoining crews, and each man was in contact with his neighbor on his own oar. The work was even less efficient than the earlier compound form. But the density of rowers per running foot of side was one man to every 6 inches. We know very well that such methods were practiced for contemporary records are ample and indisputable.[4]

These long oars, known as sweeps, were furnished to the largest battleships of the British Navy until after the Napoleonic wars. They were used for working the ship in calms. In 1816, British 100-gun ships of the line had 52-foot sweeps with four or five men on each side of each.[5]

---

[3] See Fincati: *Le Triremi;* also Vice Admiral Paris: *Souvenirs de Marine,* vol. V.

[4] See the models in the Louvre and in the Arsenal, Venice.

[5] Steel: *Elements of Seamanship,* vol. 1, p. 180. Edition of 1821.

From the certainty of medieval systems of propulsion, we must now go back to consider the ancient Greek system, and how they increased the density of rowers without undue sacrifice either of rowing efficiency or of indispensable nautical qualities.

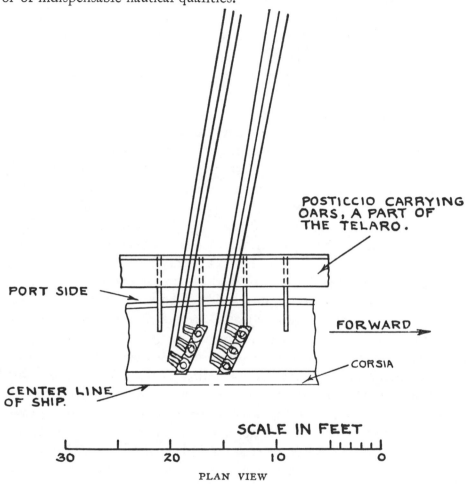

PLAN VIEW

Showing Three Oars to Each Bench, Zenzile System

We have seen that a boat of 48x6 feet would be the fastest that could be propelled by the simple system of oars, i.e., one man and one oar on each side to each thwart, with 36 inches between thwarts. But such boats would be too crowded with their rowers. To have larger boats, with more rowers per running foot of side, we need wider ships. If we take 18 inches as the width of a man, the minimum width for an efficient compound system of oars with two men to one oar, or two oars to each thwart, will be 9 feet. Such ships, based on two men (double compound) were called biremes, dieres, dicrotes. The 9-foot boat would scarcely be less than 6 beams nor more than 8 beams in length, and when light would draw not less than 0.2 her beam and when deep, not over 0.3 her beam.

The shortest of these boats, 54 feet, might have 13 oars on a side, with two men to each oar, except on the forward pair, which would have only one man each on account of the reduced beam near the bow. With a 9-foot beam, the inboard length of the oar would be 4.5 feet, and the second man would be 18 inches from the end. While the inboard man would pull his full stroke, the second man could only do two-thirds a full stroke and he could scarcely pull harder, so that the two men would do only one and two-thirds units of man power. As this is $\frac{1}{7}$ e.hp., the boat's whole crew would develop $[(24 \times \frac{5}{3}) + 2] \times \frac{1}{7} = 6.0$ e.hp. The boat being light, i.e., at $\frac{9}{5} = 1.8$ feet draft, her displacement would be about 13.75 tons. Her wetted surface with keel would be 482 sq. ft. and her e.hp. would be good for 7.3 knots. For the larger ship of 8 beams in length and 0.3 beam in draft, there might be 17 thwarts on a side, accommodating 68 of the rowers, who would develop 8.1 e.hp. while the boat would displace 27.5 tons with 739 sq. ft. of wetted surface and the e.hp. available would be good for about 7.3 knots.

Thus the compound system of oars enables the large craft when deep to equal the speed of the smaller craft when light, both of 9-foot beam.

In the arrangement above described, the long oars with 2 men to each oar make the arrangement known to the later Italians as *scaloccio*.

By the *zenzile* method, with two oars to one thwart, the early Italians were able to get one rower to each 21 inches of ship's side, each man working his own oar, which was not very long. Thus, the 72-foot boat, which we were just considering, with 17 thwarts when fitted for scaloccio rowing, would have only room for 14 zenzile thwarts (and a little more) with the same number of men per thwart. But as the outboard man would be able to apply nearly full power to his oar, we should have 56 men each developing a nearly complete unit of rowing work, $\frac{1}{7}$ e.hp., or 8.0 in all. This is almost the same as the *scaloccio* system, developed in the same length of side, with 12 more men.

Ancient Ships

So far as we can see from the innumerable sculptures and records of the ancient system of rowing, they did not employ the zenzile system of the Italians, but a modification of it.

It is clear that they had two or three rows of oars at different levels, and the rowers of each rank had only 36 inches between them. The lower row of men had shorter oars and necessarily must have sat outboard of the upper rank.

Early Pentekonter

But the boat of 9-foot beam and 55 to 70 feet long, discussed previously, was the minimum size; it was so small that its rowing crew alone

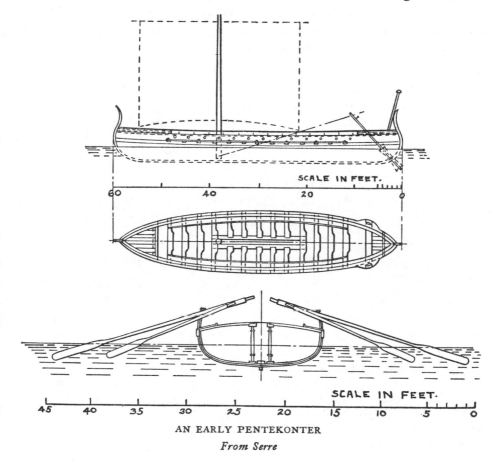

SCALE IN FEET.

SCALE IN FEET.

AN EARLY PENTEKONTER

From Serre

would have crowded it. It could only have been a dispatch boat. A serviceable fighting ship must have been somewhat wider, to give deck room for the soldiers and seamen, and deeper to carry supplies, arms, and water. I take it, therefore, that the pentekonter, which was the standard fighting ship until about the beginning of the fifth century B.C., was a diere or bireme with two men on each side of each thwart, and somewhat larger than the minimum, and I shall accept Admiral Serre's reconstruction of her. His reconstruction of Jason's *Argo*, a pentekonter (from *Revue Maritime et Coloniale*, May, 1891), is shown on p. 37. It differs from the pentekonters of the fifth century in having no spur on the bow, for Admiral Serre does not think the evidence of sketches on vases is conclusive. The bow as drawn would undoubtedly cut down an enemy, as we know from experience in collisions with boats of similar weight today.

I quote from his description. Although we cannot suppose it to be exact, yet it is an approximate solution, a seaworthy, handy, practicable boat.

The rowing space has 13 thwarts. On each of these thwarts, except the forward one, which is rather short, there are two rowers on each side (to each oar). The oars shipped on tholepins 0.80 meter (31.5 inches) above the load water line are 6 meters (19.7 feet) long. The width of the boat is that of our large launches, 3.6 meters (11.8 feet); draft 0.55 meter (21.7 inches). Amidships a fore-and-aft plank (the gang-board) a foot wide gives a passageway from end to end.

As the boat was meant frequently to be hauled up on the beach, there were two side keels besides the center one to take on rollers. Inside the boat, above the side keels, were two lines of stanchions tying the thwarts to the bottom of the boat and stiffening the whole structure.

The high decked foresheets protects the hawsers and the provisions. The stern sheets was the captain's quarters and the armory. The total length is 18 meters (59 feet), rowers space, allowing 0.92 meter (3 feet) between tholepins, is 12 meters (39.3 feet). The displacement, with midship section of 1.8 sq. m. (19.4 sq. ft.) is 22 tons, made up as follows: 60 men with clothes, arms, provisions, and water for 8 days, 9 tons (330 lbs. a head); equipment, 3 tons; weight of hull, 10 tons. The area of midship section for each rower is 3.6 square decimeters (56 sq. in.). This is about the same as for our launches when light (French Navy, 1880) with two men to an oar.

The pentekonter, being larger and longer, the oars better arranged, and the sum of the blade surfaces being more than three times that of the midship section, the craft should have a high speed with a maximum approaching 6 knots.[6]

The mast is vertical, stepped forward of amidships, its heel ships in a socket which holds it when handling it. It may be lowered by its stays while its heel is steadied in a mast box built between the thwarts, until the head rests on a pillow block on the after deck. This mast carries one or two square sails, jibs,[7] and a large lug sail (*aurique*) similar to those still used in the Archipelago. The stem and sternpost are carried above the decked ends. They give a hand-hold when the ship rolls. The tack of the jib is secured to the stem. An awning stretched from poop to forecastle with side curtains shelters the crew at night. a weather cloth on the windward side, above the gunwale from poop to fore-castle, keeps out spray when the sea is rough.

The officers and leading men have their battle stations on the high decked ends.

The rowers have offensive and defensive arms at hand and their fighting stations are by their respective oars.

The arrangement of the oars is shown on p. 40. The long oars manned by two men are attached by grummets to the tholepins. The pins are 0.8 meter (31.5 inches) above the water which is a suitable height for an oar 6 meters (20 feet) long, the ratio of height above water to length is 13 per cent. The tholepin divides the length of the oar in the ratio 27 to 73 which is good for seated men and rapid stroke. The stroke is 30 a minute and there is a man to every 18 inches of side. The depth of the stroke up and down is 18 inches and the length horizontal is 20 inches, quite practicable for this style of work.[8]

The thwarts, as in all undecked boats, serve as cross ties. They are there-fore at right angles to the keel, but their width is 7 inches at the side and 12 inches amidships. They have considerable crown, so that the two rowers are relatively in good positions, as the inboard man sits higher and farther aft than his mate. The oar is nearly level during the recover, which makes it serviceable in nearly all weather.

There is little to improve in this arrangement of rowing for full speed, but at reduced speed and for current service, it would not be so good. So suit-able arrangements were made. At 27 inches above the water line, that is, half-

[6] This craft being nearly 12 feet wide, the oars are longer than in the boat of 9-foot beam before mentioned; consequently the length of stroke of the outboard man sitting close to the inboard one will be a greater proportion of his full stroke and will be 0.73 of the inboard man. As the oar is not heavy for two men to handle, the 50 men will develop $[(24 \times 1.73) + 2] \times \frac{1}{7} = 6.2$ e.hp. The wetted surface by the usual rule is 608 sq. ft. Consequently her maximum speed for a short spurt would be 6.9 knots.

[7] Admiral Serre's views as to jibs are not generally accepted, as jibs are said to be only a couple of centuries old.

[8] A very short stroke for full speed.

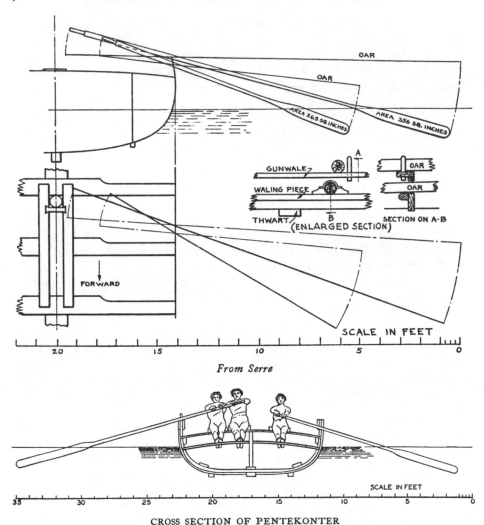

From Serre

CROSS SECTION OF PENTEKONTER

Showing Two Men on Long Oar Port Side for Speed, One
Man on Short Oar Starboard Side for Endurance

There are three ways of rowing the *Argo*: p. 37 shows two men on same thwart rowing two oars; p. 40 shows two men on same thwart rowing one oar (port side, preferable); p. 40 shows half crew working, one man on thwart rowing one oar (starboard side).

way between the gunwale and the thwarts, a row of ports was cut for oars,[9] only 4 meters (13 feet) long, manned by single rowers. The ratio of length

[9] The Gokstad Viking ship of the ninth century now at Oslo has oar ports cut through the side with shutters.

to height is 16 per cent and the oar is divided by the port in the ratio 28 to 72. The angular movements of the stroke, both vertical and horizontal, are greater with less linear movement than the long oar and the blade has a relatively greater surface. All these conditions are highly suitable for a slow long and continued stroke in smooth water.

The relative position of the two oars of a group and the inside waling piece which carries the rowlocks are shown on p. 40. By the presence of this waling piece, a unireme pentekonter (single row of oars) may be changed into a bireme (double row of oars).

The Hecatonter

The ancient records mention also hecatonters, or ships with a hundred rowers. If these were of the same type as the pentekonter with two men to each oar, the rowing space must have been 75 feet long and the ship could not have been less than about 100 feet long. As we have just seen, the pentekonter was 12 feet in beam in order to place four men abreast each other and be able to handle their oars efficiently. Moreover, as it was not good practice to build a wooden craft with more than 8 beams in her length, we see that the hecatonter was the largest possible diere that could maintain the speed of smaller ones. If the ship were to be made longer, structural strength would require her also to be wider and deeper. But for a given cross section (the minimum for 2-man oars) an increase of length would bring little increase in speed.

A hecatonter of 100′x12′x21″ and 55 per cent block coefficient would displace 33 tons and by the rules previously given could make 12.3 e.hp. and 7.9 knots for a short spurt. The same craft loaded to 3.0 feet draft would displace about 60 tons and with 100 rowers would reach a speed of 7.3 knots. As the hecatonter must have been at least 8 feet deep for necessary strength and her oars cannot have been carried over 3 feet above the water, they must have been shipped through ports cut through the side, like the ones of the Viking ships[9] known to us.

Yet, such a craft would attain its speed at the expense of other most desirable qualities and it is evident that the pentekonter must have been better for general service as they were more used. The hecatonter was a luxury craft rather than for service, like the very long Swedish church boats of the last century, whose models may be seen in Swedish museums.

The Triere

So the desire for larger craft led to the invention of the "triere" whereby the number of rowers per running foot of side was increased and so permitted increase of size without serious loss in speed.

All the evidence from ancient writers, from coins, sculptures, paintings, and inscriptions is that in the triere oars were in three rows, one above the other. The celebrated relief from the Acropolis of Athens shows three rows of oars one above the other, and the interval compared to the figures of the men (see opposite page) shows that each man had 3 feet in his own row. Although only the upper row of men is seen, the vertical distance between the rows of oars is 12 or 13 inches.

Taking any group of three rowers on different levels, the upper man (thranite) sat well inboard pulling a long oar. The man in the middle rank (zygite) sat 14 inches lower, 18 inches outboard, and 9 inches forward. Thus his head was between two oars worked by the men above him. Similarly, the man in the lowest rank (thalamite) pulled the shortest oar and was 14 inches lower, 18 inches outboard, and 9 inches forward of his zygite neighbor, so that his head was under the oar of the thranite of the next group forward.

We cannot doubt that this manner of rowing was used. The evidence is too strong to reject. But since the oars were of different length and weight, the highest efficiency could scarcely be reached with the same length and rapidity of stroke for all sizes of oars. We know that a racing stroke for a 12-foot oar is 36 and even 40 a minute, whereas the renaissance 36- to 42-foot oars, with as many as 5 men to each, never made over 26 strokes a minute. Particularly, were the sea to become rough the three ranks would almost certainly embarrass each other. It is therefore probable that the ancients did not go into battle nor maintain their ships under service conditions with one man to each oar. I prefer to agree with Admiral Serre that the "simultaneous" stroke, as he calls it, with every oar manned, was a parade and review stroke like the Prussian "goose step," not very efficient, but showy and used for ceremonies, when the people on shore cheered the fleet as it entered or left port.

The arrangement of oars for battle and for general service, according to Serre's solution, entailed only simple changes from the "simultaneous" arrangement. For battle, the zygite benches (which were movable) were

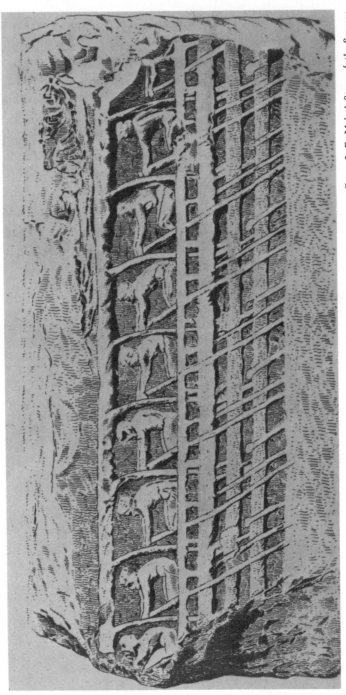

A BAS-RELIEF FOUND ON THE ACROPOLIS AT ATHENS

Representing the midship part of a triere of the approximate time of the Peloponnesian War. Note that all oars are manned but only the upper rowers are shown. There is a catastroma over the rowers.

raised a few inches and the zygite and thalamite rowers sat with the thranites at the long thranite oars. With three men at each oar the stroke was quick and the greatest speed could be reached. However, a certain loss of efficiency was unavoidable. The thranite rower, the heaviest of each crew of three, took his full reach, but the other two could not do so because they were nearer the tholepin, about which the oar swung, and so their work was proportionately reduced. The greater the inboard length of each oar, the more nearly the effort of the outboard men approached that of the inboard one. With a loom 6 feet long and the men 18 inches apart, the respective pulls would be as 1.0, 0.75, and 0.5, and the whole effort of the triple crew would be 2.25 units. As each unit of work (for the inboard man) is $\frac{1}{7}$ e.hp., each oar could develop 0.321 e.hp.

For a long effort of 2 or 3 hours, men can develop only about one-fourth of that of which they are capable for a short spurt of, say, 20 minutes, and the crew of three men will develop about 0.088 e.hp.[10]

For an effort of 5 or 6 hours, the crew would go into watches and to increase efficiency the oars should be shorter. In two watches the rowers would man three-fourths of the zygite oars with two men to each oar and each oar would develop about 0.065 e.hp. For an all-day trip, the rowers would be in three watches, manning the thalamite oars with one man each and each oar would develop about 0.035 e.hp. These units of work for oars under varying conditions will be used later to estimate speeds of differing types of ship.

The advantage of three rows of oars is very evident to all seamen who are acquainted with the difficulties of rowing in rough weather—short thalamite oars for smooth water and long sustained effort; zygite oars with two men on each for rougher water and moderately long distances; and long thranite oars with full crew for battle. In very rough water the rowing battle ships could not row and could survive with difficulty.

Having considered the oars in some detail, we are now able to discuss what sort of a ship the triere must have been to use such oars.

The triere, like the diere, needed considerable width to give stability

---

[10] The zygite and thalamite who could not exert their full capacity at full speed on account of their short stroke will be able, at reduced speed, to deliver somewhat more than one-quarter of what they did at full speed by a stronger pull than the thranite.

when the fighting men were moving from side to side. Whereas, in modern small boats, the crews are trained to avoid standing in order that the center of gravity may be kept low, in ancient ships (rowing) the oarsmen had to sit higher the larger the ship was, in order to be properly placed at the successive rows of oars. Consequently, the minimum width of a triere, seating two more rowers in the width of the ship than the diere, must have been at least 13 feet, in order to provide stability and that the length of the oar inside the tholepin might be enough for the inboard rower to render a good share of the work.

It is alleged that trieres were built as early as the seventh century B.C., but they did not come into general use until the beginning of the fifth century. Until then, pentekonters had been the predominant type of large men-of-war. We know that in the Peloponnesian War Athenian trieres had crews of 200 men, but it would be an error to believe that the earliest ones were as large. Progress is slow, so it is proper to believe that the trieres of Salamis were not unlike the pentekonters they superseded. Probably the chief change in design from the pentekonter was the provision of a complete deck under the rowers. The protective deck above the rowers (catastroma) did not appear in the early trieres.

Let us work out the minimum size of a triere. We have already decided on a beam of 13 feet at the water line. The minimum length for this beam would be about 6 beams or, say, 75 feet. This would give room for 15 thranite oars on a side or 90 rowers in all. Add to these 10 officers and seamen and 20 soldiers to make up a total crew of 120 men. From the working drawings of rowing craft of the sixteenth, seventeenth, and eighteenth centuries which have been preserved, we know that the hull weighed not over 50 per cent of the load displacement, the equipment (masts, sails, anchors, oars, etc.) about 17 per cent, and the crew, provisions, and other cargo about 33 per cent or a little more. Sixteenth century galleys carried provisions and water for several weeks and artillery but the ancient men-of-war carried only a few days' food and water. Contemporary writers mention that ships took on board 2 or 3 days' supplies and went on service. We allow 5 days' water and provisions making the weight for each man 270 pounds;[11] 120 men make the

---

[11] Weight of man, 150 lbs.; clothes, 12 lbs.; arms and armor, 28 lbs.; food, 3 lbs. a day; firewood, 2 lbs. a day; water, 1 gal. a day, weighing in casks or earthenware 11 lbs.—for 5 days, 80 lbs., a total of 270 lbs. per man.

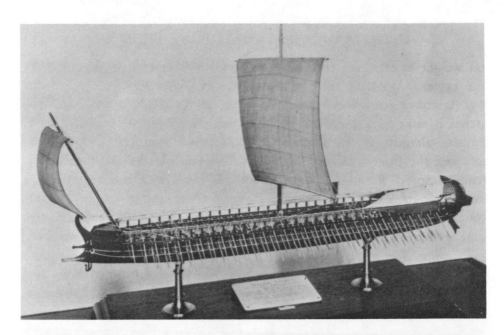

Top: Model of Triere, date of Peloponnesian War, by C. Busley. Extreme length 36.5 m; Beam at water line 4.27 m; Draft 0.93 m; Displacement 82 tons; Crew 200 men; Rowers 170; Seamen, Soldiers and Officers 30. Is without a catastroma. Has an awning. Courtesy of Deutsches Museum, München.

Bottom: View of Admiral Serre's triere, time of the Peloponnesian War. Length 40 m; Beam 4.4 m; Draft 1.1 m; Displacement 129 tons; Water and rations for 20 days; Crew 200 men in all; Rowers 144 men. Courtesy le Musée de la Marine, Louvre.

total weight of crew and rations 15.0 tons and the load displacement a scant 45 tons. With 15 oars on a side at full speed the e.hp. would be 9.63. At cruising speed with full crew the e.hp. would be 2.64; in two watches it would be 1.47 and in three watches, 1.05. From data and formulas already given, the corresponding full speed would be 7.2 knots and the three cruising speeds 4.8 knots, 4.0 knots, and 3.5 knots. Squadron speed would be less, for some ships would always be foul-bottomed. Such a craft would have a raised poop and forecastle for the pilot and the fighting men. As the rowers were unprotected overhead they must have worn some defensive armor which interfered perhaps with their rowing. Their arms of attack lay beside them and ancient sculptures show that the shields of the rowers were placed along and above the gunwale, when not in use, to offer some protection from missiles. As the space below the deck was occupied by stores, men had to sleep on deck; and an awning was an important part of the ships' outfit in order to have partial shelter from the weather.

The Trieres of the Peloponnesian War

The early trieres of Salamis were soon improved upon. Cimon, son of Miltiades, led the Athenian fleet to victory at Eurymedon in 466 with larger vessels, whose rowers were protected from the enemy by a deck (catastroma) above them, which also afforded high positions for the seamen and soldiers, who no longer stood along the sides between the oars to the embarrassment of all.

We are told that these large trieres were manned by 200 men, of whom 18 were soldiers. About 20 more must have been needed as officers, row masters, and seamen, leaving 162 available as rowers. We may attempt to reconstruct such a ship of the minimum size.[12]

---

[12] 162 rowers will man 27 oars on a side, making a rowing space 81 ft. long. To this we add 24 ft. for the ends of the ship, giving her a total length of 105 ft. The catastroma with the men on it raises the center of gravity, in spite of training the men to sit on the deck when casting their javelins, so she should have a 14.5-foot beam at the water line for stability. 200 men with 5 days' food, water, and firewood at 270 lbs. each make 54,000 lbs. and will be 35 per cent of the total displacement, making the latter 69 tons. At a block coefficient of fineness of 52.5 per cent the draft will be 3.0 ft. and the wetted surface, 1,390 sq. ft. Fifty-four 3-man oars will develop 17.33 e.hp., giving a speed for a short spurt of 7.8 knots and corresponding cruising speeds of 5.3, 4.3, and 3.7 knots for whole crew, and in two and three watches. (A smaller ship than Serre's on account of fewer rations, but otherwise similar.)

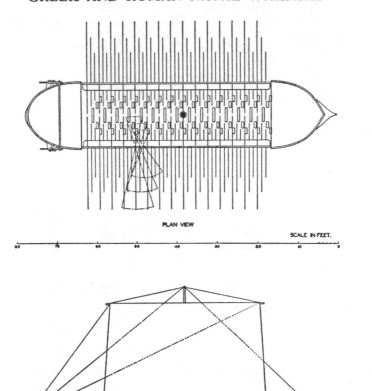

PLAN VIEW

SCALE IN FEET.

OUTBOARD PROFILE

SCALE IN FEET

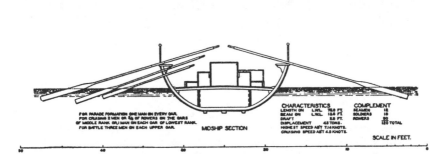

FOR PARADE FORMATION ONE MAN ON EVERY OAR.
FOR CRUISING 2 MEN OR 2/3 OF ROWERS ON THE OARS
OF MIDDLE RANK. OR, 1 MAN ON EACH OAR OF LOWEST RANK.
FOR BATTLE THREE MEN ON EACH UPPER OAR.

MIDSHIP SECTION

CHARACTERISTICS		COMPLEMENT	
LENGTH ON L.W.L.	76.0 FT.	SEAMEN	12
BEAM ON L.W.L.	13.5 FT.	SOLDIERS	18
DRAFT	2.9 FT.	ROWERS	90
DISPLACEMENT	43 TONS.		120 TOTAL
HIGHEST SPEED ABT 7.14 KNOTS.			
CRUISING SPEED ABT 4.5 KNOTS.			

SCALE IN FEET.

RECONSTRUCTION OF A TRIERE OF THE EARLY PART OF THE FIFTH
CENTURY B.C.

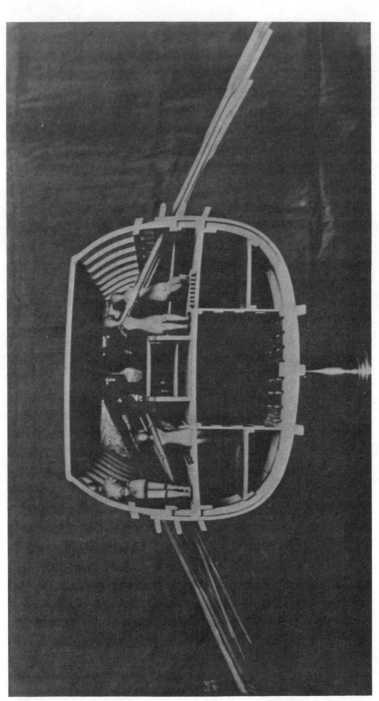

ADMIRAL SERRE'S ARRANGEMENT OF OARS IN A TRIERE

PORT SIDE: thalamite oars only, manned for a full day's voyage. Port side, Forward: (faint) all oars manned by full crew, 1 man each, for parade.   STARBOARD SIDE: zygite oars only, manned by 2 rowers each. Starboard side, Forward: (faint) thranite oars manned by full crew, 3 men each oar.

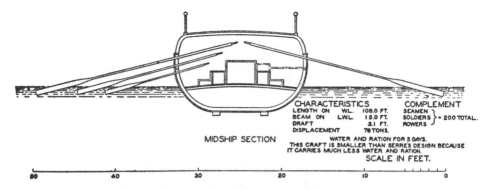

CHARACTERISTICS		COMPLEMENT	
LENGTH ON WL.	108.0 FT.	SEAMEN	
BEAM ON LWL.	15.0 FT.	SOLDIERS	= 200 TOTAL.
DRAFT	3.1 FT.	ROWERS	
DISPLACEMENT	78 TONS.		

MIDSHIP SECTION

WATER AND RATION FOR 5 DAYS.
THIS CRAFT IS SMALLER THAN SERRE'S DESIGN BECAUSE
IT CARRIES MUCH LESS WATER AND RATION.

SCALE IN FEET.

CATAPHRACT TRIERE OF PELOPONNESIAN WAR

This vessel is similar in general appearance to Admiral Serre's model. There may have been a somewhat raised poop or perhaps only a platform to let the helmsman see clearly ahead.

She would have a displacement of 69 tons with a length of 105 feet, beam at water line of 14.5 feet, and a draft of 3.0 feet. Her speed would be rather high, about 7.8 knots, when racing, and over 5 knots when cruising for not over 3 hours with all the rowers at work.

The cross section shown is of a slightly larger hull.

Photographs of Admiral Serre's triere of the date of the Peloponnesian War, showing cross section and crew are shown opposite.

In the National Museum at Munich is a model of another type of reconstruction of the Peloponnesian triere by Carl Busley, Chief Constructor of the German Navy, which is fully described in *Technische Gesellschaft fur Schiffbau*, 1919. It is without the catastroma, and the

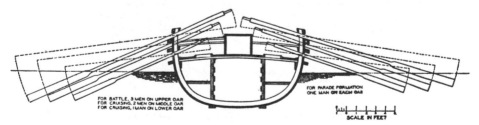

FOR BATTLE, 3 MEN ON UPPER OAR
FOR CRUISING, 2 MEN ON MIDDLE OAR
FOR CRUISING, 1 MAN ON LOWER OAR

FOR PARADE FORMATION
ONE MAN ON EACH OAR

SCALE IN FEET

MIDSHIP SECTION OF AN EARLY APHRACT TRIERE

Arrangement of Oars According to Admiral Serre

This cross section differs from the preceding in placing the lower rowers in a standing position on the partial lower deck and with their bodies rising through a hatchway. When all rowers were on the upper oars, the benches for the outboard rowers were raised,

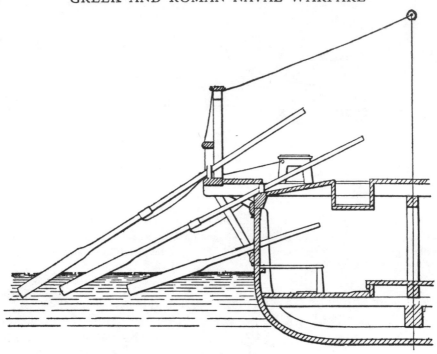

CROSS SECTION

CHARACTERISTICS		COMPLEMENT	
LENGTH ON WL.	115FT.	CAPTAIN	1
BEAM ON LWL.	14FT.	OFFICERS	11
DRAFT	3FT.	SOLDIERS	18
		ROWERS	170
			200 TOTAL

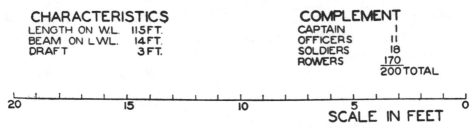

SCALE IN FEET

DRAWING OF MODEL OF A TRIREME IN THE GERMAN
NATIONAL MUSEUM AT MUNICH

Reconstruction by C. Busley, due to "Jahrbuch der Schiffbau Technischen Gesellschaft," 1919
Cross section of ship, model of which appears opposite page 45.

thranite oars are carried on an outrigger platform extending beyond the ship's side.[13]

---

[13] Length at water line, 114 ft.; beam at water line, 14 ft.; draft, 3 ft.; displacement, 82 tons. The beam across the outriggers between tholepins is 18.4 ft. With 170 oars as Busley gives her, she ought to have nearly 25 e.hp. but the oars are short and I do not think they would be as efficient as in the other arrangement described above. Even so, she would probably be as fast.

Top: Stern of a ship cut in rock at Lindos, island of Rhodes, shows rounded stern fit for hauling up on the beach, also outrigger for oars; steering rudder laid level for beaching and couch for pilot to observe the stars.

Bottom: Stone ship on island in the Tiber at Rome, showing outrigger for oars at *B*. From engraving by Piranesi in 18th century when the ruin was in better condition than at present.

Dispatch Boats

Here we may mention dispatch boats which were used for so many centuries for admirals and their aides to move up and down the line before and during battle, as well as for reconnaissance and message bearing. We probably have the partial model of one of the late fourth century B.C. in the pedestal of the famous Victory of Samothrace, at the Louvre.[14] Although this pedestal has been regarded by most commentators as a reduction of the largest type of vessel, yet it is a more artistic idea to place a Victory on a dispatch boat moving along the line of heavy ships and encouraging the combatants, precisely as every naval commander was accustomed to do before battle. The casts from ancient medals showing this statue, which are to be seen beside it at the Louvre, have the figure standing on the forecastle and blowing a trumpet, a customary use of a

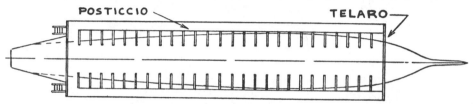

PLAN VIEW SHOWING MEDIEVAL ROWING FRAME

Length of rowing frame 119 feet. *Telaro* was the whole frame. *Posticcio* carried the oars and rested on the knees as shown, latter also bore the platform for soldiers.

dispatch boat, as a repeating ship for signals. The pedestal itself shows that the ship was fitted with sponsons to serve as outriggers for tholepins. The arrangement accomplishes the same purpose as the *telaro*[15] of the medieval galleys (see diagram). The stern of a ship with a similar outrigger, probably a triere, is shown in a relief at Rhodes, of which a photograph is given in the *Geographical Magazine*, December, 1926. The stone ship on the island in the Tiber at Rome shows the same sponson, so we may believe that the sponson was a feature which lasted through a long period.

With these three ancient sculptures as guides, we may attempt a reconstruction of a late pentekonter with a crew of 55 men. With 4 days'

[14] The most recent opinion is that this statue commemorates the Battle of Cos in 258 B.C. and was erected by Antigonus Gonatas.

[15] The *telaro* was a rectangular frame for carrying the oars. It was firmly secured to the deck and its longitudinal timbers were outside the hull.

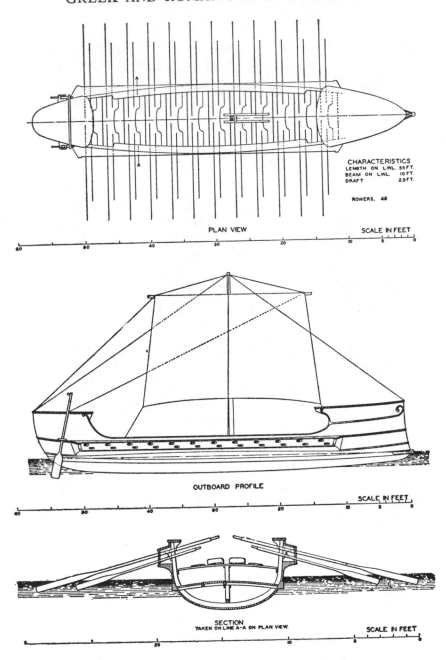

CHARACTERISTICS
LENGTH ON L.WL. 55 FT.
BEAM ON L.WL. 10 FT.
DRAFT 2.5 FT.

ROWERS, 48

PLAN VIEW   SCALE IN FEET

OUTBOARD PROFILE

SCALE IN FEET

SECTION
TAKEN ON LINE A-A ON PLAN VIEW.   SCALE IN FEET

RECONSTRUCTION OF A DISPATCH BOAT BASED ON THE PEDESTAL
OF THE WINGED VICTORY OF THE LOUVRE

PEDESTAL OF VICTORY OF SAMOTHRACE AT THE LOUVRE, SHOWING OUTRIGGER FOR OARS

provisions and water the load would be 14,500 lbs.; and allowing 67 per cent for hull and equipment the load displacement would be 19.6 tons. The length of the rowing space for 25 rowers on each side on 13 benches (2 men only on forward bench) would be 39 ft.; so the whole length would be about 55 ft. The necessary beam for stability would be 10 ft., from which follows a draft of 2.5 ft. The great importance of this pedestal in tracing the history of classical shipbuilding lies in the outrigger which allowed proper length to the oars with a minimum beam.

With 50 rowers the e.hp. would be 7.1, giving a maximum speed of about 7.5 knots for a short spurt and of about 5 knots for 2 hours with the full crew before exhaustion. With a single mast and sail area equal to that of the rectangle about the water line, she could make over 8.0 knots under favorable conditions.

Dispatch boats with only 20 oars probably had only one rank of rowers on each side and were undecked amidships with decked ends for storerooms. They would scarcely be as speedy as pentekonters.

Sails

These ships, although depending on oars for battle, were equipped with sails for general service. In cruising, oars were used only in calms and light breezes. Occasionally, in emergencies, oars were used at the same time as sails, as for instance, at the Battle of Lepanto, after the close of the battle, some escaping Turks used both oars and sails.

Ancient writers and sculptures and paintings do not give us very precise information as to sails. For that we must turn to Middle Age and later accounts, for of these times we have precise records. The galleys of the Middle Ages carried a sail area equal to about 1.5 times the rectangle circumscribed about the water line. Ancient ships cannot have carried more, and in fact they seem to have had somewhat less. This would entail no less speed in fresh winds when sail would have to be reduced in any case.

As for the type of masts and sails carried by ancient Greek men-of-war, classical scholars and archeologists agree that there was a great mast carrying a square sail and, in later B.C. times, a topsail above it. It is not apparent when the tricre first began to carry more than one mast, but probably it was before the end of the fifth century B.C. We may take it that then the mainmast carried one-half the sail area and the other two masts one-quarter each. The foremast and mizzenmast probably carried triangular fore-and-aft sails of the type known as lateen rig. Admiral Serre thinks ancient ships also carried jibs and staysails, but I do not think he proves the point. These seem to have been a comparatively recent invention. Seemingly, square sails came first and lateen sails later. It was usual for a fleet contemplating battle to land the mainsail and yard and as much stores as were not immediately necessary in order to gain speed and handiness. Smaller sails were retained as a precautionary measure in case of a disaster.

Speed under Sail of Ancient Ships

As for the speed of ancient ships we must be guided by the records of the last three centuries. In the year 1626 off Provence, a papal squadron of galleys made 12 knots under sail, running free, but this must be taken as the limit of speed, for they carried away gear and reduced sail. Also in the year 1629, a papal squadron got under way from Civita Vecchia and with off-shore breezes proceeded to Leghorn where it stopped an hour and reached Genoa in 30 hours. The speed was 8 knots.[16] The Viking ship discovered over 50 years ago at Gokstad in Norway was reproduced and crossed the ocean under her own sail to the Chicago Fair in 1893. During the voyage she reached a speed of 11 knots, yet was only 76 feet long.

As for the ancient round sailing ships, i.e., ships of 2.5 to 4 beams in their length, they also could make about the same speed as recent ships. Five knots or a little less has long been recognized as the average speed, day in and day out, for sailing ships. As an example the U.S.S. Constitution, 175 feet long, has a record of 13.5 knots under sail, and yet in 495 days at sea she averaged only 105 miles a day, or less than 4.5 knots. Shorter ships could not make quite so much. The U.S.S. Dolphin, a brig, 88 feet in length, made 10.6 knots running free. Smaller ships of 50 to 60 feet in length and displacing 100 to 200 tons might make 8-9 knots under the most favorable conditions. Ancient ships probably did just about the same.

Such data as we have from classic writers agree with performances

---

[16] Both instances from Guglielmotti's *History of the Papal Navy.*

of recent ships. Thucydides (II-97) mentions a voyage of 500 sea miles under sail in 4 days and nights, i.e., 5 knots. Livy (XLV-41) says a Roman squadron ran 110 miles (from Brundisium to Corcyra) in 9 Roman hours or 11 hours[17] of present reckoning, i.e., 10 knots.

Speed under Oars

Under oars, we know that galleys of the seventeenth and eighteenth centuries could reach 7 knots for short spurts, and could make about 4.5 knots with all hands for 2 or 3 hours. With the rowers in three watches they could make about 3 knots for an all-day voyage if the bottoms had been recently cleaned. Ancient rowing craft carried less stores and more rowers per ton of displacement and were consequently rather faster than recent galleys.

Diodorus (20-5-6) says 60 trieres took 144 hours to make 260 miles —less than 2 knots. The Athenian fleet in a hurry at the siege of Syracuse made 31 sea miles in 10 to 12 hours—3 to 2.5 knots (Thucydides: VI-65). Xenophon (Hell. 1-1-13) says Alcibiades with 86 ships made 50 miles in 18 hours. Longer voyages were very much slower, owing to frequent stops and delays whenever the wind was contrary.

PRINCIPAL AUTHORITIES CONSULTED FOR THIS APPENDIX

Cartault, A.: *La Trière Athénienne*, Paris, 1881.
Corazzini, F.: *Marina Militare Italiana Antica*, Leghorn, 1882.
Crescentio, B.: *La Nautica Mediterranea*, Rome, 1602.
Fincati, L.: *Le Triremi*, Rome, 1881.
Giomo, G.: *Le Galere Grosse Veneziane*, 1593, Venice, 1895.
Jurien de la Gravière, J. B. E.: *Les Derniers Jours de la Marine à Rames*.
Pantera, Pantero: *L'Armata Navale*, Rome, 1614.
Paris, E.: *Souvenirs de Marine*, vol. 5, Paris, 1892.
Serre, P.: *Marines de Guerre de l'Antiquité*, Paris, 1885.

The works on recent types of rowing men-of-war give us much information as to dimensions, size of crews, weights of hulls, etc., which is applicable to estimates of what ancient ships might or did do.

---

[17] The Romans divided the time from sunrise to sunset into 12 hours. The passage was made on June 7 when 9 Roman hours were 11.1 hours of our measurement.

CHAPTER III

GRECO-PERSIAN WARS—SALAMIS AND MYCALE

WHEN the Egyptian insurrection had been suppressed (484 B.C.), Xerxes consulted his council and, after hearing advice pro and con he decided to proceed with the matter of Greece as his father had intended to do. In the meantime, the political situation throughout Greece was much altered, and particularly so in Athens. The Democratic party in Athens, which had been in opposition to the government in 490 and had sympathized with the Persian invaders, had learned a startling lesson by the destruction of Eretria. It came to power in 489, and in the next few years became so strongly national as to be a chief element in the salvation of Greece, in the war of 480-479. As it became apparent that Marathon was not conclusive and that Persia was still to be dreaded, the man whose statesmanship and military and naval skill were to save Greece became prominent in Athenian affairs. Themistocles advocated a great navy and originated the sea power of Athens based on her fortified port, her commerce, and an unequaled navy, which led her to the headship of Greece in the next fifty years. Money was then a new invention and was assuming an importance in business which made the demand for silver greater than it had been in previous centuries. Athens had long enjoyed a revenue from the state-owned silver mines at Laurium in South Attica, and at this period a resort to deep levels (300 feet) brought a great increase in the state's income. It was urged that the silver revenues should be divided among the citizens as a bonus; but Themistocles proposed and carried a decree that this income should be devoted to building 200 trieres, for he saw that Greece must take heed of the development of the Persian navy.

Persia began her greatness as an inland power, but to overcome the Ionian revolt she had been obliged to rely on the fleets of the recently acquired provinces of Egypt, Syria, and Asia Minor, and at Lade in 494, after five years of effort, they had terminated the war. It was the fleets of these provinces which had brought the Persian army to the shores of

Attica in 490, and one after another the islands in the Aegean were falling to Persia. It was sea power that threatened Greece. Herodotus says that Themistocles advocated the great Attic fleet for a war with the neighboring island of Aegina. But 200 ships was a much greater number than was necessary for such a purpose; and a man of such far-reaching views as Themistocles must have been convinced that the Great King's war against Greece could not be long postponed.

SIZE OF EARLY TRIERES[1]

The size of these trieres of Themistocles needs further examination. Trieres were then just coming into general use. It is not likely that shipbuilders went at one step from the open pentekonter 60 feet long, to the triere with a deck above the rowers as in the Peloponnesian War, which is thought to have been about 110 feet long and proportionately heavier. Ship construction progresses slowly. It took Great Britain 60 years to go from the iron armored *Warrior* of less than 10,000 tons to the *Hood* of some 40,000 tons, and changes come faster now than they did 2,000 years ago. We may be sure that the trieres of 490-480 were not so large as their successors of 430-415 when the type was fully developed and still larger craft of new types were not far in the future. It is this very change in the progress of shipbuilding and other arts which lends interest to this study of early naval evolution.

---

[1] The price of these early trieres is alleged to have been a talent apiece, and this fact throws some light on their size. The labor price of naval shipbuilding in wood seems to have been fairly constant in different countries in recent centuries before the advent of steam machinery; that is to say, the price per ton of displacement divided by the shipwright's daily wage seems to have varied little. It was somewhat higher for large ships than for small ones at the same time and place; but we find from various accounts in England, France, Spain, Italy, and the United States, that in the seventeenth and eighteenth centuries the price per ton of displacement was from 100 to 120 days' wages for a shipwright.

The rate of wages in ancient Athens is not very precisely known, but early in the fifth century laborers seem to have been paid about three to four obols per day. The wages of a master workman may have been one drachma (6 obols). There were 6,000 drachmas in one talent ($1,185); and as that was the cost of Themistocles' trieres, there was the price of 9,000 to 12,000 days' labor in each ship. At 120 days' labor per ton, the deep load displacement of an early triere would come to 75 or 100 tons as a maximum. But including the cost of masts, oars, and other necessary things, and making allowance for some progress that hand machinery had made from 500 B.C. to 1600 A.D., and with consequent greater efficiency of labor, we may believe that trieres at one talent each were very much less than 75 tons each. (See Charnock, Serre, Artiñano, Guglielmotti, and the cost of the U.S.S. *Constitution*.)

MAP 4. CAMPAIGNS OF THERMOPYLAE AND SALAMIS

Preparation for War

The Egyptian revolt was suppressed in 484. The Persian preparation for the invasion of Greece began either at the close of the Egyptian
revolt or possibly the next year, in 483. So at least three full years were
occupied in arranging for the draft of men, in accumulating stores along
the line of march of the army in Thrace and Macedonia, and also in
digging a canal across the peninsula of Athos in Thrace to avoid rounding
it in bad weather. The canal was wide enough to admit two trieres abreast
and must therefore have been at least 100 feet wide and as much as 4 feet
deep. Its length was about 1.5 miles and the land was low. Herodotus
suggests that this great work was one of ostentation rather than of necessity.

As the Persian force was too large to be readily transported by sea
as the expedition of 490 had been, it was planned to bridge the Hellespont
and march the army through Thrace and Macedonia, both of which
were already under Persian rule, and so arrive in Greece from the north.
During this march along the coast, the huge army would be supplied
from the depots already established in Thrace and Macedonia and also
by the transport ships plying between the moving army and the sources
of supply in the Euxine and on the coasts of Asia Minor and in Syria and
Egypt. These supply ships were to be covered and protected by the
combatant fleet. The plan was one calling for the closest co-operation
between the fleet and the land forces, for the army was too large to live
on local supplies, and a naval defeat would entail a fatal interruption
of the army line of communications with the Persian bases. At the very
highest, the total Persian numbers may be estimated as perhaps 180,000
troops and camp followers and 130,000 men afloat, besides supply crafts'
crews, not over 350,000 in all (see appendix 2 to this chapter).

Persian Army Begins Its March (see Map 2)

In the fall of 481, the Persian army, which had been mobilizing in
Cappadocia, began to move towards Sardis, the capital of Lydia in western Asia Minor and, by the spring of 480, it was ready to open the campaign against Greece. The naval contingents from the maritime satrapies
were to assemble at the entrance to the Hellespont. The King now sent

envoys to the various states of Greece to demand earth and water as a token of submission. About April 15, 480, the army left Sardis and took about a month to arrive at the Plain of Troy on the Hellespont (140 miles), a few miles below the site of the two pontoon bridges, each of which used over 300 ships to support the huge cables on which the roadway was built. Here Xerxes spent about a month, reviewing the fleet and army, and began his advance into Thrace about June 15. About 80 miles from the bridges, the King halted the army, at the mouth of the Hebrus river (now Maritsa) to number the army, and Herodotus puts the result at the incredible figure of 1,700,000 fighting men. Apparently, also, the final organization of the army took place at that time. The pause was employed by the fleet in pulling the ships on the beach and overhauling them. Middle Age writers on naval matters tell us that only a few weeks in the water was time enough to foul the uncoppered bottoms and to check speed to a considerable amount. And speed was no less important then than it is now.

At the Hebrus the fleet was again reviewed by the King and organized in four great squadrons. Herodotus says there were 1,207 ships which came from Asia, and 120 were added from Thrace after it was overrun. The national armaments readily lent themselves to the organization of the fleet in two squadrons armed after the Greek fashion and two others light-armed, which more resembled the typical Persian style of armament (see appendix to this chapter). In addition to the provincial crews, the ships each had a detachment of Persian soldiers on board. As it was a Persian expedition and the admirals of the fleet were brothers of the King and princes of the Empire, with Persian soldiers on every ship, it is clear that the leaders would be inclined to fight after the Persian manner, that is, with missile weapons (which were also the national weapons of half the fleet) and by envelopment of the hostile flanks. To the Greek fleet, on the other hand, with heavy-armored spearmen and with inferior numbers, was indicated a boarders' fight instead of a missile fight, and a protection of the flanks to prevent envelopment. But the latter point of naval tactics was not at first understood by the Greek leaders.

From the Hebrus the army moved on to Therma (now Salonica). A part of it swept north through the mountains, but most of it must have kept near the coast. The fleet passed through the canal cut across Athos

Peninsula, and picked up local ships and troops on the way. It arrived at Therma before the army and distributed itself along the coast as far as the river Axius (now Vardar). Upon Xerxes' arrival at Therma, he went on board a ship of Sidon and, escorted by the fleet, he personally proceeded south about 40 miles to the mouth of the river Peneus, where the valley of Tempe was of military importance. During this trip of the King, a division of the army was engaged in opening a practicable route (or routes) through the mountains into Thessaly. The new crops were now available in this rich country. It was the middle of August when the main army moved out by at least two routes on the next stage of its advance, which was to bring it into contact with the Greek lines of defense.

GREEK PREPARATIONS

Let us now turn to the situation in Greece. For some years previous to Xerxes' invasion, the policy of Athens had been dominated by Themistocles. He did not think that Marathon had ended the Persian intentions of conquest. He had been able to persuade his own city to devote the income of the mines of Laurium to the up-building of a great fleet; but it had not been possible for him to arouse the rest of Greece to a realization of the danger. Athens had created a myth about the campaign of 490 in which she had beaten the invader and, as a result of the myth, she and all Greece with her under-estimated the vast might of Persia. When the invasion was seen to be imminent, a council of the Greek states was called to meet at the Isthmus of Corinth to discuss plans for resistance. There were two general plans. It was desirable to yield as little territory to the enemy as possible. For that reason, a northern line of defense was preferable to bring the greatest numbers to the side of the national defense. On the other hand, the numbers of the Persians were so much greater that it seemed that the Isthmus of Corinth was the only place which could be held with certainty by the army. For this reason the Peloponnesians, who included among them the professional army of Sparta, wanted to entrench the isthmus and fight there. The states of Central and Northern Greece, on the other hand, wished to save their lands and cities by holding a northern position. Whatever line should be selected, it was necessary to support it by the fleet, for otherwise the hostile fleet could place a detachment of its army in the rear of the Greeks and render their chosen position untenable.

It does not seem that the Spartans, who were the best soldiers in Greece but narrow in their outlook, thoroughly comprehended the impotence of the Greek land defense should the Greek fleet fail to check its opponent. But the Athenians alone had nearly half the Greek ships. Thucydides tells us that the whole available force of Attica was embarked (180 ships, less than 22,000 men). In the end Athenian policy, boldly directed by Themistocles, was able to govern the allies, for he had early seen the part the fleet was to play and had not hesitated to venture all. In previous years he had persuaded his countrymen to build a great fleet, and now at the Council he convinced the allies that if they did not agree to his proposed use of the combined Greek fleet, they would be overcome through lack of Athenian aid, for Athens insisted on a northern line of resistance. The Persian fleet covered the movements of the supply ships. Thus a defeat of that fleet would entail the retreat of the army through failure of sea-borne supplies. The test of sea power would dominate the situation.

When the Persians reached the Hellespont (May), the Thessalians sent to the Council at the isthmus for aid. The Greeks decided to endeavor to retain Thessaly by defending the pass of Tempe, about 60 miles march south of Therma, and sent 10,000 heavy-armed troops by sea up the Euripus (between Euboea and the mainland) to Halus on the Pagasean Gulf, where they disembarked. From there they marched to Tempe, where they encamped and were joined by Thessalian cavalry. But in a few days, Alexander, King of Macedon, a Persian vassal but a Greek well-wisher, sent to them recommending their departure. It is probable that after their arrival they learned that there were other routes besides the pass of Tempe across the mountains, and by these their position could be turned.

The expedition returned to the isthmus as it had come, and the Thessalians, seeing that they alone could not guard their country, sent earth and water to Xerxes at Therma in token of submission.

The Stand at Thermopylae—Artemisium

After the expedition had returned from Tempe, the Council of allies at the isthmus selected the pass of Thermopylae as the proper place to withstand the invasion. It was on the only practicable road for an invading army to enter Central Greece, and on several occasions in subsequent centuries it again proved a key position. Moreover, the situation of the pass was such that the fleet could co-operate most effectively with the army at the pass. Unlike the sailing ships of recent centuries, which could maintain themselves at sea for months, the Greek rowing men-of-war very seldom spent a night at sea. Consequently, a secure base for the fleet had to be found very close to its intended field of action (see Map 5).

Thermopylae was an excellent position for joint defensive action by land and sea. It lay at the entrance to Central Greece on the seashore, on the Malian Gulf, where a mountain chain forbade all passage to an army except by the narrow passage along the seashore, which at its narrowest points was less than 50 feet between the sea and the mountain side. The gulf opened into the Euripus, the channel separating the island of Euboea from the mainland. The north end of this island offered to the Greeks the necessary fleet base and roadstead secure from land attack. As long as the fleet could remain at the Artemisium Strand on the north reach of the Euripus, the vast numbers and the cavalry of the Persians could not act advantageously against the army at Thermopylae, which need fear nothing but a frontal attack on a 50-foot front. The retirement of the fleet would render necessary the abandonment of the pass, since the overwhelming numbers of the Persians could then be thrown by water directly against the flank and the line of supply and retreat of the army. On the other hand, the maintenance of the position at the pass was equally essential to the fleet, for if the pass were open to the enemy, he could then get into Euboea and drive the fleet away from its camp on the beach of Artemisium. The decision to hold the line Thermopylae-Artemisium was not reached without dispute.

The Peloponnesians were with difficulty persuaded that a defense at the isthmus line was hopeless without the presence of the Athenian contingent with the rest of the fleet to forbid the free use of the sea by the enemy. They were at last made to see that, unless they aided in making a first line of resistance in the north on the chance of saving Central Greece from the enemy, they ran the risk of losing the aid of the Athenian navy in holding their own final line at the isthmus. For this concession, the Spartans required that the commander in chief of the allied fleet should be the Spartan Eurybiades. Accordingly it was agreed to hold the northern line.

Opening of the Campaign

The chronology of the active campaign of six weeks during which the contact and decision took place is given with precision by Herodotus, except for two gaps of several days each. There is a discrepancy of one day in adjusting the diaries of the fleet and army. The date of the concluding battle at Salamis is approximately fixed as being "a few" days earlier than an eclipse of the sun which astronomy tells us occurred on October 2 of our calendar. In the following account the dates follow from the assumption that the battle took place on September 23.

As previously mentioned, a division of the Persian army left Therma soon after August 1 to open a road over the mountains into the plains of Thessaly, during which time the King paid his visit to Tempe. This news got to the isthmus in about five days, and the allied fleet under the Spartan Eurybiades and the army detachment under the Spartan King Leonidas moved north about the eleventh. They probably arrived at their respective stations not later than the eighteenth. Leonidas started from the isthmus with about 3,000 heavy-armed Peloponnesians, including his own 300 Spartans, and some light-armed troops. He was joined by over 2,000 more heavy-armed troops from Central Greece. They took position at the narrows of the Thermopylae Pass directly on the shore, and at the town of Albenoi just in the rear they established their base of supplies, where the Greek transport ships could have access as long as the Greek fleet could maintain itself at Artemisium. At the narrowest part of the pass the Phocians had built a wall and gate many years before to hold the entrance against invasion by the Thessalians. This wall the Greeks now repaired.

In conjunction with the army the Greek fleet arrived at Artemisium with contingents from 13 states, as follows: Athens, 127, partly manned by volunteers from Plataea; Corinth, 40; Megaris, 20; Chalcis, 20 (ships loaned by Athens); Aegina, 18; Sicyon, 12; Lacedaemon, 10 with the commander in chief; Epidaurus, 8; Eretria, 7; Troezen, 5; Styra, 2— all trieres—Ceos, 2 trieres and 2 pentekonters; Locris, 5 pentekonters—271 trieres and 7 pentekonters. The position of the fleet at Artemisium was about 40 miles east of the army at the pass. The hills above the army camp permitted a view along the Euripus as far as Artemisium, and smoke signals transmitted preconcerted announcements between the two forces in good weather which was usual at that time of year. Besides, each commander kept a swift dispatch boat in readiness to forward detailed information (a matter of from 4 to 12 hours or more according to the currents and weather). Artemisium was opposite the entrance to the Gulf of Pagasae (see Map 4), which the enemy would wish to use, and its occupation protected the island of Euboea from the enemy. On arrival with the fleet at Artemisium, Eurybiades threw out a patrol guard of three ships towards the enemy; they based on Skiathus and probably lay far to the north, near the Peneus River.

At the same time arrangements were made at the entrance to the straits for a lookout and signals from the island of Skiathus, which was visible from the fleet camp and itself commanded a view of the coast of the Magnesian promontory and all approaching ships.

The events at Thermopylae which are now to be recounted have been an epic in history ever since. The heroism of Leonidas and his 300 Spartans was no doubt a great factor in raising the morale of the Greeks for the later fight at Salamis and affected all the subsequent wars between Greece and Persia until Alexander's conquests a century and a half later. But we are studying the military conduct of the campaign and it is worth while endeavoring to see how far the hero legend has concealed the facts. It is clear that the Peloponnesians were not anxious to make the first line of defense anywhere than at the isthmus. The Athenians were all for the strategic advantage of the northern line. In this diplomatic conflict, it is not improbable that the Spartans were disinclined to make a strenuous attempt to cover the central states by a Peloponnesian army. They said they would send re-enforcements north after the great festivals they were celebrating, but none at all were sent, although Leonidas asked for them.

It is likely that Sparta played a double game. She sent her King and his 300 as the price by which she secured the command of the fleet as well as that of the army which all readily conceded to her. No doubt she further hoped that the choice troops she did send would induce the central states to send full levies of their own and complete the necessary numbers. Nor is it to be supposed that the Spartan Council meant deliberately to sacrifice their own King at Thermopylae, for while the fleet held its position the army detachment could retire by the main road at any time.

Even if the fleet should be defeated, dispatch boats and smoke signals would give Leonidas good warning, and even at the worst he and his people could escape over the hills without affording an opportunity for organized pursuit. So we may take it that the advance of the army detachment to Thermopylae had a Spartan political objective and that of the fleet to Artemisium had a serious Athenian military objective, although each movement was necessary to the other as complementary parts of a single operation of the national defense.[2] This assumption is strengthened by the anxiety of the Spartans to return to the isthmus during their entire stay at Thermopylae. They did not think much would be accomplished there.

About August 13, the Persian army marched out of Therma, bound for Thermopylae. The right wing swung to the west about 40 miles from the sea and went direct to the Malian Gulf and Thermopylae, where it arrived on August 26, but the left wing, which the King accompanied, kept by the sea to the pass of Tempe and after passing through it, turned again parallel to the coast to the city of Larissa and so to Halus on the Pagasean Gulf where it would meet the fleet and, no doubt, resupply itself.

The Persian fleet did not leave Therma at the same time as the army, but instead sent forward a reconnoitering squadron of ten ships to look into the Euripus. This squadron ran into the three Greek ships in observation and cut them off, forcing one ashore at the mouth of the Peneus and capturing her, although the crew escaped on shore and returned home. The other two were chased south and captured within sight of the Greek lookouts on Skiathus who reported the incident by smoke signal to the fleet. The bravest of the crew of one of the prizes was sacrificed on the bow of the captor to secure a favorable omen, and the captain of the other, who also had shown great bravery and was desperately wounded, was carefully tended by his captors and was exhibited through the fleet as an example of worthy conduct. He was recaptured from the enemy in the final battle, and probably told his story to Herodotus.

The Persian scouts proceeded onward and entered the Artemisium channel where three of them were wrecked on the Rock Myrmex at its entrance. The remaining ships marked the dangerous sunken rock with a stone beacon for the guidance of the fleet and returned to Therma. They must have had a good look at the Greek fleet and in any case they heard of it from the prizes. Eleven days after the army had gone, the fleet arrived at Cape Sepias, having probably left Therma the day before (al-

---

[2] See Grundy: *Great Persian War*. London, 1901, p. 273.

though Herodotus says the fleet took only one day), probably under sail, and that night, the twenty-fifth, it anchored in eight lines off the beaches along the end of the Magnesian promontory, for lack of room to haul up on the beaches.

MAP 5. THERMOPYLAE AND ARTEMISIUM

Besides the 1,324 trieres, there were probably some hundreds of transports under convoy for the supply of the army at Thermopylae. During the night a very heavy easterly on-shore gale arose unexpectedly and did great damage. Ancient craft were not weatherly. Many were unable to gain sea room and were driven on shore and lost. Of course, most were saved by drawing them on the beaches at the first sign of the storm and made safe there, as was the practice of the time. It was the outer ships which were in trouble. Herodotus says that 400 trieres were lost and an untold number of transports, and that the wrecks strewed the coast for 40 miles above Cape Sepias. We may believe Herodotus when he says that the number of transports lost was unknown, for doubtless they were coming and going every day. But the loss of one-third of the fleet seems very great and it is more probable that the wrecks on the beach numbered 400 in all. Half the number, or 200, seems ample to allow for the loss in trieres which, although more numerous than the transports, were doubtless better placed and better cared for.

The Greek fleet suffered no damage in the storm. Herodotus says that when their patrol ships were captured off the Magnesian coast they were so alarmed that they abandoned the Artemisium position, in order to guard the narrow channel at Chalcis, but this seems unlikely. They had a commanding position which they had deliberately occupied, and they would scarcely abandon it for an affair of three ships. But undoubtedly the gale swept down the Euripus, and ships not already beached would have to seek shelter. This could be found for easterly winds at the roadstead of Oreus in front of the city of Histiaea and only two or three miles from the Artemisium Strand, but it may be that some ships went farther and passed by Thermopylae and so gave rise to the report that they had abandoned Artemisium. However it may be explained, the Greek fleet took no damage.

The gale lasted three days during which time the Persian crews on the beaches rescued property and threw up entrenchments around their beached ships to protect themselves from attack by the inhabitants. As early as the first day the Greeks learned of the Persian disaster from their lookouts on the hills. The morning of the fourth day, August 29, was fine and the Persian fleet resumed its movement.

Apparently, when the Persians learned of the presence of the Greek fleet at Artemisium, the admirals resolved to send an enveloping squadron around Euboea to come up the Euripus and prevent any withdrawal of the enemy. It seems that both in strategy and in tactics the Persians favored envelopment. They had the numbers. If successful, envelopment prevented escape and, moreover, it was tactically favorable to missile action, in which the Persians were superior. Accordingly, the main body of the fleet rounded Cape Sepias and, after a voyage of 25 or 30 miles, occupied berths in the Pagasean Gulf at Aphetae, while a detachment of 200 ships was sent outside Skiathus keeping well away from the coast of Euboea while making the circumnavigation. Although the details of the circumnavigation voyage are not given, it is possible that a night was spent at Scyrus (see Map 4), for ships did not like to be at sea at night when it could be avoided. It was a few days before new moon, not very good for night sailing.

The Greek fleet resumed its station at Artemisium this same day but, apparently, neither sighted the other's movement. Later in the day, however, a belated division of 15 Persian ships rounded Sepias and by some error failed to follow the fleet into its anchorage, but saw the Greek fleet on the far side of the channel and steered for it instead and was captured before it could withdraw.

BATTLES AT ARTEMISIUM

The following day, August 30, was a day of leisure for the Persians at Aphetae, and the admirals inspected the fleet while waiting for the enveloping squadron to place itself. A Greek diver Scyllias, with the Persian fleet, who had been working on the wrecks at Sepias, employed this opportunity to escape and inform the Greek leaders of the particulars of the disaster, and especially of the voyage of the circumnavigating squadron. A council was held upon the receipt of this news, and it was first resolved to move to the southward that night and fall upon the detachment going around Euboea. However, this plan was soon abandoned, as it left the Greek army at Thermopylae open to attack by land and sea. Instead, Themistocles was able to persuade the council, after bribing Eurybiades, the commander in chief and the Corinthian admiral,[3] to the bolder course of taking advantage of the scattered situation of the enemy at Aphetae. There were as many as 900 trieres there, besides many transports, and these were distributed in several of the harbors which open into the Gulf of Pagasae. It is possible that the fighting ships were in the bay to the west

---

[3] Modern commentators think the bribery story is without foundation.

of the entrance and the transports had gone farther up the gulf to supply anew the eastern wing of the army which passed with the King through the city of Halus.

The Greek plan was to use their whole fleet at their own time against a divided enemy. So the Greeks crossed the straits, a distance of about 8 miles, and sought an action in the afternoon, so that night would put an end to the fight before the enemy could bring up all his 900 ships against the Grecian 271.

As Herodotus puts it, they wished to try the Persian mode of fighting, and practice the maneuver of cutting the line. Cutting the line, the *diekplous*, was something wholly different from the maneuver known in the eighteenth century as cutting the line. The later maneuver was a passage through the enemy's line for the purpose of getting to leeward of some of his ships so that they could not withdraw at pleasure by simply putting their helms up and running free. It was a maneuver of position only which expressed a resolution to fight to a finish. The *diekplous*, if well executed, was itself an injury to the enemy. As opposite ships passed each other in this maneuver, each tried to rake off the oars of the other by scraping the hostile side with the round shoulder of his own bow and save his own oars while doing so. For this object the catheads were long and heavily strutted. While passing each other, the enemies fought as they could, each with the national weapons.

It was the Greek tactics to seek a close fight. For them was the ramming collision and the boarders' fight, in which the brass armor and the 8-foot spear and short sword of the Greek would give him an advantage over the quilted linen coats of the Persian archers. The Persians came out full of confidence and met the Greeks in succession as Themistocles intended. At first the Greeks had the advantage and captured 30 ships but, as the hostile numbers increased, the Greeks formed in a circle with their bows outward, and the Persians surrounded them expecting an easy victory but, in a quite technical sense, the Greek circular formation prevented envelopment; that is to say, there was no exposed flank for the Persians to attack on both sides, for the flanks and rear of every Greek ship were protected by his neighbor and the Persian numbers were of no great help except to relieve exhausted crews.

When the Grecian ships moved forward to ram or board, it is probable that the effort was not to accomplish a complete *diekplous*, but was either a direct ram thrust or an arrested *diekplous*, for, were any Greek ship to succeed in passing through the hostile line, she would find herself surrounded by the second line of the enemy. After the first success of the Greeks, the increasing number of the enemy caused the fight to become equal until night came and put an end to the struggle.

Both sides returned to their respective camps, leaving the Persians much surprised at their failure to accomplish anything. On the other hand, the Greeks had no cause for encouragement. They had ascertained that, ship against ship, and Greek spearman against Persian archer, they were superior, but to foes as brave as they and much more numerous, they were unequal, even with the advantage of arms. It was night that had extricated them from misfortune and the squadron rounding Euboea would prevent their escape to the south the next day. But fortune was about to change.

> Evening had barely closed when a heavy rain began to fall, which continued the whole night (August 30-31), with terrible thunderings and lightning from Mount Pelion: the bodies of the slain and the broken pieces of the damaged ships were drifted in the direction of Aphetae and floated about the prows of the vessels there disturbing the use of the oars. The barbarians, hearing the storm, were greatly dismayed, expecting certainly to perish, as they had fallen into such a multitude of misfortunes. * * * If, however, they who lay at Aphetae passed a comfortless night, far worse were the sufferings of those who had been sent to make the circuit of Euboea; inasmuch as the storm fell on them while out at sea, whereby the issue was indeed calamitous. They were sailing along near the Hollows of Euboea [southern end], when the wind began to rise and the rain to pour. Overpowered by the force of the gale and driven they knew not whither, at last they fell upon rocks, the gods so contriving in order that the Persian might not greatly exceed the Greek, but be brought nearly to its level. This squadron, therefore, was entirely lost about the Hollows of Euboea. (Herodotus: VIII-12-13)

Before the day of August 31 was far advanced, a squadron of 53 Athenian reserve ships arrived at Artemisium from Attica, and about the same time news came by signal of the loss of the circumnavigating squadron off the Hollows. This news changed the situation of affairs and put spirit into the allied crews. It was resolved to repeat the action of the previous day, crossing over late in the day, striking a blow, and getting away under cover of darkness. The Cilician squadron of 100 ships seems to have occupied an advanced position as outposts and on this the Greeks fell and sank a number of ships, but there was no general fight, and the fleet returned to Artemisium as darkness came on.

On the third day, September 1, the Persians did not wait to be attacked as before, but came out about noon and crossed over to the Greek position on the south shore, where the Greeks lay awaiting them. Again, as on the first day, the Persians extended in crescent formation and attempted envelopment. It is doubtful if they succeeded in this attempt. The Greeks probably supported their flanks on the shore so that the enemy had no room to pass inside and attack from the rear. As Herodotus says, in their desperate efforts the Persians pressed too hard to get into the fight, and the vessels fell into disorder and fouled each other; yet still they did not give way, feeling it a disgrace not to overcome so inferior an enemy.[4]

---

[4] In view of the inconsistencies in Herodotus' story of the fights at Artemisium as repeated above, commentators have felt at liberty to do more or less reconstruction, for some part, at least, of Herodotus must be cast aside. One of the most ingenious of these reconstructions is that of Professor J. A. R. Munro in *Cambridge Ancient History*, vol. 4, who makes a plausible account of occurrences without inconsistencies as to relative times.

To the present writer this version seems more plausible than that of Herodotus.

After an acute analysis, Munro holds that there was only one gale, and that of 24 hours only. He believes that Herodotus confused the accounts that he got from different participators as to different phases of the action, and that in reality, from the first news of the Greek stand, the Persians had decided to attack the Artemisium-Thermopylae position by their favorite maneuver of envelopment on a grand scale. (This may well be, since the army started from Therma to march to Thermopylae 10 days ahead of the fleet, and the King must have learned of the enemy's position several days before the army got to Thermopylae.) Accordingly, it was arranged to start the main body of the Persian fleet in time to arrive at Artemisium about the same time the army was due at Thermopylae. The enveloping detachment of the fleet, the Cilician squadron, which was to pass east and south of Euboea, probably got off a little earlier than the main fleet. Either the Greeks foresaw the probability of such an enveloping movement, or it was imperfectly concealed from them as the Cilicians passed outside Skiathus. At any rate, the Athenians detached 53 ships from their squadron of 180 and sent them to hold the narrow channel at Chalcis before the gale arose.

After the arrival of the main Persian fleet at Sepias (on August 25) and while the Cilicians were still off Euboea, the gale came up and injured the Persians only, as the Greeks were in sheltered waters.

The Persian main body at Sepias needed time to straighten things out after the gale and the last of the ships there did not get to Aphetae till the fourth day, i.e., 3 days after the gale, August 29.

In the meantime the Greek squadron at Chalcis learned by signal from the local lookouts on the hills that the survivors of the Cilicians had passed around Euboea and had arrived in the Hollows (August 26-27); so the Greeks ran down there and destroyed them, returning to Artemisium the day after the first engagement there (August 31). What Herodotus says happened to the Cilicians at Aphetae in the second day's fight occurred 3 days earlier at the Hollows.

The Greeks suffered much both in ships and men, but the Persians experienced a greater loss. Among the King's ships the Egyptians did best, and took five prizes with their crews on board. The action was not decisive, and both sides gladly terminated the action and returned to their anchorages. The Greeks, indeed, retained possession of the bodies of the slain and the floating wrecks, but they had been roughly handled, especially the Athenians, half of whose ships had been damaged.

If we now examine the tactical lessons of these 3 days, it appears that the Greek individual superiority in weapons was not enough to overcome the Persian advantage in numbers. The Greeks could not win in open water, for they would be overwhelmed by envelopment. Moreover, the greatly superior numbers of the Persians undoubtedly enabled them to fight in relays. The effort of battle was a most exhausting one for fighters and for rowers also. If all the Greek ships could be compelled to fight at one moment, the Persians could hope to conquer them in the end through physical weariness. Such was the situation at Artemisium on the late afternoon of September 1, but the question of future fleet action was not decided by events there, but at Thermopylae.

Battles at Thermopylae

It will be remembered that the Persian army had arrived opposite the Greek position in the pass on August 26 and occupied the Malian plain whose area, as Herodotus says, was 22,000 plethra (about 5,200 acres). As the Persians approached Thermopylae the Greeks became alarmed and Leonidas was only able to retain them there by sending messengers to the isthmus to ask for re-enforcements from the main army lying there, but none were sent. On his part, Xerxes sent a rider ahead to reconnoiter and the horseman, on his return, told the King that the Lacedaemonians were outside the wall, exercising at gymnastics and combing their long hair. Xerxes applied to Demaratus, an exiled King of Sparta, who was with him, to know the meaning of what the scout had seen and was assured that the Spartans were accustomed to dress their hair when foreseeing danger; and

---

However, the acceptance of this hypothesis transferring the time and place of the Cilician disaster does not in any way affect the two other battles at Artemisium, nor the conclusions which the Greek leaders must have drawn from their outcome, namely, that envelopment of the less numerous Greek fleet had to be prevented.

that those in front of him would dispute the pass notwithstanding the vast numbers who would attack them. But so incredulous was the King that he waited 4 days without action, believing the Greeks would abandon their position without fighting. In the meantime, the rear of the army was closing on Thermopylae. It is not unlikely that the Persian army utilized this delay to get in touch with its fleet, which had arrived in the Gulf of Pagasae on August 29 and was distant only 3 days' march for the army wagons. Besides, the King may have hoped that the fleet might appear at Thermopylae and thus obviate the necessity of assaulting such a strong position.

On the fifth day, August 30, the Persians attacked the enemy's position at the old Phocian wall. The attack was made by the Medes and Cissians who were esteemed second only to the Persians themselves. Like the Persians, they were armed with helmet, shield, and light body armor for defense. Although the bow was their principal weapon, they did not rely upon it on this occasion, as the Greeks seem to have expected, but charged and used their secondary weapons, a short spear and dagger. They were re-enforced and the attack lasted long, but, in spite of their bravery and heavy losses, they could make no impression on the panoplied Greeks whose spears outreached theirs. Finally, the King put in his own body guard, the "Immortals," but they also failed to make headway and the day closed.

The battle discipline of the Greeks was remarkably good. They did not confine themselves to defense, but counter-attacked and then retreated to draw the Persians back to the narrows of the pass and strike them down when they were crowded there.

The next day, August 31, the Persians attacked again, believing that the small number of the enemy would be incapacitated by wounds and fatigue; but the day brought them no better fortune and again they retired unsuccessful. But, as the leaders discussed their procedure with anxiety, Ephialtes, a native of the neighborhood, offered to guide a party up through the narrow gorge of the Asopus stream which flowed out of the hills through the Persian camp. The length of the march was about 17 miles through a ravine with vertical walls, where, in places, only a single file could pass, and opposition would be fatal to all. Leonidas had stationed his Phocian contingent of 1,000 men at the top of the ascent, about 3,500 feet above the sea, to block the exit from the ravine should the enemy attempt it, and these men had taken no part in the fighting at the pass.

The situation was grave for the Persians. The Greeks had given a severe blow to the fleet the day before and had struck the Cilician ships that day, although probably the latter news had not yet been received by the King. The army needed supply and the fleet's delay in forcing its way down rendered it necessary for the army to make this difficult attempt at once. If successful, it would only be necessary to send a detachment of the army to Chalcis and the threat against the line of supply of the Greek fleet would cause its immediate retirement. So the King resolved to send on this task the 10,000 "Immortals," who, as Herodotus says, surpassed all the rest of the army, not only in magnificence but also in valor.

They started at dusk and pursued their difficult path through the night, arriving near the camp of the Phocian defenders of the ravine about daylight on September 1. The latter were not keeping a proper outpost at the exit and the enemy was concealed from sight by the thick groves of oak, but the trampling of their feet on the leaves alarmed the Phocian defenders of the pass who ran to arm themselves and, while still unready, the enemy appeared. Hydarnes, commanding the "Immortals," was somewhat taken aback at the sight of opponents, but ascertaining from his guide who they were, he formed a line with those who had issued from the ravine and opened a heavy fire (arrows) on the yet assembling Phocians who hastily retreated up the mountainside and there made a stand, but left the path open which led to the sea and to the rear of the main Greek position. This route Hydarnes followed, neglecting the runaways, but there must have been some delay to assemble the long column which had been struggling up the ravine all night.

In the meantime fugitives had run to Leonidas and told him that the enemy had reached the top of the path. He had already been informed the night before by deserters that the column was on its way, and now learning that the Phocians had failed him, he made preparations for his last effort. An oracle had stated that the death of a Spartan King would secure victory for his people; and as Herodotus puts it, Leonidas made his last stand in reliance on the oracle that his sacrifice would effect final triumph. But modern criticism does not accept this view, which it regards as a legend put forth by the Spartans to conceal their own political shortcoming in not keeping their promise to send additional forces to Thermopylae and stop the invader there. What Leonidas actually did was not in accord with the hypothesis of sacrifice, but rather supports the idea of the miscarriage of a last desperate attempt to maintain his position, repel the enemy, and gain a victory. To fulfill the oracle it was only necessary to retain with him his own 300 Spartans, but instead, he divided the 4,000 heavy-armed troops that he had remaining (the Phocians having already been sent to hold the upper path) into two parts. With 1,400 men, including the renowned 300 Spartans, he held his position in front of the enemy and the rest he sent to the rear. These latter reported at home that they were told to save themselves, and no one survived to contradict them; but it seems more probable that they were sent in haste to climb the hill and meet the Persians in the forest path, and stop them in a place where 2,500 determined men might hope to check the advance of a far greater number. Whatever may have been Leonidas' intention, the detachment he sent off did not meet the enemy under Hydarnes, but escaped along the main road.

These retreating contingents had some reason for ill-will; they had been promised support from the troops gathering at the isthmus, they had fought well on the preceding days and now they were abandoned by those at home who should have aided them. If this is the real story of the occurrence, as many students think, the fact that it is not given in history is explained by the desire of the Spartans to hide their own broken promise by accepting the account which those who abandoned Leonidas gave of their own conduct. By this silence, the Spartans were able to secure for themselves a prestige based on the devotion of Leonidas and his 300, which was of inestimable and enduring political value to them in their future relations, both with other Greek states and with foreigners.

Thus Leonidas at daylight made his trenchant decision while Xerxes offered a solemn libation and, then, about an hour before noon, the barbarians under Xerxes advanced at the hour suggested by Ephialtes,

and the Greeks with Leonidas, as though going to meet their death, came out much more into the wider part of the pass than they had hitherto done. Up to this time, they had held their station within the wall, and from this had gone out to fight where the pass was narrowest. On this occasion, however, the battle took place outside the narrows; and numbers of the Persians fell. For the commanders, standing behind their companies, with whips in their hands, lashed on every man, continually urging them forward. Many of them fell into the sea and were drowned, and a still larger number of them were trampled to death by their own comrades, but no one heeded the dying. For the Greeks, reckless of their own safety and desperate, since they knew that as the mountain had been crossed, their destruction was nigh at hand, exerted themselves with the most furious valor against the barbarians. By this time the spears of the greater number were shivered and with their swords they hewed down the ranks of the Persians; and here, as they strove, Leonidas fell, fighting bravely, together with many other famous Spartans, whose names I have taken care to learn on account of their great worthiness. * * * There fell too, at the same time very many famous Persians, among them two sons of Darius, * * * brothers of Xerxes. And now there arose a fierce struggle between the Persians and the Lacedaemonians over the body of Leonidas, in which the Greeks four times drove back the enemy, and at last, by their great bravery, succeeded in bearing off the body. This combat was scarcely ended when the Persians with Ephialtes approached; and the Greeks, informed that they drew near, made a change in the manner of their fighting. Drawing Lack into the narrowest part of the pass and retreating even behind the cross wall, they posted themselves upon a hillock where they stood altogether in one body except only the Thebans. * * * Here they defended themselves to the last, such as still had swords using them, and the others resisting with their hands and teeth; till the barbarians, who in part had pulled down the wall and attacked them in front, in part had gone round and now encircled them upon every side, overwhelmed and buried the remnant beneath showers of missile weapons. (Herodotus: VII-223-25)

Such was the course of the most renowned of ancient battles, but in this study of naval tactics its interest is in the resemblance of its tactical features to those of the naval battle fought the same day at Artemisium. The courage on both sides was equal, the Greek arms were superior, but the disproportion in numbers was more than superior arms could overcome. In the sea fight, with odds of less than three to one, the contest was terminated by exhaustion and mutual consent; but at the pass, there were no reliefs ready to step into the front rank of the Greeks as there were for the Persians. For the latter, there was greater slaughter at first, but when the Greeks were weary their own end came. The land fight was prolonged because the Greeks obliged the enemy to act in a manner unfavorable to his armament. The habitual Persian effort was to surround the enemy and open with archery. But here the way was narrow; on one side the steep hill and on the other deep water by the roadside. Seemingly, archery was comparatively ineffective in a strictly frontal attack. The rate of an archer's fire in the Middle Ages was about 4 to 6 rounds a minute, and the rear ranks could scarcely see to take effective individual aim. It was probably much the same for the Persians. But this time the Persians used their swords and the Persian crowd became the Grecian opportunity. As the Grecian front was narrow, a few could hold it and be relieved when exhausted; just as on a greater scale, both of time and numbers, in the recent great war, one division from time to time relieved another in the front line. Nevertheless, after a while, the front-line Greeks had to be relieved by men already weary, but the Persian numbers were inexhaustible in spite of slaughter. We must believe that the degree of success which the Greeks had obtained in these three days' fight by sea and land against greatly superior strength was tactically highly suggestive to Themistocles, who, as Thucydides says, was unsurpassed in wisdom by any of his contemporaries. The Persian victory at Thermopylae, together with the first and third days' battles at Artemisium, probably taught the Greeks how to reach their final victory at Salamis. It was through refusal of any opportunity for hostile envelopment by superior numbers.

The opening of the pass could not be followed by an immediate advance of the Persian army, for it could not move until transport ships could get to it with food, and they did not pass the Greek fleet which had fought a drawn battle that same day. In regard to this it is hard to see why the Persian admirals did not send transports to Thermopylae in rear of the Persian men-of-war while they were engaging the Greeks on the third day, but no mention is made of such action, and we must regard the omission as due to Persian over-confidence.

PLANS FOR THE PERSIAN ADVANCE

The victory of Xerxes had been gained at appalling cost, and he anxiously inquired of Demaratus, who had gained his confidence, how many remaining Greeks there were of like valor with those who lay dead before him. There were 8,000 Spartans, Demaratus replied, equal to those with Leonidas; the other Lacedaemonians, although brave, were not equal to the Spartans, and he suggested that the easiest way to overcome Greece would be to send 300 ships to the island of Cythera on the south coast of the Peloponnese. He pointed out that, should this diversion be made, the Spartans, finding the enemy so near them, would desert the isthmus and its fortifications to guard their own lands, and those defenders remaining there would be unequal to opposing the Persian army. Afterwards, so Demaratus thought, the Spartans alone could not resist, and thus all Greece would be overcome.

This was a plausible argument, and a sound one too, provided the Persian fleet was strong enough to divide, but Achaemenes, brother of the King and commander of the Egyptian squadron, did not think so and hastened to make the proper strategic answer, based on the army's dependence on the fleet. He said:

> If in this posture of our affairs, after we have lost 400 vessels by shipwreck, we now send away 300 more to make a voyage around the Peloponnese, our enemies will become a match for us. But let us keep our whole fleet in one body, and it will be dangerous for them to venture on an attack, as they will certainly be no match for us then. Besides, while our sea and land forces advance together, the fleet and army can help each other; but if they be parted, no aid will come either from thee to the fleet or from the fleet to thee. (Herodotus)

The argument was probably advanced after the fleet arrived at Thermopylae.

Xerxes accepted the advice of the admiral, his brother, rather than that of the Greek exile, but it is worth while to speculate on the possibilities of Demaratus' plan. He was a soldier of a country predominantly military in thought and organization. His plan was eminently calculated to open the way for the Persian army to march through Greece with little opposition. But the supplies of the Persian army came from over seas; and upon the fleet's ability to protect the transports depended the army's existence. The Greek forces ashore and afloat were likewise partially dependent on over-seas food, for Greece was a commercial nation, relying on manufactures and trade to pay for imported grain. Unless the Persian squadron at Cythera were likely to affect Greek imports, it was clearly inadvisable to let this diversion dominate the rôle of the fleet. Greece imported grain from Sicily in normal times as well as from the Persian dominions. At this time, Sicily, at all times a granary, was occupied by an invasion by Carthage, which was not improbably instigated by Persia. But western supplies could not have been altogether cut off by the fleet at Cythera, which could not interfere with traffic passing to the isthmus by the Gulf of Corinth, although the Persian army could cut off such trade after seizing the isthmus.

Moreover, it may well have been that the transports bringing Persian supplies were not always loyal and may have sold to the Greeks. Pirates lay in wait at every promontory and, with the fleets of all maritime states of the Levant assembled for the war, it was easy for any trader to handle his cargo as he liked and cover himself by a tale of piracy. We may also recall in this connection that when the United States was at war with Great Britain, in 1812-14, New England ships supplied the Duke of Wellington's army in Spain.

THE RETIREMENT TO SALAMIS

We now turn once more to the fleets. At the close of the fierce Persian attack on September 1, the Greeks were much discouraged, but Themistocles called the captains together on the beach at Artemisium and told them that he had a plan whereby he hoped to detach the Ionian and Carian ships from the Persians, and, if this could be done, the Greeks might well hope to overcome the remainder. He did not explain his intentions further, but assured them he would secure a safe retreat. His plan, which he put in effect that night, was to inscribe the rocks with appeals to the Greeks in the Persian fleet to desert from it. Even if they did not heed the exhortation it would arouse the distrust of the Persians. In the meantime, following an old stratagem, he advised the Greeks to slaughter the cattle which the natives had brought there, and kindle the camp fires as usual. While this was being done, a scout, who had been stationed at Thermopylae with a 30-oared boat, arrived, probably about sundown, bringing news of the disaster there. It was now obvious that the fleet could no longer delay, for the Persian army might soon cross to Euboea and fall on the naval camp; so it withdrew that night to Salamis, where it probably berthed not later than the fifth.

As soon as the Greeks were off, a man of Histiaea (west of Artemisium) crossed to Aphetae and informed the Persians, who refused to believe him until after they had sent out scouting ships to verify the report. This is evidence that the last fight had been an equal one.

By sunrise, September 2, the scout reports were satisfactory, and the Persian fleet moved to Artemisium, where it stayed till noon, and then went on to Histiaea. No doubt the supply ships were pushed on to Thermopylae to enable the army to renew its supplies before resuming its

MAP 6.

march. Soon after arrival at Histiaea, a herald came from the King at
Thermopylae directing that all those of the fleet who wished to visit the
field of battle should be given leave to do so. The scene had been staged
for the visit by burying all the dead Persians except a thousand, while

leaving exposed the bodies of all the Greeks, including the helots. Permission was no sooner granted than there was a rush for the boats, and all who could get conveyance crossed the straits to the mainland and the day was given over to sightseeing. The next day, September 4, the sailors returned to their ships and the army began its march on Athens.

THE GREEKS AT SALAMIS

The situation which the Greek fleet found on its arrival on the Attic east coast was most disappointing to the Athenians, who had believed that they would find the whole army from the Peloponnese to have marched into Boeotia to meet the enemy there. But it was not so. It became evident to the Athenians that Leonidas and his troops had been sent north, not with the purpose of securing Central Greece, but merely to delay the enemy and obtain the aid of the Athenians while the mobilization at the isthmus and the fortifications there should be completed. So while the other contingents went on to Salamis, the Athenians stretched their ships along their own coasts and made proclamation that every Athenian should save his children and household as best he could. The Plataeans, who had helped to man the Athenian ships, disembarked here to attend to their own households. So the fugitives from Attica were ferried to Salamis and Aegina, but most to Troezen in the Peloponnese.

The whole fleet was then assembled at Salamis and probably beached on both sides of the town of Salamis. There it was joined by the reserve ships which had been assembling at Pogon, the port of Troezen in northeast Peloponnese, bringing the number to 310 in all.[5] The Persians probably had about 800 at this time.

---

[5] There is some dispute to this day about the number of Greek ships present at Salamis. Herodotus, our principal ancient authority, gives two lists, one of the ships at Artemisium and one of the ships at Salamis. He makes no mention of the sum of the Greek losses at Artemisium, and it seems to me that his two lists are best reconciled by supposing that Herodotus had the roster of ships before him, and to the list of Artemisium he added the reserves from Troezen without deducting the losses at Artemisium. Trieres to the number of 324 went to Artemisium and 42 joined at Salamis (there were besides 9 pentekonters at Artemisium, but only 7 at Salamis); 15 Persian ships were captured going to Aphetae; 30 more Persian ships were captured on the first day; and after the third day's fight on the Grecian side of the Artemisium channel at least some of the Persian wrecks may have been recovered with those of the Greeks and repaired for service.

Nevertheless, with two deserters' ships added to the above numbers making a list of 413 ships in all and 368 crews, Aeschylus tells us that only 310 Greek ships were present in the

When the Greek fleet had assembled at Salamis, Eurybiades called a council of war. The discussion was as to the place of making further naval resistance. While in session, the Council heard that the enemy had burnt Thespiae and Plataea and had entered Attica and was burning and ravaging (September 9). The majority wanted to remove to the isthmus, on the ground that Salamis was an island from which escape was impossible in case of defeat, but from the isthmus they could get to their homes. The Peloponnesians failed to see that if the fleet retired to the isthmus, the Persian fleet could ferry its army across to the Peloponnese and get behind the fortifications of the isthmus. Moreover, the fleet was necessary at Salamis to protect the refugees on the island.

The next day, probably, the Persians began the siege of the citadel of Athens which was not very well defended, although it took the Persians some days to get possession. On this day, also, September 10, the Persian fleet arrived from Histiaea at Phalerum, the port of Athens, and fleet and army were again in mutual support. During the siege the Greek fleet remained at Salamis, with the Peloponnesians still anxious to depart to the isthmus, yet held where they were by the force of Themistocles' personality, for the situation at the meeting of the General Council was a peculiar one. The commander in chief had no plenipotentiary powers, but needed the consent of the chiefs of the 21 contingents as to his general policy before he could take measures for its execution. The circumstances were not unlike those on the western front in the late war, when General Foch was in command of the allied armies but had to be very cautious in ascertaining that his wishes would be acceptable to the national generals before he announced them as orders, as otherwise he might have found an army withdrawn from his command.

Of the 310 ships present more than half belonged to Athens, Megara, and Aegina. None of these states lay behind the isthmus. None of them could hope to profit by a further retreat and all were eager to fight where

---

final action. If we trust Aeschylus as a participant, it seems the Greeks must have lost 58 crews (about 7,000 men) and possibly 103 or more ships before arrival at Salamis.

As for the Persian fleet, it probably suffered more than its enemy. Besides the 45 captured ships, its losses on the third day's fight on the southern side of the channel are alleged to have been heavier than those of the Greeks. So we may well place the Persian loss in three days of battle at about 100 ships. Adding this figure to the 400 lost in bad weather at the Magnesian Promontory and at the Hollows, we have it that the fleet which left Therma over 1,300 strong was reduced in a week to about 800.

they were. So Themistocles was able to prevent the Peloponnesians at Salamis from resolving to depart. For, as Thucydides says,

> The Athenians contributed three most important things, namely: the most ships, the most able general and unshrinking zeal (I-74).

And of the Athenian leader he further says:

> Themistocles was one who displayed genius in the most unmistakable way, and in this respect calls for admiration in a special and unparalleled manner. For by his native intellectual power, unaided by study or by the teaching of experience, he was capable of giving the ablest opinion in emergencies admitting only the briefest consideration, and he was skilled in forming a judgment upon coming events, even to the most distant future. Whatever came within the range of his practice, he could explain; and he did not fail to form an adequate judgment upon that which lay beyond his experience. He possessed a peculiar power of foresight into the good and evil of the uncertain future. Speaking generally, by the very power of his genius, in spite of the slightness of his application, he was unsurpassed in devising intuitively what was required in an emergency (I-138).

These great qualities of Themistocles, in addition to great martial resolution, have put him above other admirals that history has made known to us, unless perhaps Marcus Agrippa was his equal.

The Corinthian Admiral Adeimantus seems to have opposed Themistocles at every occasion. Athens and Corinth were in rivalry for the trade of the west, and the growth of Athenian naval power in the years just passed was no doubt a cause for Corinthian jealousy. It was to the credit of Eurybiades, the commander in chief, that he was able to control these national jealousies and himself to choose the better part and be guided by the great Athenian.

On September 21 the Acropolis was seized and Xerxes sent a messenger to Susa to announce his success in gaining what had been the nominal object of the expedition. On hearing of the capture, the Greeks met in Council on board ship to determine their future action, and again the desire of the Peloponnesians to go to the isthmus and make the final stand there was made evident. There was much discussion by the Corinthians and others, in which they seem to have talked themselves out and dispersed. Themistocles then sat with Eurybiades and secured his consent to remain and fight at Salamis. Eurybiades then reconvened the Council and Themistocles talked individually with the admirals.

THEMISTOCLES

Then, in a public address, Themistocles delivered his strategic and tactical views which Herodotus has reported as follows:

With thee it rests, O Eurybiades! to save Greece, if thou wilt only hearken unto me and give the enemy battle here rather than yield to the advice of those who would have the fleet withdrawn to the Isthmus. Hear now, I beseech thee and judge between the two courses. If you engage off the Isthmus, you will fight in the open sea, and it is highly inexpedient for us to put out thither, because our ships are heavier and fewer in number; and, again, you will lose Salamis, Megara, and Aegina, even if you are successful in other respects. For the Persian land army will accompany its fleet, and so you will be responsible for bringing them to the Peloponnese, and you will place the whole of Greece in peril. But if you do as I say, you will find the following great advantages in my plan. In the first place, by engaging in the strait with few ships against many, we shall win a great victory if the war takes the course that may be expected; for it is in our favor to fight in the narrow seas, just as it is in theirs to fight in the open. Again Salamis, in which we have deposited our wives and children, will not fall into the hands of the enemy. And there is this further advantage in the plan, and one by which you set most store. Whether you remain here, or whether you fight at the Isthmus, you will be just as much fighting on behalf of the Peloponnese; and you will not, if you are wise, attract the enemy toward the Peloponnese. If matters turn out as I expect, and we win a naval battle, the barbarians will never reach the Isthmus, nor advance farther than Attica, but will retire in disorder; and we shall be the gainers by the salvation of Megara, Aegina, and Salamis, at which, according to an oracle, we should defeat the foe. When men form reasonable plans, they usually succeed, but when they form unreasonable ones, the god refuses to fall in with human fancies (Herodotus: VIII-60).

At his close he was violently assailed by the Corinthian Adeimantus who bade him hold his peace, as he had no fatherland (alluding to the destruction of Athens) and protested to Eurybiades that he should not put the question at the demand of one who represented no state. Themistocles made a bitter reply, and maintained that the Athenians had a state more powerful than Corinth so long as they manned 200 ships, for none of the Greeks could resist their attack.[6] After this declaration, he appealed to Eurybiades, speaking more earnestly than before, saying,

If you remain here and play the man, all will be well; but if not, you will bring about the overthrow of Hellas. For the decision of the war lies with the fleet. Therefore be persuaded by me.

---

[6] It is possible that the 200 ships to which he alludes includes those of the Megarians and Aeginetans for whom he was speaking, as well as for Athens.

Themistocles' argument was accepted and the Council resolved to fight at Salamis. But Herodotus tells us that during the discussion Themistocles feared the Council would not agree with him and resolved to take means to force a battle in closed waters at Salamis. A victory here and here only would save the refugees. He therefore sent his faithful slave, Sikinnos, on a secret message to Persian headquarters to urge the King to make an immediate attack before the Greek fleet should break up and depart. The King was guided by this advice, as Herodotus says, and ordered the attack.

If such a step was really taken by Themistocles, as is probable, the message must have taken the form of the clever circulation of a rumor in the Persian camp, for a direct messenger to any prominent leader would have been held prisoner to be answerable for the truth of his story, whereas, Herodotus says, Sikinnos returned to Themistocles.

Although Themistocles pointed out to the Council that a successful naval battle at Salamis would forbid any attempt by the Persian army to go to the isthmus, it is not clear why the Persians might not have blockaded the Greeks in Salamis harbor and threatened to land troops on the island behind the line of blockade. The situation was the same as existed three weeks earlier at Artemisium. We may believe that the Persian conduct in this respect, at Artemisium, caused Themistocles to feel some assurance that the Persian fleet would not attempt to slip the transports past the Greek position at Salamis. Persian pride was no doubt involved in the royal decision.

THE PERSIANS IN ATTICA

After the Persian fleet regained touch with the army, on its arrival at Phalerum (September 10), the King went down to the shore and called a meeting attended by the vassal sovereigns and captains. These all favored an attack on the Greek fleet, except Artemisia, Queen of Halicarnassus, whose five ships were among the best in the fleet. The Queen recommended to let time work. As Herodotus reports her, she said to the King's ambassador:

Say to the King, Mardonius, that these are my words to him: "I was not the least brave among those who fought at Euboea, nor were my achievements there among the meanest; it is my right, therefore, O my lord, to tell thee plainly what I think to be most for thy advantage now. This, then, is my advice.

Spare thy ships and do not risk a battle; for these people are as much superior to thy people in seamanship as men to women. What so great need is there for thee to incur hazard at sea? Art thou not master of Athens, for which thou didst undertake the expedition? Is not Greece subject to thee? Not a soul now resists thy advance. They who once resisted were handled even as they deserved. Now learn how I expect that affairs will go with thine adversaries. If thou art not over-hasty to engage with them by sea, but wilt keep thy fleet near the land, then whether thou abidest as thou art, or marchest forward towards the Peloponnese, thou wilt easily accomplish all for which thou art come hither. The Greeks cannot hold out against thee very long; thou wilt soon part them asunder and scatter them to their several homes. In the island where they lie, I hear they have no food in store; nor is it likely, if thy land force begins its march towards the Peloponnese, that they will remain quietly where they are, at least such as come from that region. Of a surety *they* will not greatly trouble themselves to give battle on behalf of the Athenians. On the other hand, I tremble lest the defeat of thy sea force bring harm likewise to thy land army" (Herodotus: VIII-68).

The Queen added something in derogation of the fighting qualities of several of the subject contingents.

Xerxes was pleased with the words of Artemisia more than with those of other speakers; but, nevertheless, he followed contrary advice, for he thought that here at Salamis where he meant to witness events in person, men would fight more courageously than had been the case at Euboea where he was absent. Another reason for his pressing matters which is not mentioned in the histories, yet which must have been in the minds of all the seamen, was the advanced season. It was a proverb of the Middle Ages in regard to galley warfare, that in the Mediterranean there were only four good ports for a fleet, namely, June, July, August, and Port Mahon. It was now the time of the equinox, and the season of settled good weather was past, not without disastrous tempests in August. So Xerxes resolved for battle instead of delay, and the allied Greeks, driven by a great and commanding personality, were forced to forget their differences and await an attack where the locality favored them.

BATTLE OF SALAMIS

The second session of the Greek Council, on the twenty-first, at which the decision was made to remain, was probably not finished till after night-fall, and the chiefs departed to make preparations for the battle. But at sunrise, on the twenty-second, an earthquake was felt, which caused the Greeks to resolve to approach the gods with prayer and, accordingly, a ship was sent to Aegina to pray there for aid. Portents were seen during the day which were held to indicate Greek victory, and no doubt they were as reliable as the angels of Mons who appeared to the British army in 1914.

On September 22, when darkness was setting in, the Persian fleet began to move out of Phalerum Bay in accordance with the resolve of the King to seek the enemy and force an action, and hastened by the false report that the Grecians were about to break away. As was said before, the Grecian ships were a little over 300 in number and the Persians may have been about 800 in four divisions. But there is an allusion in Herodotus, VIII-76, which may mean that part of the Persian fleet was occupying a position over 30 miles in the rear at the island of Ceos, who were probably a guard for the line of communication. These did not pass beyond Munychia, at any time.

The persistence of Themistocles in remaining at Salamis on the defensive was now bringing about the decisive battle under tactical conditions favorable to the Greeks; that is to say, in the narrow waters between Salamis and the shores of Attica, the Persians could not accomplish envelopment and bring all their ships into action, as they had done at the close of the first day at Artemisium when the Greeks were indebted to darkness that the fight was a drawn one. Moreover, the narrow waters gave the Greeks a still further advantage in the fact that the line of contact was so short that the Greeks themselves, like the Persians, were obliged to form in several lines, of which only the front line was engaged at any moment. Thus the fighting ships in the front could be relieved from time to time by those waiting in the rear, and the excess of numbers of the Persians was less available for exhausting the physical strength of the enemy.[7] The location of the battle was such that the superior armament of the Greek warriors was the conclusive factor.

The place in which Themistocles had persuaded Eurybiades and the Peloponnesians to make their stand is worthy of description.[8] The town

---

[7] The detailed accounts of battles of the Middle Ages mention pouring fresh reserves into ships locked in close combat, and this could have been done at Salamis, even if the ships themselves could not back out of the line to be replaced by fresh ones.

[8] Modern commentators differ much as to the position of the Greek fleet, placing it from the Bay of Eleusis to the eastern part at the strait. If it had not been well to the eastward, it would not have protected the women on the island.

of Salamis, on the island of that name, stood on a round promontory facing the channel leading between the island and the mainland, which connected the waters of the Bay of Eleusis with those of the Saronic Gulf. Adjoining the town and to the south of it was a small harbor whose southern side, the Peninsula Cynosura, was extended for about 2 miles parallel to the ridge of Mount Aegaleos whose base, running east and west, less than a mile away, formed the other shore line of the strait. Between Cynosura and Mount Aegaleos was the water in which Themistocles desired to be attacked, and here Xerxes had resolved to gratify him. The entrance to the strait led northward, and then the channel turned west. Right in the mouth of the entrance lay the little rocky island of Psyttalia, about a mile long. It might be an important position from which to aid the ships or pick up swimmers from the wrecks.

Night had fallen when the Persian fleet arrived off the entrance to the strait. The fleet lay to, or else each ship dropped an anchor under foot to hold her position. We must recollect that above all things it was necessary for the leaders to save the strength both of rowers and of soldiers for the effort of battle. Consequently, the ships' movements were very slow, both on the day preceding the battle and while maneuvering, immediately before the battle. Certainly the speed was not over 2 miles an hour. During the night the Persians landed a large body of troops on Psyttalia to take possession of the wrecks, to aid their own men, and to destroy those of the enemy who might land there. One division, the Egyptian, moved during the night to block the western entrance to the Bay of Eleusis by the Strait of Minoa, and the other three divisions, which we may take to have been each 200 strong, took station south of Psyttalia each in a single column for entrance in the morning. The three lines thus were stretched parallel to each other, reaching from Salamis to the Piraeus in a formation which must have been nearly 4 miles long.

There has been much dispute by modern students of the early authorities' statement as to how the fleets were formed and brought into contact. I shall not attempt to weigh the different versions, but give that which I think the accounts will bear and yet comply with seamanlike requirements. The three Persian divisions present were (1) that of the Ionians, armed after the Grecian fashion and commanded by Ariabignes, brother to the King, which was the left wing in the battle and during the night was probably the northern line; (2) that of the Phoenicians, light-armed, which was the right wing in battle and was now probably the southern line; and (3) the other light-armed division which had included the Cilicians and which was the center of the battle and was the center line during the night.

During the night, while the Persian deployment was taking place, there was again discussion and anxiety among the Greeks as always must occur among those who are expectant and have yielded the initiative. As Herodotus says,

> Among the captains at Salamis the strife of words grew fierce. As yet they did not know that they were encompassed, but imagined that the barbarians remained in the same places in which they had seen them the day before.

At this moment, Aristides, an Athenian and political enemy of Themistocles, arrived from Aegina. He had recently returned from exile to which Themistocles had sent him three years before. Aristides now had forgotten his feud and informed Themistocles that he had sighted the Egyptian ships going to the western entrance. Possibly they had chased him through the west passage, although he may have been lucky enough to get through or around the main fleet. The two then went before the Council, and Aristides told what he had seen, but he was doubted. Then an Ionian triere, deserting from the Persians, came in to confirm Aristides' news and, all change of plan being now impossible, the Greeks made ready for the coming fight. At dawn all the men-at-arms were assembled on the beach and the various leaders addressed them, Themistocles last. They then all embarked and put out into the strait with all the fleet. Herodotus does not positively so state, but it is probable that the Corinthian squadron of 40 ships had been sent in good time to check the Egyptian fleet at the western entrance to the Bay of Eleusis. This squadron undoubtedly fought on that day, although seemingly not in the main action.

Persian Formation

In the meantime the Persians were entering the bay. It would have been useless for the Persians to have used the channel to the west of Psyttalia. They must have known that the enemy would not expose his flank and rear by coming to Psyttalia, and that therefore he would await the attack north of Cynosura. Besides, two lines of advance would interfere with each other on the turn. So it seems proper to believe that all the Persian fleet passed east of Psyttalia going north, and then turned westward. Thus they would have more time for alignment after sighting the enemy. The maneuver is easy to reconstruct in a probable manner by

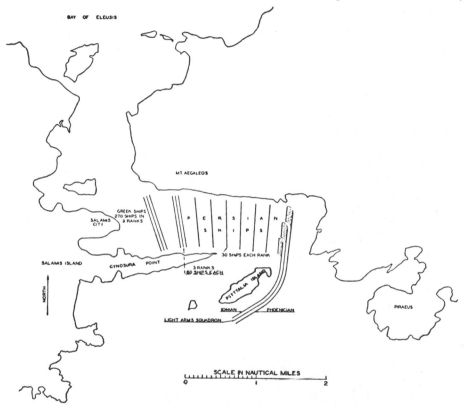

MAP 7. BATTLE OF SALAMIS
The Greek and Persian fleets facing each other just before contact.

maneuvers which steam vessels would use now with the same purpose in view, and which are laid down in the signal and drill books of the U. S. Navy today and are similar to the maneuvers actually used by the Christian fleet at the Battle of Lepanto. I suggest, therefore, that the Persian fleet at break of dawn about five o'clock, formed in three columns, some 20 yards distance between columns and about 40 yards distance between ships in column (i.e., 15 yards of open water between bow and stern of neighboring ships) and stood north at a speed not over 2 knots towards the ridge of Aegaleos. The Phoenicians in the eastern column were in advance of the center column by about 400 or 450 yards and this, again, was ahead of the Ionians in the western column by another 400 yards. The post of honor was on the right and in the advance. We may presume, therefore, that the Phoenician commander was also in general command and that as he approached the northern side of the strait he made a pre-arranged signal meaning "ships left" to the 10 leading ships of the three divisions. This maneuver would give a line of 30 ships at 40 yards distance, in three echelons moving west. The speed of this first line would be reduced to 1 knot after bringing the echelons into line. The rest of the ships still in column would continue to move north at 2 knots until the leader neared the shore, when the next 30 ships would "left turn" and follow the leading line and close with it to 40 yards before reducing speed. By such a "movement in succession," as the phrase goes, the fleet would be formed in a solid rectangle of 30 ships front and 20 ranks deep. The maneuver is after the fashion of the well-known infantry evolution, in which a regiment in column of fours marching north converts itself into a column in company front marching west. By about 7:00 A.M. the leading line of ships would be passing the tip of Cynosura Point, at 1 knot speed, and would need to have the distances between neighboring ships reduced by the second rank coming up into the first line's intervals and making the distance from ship to ship 20 yards.

Probable Position of Greek Fleet

In the meantime the Greek fleet would have placed itself in the most suitable position. Let us see what that would have been. The tactical situation which Themistocles had induced Eurybiades to occupy was one in which the flanks were covered, thereby preventing the Persians from putting more ships in action at a given moment than the Greeks. This was accomplished by allowing the enemy to advance unopposed as far as Cynosura. But an additional factor now makes itself evident. Both shores were lined with troops whose missile aid would be important. The Persians would not wish to approach Cynosura and the Greeks would avoid Aegaleos. Consequently, the Greek left wing would be beyond effective bowshot (200 yards) of the southwest tip of Aegaleos, and any Persian ship attempting to creep past would expose her broadside to the ram. It is not unlikely that the Grecian right wing might be in a more easterly position than the northern one. As Aeschylus says, "the right wing led." The available space across the strait at the point mentioned is about 1,600 yards, giving 80 ships in the front line and three Greek lines in all with a few more ships in reserve. (The 40 Corinthians having probably gone to the Strait of Minoa to check the Egyptians.) By the actions at Artemisium the Greeks were satisfied as to the individual superiority of their ships, and they may have been willing to advance the right wing somewhat, under cover of their archers on the peninsula, and so make their front line run from south southeast to north northwest. This would let them put a few more ships in the front line.

As I have said before, the Persian advance must have been very slow. Besides visual signals and trumpet calls, small fast dispatch boats took the admirals or their aides up and down the line to encourage the crews and to pass orders. The commander in chief, leading on the right, was in communication with the King on shore at Mount Aegaleos. The 30-oar scouts had no doubt been close to the enemy line and reported what they saw. So that if the Greeks did advance their right wing, as Aeschylus says, there can be little doubt that the Persians advanced theirs correspondingly and, having thus increased the length of their line so as to make it perhaps 1,500 yards long, when they turned slightly to face the enemy, they perhaps summoned the third rank as well as the second to join the first before closing with the enemy, although there may not have been room for all the third line to get in. Diodorus mentions confusion. The collision cannot have taken place before eight o'clock and then the westerly morning breeze was blowing and embarrassing the high-sterned Persian ships more than it did the Greeks. Probably it was most troublesome when both fleets were facing each other, 400 or 500 yards apart, making the last adjustments of line and passing the last orders before advancing slowly to collision. It must be realized that these ships of some 50 tons displacement had sides not more than 2 inches thick and that very little momentum was needed to drive the bronze ram point through such light material. Consequently, a captain would prefer to keep his ship under control at slow speed which was enough to strike a piercing blow, rather than put her at full speed and make himself incapable of stopping or turning in a short space. Besides, his crew had physical strength for no more than one prolonged spurt and the battle might last all day. No admiral could afford to open the battle at a

speed more than what he could sustain for the day. Of course, at any moment, a captain might call on his rowers for a few minutes of violent exertion, but it could not be maintained, even under the lash of the Middle
Ages.

There is mention of the Greeks having fallen back just before the
enemy closed with them, and commentators have made much of the incident, but seamen will require no elucidation. It was essential to the Greek
plan of action not to advance beyond a certain line, and yet they did not
mean to lie far in the rear of it. Every one knows that ships at rest in a
breeze cannot preserve their alignment. Consequently, when the alignment
was disturbed by the morning breeze or the current, it was necessary to back
water and then correct the alignment as the ships once more came forward.

Not until the hostile lines were within 200 or 300 yards of each other
would they increase the stroke and select their opponents. In an advance
of 50 yards the speed might reach 4 knots.[9] The faster speed was largely
for psychologic effect. The Persian bowmen were naturally the first to
open. Although the panoplied Greeks were well protected, the 4 archers
to each ship could make only a poor return fire. In the struggle of ship to
ship the Greeks depended not only on their 18 soldiers per ship and the
ship's officers, but on their rowers who also were at least partially armored
and had their spears and shields beside them ready to use as soon as they
trailed their oars upon collision.

Of the two maneuvers which have been handed down to us, the *diekplous* and the *periplous*, we may not think that either was much used that
day, for if any ship were to pass through the hostile line, as she struggled
clear, she would find herself at the mercy of the rams of the second line.
Most of the contacts, we may presume, were either clean ram strokes, of
which probably there were not many, for lack of room, or incomplete
diekploi in which the two enemies remained alongside each other until, in
the majority of cases, the issue was decided by the superiority of the heavy-
armed spearmen over the lightly protected bowmen and javelin throwers.
The fight lasted all day under the eyes of the King, who had seated himself
on the slopes of Mount Aegaleos to reward the brave and punish the

_____

[9] A slight calculation shows that starting from rest a 50-ton triere with 90 rowers might
reach a speed of 4 knots in 50 yards and 40 seconds—a little more or less according to the
effort on the oars.

slackers. But the presence of the King perhaps was not as helpful as he meant it to be. Under his eye, the Persians in the rear pressed into the front line and the crush was embarrassing. The oars were broken, and the ships in thus losing their mobility were the easier rammed by the Greeks who were less numerous and presumably did not press each other so much. Consequently, some probably were able one by one to withdraw from the fighting line and be replaced by fresh ships from the lines in the rear, as happens in infantry action. Also, fresh men were no doubt fed into the front ships. We may take it that at first there were three or four lines of Greek ships and six or eight of the Persians, after the rear ships closed up, according to the obliquity of the battle line with the trend of the channel, and all ships were never engaged at one moment.

Slowly the Persians were pushed back, although we are told that here they fought better than at Artemisium. Although some of the Ionian Greeks were not devoted to the King's cause, yet most did well, and one Ionian encounter observed by the King cleared them all from a charge of treason brought by some Phoenicians who had escaped from their ships to the shore at the King's seat. While the Phoenicians made their allegation, a Samothracian ship within sight of the King struck and sank an Athenian (ram stroke?), but herself was instantly struck and crippled by an Aeginetan (incomplete *diekplous?*). Whereupon, the Samothracians who were expert with the javelin, cleared the deck of the Aeginetan and then boarded and captured her. Seeing this gallant action by a subject Greek and being by this time in a bad humor, the King ordered the accusing Phoenicians to execution, and the Ionians retained their credit.

As the Persians were pushed towards Psyttalia and uncovered the channel to open water, they seem to have been insufficiently in hand to extend their left wing and did not use their numbers to outflank the Greeks, as they did the third day at Artemisium. On the contrary, they allowed the enemy to control the passage to Psyttalia, and Aristides took advantage of the opportunity to gather the heavy-armed troops, who were on the shore of Cynosura covering the fleet's southern flank. These men were now unoccupied and Aristides ferried them over to Psyttalia where they destroyed the Persians and facilitated the further advance of the Greek right flank.

By the time the action had moved abreast of Psyttalia, in the afternoon, the victory must have been decided and the Persians who, until then, had kept their rams turned to the enemy, now began to turn to the south and slip away from the scene while the Athenians pressed those who continued to resist towards the shore, and the Aeginetans on the south dealt with those who were escaping to take refuge in their former anchorage in the Bay of Phalerum where they were supported by the Persian army. (See appendix 1 to this chapter for Aeschylus' account of the battle.)

The tactical pursuit was not carried far, but the victors recovered all the wrecks which had not drifted too far away and made ready for another action. Many of the wrecks drifted to the shore of Colias, near Phalerum, by a west wind, where, of course, the Persians got them. Most of the ship construction was of light wood, and as the ships were stripped for action for greater mobility, those disabled by the ram, usually did not sink, but became water-logged and capsized, and remained floating bottom side up; a prize for the side which remained on the scene, to be towed to shore and repaired. The loss of the Greek ships was said to be 40 and that of the Persians 200 sunk, besides those taken with their crews.

The King and the Fleet Return to Asia

The King, who was greatly discouraged by his defeat, nevertheless made preparations for another engagement by sea, but he feared lest the Greeks might push on to attack his communications and even break the bridge at the Hellespont. Mardonius, a cousin and brother-in-law of the King, was afraid that having proposed the campaign the King might now hold him responsible for its failure. He therefore assured the King that the Greeks would not dare to attack the army after the result of Thermopylae. The defeat, he said, had occurred to the subject allies; but the Persians were yet unconquered and unconquerable. He therefore urged the King to depart home if he thought fit, with the bulk of the army, and leave Mardonius with a selected force of the best troops to winter in Europe and undertake a campaign against Greece the next spring. Artemisia had further established herself in the confidence of the King by her gallantry in the fight at Salamis, which the King had noted himself, and when the King sought her advice, she confirmed that of Mardonius and solaced him with the thought that by destroying Athens he had fulfilled his announced purpose when undertaking the expedition. Thereupon Xerxes sent his children in Artemisia's care by the direct sea route to Ephesus.

It would scarcely be politic to announce a great failure to such an empire as the Persian, composed of subject races held together by the armed strength of the conquerors. Besides, modern research indicates a serious insurrection at home that summer. It is therefore very probable that Xerxes was obliged to depart for Asia to forestall the news of his disaster and take measures to suppress the revolt, while the stay of Mardonius enabled the King to represent the latter as remaining to consolidate a conquest. The King delayed but a few days before dispatching the defeated fleet by night to return by the way it had come, in order to secure his crossing into Asia, and he followed with the army.

In the meantime the Greeks had been making ready for another naval battle, for they still saw the army before Athens, and were unaware of the destruction of the Persian morale.

The Greek Pursuit

On hearing of the retreat of the Persian fleet, the Greeks at Salamis pursued as far as the island of Andros, 30 miles east of the Attic Peninsula. Arrived here, Themistocles urged further chase to the Hellespont. Eurybiades, on the other hand, thought that the enemy should not be pushed to despair by cutting off his retreat, for then he would fight with a good chance of victory in order to procure himself supplies; whereas, if left alone, he would return to Asia, as his movements showed he wished to do. Thereupon Themistocles turned to his own Athenians who were still eager to pursue even alone, and pressed on them the argument of Eurybiades to "let well enough alone" and urged each man to return home and repair his house and sow his crop. For what might reasonably be attempted by the whole fleet he no doubt thought too much for the Athenian squadron only. The Greeks now laid siege to the city of Andros which had Medized during the invasion, but without success.

The Persian Army Winters in Thessaly

The Persian army marched off in its retreat through Boeotia. Mardonius resolved to winter in Thessaly, whose rich plains were the chief granary of Greece and would furnish rations for his army during the winter. On arriving in Thessaly, Mardonius chose the best troops to retain with him, while the rest went on with Xerxes, who arrived at the Hellespont 45 days later (probably early December) and proceeded to Sardis. The whole number remaining in Europe for the campaign of 479 is stated by Herodotus to have been 300,000, but he names only 5 infantry units to which some cavalry and infantry were added. Modern criticism makes the force much less. A probable estimate holds that Mardonius had one army corps in Thessaly of six myriads, including one of cavalry, and Artabazus had a similar force in Macedonia and Thrace to hold the communications (sea ports) with Asia—in all, under 100,000 men, for the ranks were probably not full. In the final battle there may have been 40,000 to 50,000 men.

The operations for the year being concluded by the retreat of the Persians and the Greek failure to take Andros, the Greek fleet divided the booty and set apart suitable offerings to the gods, after which it made sail for the isthmus, where a prize of valor was to be awarded to the man who of all the Greeks had shown the greatest merit. There were to be two prizes, a first and a second; but no first could be awarded, as every man voted for himself first. Although Themistocles got most of the second votes, envy prevented a decision. The fleet and army dispersed for the winter. As the chiefs who fought at Salamis withheld the reward to which Themistocles above all others was entitled, he went to Lacedaemonia to be honored there and was received in an unprecedented manner. The prize of valor, indeed, a crown of olive, they gave to their own leader, Eurybiades, but to Themistocles also they gave a crown of olive as the prize of wisdom and dexterity.

CAMPAIGN OF 479 B.C.

After ferrying the King across the Hellespont, the Persian fleet wintered at Cyme and Samos on the coast of Asia Minor. On the first approach of spring, the ships assembled at Samos under the command of Mardontes and Artayntes, but farther west than Samos they did not venture to go, for their presence there was necessary to keep Ionia from insurrection. Thus Mardonius in Europe was without the help of a fleet in carrying on his campaign. Mardontes had 300 ships, including the disaffected Ionian squadron, and did not think that the Greeks would venture to cross the Aegean Sea, as they would be without a base for their operations. On the approach of spring the presence of Mardonius in Thessaly roused the

Greeks to assemble 110 ships at Aegina under the command of Leoty-chides, a Spartan; for in spite of their acknowledged great services the year before, Themistocles and Eurybiades were no longer in authority. At Aegina delegates arrived from Ionia (Chios) asking for deliverance from the Persians. Apparently the assurances of the delegates were not entirely satisfactory as to the support a Greek fleet might expect on the coast of Asia, for the fleet moved only to the island of Delos, where it was in a position of observation and ready to take advantage of any opportunity.

About this time Mardonius was preparing for his campaign. His line of communications through Thrace to the Bosphorus was very long and, to us who are examining sea power, the interest of his military operations before the final battle is that they were conducted chiefly with the political objective of inducing the Athenian fleet to desert the Greek cause, and so allow him to draw his supplies directly from the Aegean ports of Asia Minor. No doubt coasting vessels helped supply in the northern Aegean. Besides, if Mardonius were to attempt to take possession of the Pelopon-nese without the help of a fleet, he would be checked by the entrenchments at the Isthmus of Corinth, and the experience at Thermopylae forbade another attempt of the sort with the whole Greek army behind the forti-fied position. Accordingly Mardonius sent an emissary to the Athenians to detach them from the Greek cause and to obtain their navy to ferry his army across the Saronic Gulf and to turn the Greek defenses at the isthmus, thus to make a marching campaign in the Peloponnese, instead of an assault at the isthmus. He offered to make good the ravages committed in Attica the previous season, and to give the Athenians additional lands if they would make peace, but he threatened them in case they refused his offer.

When the Lacedaemonians heard that Mardonius had sent to make terms with the Athenians, they also sent ambassadors to urge the Athenians to remain faithful to the Greek cause. They reproached the Athenians with having brought on the war by seeking to extend their empire and thus involving all Greece. Realizing, however, the calamities of Athens, the Lacedaemonians offered to support all Athenian women and the un-warlike portion of each household as long as the war should last. Having heard both sides, the Athenians rejected the Persian offer and promised the Lacedaemonians that they would never make peace with Xerxes. They

declined the Spartan offer of assistance with thanks, and urged the Lacedaemonians to lead their troops out into Boeotia, as by taking up that advanced position, they would save Attica from invasion.

Mardonius Moves against Athens

On learning that the Athenians would not accept his terms, Mardonius
broke camp and led his army against Athens, impressing local troops as
he advanced. Having arrived at Boeotia, the Thebans urged him to remain
there and offer bribes to the hostile leaders, by which easy methods they
assured him the Greeks might be overcome without fighting. But as
Herodotus says, Mardonius was anxious to inform the King at Sardis by
fire signals from island to island that Athens was taken, and so he declined
the advice, and advanced into Attica.

On seeing that the Lacedaemonians were not coming north to meet
Mardonius, the Athenians recalled their squadron from the fleet at Delos
and withdrew the population, some to the ships, but most to Salamis as before, where the Persians being without ships could not reach them. At the
same time, the Athenians sent a message reproaching the Peloponnesians
for remaining behind the isthmus wall instead of advancing into Boeotia to
cover Attica as they had promised. They reminded them that if no aid
came from Sparta, Athens must seek her own salvation. In the meantime
the Persians advanced to Athens but did no injury to the country. The
Spartan rulers delayed ten days without replying to the Athenian envoys.
It is probable that they were not wholly confident as to the fidelity of
Athens.

PLATAEA

Aristides had succeeded Themistocles in authority and was now in
command of the Athenian troops, and he belonged to the party unfavorable
to Sparta. The Spartans could not afford to leave the strong line of the
isthmus until they had convinced themselves that Aristides and his party
were worthy of reliance. Finally, just as the Athenian envoys were going
home, disappointed, the Spartans perceived that if they left the Athenians
to make their own terms with the enemy, it would not be long before the
Athenian fleet would be escorting the Persian army across the Saronic Gulf
to the rear of the wall on which they were so confidently depending. Per-

haps Mardonius had given indications that it was his intention to occupy all Central Greece permanently and Sparta understood that if this occupation took place and the Athenian fleet should be disposed of, the independence of Peloponnese could not last long. Thereupon, that very night, the Spartan ephors sent forward a large detachment of their army and the next morning they announced their action and the Athenian envoys left Sparta in company with another large force for the establishment of a line of defense in Boeotia. News of the Spartan decision and advance was sent to Mardonius at Athens by the Argives who were ill-disposed to the Spartans and had promised Mardonius that they would stop the Spartans from crossing their territory on the way to the isthmus, but now, they said, they were too weak to do so.

Hitherto, Mardonius had refrained from injury to Attic property, but finding that he could make no arrangements with the Athenians, he ravaged their country and leveled the city, as he withdrew into Boeotia. It is probable that Attica had been occupied only by a small part of the Persian army; for as the army was without sea transport, it was inadvisable to extend the main line of supply beyond Boeotia until Mardonius was sure of using the Attic fleet. But Persian transport ships probably came to the ports of Boeotia.

Mardonius retired towards Thebes where he took up position north of the Cithaeron range, about 4 miles south of the city along the Asopus stream, and there he built a square rampart about 2,000 yards (10 stadia) on a side for protection to his trains and army if necessary.[10] The Lacedaemonians did not pass beyond the isthmus wall until they were joined by the other Peloponnesians. But then, finding the sacrifices favorable, they set out in one body and went as far as Eleusis where they were met by the Athenian contingent; and the sacrifices being again favorable, the united force continued on under the command of the Spartan Pausanius, regent for the son of Leonidas. It is noteworthy how much reliance the leaders put in the soothsayers and sacrificial divination. It seems likely that the priesthood was in close touch with the plans of the rulers, and that the divinations were a means of propaganda for which today we have other methods.

---

[10] Large enough for 150,000 men if crowded. According to Polybius the Roman legionary camp of 726 yards on a side accommodated about 20,000 men.

The Greek army moved through the passes of the Cithaeron and took up a position east of the city of Plataea, at the foot of the rocky slope of the hills where the ground was not favorable to cavalry attack. Here they were about 3 miles from the Persian entrenchment on the Asopus and separated from it by a range of low hills. Herodotus says the Greeks had 110,000 men present and the Persians three times as many. Modern commentators think these figures much too large. Delbrueck estimates the Greeks had perhaps 20,000 hoplites and as many more light-armed, and the Persians and Medized Greeks had a somewhat less total, that is, approximately, an army of 6 weak myriads, but with a strong cavalry contingent.

The strategic situation was that the Peloponnesian forces had been obliged to defend Central Greece in order to prevent the surrender of the Athenian squadron to the Persians. Had this occurred, the Persian fleet would have crossed the Aegean and enabled Mardonius to enter Peloponnese at any selected point.

The battle of Plataea deserves some notice from naval students because tactics was then developing as an art, and military tactics led naval tactics for many centuries. As at Marathon, the Greeks had little cavalry and were weak in their missile armament. The Persians were strong in cavalry and habitually relied on a battle of envelopment by their swiftly moving cavalry.

On the sixth day after the two armies arrived in position, Mardonius ordered his cavalry to attack, hoping to draw the Greeks out of their strong position in the foothills to a place where they could be got at. In their effort to draw the Greeks out on the plain, the cavalry seems to have gone too close to the Greeks, contrary to its usual custom, and was beaten off with much loss and the death of its leader, Masistius. The Greeks got an exaggerated idea of their own efficiency against cavalry and ventured across the valley to a position with better water supply. Then Mardonius sent his cavalry behind the Greek position to seize the mountain pass by which the army was supplied, and a day or two later the cavalry was able to separate the Greeks from their water. The Greeks had to retire during the night, and Mardonius attacked desperately as they drew back, first with cavalry to delay and then with infantry as it came up. When the Greek army began its movement to the rear, it had been defeated but not broken as Mardonius assumed. His rash and disorderly charge in this belief that the Greeks had been routed caused the Persian ruin in the close encounter, where Mardonius himself lost his life. After the death of Mardonius, his army broke and fled to the entrenched camp only a short distance away, but the Greeks stormed it and all within were slain. The remnants of the army escaped into Thessaly and under Artabazus, together with the troops on the line of communications, attempted to return to Asia, but most were lost in Thrace.

MYCALE

The victory of Plataea was the complement of that won on the same day, as is said, on the shores of Asia Minor. It was not enough for the safety of Greece to hurl the Persians back upon Macedonia and Thrace. The battle at Salamis the year before had shown the dependence of the mighty invasion upon sea power, and indicated the line of the Bosphorus and the Hellespont as the proper one for the Greeks to hold for safety.

While Mardonius was advancing from Thessaly, the Attic squadron was needed on its own coast for local transport service, and the rest of the Greek fleet at Delos could do no more than remain there to watch the growth of Ionian unrest and prevent the Persian fleet crossing to aid the army. Nevertheless, as was said before, it probably could not entirely stop some sea-borne supplies to the Persians in Boeotia. But when the northward movement of the Peloponnesian army freed Attica from the enemy and the Persian fleet remained inactive in Asia Minor, then the Attic contingent of the Greek fleet was able to join the others at Delos, and the united force of 250 ships was now itself able to think of taking the offensive. This it had hitherto been unable to do because of lack of a suitable base on the Asiatic shores. Only the year before, just after Salamis, the victorious fleet had been unable to seize Andros, and in 479 it could not hope to get a footing in Asia without local help.

At this moment an embassy arrived from the great city of Samos where the Persian fleet then was, to say that if the Greeks would come over, they might count on a Samian revolt, and that the Persian fleet would not await them there. The admirals and envoys exchanged oaths and the latter returned immediately, but the fleet waited till the next day when the omens were found favorable and the fleet went forward to Samos about 70 miles away. Upon arrival on the Samian coast, the Greek fleet made

ready for battle, but on hearing of its advance, the Persian admirals
Mardontes and Artayntes had held a council and, as the envoys had predicted, decided to abandon Samos and retire to Mycale, a few miles away
on the mainland. Being resolved not to risk the Persian fleet in a general
action, they sent the Phoenician squadron home and the other ships they
hauled up on the beach and built a stockade of trees and stones around
them, and summoned aid from the troops garrisoned about the neighboring provinces. Here they were prepared either to win a battle or to stand
a siege. The fate of the fleet was to be decided on shore.

The Greeks were much disappointed on finding the Persian fleet had
gone to the mainland, but after some hesitation they followed, in the hope
of inducing revolt among the active troops. It must be remembered that the
Greek hoplites in the fleet were only 14 per ship, with 4 archers, so that
they had only 3,500 heavy-armed to land against a great body of Persian
troops who were within call although not immediately available. The
Greek mariners and rowers were not wholly unarmed, and they would increase the strength of the landing troops, but still the odds against them
were great if the Ionians were to remain faithful to the Great King.

When the Greek fleet arrived off Mycale, it approached the Persian
ships drawn on the shore, and Leotychides summoned the Ionians among
them by herald that when the Greeks joined battle with the enemy they
(the Ionians) should remember freedom. After this address Leotychides
brought his ships to the land and, having disembarked his men, they prepared for battle.[11] The Persian leaders were greatly suspicious of Ionian
fidelity by this time, and Leotychides spread a rumor of Greek success at
Plataea. The Persians took away the arms of the Samians and reported
Xerxes was coming with a great army. The Persians then advanced to
attack the Greeks, despising their small numbers. Although the Ionian
Greeks had decided to desert and go over to their countrymen, the
latter did not understand this and fell into irresolution and debate. However, the approach of the Persians obliged the Greeks to fight; and they
did so bravely. When the Ionians took part against the Persians, the hopes
of the Greeks revived and those of the Persians flagged, and the latter were
pursued with slaughter to their tents. The Aeolians and other Asiatic

---

[11] The accounts of Herodotus and of Diodorus are not in complete agreement and in the
main this account follows Obst's analysis.

Greeks then joined in the pursuit. Some of the Persians got over the mountains to Sardis and others took refuge behind the ships' stockade.[12] Thus, on this day, the Ionians revolted a second time from the Persians, and the Persian fleet had been destroyed by a battle on shore. The Greek fleet now sailed away to Samos, and there took council as to the future of the Ionian Greeks. After some discussion as to whether those of the mainland would emigrate, the proposal was rejected and the islanders and the Milesians were received into the League of the Allies.

CONCLUSION OF THE WAR

This campaign was the beginning of the predominance of the sea power of Athens. She perceived what might be done for her greatness by controlling the commerce of the Aegean with her allies. But the Spartans were not so broad-minded and did not care to undertake further accomplishments. So the Spartan ships under Leotychides sailed home, while the rest, including the new allies, all under the lead of the Athenian Xanthippus, went on to the Hellespont, whose control not only would secure Greece, but also would ensure them the commerce of the Euxine Sea. On arrival there they sat down to the siege of Sestos, which was the strongest fortress in all that region, and after long operations they captured the city and thereby held the key to the Euxine. So ended the Persian invasion of Greece in the establishment of the commercial and naval supremacy of Athens among all the Greek states.

SUMMARY

In the foregoing account much attention has been paid to the land warfare since army tactics was the basis of the fleet maneuvering, for military tactics and military tradition preceded naval tactics.

---

[12] Herodotus describes an attack of the Athenians on the stockade sheltering the Persian ships and their destruction, but Diodorus speaks only of the battle in the open. As the Greeks had only a few heavy-armed soldiers on each ship, it is scarcely possible that the European Greeks could have won without help from the Asiatic and insular Greeks who deserted the Persians. Much less could they have stormed the stockade. Consequently, Obst accepts Diodorus' version on this point and believes that Herodotus put forth an account unduly magnifying the Athenian share of the victory.

Nevertheless, it is quite possible to believe that after the Persian forces had scattered, those who had taken refuge behind the stockade agreed to surrender and that, as Herodotus says, the Persian ships were destroyed before the Greek fleet victoriously sailed away.

In reviewing the campaigns of 480 and 479, it is not immediately apparent why the King resolved to attack the Greeks in the narrow waters of Salamis. The Persian fleet might have taken position outside the entrance to the straits and passed the transports behind it to supply the army at the isthmus. This would have compelled the Greek ships to fight outside or yield. But it is probable that the explanation may be looked for in the resolution of the King to uphold Persian prestige among his subject nations by accepting battle on the enemy's terms and defeating him. Such was the case at the siege of Boston in 1775, when the British made a frontal attack on Bunker Hill for the express purpose of showing contempt for the American militia and suffered most severely for letting their disdain find tactical expression. At Salamis, the tactical effort was mainly against personnel. I do not mean to minimize the use of the ram, for both sides used it and many ships were pierced or crushed by collision, but it does not seem to have been the principal weapon. In the sea fights, as in those by land, it was to the advantage of the Persians to surround the enemy and thus give themselves the opportunity to employ all their forces against smaller numbers. At the same time, as much as possible, it was to their advantage to refuse to close; and thus make a long-range archers' fight. Tactically, both Thermopylae and Artemisium were trial battles. At Artemisium the genius of Themistocles taught him the tactical lesson to avoid envelopment and seek close action, but the Persians did not see it. At Thermopylae, neither side seems to have drawn tactical conclusions from the result of the battle, although 2,000 or 3,000 Greeks fought there for two days and escaped to the isthmus to tell their experiences. So at the decisive sea battle at Salamis the diplomacy and personal force of Themistocles enabled him to hold the Greek fleet in a position where all the tactical advantage fell to it, and the Persians, who had learned nothing from the three days' fight at Artemisium, accepted the Greek terms of battle, a close fight in narrow waters. At the decisive land fight at Plataea, it was quite otherwise. The tactical lessons of Thermopylae were not applied by either side, although it is to be remembered that neither at Marathon nor at Thermopylae had Persian cavalry met the Greek spearmen. At Plataea they felt each other out. At first, the Greeks feared to expose themselves to the cavalry, and Masistius made an unwise use of his arm in charging home whereby he lost his life and the cavalry was defeated.

This caused the Greeks to lose their fear of horsemen and change their position, and Mardonius then used his cavalry properly. But when the Greeks fell back, under the cavalry threat against the water supply, Mardonius on his part overrated his success and lost his life and his army. From Marathon to Plataea, ashore and afloat, success turned on suiting the attack to the national arms, and the tactics of the fleet was best when it followed the national army tactics. . . . In the next chapter we shall observe how the growth of ship skill in the Athenian navy alone among its contemporaries led to the development of a particular form of naval tactics, which was good only so long as the Athenian skill in ship handling continued to exceed that of its adversaries. It lasted scarcely a generation.

PRINCIPAL AUTHORITIES CONSULTED FOR THIS CHAPTER

ANCIENT

Herodotus.
Thucydides.
Diodorus Siculus.
Plutarch: *Themistocles, Aristides.*

MODERN COMMENTATORS

Bury, J. B.: *History of Greece.*
Delbrueck, H.: *Geschichte der Kriegskunst.*
Giannelli, G.: *La Spedizione di Serse da Terme a Salamina.*
Goodwin, W. W.: *Battle of Salamis.*
Grundy, G. B.: *The Great Persian War.*
Hauvette, A.: *Hérodote, Historien des Guerres Médiques.*
Jurien de la Gravière, J. B. E.: *La Marine des Anciens.*
Kromayer, J.: *Antike Schlachtfelder, Perser Krieg. Schlachten Atlas.*
Macan, R. W.: *Herodotus.*
Munro, J. A. R.: *Cambridge History*, vol. 4.
Obst, E.: *Der Feldzug des Xerxes.*

APPENDIX 1 TO CHAPTER III

AESCHYLUS' ACCOUNT OF SALAMIS

An eyewitness of the event has given an account which is worth quoting, for Aeschylus' play of "The Persians" is unsurpassed as literature and is full of tactical detail.

Xerxes * * * published this order to all his captains, that when the sun should have ceased to illumine the earth with his rays, and darkness tenant the temple of the firmament, they should draw up the squadrons of the ships in three lines, to guard the outlets and the murmuring passes of the sea and others in a circle around the Island of Ajax (Salamis); so that if the Greeks should elude fatal destruction, by discovering any path of escape for their ships by stealth, it was decreed that they all should be deprived of their heads. To this effect he spoke from a frantic spirit, for he knew not what was ordained of the gods. And they, without disorder and with obedient mind, both provided supper for themselves, and the mariner lashed his oar to the well-fitted thole pin. And when the light of the sun had waned, and night had come on, every man, master of an oar, went on board ship, and every one that had sway over arms; and one line of ships cheered on another line, and they made sail as each had been appointed, and all night long the commanders of the ships were keeping the whole naval host occupied in sailing about. And night withdrew, and the force of the Greeks by no means made a stealthy escape in any direction. But when day, drawn by white steeds, had occupied the whole earth, of radiance beautiful to behold; first of all, a shout from the Greeks greeted Echo like a song, and Echo from the island rock at the same time shouted forth an inspiring cry; and terror fell on all the barbarians, for not as in flight were the Greeks then chanting the solemn paean, but speeding on to the fight with gallant daring of soul. And the trumpet, with its clang inflamed their whole line; and forthwith at the blow of the dashing oar, at the word of command they smote the roaring brine. And quickly were they conspicuous to view. The right wing, well marshaled, led on foremost, in good order; and secondly, their whole force was coming on against us, and we could at the same time hear a mighty shout: "Sons of the Greeks! On! Free your country, and free your children, your wives and the abodes too of the gods of your fathers, and the tombs of your ancestors; now is the battle for them all!" And sooth to say, a murmur of the Persian tongue reached them from our line, and no longer was it the moment to delay but forthwith ship dashed her brazen beak against ship. And a Grecian ship commenced the engagement and broke off the whole of the figurehead of a Phoenician ship and each commander severally directed his bark against another of the enemy's. At first, indeed, the torrent of the Persian fleet bore up against them but when the multitude of our ships were crowded in the strait and no assistance could be given to one another, but they were struck by their own brazen beaks, and were smashing their entire banks of oars, and the Grecian vessels, not without science, were smiting them in a circle on all sides, and the hulls of our vessels were upturned, and the sea was no longer to behold, filled as it was, with wrecks and the slaughter of men. The shores, too, and the rugged rocks were filled with the dead; and every ship, as many as there were of the barbaric armament, was rowed in flight without order. But the Greeks kept striking, hacking us as it were tunnies or any draught of fishes, with fragments of oars and splinters of wrecks; and wailing filled the ocean brine with shrieks, until the murky eye of night removed it. * * * Many of the Persians in the very bloom of life, most valiant in their spirit, and distinguished by their high birth, and ever foremost in faithfulness to our monarch himself have fallen foully by a most inglorious doom. * * * There is a certain island, lying off the shore of Salamis, small, a dangerous station for ships, which Pan, who delights in the dance, haunts on the beach. Thither Xerxes sends these men that when the foemen, wandering out of their ships should make their escape to the island, they might slay the soldiery of the Greeks and rescue their comrades from the streams of the sea; ill-knowing of the future. For when God gave the glory of the day to the Greeks, on that very day, having fortified their bodies in their armor of well fitting brass, they leaped out of their vessels and encompassed the whole island around, so that they were at a loss whither they should betake themselves; for often were they smitten by stones from the hand, and arrows falling on them from the bow string destroyed them. And at last, having charged them with one onslaught, they smite, they hew in pieces the limbs of the wretches until they had utterly destroyed the life of all of them.

And Xerxes shrieked aloud when he saw the depth of his calamities; for he had a high seat that afforded a clear prospect of the whole armament, a high hill near the ocean brine; and having rent his clothes, and uttered a shrill wail, after issuing orders to the land forces, he dismissed them in disorderly flight.— Buckley's translation.

THE FORCES EMPLOYED IN THE PERSIAN WAR 480-479 B.C.

Our principal authority for the great campaign of Xerxes against Greece is Herodotus, who says that the total force led by Xerxes, including fleet, army, and camp followers of both sexes, was over 5,000,000 souls. It has been recognized that such a number was impossibly large and, at the same time, it has been admitted that precision was impossible of attainment. Nevertheless, the situation has always been recognized as so important in the history of European civilization, that discussion and criticism have never been wanting with the object of making some approximation. For the history of naval tactics the point is no less important. In the tale of Herodotus, we get our first detailed information on naval strategy and tactics. Even if much is inaccurate and unacceptable, we must yet do our best to analyze what we have and turn it to account. Moreover, the operations, both ashore and afloat, cannot fail to be affected by the size of the forces to be fed and supplied. This appendix will, therefore, be devoted to a study of the matter, to see what figures may reasonably be set as upper and lower limits of the Persian and Greek forces in opposition to each other. There are two lines of approach. The scholars who have studied Herodotus and the other ancient writers have been able, by the methods of the "higher criticism," to make their story bear meanings quite different from what the words seem to tell. Herodotus himself is made to elucidate his own text. It is true that the critics do not all thoroughly agree in their opinions; but, nevertheless, they are very plausible and we must go a part of their way with each of them. Secondly, the fundamental facts of physics, of economics, and of existence have not altered since the days of Xerxes, and we can estimate the limits of accomplishments for men of that day in the light of what men can do today.

PERSIAN ARMY

First as to the number of men in the Persian army: Herodotus says that there were 1,700,000 soldiers who were estimated by counting off

10,000, crowding them close together, and then building an enclosure around them. This enclosure was then filled 170 times as the army passed through it. This direct statement is challenged by the present day students who dwell on his account of the army organization, which was on the decimal system: decad—squad, 10; hecatonad—company, 100; chiliad —regiment, 1,000; myriad—division, 10,000. Herodotus also mentions larger army units of 6 myriads—army corps as we would call them today. Further, he mentions that in this vast assembly, composed of so many different races, the smaller units were racially homogeneous and commanded by their own countrymen, as was most natural. He then goes on to name 29 Persian archons or commanders over whom were 6 commanders also Persians. Besides, Hydarnes commanded the royal body guard known as the "Immortals," a myriad of Persians. As Herodotus understood the Persian organization, the 29 archons whom he named commanded the army corps of 6 myriads each; but the modern commentators hold that he was mistaken, and that the Persian archons were only myriarchs, like Hydarnes, the guard commander. Herodotus puts the Persian cavalry at 80,000 and names 6 cavalry generals, who seem to have been of the same rank as the 29. Thus modern criticism believes that the cavalry was not 8 myriads strong, but 6 only under the 6 named cavalry myriarchs and that the whole Persian levy consisted of 6 army corps, each 60,000 strong, composed each of 5 infantry myriads and 1 cavalry myriad, 360,000 in all.[1] However, Munro believes that only 3 out of the 6 army corps in the Persian levy went into Europe as the invading force and supports his opinion on the ground that only 3 army leaders are clearly mentioned by Herodotus as having done service there; namely, Mardonius, who remained in Thessaly in the winter of 480-479; Artabazus, who commanded the lines of communication through Thrace; and Pharnabazus, who returned to Asia with Xerxes. Grundy thinks that the Persian troops employed on land must be estimated at over 500,000. Delbrueck thinks that at Plataea there were about 15,000 to 25,000 Persians and Medized Greeks with as many more light-armed troops. Daniels thinks that Xerxes brought only 20,000 Persians into Greece and that no more than 18,000 allied Persians and Greeks fought the free national Greek forces at Plataea; but he adds that Xerxes' fighting men were a selected group and

---

[1] See J. A. R. Munro: *Journal of Hellenic Studies*, 1902.

that they were accompanied by a train of 40,000 to 50,000 men, making a force of 60,000 to 70,000 men with a proportionate number of horses. Hauvette[2] agrees with Munro that the 29 archons commanded myriads, but he does not believe that every titular myriad actually numbered 10,000 men in the ranks. The guard of "Immortals" was the only myriad which Herodotus expressly states was always maintained with full ranks.

But the text of Herodotus may be compared with such economic and military data as is possible to derive from other sources. For one thing, Herodotus tells us that when the Persian army reached the pass of Thermopylae, it camped on an area of 22,000 "plethra." A plethron is 0.2357 acre, so the camp covered 5,185 acres. *The Soldier's Pocket Book,* by Field Marshal Lord Wolseley, calls for 17.5 acres for an infantry battalion of 1,096 men or about 16 acres per 1,000 men. For cavalry he asks 25 acres per regiment of 662 men or 37.7 acres per 1,000. But for large forces more space per man is occupied. But if we assume that Xerxes' army before Thermopylae, which was neither pressed for room nor by the enemy, was about one-sixth cavalry and (being a very large body) used about 25 per cent greater area than the British rule, i.e., an average of 24.5 acres per 1,000, we get a figure of about 200,000 for Xerxes' total land force, including his train and non-combatants. (This assumes that the ancient army train was not materially larger than a modern regimental train, there being no artillery supplies.)

Another mode of estimate is through the transport fleet. Herodotus says there were 3,000 small craft of 30 oars, 50 oars, horse transports, and supply ships; and although the figure may not be very accurate, yet we may take it at face value and proceed.[3] The army was too large to draw more than a small part of its current supply from the country. It kept closely to the coast for the most part of its movement and was never long separated from the fleet. Greece and the Persian army relied for imported grain on regions as far away as Egypt and the present Ukraine—about 1,000 miles distant. We may assume that the average length of voyage

---

[2] *Hérodote, Historien des Guerres Médiques.*

[3] The 30-oared and 50-oared boats were no doubt dispatch boats such as were used all through the Middle Ages for communication with the fleet and the shore. The horse transports were probably not very numerous, as the army crossed the Hellespont by the bridges. The whole 3,000 is here assumed to be for supply. Herodotus estimates crews of all at 80 men each, i.e., pentekonter crews. This seems to me much too high.

was about 500 miles. The speed of sailing ships is about the same now as then, for obvious reasons. Briefly, the winds and seas are unchanged, and ships of equal size can carry about the same amount of sail. Consequently, they will make about the same speed. This averages under 5 miles an hour or, say, 100 miles in 24 hours. But as a general rule, ancient mariners were averse to voyaging at night. The long ships, the trieres, usually drew up on the beach and the sailing ships, if at sea, frequently lay to, in order to avoid running upon dangers then unmarked for navigation, as well as to keep clear of strangers, for every ship might prove to be a pirate. Hence, we may allow Xerxes' supply ships a daily movement of 50 miles, which, with a mean length of voyage of 500 miles and 5 days at each terminal for the turn-around, calls for a round trip a month. This would give a daily arrival of 100 ships. As for their size, we know that in 421 B.C. the Lacedaemonians made a treaty with Athens not to employ on their own coasts any ship larger than 500 talents burden (i.e., 13 tons). If we take it that the maximum size permitted to the Lacedaemonians was the average size 60 years earlier, the daily supplies arriving for the fleet and army would be 1,300 tons. The ration in those days was no doubt less than the abundant one given to our army today, but the men needed supplies other than food alone. The U. S. Army Quartermaster's Department now allows 311 rations per ton, packed for over seas. If we assume that the ancient Persian's total daily consumption of all supplies was equal to the American's ration alone, we shall conclude that the whole Persian fleet, army, and train and camp followers numbered about 400,000 souls.

The time required to cross the two bridges over the Hellespont affords means of estimating the size of the army. Herodotus gives two different times for the crossing. In VII-55 he puts the time at 2 days and in VII-56 he makes it 7 days. The *U. S. Field Service Regulations* tell us that 175 infantry in column of fours can pass a given point in a minute. But large bodies do not move so fast. A French military work on the battles about Metz, in 1870, states that the French army crossed the Moselle on the night of August 14-15 in from 9 to 10 hours. There seem to have been seven bridges, including pontoons, and the rate of passing was 1,500 to 1,650 men per bridge per hour, including therein the artillery and so much of the train as was on the right bank of the river. Applying the higher rate to the two Hellespont bridges, for 48 hours the people passing would be 158,400 in all. This is quite a different figure from the preceding estimates, but nevertheless it is of the same order of magnitude. A modern German army corps of 35,000 men occupied 30 miles of road space with its train. At 2 miles an hour it would be 15 hours in passing a given point. This would allow 224,000 to cross the bridges in 2 days.

The number of men that a country can support under arms in proportion to its population is larger now than it was in ancient times when there was no power machinery and the margin of production beyond bare necessities forbade the maintenance of large armies. The proportion of inhabitants that Xerxes could levy in his dominions was probably not very different from that which equal populations could furnish at all times until the last century, when machinery enabled nations to maintain and arm larger armies than ever before. We can estimate what forces he could muster by ascertaining what was done on other occasions with similar populations.

In 31 B.C., at the campaign of Actium, the eastern forces under Antony amounted to 100,000 infantry, 12,000 cavalry, 800 supply ships, and 500 very poorly manned fighting ships; although many of the latter were of the largest size. A number were destroyed for lack of crews and under 200 seem to have been in the battle. Antony's fleet was drawn from the same regions as that of Xerxes. We may assume, then, that after the great losses of the winter of 32-31, Antony's fleet, very short-handed, did not have more than about 50,000 seamen and rowers, making a total for fleet and army of 162,000. The opposing western forces under Octavianus Caesar amounted to 80,000 infantry, 12,000 cavalry, and, at the most, nearly 300 well-manned but moderate-sized ships with crews (excluding soldiers) of perhaps 50,000 to 60,000 men. In all, Octavianus had about 150,000 men. The whole assembly was about 310,000 strong. Beloch gives the population of the Empire in 14 A.D. as 54,000,000. The long peace of a generation had probably much increased the population since Actium. If we take the population in 31 B.C. as 45,000,000, we have about 0.7 per cent present in the campaign (local garrisons were additional).

A final comparison for the size of the Persian effort may be taken from the war of the French Revolution, the last great war before steam machinery affected the character of war. In 1795, France had a population of 27,000,000 and her forces under arms numbered 531,000, or 2 per cent;

but the following year she was able to strike Germany with only 150,000 under Jourdan and Moreau, and Italy with 40,000 under Bonaparte. In a little time the troops in Germany were no more than 95,000; that is, the forces available for employment abroad were only 0.5 per cent. Turning back to Xerxes and the Persian Empire, its population is placed by Beloch at this time at 45,000,000. Guided by the foregoing examples, if we take 0.7 to 0.9 per cent of the population as all that Xerxes could muster for fleet, army, and train, we arrive at a maximum of 400,000 available for long and distant service, and probably less.

Persian Fleet

We may now take up the estimate of the Persian fleet. Commentators have remarked on the great number of ships and have thought them excessive, but an error is less likely in counting some hundreds of ships at an anchorage than it is in estimating how many thousands of men are occupying an extensive camp. Herodotus says that there were 1,207 fighting ships and 3,000 transports and small craft. The last figure is no doubt a round number, but, as was seen previously, it is one in keeping with other data as to the size of the expedition. As for the list of fighting ships as furnished by each province, this also is one which the various points mentioned by Herodotus seem to confirm. He not only gives the number in each provincial contingent, but he also gives the nature of armament of the provincial crews. (This is aside from the soldiers of Persian or Median blood which were added to the local crews.) As Herodotus describes the fleet and its organizations and its armament, the 1,207 ships were in four divisions, each commanded by a Persian of high rank.

Achaemenes, brother to the King, was ruler of Egypt and commanded the 200 Egyptian ships. Another brother, Ariabignes, commanded the 170 Carians and Ionians. It is natural to suppose that the four squadron commanders would have approximately equal commands, i.e., of about 300 ships each. The Phoenician contingent was of that size. Further, it is in every way probable that the squadrons would be organized as far as possible by their arms and language, as stated by Diodorus. This suggests the following probable arrangement in which it will be seen that squadrons *A* and *B* are light-armed with missile weapons and squadrons *C* and *D* are heavy-armed with spears. And in squadrons *A* and *C* the contingents in each all spoke a common language.

		Ships	*Province*	*Armament*
A.	1.	300	Phoenicia	Helmets, linen breast plates, light shields, javelins.
B.	2.	100	Cilicia	Helmets, woolen tunics, rawhide shields, javelins and cutlasses.
	3.	50	Lycia	Greaves, breast plates, bows, reed arrows, javelins.
	4.	150	Cyprus	Tunics. Otherwise clad like Greeks.
C.	5.	70	Caria[4]	Greek armament (i.e., heavy armor and spear) and falchions and daggers.
	6.	100	Ionia	Greek armament.
	7.	100	Hellespont	Greek armament.
	8.	30	Doris	Greek armament.
D.	9.	200	Egypt	Plaited helmets, concave shields, spears for sea fight, pole axes, long cutlasses, and most had breast plates.
	10.	60	Aeolia	Greek armament.
	11.	30	Pamphylia	Greek armament.
	12.	17	Islands	Greek armament.

1,207

As a check on the numbers of ships in Xerxes' expedition, we may examine what Herodotus tells us about the naval forces which took part in the Ionian revolt against Persia in the years 499-493 B.C. The principal naval campaign in 494 brought out their maritime strength. At the battle of Lade on the coast of Asia Minor, about 60 miles south of Smyrna, the Ionians mustered 353 ships, and Herodotus gives the list of each state's contingent. The Persian force he names in gross as 600, and says it was composed of Phoenicians, who showed the greatest zeal, but also Cyprians, Cilicians, and Egyptians. In 480, Xerxes drew most of his fleet from the regions which had been hostile to each other in 494. From the four provinces of Phoenicia, Egypt, Cilicia, and Cyprus which had furnished his father with 600 ships, Xerxes obtained 750. In the Ionian rebellion of 494, the Ionians themselves had furnished 283 ships and Aeolian Lesbos, 70. These now sent only 160. The rest of Xerxes' 1,207 came from those provinces of Asia Minor which had not been represented at Lade. As every province and city state needed a fleet to defend its local commerce, in proportion to the value of that commerce, there is nothing irreconcilable in the figures given by Herodotus for the size of the fleets, since it is more than likely that the Ionians were forbidden to maintain as large a fleet as

[4] The Cnidians and others in Caria were Greek but not so the Carians in general.

that which they had at Lade. For a further check, we may compare Xerxes' fleet with that of Mark Antony at Actium, in 31 B.C. Both were drawn from the same regions. The later ships were much larger and therefore more costly, and although no more than 500 in number, yet the whole number of men needed to man the two fleets fully was probably about the same. However Antony could not man all his 500 ships, owing to his poverty and the prevailing pestilence, and yet the population and economic conditions were not widely different.

If we take the crew of each early triere at 120 men, we have 144,840 as the number of men embarked in the fleet from Asia: later, 120 more ships were contributed by the European regions through which the Persian army passed, bringing the number of ships to a total of 1,327 and their crews to 159,240 as the maximum. But Herodotus, VIII-60, says the Greek ships were heavier, so it is probable that many of the Persian ships were pentekonters of only 75 to 80 men each and the average number of men per ship may have been only about 100, or 130,000 men in the fleet.[5]

Returning now to the estimate of 400,000 men as the largest number of men that the population could support, in addition to garrisons, for a long period of active military service, we have 270,000 as the maximum size of the army, inclusive of non-combatants, which entered Europe. Assuming as correct the opinion of learned scholars that the whole Persian levy consisted of 6 army corps of 6 (nominal) myriads each, we may believe that Xerxes crossed the Hellespont with 3 army corps. As the ranks are never filled to the nominal strength, we may further believe that, including camp followers, the force numbered scarcely 180,000 men and the whole fleet and army little exceeded 300,000 souls. This number takes no account of the fleet train of 3,000 ships which may have had 10 or 15 men each. Adding these, the entire Persian force may have been 350,000 men, all depending on sea communications for daily supplies.

GREEK FORCES

In the main, the population of Greece was a free and self-governing one, which turned out a larger percentage of its number for national defense (under short-time service) than did the enemy. Although there were

---

[5] Munro, in *Cambridge Ancient History*, vol. 4, thinks that the Persian fleet in all did not exceed 730 ships.

slaves, they formed a smaller percentage of the inhabitants than they did later, and only in Sparta do they seem to have been a source of uneasiness to the ruling class.

Citizens were borne on the conscription rolls and, from the data which have been preserved, it seems that about one-half of those on the rolls served in the field army and the other and older half formed the local defense force. There were also a large number employed on ship board, specially in Athens. Not all of these latter were citizens and there are modern commentators who believe that the entire army was not available when the fleet was fully manned. In the campaign of Plataea in 479, Herodotus says the Greeks had 38,700 heavy-armed troops and 35,000 helots accompanying the Spartans, besides 34,500 other light-armed troops, which with another body of 1,800 unarmed men made up a total of 110,000 men. The numbers in the fleet at Mycale are not clearly told by Herodotus, but if it was 250 ships, as Diodorus says, there would be (at 120 men to the ship) a total of 30,000 afloat.

Modern critics, however, are inclined to reduce Herodotus' figures. First, it is said that he gives the enrollment figures and that never are all the enrolled men present for service.

(In the Civil War of this country it was the experience that of all the enrolled men in any military organization only about two-thirds were habitually present for duty.) Moreover, it is alleged that the 7 helots who are said to have accompanied each Spartan were not fighting men, but in the service of supply, if in service at all. Making these allowances, we have for the force turned out in 479 about 25,000 heavy-armed troops, about as many light-armed, and with 30,000 in the fleet, we have a total of not over 80,000 men under arms. The population furnishing these men, including slaves, did not exceed 1,000,000, if so many. This large available percentage, so much greater than that of the Persian population, may be attributed to the fact that the Greeks were engaged in defending their own territory, that most were free men, that the slaves were not a disturbing factor in the situation, and that the army was out only for a season's operations, whereas the Persian army was out for a much longer time, a permanent force.

CHAPTER IV

THE PELOPONNESIAN WAR

PRELIMINARY DISCUSSION

HERODOTUS has told us of the repulse of the Persians, and Thucydides of the Peloponnesian War a half century later. In the interval there was great development in naval tactics, but the steps in it are not known to us. Nevertheless, it is apparent that this development was the result of the leading position in commerce and in politics which Athens assumed in the Levant and the islands of the Aegean Sea through her preponderant navy.

The Persian and the Peloponnesian Wars both turned on sea power. Unlike the Persian War, the Peloponnesian one was not for territorial expansion of an already great Empire, but was waged rather for commercial control of far extended lines of Athenian trade and for the profits that went with good business management and such preponderance or monopoly of trade as could be established.

Let us glance for an instant at the economic conditions of the Greek world in the fifth century B.C., for after all, these are the principal causes of international disputes and wars. At first Greece was chiefly agricultural and was economically self-contained, but in the eighth century she began to be over-populated and, as Plato says, she avoided revolution by throwing out colonies to the shores of Asia Minor, to Sicily, to Italy, and as far as Massilia (now Marseilles). With these the mother states continued to retain friendly relations. The colonists did not penetrate deeply as territorial conquerors, but maintained themselves as seaport city states and centers of trade to draw the products of the back countries and distribute them through the Mediterranean world by shipping. The commercial relations with the colonies enabled the still growing population of the homeland to support itself increasingly by manufactures which were exported to pay for imports of grain, so that even the non-maritime states shared in the general prosperity developed by mercantile connections.

In this colonial and commercial expansion of Greece with chains of communication reaching from one market city to another, business fell into two rival commercial leagues. Every city maintained a fleet to protect its commerce from pirates and from the attacks of the other League. Indeed, the line between piracy and what is now known as privateering was not sharply drawn. Piracy was in large measure a means of dealing with commercial competition.

Athens, whose great navy we are about to examine, took no part in the early colonization, for she was still comfortably agricultural; but early in the sixth century Solon's legal reforms induced her to turn strongly to commerce as the basis of the national prosperity. Athenian agriculture was then transformed by a development of orchards and vineyards at the expense of grain fields, and therewith came a growth of manufactures and shipping wherewith she bought a large part of her grain supply. Athens became commercial and wealthy. By the time of the Persian War in 480 Athens had a great trade in the Euxine and the greatest navy in Greece to protect her commercial interests which lay chiefly eastward. Corinth was Athens' principal commercial rival, with connections mostly with the Greek colonies in the west. She was the leading commercial state in the Peloponnese, where her political interests also lay.

The year after the victory of Mycale and the seizure of Sestos, the allied Greek fleet pursued its advantage and conquered both Cyprus and Byzantium. The possession of the latter assured Greek control of the wheat trade of the Euxine and was a step in the growth of the Delian League which was the outcome of the original anti-Persian League, having its treasury and headquarters in the little island of Delos. In this new Delian League Sparta had no share. She resolved to rely on her army, and left the Aegean to the control of the maritime states. Sparta was military, self-contained and self-centered with little commerce and little inclined to reach out for it. Like Sparta, Corinth withdrew from the League. She continued to predominate in western trade. Until the victory over Persia, Athens had competed more or less with Corinth for the western trade, but the two powers remained good friends. Thereafter, as the possessor of the greatest navy, Athens was the natural leader of the newly formed Delian League, and the great naval and commercial development of Athens threw her into intensest rivalry with Corinth.

In the Delian League all the member states had a share in the maintenance of the allied fleet, which protected their merchant shipping and assured them entry into ports which might otherwise have been closed to them. As for ships and men, many of the smaller states commuted by a money tribute to the League treasury which Athens managed, and supplied each city's quota of ships from the tribute money. During its first years the League grew slowly, but in 466 Cimon, son of Miltiades, won a great double victory by sea and land over the Persians at the mouth of the River Eurymedon on the south coast of Asia Minor, and thereafter the power of Athens increased rapidly.

Cimon's Development of the Fleet

We know nothing of the plan of battle or the tactics at Eurymedon, but in his *Life of Cimon*, Plutarch tells of his attention to the exercise of the fleet, so that the captains and crews became far more expert in handling their vessels than those of other states. The League fleet was by this time transformed into one mainly Athenian, although the expense fell largely on the other members of the League. It continued duly to protect and develop the commerce of all but, of course, the profits of empire flowed chiefly to Athens, since she had directive power through the fleet. From the first, the League had control of the eastern trade of Greece, and Athens soon began to expand her business within Corinth's area in the west, acquiring memberships in the League along the Gulf of Patras, and thereafter an Athenian squadron was usually based at Naupactus to safeguard and escort merchant craft.

Development of Athenian Empire by the Fleet

In 459 the city of Megara (see Map 6) on the Isthmus of Corinth had a dispute with Corinth and applied to Athens for aid. The latter occupied Megara and its two seaports, Pagae and Nisaea, on opposite sides of the Isthmus and then built walls from Megara to Nisaea, manning them with an Athenian garrison. In this way Athens had a port on both sides of the isthmus and a short portage enabled her shipping to avoid the dreaded passage of west-bound ships around Greece, putting her western commerce in equal competition with that of Corinth. Thus began the active bad feeling of Corinth against Athens which led to immediate war and a generation later to the great war against the Peloponnesian states.

We know little of the war of 459. At first, Athens had a firm grip on western trade, holding (see Map 2) Megaris, Naupactus, Zacynthus, and Cephallonia as intermediate bases. In 453 the war died away and was followed by a truce, at the close of which in 446 a definite peace was signed to last for 30 years, by which Athens lost most of her gains since 459. Athens' foreign policy was now much less arrogant but, nevertheless, she still retained a strong desire to hold her western markets. Within the League her policy altered in the opposite direction. Before the war Athens used the allied fleet for League purposes, but afterward to establish the Athenian Empire. The Athenian fleet supported by the tribute money of the League was used to enforce the loyalty of the minor members of the League.

After the war, it was necessary even in peace to keep a large fleet distributed at various bases to protect shipping and prevent insurrection. In the course of time 100 ships were held in commission for eight months every year. Cimon had formed the naval school of maneuver, and a generation later Pericles continued and developed its traditions. The Peloponnesian League had its ships, too, which did their share in protecting their own trade and that of their allies from the depredations of pirates and the other League. Yet the other navies do not seem to have felt the necessity for drill and efficiency in peace that Athens did. The constant service of the Athenian fleet, in enforcing loyalty on reluctant allies, made it far superior to the enemies it was to encounter on the outbreak of the Great War.

Training of the Athenian Navy

The Athenian ships were not so heavily equipped as the others and their superiority depended both on their lightness and better construction and on the skill of the captains and the skill and endurance of the rowers. Their technique in handling the vessels was better. They could turn quickly for the new attack (*anastrophe*) after executing the break-through (*diekplous*). When wishing to back water (row astern), it is probable that each rower passed easily under his oar to the thwart in front of him, and seated there, facing forward, he could exert himself as effectually as before. It is to be noted all through the history of rowing ships-of-war that on occasions when it was desirable to retreat when close to the enemy, they were averse to turning their bows away from him.

The advantage in speed of these highly trained Athenian crews over their opponents cannot have been very great; perhaps half a knot at extreme speed for half an hour and less over long distances, combined with better long-time endurance through much rowing practice. This superiority enabled the Athenians to delay action while exhausting the enemy by making him move. Then they could attack or refuse battle. They could ram and back away with only a moderate risk of being held against their will for a boarders' fight. Moreover, they could move to the end of the hostile formation, and by envelopment (*periplous*) they could attack from both sides with advantage. Above all, the admitted superiority of the Athenians gave them a moral advantage which was worth as much or more than the physical one. Instead of desiring a battle at a fixed point with covered flanks which Themistocles had sought and obtained at Salamis, the fleet which Cimon had formed and bequeathed to Pericles was one which preferred the open sea where it could make the enemy move, knowing that exhaustion would come to the enemy sooner than to itself.

THE BATTLE AT THE SYBOTA ISLANDS

The thirty years' peace, declared in 446, lasted till 432 before it was broken. The Peloponnesian War which then began was brought about by jealousy of the growth of Athenian sea power and trade; but the putative cause was an active dispute between Corcyra (now Corfu) and Corinth. Although Corcyra had been founded as a Corinthian colony, there had long been bad feeling between them. Corcyra was a most important station on the great Greek trade route to Italy, whose good will was essential both to Athenian and Corinthian shipping. Corinth found cause of quarrel with Corcyra in 436, and next year sent a fleet and army to attack her. The expedition was defeated with loss, but we have no details of the naval tactics. Corinth spent over two years in preparing to renew her effort, and in the meantime Corcyra applied to Athens for help, while Corinth sent an embassy there to set forth her side. Athens could not willingly see Corcyra overcome by Corinth, for that would cripple Athenian trade with the Western Mediterranean, obstructing her supply of Sicilian grain and making her too dependent on the Euxine as the main source of supply. On this route lay Byzantium, which had recently been in revolt and was near the Persian strength and could appeal to it. Athens was far from wishing to break the peace; but, in order not to neglect the control of the western route and its traffic, she made a defensive alliance with Corcyra, and sent 10 ships there with orders not to fight the Corinthians, unless the latter should attack Corcyra.

In 433 the expected Corinthian expedition set out. Corinth sent 90 ships of her own, and her allies provided 60 more. In September, the allied fleet beached and camped at Chimerium, a port near Parga in modern Epirus, about 20 miles from the southern end of Corcyra. Many of the local barbarians joined the allies at their camp. Learning of the enemy's approach, the Corcyraeans manned 110 ships[1] and set out with the 10 Athenians and encamped on one of the Sybota Islands on the mainland side of the channel abreast the southern point of Corcyra. Corcyraean troops with some allies were on their own island abreast their ships.

After making their preparations, the Corinthians embarked three days' supplies, and got under way by night. In the morning they sighted the enemy also under way and approaching. Both fleets formed line of battle. The Corinthians put their allies on the right of their line, near the shore, and themselves occupied the left. The Corcyraeans formed in three divisions and had the Athenians on their right on their uncovered seaward flank where there was room for the Athenians to exercise their maneuvering skill. The Athenian division, under its instructions from home, was unwilling to engage and at first remained in observation only; but nevertheless, the prestige of the Athenian fleet and the danger of precipitating a war with Athens seems to have caused the left of the Corinthian line to have exercised some restraint in attacking the Corcyraeans.

The description in Thucydides is very full. He says:

As soon as the signals on both sides were raised, they closed and fought, both sides having many heavy-armed (armored spearmen) on deck and many archers and javelin men, as they were still equipped in the old fashion.[2] And

---

[1] We cannot fail to be struck by the enormous capital invested in the Greek navies for the insurance of the profits of municipal transportation and municipal industries. Here were 270 ships besides the Athenian fleet at home which was almost as great, although not all ships were in commission.

[2] The old fashion returned to favor before the end of the Peloponnesian War.

the battle was well contested, not so much in point of tactics, but more like a land fight. For whenever ships collided, they did not easily get clear again, owing to the number and confusion of the ships, and because they trusted for victory in a greater measure to the heavy-armed on deck who set-to and fought while the ships remained stationary. There was no breaking through the line, but they fought with fierceness and with strength more than with nautical skill. On all sides, then, there was much confusion and the battle was a disorderly one. If the Corcyraeans were hard-pressed at any point, the Athenian vessels coming up, struck fear into the enemy, but did not begin fighting, in deference to the orders from Athens. On the shoreward flank the Corcyraeans overcame the allies of Corinth, and twenty of the victors pursued to the deserted Corinthian encampment at Chimerium, where they landed for pillage. Of the remaining combatants, the Corinthians originally had the superiority in numbers and now profited by this advantage to gain a victory. But the Athenians, seeing the Corcyraeans hard-pressed, now assisted them more unequivocally. Although at first they had refrained from ramming any vessel, now, when the rout had clearly taken place and the Corinthians were close to them, then, indeed, everyone at length set to work, and there was no longer any distinction, but it had come to such urgent necessity that the Athenians and Corinthians attacked each other.

It is not difficult to realize the change from the tactics of Salamis to the new style, practiced only by the Athenians, of which we shall have fuller accounts a few years later. At Salamis the rowers were exposed, except for their shields along the ship side. But when the ships were once in contact the rowers dropped their oars and took part with the soldiers in the fight. By the time of Sybota, the motive power was better safe-guarded, for the rowers were under the catastroma. But at Sybota all except the Athenians still fought an infantry fight with ships filled with soldiers. Only the Athenians had adapted their tactics to the invention of the catastroma by reducing the soldiers on board. The Athenians with their protected rowers were depending on maneuver and the ram, on speed and the endurance of the rowers, with only a few soldiers to repel boarders. The reduction in soldiers and of the rations for them in the cargo was a chief factor in making the Athenian ships lighter, and therefore not only faster, but quicker in turning. If, unfortunately, an Athenian ship remained jammed in collision with an adversary, the rowers could then come on deck with their arms and take part in the battle with the soldiers and seamen already there.

Moreover, it appears that at Sybota the lines of ships in general were compact, since after ships fouled each other they did not readily get clear. The Athenians, on the contrary, were in more open order to have maneuvering room. This is in accord with what Captain Pantero Pantera of the Papal Navy tells us, writing in 1614, that some seamen preferred very close order for galley fleets, and others an open order, giving more room for maneuvering the individual ships within the limits of the formation.

After routing the Corcyraeans, the Corinthians killed the swimmers surviving from the wrecks, and in their haste they included some belonging to their own defeated right wing. They then picked up the water-logged wrecks and towed them to Sybota, where their barbarian allies had taken possession of the enemy's camp. After this, the day being late, the Corinthians once more formed line for battle, and the Corcyraeans with the Athenians drew up and faced them, fearing lest the enemy might land on the island of Corcyra. As the two fleets approached each other and the paean was sung, the Corinthians began to row astern, for they observed a re-enforcement of 20 Athenian ships in their rear, approaching from the south, which Athens had sent in the fear that the original 10 were not enough to preserve the peace. As the day was now nearly over, the Corinthians withdrew to Sybota for the night, while the Athenians and the Corcyraeans encamped at the southern point of Corcyra and the next morning crossed to Sybota. On their approach the Corinthians formed their line, but did not attack as they feared the 30 Athenian ships in spite of their own great success against the Corcyraeans the previous day. After a parley it was agreed the Corinthians might return home.

Both sides claimed the victory, the Corinthians because they had destroyed 70 ships against a loss of 30 of their own, and the Corcyraeans because the Corinthians went home after the arrival of the second Athenian squadron, and because they had salvaged all the wrecks and the dead that drifted their way. As ships were lightly loaded and probably not very stable, particularly after they were bilged by a ram stroke, they frequently remained floating although useless, with or without having capsized, and naturally many such were capable of repair. Although on this occasion the Corinthians claimed to have recovered more ships than their enemy, yet the Corcyraeans were last on the scene of battle, and may actually have suffered no greater permanent loss of ships.

Before passing from this incident, let us note the political error of the Athenians who did not want war, in failing to send at the first a sufficient squadron to impose peace. A boy cannot do a man's work. The course of affairs on the second day showed that 30 Athenian ships could have prevented battle. The Athenian detachment present on the first day also made a political error in waiting till the course of battle had definitely turned against its allies, instead of taking part from the first moment. Athenian victory at Sybota might have saved Greece from the war or, at all events, delayed it. A much similar error was made by Great Britain on August 3, 1914, when the British commander in chief in the Mediterranean by radio asked London's permission to destroy the *Goeben* and, being refused, then lost touch with the enemy which escaped to Turkey and induced her to make war. Until the day of radio, every commanding officer had to be a diplomat and statesman as well as a military man, and woe to his country when he was unequal to his task. Constantly they had to make far-reaching decisions of national policy because the local tide of events was too swift for delay; but now responsibility is more centralized, as the British example shows, and perhaps with no great advantage, as it also shows.

OUTBREAK OF THE PELOPONNESIAN WAR

Immediately after the Battle of Sybota, Athens began to suspect the fidelity of the city of Potidaea on the peninsula of Pallene in Macedonia. Although Potidaea was a tributary ally of Athens, it had begun as a Corinthian colony, and Corinth was inclined to support it in opposing the hard terms imposed by Athens. Athens besieged Potidaea (432-430 B.C.), and Corinth sent troops to aid it. The King of Macedon was also favorable to Potidaea. During the progress of the long siege Corinth called on the other Peloponnesians to support her. It was a question how many states would comply. Pericles, the leading statesman of Athens, preferred not to delay action and issued the Megarian Decree excluding Megara, whose ships had fought at Sybota as Corinthian allies, from all ports and markets of the Empire. To Megara the decree meant something like starvation, and there was the possibility that it would submit, in which case Athens would again control the isthmus and have direct commercial access to the Corinthian Gulf. This Corinth could not tolerate, so she asked the other Peloponnesian states, and chiefly Sparta, to take up her cause and that of Megara. Sparta was not ready to go to war immediately, for she fully realized that the allies needed time and money to prepare and knew that Athens was more ready, having great sums available from unexpended tribute, and also because the control of the sea gave the city of Athens a great advantage. Nevertheless, Sparta allowed herself to vote at an assembly that Athens had violated the treaty of 446, having been pushed by Corinth into a warlike frame of mind before it was wise to begin hostilities. Consequently, Sparta opened negotiations until she felt ready and then sent an ultimatum which it was impossible for Athens to accept. Athens replied by offering to arbitrate in accordance with the treaty which Sparta had just declared broken. Sparta refused and the war became general early in 431.

Relative Strength of Opponents

In spite of the attention paid by modern commentators to relative strength, the estimates of the population engaged in this war are not very precise. G. B. Grundy thinks that all Greece had about 3,000,000 inhabitants at the beginning of the war. Beloch estimates the whole population of the Peloponnese at 890,000, and among its forces the Spartan army of 5,000 or 6,000 was the most renowned in Greece. On the other side Attica had about 150,000 freemen and 200,000 slaves with 44,000 men of military age. At the beginning of the war, the Athenian Empire had a population of over 2,000,000. It included the islands of the Aegean Sea and the fringe of coast land of Asia Minor, reaching from Rhodes to the Bosphorus. On the European side it included the coastal cities from Byzantium westward along the shores of Thrace. Thessaly was an ally, but not Macedonia.

In this war for the control of trade, although Athens was mistress of the Aegean Sea, yet her nominal allies in the League and actual subjects were not all well disposed to her. She ruled them through her fleet which could apply either military or economic pressure at will. The tribute which these states paid as commutation money for their ship contingents due to the League enabled Athens with one-sixth of the population of her Empire to man a fleet of 250 ships with 50,000 men, among which, of course, many were hired foreigners and many slaves. On the other hand, this great fleet (not all were commissioned in time of peace) was not wholly a burden, even to the tributary states. It kept piracy down and was of great service to general good order and prosperity, even if Athens frequently abused the power it gave her.

OUTLINE OF THE STRATEGY OF THE WAR

As for the military situation, Sparta had an army of professional soldiers, the finest in Greece, whereas Athens had an unequaled navy and a great accumulation of tribute money in the treasury. Neither side grew enough food supply for its own use. Both needed to maintain communication across the sea. At the beginning of the war Spartans assumed that they could force a decision, as in previous times, by ravaging the Attic vineyards and olive orchards. Such had been the normal course of Greek warfare, but during the half century since the great Persian campaign there had been changes in the military situation of Athens as well as in her maritime one. In general, although Greece depended largely on commerce, yet agriculture had been one of the chief components of national industry. Consequently, when a hostile force invaded another state's lands, a battle always ensued because the wasting of the fields was a loss of food for that year and the means of purchasing supplies for next year. This general situation, which had long existed, was greatly modified for Athens in recent years by two things. As her commerce increased, she had substituted olives and vineyards for export for much of her grain crops, so that her own grain was not sufficient for her existence. Besides, the successive steps in the fortification of the city after the Persian War altered her military situation.

As Attic agriculture shrank, Themistocles began the greatness of Athens by advising his countrymen to base it on the sea-borne commerce of the Aegean protected by a predominant navy, telling them that, when they were hard pressed by the enemy, they should take shelter behind the walls of the seaport of Piraeus and depend on their commerce and their navy to outwear the hostile army which could only remain in Attica for a short summer campaign. Pericles went further than Themistocles in following this policy. He built the long walls, 4 miles long and 200 yards apart, joining Athens and the Piraeus. As the day of effective siege work had not yet come, these long walls could be defended by a very small garrison when Attica was invaded, and all the population of the country-

side could come within without causing intolerable discomfort, and yet
Athens itself would be in communication with the sea. Thence forward, as
an imperial city supported by commerce and her own manufactures besides
the tribute of the subject allies, Athens was able, in time of war, to endure
the annual destruction of the Attic crops while her navy of 250 or 300
trieres protected her commerce, supplied her if besieged, held down her
allies, and gave her the means of counter-attack at pleasure. The tribute
helped to support a somewhat indigent peasantry which manned the fleet
and army and ruled the Empire by its votes.

The access to the sea in time of war, which Pericles provided for
Athens, introduced a new strategic idea into warfare through the maintenance of economic power by far-flung trade. So as the war developed,
the enemy was surprised to find that the destruction of local vineyards was
not economically ruinous to the Athenian state, nor could the Attic farmers
who were the mainstay of the state be reached by the invaders. On the
other hand, although Pericles had made the defense of the city entirely
effective, any counter-attack by means of a mere blockade of the Peloponnesian coasts was not sufficiently damaging to bring a prompt decision in
favor of Athens. Athens was determined to maintain her trade interests in
·the west, yet her situation with regard to commerce in that direction was
not as good as it had been after she seized Megara, for Megara had been
surrendered by her at the peace of 446. Nevertheless, the Athenian squadron permanently based at Naupactus at the entrance to the Gulf of Corinth
and the friendly cities of Corcyra and Messana in considerable measure
covered the trade to the Adriatic and to Sicily. On the whole, Corinth was
better situated than Athens with regard to western trade and at the far
end of the line the great city of Syracuse was her colony and sympathetic
to her. In this region, where Athens was the weaker, war was unavoidable.

For Athens to maintain her sea power in the west, it was desirable
for her to have seaports at short intervals around the Peloponnese, owing
to the limited endurance of the ships of the time, both as to supplies and
man power at the oars. These she did not have at first. In the meantime the
Athenian fleet raided on the coast of the Peloponnese. One of these raids
was led by Pericles himself. But no serious move into the interior was ever
made. Had Pericles taken advantage of his maritime strength and mobility,
to throw a formidable landing force into Sparta early in the war, he would

almost certainly have caused the withdrawal of the hostile army from Attica, and perhaps have terminated the war in his favor by a negotiated peace. Instead, as her chief military effort, Athens merely did what she could to hold a line to the Gulf of Corinth through the state of Megaris, which region was equally important to the Peloponnesians, as they found through it a route to the north and their ally Boeotia. After a year or two without decisive results, the plague broke out in Athens (probably due to the country crowds seeking shelter), greatly weakening the state, and Pericles died of it in 429.

A more active course was then followed by the new Athenian authorities. They tried to secure a hold in Acarnania, north of the Gulf of Patras, and sent fleets to Sicily to support their allies there. Besides, they gradually seized a line of bases around the Peloponnese at Methone, Cythera, and Pylos, which cut off the Egyptian trade to the Peloponnese and gave Athens a better hold on the routes to Italy. To counter this, the Spartans sent an expedition by land into Thrace to take the seaport cities which formed the Athenian line of communications with the Euxine. The success of this expedition in 422 perhaps alarmed Athens more than need was, but, in view of her failure to reduce her enemies by sea power, she was disposed to peace and, after the war had languished another year, she made peace in the spring of 421 B.C. Yet the war had not yet been fought to a finish.

Naval Actions in the Gulf of Corinth

The important naval events in the war, whose general strategic course has just been sketched, arose out of the struggle to control the lands on the northern side of the Gulf of Corinth. The Athenian naval base at Naupactus with its squadron was a constant threat to Corinthian trade out of the gulf, and caused the Peloponnesians to wish to hold Acarnania on the north of the Gulf of Patras, not only to isolate Naupactus, but also as an alternative although difficult trade route to Adriatic waters and so to Western Europe. On the other hand, the primary duty of the Athenian fleet was in the Aegean Sea to control the tributary allies and the commerce eastward. Thus the fleet was not strong enough to stop Corinthian western trade altogether. Nevertheless, Athens sent a squadron of 20 vessels under Phormio in the winter of 430-429 to lie at Naupactus and operate thence against the hostile communications in and out of the Gulf of Corinth. The following summer the Ambraciots and Chaonians in northwestern Greece asked the Spartans to send them a force which, added to their own, would operate against Acarnania, lying between them and the Gulf of Corinth (see Map 2). If successful, they might then hope to occupy Zacynthus and Cephallenia, allies of Athens, and so stop the Athenian route around the Peloponnese to the western seas.

The Spartans sent 1,000 heavy-armed troops under Cnemus, their admiral in those parts, with orders to assemble his fleet and army at Leucas and invade Acarnania. While the main Corinthian and allied fleet was

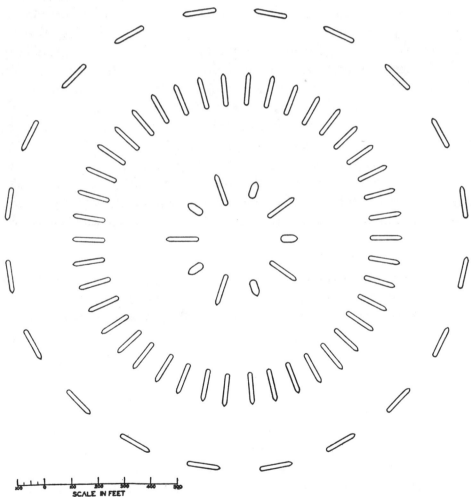

SCALE IN FEET

PHORMIO AND MACHAON OFF PATRAS

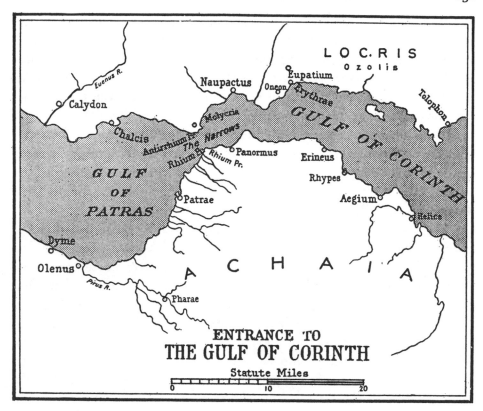

MAP 8.

mobilizing within the Gulf of Corinth, Cnemus committed himself to a premature invasion. The Chaonians did not follow the plan and were defeated. The whole expedition then retreated and re-embarked. Not until then did the Corinthian fleet under Machaon appear.

BATTLE OFF PATRAS (OR CHALCIS)

There were 47 trieres, besides small craft, probably supply snips, commanded by a group of admirals. The battleships had no desire to meet the enemy at sea, as they were equipped for land service, that is, they were going to annoy the coast and carried troops for disembarkation and were heavily laden with army supplies. As the expedition moved westward along the southern coast of the Gulf of Corinth, Phormio was made aware of its approach and moved abreast it on the northern side, wishing to attack outside the gulf in open water. As the Corinthians attempted to cross over to the northern shore, when in mid-channel abreast Patras, Phormio turned against them with his 20 ships. It was early in the morning and the usual easterly morning breeze had not yet arisen; the sea was calm. Being heavy with equipment, the Corinthians knew they were even less capable than usual of maneuvering on even terms with the highly trained and swift Athenian ships. Accordingly, they copied the Greek formation on the first day at Artemisium. They put 42 trieres in a circle, heading outward ready to ram. The small craft and a reserve of 5 trieres were held in the center. The latter were to attack any hostile ship which might drive through the circle, which might be 300 yards or more across.

Seeing the enemy thus immobile, Phormio drew near in column of ships, no doubt at a moderate speed not exceeding 4 knots, for he needed to preserve the strength of his rowers, and began to circle round the adversary distant one or two ships' lengths, feigning attack, and waiting for the morning breeze to spring up and throw them against each other, for ships cannot maintain relative positions unless in motion. In thus exposing their broadsides to the enemy's rams, the Athenians ran no risk whatever. The Corinthian ships of over 100 tons displacement would be slow to get in motion, needing perhaps 20 seconds to advance the first 32 feet. In this time the lighter Athenian ships, already moving at 4 knots, would go 135 feet and could accept or refuse contact. Let Thucydides himself tell the story:

On the other hand, the Athenians ranged in a single column kept moving round them, continually brushing past them, and making show of an immediate attack, though they had been previously directed by Phormio not to do so till he himself gave the signal. For he hoped that their order would not be maintained like that of an army on shore, but that the ships would drift foul of each other, and that if the usual morning wind for which he was waiting should spring up they would not remain in their formation. He thought, too, that it rested with him to close whenever he pleased, as his ships were the better performers, and that the wind would favor his intentions. So when the wind came upon them and their circle was contracted, being thrown into confusion both by the wind and by the small craft dashing against them, and when ship was fouling ship and the crews were shoving clear with boat-hooks and what with shouting and efforts and abuse of each other, they did not hear a word of command either for battle or for the oars, and through inexperience they could not manage their oars in the swell, thus putting the ships out of control; then, at the favorable moment, Phormio gave the signal. And the Athenians charged and first sunk one of the flagships and then destroyed all wherever they went and reduced them to such a condition that they no longer thought of resistance but fled to Patrae and Dyme in Achaia and then to Cyllene. The Athenians, having taken 12 ships and picked up most of the men from them, went to Molycria and having erected trophies and dedicated a ship to Neptune, they returned to Naupactus.

Cnemus after his defeat at Stratus came also to join the defeated fleet with the ships from Leucas.

The battle marked the high-water point of superior mobility in naval tactics. Neither before nor afterwards was a victory ever won owing so entirely to movement. Always the end of any formation afloat or ashore is particularly vulnerable because elsewhere each unit is supported by a friend on each side, but the end can be attacked by superior numbers. Through trying both to cover their non-combatant ships and to avoid exposing a flank by forming a circle, the Corinthians immobilized their ships and gave the enemy the choice of time and point and method of attack. After ramming the Athenians could not remain in contact with the enemy for a boarders' fight, since the Corinthians were carrying soldiers in addition to the crews. As the Corinthians were able to repel an attack on personnel, Phormio made his effort against ship structure. He struck and backed away, while the enemy was in confusion. As for the Spartan strategy, Cnemus began with a tactical effort in Acarnania depending for success on contemporaneous support from the fleet at another point, but he did not wait for the fleet to appear. He was consequently defeated, and the tardy fleet, which was unequal to its task, also suffered in meeting the better trained Athenians.

For their part, the Peloponnesians did not attribute their defeat to the inferiority of their fleet but to the misbehavior of Cnemus. Without depriving him of command, they therefore sent him three counselors, who brought him orders to call on the different states for more ships and to refit those already at hand and seek another engagement.

BATTLE OF NAUPACTUS

After the action in the Gulf of Patras, Phormio sent home for more ships, which were sent as requested, but with orders to undertake a secondary operation on the way around the Peloponnese, which delayed them. While the re-enforcement was ravaging in Crete, the Peloponnesians at Cyllene remobilized their fleet and started north with 77 ships and brought to at Panormus just within the entrance to the Gulf of Corinth on the southern side, where the army had come to support the fleet. Phormio left Naupactus with the same 20 ships which had fought off Patras, and took position opposite the enemy on the northern side where the local inhabitants were friendly and had assembled soldiers to support them. Their position was just outside the narrows. Seeing this, the Peloponnesians also came outside the narrows on their side and the fleets easily observed each other, as the opposite points of land are only a couple of miles apart. For about a week the two fleets occupied these positions and exercised daily, the Peloponnesians wishing for battle inside the narrows, where the shores were not far distant and where they had the support of the army in case they should have to beach their ships on account of disaster. Phormio, on the other hand, wanted to draw the enemy outside the narrows where he had plenty of sea room and had defeated them only a few weeks before. But the Peloponnesians feared undue delay, whereas it pleased the Athenians, for both were aware of the approach of the other squadron of 20 ships from Athens. So Cnemus and his counselors assembled their men and told them that they would avoid the previous mistakes in tactics and would rely on their own greater courage to win the battle. Phormio, seeing that his men also were somewhat lacking in confidence in face of odds of nearly 4 to 1, assembled them and said:

> I have called you together because I do not wish you to dread what is really not to be feared. For, in the first place, these men, because they have been previously overcome by us and do not think themselves a match for us, have equipped this great number of ships instead of a force that would be merely equal to us. In coming against us they chiefly rely on the fact that it is their natural character to be courageous; they feel this confidence for no other reason than that they are generally successful on land, and they think it will be the same at sea. But this, in all reason, will be our advantage here, as it is theirs on shore. For in valor they are not at all superior to us, but from our being more experienced in one particular service, we are the more confident regarding it. * * * Many armies ere now have been overthrown by an inferior force through lack of skill and others through want of daring; with neither of which have we now anything to do. As for the battle, I will not, if I can help it, fight in

the strait, nor will I enter in there at all, being aware that with a few well managed swift ships against a large number of badly handled ones; want of sea room is a disadvantage. For one can neither move up as he ought to the charge, having a view of the enemy from a distance, nor retire at the proper time if hard pressed; and there is no breaking through the line and returning for a second charge, which are the maneuvers of the better handled ships, but the sea fight must in that case resemble a land fight, and the greater number of ships gain the advantage. On these points I shall exercise as much forethought as possible, and do you, retaining good order in your ships, be quick in receiving the word of command, especially as we lie so close to the enemy. During the action, attach the greatest importance to order and silence, which is good for all operations of war and in particular for naval action, and so repel your enemies in a way worthy of your former achievements. (Thucydides: II-89)

But as time went on and the Peloponnesians saw that the enemy would not attack, they decided to threaten Naupactus and oblige him to give battle before he was re-enforced. They were lying at anchor in four lines with the best ships to the eastward. In the morning they got under way and without altering their formation moved towards Naupactus on their own side of the straits in four columns in line abreast with the fastest ships leading. Thus the leading ships were in the most favorable position to interpose between the enemy and the port which he was obliged to defend. As the Peloponnesians hoped, Phormio embarked his crews in the greatest haste and hurried towards Naupactus while the local troops with him moved along the shore abreast of him.[3] When Cnemus saw the enemy within the gulf in a single column (probably less than 1,500 yards long) coasting near the shore and, as he thought, within striking distance, he turned his ships simultaneously to the left and charged in four lines, with a front probably about the length of the hostile column. Owing to his misjudgment of pace and distance, 11 of the Athenian ships passed his right flank and proceeded eastward; but the 9 others were forced to run ashore, where some were seized, and those of the crews who had not swum out of them were killed. Several ships were saved by the local troops who came up and, dashing into the sea in their armor, boarded them and fighting from their decks rescued them from the enemy before they could be towed away.

As for the escaped ships, they kept on to Naupactus, with one ship

---

[3] A maneuvering speed in presence of the enemy of scarcely 3 knots.

much in the rear and closely followed by a Leucadian vessel far in advance of her comrades. As this fleeing Athenian passed a merchant vessel anchored far out from port, she used it for a base of maneuver and turning round it, rammed and sunk the self-confident enemy; whereupon the Peloponnesian pursuers were shocked by this unexpected incident and checked themselves as they crowded on in disorder. Some, through local ignorance, even grounded on the outlying shoals. Thereupon the Athenians took courage and shouted for battle, and rushed upon them. In consequence of their blunders and their present confusion, the Peloponnesians made short resistance and returned to Panormus after the Athenians had taken six prizes, and also rescued the ships which the enemy had taken earlier and begun to tow away. As the Peloponnesians were afraid to remain longer in presence on account of the over-due Athenian re-enforcements, they returned to their bases and the campaign ended. Upon the arrival of the expected ships, Phormio established complete control in western waters.

This battle, like the other one, was tactically an effort on the part of the Corinthians to make it a boarders' fight while the Athenians wanted a maneuver fight. Each was partially successful, but the maneuvering advantage of the Athenians was never afterwards displayed to so great an extent as under Phormio. The Corinthians made it a point to deny them opportunity.

The Athenian naval tactics of the day were based on three assumptions: better trained crews; faster, handier ships consequent upon fewer soldiers; and liberty of choice of the open sea for the place of battle. If any assumption was not fulfilled, the system of tactics would fail as Phormio found to his cost at Naupactus.

Naval Operations in 428-427

However, although the Athenian fleet had clearly shown its predominance, it had a great task and the enemy was still formidable at sea. During the succeeding year (428) the city of Mytilene in the island of Lesbos revolted, and the Athenians were engaged in its siege till the spring of 427 B.C., when the Peloponnesians sent 40 ships to raise the siege. They delayed on the way and arrived a few days too late and were immediately chased away without a battle, and at last reached Cyllene in their flight.

SECOND BATTLE OFF SYBOTA ISLANDS

At Cyllene were 13 ships of the Leucadians and Ambraciots, and it was resolved to attack Corcyra, where a party was anxious to revolt from Athens. It was the easier to undertake this operation as the Athenian station fleet at Naupactus was now reduced to 12 ships. Civil war having broken out among the Corcyraeans, the Athenian squadron from Naupactus proceeded there to restore order. Before this had been accomplished, the Peloponnesian fleet from Cyllene, numbering 53 ships, came up and spent the night at Sybota on the mainland opposite Corcyra. In the morning it got under way, while the Corcyraeans in great confusion manned 60 ships and went out in succession as they were ready, although the Athenian admiral urged them to let him first meet the enemy and by his maneuvering gain time for the Corcyraeans to take up an orderly formation. The Peloponnesians assigned 20 ships to meet the Corcyraean fleet, and the other 33 faced the 12 Athenians, which included the 2 celebrated ships *Paralus* and *Salamina*. The Corcyraeans were easily outmatched, as they attacked in succession, but the Athenians by their greater skill and speed avoided the enemy's center and enveloped one wing and sank a ship; whereupon the Peloponnesians abandoned any effort to attack and threw themselves into the circular formation which had been so disastrous to them two years before. Again the Athenians began to circle the enemy, but before they were ready to attack, the other division engaged with the Corcyraeans withdrew from action and came to help their comrades. Seeing their approach the Athenians rowed slowly astern, and gave the Corcyraeans a chance to get back to port. The Corinthian victors, however, did not venture to attack the city but were content to retire with 13 prizes to their berth at Sybota. The next day the approach of 60 Athenian ships was signaled to the Peloponnesians, who thereupon, in the greatest haste and by night, abandoned their position and, hugging the shore, hauled their ships over the isthmus at Leucas and escaped to their bases.

CAPTURE OF PYLOS

There was little more of striking naval interest until peace was made in 421, although Athenian squadrons were busy everywhere from Sicily to Asia Minor covering Athenian trade, escorting and supplying military expeditions, and landing raiding parties from their own personnel. Every-

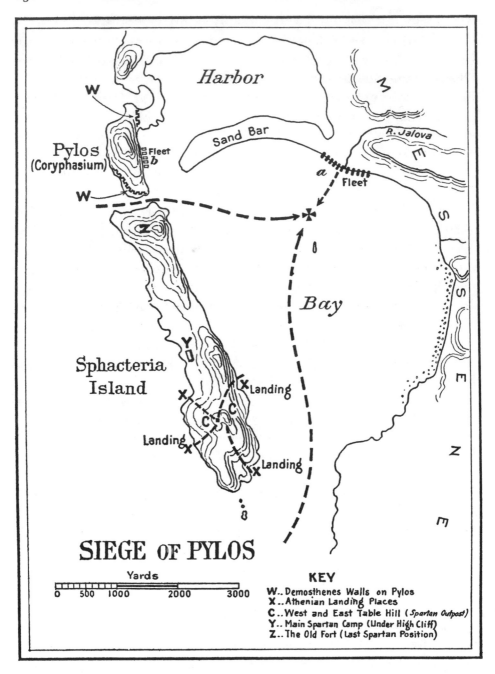

Harbor

Sand Bar

R. Jalova

W

Pylos
(Coryphasium)

Fleet
b

a
Fleet

Z

Bay

Sphacteria
Island

Y

X Landing

X

C C

Landing X

X Landing

SIEGE OF PYLOS

Yards

0   500   1000   2000   3000

KEY

W.. Demosthenes Walls on Pylos
X.. Athenian Landing Places
C.. West and East Table Hill (*Spartan Outpost*)
Y.. Main Spartan Camp (Under High Cliff)
Z.. The Old Fort (Last Spartan Position)

MAP 9.

where they met more or less resistance from the hostile naval forces, but the Athenian hold on the Aegean Sea was unshaken, and in western waters some gains even were made. The Athenian seizure of Pylos deserves some notice, less for the strictly naval operations than for the development of military tactics which later had their effect on naval warfare.

In the fall of 427, the Athenians sent a squadron of 20 ships to the Strait of Messana to prevent the importation of grain into the Peloponnese. With the help of their allies in the region the Athenians took Messana. The next year (426) Athens decided to re-enforce its squadron operating in Sicilian waters, and manned 40 ships to go there with orders to support the government of Corcyra against insurrection, while on their way to Sicily. When off the west coast of the Peloponnese, the squadron heard that a Peloponnesian squadron of 60 ships was already at Corcyra. While the Athenian leaders deliberated as to their course, a gale blew their ships into the harbor of Pylos (see Map 9).

The harbor is formed by a deep indentation in the coast, which is protected by the narrow precipitous island of Sphacteria about 5,000 yards long. Channels on both sides of the island are navigable; the southern one is 1,200 yards wide, the northern one about 130 yards. Pylos is a rocky peninsula nearly a mile long forming the north side of the north entrance and is joined to the low mainland by a sandy neck. Both Pylos and Sphacteria have foul beaches or cliffs along most of their lengths so that landing is impossible except at a few points and even these are difficult. Inside, the harbor is divided by a low spit which almost cuts off the northern part from the rest. The shores of the mainland are low in the northern part, but to the south they are rocky. Good water for a large fleet is to be found at the stream which enters on the east side.

Demosthenes, one of the Athenian admirals, besought his colleagues to fortify the rocky point of Pylos, for which ample material was available, and hold the harbor as an important way station. The others declined to do so, but the fleet was held by contrary winds and, in the meantime, the soldiers, lacking occupation, themselves undertook the work of fortification and made the place quite strong with works at the northern end and on the southwest side outside the channel. After 6 days the main body of the fleet moved on, leaving Demosthenes with 5 ships (at *b*, Map 9) to hold the position.

The Lacedaemonians were at first inclined to treat lightly the occupation of Pylos, as they thought they should have no difficulty in driving the Athenians out. Nevertheless, when the news got to the Spartan army then invading Attica, the King promptly withdrew his forces to recover Pylos from the enemy, and recalled the 60 ships from Corcyra to Pylos. Demosthenes anticipated the enemy's action by sending 2 of his 5 ships to recall the Athenian squadron from Zacynthus, where it had arrived on its way to Italy. The Spartans had news of the recall and, in order to bar the entrances to the harbor, they occupied Sphacteria with a detachment of 420 hoplites (heavy-armed spearmen) and meant to anchor a line of ships across the entrance channel, but this they neglected. The Spartans were then ready to assault Pylos from the sandy neck, thinking that the Athenians would be able to get no assistance from their ships as no landing could be made on the precipitous seaward side of the position. Demosthenes drew his 3 ships on shore inside the harbor and put everybody in the fortification, except a few men outside the wall where he thought the enemy might try to land. The Spartans then made simultaneous assaults by sea and land on opposite sides of the rock of Pylos.

The soldiers at the northern end found the ground very precipitous and could not get in. On the southwest side, where 43 ships attacked, the shore was not very steep, but the bottom was rocky and the ship captains feared to drive in and land their men. At last, Brasidas, captain of a triere, said it was a time to sacrifice ships to make a landing, and obliged his pilot to run ashore, but even he was repulsed and badly wounded. His shield slipped overboard and was afterward thrown on the beach by the waves, whence our Athenians recovered it and set it up as a monument of victory. The Spartans then suspended their attacks for two days while getting timber for siege engines, and moored their ships at *a*, Map 9.

BATTLE IN THE BAY OF PYLOS

In the meantime the Athenian fleet returned from Zacynthus, having increased its numbers to 70 vessels, and found the harbor occupied by the enemy, so it retired for the night to an island not far away. In the morning the Athenians charged through both entrances to the harbor while the Spartans were standing by their ships and making ready to launch them. Many of the Spartan vessels got off into deep water, but these the Athenians soon put to flight after damaging many and capturing 5. The Athenians pursued to the shore where some vessels had not even left the beach and hoped to tow all away, but the whole Spartan army hurried to the shore, and after a long fight they saved all their empty ships, except the 5 first taken in the open harbor. The Athenian fleet was now in complete control of the harbor, and the Spartan troops on Sphacteria were isolated.

In their anxiety to save these, the Spartan generals consented to an armistice on condition of temporarily yielding in pledge all their ships which were present, until the whole affair could be referred to Athens with a view to arranging a permanent peace. Should no peace be made the ships would be returned and the armistice ended. In the meantime the Spartans on Sphacteria would be rationed each day. In the discussions at Athens the terms of the Lacedaemonians were rejected and the armistice ceased; but the ships were retained contrary to the armistice terms.

Sphacteria was now closely blockaded for several weeks under difficult conditions. The Athenian vessels had no place available to haul their ships ashore and only one small well on Pylos for 14,000 men. The ships took turns in going off to eat their meals on shore and get water while the rest lay at anchor on both sides of Sphacteria. On the Spartan side great efforts were made by night to supply the garrison by men in small boats and by swimmers, and these had so much success that it was feared at Athens that the blockade might last until the bad season compelled its abandonment.

Accordingly, a large expedition was sent from Athens to land on Sphacteria and make an active assault. The main body of the Spartans on the island was at its center where there was a fortification and a well. An outpost of 30 men was stationed at a hill at the southern extremity under which were two small landing points, one within the bay, the other outside. After the heavy-armed troops from Athens had arrived, 800 of them were placed in a few ships, and a little before dawn these men were thrown on shore at both landings. Hastening up the hill, they seized the outpost unaware and slaughtered the men within.

Being now in possession of the landings and their covering hill, the Athenians put ashore two-thirds of the rowers of the fleet, leaving only just enough men to handle the ships, and also 1,600 light-armed soldiers, making in all over 10,000 troops to oppose 400 Spartans.

The Spartan main body saw the loss of the outpost and drew out in phalanx to advance against the enemy. The Athenian heavy-armed troops who had first landed also formed a phalanx, and the two bodies stood facing each other. The Athenians refused to move; the ground was too rough to maintain the rigid formation which made the phalanx formidable. In the meantime the Athenian auxiliary light-armed troops with missile weapons were swarming up from the landing points and surrounded the Spartans. The latter could neither get at their light-armed enemies nor neglect them to advance and attack the waiting hostile phalanx. They were much distressed and found it impossible to retain their main position in the center of the island, so they fell back to a strong position at the northern end of the island where most of them arrived.

It was a great day in the history of European warfare. The Spartan phalanx had not been able to hold its position against the light-armed troops. In the final stand in the north the Spartans put up an excellent defense, but they did not occupy the very highest points of a precipitous rock behind them, and after a while some Messenian allies of the Athenians found a circuitous way practicable for light-armed archers and javelin men to reach the summit and shoot inside the Spartan position. The garrison could not reach its enemies and was granted permission to surrender by the generals on the mainland. There were 292 survivors. Sparta's military prestige suffered very much.

This battle has been narrated at some length because it was a typical one of the time in the struggle on the beach for the capture of the Spartan fleet, and secondly for the stripping of the Athenian fleet to get a landing force. Above all, it was noteworthy for the novel employment of auxiliary troops. Before this occasion, Greek battles had been decided by the charge of the phalanx of many ranks of heavy-armed spearmen, and the light-armed auxiliaries merely foraged and reconnoitered before battle and threatened the flanks in battle. Here the missile weapons took the active part, while the Athenian phalanx stood in readiness.

CONCLUSION OF THE FIRST PHASE OF THE WAR

The war continued for some years longer on fairly equal terms. Athens held her allies in the Aegean Islands and on the shores of Asia Minor, but in 424 her Sicilian allies made peace with Syracuse, and so deprived Athens of a naval base in that region. She withdrew her squadrons in consequence, and in so doing relieved pressure on Corinthian trade in the western Mediterranean. Then the Athenian armies were unsuccessful on the mainland. They suffered a severe defeat at Delium in Boeotia, and Brasidas, who had so distinguished himself at Pylos, had much success in Thrace where his capture of Amphipolis in 422 deprived Athens of an important intermediate base on the line of trade to the Euxine. In an Athenian attempt to recapture Amphipolis from the Peloponnesians both Brasidas and the Athenian general Cleon lost their lives in a battle under the city walls. As they were the chief supporters of the war in their respective countries, it was now possible to negotiate a peace. Sparta was discouraged by the failure of her traditional way of making war, the destruction of crops and orchards leading to a battle. Besides, Athens still held the prisoners of Pylos, so the two powers made a peace taking effect in the spring of 421 and an alliance to last 50 years, each promising to aid the other in case of an attack by a third state, and in such case neither would make peace without the other. Besides the treaty provided for settling disputes by justice and under oath. It restored all the prisoners taken on both sides and also many cities and regions which had been occupied during the war.

Reviewing the development of naval warfare in these 10 years we see for the first time a great war maintained on one side entirely by sea power. Primarily, the war was one between Athens and Corinth for the control of western sea-borne commerce and the profits thereof. As her ally, Corinth secured Sparta with the finest army in Greece. The war ended because Sparta was getting nothing by her efforts. On the other side, Athens had not been able to establish predominance in trade in and across the Adriatic. Yet the war was not fought to a finish, for neither side was near exhaustion.

As for tactics, the Athenian fleet had shown its great superiority over the Corinthians and their allies in the sea battle of movement and skillful ship handling; but never again was the ram as effective as in Phormio's two great battles, whose memory was revived in the nineteenth century to justify the use of the ram in steam naval tactics. Phormio used the ram as the main weapon of the fleet, directed by the commander in chief. His successors used it as a single-ship weapon upon the opportunity of each sea captain. In addition the precedent was set on Sphacteria for the greater employment of missile weapons in purely naval actions in the next hostilities.

The Interval between Hostilities

Although Sparta had made peace, unfortunately she could not make her allies carry out the terms to which she had pledged them, for they gained nothing by the treaty. Athens still retained sea power through her unrivaled fleet and the walls linking Athens to the port of Piraeus. During the 10 years of war the merchant ships of Corinth, which supplied her allies with grain from Egypt and Sicily, had enjoyed on the sea only the privileges of pirates, and even now things were not satisfactory; for Athens still had control of important fleet bases on the route to the west and did a great business in Corinth's area of trade. In making the treaty, Sparta and Athens both hoped that their alliance would keep the rest of Greece quiet, but this proved not to be the case. Sparta could not convince either Athens or the rest of the Peloponnesians of her good faith. A new series of alliances was made in 420, and Greece was again divided into two opposite camps; but on neither side were the leaders anxious for hostilities, and general war was delayed until 418 when Sparta and Boeotia shattered the alliance headed by Argos and Athens at the battle of Mantineia in Arcadia. The Spartan hegemony in the south was re-established.

There were minor hostilities for a couple of years, and then Athens decided to make a great effort in the west to control Italian and Sicilian trade. At the time of this decision Athens was in complete control of commerce in the Aegean and was engaged in no serious hostilities.

The Sicilian Campaign of Athens—Its Origin

The great event of the second part of the war was the Athenian siege of Syracuse in 414-413. The bad relations were not of sudden growth, but had existed since the beginning of the war. Syracuse was a Corinthian colony whose importance had grown rapidly in the past 30 years. She had a strong navy and her Peloponnesian friends hoped for her aid in 431. At least, her benevolent neutrality would facilitate the important grain trade of Sicily with the Peloponnese; but Athenian diplomacy encouraged other Sicilian states to resist Syracusan growth and made treaties to check Corinthian trade. In September, 427, Athens sent 20 warships to Sicily in observation of events; for if the Athenian group were to collapse, the

MAP 10.
LOWER ITALY

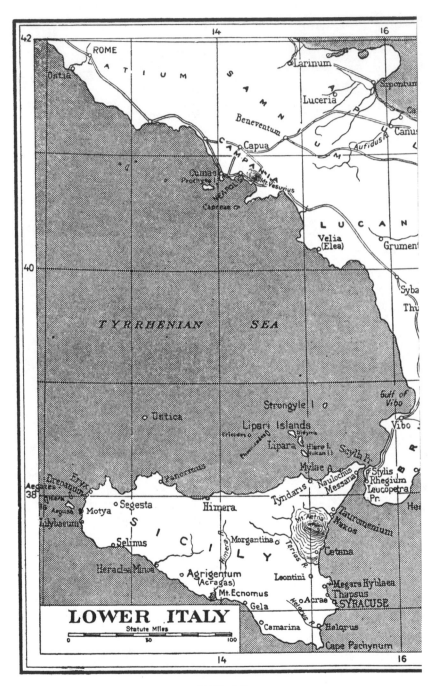

MAP 10.

Note: Hiera, Aegusa, and Phorbantia group are the Aegates Islands.

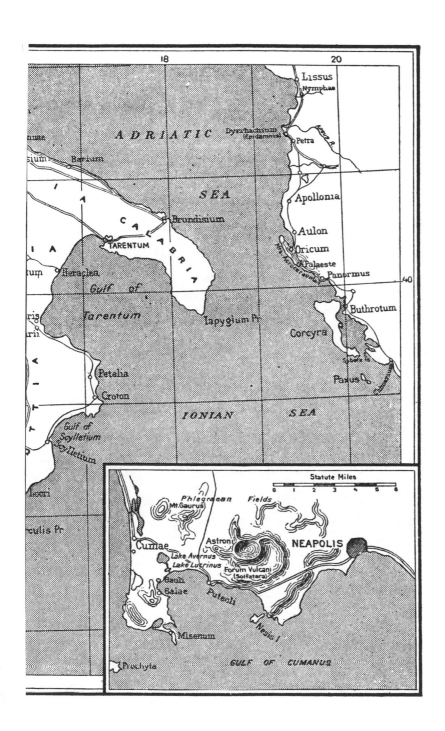

Syracusan navy might be added to those of Peloponnesus. However, the small force sent showed that the Athenian government had no purpose in its dispatch beyond the maintenance of political equilibrium.

A by-product of hostilities in Sicily was the cessation of exports of grain to the Peloponnese. While the Sicilians were fighting each other instead of working in the fields, there was some obligation on the Peloponnesians to work in the fields instead of fighting. Hostilities in Sicily were helping Athens.

But to the demagogues in Athens, their little squadron in Sicily meant more. They regarded it as the first step on the road to a new empire. The Athenian squadron established itself at Rhegium and enjoyed some minor successes, but after a year it became apparent that the Syracusans and their allies were making headway, and Athens sent out 40 more ships; but still the naval engagements were indecisive, and her Sicilian allies began to see that the policy of Athens was egotistical, and they became cool. Hermocrates, the Syracusan leader, realized that a peace keeping Athens out of the west would be better than a war hard to win. Thus the Sicilians came to a general peace among themselves in 424, and the Athenian squadron was obliged to withdraw, as there was now no cause for its presence. But the impression remained among the Athenian people that Syracuse was not a very formidable enemy and that Sicily was a valuable prize.

During the years of comparative naval inactivity from 421 to 416 Athens strengthened her Empire and embellished·the city. Oceanic traffic was regulated for the good of Athenian markets and the state recuperated.

But in 416 the situation in Sicily drew attention there once more, and public opinion was guided by the idea formed 10 years before that Syracuse was an easy mark. An Athenian ally was again oppressed by Syracuse. First, it had been Leontini which was laid waste; now it was Segesta. Selinus and Segesta, about 30 miles apart, had adjoining lands and boundaries, and mixed marriages made trouble. Syracuse supported Selinus, and Segesta appealed to Athens. Envoys sent to Athens said that if Syracuse were permitted to become mistress of Sicily, she would some day send fleets to the Peloponnese to destroy the Athenian Empire; they said also that Segesta would furnish money for the Athenian campaign. The Athenians sent back to see the money. Although the government acted thus discreetly, the Athenian people were under the spirit of adventure, and they knew little of the size of Sicily or its number of people. To some, the real object was no more than to keep alive the local opposition in Sicily to imperial Syracuse, and to maintain Athens as a great factor in western trade. They thought that if an expedition was not successful it could withdraw, as in 424.

The envoys returned from Segesta with 60 talents to pay a month's wages for 60 ships, and the mistaken statement that there was plenty more. It was voted to send 60 ships under Nicias, Alcibiades, and Lamachus. Instructions were to aid Segesta and rebuild Leontini, and then to settle matters to the best interest of Athens. Of the three generals, Lamachus was an able soldier, but of no political weight in Athens, while Nicias and Alcibiades led their respective parties. Nicias was old and far from anxious to undertake the expedition. He was content to maintain Athens as she was. Alcibiades, young and enterprising, was anxious to establish a new empire and to be himself the foremost man of his time.

By his effort to have the adventure called off, Nicias made the people realize it was a great task. He pointed out that a great war in Sicily was rash while unfriendly states nearer home were planning to fall on Athens; and that it was folly to seek for new subjects while old ones were still in revolt. He said, too, that the Sicilians would not be so easy to conquer as the nearer enemies of Athens, for nature had divided the Ionian from the Sicilian seas and put the islanders far away. In rebuttal Alcibiades urged that his abilities gave him a right to lead. He pleaded for union in action and that Athens should strike down enemies before they declared themselves such. In Sicily, he said, there was no union, rather a lack of national spirit. He alleged that without imperiling the situation at home they could send out enough ships to defeat all the fleets of Sicily, and he held out hopes of securing there a great increase to the Athenian fleet with which to overwhelm the Peloponnese. It was evident from the course of the past 5 years that Sparta was reluctant to take up arms again, and she was no longer desirous of supporting Corinthian interests in Sicily.

DEPARTURE OF THE ATHENIAN FLEET

As a result of Nicias' warning of the magnitude of the task, the people authorized an increase in the force at first contemplated to 100 trieres and 5,000 hoplites, and 3,000 talents were set aside from the treasury. For several months there was preparation, and in early June, 415, the fleet was ready with the finest ships' crews and the best soldiers.

Now when the ships were manned and complete with stores, silence was proclaimed by trumpet, and they offered the usual prayers before departure, not singly, ship by ship, but altogether, responding to a herald, having mixed bowls of wine throughout the fleet and both seamen and officers making oblations with gold and silver goblets. They were joined also in their prayers by the multitude on shore, both the citizens and whoever else there was that wished them well. When they had sung their hymn and finished their libations, they let go their lines, and, having left port in column, they then raced each other as far as Aegina [15 miles]. And thus they hastened to Corcyra where the allies joined them. (Thucydides: VI-32)

SYRACUSAN DEBATE ON THE WAR

At Syracuse Hermocrates came forward at a great popular assembly to confirm the rumors of the Athenian expedition, saying that although the expedition was nominally to aid Segesta, really the object was to conquer all Sicily and chiefly the Syracusans (as was the case). He urged that the Syracusans should not fear the Athenians too greatly, for in spite of the large size of the expedition there were more soldiers in Sicily, and the distance from home would be a great handicap to the enemy. So he recommended alliance with other Sicilian cities and with Carthage, and even with Corinth and Lacedaemon (see Map 4), begging them to aid in Sicily and stir up war in their own parts. All the Sicilian cities which could be induced to join them should be urged to commission all their present ships, and with two months' provisions send them to meet the Athenians at Tarentum and the Iapygium Promontory (heel of Italy), and there

show them that they will not be able to fight in Sicilian waters before they have fought for their own passage across the Ionian Sea. We should strike them with the greatest fear, for we set on them from a friendly country, acting as its guardians (for Tarentum is ready to receive us); but they will be crossing the open sea which is wide, and their great armament would hardly keep well together in so long a voyage and would be open to our attack while it comes on slowly and in isolated groups. But supposing on the other hand that having lightened their ships they should attack us with the best ships in a more compact order, then, if they use their oars, we shall fall on them when they are weary, or if we do not wish to attack, we may retire to Tarentum. While they, having crossed with few provisions, to be ready for battle would be at a loss what to do in uninhabited regions and would either be blockaded if they stayed at one place or if they attempted to move along the coast, would leave their other ships [transports] and would be dispirited, not knowing whether other cities would receive them or not. I, therefore, am of opinion that being deterred by this consideration, they will not so much as leave Corcyra. We should be reported also as more ready than we are, for men's feelings are affected by what they hear. If they saw us acting with courage beyond their expectations they would be the more dismayed. (Thucydides: VI-34)

The proposal to go to Tarentum turned on the tactical features of trieres already alluded to. Militarily, this proposal had great merit, but politically it was impracticable, for not even the Syracusans could be aroused to their danger, for the people of Syracuse were at odds with one another, some maintaining the Athenians would not come, and others that they would suffer greatly, and few believed with Hermocrates that they would come and prove dangerous. Athenagoras, leader of the popular party, said,

whoever does not wish them to come is a coward or no friend to his country. Those who speak of danger wish to get authority in their own hands for the emergency, for they would not come here, leaving the Peloponnesians behind them.

He praised the strength of Syracuse, saying the Athenians would not be able even to effect a landing. After the generals had promised to examine the state of supplies and send to other cities for observation of events in them the assembly broke up.

STRENGTH OF THE ATHENIAN EXPEDITION

By this time the Athenians were at Corcyra, where a review was held and the fleet organized in three divisions, so that moving independently they might not overcrowd individual ports and more readily get water and provisions. Three ships were sent forward to reconnoiter and return to report as to which cities would receive them. When the fleet sailed for Sicily, late in June, 415, there were 134 trieres in all and 2 pentekonters, of which 100 were Athenian and of these 40 were fitted as troop ships; the remainder of the fleet were Chians and the other allies. Of hoplites there were 5,100, of which 1,500 were Athenian and 700 *epibatae* (heavy-armed for ship service). The rest were sent by the subject allies and by the Argives (500) and by the Mantineans (250). Of archers there were 480 and also 700 Rhodian slingers and 120 light-armed Megarean exiles and one horse transport carrying 30 horses. With the fleet went a train of 30 ships carrying provisions and the bakers, stone masons and carpenters with tools, for fortifications and also 100 boats pressed into service, as were the ships of burden.[4]

Arrival in Italy—Uncertainty of Leaders

After crossing the sea to the Iapygian foreland and to Tarentum by divisions, as they could, the leaders found the cities would not give them a market nor the protection of their walls, but only water and anchorage, and Tarentum and Locri not even these. The fleet came to Rhegium, which remained neutral, giving a market but not admitting men within the walls, and waited there for the return of the advance ships, which announced on arrival that only 30 talents were to be found at Segesta.

Much alarmed by the arrival of the expedition at Rhegium, the Syracusans were preparing to meet the attack of the Athenians who, on this news from Segesta, held a council. Nicias wanted to sail for Selinus, as the action of that city was the nominal cause of their coming, and after bringing the Selinuntines to terms they might cruise along the coast of Sicily, display the power of the Athenian state, and go home. Alcibiades thought they ought not to return home with so large a force without some noteworthy act. They should send heralds to the Sicilian cities to establish friendship and get grain and troops, and particularly control the harbor of Messana. After this, they would know whether to attack Selinus and Syracuse. Lamachus urged that they ought to sail direct for

---

[4] The 30 ships carried two months' provisions. Further maintenance depended on local markets. There were also a large number of ships and boats which went along to supply the army as a personal adventure. Including everybody, there must have been nearly 30,000 souls. Taking Herodotus' estimate of one choinix (1.94 lbs.) of wheat per man per day, the 30 ships carried 3,492,000 lbs. of wheat, or an average of 52 tons each. They probably carried other military supplies in addition, perhaps 30 to 50 tons each, and their average displacement might be 200 tons, say from 150 to 250 tons each. Taking the usual proportions of round ships, the dimensions of the smaller size would be roughly about 19 ft. wide and 57 ft. long. The larger size would be roughly 22 by 66 feet. The horse transport for 30 horses is convertible into man transportation at the rate of 1 horse to 5 men. Add 50 men for the crew and horsemen and we have it that this transport carried the equivalent of the triere crew of 200 men and probably considerable cargo besides.

Syracuse, and fight under the walls of the city while the people were un-prepared and terrified. As for a naval base, he said that after withdrawing the fleet from Syracuse (after landing the army) it could go to Megara and establish itself there where it was at no great distance from Syracuse either by sea or land. As Lamachus was not important politically, although an able soldier, he finally thought best to cast his vote with Alcibiades.

Messana refused to admit the men of the fleet within its walls, so the generals took 60 ships to Naxos where they were well received, and then went on to Catana whose people would not admit them. The squadron advanced to Syracuse where a reconnaissance force of 10 ships entered the Great Harbor to observe conditions and the readiness of the Syracusan ships, while the herald made proclamation that the fleet had come to right the Leontini. On returning to Catana, Alcibiades was allowed to address an assembly of the people, and while he did so a party of his soldiers en-tered the town. The majority of the assembly was overawed and voted to make an alliance with Athens while the opponents of the measure fled from the city. The base of the expedition was then transferred to Catana where it remained till the end. The harbor was admirable as it is today. Time was now wasted in a useless voyage to the south coast and back to Catana while Syracuse was preparing.

RECALL OF ALCIBIADES

The sacred ship *Salaminia* now arrived from Athens to bring Al-cibiades home to stand trial for sacrilege. Before he left Athens, his po-litical enemies had made the charge, and he had pressed for immediate trial while he had the votes of the army at hand to acquit him, but his opponents delayed action till the expedition had gone. He deserted the ship on the way home and was sentenced to death in his absence. He went to Peloponnese where he gave much information about the intentions of Athens which helped to induce Sparta to declare war.

Following the departure of Alcibiades, the expedition was reorganized in two divisions under the two remaining generals, and more time was wasted by a cruise along the north coast of Sicily, nominally to discover the state of affairs, but really made because Nicias was averse to any seri-ous military action, and he controlled Lamachus because he alone was

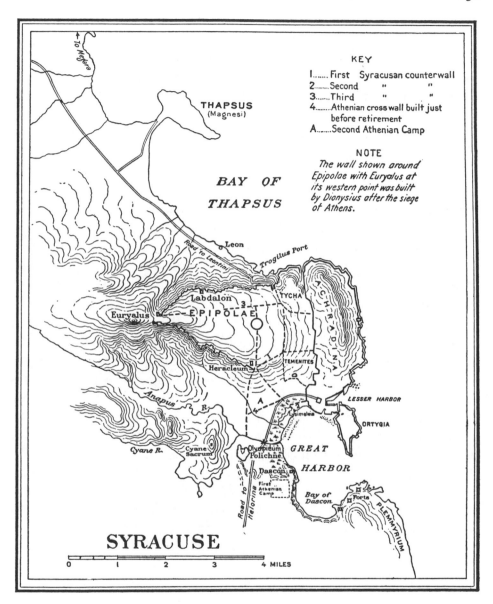

KEY

1...... First Syracusan counterwall
2...... Second   "   "
3...... Third   "   "
4...... Athenian cross wall built just
        before retirement
A...... Second Athenian Camp

NOTE
*The wall shown around
Epipolae with Euryalus at
its western point was built
by Dionysius after the siege
of Athens.*

THAPSUS
(Magnesi)

BAY OF
THAPSUS

To Megara

Road to Leontini

Leon

Trogilus Port

Labdalon

Euryalus

EPIPOLAE

TYCHA

ACHRADINA

Heracleum

TEMENITES

Anapus
R.

A

LESSER HARBOR

Cyane R.

Cyane
Sacrum

Olympieum
Polichne.

Dascon

First
Athenian
Camp

Lysimelea

ORTYGIA

GREAT

HARBOR

Bay of
Dascon

Forts

PLEMMYRIUM

Road to Helorina

SYRACUSE

0   1   2   3   4 MILES

MAP II.

politically important at home and with the army. The summer of 415
was now at an end, and nothing had been done except seizing the base at
Catana.

FIRST ATTEMPT AGAINST SYRACUSE

As winter approached, the Athenians began preparations for an attempt upon Syracuse. By this time the spirit of the Syracusan people was rising; of which the Athenian generals took advantage. They put out a false story to induce the Syracusan army to appear before Catana, expecting to seize it by treachery within the walls. When the Syracusans drew near hoping for entrance at dawn, the Athenian army embarked in the fleet and made a night passage to Syracuse, entering the Great Harbor and landing south of the city about dawn where it occupied a good position on the plateau and fortified it. In the meantime, the Syracusan army returned in haste from Catana, and there was a battle in which the Athenians had the advantage. But Nicias was averse to forcing a decision, and the Athenians departed by sea to Catana and Naxos to spend the winter, sending to Athens for money and cavalry to join them in the spring. Nicias' failure to try to accomplish anything against Syracuse during this first season was most disastrous. His withdrawal is inexplicable on military grounds, but probably he hoped to cause the Syracusan allies to fall away by diplomacy, backed by the display of Athenian strength.

Hermocrates came forward in the Syracusan assembly to urge reorganization and re-equipment of the army during the winter, and was himself elected one of the generals. The city built a wall along the whole side looking to Epipolae and fortified Megara as an outpost to the north besides the Olympieum overlooking the harbor. Palisade obstructions also were put along the shore at places favorable for landing.

THE FIRST WINTER

The Syracusans and Athenians both sought allies during the winter. The Syracusan envoys to Corinth and Sparta were successful at both places. At Sparta Alcibiades appeared and exposed the imperialistic intentions of Athens, urging that were the Syracusans to be defeated, the whole Grecian race would be subdued to Athens. Particularly, he recommended Sparta to send a force to seize Decelea in Athenian territory, which having taken and fortified they would be able very greatly to annoy Athenian sea trade, which passed overland from Oropus to Athens, and also to interfere with the agriculture of Attica. But this recommendation was not carried out for a year. However, the Syracusan envoys arranged with the Corinthians to send them help (ships) and before returning they chose a brilliant Spartan general, Gylippus by name, to take command at Syracuse. At the same time the Athenians received the messengers from Sicily and resolved to send both supplies for the army and more cavalry as requested. And so the winter of 415-414 ended.

THE SIEGE OF SYRACUSE BEGINS

At the beginning of the spring of 414, while waiting for cavalry, the Athenians at Catana undertook some minor raids by sea and land, on one of which they took Megara from the Syracusans. Hearing that the Athenian cavalry had come, it being now almost summer, and the enemy about to take action, the Syracusans decided to hold the heights of Epipolae to the west of the city as being necessary to them. So at daybreak sometime in May they marched out to the meadows south of Epipolae and the new generals held a review of the troops. The Athenians on the same instant had brought their entire force to Leon, less than a mile from Epipolae on its other side and, after landing the soldiers, placed their ships at Thapsus (see Map 11). The fleet secured itself and the possible retreat of the army by throwing a stockade across the isthmus, while the troops hastened to Epipolae and ascended it before the Syracusans could get there from the review. An engagement followed on the plateau in which the Syracusans were defeated, and the Athenians the next day fortified the strongest part of Epipolae at Labdalon. The Athenians were supplied from Thapsus to the north, and Labdalon covered them from the attack from outside the city. Soon after additional cavalry arrived for the Athenians from their Sicilian allies, for success makes friends. So in order to isolate the city they began a fortification which was to extend from the sea near Leon across Epipolae to the Great Harbor, parallel to the wall the Syracusans had made the previous winter.

As the Athenians were only working on the northern half and on the citadel (circle) in the middle of their projected wall of blockade, Hermocrates, who was the most aggressive of the Syracusan generals, proposed a counter-wall at right angles to that of the Athenians to prevent them from carrying it further south. (See 1, Map 11.) This would keep open communication with the country. When the Syracusans thought their wall so far advanced as to permit it, a part of them returned into town, leaving a guard. The Athenians, having cut the city aqueduct, charged the counter-work with 300 men and destroyed it, while the rest of the army advanced towards the city to prevent interference. The next day the Athenians went to the southern edge of the Epipolae cliffs overlooking Lysimeleia marsh and began a wall from that point to pass through the marsh to the Great Harbor by the shortest line. Again the Syracusans answered by a counter palisade and ditch (see 2, Map 11) running out from the city through the marsh. Again the Athenians attacked at dawn, laying a line of house doors and planks across the firmest part of the marsh, and drove the Syracusans away, but at a rally of the Syracusans, Lamachus was killed, and thereby the Athenians suffered greatly in their leadership, for Nicias was now sole leader and ill with kidney trouble besides being disinclined to the whole campaign. The Syracusans after their rally went up on the heights and destroyed some of the Athenian works, but, getting up from a sick bed, Nicias repulsed them.

THE ATHENIAN FLEET ENTERS GREAT HARBOR

At this time the fleet came round into the Great Harbor from Thapsus. The camp, fleet base, and the source of army supplies was now within the Great Harbor, and the army built a double wall from Epipolae and the cliffs down to the sea. Thucydides says it was to circumvallate the city, but we cannot doubt the western leg of the wall was also to protect the Athenian camp (see A, Map 11) and ships from the enemy at the Olympieum. The area between the two walls must have included at least 400 acres, even if some of the seamen were quartered on board ship on the beach; and the camp must have been on the first rise about the marsh. Of course, a part must have included the lowland which later proved unhealthy, for the fleet and army had to keep in close touch, and this position gave the army short lines to build and maintain. Unfortunately, the piece of wall running from the central fort to the sea on the north was never completed. Appearances now favored the Athenians and provisions came freely to them from all Sicily, while the Syracusans began to think of capitulation.

GYLIPPUS BECOMES GENERAL IN SYRACUSE

At Leucas, Gylippus with the Corinthian ships heard they were thus inclined. He had little hope of saving Sicily, but wished to organize south Italy for resistance to the Athenians. He hastened on with 4 ships only, and learned that the investment was not entirely completed towards the north, and that he might enter Syracuse. He therefore sailed for Himera on the north coast of Sicily, to gather forces and then march to Syracuse overland with an army. Although Nicias made light of Gylippus, he took the precaution to send out 4 ships to intercept him, but they were too late to catch Gylippus, who got safely to Himera. There Gylippus armed his own crews, and with 700 of them and 2,000 light- and heavy-armed local troops and 100 horsemen he advanced upon Syracuse about 130 miles away by road.

Syracuse was now on the point of surrender, but Gylippus had not failed to send a Corinthian ship there to urge hope and delay. The Syracusan army sallied out to meet Gylippus, who arrived just as the Athenians were about to complete the last bit of wall down to the northern sea. After joining the townsmen and facing the enemy with the combined army, apparently with his back to the sea, Gylippus sent to offer the Athenians 5 days' grace to withdraw without penalty. Of this offer, Nicias took no notice, and Gylippus then marched his united force by the left flank and bivouacked inside the Athenian lines at the fort of Temenites. The next day he took a position for battle and, under cover of this threat, sent a body of men to capture the detached fort of Labdalon which more or less commanded the road into the city. This done, he began a third defensive cross wall, north of the Athenian stub wall to prevent its extension, and secure his own freedom of communication with the interior of Sicily. There was now some fighting, and the Athenians held their positions without improving them.

NICIAS TRANSFERS HIS BASE TO PLEMMYRIUM

It was the turn of the tide in the progress of the siege whose end was yet far off. Nicias felt this; he had previously enjoyed freedom of movement over the heights, and no doubt used the harbor of Thapsus at pleasure, although his main fleet was in the Great Harbor.[5] Now all was changed: it was imperative to hold undisputed entrance into the Great Harbor past the hostile squadrons outside the city in the Little Harbor. Nicias therefore sent a body of troops to fortify the peninsula of Plemmyrium at the harbor mouth, opposite the city. When he had established three forts there he transferred most of his ships and the army base of supplies to their protection.

This took many men out of the unhealthy part of the camp, and gave him control of the entrance and ability to fight in the open sea, as was best for Athenian tactics. The supply ships may possibly have made some use of the eastern shore of Plemmyrium outside, although the bottom is foul; but an outside position would be embarrassing as soon as the enemy should undertake naval operations.

By thus going to Plemmyrium Nicias made a compromise. His lines of defense were somewhat longer, but the fleet was better placed to sally out of harbor to the open sea and have the room necessary for the maneuvers which were the peculiar excellence of the Athenian fleet. On the whole, the position was inconvenient, for there was little water on Plemmyrium and when the crews went into the country to gather firewood, the Syracusan cavalry, having possession of the back country, cut them off, sallying from a strong cavalry post which was maintained at Olympieum. From this moment the Athenian crews began to waste.

GYLIPPUS MAKES SYRACUSE SECURE FOR THE WINTER

Hearing of the coming of the rest of the Corinthian fleet, Nicias sent out a division of 20 ships to meet them along the South Italian coast and the Straits of Messana. Gylippus now continued his cross wall using the materials collected by the Athenians, and on a favorable opportunity brought about an engagement between the hostile lines, but found he had no good opportunity to use his superior cavalry and missile throwers, and was defeated. He addressed his people telling them that it was his tactical error and that he would correct it. The Athenians, seeing that the hostile

---

[5] The fleet had been better placed at Thapsus for its own freedom, but transporting stores across Epipolae was troublesome.

counter-wall was about to pass the end of theirs, offered battle, and Gylippus led his men out into the open country beyond both walls and put his cavalry and light-armed men to his right. In the action which followed Gylippus had maneuvering space. His cavalry attack on the left flank of the Athenians drove them in and decided the battle for the Syracusans. Soon afterward the 12 Corinthian ships got in, having eluded the hostile ships looking for them, and their crews went to aid in the wall building.

Since the Syracusan fleet had not enough men to fight and the city was temporarily safe, with open communication to the island, Gylippus now went away to drum up allies and recruit men for fleet and army. Requests for aid were again sent also to Sparta and Corinth, and the Syracusans began to man and drill their fleet. It was now November, 414. Seeing his own strength diminishing and that of the enemy increasing every day, Nicias wrote to Athens telling of his difficulties and asking further aid. Then putting himself on the defensive he thought little of aggressive measures.

On the arrival of Nicias' messengers in Athens at the close of 414 B.C., his letter was read to the assembly. It recounted that after building the lines within which they were then lying, and after they had beaten the Syracusans in many engagements, Gylippus came with re-enforcements and, although he was defeated on the first day, in the action on the following day his flank attack with cavalry and dartmen had driven the Athenians within their walls where they still lay. Owing to the necessity of keeping a large number as a garrison for the walls, Nicias was unable to undertake further activities. He heard that Syracuse had sent to the Peloponnese for additional troops and a fleet, intending to assail them by sea and land. He reported that, as the enemy well knew, the Athenian fleet originally had been in fine shape both as to ships and men, but now the ships were deteriorating and the crews diminishing. He could not allow many ships to go on the beach for overhaul, because the ships of the enemy were as numerous and continually threatening. The latter were seen practicing, and it rested with them to make the attack when they pleased, and they could beach as many ships as they pleased since they were not blockading others. (This was the situation of the British and German fleets before Jutland. The Germans could and did get all their fleet ready for action at a given date; the British did not know when the sortie would come, and so always had some ships under repairs.) Nicias went on:

> We, on the other hand, cannot enjoy this advantage, even if greatly out-numbering them in ships, and if not compelled as at present to keep all of them on guard duty. For if we relax our vigilance in a slight degree, we shall have no provisions, since even now we have difficulty in getting them past the city. On this account our crews have wasted and are still wasting, as some of them on account of distant foraging and watering are cut off by their cavalry, our servants, having been placed on an equal footing, are now deserting, the pressed foreigners are leaving, and some are putting Hyccarian slaves in their place, and have thus destroyed the perfection of the navy. For you know that there are few seamen who can get the ship under way or keep the rowers working in stroke. I, their general, cannot stop these abuses for the temper of the men is difficult. If the Syracusans can induce the cities which supply us with food to turn against us, we shall lose through starvation without a battle. The force you sent was sufficient for the purpose as then seen, but now that all Sicily and the Peloponnese is against us you must send re-enforcements, or recall us. And I am not equal to the command for I am ill.

It was a despairing message, but the Athenian assembly foolishly re-tained him in command, while appointing two men then with him to ease his burden of responsibility. Demosthenes and Eurymedon were made his colleagues. The latter at once went to Sicily at the winter solstice with 10 ships and 120 talents of money. Demosthenes who was a brilliant soldier stayed to raise troops, ships, and money. The Athenians also sent 20 ships to cruise around the Peloponnese to see that nothing got over to Sicily from Corinth and the Peloponnese.

CORINTH AND SPARTA AID SYRACUSE

After hearing the autumn reports from Syracuse, the Corinthians thought they had been slack and decided to do more for Syracuse. They sent 25 ships to fight the Athenian squadron at Naupactus and check the movement of Athenian transports. The Spartans prepared to invade Attica, hoping to stop the departure of troops for Sicily, but were doubtful about it, as they were technically at peace with Athens. But after the Athenians with 30 ships had raided in the Peloponnese and refused arbitration there-on, the Spartans became eager for hostilities and entered Attica early in the spring of 413 and seized and fortified Decelea as Alcibiades had ad-vised them to do. At the same time Sparta sent some of her best helots and freedmen to Sicily. There were 700 of these, 300 Boeotians, 500 Corinthians, and 200 Sicyonians; all were heavy-armed. The 25 ships of the Corinthians manned during the winter now took position on the shores opposite the 20 Athenian ships which were stationed at Naupactus until the heavy-armed Spartans should get to sea on the transports and pass on.

About the same time of the spring of 413, Gylippus returned to Syracuse with troops and, calling the Syracusans together, said they should now try a fight at sea, for they now had men to man the fleet and he thought the result would be worth the risk. Hermocrates joined him in so urging, saying that the depression of the Athenians would more than counter-balance any lack of Syracusan skill.

THE FIRST NAVAL BATTLE AT SYRACUSE

When the fleet was ready, Gylippus took the whole army by night and placed it in concealment to attack the forts which protected Plemmyrium during the naval action. According to the plan, 35 ships issued from Syracuse into the Great Harbor, while 45 put out from the Lesser Harbor, where their arsenal was, and went around into the Great Harbor to make a junction and threaten Plemmyrium from the sea. The Athenians at once manned 60 ships and sent 25 against those in the Great Harbor, and with the others met those coming around the city, and these fought a long action in the entrance to the Great Harbor. In the meantime Gylippus, while the Athenian garrisons had gone down to the shore to see the engagement, surprised the forts at daybreak by assault and took all; the last two did not offer resistance as their men fled. The soldiers out of the first fort escaped with difficulty to their boats and merchant ships, but men from the other two suffered less, for by this time the Athenian ships were repulsing the enemy. As the account says, Syracusan ships that first broke through the Athenian line fell into disorder and got foul of each other, and were then overcome by the Athenians who routed them and also those that came from the Great Harbor side of the city. These had at first been successful over the Athenians opposing them. The Syracusans lost 11 ships and the Athenians 3. It looks as if the right wing of the Athenians must have obtained sea room outside the harbor and were able to envelop the enemy.

But although the Syracusans were defeated on the sea, they had secured the three forts, one of which they destroyed and the other two they
garrisoned. At the forts the Athenians lost many killed and prisoners and
much property, partly belonging to the state and partly to the merchants
who were the sutlers to the expedition. Three trieres drawn up on the
beach were also taken. As Thucydides says, the loss of Plemmyrium was
the principal cause of the failure of the expedition, for the entrance to the
harbor was no longer secure, as the Syracusan ships were between the
original Athenian base at the camp and the deep sea, making it difficult to
get supplies, and besides the morale of the Athenians suffered greatly,
when the fleet was thrown back on the army camp by Lysimeleia after its
own success in battle.

The Syracusans now sent out a squadron of 12 ships to Italy to intercept hostile ships on their way with treasure to the Athenians. These they
captured and also destroyed timber meant for the Athenians. They then
returned to Syracuse escorting troops, and although the Athenians had
20 ships lying at Megara, 7 or 8 miles north of Syracuse, to catch them,
only 1 was captured.

The Syracusans built obstructions in the harbor by the old docks, consisting of piles driven in the sea, so that the ships behind them might lie
at anchor ready to move without the labor of launching them from the
beach. Behind these piles the Athenian ships could not pass without delay,
and while doing so the enemy could overwhelm them. But the Athenians
brought up a ship of 10,000 talents (257 tons) burden or about 600 tons
displacement (probable dimensions, say 90'x30'x12') carrying wooden
towers and screens and with their boats fastened ropes to the piles and
raised them with windlasses. Even more dangerous piles which did not
project above water were sawed off by divers. There was much skirmish-
ing while this work was in progress, for the obstructions were within range
of the docks and missile action was constant between the ships and the
men on the docks; yet most of the piles were raised. The Syracusans reported to all their allies that they were succeeding and asked for help
before the Athenian succor could arrive.

In the meantime the Athenian re-enforcements under Demosthenes
got off. They amounted to 60 Athenian and 5 Chian ships and many
troops. On the way they joined temporarily with another Athenian squad-

ron to ravage in the Peloponnese. At the peninsula opposite to Cythera, they fortified a post to check Corinthian commerce and to receive Spartan helots who might wish to desert.

The sea power of Athens was cause of great wonderment to all Greece, for whereas it had not been thought that Athens could withstand invasion for more than 1 or 2 years, or 3 at the most, this was now the seventeenth year of the war, and she was acting in two wars at once. Yet money was scarce in Athens and, instead of the tribute, she was obliged to rely on a tax of 5 per cent on all sea-borne goods.

When Demosthenes with his relief expedition had gone as far as Zacynthus and Cephallenia, he picked up some troops, and while there Conon, commanding the 18 station ships at Naupactus, crossed with the news that he was expecting the 25 Corinthians opposite to attack, and he wished some of the ships meant for Syracuse. This way station had to be maintained, and so he got 10 of the best, while Demosthenes collected other ships and men and proceeded as far as Thurii and waited there to gather additional forces (see Map 10).

BATTLE IN THE GULF OF CORINTH, AT ERINEUS

We must interrupt our account of the siege of Syracuse to tell of the battle in the Gulf of Corinth for it had a marked effect on Syracusan naval tactics. After Demosthenes and Eurymedon had passed on to Italy, the Corinthian squadron opposite Naupactus under Polyanthes got some more trieres, so that it was now nearly equal to that of the Athenians, and prepared itself for a battle under conditions which should not give an opportunity to the Athenians to make use of their greater speed and better skill and training. Polyanthes wished to avoid the *periplous*, the envelopment of the flank, by the enemy in column, which would then turn into line to ram either singly or simultaneously.

The Corinthian preparation was both structural and tactical. Polyanthes brought up the army to support the fleet, for the ships were so light of draft that men could wade out to them while they yet had water under them and were afloat and mobile. The fleet then took position in a re-entrant bay of the coast off Erineus, and the troops occupied the headlands on the two flanks of the fleet. It was a reversion by the Corinthians to the situation at Salamis, for the same reason—to avoid envelopment.

But whereas at Salamis the Greeks made a spearmen's fight against the archers, with comparatively little ramming, for this occasion the Corinthians wished to disable the enemy's ships without making much demand on nautical skill in which they were somewhat lacking. Accordingly, they strengthened their *"epotides"* so as to be sure to crush the lighter bows of the enemy. The *epotis* seems to have been a cathead or other form of cheek piece on the round of the bow, so placed as to crush in the bow of the enemy and sweep away his oars. It may well have reached out above the water line far enough to fend off the hostile ram in a bow to bow collision. It also served to carry the anchor.

I think it probable that neither side habitually maneuvered at the highest speed for a ram stroke. When the enemy offered a favorable presentation, even a slow speed would carry the sharp metal beak through the slight side of the enemy. At high speed a ship was more likely to injure herself in the collision and, moreover, correction of an error in judgment in the approach was more difficult. Besides a deeply driven spur could not be withdrawn so readily, and always high speed soon exhausted the rowers.

So then, the Corinthians strengthened their *epotides,* protected their flanks by the shore and the soldiers there, so that the *periplous* was impracticable. Thus they awaited a frontal attack. With 33 ships under Diphilus the Athenians accepted the invitation and faced the Corinthians who now had nearly as many ships. At first the Corinthians remained stationary under the flanking headlands, but when a favorable opportunity appeared, the signal was made to advance, and the ships closed and fought obstinately for some time on equal terms. At last they separated without pursuit or loss of prisoners by either side, for the Corinthians swam out of their injured ships to the shore and no Athenian ship sank or capsized. The Athenians sank 3 enemies, but themselves had 7 ships disabled through having their bows crushed in by the heavy Corinthian *epotides.* Both sides claimed the victory, since all the wrecks drifted out to sea and were recovered by the Athenians, while on their part the Corinthians were much pleased at not having been decidedly beaten and had disabled more ships than they had lost.

Polyanthes deserves a high place in the history of naval tactics which he has not received. Between the battle of the Eurymedon and the beginning of the Peloponnesian War, Athenian seamen built up a system of ram tactics based on light speedy ships carrying few soldiers, avoiding the infantry fight afloat which Thucydides described as the "old style." This system came to full flower in Phormio's two great battles at Patras and Naupactus; but the system required maneuvering room and was inapplicable in closed waters. It could be successful only in special conditions. This fundamental fact Polyanthes had the ability to perceive and he forced a fight in closed waters as Themistocles had done before him. He restored the norm of naval fighting to the infantry soldiers' battle and again placed the ram in the secondary position which it held for 2,000 years until the end of rowing battleships, when the ram disappeared.

SECOND NAVAL BATTLE AT SYRACUSE

The new structural arrangement seems to have been promptly reported to Syracuse, where the conditions favored its employment by the besieged. Knowing that the great re-enforcing squadron was already in Italy, the Syracusans were desirous of striking a blow before its arrival. As a result of their own experience and the reports from the action in the Gulf of Corinth, they cut down their bows to reduce weight (they were going to fight in smooth water), strengthened them greatly by fixing stout *epotides* and bracing them heavily both inside and outside the hull for about 9 feet from the stem.

> For the Syracusans thought that in this way they would have an advantage over the Athenian vessels which were not built in the same manner to resist them, but were lightly built in the bows (because they did not intend so much to strike bow to bow as on the enemy's side, after a turn), and moreover because the battle would be fought in the Great Harbor, against a great number of ships in no large area (an oval of about 2,000 by 4,000 yards) they thought it would be in their favor. For by striking stem to stem, the Syracusans would crush the enemy's bows. Nor would the Athenians with their small sea room be able to practice either the envelopment (*periplous*) nor the cut-through (*diekplous*), the two maneuvers in which they most trusted, for Syracusans would prevent the cut-through by their own effort and for the envelopment there was no room. And what was before thought to be a want of skill on the part of captains, namely, to collide bows on, now was the very method the Syracusans would adopt, for by so doing, if the Athenians refused to accept the ram, they could only back towards the shore just astern and most of that was held by the hostile troops. (Thucydides: VII-36)

If ships fouled each other in these narrow waters, they would fall into confusion which was most objectionable to the Athenians. And the Athenians could not readily get sea room by going outside, for on both sides the Syracusans held the entrance, which was less than 1,200 yards wide. So the Syracusans made ready to attack by sea and land.

By this time the Athenians seem to have lost over a quarter of their force, and the Syracusans had been getting allies and ships from Sicily, Italy, and Greece, so that they were somewhat stronger than their enemy both ashore and afloat.

The troops in the city Gylippus led out to face the Athenian wall which looked towards the city, while those by the Olympieum advanced against the other Athenian wall.

Thereupon the ships of the allies came out. The Athenians first thought the attack was by land only, and much confusion arose when the hostile fleet was seen. Men must have had to be withdrawn from the walls, but the Athenians manned 75 ships and met the 80 ships of the enemy. The Syracusans made no determined attack, and after backing and advancing for the greater part of a day, one or two Athenian ships were sunk, and ships and troops withdrew on both sides. Nicias expected the action to be renewed, and he caused all ships to be repaired, and stationed merchant ships about 200 feet apart outside the line of pile obstructions which he had caused to be driven in the sea, making an enclosed harbor to protect his ships. The Athenian fleet had lost its professional confidence through the half-hearted behavior of Nicias, who looked for success to an imposing display when he first arrived rather than to immediate battle.

THIRD NAVAL BATTLE

Nothing was undertaken by the Syracusans the following day, but on the next the Syracusans acted as before, by sea and land, until noon. Nothing decisive occurred. Then Aristo, a Corinthian, and the most able shipmaster there, persuaded the generals to order the noon market to be held on the beach instead of inside the city. Thereupon the Syracusan ships backed water, and when they had drawn away from the enemy, the latter thought the engagement was over and landed leisurely and dispersed to look for dinner. The Syracusans also had dinner, but alongside their ships without dispersal, and when refreshed, they immediately re-embarked and crossed the harbor for battle, while the Athenians, in confusion and most of them fasting, put out to meet them. For some time they remained in line without action, but after a while the Athenians would delay no longer and advanced cheering. But the Syracusans met the Athenians bow to bow as they had planned and stove in the Athenian foresheets, as the Corinthians had done at Erineus.

At the same time the Syracusan dartmen on the decks did much damage, and small boats filled with javelin men got under the oars of the Athenians and checked their movements, striking at the rowers. Here we have the light-armed troops becoming prominent at sea, as on shore at Pylos. The style of naval fighting is following army progress. After desperate fighting, the Syracusans were victorious, and the Athenians retired between the merchant vessels to the shelter of their harbor obstructions. There the pursuit was stopped, but two Syracusan ships which came too close to the big Athenian merchantmen, which had dolphins (falling weights) suspended from their yards, were destroyed, and the crew of one of them was captured. The Syracusans had sunk seven ships and disabled many more. They were much encouraged and began to believe they would be victorious in the end, and prepared to attack again by sea and land.

THE ATHENIAN ATTACK ON EPIPOLAE HEIGHTS

At this time, July, 413, Demosthenes arrived at Syracuse with 73 ships (51 Athenians) and about 5,000 heavy-armed Athenians and allies, and 3,000 dartmen, slingers, and archers, besides the camp followers. There must have been nearly 25,000 men in the relief party. This created much consternation among the Syracusans and gave confidence to the besiegers. Nicias was no doubt pleased to throw responsibility on Demosthenes, who wished to take advantage of the situation to attack at once. He decided to move against the Syracusan counter-wall, which ran along the top of Epipolae and assured the city's communications with the exterior. It was to be a night attack. Going out with the masons and carpenters and five days' provisions and stores of arrows, after the first watch he took the whole mobile force and advanced (July, 413) against Euryalus, a fort at the western end of Epipolae. The fort was seized, and most of the garrison fled and gave the alarm. The first comers of the Syracusans were repulsed, and the Athenians began to pull down the counter-wall.

The Syracusans rallied in a second movement, and then the advancing Athenians fell into confusion, and lost their watchword to the enemy who used it. Besides the Athenians proper were dismayed by the Doric paean of their Argive allies which they took for hostile and began to retreat, and many fell over the cliffs, and others lost their way on the way back to the camp. The great re-enforcement had failed to change the situation.

Demosthenes Wishes to Abandon the Siege

The Syracusans now hoped even to take the Athenian lines by storm. After this engagement, seeing that they had failed and the troops were dispirited, the Athenian commanders were divided in opinion. The season was unfavorable to the health of the men, they were camped in a marshy place, and there was much sickness. Demosthenes recommended going back to Attica immediately, for the army would do better work at home against the Spartan fort at Decelea than in seeking victory at Syracuse, and they still had a superior fleet. Nicias admitted the situation was bad, but did not wish to say so publicly, nor to accept the shame of retreat. He was too ill to act or to give up. He said the enemy was badly off, too, for they had no money, and there was a party within wishing to surrender. He refused to withdraw without a vote of the people at home. Besides, he said, the soldiers who were now clamoring to go home would deny it on arrival. Demosthenes replied that at least they should remove to Thapsus, where they could forage in the country and have the open sea before them for fleet maneuvers. Eurymedon supported him, but Nicias overbore them, and they lingered. Nicias thereby lost the chance of successful retreat. Gylippus returned with troops from a trip through the island and prepared for immediate attack. The Athenian generals now repented of not having moved before, and were making ready to do so when an eclipse of the moon (August 27) caused Nicias, who was very devout, to insist on a delay of 27 days.

The Fourth Naval Action

The Syracusans were encouraged when they heard this and wanted a sea fight. They manned and exercised their ships for some days. They then made an attack on the Athenian lines with heavy-armed troops and with cavalry, and obtained a minor success. The next day, about September 7, the Syracusans came out with both fleet and army. The latter at first did nothing, but the Syracusan fleet of 76 was opposed by 86 Athenians in the harbor. The Athenian right wing, commanded by Eurymedon, extended far south in the intention of enveloping the enemy, and he got too near shore. So, after defeating the center of the Athenians, the Syracusans turned on Eurymedon and the ships with him and drove them on shore at the bottom of the harbor, and he was killed. Seeing the plight of the Athenian ships, of which some were driven on shore outside of the stockade, Gylippus[6] with some of his army hastened to man that region of the shore in order to make the work of hauling off the prizes easier for the victor ships. But as these soldiers came on in disorder they were repulsed by the Athenian troops who drove them into the marsh (south of the Anapus) and saved the greater part of their ships, although they lost 18 whose crews were put to the sword. Thereupon the Syracusans filled an old merchant ship with combustible and started it as a fire ship with a fair wind towards the Athenian ships near the beach. This the Athenians managed to turn aside.

The Athenians Decide to Withdraw

After this victory the Syracusans felt able to move freely about the harbor, and they began to close the Great Harbor mouth by building a boom supported by anchored ships of all types. On seeing this work, the Athenians held a council. They were short of provisions, having sent to Catana to stop their issue when they were expecting to leave before the eclipse, and no more supplies could come in without opening the passage to the sea. They therefore abandoned the upper part of their lines and built a cross wall (see 4, Map 11) between them enclosing enough space for their stores and the sick. It was the end of the pretense of investment and of the hope of victory.

They then manned all their ships, intending to go to Catana if they broke out, but if otherwise, they would abandon the ships on the beach and retreat by land to some friendly town. Thucydides says there were still 40,000 Athenians and allies present, but they were only able to man

---

[6] Gylippus' party must have come down from the Olympieum fort and run between the marsh and the sea.

110 ships after putting on board all who seemed fit for service and including many bowmen and javelin throwers.

The Last Naval Engagement

As the men were discouraged by their defeats on the water, Nicias made an address appealing to their experience and usual good fortune, but he was obliged to remind them that they were now going to fight, not in the old way that had brought success to Phormio in the open sea, but after the Corinthian method. They had embarked many bowmen, such as they would not employ on the open sea, for they would have slowed the ships by their weight, but here they would be of service. Moreover, they had provided grappling hooks to prevent the enemy from backing off to strike again. For in this way the heavy bows of the Syracusans would best be countered. Nicias also forbade masters to withdraw from contact with the hostile ships, once they had come together, until the enemy was overcome. As Nicias said, it was to be fought out as a land battle on ship board. To the seamen he pointed out the large number of their ships and the superior resources on their decks. He reminded the allies of their reputation throughout Greece, and to the Athenians he said that if defeated now, there were no such ships nor men remaining at home and that in case of defeat that day not only would they be at the mercy of the Sicilians, but they would expose those at home to Spartan conquest. However well meant, Nicias' speech can scarcely have been reassuring. His appeal was to the courage of despair rather than to that of the old Athenian confidence.

Thus, for the final battle, the Athenian fleet renounced the mobility of Phormio's tactics and reverted to the close fight of Salamis, with the difference that instead of spearmen, it relied greatly on the light-armed missile throwers who had brought the army success at Sphacteria under the same Demosthenes who now commanded here.

The Syracusans knew that the Athenians were coming out and heard of the grappling hooks, so they covered the bows with hides to deprive the hooks of a hold. Gylippus, too, addressed his fleet, saying fine things of their valor and skill and reminding them that the Athenians were about to copy their tactics of an infantry battle at sea, with which they were not familiar, so that the new hands on board would not even know how to discharge their missile weapons without making their ships roll and stumbling themselves. Moreover, as he asserted, 110 ships could not get into action together on account of the lack of space.

The Athenian fleet was to be under the direction of Demosthenes, and Nicias, wishing to do something more, again called all the ship captains together and, using every imaginable appeal, made them another address which "was not so much satisfactory, as one with which he had to be content" (Thucydides). He then led the army remaining on shore (perhaps 12,000 to 15,000) down to the beach and stretched it along as far as possible to aid the ships that might be driven ashore (probably from near the city to near Dascon).

The fleet put out and made for the entrance to tear away the obstructions. The Syracusan fleet was inside the Great Harbor and had about 75 ships as before, of which one division went to defend the block ships at the harbor mouth, which were no doubt themselves manned by soldiers, and the rest opened out to surround the enemy when engaged at the obstructions across the entrance, which were the Athenian objectives. Like the Athenians, the Syracusan troops made ready, distributing themselves along the south shore and at Plemmyrium, to act for or against the ships driven near them on the beach.

When the Athenian ships came out they reached the obstructions at the first rush and endeavored to clear them away. Then the Syracusan squadrons attacked from all sides, and the engagement extended over all the harbor, as the Athenians were obliged to turn away from the boom to face the hostile ships.

It is evident that while the whole fleet moved out to the obstructions, one division must have attempted to break through while another and probably larger one faced west and covered the others. Gradually, as it seems, the struggle worked back into the middle of the bay, and the lines of combatants fell into confusion. It was the Syracusans who now had space at command.

Great eagerness was shown on both sides by the seamen and the masters did much maneuvering, in rivalry with each other. The soldiers exerted themselves that the operations on deck might not fall short of the skill of the shipmen. As a great number of ships were engaged in a small space, the *ram attacks were few*, as there was no space to back water nor to charge through the hostile line. But chance collisions were more frequent, as one ship happened to strike another either in flying or in attacking a second. So long as a ship was approaching another, those on her deck plied their arrows, javelins, and stones in abundance, but when in contact, the hoplites (*epibatae*) fighting hand to hand, tried to board. In many cases it happened that for want of room a ship was charging the enemy and at the moment was herself attacked by another. And thus the masters had to guard against attack while they were thinking of striking another. The admirals on each side, if they saw any captain anywhere backing astern unnecessarily called out to him by name and asked, if Athenian, whether he was retreating because he considered the land in possession of his bitterest foes as more his own than the sea which Athens had won with no small trouble; or if Syracusan, whether they were themselves flying from the flying Athenians, whom they knew to be anxious to escape from them in any way whatever? The troops, too, on shore suffered a great agony and conflict of mind, for since the Athenians had staked all on their fleet their fear for the future was like none that they had ever felt before, and from the unequal nature of the struggle they were obliged to have an unequal view of it from the beach. And thus among the Athenians there might be heard at the same time every sound, both wailing and shouting, "They conquer!" At length, after the battle had long continued, the Syracusans and their allies routed the Athenians and pressing on decisively with much shouting pursued them to the shore, and as many ships as were not taken afloat put in to the land at various points and rushed to the camp, while the soldiers deplored the event and went, some to help the ships and others to guard what remained of their wall and the greater number began to think of themselves and their own preservation (Thucydides: VII-70-71).

The Syracusans having gained the victory, took up the wrecks and the dead and went to the city.

The Retreat by Land

The Athenians were not thinking of their dead but wished to retreat that night. Demosthenes urged on Nicias that as they had 60 ships left to the enemy's 50 (a loss of 50 to 25) they should attack again and Nicias agreed, but the seamen refused, being utterly dispirited (like the German seamen in November, 1918). So it was agreed to retreat by land. Hermocrates suspected that the Athenians would go off by land and urged that the Syracusans should issue that night and occupy the roads, but the magistrates thought the people would not leave their feasting, so Hermocrates sent a deceitful message to the Athenians which led them to delay until the third day after the fight. By this time the Syracusans were ahead of them on the roads, and had towed most of the Athenian ships from the shore were they had been abandoned after the fight. Some few remaining ships the Athenians had burnt themselves. When the army marched away, it was pursued by Gylippus and after marching and counter-marching, with constant fighting and great losses, for 7 days, it had gone only about 15 miles from Syracuse when the last organized body under Nicias surrendered. Against the wish of Gylippus, Nicias and Demosthenes were both put to death (possibly after torture), and the main body of prisoners confined in the quarries of Syracuse, where they were badly treated. About 7,000 surrendered to public authority and others escaped to Catana, but Thucydides says these formed a small part of those who marched away from Syracuse (latter part of September, 413).[7] Many surrendered to individual pursuers to be sold as slaves and many were killed.

THE CONTINUATION OF THE WAR

For long the Athenians could not believe the story of the defeat of their great expedition. Not only did the members of the public suffer on account of their personal losses, but it seemed impossible longer to carry on the war with so many men lost in the strength of their youth, and with no more good ships and no money in the treasury. The political situation had grown worse during the expedition. As already mentioned, Athenian squadrons on the way stations to the west had raided in the Peloponnese late in 414, and offended Sparta which claimed infraction of the treaty with Athens. Early in 413 the Spartans made war and the army invaded Attica and seized and fortified Decelea about 15 miles north of Athens. The position dominated the Attic plain and lay across the lines of traffic from the Euripus to the city. When the disaster at Syracuse came 6 months later, it was thought at Athens that the Syracusans would come at once to aid the Spartans to blockade the city completely. Nevertheless, it was determined to equip such a fleet as was possible and put matters on a secure footing among the allies, and so the winter of 413-412 approached with all the Greeks much excited about the plight of Athens. Those cities which had been neutral thought it was now time to get some credit by

---

[7] The first expedition numbered nearly 30,000 men, the second about 23,000, and 5,000 more allies joined the Athenians at various times, making 55,000 to 57,000 in all; 40,000 remained for the last naval battle, and perhaps 35,000 began the fatal retreat.

joining the war. The allies of Sparta wished to end matters and many of the Athenian allies hoped they might now break away.

So the Spartans resolved to prosecute the war vigorously in the spring of 412. Even during the winter they raided northward from Decelea and issued a requisition upon their alliance for 100 trieres, of which the Spartans were to furnish 25. The Athenians also got timber for shipbuilding and fortified Sunium in their own territory for the better protection of their passing grain ships. They abandoned the fort at the southern peninsula of Sparta, which they had established to control Peloponnesian trade, but did not altogether renounce their pretentions in western waters, for they maintained the squadron based on Naupactus and the western islands.

As for Athens' general situation, it was possible for her fleet to restore her dominion if it was not required to maintain a war for additional conquest. The Athenian Empire was not altogether a bad thing for the subject allies. Sometimes, no doubt, the great fleets abused their power, but at least they kept down piracy, and on the whole the services of the Athenian fleet to general prosperity in the past 60 years had been very great in maintaining order and promoting trade. That business was not bad during these years of war is shown by the enormous forces that these small states were able to keep in operation. Unfortunately Athens had lost her prestige at Syracuse and could not sustain a great war if there was serious defection among her subject allies, for their tribute was a necessary condition of her own power. Just as England and France fought in the eighteenth century for the control of the revenue of the sugar islands, so Athens fought for her islands with the difference that for Athens loss of control would be fatal.

Not only was Athenian trade embarrassed by the Peloponnesian fleet, but the cities in revolt on the shores of Asia Minor (see Map 2) drew much of their business from the country behind them. The Persian satraps could therefore curtail Athenian shipping business even without the activities of the Peloponnesian fleet. Nevertheless, Athens made a wonderful effort to continue "business as usual." An essential thing for her was to retain the Euxine commerce. In great degree the war turned on the efforts of the enemy to cut Athens off from the use of the Hellespont, while she tried to hold way ports and a fleet there to help her merchant ships through it.

The course of the war of Athens against Sparta and her Peloponnesian allies depended largely on the resources of the great Persian Empire. This was outwardly as great as in the early part of the century under Darius, but the central management was weak. The satraps in northwestern and southwestern Asia Minor, Pharnabazus and Tissaphernes, were bidding against each other for the services of the Peloponnesian allies to control the Greek cities of Ionia and divert their tribute to Athens into their own provincial treasuries and so pay their own dues to the Persian King. For such aid the satraps would finance the Peloponnesian fleets and armies, and the allies be rewarded by the destruction of Athenian power within Greece.

ATHENS' RECOVERY

The year 412 opened by a revolt in the island of Chios where Tissaphernes urged the islanders to seek Spartan aid. Spartan rulers were indisposed to do much, but Alcibiades encouraged them, saying that he would go to Ionia and easily persuade the Greek cities. As he had promised, the revolt flamed as soon as he exerted his eloquence and spread rapidly. Miletus was among the insurgent cities and became thenceforward the principal Asiatic naval base of the Peloponnesian allies. Late in 412 the Syracusans sent a squadron under Hermocrates to join the Spartans.

With the greatest courage Athens fitted out a considerable fleet with money held in reserve. Tissaphernes now made an alliance with the Spartans on the basis that all Ionian cities formerly belonging to Persia and now to Athens should pay tribute jointly to the King and to Sparta, and that the war should be carried on in common by the two allies without either making peace separately. Tissaphernes was to pay the Greek forces. Thereafter, without any important battle, the war took the form of constant movements of detachments of the fleets to hold different points controlling sea communications which were the economic life of Athens. As time passed the Chians, who always had a fleet even when in alliance with Athens, undertook to attack Lesbos and then the Hellespont while the land forces of the Peloponnesians, who were at Miletus were to reach the Hellespont overland. If successful this would have been a very severe blow to Athenian trade with the Euxine, but the Athenian fleet recovered Lesbos and was able to block hostile movement to the Euxine.

The Athenians then sent a fleet and army to occupy Samos, which they afterwards held as their Asiatic base till the end of the war, and so were in close contact with the hostile fleets based on Miletus and other points in the southeastern Aegean. Thus the year closed. In its comparative inactivity Athens had made considerable recovery from the disaster at Syracuse. She still controlled her trade with the Euxine and the Levant, which could not be interrupted while the Peloponnesian fleet at Miletus was held there by the Athenians at Samos.

Year 411 b.c.

During the winter of 412-411, the Spartans sent additional ships across the Aegean and, after an unimportant naval engagement, they went to Rhodes and induced that great commercial and naval center to abandon the Athenians, believing that thereby they would be more independent of Persian aid.

About this time Alcibiades lost the confidence of the Spartan government which sent orders to Ionia to put him to death. He was able to escape to Tissaphernes, who liked him and listened to his advice. His wonderful diplomatic ability was once more employed in favor of his native city. He suggested to Tissaphernes to halve the pay per diem with which the Persian was subsidizing the Peloponnesian fleet, and also advised him not to be in too great a hurry to bring up the Phoenician fleet which he was equipping, nor to give more pay to the Greeks for soldiers, nor to allow command by sea and land to fall into the hands of one belligerent, but rather to let the sway be divided between the two. Thus, Alcibiades said, the Great King would hold the balance of power while the Greeks wore themselves out. Yet he represented the Athenians as the more desirable winners. Tissaphernes carried out these recommendations by telling the Spartans to wait for the Phoenician fleet and, by giving little pay for their men, he took away the vigor of their navy, and Athenian commerce was not too much disturbed.

The Athenian troops at Samos thus became convinced that Alcibiades was still a friend of his country, and he gained much influence with them. A revolutionary party grew up in the camp, which communicated with Alcibiades and started a club to favor his recall from exile and to form a new government at home. A deputation from the army went to Athens with this object, which stirred up dissension and was successful in having new commanders sent to Samos. In Asia there was much conspiracy and treachery between the parties to the war, and Alcibiades tried unsuccessfully to make Tissaphernes come out in favor of Athens.

While all this was going on more Athenian ships were sent to Samos, and it became possible in the spring of 411 to send a force of 30 ships and a number of troops to blockade Chios, while the rest of the fleet contained the hostile squadron at Miletus. The enemy countered by sending a Spartan force north by land to induce revolt at Abydos on the Hellespont. It was impossible to neglect this blow at the Euxine trade, and 24 of the Athenian ships besieging Chios went at once to Abydos; but, not being able to save it, they occupied Sestos opposite to Abydos in order not to lose control of the straits.

During the summer of 411 military operations were checked by internal dissensions at Athens. The oligarchic party there seized the government and then offered peace to the enemy. The fleet and army at Samos refused to adhere to the new government, saying that there were few citizens at home to authorize a change and that the men at Samos were the true state. At Miletus the Spartan forces were indignant with Astyochus, their admiral, for not taking advantage of the enemy at Samos, saying he would not fight previously when he was stronger, nor would he then when the enemy was in insurrection. Astyochus put to sea, but the Athenians refused to meet him. Soon the Athenians were re-enforced, but then Astyochus refused to go out and meet them. Alcibiades' advice to Tissaphernes now bore fruit, and lack of pay in the Peloponnesian fleet induced the dispatch of 40 ships northward to Pharnabazus who offered to supply them. A gale drove most of them back and only 10 got through, where, in August, 411, they were able to bring about the defection of Byzantium.

Alcibiades now ventured to Samos and completely gained the confidence of the forces there, whereupon they elected him general, and he took command at Samos. He kept the army from returning to Athens to eject the government while foreign enemies remained behind them, and then returned to Tissaphernes, playing the Athenians against the Spartans. As the latter at Miletus had been getting no pay from Tissaphernes, it became evident that, unless the fleet fought a battle or went where it could get supplies, the men would desert. Indeed, they soon after turned against their admiral Astyochus, and he took refuge in sanctuary. Mindarus arrived from Sparta as his successor.

Negotiations continued between the government of Athens and the fleet and army at Samos, and Alcibiades prevented civil war. Tissaphernes now went to Aspendos on the coast of Pamphylia where he had nearly 150 Phoenician men-of-war. He did not bring them up to throw into the conflict, and Thucydides says Tissaphernes merely threatened with them to make the Greeks wear themselves out. Alcibiades advised the city to continue the war, and gave hope of reconciling the men at Samos and the government at home.

Battle off Eretria (see Map 6)

Just then 42 Peloponnesian ships, invited by insurgent Euboea and on their way to Oropus, passed in front of the city, and the Athenians, greatly alarmed, ran to the walls, manned the ships afloat, launched others, and followed the enemy to Eretria opposite Oropus, where they joined the Athenian ships already there, making 36 in all. For Athens could not permit the loss of Euboea, by which all its trade passed. They were immediately forced to a battle. The Spartan admiral, Agesandridas, expecting the Athenian ships to follow him, had made an arrangement with the Eretrians that when the Athenians should arrive there the usual market for the men's dinner should not be held at the market place near the ships, but in the houses at the outskirts of the town, so that the men were drawn away from their ships. After the Peloponnesians had their dinner at Oropus, signal was made from Eretria about 6 miles away that the Athenians were dispersed, and they crossed to surprise them. When the enemy was seen by the Athenian admiral, Thyochares, he called his men whom he thought were near, but they had straggled, as arranged by Agesandridas, and the ships put out to sea unprepared and were defeated. Twenty-two ships were made prize and men that escaped to Eretria were killed. The rest got away.

On hearing the news, Athens called an assembly, deposed the new government, and recalled Alcibiades. The oligarchical sedition was at an end. In spite of the poverty caused by the war and interrupted business, the state was still strong. Although the Athenians were greatly alarmed by this disaster, which seemed to them even worse than that of Syracuse, the Spartans were not bold, but "proved themselves once more to be very convenient enemies for the Athenians to be at war with."

Operations Shift to the Hellespont

About the same time (September, 411) as Mindarus realized that Tissaphernes was neither giving him supplies nor aiding him with the Phoenician fleet, and as Pharnabazus was calling him north with handsome offers, he left Miletus with 73 allied ships to go to the Hellespont. Of these 20 formed a squadron from Syracuse, which had come out a year before. Sixteen ships had preceded him.

This brought about a complete change in the situation. As long as the Peloponnesian allied fleet lay at Miletus depending on insufficient supplies from Tissaphernes, the Athenian fleet at Samos gave fairly adequate protection to the Athenian trade in the Aegean and in the Euxine. When Mindarus threw himself on Pharnabazus for support and moved north, the Athenian fleet had to follow and defeat him to preserve the Empire, for the trade with the Euxine was vital.

Bad weather compelled Mindarus to put in at Chios. When Thrasylus, commanding the Athenian fleet at Samos, heard that Mindarus had left Miletus, he followed with 55 ships, hoping to get to the Hellespont first. Finding Mindarus was at Chios, he posted scouts at Lesbos and also opposite on the mainland and delayed to get provisions at Methymna, and then had to check a revolt at Eresus in Lesbos. Here he was joined by Thrasybulus with 12 ships from Samos and elsewhere, so that there were now 67. In the meantime Mindarus spent two days collecting provisions, and then slipped past Lesbos and arrived at Rhoeteum in the Hellespont.[8]

An Athenian squadron of 18 ships was at Sestos, and when its friends gave notice by fire signals and it saw more numerous lights on the other

---

[8] Starting from Chios at dawn, the fleet dined at the harbor of the island of Carteria off Phocaea, passed Cyme, supped and slept on the mainland by the islands of Arginussae, and went on before dawn to Harmatus, opposite Methymna, where it dined and reached Rhoeteum before midnight. Stragglers got only as far as Sigeum that night (see Map 2, p. 14). A distance of 142 sea miles was done in two days and part of the second night with two noon-day stops and one night stop for sleep, say 44 hours in all and perhaps 32 hours under way, making an average speed of about 4.5 knots. It was too fast to have been done without some help from sail for at least part of the voyage, but the itinerary gives an idea of how the ancients navigated.

side, it knew the Peloponnesians were entering the Hellespont. That same night, moving as promptly as possible and keeping close along shore, the Athenians reached Elaeus, wishing to be near the open sea. They had eluded the 16 hostile ships at Abydos, but were seen at dawn by Mindarus'

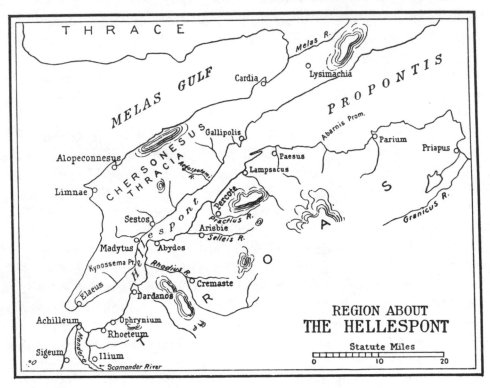

MAP 12.

ships at Rhoeteum and chased from Elaeus. Four were taken and the rest escaped to Imbros and Lemnos. Mindarus then attacked Elaeus where the Hellespont squadron joined him, but when the town did not surrender, he sailed away to Abydos.

As soon as the Athenian besiegers at Eresus heard that Mindarus had passed, they followed at once and took two Peloponnesian ships that had been separated at sea from their fleet, and arrived at Elaeus the second day, bringing with them the ships that had escaped to Imbros. They were five days at Elaeus making ready for battle.

Battle of Kynossema (see Map 12)

The Athenians then set out in column of ships to reach Sestos and command the Hellespont from there. They had 76 ships, led by Thrasylus with Thrasybulus commanding the rear. They hugged the European shore as far as the point of Kynossema, now Kilid Bahr. The length of the column was probably something between 2 and 3 sea miles, with a distance between ships from bow to bow of 60 to 70 yards. The Peloponnesians put out from Abydos with 86 ships, intending to get below the enemy and envelop his rear and drive his center on shore to which the latter was very close. Thucydides says the Peloponnesian fleet reached from Abydos to Dardanos. As the distance is 7 or 8 miles, his statement must be taken as indicating the region of maneuver rather than the length of column. Mindarus in mid-stream led with the fastest ships, and the Syracusan squadron brought up the rear.

The battle which ensued is difficult to understand without considering the current which played an important part. Above Kynossema the down current, usually 2.5 knots strong, sweeps the whole channel, but below the point the bend in the channel throws the down-current towards the mid-stream, and an up-stream eddy of half a knot runs along the European shore. The difference between the two currents was equal to the speed of the individual ships. Until the ascending Athenians came to Kynossema, they hugged the European shore and had an easy time at the oars. After the van rounded the point, its ships had to work hard to make headway, and naturally the center and rear avoided crowding the ships which had turned into the adverse current, and were lost to their sight. The result was that the vessels were widely spaced about the point of Kynossema.

Now came Mindarus flying on the favorable current with an evident intention of using his greater numbers to envelop the rear of the Athenians and prevent their escape to Elaeus. Thrasybulus, commanding the rear, checked his squadron's advance to frustrate Mindarus' enveloping movement (perhaps he backed down stream a little), and then all the Peloponnesians turned into line and charged the enemy, who also swung their ships to face him. It seems that Mindarus misjudged his pace and turned too soon, for Thrasybulus was not advancing, and besides the Peloponnesian ship captains were anxious to strike the hostile line at the center where the ships were farther apart. Here the Peloponnesians were successful, and the few Athenians near the point were forced to back ashore, and the opposing ships landed men to follow up their success, so the Peloponnesian numbers were reduced at the height of the battle. Thrasylus in the van, now the left of the line, could not aid the vessels on shore, for he was fully occupied with the Syracusan squadron which equalled his own in numbers, but in the end he was able to overcome it. Probably most of the ships of both fleets above the point drifted below it and into the area of Mindarus and Thrasybulus where the battle was decided.

As Diodorus tells us, victory was gained through the seaman-like skill of the individual Athenian ship captains. Below the point the two lines of ships were in opposite currents giving unusual opportunity to the best managed vessels. The Peloponnesians were clearly the attacking party, and we may imagine that Thrasybulus held his ships within the up-stream eddy. Then as the enemy crossed the dividing line between the two currents, ships' heads were thrown upstream and their sides turned momentarily to the Athenian rams. It was a chance which was improved in enough cases to turn the scale of victory, and Mindarus' squadron was routed. The successful Peloponnesian center had lost its formation and, after driving its opponents to the shore, was now struck with panic on seeing Thrasybulus coming at it. It fled with scarcely a blow. The Syracusans had already been repelled by Thrasylus, and they hastened their flight on seeing their allies were defeated too. The Athenians were able to capture a few ships only, for the opposite friendly shore was near, and Mindarus made his way back to Abydos. The Athenians lost 15 ships and the allies 21.

We may compare this battle with that of Phormio at Patras. Phormio was the only admiral who ever used his rams as a tactical unit in his own hand. At Kynossema and ever afterward the ram was the weapon of individual captains as opportunity offered itself.

The Athenians were greatly elated by their success, and their morale, which had so suffered since Syracuse, was restored. Still, they did not secure the complete control of the sea, for while they ran by Mindarus at Abydos and went up to Cyzicus and recovered that city as an ally—going on to take 8 ships forming the squadron at Byzantium—Mindarus went down to Elaeus and recovered such ships as were captured from him at Kynossema and were not burnt on his approach. He also sent to Euboea to call up 50 ships from there, but they were lost in a gale as they rounded Athos.

Battle off Abydos

One more serious naval action was fought before the end of 411. Dorieus with 14 Rhodian ships arrived at the entrance to the Hellespont to re-enforce Mindarus. Here they were seen by the Athenian lookout on the opposite side, and 20 ships put out to attack the Rhodians, who fled to the shore not far from Rhoeteum and beached their ships, fighting from them and from the shore until the Athenians sailed away to join the rest of their fleet at Madytus. Mindarus was doing sacrifice at Ilium and saw the action on the shore below him. He hastened down to get his own fleet out to the aid of the Rhodians (it must have been at Rhoeteum), but he was too late to catch the enemy and followed him up the Hellespont. Near Abydos the two main fleets met, the Athenians opposing 74 ships to 97 of the Peloponnesians. After fighting for sometime without reaching a decision, 18 ships were seen approaching from the open sea giving hope to both sides.

When their recognition signal became distinguishable, it proved to be Alcibiades' purple flag, and the Peloponnesian fleet fell back to the shore of Abydos, and beached the ships. Here Pharnabazus with his army came to their aid, and, riding into the water, the satrap directed his cavalry and infantry to repulse the Athenian ships without success. At the close of this amphibious battle, the Athenians had taken possession of 30 empty ships and made off with them to Sestos. Important as the victory was, it effected no strategic change in the situation which remained unaltered for nearly a year longer.

YEAR 410. BATTLE OF CYZICUS

During the winter of 411-410, the large Athenian fleet at Sestos was obliged to disperse. It had to collect money for support, and supplies must have been scanty there. The trade through to the Euxine had been the great dependence of Attica for many years, but it was now difficult to get anything past Byzantium, since it had revolted the previous summer. Mindarus consequently had the best hold on the region, as his force was supplied by Pharnabazus from Persian resources, and the Persian army guarded the Asiatic shores. Mindarus was also the first to get re-enforcements from home in the spring of 410, so the Athenians at Sestos felt it necessary for safety to launch the few ships which had been hauled out and run them down the Hellespont and base them at Cardia on the other side of the Chersonese and call for more ships.

At the beginning of spring Mindarus entered the Propontis, landed his men, and besieged Cyzicus (see Map 2). This city was then an island; now an isthmus of sand joins it to the mainland. Pharnabazus went there with an army to aid Mindarus, and they took the city. In the meantime the Athenian fleet detachments, which had scattered for maintenance during the winter, assembled at Cardia and entered the Hellespont under the command of Alcibiades to rescue Cyzicus. The Athenians passed Abydos by night, so that the Peloponnesians should not be able to count their numbers, and went to Proconnesus in the Propontis, about 20 miles from Cyzicus, and spent the night, having first seized all small craft to stop news passing to the enemy. Alcibiades pointed out to the crews that they had to fight, for they had no money, and the enemy had plenty from the King. In three squadrons of 86 ships the Athenian fleet sailed for Cyzicus in thick and rainy weather. On arriving near the port the weather cleared, and Alcibiades saw that by good fortune he was between the port and the hostile fleet of 60 ships which Mindarus had taken out merely for exercise. The Peloponnesians felt their great inferiority in numbers as well as in skill, and retired to the nearest point of shore where they moored their ships together, as Xenophon says, and awaited the attack.

Alcibiades matched the enemy ship for ship with a few to spare. Then he led the remaining 20 vessels past the fight and landed their crews with whom he attacked the beached ships from the shore. Although Xenophon does not say so, it is clear that in this way Alcibiades could throw a great number of men (archers, slingers, and dartmen) against a few ships at the end of the allied line, which were already occupied by op-posing ships, and so start to crumple the hostile formation. It was a new variation on the always recurring attack by envelopment. To meet this serious danger Mindarus drew a landing force from his hard-pressed crews and attempted to drive Alcibiades away. Mindarus lost his life in the clash between the two landing forces, and an overwhelming success followed for the Athenians.

The Peloponnesians seem to have abandoned the ships and escaped to the city of Cyzicus, leaving all the empty hulls to be towed to Proconnesus by the victors except a few which were burned by their fleeing crews. The next day the Athenian fleet returned to Cyzicus to find it evacuated by its Persian garrison and the defeated crews. Alcibiades inflicted no damage on it, but fined it for its defection the year before. Mindarus' unfortunate successor sent the despairing message to Sparta, "Ships gone; Mindarus dead; men starving; do not know what to do."

This sweeping success entirely changed the face of affairs. The victorious fleet now controlled the Hellespont, Bosphorus, and the Propontis with the all-important Euxine commerce. It occupied some cities, levied on others, and fortified Chrysopolis, opposite Byzantium. Leaving a squadron of 30 ships at Chrysopolis to assure the passage of Athenian commerce and collect a toll on the traffic, the main fleet withdrew to Sestos.

Although Pharnabazus provided money to build a new fleet for the allies, they were much discouraged, and Sparta sent to offer peace, but the Athenians were so much uplifted by their victory that they refused to agree. Indeed, a peace at that time could have had nothing durable about it, for the two rival systems of government and of commercial supremacy had not fought the war to a finish. Nevertheless, Sparta had to delay aggressive operations for the next year in order to recover her strength.

YEARS 409 AND 408 B.C.

Nothing much of naval importance happened in the year 409. A minor squadron under Thrasylus gained a victory over a Syracusan squadron in Lesbian waters, indicating that Athenian maritime skill was completely restored in spite of the loss of seamen and pilots at Syracuse four years previously Thrasylus then joined the main fleet under Alcibiades in the Hellespont, and they raided and gathered tribute during the summer. Late in this year Alcibiades completely regained the Bosphorus by retaking Byzantium, and Athenian commerce profited. His success caused the people of Athens to overlook his desertion from the Sicilian expedition six years before, and they elected him general for the year 408. After some hesitation he ventured once more to enter Athens. Soon afterwards he sailed with fleet and army to the coast of Asia Minor and carried on the war from Samos as his base. The movement of Alcibiades to this point, to face the hostile fleet slowly regrowing with the Persian money, shows that Athens was now fairly free in trade connections with Thrace and the Euxine, and not badly off in spite of the hostile garrison in Decelea; yet her demands for tribute from her allies to support the war tended to alienate them.

Year 407 b.c.

Towards the end of 408, Sparta had somewhat recovered from her exhaustion of 410 and appointed Lysander, a most able general, to command the allied forces in Asia Minor for the year 407. He spent the year in working up his strength. After assembling what ships and soldiers he could find, he went to Rhodes, where he got more ships and also could receive supplies and money from Cyrus, the new Persian satrap, son of the King.

The neighboring towns also afforded him support, and early in 407 he moved to Ephesus, where he arranged with Cyrus for higher pay (4 oboli or 13¢ a day) for his sailors. Here he hauled his 90 ships on the beach for overhaul and for refreshment for the crews. He was not strong enough to challenge the supremacy of Athens on the seas.

Alcibiades was at Samos, only 20 miles away, and crossed with the fleet to Notium on the mainland a few miles west of Ephesus. Hearing that Thrasybulus had left the Hellespont and was fortifying a post in Phocaea, Alcibiades thought he could take advantage of Lysander's passivity, and went to join Thrasybulus with a small part of his fleet and the two raided about Cyme near there (for supplies were scarce), having left orders with Antiochus, his second, at Notium, not to engage the enemy during his absence. Antiochus, however, passed in front of the hostile fleet with only two ships, jeering at them. Lysander launched a few ships and finally all the ships of both fleets became engaged in succession (Plutarch), but the Peloponnesians were more in hand and Antiochus lost his life and 15 or 20 ships. Whereupon Alcibiades came back in haste and offered battle, which Lysander refused.

The city of Cyme sent envoys to Athens to complain of Alcibiades, and what with his losses through Antiochus, he was deprived of his command and departed to his castle in the Chersonese. Conon took command of the Athenian fleet, and was able to man only 70 ships instead of 100 as previously, although the Athenian fleet was still superior at sea. This was the end of the year 407, and Lysander, whose year of office had run out, was replaced by Callicratidas. On turning over the command, Lysander said that he did so after a victory and while in command of the sea. "Then," said Callicratidas, "take the fleet and sail from here to Miletus passing the enemy at Samos and I shall admit your claim."

Campaign of Arginussae 406 B.C.

Callicratidas then got together 50 ships more from the allies, and having 140 he broke off relations with Persia on account of delay in getting money and made preparations for meeting the enemy. He now felt strong enough to move upon Athenian Methymna in Lesbos, where he was followed by Conon with his inferior force which was, however, in extremely good shape.

As Diodorus says, none was ever superior. When Conon found that Methymna was taken, he lay to over night, and in the morning, seeing a double force in front of him, he took refuge in Mytilene. On the way, there was a chance engagement by which Conon lost 30 ships, but he got into Mytilene with the other 40.

By this time Callicratidas had 170 ships. He now blockaded the harbor and city by land and sea, while Conon obstructed the mouth to prevent the enemy from breaking in. He also prepared two of his best ships with special crews to send home for aid. Then, on the fifth day, when it was noon and the blockaders were paying little attention and were getting dinner, the two ships made a rush, one towards the Hellespont and the other for the open sea. There was hasty effort to pursue, and the one going out to the north got to Athens, but the one going to the south and the open sea was captured about sunset.[9] An Athenian squadron of 12 ships going to Mytilene to aid Conon lost 10 before getting in. But Athens made a great effort, and after 30 days dispatched 110 ships manned in her necessity by slaves as well as by freemen. They went to Samos and got 40 more from that city and other allies, and then sought the enemy.

---

[9] As the chase was a long one and the Athenian ship of the best, we may suppose the pursuers followed the well-known hunters' practice of keeping the chase pressed by one ship at a time, while the main body followed more leisurely.

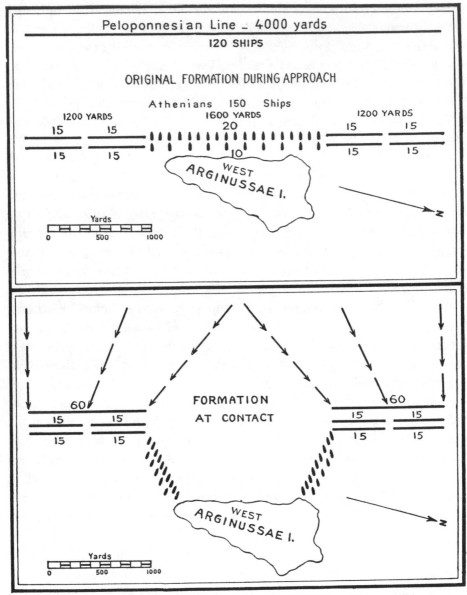

Peloponnesian Line ⸗ 4000 yards

120 SHIPS

ORIGINAL FORMATION DURING APPROACH

Athenians　150　Ships

1200 YARDS　　　1600 YARDS　　　1200 YARDS

15　　15　　20　　15　　15

15　　15　　10　　15　　15

WEST
ARGINUSSAE I.

Yards
0　　500　　1000

N

FORMATION
AT CONTACT

60　　　　　　　60

15　　15　　15　　15

15　　15　　15　　15

WEST
ARGINUSSAE I.

Yards
0　　500　　1000

N

MAP 13. BATTLE OF THE ARGINUSSAE ISLANDS

BATTLE OF ARGINUSSAE

On hearing of their arrival at Samos, Callicratidas left 50 ships to maintain the blockade of Mytilene and with the other 120 moved to the point of Malea, 3 or 4 miles south from the city, in order to meet them. The Athenians seeking him took supper the same night at the Arginussae Islands about 7 miles away on the mainland side of the channel. Seeing their fires on the opposite coast, Callicratidas got under way about midnight, but a squall of rain and wind held him till daybreak, when he crossed over and formed in a single line of ships. The Athenians drew up not far from the Arginussae Islands which were in the rear of their center, and gave the name to the battle.

The circumstances of the battle were quite different from those of Kynossema. There the victory was greatly owing to the individual skill of the Athenian pilots in handling their ships to strike with the ram and avoid it for themselves. But here Athens had a scratch fleet of old ships patched up to meet a grave emergency, and the crews were likewise a hasty assemblage. The Peloponnesian fleet of only 80 per cent in numbers had individually better ships. The omens of the sacrifice, which were of such importance to the Greeks, were not wholly satisfactory to either side. To Callicratidas the augurs predicted death, but he answered that the glory of Sparta would not be obscured by his death. To the Athenians the priests said that they would be victorious, but 7 out of 8 generals (*strategoi*, the military commanders appointed by the people) would lose their lives. The generals announced victory to the fleet, but concealed the prediction of their own deaths.

The Athenians made use of the islands as a background of maneuver. The outside and westward island is about 1,600 yards long. Apparently it formed the center of the Athenian line of battle, for we are told its presence compelled the Peloponnesians to fight in two bodies. Knowing themselves to have the worse ships, the Athenians formed in a double line. Each of the eight admirals had 15 ships in his squadron. Four squadrons composed each wing; two in the front line, and two in their rear. The center was composed of 20 ships in the front line and 10 in the rear. There were thus 80 ships in the front line and 70 in the rear one. The Peloponnesians in a single line of 120 ships attacked their enemy, and yet they drew into two groups and fought in two places. The 30 Athenian and allied ships forming the center suffered very little in the battle. So much we learn from Xenophon and Diodorus about the tactics of the battle.

In seeking, with the help of the map, to understand what happened, we may infer that the 20 ships forming the front line of the center were about 80 yards apart and extended the length of the island and were 200 or 300 yards in front of it. The supporting rear line of 10 ships had twice the distance between ships. The 60 ships in two lines in each of the wings prolonged the lines of the center, and may well have had an unusually great distance between ships, say 40 yards, since the rear ships would be able to attack with advantage any hostile ship which might pass through the front line or become held there. The length of the whole Athenian line would then be about 4,000 yards before beginning the battle. The Peloponnesians had better ships and better trained rowers. It was their cue to maneuver, to envelop the flanks of the enemy, and to charge through his line, sweeping away his oars. Against such an attempt the Athenian formation was a very strong defensive one for ships that did not handle well. Callicratidas could not envelop the hostile flanks without making his single line very thin (over 35 yards between ships).

In consequence, what he did was to divide his fleet and shorten his fighting line by the length of the island, making the distance between ships perhaps 20 yards and each wing 1,200 yards. We must here recall that the 30 ships of the Athenian center suffered very little in the battle, as they were detailed after the battle to pick up wrecks. We may therefore conjecture that as the Peloponnesian line approached and was a few hundred yards distant, the Athenians gathered way for the contact, and then the Athenian center divided into two parts which withdrew from the front of the island and formed guards for the inner flanks of the two wings, preventing the envelopment of these advancing ships. This would explain how the center did not get into serious action. Possibly some of the center ships may have strengthened the second line of the wings, and given these an opportunity of enveloping the outer flanks of the Peloponnesians. I confess that the above account is a surmise, but it is in accordance with what our two ancient sources tell us.

Now let us quote the account of the battle as given by Diodorus:

When Callicratidas saw that they could not reach so far as to equal the line of the enemy, because the islands stretched out so far, he divided his navy into two parts and fought in two places. This amazed the beholders from all parts, as if four fleets with no less than 300 sail, close together, were hotly engaged. For this was the greatest sea fight that was ever fought by Grecians against Grecians that any history commemorates. And now at one instant, all the trumpets were commanded by the admirals to sound a charge, and the crews on both sides set up a great shout in their turn, one against another, and plying their oars with great heat and earnestness every one strove who should be the first in making the onset. For there were many that by the long continuance of the war, were well instructed for fights at sea, and the battle was very hot and obstinate on both sides, in regard that the best and stoutest men were got together to fight in order to get or lose all at once. For none doubted but this battle would put an end to the war, whichever side so ever got the victory. But Callicratidas, knowing by the predictions of the augurs that he was to die, endeavored to make his death honorable and glorious. Therefore he made fiercely upon the galleys of Lysias, the vice admiral, whom he sunk with those next to him at the first charge. Others he disabled, striking them through with the beaks of his ships, and others he made useless for fight by brushing off their oars. At length he struck the ship of Pericles [son of the statesman] with such violence that he tore off one great part from another. But the fore part of his own ship was so fixed by the fierceness of the stroke in the prow of his enemy's ship that he could not clear himself off. Upon which Pericles cast grappling irons into Callicratidas' vessel, and so forced him up close, side by side. Here it is reported that Callicratidas, after he had behaved himself with great gallantry a long time and received many wounds in all parts of his body, at length wearied out, fell down dead.

The right wing of the Peloponnesians then fled, but the left wing held out longer; yet in the end all were routed and pursued with much loss. The Peloponnesian allies lost 70 ships, but the Athenians only 25.

At the close of the action 47 Athenian ships, including almost all those of the center, were detailed to recover the wrecks and the dead. It was the intention of the Athenian leaders to proceed with the rest of the available ships, about 75, to raise the siege of Mytilene and attack the covering squadron of 50 ships. Unfortunately, bad weather came on and the victors neither salved the wrecks nor caught the squadron, for Eteonicus, commanding it, was far from unmindful of the battle, and sent out a dispatch boat to see how it went. When the boat returned with bad news, he got ready to move, but sent out again, telling the captain to return with the crew wearing garlands and shouting victory. When the boat returned a second time Eteonicus offered sacrifice for the victory and sent word to the fleet and the merchantmen to get under way and go around the island, while he with the army marched across to Methymna to embark, and so all departed to Chios, without any confusion or panic arising out of the defeat.

The people of Athens heard with delight of the Battle of Arginussae, but were much disturbed by the failure to recover the bodies of the drowned for burial. Political differences in Athens led to the preferment of charges against the admirals, followed by an illegal trial, by which six generals who were within reach were executed, and thus the prediction that they would lose their lives was fulfilled.

Campaign of Aegospotami 405 b.c.

After this defeat the Spartans could continue the war only as dependents of Persia, so they again asked Athens for peace, offering to surrender Decelea (see Map 6), their fortified post in Attica, and as to other places, they suggested both sides should retain what they held. Athens had spent all her money and resources to make the Battle of Arginussae possible, and she was now obliged to raid for the daily supplies of the fleet at Samos without being able to undertake the serious work of settling with her rebellious subjects in slow succession. She, too, needed peace, but she put her terms high. Her counter-offer was that Sparta should restore the cities she had captured. Rather than do this, Sparta came to a new arrangement with Persia. This was the political point of the situation which Athens had overlooked. Lysander was again sent across the Aegean early in 405 to command the fleet, and renewed his friendship with Cyrus, who gave him money, with which Lysander reconstructed the fleet and got men, even shipping deserters from the enemy, and restored fleet morale. With Persian resources to back him, he planned to drive the needy Athenians to despair by attacking the extremities of their possessions. First he went to the Ceramic Gulf (southwestern part of Asia Minor) where he took Cedreae, an ally of Athens, and then to Rhodes.

By this time Lysander had a fleet stronger than the enemy's, but still he did not seek battle. Instead, he went to the Hellespont (see Map 12) and put himself on the enemy's most important line of communication (September, 405). Here he assaulted and took Lampsacus, well up the Hellespont and waited developments. He knew he would draw the Athenian fleet after him and oblige it to fight him. As soon as that fleet at Samos, commanded by six generals, heard that Lysander had passed on his way north, it followed as far as Elaeus on the Chersonese, having 180 ships. There, while at breakfast, they heard of the assault of Lampsacus and immediately went to Sestos, where they provisioned and went on some miles farther to a bare beach at the Aegospotami, the Goat River, on the opposite side to Lampsacus and 5 miles below it, having neither protection nor a market.

BATTLE OF AEGOSPOTAMI

The next morning Lysander manned his ships and waited for the enemy abreast his own camp. The Athenians also manned their ships and went up the stream until opposite, but took no action, and when the day was spent both returned to camp and beached their ships. But Lysander sent two fast ships to see that the enemy really landed for the day, and did not break his own battle formation until he was assured. Both fleets followed this course for several days, and Alcibiades came down from his neighboring castle to warn the Athenians not to be deceived and to go to Sestos, where they would have both a harbor and a city with a market. But they sent him away.

On the fifth day the Athenian fleet, after a visit to the hostile position, returned as usual and the crews dispersed to buy provisions which were becoming more and more difficult to obtain. Lysander told the scouts who followed them to return as soon as the enemy's dispersal was apparent, and make signal when halfway back. On seeing the glittering shields at the scout mastheads, Lysander moved against the fleet whose crews were absent while he sent a body of troops in transports across the Hellespont to march down the shore on the Athenian encampment. He took the Athenians entirely unawares and had no difficulty in taking the whole fleet except 9 ships, whose crews were near enough to get on board and escape down the stream.

In an hour the issue of 27 years of war was settled. With the hostile fleet in control of the sea, the profits of commerce passed away from Athens, leaving her without economic resources; but it was necessary to impose the peace on Athens. This was not difficult when the fleet was no longer in existence to keep the seas open for supply. As the first step, Lysander told all Athenians abroad for any reason whatever that they should return to Athens under penalty of death where they were. The sea was soon filled with ships, no longer bringing supplies for Athens, but mouths to be fed. The city was filled with wailing, yet nevertheless the people decided to resist to the utmost, for they did not realize what it was to have no fleet and consequently no business. The King of Sparta arrived with his army in November and surrounded the city and then Lysander came with the victorious fleet to close the seas. The terms offered were the destruction of the Long Walls. The city refused and famine began its slow work. On April 5, 404, the city capitulated. The terms then were the destruction of 2,000 yards of each of the Walls, the dismantling of the Piraeus, the cession of subject cities, the return of exiles, and the delivery of all trieres, except a number to be settled by Lysander, who, in the end, allowed 12 to be retained. Lysander and his forces entered the city, and the walls were pulled down to the music of flute girls.

So was finished the first empire founded on maritime trade and sea power. Politically it failed because Athens, the imperial city, took to herself too much of the profits of business and caused discontent among the subject allies. Strategically she did very well, until she over-extended herself in the campaign against Syracuse in the far west.

Even after Syracuse, Athens was able to maintain herself through her commerce in the east, until her fleet was lost through negligence without a real battle. It was the money of the vast Persian Empire which at last turned the scale against the commercial resources of Athens.

REVIEW

In less than a century between Marathon and Aegospotami we may see all types of naval warfare. At Marathon the navy merely covered the sea communications of the invading army and had only to hold down the sea raiders and pirates of whom the seas were always full although unmentioned by history on this occasion. Ten years later, the Great King undertook a huge over-seas invasion whose success depended on the mutual support of the army and navy. It was a contest of superior Greek weapons against greater Persian numbers. At the trial battles of Artemisium it was made apparent that the balance of strength was on the side of the Persians. They had the opportunity to bring greater numbers into action. The warlike and diplomatic genius of Themistocles enabled him to bring about battle in the position at Salamis where weapons and not numbers were decisive and the Greeks won. Yet on both sides the battle was fought chiefly with hand weapons. In the next two generations the obscurely known labors of Cimon and his successors brought another, although not a new weapon, the ram, into chief importance. With rowers protected by the catastroma and not required to drop their oars to fight, by constant drill and exercise, the Athenian fleet slowly became superior in maneuvering power to the ships of other Greek states. As the fleet gained in maneuvering skill, the ram became more important as a weapon and the soldiers on board could be and were reduced. With the consequent saving of weights on board, ships became still more handy, so that at Sybota before the opening of the Peloponnesian War the Athenian fleet had established the prestige of invincibility at sea through skill with the ram as against numbers of skilled spearmen on ship board. With this prestige Athens entered her great war and Phormio maintained it in his brilliant battles at the entrance to the Gulf of Corinth. But the Athenian exclusive reliance on the ram and consequent reduction of soldiers in the crews was very faulty as a rule of battle. Success with the ram depended on ample sea room both for maneuvers and for feints which utilized the greater endurance of Athenian crews at the oar in order to exhaust the enemy before closing to deliver the fatal ram stroke. Without maneuvering space the Athenian lack of soldiers on board would be ruinous. It was Polyanthes' great merit that he saw the Athenian mode of fighting was not generally applicable, and he forced the enemy to make a frontal ram attack for which he had prepared his own ships in advance. Phormio showed that under special conditions the ram might be made the sole weapon of victory. Polyanthes showed that as a general rule the fighting man is the chief means of victory and never afterward did fleets rely wholly on the ram. It was thereafter always a subordinate, although an important weapon.

The campaign of Syracuse has been criticized unfavorably by some modern historians as a foolish adventure at best, in which success should never have been expected. Really the Athenian fault was in vesting the command in an elderly statesman who was politically opposed to the effort and who was physically incapable through disease of assuming the responsibilities of office, yet able to withstand his abler colleagues through political prominence. The second expedition to Syracuse has also been condemned as a repetition of folly. This too seems to me an ill-founded charge. When a nation has undertaken a great matter it must not too easily renounce its purpose. War is uncertain and when Demosthenes sailed from Athens he had an excellent prospect of succeeding. The government's fault lay in giving him minor tasks to execute on his way. Thus his arrival was much delayed while the Syracusans were improving their situation. As for Demosthenes' unsuccessful assault he had to take some action and his effort was near success. He was unfortunate rather than foolish in his venture.

Although we may not condemn the Syracusan expedition on military grounds, we may well doubt the political wisdom of a democratic city state endeavoring to hold a great tributary city so far away from Aegean waters where Athens' real power lay. Such a conquest could scarcely be permanent.

In the naval battles within the harbor the Syracusans learned from Polyanthes how to nullify Athenian skill in ship handling and before the siege was over Demosthenes too had gone over to the old form of sea fighting with many soldiers. The Athenians still had the advantage in numbers of ships and there is little apparent reason for their failure except that the advantage of morale which they had enjoyed for so many years had passed to the other side.

Besides we should not overlook the point that the Syracusans introduced a new form of attack, always an advantage. Syracusan small boats got under the Athenian oars, and shot up the rowers on their benches. Perhaps the diversion was not very serious but it must have been most disconcerting and still more reduced Athenian morale.

After Syracuse the character of the fighting changed again. There were no more great invading expeditions. The war became wholly one against commerce, and turned on holding maritime bases and covering one's own shipping while striking at that of the enemy. Tactically, in the last years of the war, the soldier remained prominent as at Syracuse and the ram was secondary, but there was still room for skillful ship handling when fleets faced each other as was shown at Kynossema. Yet there were no more maneuvers of whole squadrons in motion to use the ram as at Patras. Fleets settled down to battles of position, like armies, with frontal attack and envelopment; and these methods lasted until the advent of sail power.

PRINCIPAL AUTHORITIES CONSULTED FOR THIS CHAPTER

ANCIENT AUTHORITIES

Thucydides.

Diodorus Siculus.

Plutarch: *Nicias, Alcibiades, Lysander, Pericles.*

Xenophon.

MODERN COMMENTATORS

Adcock, F. E., and Ferguson, W. S., *Cambridge Ancient History*, vol. 5.

Bury, J. B., *History of Greece.*

Delbrueck, H., *Geschichte der Kriegskunst.*

Grundy, G. B., *Thucydides and the History of His Age.*

Henderson, B. W., *The Great War between Athens and Sparta.*

Jurien de la Gravière, J. B. E.: *La Marine des Anciens.*

Kromayer, J., *Schlachten Atlas.*

CHAPTER V

DIONYSIUS—SICILY AND CARTHAGE

GENERAL CONDITIONS

AFTER the close of the Peloponnesian War, the development of naval construction shifted from Greece to Sicily. As a result of her great effort against Athens, the power of Syracuse over the rest of Sicily greatly increased, and under the tyrant Dionysius (406-367) great changes in army and navy organization and tactics were introduced. These did service in the defense of Syracuse against Carthage.

Carthage was founded before 800 B.C. and the vigorous Greek colonization movement of the eighth and seventh centuries to Italy and Sicily affected Carthage as it threatened her commercial expansion throughout the Western Mediterranean. By 500 B.C. Carthage had established herself firmly in the extreme west of Sicily and was desirous of extending her control over all this fertile island. At the time of Xerxes' expedition, a simultaneous attack by Carthage upon the Greeks of Sicily met an overwhelming defeat at Himera on the north coast at the hand of Gelon, tyrant of Syracuse, and Greek Sicily was free from Carthaginian incursions for 70 years.

The Athenian expedition to Sicily (see Map 10) revealed the island as full of dissensions and Carthage found an opportunity to increase the area under her commercial control. Segesta appealed to Carthage in regard to her old quarrel with Selinus in the year 409, and a Carthaginian army answered by the destruction of Selinus. The Carthaginian general, Hannibal, then went to Himera to revenge the defeat of his grandfather there in 480 and destroyed the city with great cruelty. By this time the somewhat unready Greek democracies of Sicily were aroused and Hannibal retired to Africa.

In 406 Hannibal reinvaded Sicily and besieged Acragas (now Girgenti) on the south coast. A large Greek army from Syracuse and other towns failed to relieve it. One of the Syracusan army leaders was Dionysius who came to the front in the political discussions at Syracuse following the failure to save Acragas and in 405 was able to make himself sole general with supreme power. By successive steps he posed as champion of Greek liberties against the Carthaginians.

Dionysius' first adventure in the rôle of savior failed to relieve the city of Gela when the Carthaginians proceeded to besiege it after their conquest of Acragas. It was thought he did not really wish for victory and a large part of his force deserted him. Still, he held his own against the enemy and then made a treaty favorable to the invader, yielding the western half of the island, but securing himself by the assurance of Carthaginian aid to support him as the ruler of Syracuse.

While Dionysius thus made it his first care to secure his own authority, he had no idea of yielding Sicily to the barbarians. He employed the next few years of peace in strengthening and reorganizing the naval and military bases of his authority. He fortified the city anew with works making the island of Ortygia an impregnable citadel. These included the Lesser Harbor which was made the naval base with a mole across the entrance so that only one ship could enter at a time. Within it he built slips for 60 ships. Dionysius also extended the area within the city walls, building, as is said, a wall over 3 miles long in 20 days with 60,000 men and 6,000 ox teams.

Dionysius was also aware of the developments of the Peloponnesian War as to the increased importance of light-armed troops (*peltasts*), and he perceived further that the more complicated drill and training for the *peltast* required that the amateur citizen soldier should be replaced by a professional man; so he founded his tyranny on an army of mercenary professional soldiers. He built a great navy and taught all how to act in unison, army and navy, horse and foot. His engineers invented mechanical artillery, able to throw stones of a couple of hundred weight for 200 yards. For the first time he built ships larger than the standard triere with better protection for the rowers and no doubt the new artillery was installed on their upper decks. Although Diodorus does not expressly say that the penteres carried the new armament, there was otherwise little use in building large ships. The new army and navy, as well as the personal security of the tyrant, were all based on the great fortifications which surrounded the entire city, and with these he set out to establish an empire in Sicily and South Italy.

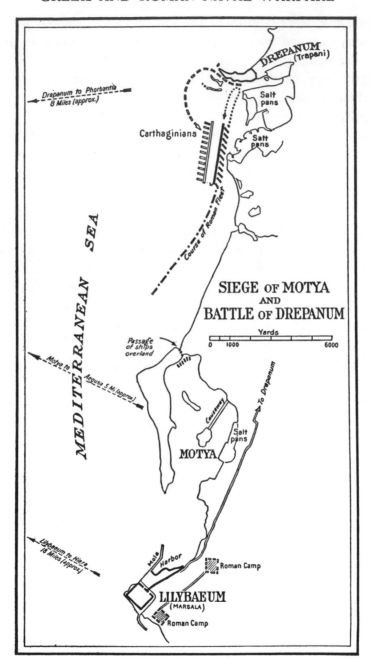

MAP 14.

After Dionysius felt himself reasonably safe in his position as ruler of Syracuse, had made the city a secure fortress, and had mastered much of Greek Sicily, he set out to drive the Carthaginians from the whole island and hold it for himself and for the Grecian world of trade and culture. In this great but gradual extension of power by the tyrant it is important to note that, as an administrator, the great fleet and army that he built up to maintain his own power were economically valuable to his subjects because he kept good order wherever his arm reached and, although sometimes cruel, did not abuse his authority wantonly. In particular, the fleet was used to suppress piracy which was so prevalent both in the Tyrrhenian and the Adriatic Seas. Through the maritime good order thus maintained, he was enabled to draw huge taxes from the cities whose trade he protected at the price of their submission to him.[1] Besides, he saved Greek Sicily from slavery to Carthage.

DIONYSIUS' FIRST WAR WITH CARTHAGE

In 398 B.C., at the head of a great army, alleged to be over 80,000[2] men, Dionysius moved through Southern Sicily, delivering the Greek dependencies of Carthage, to lay siege to Motya, an island city within a harbor in the western end of Sicily and the military and commercial base of the Carthaginian occupation. The army's movement was supported by a great fleet of 200 ships of war, many of the new type and by 500 ships of burden with siege engines, catapults, provisions, and stores.

The island on which Motya stood was about half a mile in diameter in the center of a bay 2 miles wide and even longer. It was joined to the mainland by a causeway which has now become an isthmus in the course

---

[1] See *Piracy in the Ancient World*, pp. 128, 159, by H. A. Ormerod.

[2] In his *Population et Capital dans le Monde Mediterranée Antique*, Cavaignac estimates the cost of 100,000 men in fleet and army at 2 obols per day per man and 2,000 talents ($2,400,000) a year. He estimates Dionysius' maximum revenue at 3,000 talents. But the army seems too big for his premise of wages and revenue. At wages of 2 obols per man, the total army and navy expenses per man and per day can have been little less than 5 obols, so that for a year's service (active for 8 months) the cost must have been 50 talents per 1,000 men. Besides there were local garrisons and coast guard squadrons and public works, so that on Cavaignac's basis of a revenue of 3,000 talents perhaps one-half may have gone to the field and cruising forces, giving a total for them of only 30,000 men in all, which we may divide roughly about half and half between army and fleet. The Carthaginian numbers were not greatly dissimilar. All Diodorus' numbers as given below, seem high.

of time. On the approach of the Greeks, the Motyans destroyed their causeway, and abided the siege. When Dionysius arrived, he drew his fleet to the shore on the northern side of the harbor; put some guard ships at the entrance and set a part of the army and men of the fleet to build a wide earthen causeway out to the island from which to attack the city upon a sufficiently wide front. The rest of the army went off to subdue neighboring cities.

On hearing of Dionysius' attack, the Carthaginians prepared an army in Africa and while doing so sent 10 ships to make a diversion upon the port of Syracuse in the hope of drawing Dionysius from the siege of Motya. Their night attack on the shipping in Syracuse was very successful but had no effect on Dionysius' operations in the west.

When the causeway was about to reach to Motya, Dionysius returned from his raiding expedition to undertake a more active form of attack against it than had been possible in previous ages which lacked the siege weapons that he had developed. Himilco, the Carthaginian commander, having mobilized in Africa about this time and hearing that the Syracusan fleet had been brought into the harbor, sailed with 100 ships to surprise it. He caught some guard ships at the harbor mouth, but after entering he found the hostile ships drawn on the beach and guarded by the army and by the new mechanical artillery.[3] The Carthaginian fleet could not maintain itself before these and its attack was repulsed. Then Dionysius, whose operations at Motya were not checked by Himilco's aid, using his numerous army, drew his ships on rollers across the low land to the open beach on the other side where he was able to embark at pleasure and so resumed command of the sea. (Such ships must have been small.) Seeing this, Himilco returned with his fleet to Carthage, leaving the city to make an unsuccessful defense against the violent attack of Dionysius, like which nothing had been seen in the Peloponnesian War. Dionysius had battering rams and catapults to use from the mole and the enemy replied with soldiers in armor who hurled firebrands on the attackers. Of particular importance were the high towers which Dionysius brought up on the mole to reach the men on the roofs of the high stone houses of the city. The de-

---

[3] We may suppose the catapults were placed on the beach between the ships, and soldiers with missile weapons re-enforced the crews of the ships; whose flanks also were doubtless protected by soldiers and catapults.

fense was able to fire some of Dionysius' wooden towers, but his progress could not be checked. The bravery of the citizens was no match for artillery and was unable to save them; the city was destroyed and the inhabitants sold into slavery, and Dionysius retired to Syracuse. The new penteres did not have an opportunity in this campaign, but the new catapults were tried out in the siege. When the fleet was ready for service the next year, the larger ships were probably fitted with them.

Carthaginian Army Attacked at Sea

All Carthage was aroused by the fall of Motya, for Carthage could not see itself dispossessed of Phoenician Sicily. Himilco was intrusted with the direction of the operations for the next year, 397 B.C. In the spring Dionysius advanced again into Western Sicily and laid siege to Segesta, while his brother Leptines, with the fleet, lay off ruined Motya to intercept invasion. Himilco assembled a fleet of transports to take a great army to Sicily together with 300 men-of-war to escort them.[4] The Carthaginian transports sailed directly for Sicily while their escort lingered on the coast of Africa. As the transports drew near the Sicilian shore with a favorable breeze, Leptines put out with 30 ships and succeeded in destroying 50 transports with about 5,000 soldiers, but the rest took advantage of a change in the breeze to escape from the oar-driven enemy, and landed the army at Panormus where the Carthaginians had a secure base.

The tactical point in this escape is one often repeated in the much later times when men-of-war were taking to sail power. When Leptines' small squadron broke into the great fleet of transports, he destroyed all he could reach, but before he could get many, the rowers were exhausted and the sailing ships were off. The wind and consequent sea were disabling to the rowing ships, owing to their low hulls and great length, while calms rendered the sailing ships comparatively helpless.

Upon the approach of the Carthaginian army from Panormus, Dionysius abandoned the siege of Segesta and fell back to Syracuse, and Himilco, returning to Panormus, supported by his fleet, marched eastward along the north coast of Sicily to Messana, the Greek city which commanded the communications with Italy, and destroyed it after a siege.

---

[4] Diodorus probably over-estimates.

Naval Battle off Catana

The Carthaginians now moved southward along the coast to attack Syracuse and Dionysius proceeded north as far as Catana to meet them with fleet and army. As Himilco drew near Catana an eruption of Aetna cut off the coast road and obliged the army to pass inland around Aetna, while the fleet with the transports was left without army support. Dionysius resolved to take the opportunity to attack the hostile fleet. Its defeat would embarrass the supply of its army, which came largely by sea, and might occasion the army to withdraw from Grecian Sicily.

Accordingly, Dionysius directed his brother Leptines to attack with his fleet of 180 ships,[5] of which many were the new construction (penteres). Leptines also was directed to keep all the fleet together while delivering the attack. Mago, commanding the fleet of Himilco, had 500 ships altogether but many, probably the majority, were supply ships and his fighting vessels were probably few more than the Syracusans. On seeing the approaching enemy, the Carthaginians were at first much alarmed, and turned towards shore to beach their ships, but then, seeing that the shore was occupied by hostile troops, they formed line to receive the enemy. Leptines failed to observe his orders to bring all his ships into action together. With 30 of his best he made a bold attack and sank several opponents, but then the more numerous enemy surrounded him and he was obliged to flee. As the rest of his ships came up in succession, they were discouraged by the admiral's withdrawal and were defeated also. Leptines lost over half his ships. The men swimming ashore out of the disabled ships were taken or killed by the Carthaginian transport ships lying between their own fighting ships and the shore, but out of reach of Dionysius' army.

This action deserves notice because it was the first we know of in which the admiral had orders about his tactics from the home office. Leptines had two classes of ships, the trieres and smaller ships and the new penteres with catapults in addition to the marine infantry. As the new ships of Leptines were built to use the catapult, the ships had to be heavier to carry it and, even if they were to have enough rowers to equal the speed of the lighter ships, they could not start and stop so quickly on account of their

---

[5] So says Diodorus; probably there were far from so many.

extra weight. Their comparative unfitness for maneuver tactics required an increase in the soldiers on board, not only to man the catapults but also to act as heavy-armed spearmen for boarding, and as light infantry with missile weapons to attack the enemy during his approach. Thus the use of light-armed soldiers continued to develop on shipboard as it did on shore, and the new weapons brought naval tactics once more to emphasize the soldier's effort against life rather than the seaman's effort to destroy ship structures by the ram. Consequently the penteres needed to have their flanks and rear covered by lighter ships as they advanced into battle for protection against ram attack in the stern. Their normal place must have been in the center of the fleet formation. Probably Leptines neglected this point and had permitted straggling.

It seems within the proper limits of inference that Dionysius meant his brother to try out the new craft in conjunction with the others, but that the admiral and the fleet were over-confident in their superiority and engaged in succession as has so often happened in history. Nevertheless, the new type must have done well for it continued to develop, although not very fast, for the difficulty of manning large ships tended to hold their numbers down.[6]

Carthaginian Siege of Syracuse

After Mago's success off Catana, Dionysius had the choice of meeting Himilco's army as it made the round of Aetna or of retiring into the fortifications of Syracuse to secure the city against debarkation of the soldiers in Mago's victorious fleet. He chose the latter course and sent to Greece (Corinth) to beg for aid against the barbarians. Soon from the battlements the Syracusans saw the Carthaginian fleet sweeping into Great Harbor, so that the anchorage was filled with transports and the beaches with men-of-war. A little later the Carthaginian army arrived and established a blockade, occupying a position about the Temple of Jupiter, and southward, somewhat farther from the city than that of the Athenians in their siege.

Here the hostile army lay for some time without making any very

---

[6] From the contemporary records of the Athenian fleet published by Boeckh it appears that so late as the year 325 B.C. it included 360 trieres, 50 tetreres, and only 3 penteres. A few years later, however, the successors of Alexander were employing a much larger proportion of heavy ships.

serious attack until ships from Corinth arrived to aid the city as had been requested by Dionysius. Soon after, disease broke out among the besiegers who were encamped in an unhealthy place and Dionysius decided to attack them. The Carthaginians had established their base and storehouses along the southern part of the bay of Syracuse from Plemmyrium to Dascon and had erected three forts on the shore and by the camp to protect the ships and the stores (see Map 11).

The plague had not only killed many of the Carthaginians, but they had become negligent, so Dionysius arranged for a simultaneous attack by sea and land. He directed his brother Leptines to move at daylight with 80 ships against the hostile fleet in the southern part of the bay, whose crews were sleeping on shore as usual, while he with the army started by night to reach position along the northern front of the enemy's camp. The action opened by a false attack on the inland end of the Carthaginian line, Dionysius followed this with a general attack on the camp and the forts defending the base and as the Carthaginians ran to defend themselves there, the fleet bore down on the Carthaginians' ships, the crews of which did not all have time to get on board. Great loss was inflicted on the unready fleet and then Dionysius led a party of soldiers upon the transports, which were beached somewhat farther north than the men-of-war, and threw fire into them. They pushed off in confusion; the bay was filled with burning ships and many were lost.

The result of this tremendous victory was that the Carthaginians offered to pay an enormous ransom to be permitted to depart, abandoning their Greek allies in Sicily. This offer Dionysius accepted, as he did not wish to destroy entirely the Carthaginian power in Sicily, for he relied on their presence to reconcile his Greek subjects to his own dominion. Thus the war ended.

Although Dionysius maintained three other wars with Carthage before the end of his life, there was no further important naval action. The fleet was used to escort the army over-seas, to suppress piracy, and to assure communications. It was indispensable to the army's movements, but it was an auxiliary. The result of Dionysius' invention of the catapult was far reaching, however, as has been said, and its influence on tactics lasted nearly 400 years. Besides it seems possible he was the first to make some practical device for the tactical employment of fire. He had great success with it at the siege. Before him fire was used to destroy vessels but not to fight them. Afterwards fire was a tactical weapon.

PRINCIPAL AUTHORITIES CONSULTED FOR THIS CHAPTER

ANCIENT

Diodorus Siculus.

MODERN

Bury, J. B.: *History of Greece.*
Cambridge Ancient History, vol. 6.
Freeman, E. A.: *History of Sicily.*
Gravière, Jurien de la: *La Marine des Anciens.*

CHAPTER VI

THE PENTERE AND ITS OARS

IN ORDER to arrive at some estimate of the size and design of penteres, we start from the idea that the word pentere as applied to a
certain class of ships embodies the conception that there were 5 men
to each oar rather than 5 rows of men with separate oars. The nature of
the motive power must have been a principal element in the design of
ancient ships, just as it is today. Consequently, a comprehension of the size,
horsepower, and management of these great oars is a necessary preliminary
to any attempt to reconstruct the ancient penteres as invented by the
engineers of Dionysius. Fortunately, we are not without the means for
such a study of oars. The data recorded by practical seamen of the sixteenth, seventeenth, and eighteenth centuries, as to the construction and
performance of the galleys under their command, enable us to estimate
closely what could be done by oars of various sizes when worked by different numbers of men per oar, and it is convenient here to consider oars of
larger size as well as the 5-man oar.[1] Barras de la Penne tells of rowing
the heavy oars and the speed reached. For 5 men the oars were 37 ft. long,
of which a little less than one-third was inboard of the tholepin. The blade
was 10 ft. long and 7 in. wide. The loom was very stout, over 6 in. in
diameter, in order to balance the blade, and, if necessary, there was a
counter-weight attached to or let into the handle. The oar was kept from
feathering by flat pieces of wood secured to it at the tholepin so that it
rested on a flat surface, and, as it was too large to grasp in the hand, there
were handles of convenient size cleated to the oar. The largest oars were
52 to 60 ft. long and were of the same type as the 5-man oar and weighed

---

[1] Some of the contemporary authorities are Pantero Pantera, *Armata Navale*, Rome, 1614;
Bernardo Crescentio, *Nautica Mediterranea*, Rome, 1602; Barras de la Penne wrote about 1700.
His manuscripts are in the Bibliothèque Nationale and Bibliothèque de la Marine, Paris. Much
of his material and his drawings have been published by Vice Admiral Paris, *Souvenirs de
Marine*; and Vice Admiral Jurien de la Gravière *Les Derniers Jours de la Marine à Rames*.
A report to the French Academy of Sciences in 1702 by De Chazeulles tells of a speed trial he
made in a standard galley of about 300 tons displacement.

between 400 and 500 lbs. They were for crews of 9 or 10 men, in double rank, facing each other over the handles (see *Souvenirs de Marine*). For the 5-man oars it was desirable to take a long, slow stroke. The maximum was 26 strokes a minute and the handle swung over a path full 6 ft. long. The work of the leader (the end man) was very heavy at full speed. As Barras describes the stroke, the men rose from their seats and the end man thrust his handle as far aft as possible, at the same time each rower took a step aft, placing the unchained foot on the raised rest (*pedagne*) in front of him, and then dipping the oar, all fell back on the seat, each pivoting about the raised foot and keeping the arms extended until the full stroke was completed. The speed of the ships was measured by noting the eddy or wake left in the water by each oar at the end of each stroke. The point among the eddies where the stroke oar next dipped was the measure of the speed at the rate of 1 knot for each eddy that the blade overpassed as it swung forward. The maximum speed covered seven spaces, but this speed could be maintained for a short time only. Both Barras and Crescentio give the same rule and, as the distance between oars was a little over 49 inches, the apparent distance run at each stroke was 29 ft. or 7.5 knots. But neither author makes allowance for slip of the oar in the water. With 1 sq. ft. of immersed blade per man, to develop the necessary resistance, the slip would not be less than 3 ft., and the distance run per stroke would be not over 26 ft., or 6.67 knots.

Barras de la Penne tells us that a royal decree of 1691 standardized the galleys of France at a length of 153.6 ft., and the other dimensions gave a displacement of about 300 tons at deep draft. The data supplied by the naval model tank in Washington show about 23.4 effective horsepower for the speed of 6.67 knots. Therefore, a 5-man oar was good for 0.450 effective horsepower at its best, as the standard galley had 52 oars. De Chazeulles in his report to the French Academy of Sciences, in 1702, says that the same galley (standard) with the same crew of 260 rowers, rowing easily at a stroke that could be maintained for "some time," made 72 toises per minute at 24 strokes. This is 4.5 knots, or about two-sevenths full power and two-thirds of full speed. We may therefore assume that at a moderate speed which a crew of one or several men per oar can maintain for several hours the power is about two-sevenths of what they can develop for a spurt of 20 minutes and the speed will be about two-thirds of full speed.

With the effective horsepower for 1 man and 5 men to an oar, it is easy to construct a graph showing approximately what power any number of men on one oar may develop, and the curve may be prolonged up to 10 men with oars about 55 ft. long, which was the limit of efficiency. The data for such a graph are given below, assuming oars of suitable lengths, but a considerable variation in the length of the oar would cause a less

Length of oar in ft.[2]	No. men per oar	E.hp. developed on each oar, full power, not over 20 min. duration	E.hp. (approx.) developed on each oar, long effort
12–14	1	0.143	0.036
19–21	2	0.243	0.066
25–28	3	0.325	0.093
31–33	4	0.393	0.112
36–39	5	0.450	0.128
40–43	6	0.499	0.143
43–47	7	0.542	0.155
47–51	8	0.580	0.166
51–55	9	0.613	0.175
54–59	10	0.640	0.183

proportional reduction in the work done, perhaps 20 per cent in length of oar, and only 8 or 9 per cent in work done.

Pantero Pantera tells us that he had been told by old seamen that, when the Venetian navy changed its rowing organization from the old way of having 3 men on each thwart, each with his own oar, to the then current way of 4 and 5 men on the same oar, it was found that the new way with 3 men on one big oar was not so good as the old way, but with 4 men on the big oar it was better. Hence, we may assume that 3 men on three 30- to 36-ft. oars (see Admiral Fincati's *Le Triremi*) could develop about 0.120 effective horsepower each, not quite as much as they would get with lighter and shorter oars, but they had more men at work on a given length of side. Since considerable variation in the length of oars was possible with much less change in efficiency, it is quite likely that Greek trieres had only 26 ft. in their longest oars, with 3 men on each. Assuming an ancient ship to be able to make 7 knots at full speed for 20 minutes, then the physical strength of man is such that she would not be able to ex-

---

[2] At end of the sixteenth century the Venetians seem to have made trial of 48-ft. oars with 5 men each.

ceed, say, 13 miles in 3 hours before exhausting the crew. With the rowers in two watches, a galley might be able to make 35 to 40 miles in 10 to 12 hours, possibly 45 miles during summer daylight. In three watches, rowing continuously, she might reach 70 miles in 24 hours with calm weather. This is confirmed by a letter of Honorato Cayetano, general of papal infantry in the campaign of Lepanto, who wrote a series of interesting letters to his family telling of the campaign (published about 90 years ago). The papal squadron made 2.8 knots under oars in a long day with calm weather. These data from records of the sixteenth and seventeenth centuries are confirmed by many references in classical writers and must be kept in mind when discussing the size of classical men-of-war and their speed and maneuvers.

Let us now consider what sort of ships the early penteres must have been. We approach the subject from what Polybius tells us, writing more than two centuries later. He says penteres in his time had 300 rowers and 120 soldiers. There must have been 50 more as officers, seamen, mechanics, and cooks, so that a crew of 470 men is a minimum for such ships as Polybius had in mind. In his *Marines de Guerre de l'Antiquité*, Admiral Serre has worked out a minimum size for Polybius' craft and gives it as 304 tons displacement, with 21 ft. 4 in. at the tholepins. The design is based on the cross section of the rowing chamber, which he makes a minimum by using somewhat inefficient oars only 30 ft. in length for 5 men. Another principal factor in his design is the provision of 20 days' food and water, which seems to me to be excessive in view of the constant allusions in classical writers to embarking 2 days' and 3 days' supplies for trieres. If we allow that Dionysius' new ships had considerably more ration endurance than trieres, it seems that 10 days would be ample increase, and Serre's displacement could be reduced by this change alone as much as 30 per cent. We can scarcely believe that Dionysius made a great jump in the size of his ships, when his engineers invented the new type to carry the new mechanical artillery. It was enough to provide a ship big enough to take the new armament without serious loss of speed, for the ship's activity in battle was no longer primary. The first penteres must have been heavier built than trieres, for two reasons: (1) they carried heavy stone throwers and, (2) they were "cataphract" (i.e., covered or fenced) in the third meaning of the word. At first it was the ship's hold that was "covered" by a deck and the triere rowers sat on it (early trieres). Then the rowers were covered by the catastroma deck and the soldiers fought on this deck. Finally, in the pentere, the upright timbers carrying the catastroma deck were planked over although probably not completely, still further covering the rowers, although somewhat at the expense of ventilation, which had been excellent in the trieres and could not be neglected in the pentere. The last type of "cataphract" was no doubt the

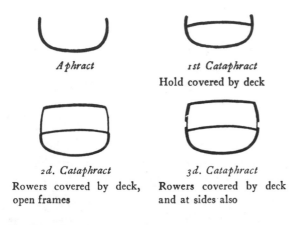

Aphract

1st Cataphract
Hold covered by deck

2d. Cataphract
Rowers covered by deck, open frames

3d. Cataphract
Rowers covered by deck and at sides also

result of the desperate battles in the harbor during the siege of Syracuse. As long as the Athenian fleet dominated the seas with ships built for maneuver the rowers were not greatly exposed, but when the "hand-to-hand" style of fighting came into its own again, at Syracuse, the rowers needed protection from the new type of fighting men, the *peltast* with missile weapons, the arrow, and the sling. (The figure shows the three meanings of "cataphract.") A device which was perhaps invented for the early penteres to increase the rowers' efficiency was the outrigger frame similar to the *apostis* of the Mediterranean rowing navies. It was certainly in use a little later, as told in the appendix to Chapter I. That the first penteres were small is indicated by the fact that they were drawn overland at the siege of Motya, just like trieres. I therefore assume a minimum size with no more rowers than the triere, that is, 150 rowers, with some 25 ship men and 75 soldiers to complete the crew. The figures (p. 211) give an outline of what they may have been: length 100 ft., beam at l.w.l. 21.5 ft., beam at tholepins 28 ft., draft 4 ft., displacement 140 tons; 30 oars, 38 ft. long, 5 rowers each; complete protection for rowers, overhead and on sides; ventilation through deck and sides for rowers; 2 ballistae forward; raised half-deck and quarter-deck aft; 2 side rudders; 1 mast with 1 yard; height of mast 45 ft. above deck; sail area 2,200 feet. From records of the seventeenth century, we may say with some confidence that such a design would have a

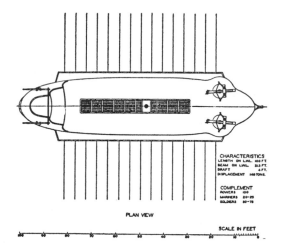

PLAN VIEW

CHARACTERISTICS
LENGTH ON L.W.L. 100 FT.
BEAM ON L.W.L. 31.5 FT.
DRAFT 4 FT.
DISPLACEMENT 140 TONS.

COMPLEMENT
ROWERS 150
MARINERS 20-25
SOLDIERS 50-75

SCALE IN FEET

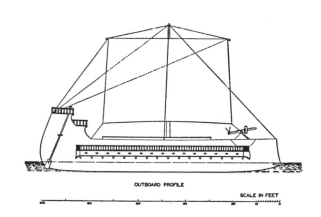

OUTBOARD PROFILE

SCALE IN FEET

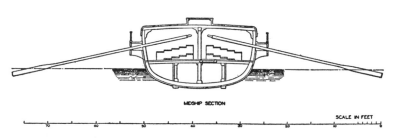

MIDSHIP SECTION

SCALE IN FEET

EARLY PART OF FOURTH CENTURY B.C. PENTERE OF
DIONYSIUS—RECONSTRUCTION

speed under oars for a racing spurt of 6.4 knots; for 2 hours with full crew 4.0 knots; when in 3 watches, 2.7 knots; best speed under sail about 10 knots in smooth water.

The new pentere bore much the same relation to the triere as the battleship of the eighteenth century bore to the frigate. The pentere was heavier and slower, but she made up for it in her artillery and her many soldiers. When penteres grew larger in the course of time, it is probable that the cross section grew very little. The principal change must have been in the length to accommodate more soldiers and *ballistae*, and with them, more rowers to maintain speed. Nevertheless, the triere remained the standard ship for long afterwards, as is shown by the inventory of the Athenian fleet in the time of Alexander the Great, already mentioned.

PRINCIPAL AUTHORITIES CONSULTED FOR THIS CHAPTER

Cartault: *La Trière Athénienne.*
Fincati, L.: *Le Triremi.*
Paris, E.: *Souvenirs de Marine.*
Serre, P.: *Les Marines de Guerre de l'Antiquité et du Moyen Age.*
    Same title: a serial in 1890–91 in *Revue Maritime et Coloniale.*

CHAPTER VII

EXERCISES AND STRATAGEMS OF THE GREEK FLEETS

AFTER the close of the Peloponnesian War we have slight tactical information as to the handling of the Greek fleets. There were great sea battles at Cnidus in 394 and off Naxos and Corcyra in 375, but we know little about them beyond the numbers of ships engaged. In his *Hellenica,* Xenophon tells several stories illustrating the methods of training and of warfare of the day which are interesting and instructive. No matter how out of date the details may be, the history of stratagems and surprises is stimulating to the imagination of every commander ashore or afloat. I shall therefore quote these incidents as pictures of the times as well as for what they may have of suggestiveness.

In 389 the Spartans urged the Aeginetans to cut off the trade of Athens, and in reply the Athenians sent 10 triremes and a force of hoplites under Pamphilus to occupy Aegina. Pamphilus built a fort on the island as a base and besieged the city by sea and land. Teleutias, brother of the Spartan King Agesilaus, hearing of the difficulties of Aegina, came to its relief and drove off the fleet but the Athenians holding the fort remained there. Teleutias was then relieved of his command by Hierax. And, as Xenophon says,

> Teleutias, under the very happiest circumstances, set sail for home. For as he was going down to the sea to embark, there was no one among the soldiers who did not grasp his hand, and one decked him with a garland and another with a fillet, and others who came too late, nevertheless, even though he was now under way threw garlands into the sea and prayed for many blessings upon him. Now I am aware that I am not describing in this incident any enterprise involving money expended, or danger incurred or any memorable stratagem; and yet, by Zeus, it seems to me that it is well worth a man's while to consider what sort of conduct it was that enabled Teleutias to inspire the men he commanded with such a feeling towards himself. For to attain this is indeed the achievement of a true man, much more noteworthy than the encountering of many dangers.

The war between Aegina and Athens ran on into the next year when

213

the Spartan Admiral Gorgopas with 12 ships was driven to take refuge in Aegina just before sunset by the Athenian Eunomus with 13 ships.

After watching the enemy for a little while Eunomus moved away. When night came on he led the way [column of ships] showing a light as the custom is, so that the ships following him might not go astray. Then Gorgopas immediately embarked his men and followed the light, keeping astern so as not to be visible, while his boatswains marked the stroke by clicking stones together instead of with their voices, and made the men employ a sliding motion of their oars [to muffle them]. But when the ships of Eunomus were close to the shore near Cape Zoster in Attica [13 miles from Aegina] Gorgopas by the trumpet gave the order to attack. As for Eunomus, the men on some of his ships were just landing, others were still securing their ships and others were even yet approaching their berths. Then, a battle being fought by moonlight, Gorgopas captured 4 trieres, and taking them in tow carried them off to Aegina, but the other ships of the Athenians got to Piraeus.

Soon after this the Athenian Chabrias landed on Aegina and surprised and killed Gorgopas with many Aeginetans in an ambush, after which the Athenians sailed the seas just as in time of peace, for the Spartan sailors refused to row for Eteonicus (the new Spartan commander) even though he tried to compel them, as he did not pay them. Thereupon the Spartans sent Teleutias to Aegina to resume his command as admiral.

And when the sailors saw him they were delighted beyond measure. And he called them together and spoke as follows: "Fellow soldiers, I have come without money, yet if God be willing and you perform your part zealously, I shall endeavor to supply you with provisions in the utmost abundance. And be well assured that whenever I am in command of you, I pray just as earnestly for your lives as for my own. * * * For I do not bid you do any of these things that you may suffer discomfort, but that from them you may gain something good. And Sparta too," he added, "that Sparta of ours, which is accounted so prosperous—be assured she won her prosperity and her glory, not by careless idling, but by being willing to undergo both toils and dangers whenever there was need. Now you in like manner were in former days, as I know, good men, but now you must strive to prove yourselves even better men in order that just as we gladly undergo toils together, so we may gladly enjoy good fortune together. For what greater gladness can there be than to have to flatter no one in the world, either Greek or Barbarian, for the sake of pay, but to be able to supply oneself from the most honorable source? For be well assured that abundance gained in war from the enemy yields not merely sustenance, but fair fame among all men." Thus he spoke, and they all set up a shout, bidding him give whatever order was needful, and they would obey.

Now he chanced to have finished sacrificing and he said, "Come my men, get dinner, just as you were about to do in any case and provide yourselves with one day's ration and come quickly to the ships that we may go to the place that God wills and arrive in good time." And when they had gone on board he departed during the night for the harbor of Athens [distant about 16 miles] now letting the men rest and bidding them get a little repose and now setting them at the oars. But if any one supposes it was madness for him to sail with only 12 trieres against men who possessed many ships let him consider Teleutias' calculations. He conceived that the Athenians were more careless about their fleet in the harbor now that Gorgopas was dead; and even if there were ships at anchor there, he believed it was safer to attack 20 ships at Athens than 10 elsewhere. For in the case of ships abroad, he knew that the sailors would be quartered on board their several ships, whereas at Athens he was aware that the captains would be sleeping at home and the men quartered here and there. He had weighed these considerations before setting out, and when distant 5 or 6 stadia [half a mile or more], he remained quiet and let the men rest.

Then, as day was dawning, he led them on, and they followed. He directed them to disable any trieres lying at anchor but not to injure any merchantmen, but on the contrary, to take the loaded ones in tow, and to seize the crews of the larger ones. He succeeded in these things and some of his men even leaped on the quay and there took merchants and owners of trading ships. Some of the Athenians upon hearing the uproar, ran from their houses to see what it was; others ran home to get their weapons and still others to Athens to carry the news. Then the Athenians, hoplites and horsemen, rushed to the rescue thinking that Piraeus had been captured. But Teleutias sent off the captured ships to Aegina under escort of 3 or 4 of the trieres while with the rest he coasted along the shore of Attica, and inasmuch as he was leaving the harbor he captured many fishing craft and ferry boats inward bound from the islands. And on coming to Sunium, he captured trading vessels also, some full of grain, others of merchandise. Having done all these things, he returned to Aegina and when he had sold his prizes he gave his men a month's pay in advance. And from that time forth he cruised and captured whatever he could. And by doing these things he maintained his ships with full complements and kept his soldiers in a state of glad and prompt obedience (388 B.C.).

In 387 Antalcides, a Spartan admiral in the Hellespont, heard of the approach of 8 Athenian ships. He manned 12 of his fastest ships, filling vacancies from others, and waited in concealment. When the enemy passed him, he pursued and they fled. He soon overhauled the slowest of the enemy with his fastest ships, but gave orders to them not to attack the rear ships but to pass them and fall on the van, while his own slowest ships were able to overtake the enemy's rear and thus all were captured.

We may compare Teleutias' manner of command with that of another contemporary Spartan admiral, one Mnasippus, who besieged Corcyra in 373, that is, he blockaded the city by sea and land.

> The Corcyraeans were suffering so greatly from hunger that on account of the number of deserters from the city Mnasippus issued a proclamation that deserters should be sold into slavery, but when the none the less they continued to desert, he even tried to drive them back with the scourge [to help exhaust supplies]. Those in the city, however, would not admit the slaves within the walls again and many died outside. Now Mnasippus, seeing these things and believing he all but had possession of the city already, was trying innovations with his mercenaries. He had previously dismissed some of them and he now owed as much as two months' pay to those who remained. As it was said, this was not because he lacked money, for most of the states had sent him money instead of men, because it was an over-seas expedition. The people in the city, observing that the enemy's posts were more carelessly guarded and that the men were scattered through the country, made a sally, capturing some and cutting down others. When Mnasippus perceived this, he put on his armor and went to the rescue himself, with all the hoplites he had, and at the same time ordered his captains to lead out the mercenaries and when some captains replied that it was not easy to keep men obedient unless they were given rations, he struck one of them with a staff and another with the butt of his spear. So it was, then, that when his forces issued from the city, they were all dispirited and hostile to him—a condition that is by no means conducive to fighting.

And so, as Xenophon goes on to tell, the men broke in action and Mnasippus was killed.

The Athenians sent Iphicrates to relieve Corcyra from the siege by Mnasippus. When Iphicrates began his voyage around the Peloponnese he carried on exercises for battle while under way.

> At the outset he left all his larger sails at Athens for he expected to fight [and they made the ships heavy] and on the way he made slight use of the smaller sails even if the wind was favorable. For by making the voyage under oars he kept the men in better condition of body and made better speed. Furthermore, whenever the fleet was going to take the noonday or the evening meal at any particular place, he would draw up the fleet in a line opposite the landing place and at a signal have them race to the shore. It was counted a great prize of victory first to get water or any other supply and be the first to get their meal. On the other hand, those who were last incurred a great penalty in that they came off worse in all these points [they had farther to go to get water, etc.] and in the fact that they had to shove off at the same time as the others when the signal was made and thus those who came in first did all at their leisure, while those that were last had to hurry.

Again, in setting the watch, if he chanced to be taking the noon meal in hostile country, he posted some on land as is proper, but besides he stepped the masts and had lookouts at their heads. These men from their height could see much farther than those on the ground. Further, wherever he slept, he would not have a fire within the camp during the night, but kept lights in front of his forces so that no one could approach unobserved. Frequently, however, if it was good weather, he would put to sea again immediately after dining, and if there was a favorable breeze they sailed without labor, while if it was necessary to row they took the work by watches. Again, when he was under way by day he would lead the fleet by signals, sometimes in column, and then in line of battle. So that while still pursuing their voyage, they had at the same time practiced and become skilled in all the maneuvers of battle before they reached those waters, which as they supposed, were held by the enemy. And although for the most part they took both their noon and evening meals in the enemy's country, nevertheless, by doing only the necessary things, he always got under way again before the enemy's forces arrived to repel him. * * *

Now I am aware that all these matters of practice and training are customary whenever men expect to engage in a battle by sea, but what I commend in Iphicrates is this, that when it was incumbent upon him to arrive speedily at the place where he supposed he should fight with the enemy, he found a way to train his men on the voyage without delaying his passage to do so. (*Hellenica*, VI-2, 27-32)

Some of the naval stratagems narrated by Polyaenus throw light on the practices of the times. Thus Timotheus, having 40 ships and wishing to send 5 of them secretly on a long trip with much provision, directed the 40 ships to embark 3 days' supplies and then shifted anchorage to a retired spot where all ships landed 2 days' allowance which the 5 then reshipped and proceeded on their way with 17 days' allowance (Bk. 3, Chaps. 10-11). This account shows that ordinarily ships did not have more than 3 or 4 days' food on board, but that at a pinch a triere could stow nearly 20 tons extra cargo, including water and 6 or 7 tons of food, but of course such an addition would make her unduly heavy for battle as well as be an embarrassment to the rowers.

Several times Polyaenus mentions that a fleet, outside a harbor and wishing to induce the enemy to come out and attack him, appeared off the entrance with a superior force but with the ships lashed together in pairs and each pair showing only one mast, so as to deceive the enemy into thinking the force was only half its real number. Then on the approach of the harbor fleet, the blockaders cast off their lines and attacked.

CHAPTER VIII

ALEXANDER'S NAVAL CAMPAIGNS

THE development of naval tactics during the second and third quarters of the fourth century B.C. is not very clearly indicated in the histories that have come down to us. Navies continued to support and defend peaceful commerce and to escort over-seas expeditions during wars, for neither in peace nor in war could the commercial states of Greece maintain themselves without their help; but no naval victory decided the outcome of any war as happened at Salamis and twice at Syracuse. Thus we take up next the Macedonian invasion and conquest of the Persian Empire, under Alexander the Great.

Philip II of Macedon, Alexander's father, who ruled from 359 until his murder in 336, established thorough control over the hill tribes of Macedon, reformed the army of the state, opened gold mines which made the state rich, subdued Thrace, and became the archon of Thessaly. In 338, after the Battle of Cheronea, he became ruler of Greece and head of the League of Corinth. As such, with a Macedonian garrison at Ambracia, he controlled the west; another garrison at Corinth held the Peloponnese; and a third at Chalcis observed Athens and the northeast. The next year, 337, at the second meeting of the League's Congress, Philip announced his intention of invading Persia, in behalf of Greece and her gods, to liberate the Greek cities of Asia and to punish the barbarians for acts of sacrilege wrought in the time of Xerxes. The federal gathering voted for the war and elected Philip as general with full powers, and arranged for contingents of men and ships. The proclaimed purposes of Philip were accepted by the Congress but it is probable that a more profound reason was the hope of the economic advantage. Greece was now united and practically under the rule of an efficient master. It was enjoying the economic advantages belonging to internal tranquillity and good order. The Persian Empire was losing its cohesion and the strength of Greece under Philip now seemed equal to extending unity of political control over Asia Minor with the consequent economic advantages to the merchants and shipping of Greece, who were to provide the armaments to extend the King's peace as far as Persia proper. Early in 336 Philip sent an advance force under Parmenio to hold the Asiatic side of the Hellespont for the passage of the main army, but he was assassinated a little later and in consequence the unity of the Greek world was on the point of breaking.

Philip's successor, his son Alexander, now only 20 years old, had first to secure his position. Alexander found the confederation of Corinth unfavorable to him, the peoples of Thrace (see Maps 1 and 2) rebelled, and Greece was urged to throw off Macedonian control and expel the garrisons. Thessaly was also rising. Alexander marched south from Pella, his capital, and Thessaly accepted him without bloodshed, late in the summer of 336. As he proceeded south, Athens sent an embassy and the Congress, meeting at Corinth, elected him general in his father's place, so he could go out against Persia as the head of Hellas rather than as Macedonian King. But it was necessary to reduce Thrace. This occupied the summer of 335. In the meantime agitation against Alexander was proceeding in Greece aided by Persian subsidies, for the new King of Persia saw the need of keeping Alexander occupied in Europe, instead of following Parmenio across the Hellespont. Thebes led in the insurrection and Alexander appeared before the city unexpectedly. He gave the citizens time to submit, but they were obstinate and the city was stormed and destroyed by the Macedonians; only the house of the poet Pindar being spared by the express order of Alexander. The winter of 335-334 was spent in preparations for the eastern adventure.

In the spring of 334 Alexander departed from Europe which he never saw again, with a force of about 30,000 infantry and 5,000 horse, leaving nearly half the national Macedonian army behind him under Antipater to hold Greece loyal. The army was not all Macedonian. There were contingents from the cities of the League and mercenary troops from all Greece. The cavalry was largely Thessalian. The apparent weak point in the arrangements was the small navy. To preserve his indispensable communications with his base in Macedonia, Alexander had at first only 60 ships, whereas the Egyptian, Phoenician, and Ionic squadrons of Persia numbered 400. It is true that the League of Corinth, of which Alexander was the elected general, had many ships. Athens alone had

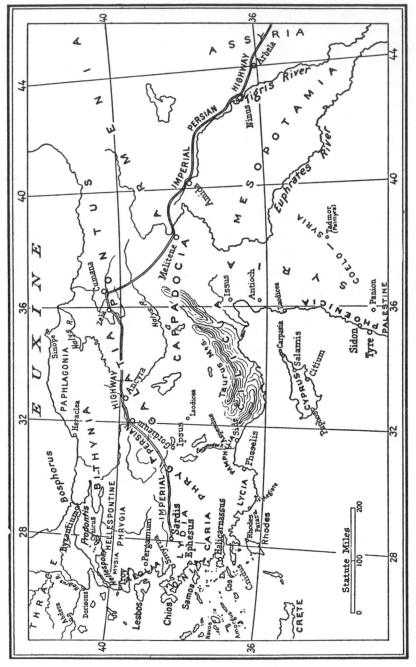

MAP 15. ASIA MINOR

200 but, in order to conciliate Greece which had so recently opposed King Philip and himself, he made no call on the League for its fleets.

The army crossed into Asia at Sestos-Abydos without resistance, while Alexander crossed at Troy to render honors to Achilles. The Persian fleet was not present in the Hellespont to defend Asia. Shortly after landing, Alexander met the enemy on the Granicus River about 50 miles from Abydos. The Persian army of about 40,000 was under the command of a group of satraps and generals among whom the ablest was Memnon, the Rhodian. The Persian fleet having failed to intercept the Macedonians at the Hellespont, Memnon proposed that the army should retreat before Alexander and lay waste the country, while the powerful fleet should operate on the coast of Greece and even escort a Persian army there to raise insurrection. In view of the state of minds in Greece, such a strategy was most promising, but the Persian leaders were chivalrous. Arsites, the local satrap, refused to lay waste his province and the council adopted the bold and simple plan of offering battle to the enemy as he crossed the Granicus while the leaders themselves were to seek out Alexander in personal combat and, by killing him, they hoped to end the war. Their scheme failed; they met Alexander in the front of battle, but were themselves slain and their army defeated.

Thereupon Alexander moved upon Sardis, the great capital of Lydia, and from there he proceeded to the Ionian coast and laid siege to Miletus. At Miletus the Greek commander of the Persian garrison at first meant to surrender, but learning that the powerful Persian fleet was approaching from Syria and Cilicia he stood a siege. In his need, Alexander was able to assemble a naval force of 160 ships which by its presence prevented the Persian fleet from throwing re-enforcements into the city, and he took it.

Alexander was nearly bankrupt. To succeed in his military effort to conquer the Persian Empire, Alexander had to restore the business of the Mediterranean, and so become solvent himself; and politically he had to make the sea-coast inhabitants satisfied. Sea power was a necessity to him.

Yet the King now dismissed all his fleet except 20 Athenian ships. His Graeco-Macedonian fleet must have cost him fully 250 talents a month. This reduction of the navy was not militarily unwise. Alexander had hostages for the good behavior of Greece in army contingents from

Greek cities as well as in the Athenian ships he retained. Moreover, the proclamation of democratic rule that he made to the Greek cities of Ionia as he came south had shaken the Persian hold on them so that their squadrons in the Persian fleet were no longer reliable. The Cyprians and the Phoenicians were also ill-disposed to Persia. But besides all this, it is probable that Alexander saw that he could best gain the necessary sea power to assure his communications with Europe by a military advance along the shores of the Levant until he had secured all the naval bases of the Persian Empire and that he could do this before the Persian fleet operating in the Aegean could inflict irreparable damage there.

Accordingly, Alexander set out along the south coast of Asia Minor while Memnon, who had now been made commander in chief of all the Persian forces by sea and land, gained minor successes in the Aegean. Memnon overran Lesbos and laid siege to Mytilene but died before its capture, and with his death the strategic effort of Persia to develop a counter-attack against Europe through mobility of sea power ended. It had been a danger that Memnon's success might start an outbreak in Greece, but the few ships that he sent over to Greece for that purpose were captured by a small Macedonian squadron. In his eastward march along the southern seaports of Asia Minor, Alexander met King Darius at Issus at the gates of Cilicia and gained his second great victory in October, 333 B.C. This battle cleared the way for the Macedonian army to occupy Syria and seize the Phoenician and Egyptian ports and thus establish its own sea power and sure communications with Macedon. Business revival was on its way, behind his advance.

Siege of Tyre

Tyre, the chief maritime city of Phoenicia, resolved to resist the conqueror, although a part of its fleet was absent, acting ineffectually against him in the Aegean, for Persia was not yet subdued and Tyre was unwilling to compromise herself by an early adherence to Macedon. The principal part of the city was on a rocky island of nearly 150 acres in area, about one-third of a mile from the shore, and was surrounded by high walls of heavy masonry. It had two harbors well sheltered, the Sidonian Harbor to the north, the Egyptian to the south. The squadron remaining on home duty numbered 80 ships. Such a strong home squadron shows the importance of the navy in those times as a defense against pirates and as the necessary protector of trade. This commercial city, while sending its contingent to the imperial navy to engage in distant service, was obliged to keep a great force at hand to cover local trade. Other maritime cities were obliged to act in the same way. Navies then were the chief guardians of peaceful commerce and business prosperity.

With only the few ships that Alexander had retained after taking Miletus, he could neither isolate the city by blockade nor reach it with his mechanical artillery. His only means of attack was to build a mole. This he did without much difficulty at first, for the workers did not embarrass themselves with armor; but as the work approached the island his men came within range of the enemy; and even earlier the Tyrian squadron could lie near the mole on both sides and annoy the workers while they were still

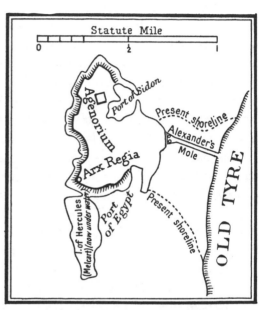

MAP 16. PLAN OF TYRE

outside the range of archers (200 yards) on the city walls. Alexander replied by building towers carrying catapults along the mole and hanging leather screens to protect both the towers and the workers from the hostile projectiles. The Tyrians arranged a fireship carrying combustible ahead of herself on her yard arm and trimmed her by the stern so that her bow would be above water. With this ship they charged the mole and set her on fire while the crew swam out of her and were covered by the missiles of their supporting squadron. The siege towers thus were destroyed.

Thereupon Alexander turned to widening his mole so that more men and more throwing machines could find place on it to face the city defenses, but he saw that he must have a fleet to overcome the local counter-attack of the Tyrian ships. He went off to Sidon to collect a fleet while his engineers made additional machines. By this time his military success along the coast of Asia Minor and his political concessions to the democratic parties in the seaport towns were reaping reward. All the Phoenician squadrons, except that of Tyre, joined him at Sidon together with ships from Rhodes, Lycia, Cilicia, and from the Kings of Cyprus. In all he gathered 250 ships, great and small, and returned to Tyre, where he assumed personal command of the Phoenician squadron by his prerogative as claimant to the Persian throne and placed himself on the south side of the mole, blockading the Egyptian port while the Cyprians and others to the north of the mole observed the Sidonian port. As soon as the new machines were ready, Alexander put some on the mole and others he mounted on ships lashed together in pairs to make more stable platforms. To meet the new attack the defenders had built similar towers and machines on their walls and had sown the harbor bed with bowlders[1] (an early forerunner of mines) to obstruct the movements of the hostile ships. But Alexander brought up sweepers to drag the bowlders away. Tyrian divers cut the anchor cables of the sweepers so that they had no purchase for sweeping. Then the Macedonians substituted chain cables which the divers could not cut and at last the rocks were out and the battleships could move to the attack of the walls.

Before these Macedonian preparations were complete, the Tyrians arranged for a final naval counter-attack. It was the custom of the times for fleets to dine on shore and take a siesta afterwards. The Tyrian ships in the Sidonian Harbor spread all their sails one morning, apparently to dry, as was still the custom a few years ago. Behind this screen, 13 ships with choice crews made ready for a surprise attack on the Cyprian fleet in the heat of the day. It was a success, some Cyprian ships partly manned were sunk and the fight grew about others on the beach as their crews ran to them.

Coming from his tent, Alexander saw the disturbance and led some of the best of the Phoenician division around the island while its main body guarded the exit from the Egyptian Harbor. He had over 2 miles to go to reach the fight and must have arrived at least three-quarters of an

---

[1] The bowlders cannot have weighed more than a few tons. Consequently, the water can little have exceeded 9 ft. The work for divers and pile drivers was not of great difficulty.

hour after the action began. The citizens on the walls saw his movements and signaled in vain to their vessels to warn them. Alexander was able to interpose between them and the harbor and the greater part were cut off. Thereafter the Tyrian ships remaining were not active.

The Macedonian engineers were now able to press the siege works without meeting flank attacks from the sea, but as the mole drew near the Tyrians threw fire and hot sand which got inside men's armor and scorched. The weakest part of the eastern wall proved to be south of the mole and there a bit of the wall was broken. Alexander prepared to assault this point from the sea. The ships carrying the siege engines were brought up to the wall and two ships, with assaulting troops led by Alexander himself, lay in readiness. Strong divisions of the fleet lay opposite the two harbor mouths to force their obstructions at the proper moment and other ships reached around the island to command all the walls with their missiles and draw off the attention of the defenders from the main attack.

Finally the breach was ready and the transports charged in and threw out their gangways to the wall. Alexander was the first to cross and enter the breach and lead his storming party to the palace but the city was entered elsewhere, also. The chains of both harbors had been broken by the Cyprian and Phoenician squadrons, the Tyrian ships had been overpowered and the victorious crews landed and pressed into the town. Of the Tyrians 8,000 were killed in the town, 2,000 were later executed, and the rest of the people, 30,000 in number, were sold as slaves. The siege had lasted for 7 months till the summer of 332.

The conquest of Tyre, which the ancients regarded as the most renowned siege known to them, was rendered possible by Alexander's fleet and was remarkable for the fact that on both sides attack and counter-attack on the military works were carried out by ships acting against infantry behind their defenses. It was largely owing to the small draft of the ships that this could be done. The men on board could be brought so close to the shore that they could step overboard in 2 or 3 feet of water, while their supporters remaining on board had the advantage of a higher position to shoot down on the enemy on the beach. The ships' tops gave high archers' stations for shooting against the walls. The naval battles of the siege were in substance those of infantry, with the ships as conveyors and artillery platforms, and the military inventions of Dionysius were developed and extended to aid the infantry assaults.

Alexander was now able to march into Egypt after an action at Gaza, and Alexandria was founded as a commercial center in a favorable position for its harbor to avoid silt from the Nile.

Egypt readily surrendered. Alexander's control of the navies and the commerce of the Eastern Mediterranean was now complete.

It was the re-establishment of business in the Mediterranean basin that restored his finances and enabled him to proceed. Leaving in Egypt a small garrison and his new organization of government, Alexander passed on to the destruction of the Persian Empire and the establishment of the Macedonian dynasty as far as India. Until his death early in 323, the question of sea power is not brought out in the histories of the time, although his Admiral Nearchus was employed to open sea routes to commerce. After Alexander's death, when his Empire was divided, sea power played a great part in the struggles of his Successors for mastery.

PRINCIPAL AUTHORITIES CONSULTED FOR THIS CHAPTER

ANCIENT

Arrian: *Anabasis.*
Diodorus Siculus.
Plutarch: *Alexander.*

MODERN

Bury, J. B.: *History of Greece.*
Delbrueck, H.: *Geschichte der Kriegskunst.*
Kromayer, J.: *Antike Schlachtfelder.*
          Schlachten Atlas.
Tarn, W. W.: *Cambridge Ancient History,* vol. 6.

CHAPTER IX

THE NAVAL WARS OF THE SUCCESSORS
OF ALEXANDER

ECONOMIC SITUATION

UPON the death of Alexander his principal generals seized the main divisions of his Empire for their inheritance and warred with each other for over 40 years in unsuccessful attempts to reunite it. In studying the ancient histories of the time and the innumerable commentaries since then, we see something of the characters and intentions of the chief actors and much of the distress caused by their constant wars. We realize that the leaders fought for selfish and personal reasons, but it is not so apparent why their peoples were willing to support them.

At the time of Alexander's death in 323, he had given political unity and fairly good order to the world about the Eastern Mediterranean. Greece had apparently been somewhat overpopulated; he had found occupation for the excess laborers in his armies, and the result of their victories had quickened the economic pulse of the world. The armies brought good order in the train of their victories and the Greek cities built up as colonies in Asia and Africa gave not only a political hold on the surrounding areas, but promoted commerce as a supporter of industry and as a chief agent in individual and national prosperity. In the usual picture that historians make of the times after Alexander, we see only the great leaders. As we readily understand, they wanted power, but their followers, whose names we do not know, they, too, looked for profit and expected to find it, although often disappointed, in the control of over-seas trade, which Alexander's conquests had done so much to facilitate and increase. The merchants of each great seaport city hoped to obtain, or to retain, a monopoly of ocean trade for their own city and its business allies. For this object they lent their support and money to the wars of Alexander's Successors, the Diadochoi.

What is known of the economic life of the peoples of those days has been recovered in great measure from the monuments and papyri discovered in Egypt. Contemporary historians did not dwell much on this subject. Plato and Aristotle wrote on the ideal city, but had less to say of the current conditions which they wished to idealize. They both were critics of the democratic city which had turned itself into a loose commercial association and cast away moral purpose. A paragraph in Aristotle's works indicates something of the situation. He speaks of the natural slave as "a man whose chief use is his body, but who possesses mind enough, not indeed to control himself but, to understand and profit by the control of a superior mind." In the histories we see the great leaders and the thousands unnamed who tilled the fields and worked the mines and manned the armies and the fleets, but we see nothing or little of the superior minds who interposed between the heads of states and the natural slaves and directed the latter, in mind and body.

We are told that the Greeks did not care for manual labor; that means of course that the "superior minds" did not care to work at handicrafts. Their field was what is known in business today as "management," which then had two sides, mutually helpful, that brought economic prosperity to the managers. They were (1) the maintenance of law and order (with peace when practicable) both in cities and on the seas; and (2) the monopoly of commerce, particularly over-seas commerce. As President Hoover said when he laid the corner stone of the new commerce building, June 10, 1929, "successful economic life underlies advancement in every other field." Then, as today, the great profits of business were on the side of the middleman, of the distributor of goods rather than of the producer, and in those times the monopoly of trading privilege was the chief way to success for those who could seize it. Our present-day methods have reduced the power of the ruler and his armed subordinates to grow rich and to confer riches by granting monopolies to their friends, although we still have "graft." But then government and prosperous business were in closer alliance. The conquests of Alexander improved the opportunities in the times of his Successors for profitable mercantile adventures by rulers and their merchant princes. Unfortunately, the expenses of establishing monopoly were great, as the historians tell us in their accounts of the wars, but they leave us to divine the hopes of economic profit which urged on the ruling classes.

The conquest of the decaying Persian Empire by Alexander was politically maintained by the train of Greek and Macedonian colonies along the trade routes connecting India and China with the basin of the Mediterranean. These cities increased trade and controlled it for Greek profit. There were two routes from India. The southern one was by sea around Arabia into the Red Sea to Berenice, a point about two-thirds its length from the entrance, and then across by caravan to the Nile and so by river to Alexandria and the sea. The other route was also by sea to the lower part of the Persian Gulf and then across Arabia by caravan to Syria and the Phoenician ports on the sea. The trade of the Euphrates Valley also went to Syria (later to Antioch) and the sea. China silks crossed the Caspian Sea to the Euxine and the shores of Asia Minor. All this great trade was distributed to Mediterranean markets by sea, while the raw products of Spain and Mauritania went in the opposite direction. The strong local governments made trade fairly safe and the fleets of the King and of the great seaport cities kept down piracy to reasonable losses that business could stand. This vast increase of business was made profitable to governments and monopolists. We read, for instance, of the guilds of Phoenician merchants established in the islands and cities of the Aegean to hold business for their city as well as for themselves. Again, we read that during a shortage of crops in Greece lasting from 330 to 326, Cleomenes, Alexander's treasurer in Egypt, who seems to have had good information service in Greece, shipped Egyptian grain to ports where the price was momentarily the highest.

At the close of Alexander's reign the political question arising out of his death was whether his Empire could hold together as an economic and political whole; or if it was to break up, was Egypt or Asia Minor to control the distribution of eastern trade throughout the Mediterranean world? If the break up should come to pass, the holders of the rival routes to the East each wanted good business connections to the West, either by ruling Greece or by alliance with the ruling authority. The purposes of Alexander's Successors were probably little different from that of the recent Farm Act of the United States in which it is

declared to be the policy of Congress to promote the effective merchandising of agricultural commodities in interstate and foreign commerce * * * by encouraging the organization of producers into effective associations * * * for greater unity of effort in marketing.

The methods of the Successors, however, are rather to be found in the practices of the present military governors of the provinces of China. There the war is burdensome, but it is not destroying all wealth nor all idealism as the vast monument to Sun-Yat-Sen shows. The style, however, of the Chinese as compared with that of the Successors is somewhat cramped by the flotillas of gunboats and the garrisons in Peking belonging to the great powers.

These remarks about the economics of the third century B.C are made to enable the reader in the following pages to see the economic objective as directing the movements of the various campaigns and particularly the naval ones. In many cases the appearance of the fleet in certain waters and its occupation of the local seaports secured the economic control of the region which usually comes from occupation of the territory by an army.

Changes at Alexander's Death

Sea power as the foundation of economic prosperity was thoroughly understood by Alexander. He intended to make Babylon a great seaport such as Chicago hopes to become, with a great canal to the sea. His sudden death at Babylon in 323 took place a few days before he was intending to set out on an expedition to the south for the conquest of Arabia, by which he would assure the junction of the trade of India with that of the Mediterranean and supervise and control it from Babylon. His death threw all into confusion, for there were no arrangements for carrying on the administration of the Empire. On his death bed Alexander had given his ring as token of authority to Perdiccas, his senior general, who was probably desirous of holding the Empire together, but others did not agree with him. Among those at Babylon who did not believe the Empire could continue to cohere was Ptolemy, a brigade commander and "body-guard" of the King, who from the first seems to have resolved to be the independent ruler of an independent state in Egypt.

But the great men of Alexander were not all in Babylon. Antipater, the last of King Philip's men, was Regent of Macedonia and Governor of Greece. The throne being vacant, it was the prerogative of the whole army including the troops in Macedonia to elect a King. While both Perdiccas and Antipater were favorable to the dynasty, it had to be decided whether the Empire was to be ruled conservatively from Macedon, or from

Babylon with oriental policies such as Alexander had initiated. There were already groupings between those who favored one policy or the other.

Perdiccas, as the holder of Alexander's signet ring, called a council of the generals at Babylon. It was agreed that if the Queen's expected child was a son he should be King. But the army could not be assembled to ratify the decision, so Eumenes, a Greek, secretary to the late King and devoted to his dynasty, arranged a compromise between Antipater's conservative party and that of the oriental-minded liberals with Perdiccas as their head, whereby Philip Arrhidaeus, Alexander's half-wit brother, and the expected heir were to be joint Kings. Antipater was to be general in Europe. Perdiccas was to be chiliarch (vizier) in Asia and general of the army there, while the regency was to be in commission between the two. The weak point in the arrangement was that the relations of Perdiccas and Antipater were not clearly defined in the agreement. Probably it was owing to this weakness that the compromise was possible. Although both regents stood for the Kings, they soon quarreled.

After some bargaining, Perdiccas allotted the Persian satrapies to be held under him. Ptolemy received Egypt, where he proceeded to establish his authority with little regard to the unity of the Empire. Antigonus, a great soldier, added Lycia and Pamphylia to Phrygia which he already held. Leonnatus took Hellespontine Phrygia. Eumenes received Cappadocia, Paphlagonia, and Pontus. In Europe Thrace was taken from Antipater and given to Lysimachus. Seleucus was given a cavalry command. In this distribution of territory we may trace the subsequent political groupings. For the moment the leaders of the Macedonian army had established two parties, each desiring rulership within the Empire and, as a third factor, Ptolemy, who meant to hold his province outside the Empire and yet was to find himself constantly called upon to exert the balance of power within the Empire to preserve his own authority and the economic leadership of Egypt in world trade.

The arrangements made at Babylon were short-lived. The individual leaders of the Macedonian armies and governors of provinces sought to improve their personal positions and a general war among them began which lasted for 40 years with only short intervals. During the first 8 years the accounts of military events are somewhat meager and the movements of individuals from side to side are confusing. At the end of the 8 years the triple division of Alexander's Empire into the great states of Macedon, Asia, and Egypt is clearly defined. The strategy of these years is apparent enough and depended on sea power to a great extent. I shall therefore attempt to give a brief summary of the more important developments.

REVOLT OF GREECE

As soon as the news of Alexander's death reached Europe, the nominally free allies of the Empire saw an opportunity of breaking from it. An assembly of the people of Athens declared their aim was the common freedom of Greece and the liberation of its cities from the regent Antipater's garrisons. Really, Athens was thinking of re-establishing her commercial connections with Samos and the trade of Asia Minor (see Maps 2 and 4). The city picked up an army of discharged veterans and manned her great fleet. It was the summer of 323 and an alliance of Greek cities was formed. Antipater did not have a strong force and was driven into the city of Lamia near the Thessalian border, where he waited for assistance from the rulers of Asia. To stop such help, the Athenians sent their fleet under Euetion to the crossing place in the Hellespont. Antipater had a considerable navy of his own and was re-enforced after some delay by a part of the imperial fleet under Cleitus. In the late spring of 322 Cleitus defeated Euetion off Abydos and the way was open for an army of time-expired veterans under Craterus to enter Europe and relieve Antipater. By a great effort the Athenians put forth another great fleet to isolate Europe from the Macedonian armies in Asia and in July, 322, again Cleitus defeated Euetion, this time off Amorgos (60 miles southwest of Samos) and destroyed forever the sea power of Athens. Cleitus then blockaded Athens and, as the Greek allies had lost the sea, the Peloponnesians could not pass Antipater's garrison at Corinth and the Greek cause was defeated at Crannon. Not only had the Macedonian fleet made possible the victory of Crannon, but thenceforward the commerce of Greece with the Western Mediterranean was under Macedonian protection and supervision. Greek merchants stood in with the Macedonian government. Antipater was firm in his European base and took the profits arising from unity of trade control from the Aegean westward.

The War in Asia

Disturbance in Asia followed that in Greece. In the spring of 322 the regent Perdiccas broke with Antigonus who fled to Antipater and reported that Perdiccas was aiming at the throne. Antipater allied himself with Ptolemy, ruler of Egypt, to preserve the Empire, although Ptolemy wished for an independent Egypt. Both Asia and Egypt wanted good connections with the western commerce controlled through Macedon, and moreover, Asiatic and Egyptian rulers wanted to control Macedon and Greece whence came the good soldiers who were the foundation of law and order throughout the area of Alexander's Empire.

Perdiccas, holding the central position in Asia Minor, had to keep Antipater in Europe and Ptolemy in Egypt from uniting their forces. Antipater made Antigonus his general in Asia and the latter's first step was to seize the Syrian trade route from the East. He took the greater part of the Macedonian fleet to Cyprus where he met Ptolemy and the sea kings of the island, and the united fleets blocked the Phoenician sea ways. The allies ruled the commerce of the Levant. As his first step in the war, Perdiccas sent his lieutenant, Eumenes, to recruit an army to oppose Antipater's entry into Asia, while Perdiccas himself marched through Syria to conquer Egypt. Perdiccas failed to make good his crossing into Egypt at the eastern branch of the Nile and was killed in a mutiny of his soldiers (year 321). As Eumenes was slow in creating his army, Antipater crossed into Asia without opposition and with little difficulty he arrived in Syria where he was met by the armies of Asia and Egypt and the whole Macedonian army being there assembled, it constitutionally elected Antipater as sole regent. Antipater then retired to Macedon with the two Kings (year 320) and there reversed Alexander's policy of a joint Empire of Europe and Asia in favor of the sovereignty of Macedon. Antipater left Antigonus to rule in Asia where he put down insurrections and by the end of 320 he had the strongest army in the Empire. The separation of the Empire into three realms all desirous of controlling commerce was now a fact although not so acknowledged. The next year (319) Antipater died and with his death the nominal bond of Empire broke. Antigonus and Ptolemy pushed the forces of disruption.

Ptolemy saw an opportunity for himself and invaded Syria, annexing the whole province and making himself master of the whole trade of the Levant, holding the route eastward through Syria as well as the Egyptian one through the Red Sea. Polyperchon, the new regent in Macedonia, aided by Eumenes in Asia, was opposed by Antigonus in Asia and by Antipater's son Cassander in Europe. The regent was fighting to maintain the Empire. Cassander wanted to rule in Macedon and Antigonus wished to hold Asia.

In 318 the war was well on. The result depended greatly on sea power. Cleitus, with the Macedonian fleet, went to the Hellespont to block Antigonus' effort to enter Europe with his great army. Nicanor, with Cassander's ships from Athens and others of Antigonus from the south of Asia Minor, went to the Hellespont in pursuit of Cleitus to open the sea for Antigonus' army. The two fleets met in the Bosphorus and Nicanor lost about half his vessels; yet, nevertheless, Antigonus put some light troops into Europe by the help of transports furnished by the city of Byzantium. He then placed good troops on the remaining ships of Nicanor for a joint attack on the Macedonian fleet. At dawn he surprised the enemy in camp with the ships drawn up on the beach in fancied security after the recent victory. The simultaneous attacks by sea and land destroyed the Macedonian fleet just as the Athenians had been destroyed at Aegospotami a century before. The naval victory was conclusive, for Antigonus could now keep Polyperchon and Eumenes apart by his fleet and deal with each separately. He hurried south against Eumenes, stopped the latter's construction of a fleet in Phoenicia, and drove him to Babylon, where he was supported by the eastern Satraps, and then early in 316 defeated him and took over his army, near the present Ispahan, and then killed him. Antigonus occupied Babylon.

In the meantime, Cassander had seized Athens with a small force in 318, and in the spring of 317 he entered Macedon and drove out Polyperchon and won Thessaly and much of Greece. He now claimed to be successor to King Philip II and was no more an ally of Antigonus. Polyperchon was rather inclined to neglect big business, to which Cassander was more favorable and to this policy the latter's success was largely due (see Diodorus, end of 18th book). With the disappearance of the regent the division of the Empire was completely effected, to last until the Romans crossed the Adriatic.

Antigonus Attempts to Dominate the Empire

The death of Eumenes left Antigonus with 60,000 troops and 25,000 talents to run his administration. He occupied the summer of 316 in securing his authority throughout Asia and drove out Seleucus, the satrap of Babylon, announcing that he ruled the whole Empire in the name of Alexander's son who was in Europe out of his control. The opposition between Antigonus and Cassander became clear as both claimed to succeed Alexander.

After leaving Babylon, Seleucus escaped to Ptolemy and persuaded him that the ambition of Antigonus threatened the power of all the other Successors. Ptolemy made an alliance with Cassander and with Lysimachus of Thrace whose possessions controlled the Bosphorus passage. The three sent an ultimatum to Antigonus requiring him to yield to them a large part of his territory, so that his remaining possessions would be cut off from the sea and from the interior of Greater Asia, thus isolating his domains from the main trade routes between the East and the West. Such an economic situation Antigonus refused to accept and he countered in 315 by sending envoys to Greece to raise an insurrection against Cassander. Besides, he sent a squadron to the Hellespont to hold the passage into Asia against any attempt by Cassander to cross. This done, Antigonus turned upon Ptolemy to regain the Phoenician seaports and the prosperous commerce they controlled. It was Antigonus' ultimate intention to cross the Hellespont with his great army and rule in Europe too, but for the summer of 315 he marched his main army into Syria and besieged Tyre, while he directed the other Phoenician cities to build him a great fleet to control the sea routes out of Syria and to interpose by sea between Ptolemy and Cassander. As Antigonus approached Syria, Ptolemy garrisoned Tyre and retired with its fleet into Egypt.

In the meantime the attempt of Antigonus to raise an insurrection in Greece was successful. He declared the cities free from Macedonia and carried out this policy honestly and considerately, following the example of Alexander. Thus Antigonus possessed seaports on the mainland of Asia Minor, connecting with those of Greece and the West, but for the moment Ptolemy had the advantage in ships ready for service. He sent 100 ships to Cyprus with 10,000 soldiers and won its Kings to his cause and there they were joined by a fleet that Seleucus had brought from

Egypt. From Cyprus a squadron of 50 ships was sent to aid Cassander to subdue the Peloponnese and the rest of Ptolemy's fleet was to hold Cyprus and the southern coasts of Asia Minor. The purpose was, of course, to operate against Antigonus' communications by sea.

By this time Antigonus had been joined at Tyre by 40 ships from the Hellespont and Rhodes and 80 more under Dioscorides, his nephew. With 120 more that he had built in Phoenicia, by the fall of 314 he had a fleet of 240 ships, including 97 trieres, 90 tetreres, 10 penteres, 3 henneres, 10 deceres, and 30 light ships. But by this time the siege of Tyre was over, the city having surrendered upon terms, and Antigonus withdrew his main army to Phrygia for the winter of 314-313, leaving his son Demetrius at Gaza to watch Ptolemy and confine him to Egypt. Antigonus now controlled the overland route to the East. He still had to secure a trade route through the Mediterranean.

Struggle of Antigonus and Ptolemy to Control the Sea Routes to the Western Mediterranean

Of the new fleet, 50 ships were sent to Peloponnese to support the insurrection against Cassander, and the rest Antigonus put under his nephew, Dioscorides, to guard the seas, that is, to gain the islands and keep open the line of communications to the west against Ptolemy's efforts from Cyprus to interrupt it. In the spring of 313 Antigonus set three expeditions on foot—one to the Thracian Black Sea coasts was to raise an insurrection to draw Lysimachus from the Hellespont; another freed Miletus and reduced Caria; the third attacked Cassander in Greece. Ptolemy was occupied with an insurrection in Cyrene, which was ultimately successful, and he could send little aid to Cassander and Lysimachus.

The military object of Antigonus was to get his main army into Europe. The insurrection he was supporting in Greece had some success and Cassander was anxious to cut off the support it was receiving by sea. As a fleet and army of Antigonus under one Perilaus were moving in company westward along the south coast of Asia Minor, seemingly for the purpose of patrol, a body of Egyptian troops was ferried over from Cyprus, escorted by a squadron under Polyclitus. He placed his soldiers in ambush along the hostile line of march and concealed his fleet also behind a neighboring point. As Perilaus came up, his soldiers were cut to pieces by the ambush and, when the fleet went to their assistance, the Egyptian fleet came round the point upon its rear and it also was wiped out. Nevertheless, Cassander was scarcely holding his own in Greece and made overtures for peace, which were refused. He then boldly invaded Euboea. Antigonus sent 5,500 men and his fleet of 150 ships to drive Cassander out of Euboea, and, as soon as he thought Cassander fully engaged there, he withdrew his fleet to the Hellespont and sought a crossing into Europe with the aid of the city of Byzantium. But he had delayed too long. Lysimachus had been absent from the Hellespont upon a successful campaign against the insurrection in the North, which Antigonus had fomented, but had now returned and was able to prevent the crossing. Although Antigonus had obliged Cassander to withdraw from Greece and his fleet controlled Central Greece, yet the former's sea power had not served to bring his great army into action in Europe.

Still, by the end of 313, Cassander was much shaken and appealed to Ptolemy to do something for his allies. In the spring of 312 Ptolemy, with 18,000 infantry and 4,000 horse, attacked Antigonus' holding force at Gaza under his son Demetrius, which had been there for more than a year. Demetrius had little over two-thirds the men, but a number of elephants. Ptolemy used a movable barrier of iron (seemingly chained caltrops) to check the elephants and defeated Demetrius, who got away to Cilicia with only a few cavalry. The retirement of Demetrius from Syria relieved Cassander and also opened the way for Seleucus (who had been with Ptolemy) to make a dash for Babylon, and the date of his entry marks the beginning of the Seleucid era in Asia Minor (October, 312). In the rest of 312, Antigonus recovered Syria and Phoenicia, but this effort in the South cost Antigonus his opportunity in Europe and the war languished.

By 311 it was clear that neither side could thoroughly defeat the other and Antigonus made peace with Cassander and Lysimachus and later with Ptolemy, but he did not give up his claim to Babylon. In four years Antigonus' main army had never been engaged and he had lost the eastern Satrapies, but had Syria, Phoenicia, and Caria instead. Cassander had lost much of Greece, whose released cities were favorable to Antigonus, but still held Athens. Lysimachus had consolidated his situation in Thrace. Ptolemy had gained Cyprus, counter-balancing the loss of Cyrene and Syria. Rhodes retained its independence and its commercial importance. Antigonus had not had sufficient sea power to force his way into Europe, and he was obliged to postpone his ambition.

Still Antigonus controlled the Phoenician trade with the East, although Ptolemy at Alexandria lay athwart his Mediterranean lines through the latter's control of Cyprus and neither had a monopoly either of Mediterranean trade or of the routes to the East. The war was a draw.

The Greek cities were Antigonus' free allies. As he could not revive the League of Corinth, he made the Cyclades into a League of Islanders with its seat at Delos and he revived the Ionian League. He desired sea power and this was his way of keeping Ptolemy out of the central base offered by Delos. He founded many cities and simpified trade arrangements, and made cities which needed corn buy up that paid as taxes by tenants of the "King's lands." Although he desired to promote prosperity, his wars and war contributions had put many cities into debt. In modern phrase, the efforts of rulers for economic advantage had led them to overdo the effort to undersell each other. The military effort to seize commercial monopoly had been too expensive

PTOLEMY EXTENDS HIS SEA POWER

Although the peace of 311 was no more than a truce, yet it formally marked the dissolution of the Empire into different states. Cassander employed the peace in recuperation of his territory, but there was no real reconciliation between him and Antigonus. The latter attacked Seleucus in 310 and 309, but was unsuccessful. On the other hand, Ptolemy attacked Antigonus, nominally on Seleucus' behalf, but also to improve his communications with the Greek world. His fleet attempted to secure Cilicia, but was defeated by Demetrius. It then went to Cyprus and made that secure for Egypt. The next year Ptolemy got some bases in Cilicia and Caria, and Demetrius made peace with him late in 309.

Ptolemy now aimed to extend his commerce by controlling Greece and with it the commerce to Italy and the West. He spent the winter of 309-308 at Cos and in the spring of 308 crossed the Aegean with his fleet and freed Andros. Then going to the Isthmus of Corinth, he announced he had come to free Greece from Antigonus. He secured Corinth and Sicyon, but made no impression on the rest of Greece which trusted

Antigonus and his liberal policy. But the latter was roused by this attempt of Ptolemy and he gave out that he would drive Cassander and Ptolemy entirely out of Greece. He did not follow his plan in the previous war and attempt himself to cross into Europe. He proposed to raise Greece against Cassander and, when he was occupied, he would turn on Egypt and, after defeating Ptolemy, he would have the control of the sea to invade Macedon from Greece.

For 10 years Cassander had ruled Athens with Demetrius of Phalerum as governor. The administration was in the interest of the wealthy and, from their point of view, the city had never been governed so well. In June, 307, Antigonus' son Demetrius sailed for Athens with 250 warships and transports, found the obstructions open at the Piraeus, and entered the harbor and made the usual declaration that he had come to give back freedom and the ancestral constitution, the formula for overthrowing a tyrant. Athens was surrendered and Demetrius entered a free city. Antigonus sent the city 150,000 bushels of grain and timber for 100 ships. Demetrius ordered all free cities to support Athens and, when it was in all respects equipped for war with Cassander, he returned to Asia to attack Ptolemy.

CAMPAIGN OF CYPRIAN SALAMIS

In the spring of 306 Demetrius sailed for Cyprus, meaning to begin by cutting off the trade of Egypt with Europe. He first summoned Antigonus' former ally, Rhodes, to join him with her fleet, but her trade with Egypt was too important and Rhodes remained neutral. He then went to Cilicia and brought his forces to 15,000 foot, 500 horse, and a strong fleet of men-of-war and transport ships. He next proceeded to Cyprus and landed at Carpasia on the northeast point and dug a trench around his beached ships. Leaving a guard, he marched on Salamis where Menelaus, brother of Ptolemy, was lying with 12,000 infantry and 800 horse. Demetrius defeated Menelaus outside the city and drove him within the walls (see Map 15). Menelaus sent to Ptolemy to tell him of events and prepared to defend the town, while Demetrius sent to Syria to get material for building the most powerful siege engines, and pressed the attack with great vigor. Ptolemy came from Egypt with 10,000 soldiers in 200 transports and 140 tetreres and penteres and landed at Paphos at the far end of the island. He advanced to Citium only 29 miles away from Salamis, and sent to his brother to direct the 60 ships lying in the harbor to join his own in his intended sea battle.

Demetrius had taken some large ships in the ports of Cyprus when he landed, and now had available for battle 118 ships. Diodorus says that of these there were 7 Phoenician hepteres, 10 hexeres, 20 penteres, and 30 tetreres, and the rest were smaller. Demetrius divined Ptolemy's intention to get his brother's fleet to join his own and manned his ships with the best of his soldiers and placed his artillery on the forecastles of his ships ready to throw darts 2 feet long and stones. He then took station off the entrance to the port, so as to prevent the two hostile squadrons from effecting their junction, and spent the night just outside of range. In the morning he left 10 penteres under command of Antisthenes to remain deployed outside the harbor entrance, to contain the 60 ships of Menelaus should they attempt to issue in column as they would be obliged to do. With the main body of the fleet Demetrius moved south along the coast, to seek the enemy, and was accompanied along the shore by a strong detachment of the besieging army to help men swimming ashore, only enough men being left in the trenches to resist a sortie of the garrison. On the other hand, Ptolemy got under way from Citium with his fleet and the troop transports, hoping to arrive at the entrance to Salamis before the enemy and land his soldiers. It seems probable that, owing to the long tongue of land reaching seaward between Salamis and Citium, Ptolemy must have left his anchorage the day before and stopped for at least a part of the night before going forward for a morning entrance into Salamis Harbor. He would not wish to keep his rowers working for many hours before battle.

Thus it is probable that a runner brought Demetrius the news that Ptolemy was coming in time for the former to take a commanding position before the port, as mentioned earlier. Demetrius' plan of battle was to make his left wing strong where he was to station himself and, if possible, drive the enemy on the beach where the ships would meet his own army. The left wing of Demetrius was therefore composed of 7 hepteres and 30 tetreres supported by a second line of 10 hexeres and 10 penteres, making 57 in all. In the center were the smallest ships and the right was under the chief pilot Plistias of Cos, presumably because this wing needed more skillful navigation, being nearest the shore.

Demetrius Poliorcetes

Prow of his ship with winged victory

FROM A COIN

Ptolemy was disappointed in getting his re-enforcing troops into port before Demetrius could meet him, for dawn showed him the enemy not far away. He ordered the transports to remain at a distance and formed his fleet in line with the heaviest ships near shore in the left wing where he commanded in person. If Ptolemy did not double any part of his line, it must have extended not less than 4,500 to 5,000 yards. The line of battle of Demetrius must have been at least 3,000 yards long, with 88 ships in the front line. But it is likely the right wing was deployed at greater intervals than the left wing to reach the shore and that Demetrius' plan was to fight a delaying action with his much extended right wing and center, while his massed heavy ships with their powerful mechanical artillery and a second line in reserve decided victory on the seaward flank. The graphic details are given by Diodorus.

The fleets being deployed, the boatswains accordingly made the signal for prayers to the gods and the crews made the invocations aloud. The two fleets being then about 600 yards apart, Demetrius gave the signal to engage by hoisting a golden shield which was seen by all [and doubtless repeated by light craft in rear of the line]. Ptolemy did the same and the two fleets closed quickly with each other, as the trumpets sounded the charge and the crews cheered. The engagement opened with archery and stones and darts from the catapults, and many were wounded during the approach. Then contact was made, the rowers being incited by the boatswains to make their greatest exertions, and the men on deck fell on the enemy with spears. The first shock was violent, some ships had their oars swept from their sides and remained motionless with their soldiers out of action. Others, after striking, rowed astern to ram again and in the meantime the soldiers attacked each other hand to hand. Some captains struck their opponents broadside to broadside, and the ships being held in contact became so many fields of battle with the boarders leaping to the enemy's deck. In some cases these missed their footing and falling overboard were drowned, while others making good their foothold killed the enemy or drove them overboard. Many and varied were the fortunes of the ships. In one case a weaker crew was victorious owing to its higher deck and in another case the better crew lost because its decks were low. For luck has much to do in naval actions. On shore valor is pre-eminent, whereas at sea many accidents occur which bring ruin to those whose valor deserves success.

Among all the rest, Demetrius standing on the poop of a heptere showed brilliant courage. Surrounded by enemies, he struck them down with his own lance and avoided the missiles showered upon him, some by dodging and some by his defensive arms. Three body guards stood by him, one was killed with a lance thrust and the other two were wounded. At last Demetrius broke the wing opposing him and turned on the center. In the meantime, Ptolemy with his heaviest ships and best crews had been successful on his flank, sinking some, taking others with their crews, and putting the rest to flight. On turning back from pursuit to finish the battle he found the rest of his fleet defeated and he returned to Citium. Menelaus at Salamis directed his squadron of 60 ships to force its way out and join the fight down the coast. This it did, driving the blockading ships back to the support of their army on shore but, when Menelaus' ships arrived in the neighborhood of the battle, Demetrius was already successful and he returned to Salamis. Demetrius sent a part of his fleet to continue in pursuit and pick up swimmers and with the rest, decorated with booty and towing the prizes, he returned to his camp and the port which he had left. The prizes were 100 transports with 8,000 soldiers, 40 long ships with their crews, and 80 others seriously injured. Of the victorious fleet, 20 were badly damaged but all were made serviceable.

Ptolemy made no further effort to retain the island of Cyprus and all its cities and garrisons yielded themselves to Demetrius, so that Antigonus and his commercial friends were now predominant in eastern Mediterranean trade.

At the first (Greek) Salamis, in narrow waters, there was little maneuvering by the high command. At the second (Cyprian) Salamis a great seaman combined maneuver with skillful use of weapons. In his strong left wing he opened the battle during the approach by heavy mechanical artillery and archery and, after closing when the boarders' fight began, his lofty decks (probably no more than 2 feet higher) gave his soldiers the usual advantage of elevation in hand-to-hand fighting. Finally, when his massed attack overcame the hostile flank, he turned on the center and rolled it up until Ptolemy saw that he could not profit by his own initial local success. The command of the sea was settled for 20 years.

Antigonus Fails in Attempt to Invade Egypt

Antigonus took the title of King and granted it to his son, that is, he claimed to succeed Alexander and to rule with his son. The other Successors, not to be outclassed, did the same, and thus terminated all pretense that they were fighting for unity of the Empire. Ptolemy not only lost Cyprus, but also his bases in Asia Minor and, as he could no longer control Corinth, he ceded it to Cassander. Ptolemy's commerce was further handicapped by his inability to secure ship timber except through Rhodes, which was playing for prosperity through commerce and neutrality.

It was now late in 306 and the season was getting bad for naval operations; nevertheless, before winter, Antigonus attempted the invasion of Egypt with 88,000 men and 83 elephants, with Demetrius' fleet of 150 men-of-war and 100 transports accompanying him to provide supplies and military stores by sea. The army left Gaza with each man carrying 10 days' rations and the train of camels with 195,000 bushels of wheat (70 days' rations) and forage for the animals. Projectiles were carried on 2-horse carts.[1] The army got through the desert with some difficulty, but Demetrius loosing from Gaza, as soon as the Pleiades had set (i.e., end of October), was becalmed and his men-of-war had to tow the transports. After this, a heavy gale threw several tetreres on shore near the city of Raphia, whose port is difficult of entrance and surrounded by marshes. Some of the transports with munitions of war were also lost, but the rest got back to Gaza. Yet some of the best ships bore up before the gale and arrived at the promontory of Casius near the Nile. This was not a good shelter for shipping, as it could not be approached in bad weather, so these ships rode out the gale with two anchors about 400 yards from the shore which was held by the enemy. Three penteres were lost here, but some of their crews got alive through the breakers. But the worst was that their water gave out. Just as they were at the last of it, the storm ceased and Antigonus arrived with his army and drove away the enemy, and camped near the Nile.[2]

Ptolemy was holding the strong places to oppose his passage of the river, and also sent men to incite desertion among the enemy, and Antigonus lost many who accepted the offered reward. When the ships that had been delayed and driven back by the storm had come up, Demetrius attempted to land troops from his ships beyond the eastern branch of the Nile, but found the shore defended with troops and artillery. He drew back at nightfall and told his ships to follow his night lanterns and went on to the Phagnatic mouth of the Nile, but at daylight he found many ships missing and was obliged to wait. In the meantime Ptolemy

---

[1] The camels to carry the wheat mentioned above cannot have been fewer than 16,000 to 20,000 and the horses for the cavalry and draft as many more. Thus the drivers and camp followers must have brought the whole number of men of the army to well over 100,000, besides not less than 30,000 in the fleet. It seems, however, from what Diodorus says later, that he may have been in error in saying that all these supplies went by camel train. The ships must have carried most of them.

[2] The ships must have carried about 10 days' water.

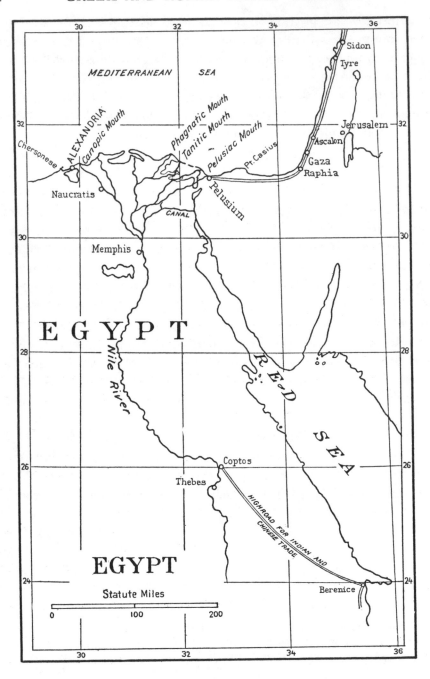

MAP 17.

arrived with his army and Demetrius withdrew with his ships to his father's camp, when a heavy gale came up and several transports were lost. Antigonus was now in a difficult situation; his army could not cross the Nile, nor could his son force an entrance with his ships. The supplies were also running short and Antigonus decided to return to Syria and wait for the flood of the river to subside. For the second time Ptolemy had made good his possession of Egypt.

Siege of Rhodes

Thus repulsed before the frontiers of Egypt, Antigonus now turned to Rhodes which, preferring neutrality, had refused to be his ally the year before when he attacked Ptolemy in Cyprus. Rhodes based its prosperity on its naval forces which suppressed piracy in all the neighboring waters and made the island an *entrepot* of commerce. It had been favored by Alexander, who had deposited his will there. The Rhodians endeavored to keep on friendly terms with all Alexander's Successors, and had been quite correct in their commercial relations, although showing some partiality for the Egyptian trade. During the Cyprian campaign Antigonus had given orders to intercept all shipping bound between Rhodes and Egypt and confiscate the cargoes, but the Rhodians had defeated the squadron sent for this purpose. Antigonus now (305) made this action a pretext for attacking the prosperous city which wished only for peace and freedom of trade, and sent Demetrius against it. At the appearance of his great force, the city offered to aid Antigonus in his war with Ptolemy, but Demetrius demanded hostages and the admission of his ships to the ports of the island. This the Rhodians refused, as they feared to lose their independence, and they prepared to meet his attack.

It was a false move on the part of Antigonus. He had not yet secured his supremacy over the Egyptian ruler and the others were ill-disposed to admit his claims. It was not the time to embarrass himself over a commercial city which would not take action against him and which wished only to carry on trade and had little military strength outside its fleet which rendered good service to all in keeping down piracy throughout its neighborhood. His proper task was to return to Greece to aid the Greeks in the war he had persuaded them to begin against Macedonian rule, which was now current.

Demetrius assembled his forces on the mainland of Asia Minor about 7 or 8 miles from Rhodes. He had 200 long ships and 170 transports with 40,000 men, among whom were a few horsemen and also contingents from the pirates of the neighborhood. Besides the great cargo ships with missiles and machines, there were no less than 1,000 small craft hoping to profit by loot, for Rhodes had not been ravaged for many years. Demetrius deployed his fleet as if he were about to engage in battle. First came the long ships with their catapults, throwing darts 2 feet long, on the bows; then came the troop and horse transports towed by smaller rowing ships; then came the pirates and all the crowd of merchantmen, so that the sea between the island and the opposite shore seemed covered with shipping. The Rhodian soldiers manned the walls while the women were on the house tops and, as the city was built like an amphitheater (sloping to the port), all could see the size of the fleet and the glittering arms reflected by the sea. After landing, the army took position near the city, but out of range and Demetrius sent the pirates to pillage the island. He cut down the trees and razed the towns and with the materials he fortified his camp with a triple ditch. Then by the labor both of the army and the seamen, he threw up a dyke about his landing place that included a port large enough to protect his ships. (Most of them were drawn on the beach.)

The inhabitants still attempted negotiations, but these failing they sent embassies to Cassander, Lysimachus, and Ptolemy, asking for help. All useless persons were sent out of the city and it appeared that they had 6,000 citizens, 1,000 strangers, and 1,000 domiciled foreigners able to bear arms. They also took slaves into service, after freeing them, and the mechanics were set to work making arms and war engines. Cruisers were sent out to cut off hostile supplies and took prizes and destroyed some of the ships drawn on the beach and ransomed their prisoners at 1,000 drachmas for freemen. Demetrius had much material for siege work. He built tortoises to give shelter against the enemy's missiles and mounted each on two ships fastened together. He also mounted two battering towers four stories high in the same way, and then built a floating boom of heavy timbers to protect the ships carrying the engines from rams. He also assembled numbers of smaller craft and decked them over in pairs, so that they might carry catapults and Cretan archers. All the means of attack were placed off the port and brought within range. When the Rhodians saw the main attack was to come from the sea, they replied with counter measures of the same sort, both on the quay walls and on board their ships in the port.

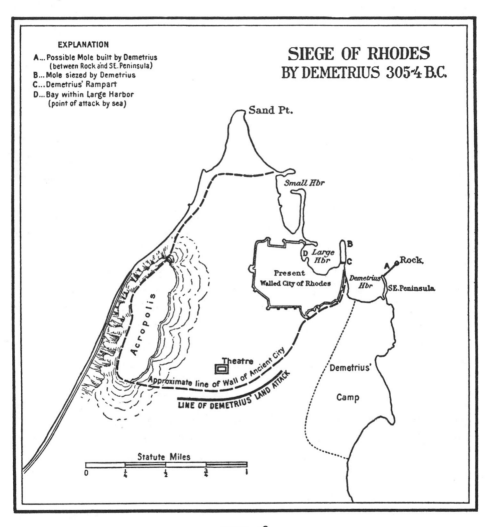

MAP 18.

One calm night Demetrius was able to throw 400 men on the principal mole less than 200 yards from the city walls, where they secured themselves behind a barricade with a great supply of missiles. At daylight Demetrius got his floating engines inside the port. Their fire drove back the workmen strengthening the walls of the city and, then using the heavier engines, he was able to make a small breach in the wall and both sides suffered severely in the day's fighting. At night Demetrius towed his engines out of range, but the Rhodians attacked them with fire and burned most of them, although some of the crews saved their ships by putting out the fire. The next day and for eight days thereafter he continued to attack the engines on the mole with heavy stone throwers (of a talent, 57 lbs.) and, having gained some success, he threw an assaulting party against the sea face of the town, but it was driven off and a number of craft, filled with soldiers, beached themselves through panic and the Rhodians burned them. During this sea attack Demetrius assaulted elsewhere on land and reached the top of the walls, but after a desperate action the attackers were thrown down. There was then a lull for a week, while both sides prepared for further effort.

Again Demetrius attacked the harbor entrance, with stone-throwing machines against the walls and with fire ships against the Rhodian ships inside the mole. The Rhodians made a desperate counter-attack and three of their best ships with selected crews broke through the boom protecting Demetrius' ships carrying the stone throwers and sank two. The third was towed away. But the Rhodians were rash and, going too far outside, were surrounded and rammed. The admiral and some captains were wounded and made prisoners, but most of the crews swam away safely, only one Rhodian ship was taken. Demetrius made another float to carry a larger engine than any previous one, but at the moment of sending it to action a rain squall swamped its tugs and it was disabled. Thereupon the Rhodians opened their water gate and fell upon the enemy party, which had been occupying the mole since the beginning. Owing to the bad weather, Demetrius could not re-enforce his men, but the Rhodians continually renewed theirs as they became exhausted, so that the 400 on the mole had to surrender in the end.

About this time Ptolemy threw in about 500 men and others from Cnossus also ran the blockade. Demetrius now resolved to make his chief attack by land and constructed his great "helepolis," or taker of cities. It was a movable tower, 75 feet on a side and 150 feet high, in nine stories somewhat pyramidal in shape and armored with sheet iron to protect it against flames. In the front face on each floor were loop holes in the walls suitable in size for the engines placed there. These ports were protected by shutters with stuffed leather pillows to deaden the blows of stone projectiles. Each floor was accessible by two wide ladders for the supply of material. Over 3,000 men inside and outside the machine were required to move it. He also made two tortoises, one to protect the men filling up the trenches and the other to protect the rams used against the walls. There were likewise covered ways for the besiegers to move in safety, and the ships' crews were now used to level the ground for the machine. In this way he brought up his machines against 7 towers and the 6 curtain walls between them. Demetrius was considered the best siege engineer of his time.

The Rhodians built inside counter-walls with materials from the temples, promising the gods to build new temples after victory, and sent out three squadrons of three ships each to raid the enemy's shipping, bringing him supplies. All had much success and brought captured supplies and valuable workmen into the city.[3] When it was proposed in the city to throw down the statues of Demetrius and his father Antigonus, which had been erected there in happier times, the assembly refused to do so, and this deference to their enemies was regarded as both magnanimous and prudent.

Demetrius then undertook mining and the Rhodians, hearing of it by deserters, undertook counter-mining and also dug a ditch behind the wall attacked. As the mines advanced, their roofs were shored up by timbering and, when they were complete, the mines were filled with fuel and fired to burn down the timbers, and the city walls above collapsed into the mine, thus making a breach for the assaulting column.

The attacking machines were all brought up, the fleet took position off the port, and a general attack was made and one of the strongest towers was thrown down. Presently the Rhodians attacked the siege engines by night, with fire, and killed many. The great helepole had been lightened of its sheet armor and was in danger of catching fire, but the water casks stored on the various floors were called into service and the fire extin-

---

[3] During the siege Ptolemy sent many ships with 400,000 bushels of grain and vegetables to break the blockade. Demetrius sent out boats to seize them, but taking advantage of a favorable wind the supplies got in. As it was unusual for ships to remain under way at night, blockades were not very effective. Cassander and Lysimachus also sent supplies which encouraged and nourished the city.

guished. Then the reserves were called up and, by great effort, the helepole was withdrawn to safety. In the morning Demetrius caused his people to collect the projectiles thrown during the night by the Rhodians and found that they numbered 800 flaming projectiles and 1,500 bolts from the catapults. So great a number in a single night made him realize the vast resources of the city.

The Rhodians constructed additional counter-works and sent out some of their best ships under Amyntas to attack the pirates on the mainland who were aiding Demetrius. Amyntas brought back a number of prizes with which he entered the harbor by night and thus once more renewed the supplies. After repairing his engines, Demetrius again assaulted the walls and threw down two curtains between the towers and caused many losses to the Rhodians. At this time Ptolemy threw into the city as much provisions as he had sent before and 1,500 men, and at the same moment Demetrius was visited by 50 deputies from the cities of Greece asking him to make terms with the city, for they wished for aid against Cassander. Doubtless the influence of commerce was also making itself felt. An armistice was arranged, but no terms were reached and Demetrius resolved on another night attack on the open breach. The select troops chosen for the assault broke into the town and then all the besiegers made a general attack. The new arrivals sent by Ptolemy finally drove back the assailants who had reached the theater, and the city was held.

Antigonus now sent to his son to make peace on favorable terms, for Cassander was besieging Athens and it was necessary to check his progress in Greece. Ptolemy was declaring he would send Rhodes 3,000 men (although not immediately) and he also suggested peace. Thus after a year's siege peace was signed in 304, on the terms that Rhodes should keep its freedom and its revenues and send auxiliary troops to Antigonus, although these were not to be employed against Ptolemy.

DEMETRIUS GOES TO GREECE

While Demetrius had been occupied at Salamis and Rhodes, Athens had been fighting a 4-year war (307-304), which Antigonus and Demetrius had persuaded her to lead against Cassander. It had not been going well for the cities of Greece after Antigonus had failed to enter Egypt. Immediately after abandoning the siege of Rhodes, Demetrius hastened with his fleet and army to Greece, where he should have gone a year earlier after defeating Ptolemy off Cyprus.

Demetrius first rescued Chalcis from its Macedonian garrison and, after defeating Cassander at Thermopylae, he obliged Boeotia to abandon him and made an alliance with Aetolia. He spent the winter of 304-303 in Athens, holding it by his sea power connecting him with his father's kingdom in Asia Minor and by his considerate treatment of Greek cities.

In the spring of 303 Demetrius marched south to deliver southern Greece from Cassander's Macedonians and recovered much of the Peloponnese. He renewed the League of Corinth and took possession of Sicyon and Corinth, putting a garrison in the latter's acropolis. He now had a strong hold on the sea route to Italy and connected it with the through line to India by Cyprus and the Phoenician seaports.

DEMETRIUS' FLEET FAILS TO HOLD THE HELLESPONT AND ANTIGONUS IS DEFEATED AT IPSUS

The loss of Greece and Epirus made Cassander's position in Macedon insecure and he made overtures to Antigonus, who replied by asking unconditional surrender. At this Cassander sent for his close friend Lysimachus, King of Thrace, and they agreed to show to Seleucus and Ptolemy how necessary it was for all of them to unite to overthrow Antigonus, who would otherwise re-establish the Empire of Alexander. Thus the coalition of 315 was renewed under Lysimachus as commander in chief. In the spring of 302 Demetrius invaded Thessaly with 57,500 men, of whom 8,000 were Macedonians and 25,000 were of the Grecian League. He had his great fleet to assure his communications with his bases in Asia. This was the main attack on Europe, which Antigonus had been trying to bring off for 15 years through sea power to cross the Hellespont.

Cassander sent part of his army to Lysimachus to attack Antigonus in Asia and, with 31,000 men, he entered Thessaly and occupied a strong defensive position. Demetrius came and faced him and then waited for an opportunity to attack and, in the course of time, must have been successful, but the decision had passed elsewhere. Demetrius' fleet failed to hold the Hellespont and Lysimachus crossed, probably through treachery in the cities on the Hellespont, and moved south along the coast of Ionia and took the cities with their fleets, as Alexander had done some 30 years

before. Seleucus started from Babylon to join Lysimachus. Antigonus
hurried into Phrygia to attack Lysimachus before Seleucus could come up,
but Lysimachus maneuvered for time and fell back towards Heraclea.
The winter of 302-1 came with nothing decided. Antigonus called on his
son Demetrius to cross to his aid.

Accordingly, Demetrius made a truce with Cassander, left a part of
his fleet with Athens, and recovered Ephesus and the Hellespontine cities
and held the passage when it was too late. Cassander sent 12,000 men
under his brother to join Lysimachus, but Demetrius' fleet caught one
of the three divisions and sank a number of ships and the soldiers. The
flagship, a hexere with 500 men, was lost. Demetrius wintered at Ephesus
and in the spring of 301 he joined his father in Phrygia, and Seleucus,
from Babylon, joined Lysimachus. The two great armies were now assembled and neither had cause to wait longer. Antigonus had about 80,000
troops and 75 elephants, while the allies had about 75,000 troops, 480
elephants, and 120 war chariots. They met at Ipsus, and Antigonus lost
the battle, as Demetrius charged too far with the successful cavalry and
could not get back to aid the main action. Antigonus was killed and his
territory divided among the conquerors.

DEMETRIUS AS A SEA KING

Demetrius fled to Ephesus with 9,000 men and with his powerful fleet
he retained the Phoenician ports and the coastal cities in Caria and Ionia,
Cyprus and the Aegean Islands, and was still President of the Hellenic
League. With this chain of seaports, he remained a sea king, controlling in
great measure the commerce across the Aegean, and supporting himself
on the profits of commerce which he took to himself. His friends in Athens
were overthrown, but he got back his squadron at Athens, his treasure,
and his wife. Most of the Greek cities repudiated him, but his garrisons
still held the fortress of Corinth and part of the Peloponnese. The Ionian
League maintained his cause and he was still a power. Cassander remained
King of Macedon, and claimed a kingdom in the south coast of Asia Minor
for his brother Pleistarchus. Seleucus took most of Antigonus' kingdom.

It is unnecessary to trace further here the course of the wars of the
Successors to their conclusion on the field of Korupedion in 281, for there
was no important development of naval tactics. It is enough to say that, in

the end, Demetrius, son of Antigonus, established himself on the throne of Macedon and, although driven out, his son, Antigonus, re-established the Antigonid dynasty. Seleucus established his dynasty in Asia Minor and Ptolemy made his in Egypt. Until Rome intervened in Macedonia and Asia, the three great kingdoms continued to dispute for predominance in the control of ocean commerce through possession of seaport bases.

The wars of Alexander and his generals have been traced here not only on account of the naval tactics which ancient writers have described to us with some minuteness at Tyre, Salamis, and Rhodes, but also because we can see in them the profits which fall to the nation commanding the sea and thereby taking the middleman's profits on international commerce. The objective of Antigonus in his wars against Macedon and Egypt was well conceived, but, in modern phrase, he held his corner on naval power too long. His delay at Rhodes took too much of his resources and his time, and the market broke at Ipsus.

PRINCIPAL AUTHORITIES CONSULTED FOR THIS CHAPTER

ANCIENT

Diodorus Siculus.
Plutarch: *Demetrius, Eumenes.*

MODERN

Tarn, W. W.: *Cambridge Ancient History*, vol. 6.

APPENDIX 1 TO CHAPTER IX

GREAT SHIPS OF DEMETRIUS AND PTOLEMY

Ancient men-of-war probably reached their greatest development under Demetrius Poliorcetes. He was an able general and admiral and a military engineer and shipbuilder as well. He built ships called 16-ers. There is dispute as to what this numeral root word indicated. As was said in the first chapter, speed was the objective of shipbuilders and this was to be reached by having the greatest possible number of men per running foot of the ship's side. There were three ways of doing this: (1) by putting several men on one oar, (2) by having several oars rowed from each bench, and (3) by putting rowers on different levels. Venetian records show that in the sixteenth century, when galleys were habitually rowed with 3 rowers on each bench, each with his own oar, experiments were undertaken. Four men and then 5 men were placed on the same bench to row 2 oars. Also 4 men on the same bench rowed 4 oars. The result of this series of trials was that, as ships grew bigger, 1 large oar with from 4 to 10 men on it was found better than 1 man to each oar. Later, as ships and oars grew larger, the crew of each great oar faced each other in double rank. The men facing forward were not as efficient as those facing aft in the usual way, but they did more than if they all were facing aft, with some close to the tholepin, pulling a very short stroke. On the other hand, when men were in two ranks on each oar, the space necessary between oars was about one-eighth greater than when in a single row. From the data available it seems that we may estimate roughly that, when an oar was manned on both sides, those who faced forward did about 0.75 the work of those who faced aft; that is, 6 men facing each other in groups of 3 did about 1.75 times as much work as 3 men on 1 oar, or about 0.57 effective horsepower. In the same arrangement 8 men developed about 0.69 effective horsepower and 10 men about 0.79 effective horsepower.

Referring to the seventeenth century big oar, its maximum length was about 55-58 ft., the height of its tholepin above the water about 7 ft., or

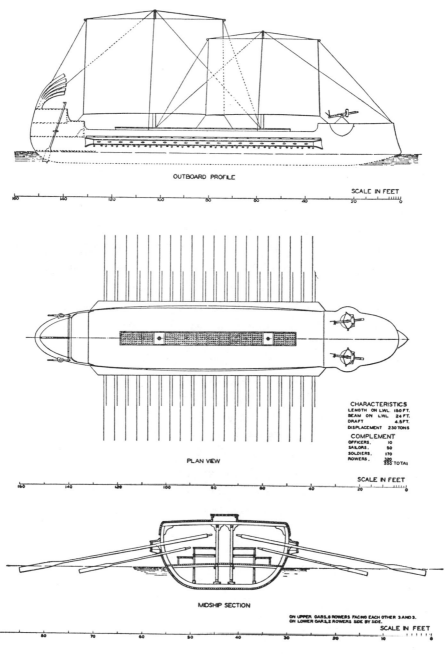

OUTBOARD PROFILE

SCALE IN FEET

PLAN VIEW

CHARACTERISTICS
LENGTH ON LWL. 150 FT.
BEAM ON LWL. 24 FT.
DRAFT 4.5 FT.
DISPLACEMENT 230 TONS

COMPLEMENT
OFFICERS. 10
SAILORS. 50
SOLDIERS. 170
ROWERS. 320
350 TOTAL

SCALE IN FEET

MIDSHIP SECTION

ON UPPER OARS, 6 ROWERS FACING EACH OTHER 3 AND 3.
ON LOWER OARS, 2 ROWERS SIDE BY SIDE.

SCALE IN FEET

OCTERE, RECONSTRUCTION

one-eighth its length. There were never more than 10 men to an oar. What was an effective arrangement 2000 years before was effective in the time of Demetrius. There is no evidence that there were ever more than 3 levels of oars and yet the root word applied to rowing systems runs as high as 40. We are therefore forced to the conclusion that the numeral root meant different things in different periods. First it meant ranks of rowers; then it meant number of men on an oar; and, lastly, as in the case of the 40-er (tesserakonter), it must have referred to the whole number of rowers on both sides of the ship in one longitudinal rowing space. As the biggest and highest placed oar we know of had only 10 men, there could not have been a rank above that in antiquity, for the oar would be impossible; nor could there be more than 2 rows of smaller oars under the big ones for lack of space. Consequently, we are driven to believe that the term 40-er meant, on each side a row of 10-man oars, underneath a row of 6-man oars, and still lower one of 4-man oars, making 40 men in one longitudinal rowing space. With these assumptions, the figures (pages 255 and 257) show an attempt to reconstruct an octere and a 16-er of Demetrius and the later 40-er of Ptolemy IV (p. 259).

For the octere let us assume a crew of 60 officers, seamen, and mechanics, 170 soldiers, and 320 rowers manning 40 six-man oars in double rank and 40 two-man oars with the men sitting beside each other at a lower level. Allowing 200 lbs. for each man and his arms and clothing, and 160 lbs. for each for 10 days' supplies of food,[1] water, and fuel, we have a total of 88.4 tons. Adding 10 tons to this for artillery and putting the weight of hull at 47 per cent and masts, sails, and equipment at 16 per cent of the total displacement, we arrive at 266 tons for the latter. As for the linear dimensions, the oars and fore-and-aft gangway would need 31 ft. across the ship between tholepins, and 90 ft. longitudinally. A suitable beam for stability would be 24 ft. at the water line. From this we get a length of 150 ft. and draft of 4.75 ft. The ship would have the outrigger arrangement for the oars as shown by the pedestal of the Victory in the Louvre. From the data previously given, the e.hp. available would be 32.8, giving a speed of about 7.3 knots, with a stroke of about 27 per minute.

---

[1] These large ships, which could not be conveniently beached like trieres, needed more food supplies on board, as the crews could not be so readily landed to search for rations.

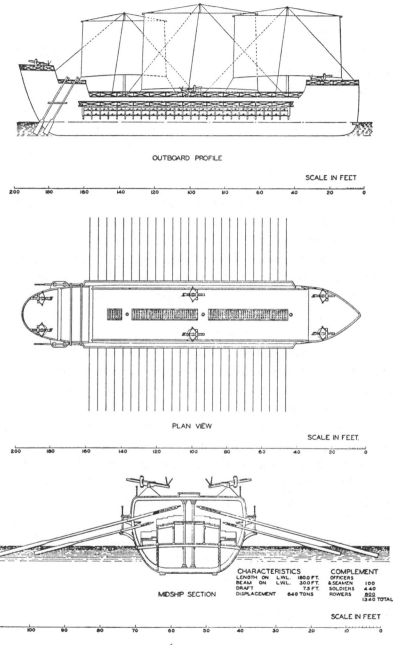

OUTBOARD PROFILE

SCALE IN FEET

| 200 | 180 | 160 | 140 | 120 | 100 | 80 | 60 | 40 | 20 | 0 |

PLAN VIEW

SCALE IN FEET.

| 200 | 180 | 160 | 140 | 120 | 100 | 80 | 60 | 40 | 20 | 0 |

MIDSHIP SECTION

CHARACTERISTICS		COMPLEMENT	
LENGTH ON L.W.L.	180.0 FT.	OFFICERS	
BEAM ON L.W.L.	30.0 FT.	& SEAMEN	100
DRAFT	7.5 FT.	SOLDIERS	440
DISPLACEMENT	640 TONS	ROWERS	800
			1340 TOTAL

SCALE IN FEET

| 110 | 100 | 90 | 80 | 70 | 60 | 50 | 40 | 30 | 20 | 10 | 0 |

RECONSTRUCTION OF A 16-ER OF DEMETRIUS POLIORCETES

With two masts carrying 3,600 sq. ft. of sail (equal to the area circumscribed about the water line) she might make 11 knots under sail under very favorable circumstances.

For the 16-er of Demetrius we assume a crew of 100 officers, seamen, and mechanics, 440 soldiers, and 800 rowers with 10 days' water, food, and fire wood. Assume also 20 tons for mechanical artillery and hurling stones, making a total weight of 237 tons. With hull and equipment at 63 per cent of the load displacement the latter will be 640 tons. Assume two levels of 25 oars on each side on each level, with crews of 10 men facing each other in groups of 5 men on the upper oars and 6 men on the lower oars similarly facing each other with 30 per cent of the length of the oars inboard. As has already been said, the 10-man oars can develop 0.79 e.hp. each, but when doing so the stroke is only about 21 or 22 a minute. The 6-man oar can render about 0.57 e.hp. at 26 strokes per minute. At higher speeds a greater proportion of the crew's strength is absorbed in swinging their oars and themselves, and at 27 strokes the big oars would probably give no more than 0.43 e.hp. and the lower oars about 0.52 e.hp. so that the horsepower available would be only about 48.0.

For the linear dimensions, assume 38 ft. beam between tholepins, and 30 ft. at the water line, which will give good stability with a large number of men moving freely on the upper deck. Proportionable length would be 180 ft., draft 7.5 ft., full speed of 7.3 knots. For a watch of 2 hours the full crew might make 4.8 knots; in two watches the speed would be 3.8 knots; and in three, 3.3 knots.

For such a wide ship a suitable sail area would be 1.25 times the rectangle about the water line, or 6,750 sq. ft., divided among 2 or 3 masts. Under the most favorable conditions this might give a speed of 11.0 knots.

The deck area of the two principal decks would be about 8,600 sq. ft., enough for quartering 1,300 men according to the practice of the Middle Ages. The rest would find room to sleep on the raised flooring for the rowers. Presumably the upper deck was protected at night by a heavy awning and there were weather curtains along its sides, as in the Middle Ages.

This great ship differs little in speed from a triere, but carries many

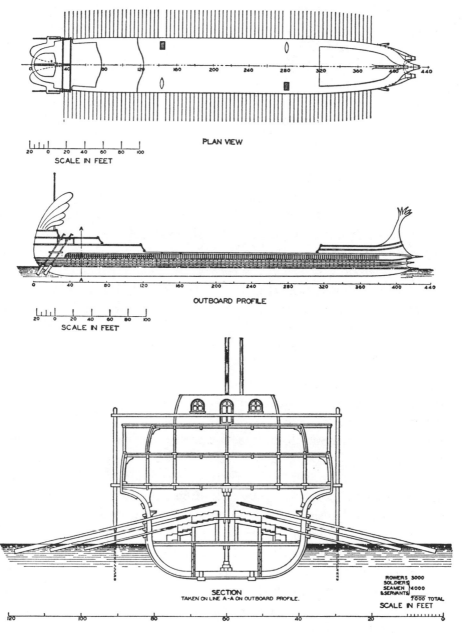

PLAN VIEW

SCALE IN FEET
20 0 20 40 60 80 100

OUTBOARD PROFILE

SCALE IN FEET
20 0 20 40 60 80 100

SECTION
TAKEN ON LINE A-A ON OUTBOARD PROFILE.

ROWERS 3000
SOLDIERS
SEAMEN } 4000
& SERVANTS
7000 TOTAL

SCALE IN FEET
120   100   80   60   40   20   0

TENTATIVE RECONSTRUCTION TESSERAKONTER OF PTOLEMY

soldiers and heavy artillery. The cost was far too great for any but a great prince and was a rarity even for such. Two centuries later the largest ship we hear of was a decere. So it seems that moderate ships were more serviceable, just as 74's were more suitable for general use than 120-gun ships in 1800.

The tesserakonter or 40-er of Ptolemy IV, according to the account of Athenaeus, was over 400 ft. long. This, of course, puts her out of the class of seagoing ships, for not until the end of the eighteenth century did any ships exceed over 200 ft. on the water line. So with the understanding that the 40-er was the luxury of an extravagant king, for trips on the Nile, and that she never went to sea for more than an hour's trip from Alexandria on a fine day, it is possible to discuss her characteristics. The description which has come to us is that she was 429 ft. in length, 58 ft. maximum beam, and her *aphlaston* (poop ornament) was 81 ft. high above the water. She had 4 steering oars each 46 ft. long and her thranite oars were 58 ft. long and balanced at the tholepins by weights on the looms. She had 2 bows and 2 sterns and 7 rams. Every part was inlaid and ornamented with encaustic paintings. The crew is given as about 7,000 men, but there are two versions as to how many of these were rowers. The larger figure, 4,000, is incompatible with the length of 429 ft. The smaller figure, 3,000, and even 3,200, is possible. Most of the remainder are said to have been soldiers; a few hundred only for the service of the ship and of the prince. To determine the ship's size, let us allow a weight of 160 lbs. for each rower without clothing and 200 lbs. for each of the rest with arms and clothing. Add 2 days' food and water at 15 lbs. gross a day, and we have a total of 665 tons. To this we arbitrarily add 300 tons for royal fittings. With an extra heavy hull of 63 per cent of her displacement on account of her great length, and only 7 per cent of stores because she did not venture far from Alexandria, we have a displacement of 3,217 tons. The great height of the *aphlaston* suggests that the royal quarters were at the stern. We may assume either that the immense width assigned was that of the under-water body and that the ship was of very little draft; or that the ship body was narrower and that the royal quarters were in a box set on the after part and were wider than the body of the ship. The drawing (p. 259) shows the upper deck overhanging the side.

On the premise that she was not seaworthy, we are free to make this latter supposition, and it is to be preferred because the narrow body and deeper draft will give more speed. We may take the water-line length as 420 ft. and the water-line beam as 44 ft. The heavy royal quarters at the stern would make the draft aft about 11 ft. and forward about 7 ft. The double bow and stern would make an unusually great wetted surface and great wave resistance and slow the ship.

As for the rowing system, the stated length of the thranite oars corresponds well with that of 10-man oars of the seventeenth century and later.

We can arrange a system of oars on three levels, the upper one with 10 men, the middle one with 6 men, and the lower one with 4 men, the crew of each oar being in two groups facing each other with 4.67 ft. between benches and occupying a length of 350 ft. With 30 per cent of the oar inboard, the stroke could scarcely be under 27 per minute. The e.hp. of the big oars would be about as in the 16-er, say 0.43, the middle oars 0.52, and the small ones about 0.42. With 3,000 rowers on 450 oars, the total e.hp. would be about 206. This would give a speed of about 7.5 knots for a spurt and for a watch of 2 hours about 5.0 knots. In two watches the crew could make about 4.0 knots and in 3 watches, about 3.5 knots.

It is important to consider this great vessel, for if we can arrive at any clear and logical conclusion about her rowing system, we can make our ideas about rowing smaller ships conformable.

APPENDIX 2 TO CHAPTER IX

COST OF WARS AT END OF FOURTH CENTURY B.C.

Little is known of the cost of government and of war in ancient times, but an estimate may be made, based on the ratio of wages and of war costs in the present day. We may assume that the wages of unskilled labor in Greece at the end of the fourth century B.C. were 1.5 drachmas a day, and that mercenary troops received 1 drachma daily for pay and rations.[2] As for naval costs, somewhat later than the time now under discussion, Rhodes rented some trieres at a monthly price of 10,000 drachmas (see *Rhodes in Ancient Times*, by Cecil Torr). No doubt Rhodes made additional charges in case of loss of ships in service. With these data as our basis, we may make some approximation to the national expenditures, by comparing modern prices and expenditures. First as to military expenditures: During the last year of our Civil War the Federal Army was about 980,000 strong and the annual cost of the army was about $1,030,000,000. The individual soldier's pay and allowances were about $400 a year. That is, the total army costs were about 2.6 times the army's wages. In the recent World War the pace was more rapid and the War Department spent nearly 6 times the soldier's pay, but this we may put aside on account of the great cost of transportation over seas and the great expenditure of ammunition. The naval cost in the Civil War for the year 1865, for a force of 60,000, was about 5 times the wages and rations. In the present time of peace, the cost of both Army and Navy are a little less than 2.5 times the pay and allowances of the men. We may take it that in classic times the expenditure of material was somewhat less in war than in 1865, but transport and train service cannot have been relatively very different; so let us assume that garrison troops were maintained at a total cost of 2 times their pay and that field armies in war cost 2.5 times their pay. As for the size of the armies, nearly all the field strength

[2] Professor Jevons in the *Journal of the Hellenic Society* for 1895 gives this figure for labor. Blumner, in his *Home Life of Ancient Greeks*, gives the wages of Cyrus' mercenaries as 4 obols a day and wages advanced 50 per cent in the course of the next century. See also, Gulick: *Life of the Ancient Greeks*.

of Alexander's Empire was assembled at Ipsus in 301 except the Egyptian contingent and there were about 150,000 present. Ptolemy was able to send about 25,000 men to Cyprus in 306, so we may call 175,000 the total field strength of the Successors. But the rule of the sovereigns was maintained and secured by local garrisons in the principal cities, and although many of these garrisons were at the cost of the locality, nevertheless, their maintenance fell on the national resources. The number of men in these garrisons was probably less than that of the field armies and, at all events, did not exceed it. At a drachma a day wages and a total cost per man and per day of 2.5 drachmas for field armies and 2 drachmas for garrisons, the annual cost of 175,000 men of each class for 365 days with the colors would be about 48,000 talents ($57,600,000).

Now for the cost of navies. At a monthly rental of 10,000 drachmas, the annual cost of a triere for a season of 8 months would be 80,000 drachmas or 13⅓ talents. But some addition must be made to this for risks of the sea and war losses, so that it is not too much to put the annual cost of a triere at 18 talents. As there were both larger and smaller ships than the triere and large sizes were far from the most numerous, we may take 18 talents as the average cost per ship and per year, with crews averaging not over 200 men. As for the total numbers of ships in commission, all navies had important local services to render in the protection of commerce against pirates and at every maritime center there was a considerable local navy whose duties kept it in home waters. Let us assume a police force of ships in home waters equal in numbers to the battle fleets available for foreign service, although no doubt the ships at home were considerably smaller in size.

As for the numbers of ships, when Antigonus besieged Tyre in 315, the Tyrian fleet got away and joined Ptolemy. So to carry on the siege Antigonus built a new Phoenician fleet and assembled other ships from as far as the Hellespont, amounting in all to 240 ships, while Ptolemy at the same time had 200 ships at Cyprus, including Egyptian and Cyprian contingents as well as the original Tyrian ships. In 306 at the siege of Salamis in Cyprus, Demetrius and Ptolemy had 318 ships present for battle, including the divisions at the city. This figure is preferable as a basis to the other, in which the whole normal Tyrian fleet appears twice. Doubling these figures to include the local squadrons, we assign the dominions of Ptolemy and Antigonus a fleet of some 600 to 640 ships. But this does not include the navies of Greece, Macedonia, and Thrace. These were small at the time and could scarcely have been more than one-fourth of those of the two great powers, or 150 to 160 for local and foreign service. The total cost of the whole fleet, from 750 to 800 ships, would be 13,500 to 14,400 talents, for not over 150,000 to 160,000 men, (for 8 months).

To ascertain the government charge upon national income, we may again get light from present day ratios. The *Monthly Labor Review* for May, 1929, gives the hourly rate of unskilled labor in this country as 45 cents, or $3.60 for an 8-hour day. The population of the United States was about 120,000,000 and the national income was about $84,000,000,000. The average yearly income was therefore $700 per capita or about 194 days wages for unskilled labor. Applying this ratio to a daily wage of 1.5 drachmas, we have the average yearly income of all classes in Greek lands as 291 drachmas, or 48.6 talents per 1,000 population.

Turning now to the size of the population, Beloch estimates that of Mesopotamia, Syria, Asia Minor, and Egypt as 28,000,000. Greece, Macedonia, and Thrace he puts at 3,600,000. Assuming that the present population of Persia and Afghanistan of 17,000,000 differs little from that of ancient times we have a total of about 48,600,000 for Alexander's Empire.

Perhaps the earning capacity of Asia was not so high as that of Europe and was no more than 40 talents per 1,000, so that the total national income of a population of between 40,000,000 and 50,000,000 would run between 1,600,000 talents and 2,500,000 talents, with an expense for military and naval forces, numbering about 500,000, of something like 62,000 talents or from 4 per cent to 2.5 per cent of the national income.

We still have to estimate the civil expenses of government, partly local and partly royal. In the United States in 1929 the local and national expenditures were nearly $11,000,000,000, about one-eighth the total income, but of this about 20 per cent was for the single item of public schools, or three times the cost of the Army and Navy. And there are many other charges on our national and local revenues which did not appear, or but slightly, on ancient budgets, as for example, interest on debts, pensions, public health, and research and aid work of many kinds. Let us reject from our expenditure such charges as these and take only the few items of roads, water works, harbor improvements, city fortification, temples, and public monuments which were the chief ancient expenditures. A rough estimate of American expenditures for general administration and public works indicates that the cost was about $2,400,000,000 or about $20 per man. At $3.60 per day this is about 5.5 days' labor per year; but a large part of this is city expenditure; the rural cost is less. Taking it in ancient wages at 1.5 drachmas a day for a larger rural population at 5.5 days' labor per year, it is 1⅜ talents per 1,000 per year. That is, for a population of 40,000,000 to 50,000,000, the civil and military expenses of government while maintaining war ran perhaps between 117,000 and 131,000 talents or from 8 per cent to 5 per cent of the whole income, as previously estimated. This is a surprisingly low figure when one reflects that the tax in kind on the farmer was usually a tithe at the least. On the other hand, the tithe fell only on a part of the people and that a poor one. The tax on business seems to have been less, whereas with us the richer classes pay proportionately more. Moreover, there was then much labor within the family which now receives industrial wages. Again, the calculation above makes no allowance for graft, which was probably then on a larger scale than is now customary. And finally, in former times, when all industry was manual, it was impossible to tax as heavily as can be done now when machinery gives such great reserves of labor which may be diverted for public service.

This cost per thousand population is not very different from the revenue per thousand population for Carthage as mentioned in the next chapter.

As the foregoing estimate is based on a comparison of day's work, it gives a measure of the burden of governmental charges upon national industry with little regard to the correctness of the assumption as to daily wages.

CHAPTER X

THE FIRST PUNIC WAR

POPULATION AND ECONOMIC CONDITION OF THE OPPONENTS

AFTER the decisive battle of Salamis (2d) in 306 B.C., there were no important naval tactical developments until Rome's first war with Carthage, beginning in 264 and lasting until 241 B.C. Like the wars of the Successors of Alexander, the Punic War developed out of an age-long effort to establish a national monopoly of maritime trade. This time the would-be monopolist was the imperial city of Carthage and the scene was the Western Mediterranean. The ostensible origin of the war was, however, quite another matter, as it came up over the occupation of Messana in Sicily by a Carthaginian garrison.

In the middle of the third century B.C., the city of Carthage was probably larger than Rome and certainly much wealthier. Her actual territory was not much over 600 square miles of plow land. Her great strength lay in her monopoly of commerce by the occupancy of outlying seaports as trading posts, through which she controlled the products and trade of the back country of each district. These outposts of international business were held by strong garrisons. All were tied together and protected by a powerful navy which maintained communications with the imperial city. Carthage was the most prosperous industrial and commercial city in the world. Along the coasts of Africa her monopoly rested on the control of ports reaching from Oea (Tripoli) to Tingis (Tangier) through which she dealt with a population of 3,000,000 Moors. Besides, she held several ports in Spain, which gave her access to the rich mines of the interior. She had five colonies in Sardinia, and she took tithes from the western half of Sicily whose crops were very rich and whose population was estimated at over 1,000,000, in all. Carthage was thus the trading center of a population of some 4,000,000 or 5,000,000, and her merchant nobles were prosperous because her fleets were strong enough to drive the shipping of other powers out of the Western Mediterranean and to restrain in considerable measure the burden of piracy, which was perennial

MAP 19.
WESTERN MEDITERRANEAN SEA

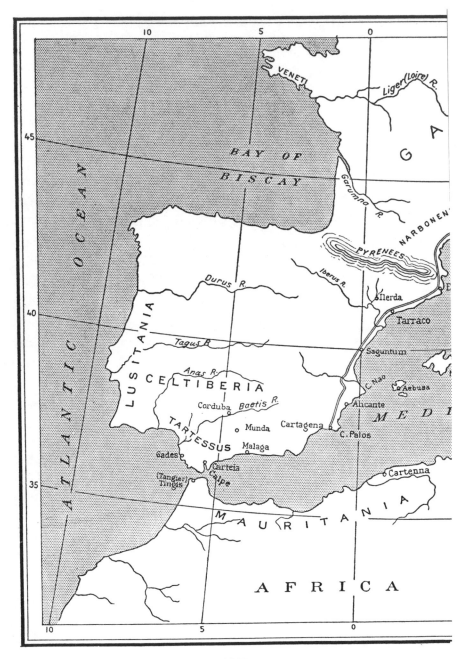

MAP 19.

WESTERN HALF
MEDITERRANEAN SEA

Statute Miles

0   50   100   200   300   400

throughout the Mediterranean and has only been completely extirpated within the last 50 years. The armed forces by land and sea, which maintained this thriving commercial monopoly of the Carthaginian nobility, were conscripts of the subject peoples and mercenaries drawn from available warlike tribes, led and directed by the Carthaginian merchant aristocracy. The expenses of monopolistic management of business were in great part paid for by tribute from the subject cities, whose peoples shared in the profits of industry, which were possible through its protection by the Carthaginian hired fleets and armies. The revenues of the state at the outbreak of the war have been estimated at 12,000 talents ($16,612,000) (see *Cambridge Ancient History*, vol. 7), or 2.5 to 3 talents per 1,000 subjects.[1]

Rome had an entirely different basis of economic and military strength. It was mainly an agricultural country depending largely, although not entirely, on other countries for commerce and manufactured goods. By the middle of the third century B.C., Rome had extended her rule over all Italy south of the valley of the Po (i.e., peninsular Italy). Apparently her hegemony was not originally established with the wish to profit economically by the forced tribute of subject peoples, as was that of Carthage. Rome found herself obliged to enlarge her boundaries from time to time to preserve peace along her borders, for the local mountain tribes were restless and the pressure of over-population drove the Gauls and other tribes to invade Italy and stir up war. As Rome enlarged the area of her rule, she bound the conquered peoples to her by alliances which required the new allies to assist her by arms in war, but left them local autonomy and did not humiliate them by forced tribute. Her rule was strict, but enlightened. Under it peace and good order with rural prosperity were more prevalent than elsewhere. Unlike Carthage, the profits of sovereignty were political rather than economic.

At the opening of the third century treaties long in force forbade the Roman ships to extend their voyages into Carthaginian reserved areas and, in return, the Carthaginians had agreed not to plunder the shores about Rome. Commerce came to Rome, but the Romans were not seeking maritime trade and neither were the Carthaginians desirous of political conquest

---

[1] The relative value of gold to silver was at this time not far from 12.5 to 1, making the present day value of 1 talent of silver about $1,384.

in Italy. But the invasion of Italy by King Pyrrhus of Epirus, in 281, and his later attack upon Sicily made a great change in the political situation of Rome and its attitude as to foreign commerce. After Rome had defeated Pyrrhus and driven him back to Epirus, she dealt with the cities of southern Italy which had supported him and, by 269, she found herself in control there and consequently responsible for local prosperity. The Italian Greeks were traders and seamen by choice, like their Carthaginian neighbors in Sicily; and in the face of their business rivalry and her own impoverished soil, Rome's indifference to commerce was about to disappear. The population of Italy south of the Po Valley was under 3,000,000, including slaves.

Situation in Sicily

For several centuries Greeks and Carthaginians had been struggling for the possession of the rich lands of Sicily, the Greeks holding the eastern part and the Carthaginians the rest of the island which, besides its own productivity, was important to them as a halfway station on the route from Africa to Sardinia. For nearly a century the Greeks had scarcely been holding their own against Carthage, and now an incident occurred which brought the Romans into the chronic dispute. Hiero, ruler and later King of Syracuse, undertook to extend his power by the conquest of Messana (see Map 10), whose position on the straits made it the natural point for communications between Sicily and the mainland, as it remains today.

Messana was governed at that time by a band of Campanian mercenaries, who had been discharged some years before from the army of Syracuse and who then seized Messana where they killed or drove away the men and seized their wives and property, taking the name of Mamertines, or sons of Mars. They established friendly relations with the Roman garrison of Rhegium, which had been stationed there at the request of the citizens at the time of Pyrrhus' invasion. The Roman troops followed the example of the Mamertines across the straits and seized for themselves the city that they garrisoned. But when Rome had cleaned up South Italy after Pyrrhus had gone home, she did not fail to restore Rhegium to its citizens, nor to execute the unfaithful garrison in the forum at Rome. It was perhaps this severe act of the Roman Senate that encouraged

Hiero of Syracuse to attack the mercenary soldiery in authority in Messana
(265 B.C.). In their distress, a part of the Mamertines appealed to
Carthage for aid against Syracuse and delivered their city to a Carthaginian garrison, while another group sent to Rome for support, thinking
that Hiero, though not a dependent of Rome, might perhaps be restrained
by her.

The Romans deliberated long upon this request. They did not wish
to aid the Mamertines, who had committed much the same faults for
which they had executed their garrison at Rhegium. On the other hand,
the Romans did not care to see the Carthaginians firmly established in
the eastern part of Sicily, in control of the straits and threatening the
commerce of the new Roman allies in South Italy with a hostile monopoly
of trade in Sicily. In the end, the Senate refused to decide this far-
reaching question, which would evidently affect the whole future of the
republic, and it was settled in favor of intervention by a referendum vote
of the people (264 B.C.).

Roman Occupation of Sicily

Accordingly, a consular army went down to the straits and succeeded
in crossing to Sicily. Although without a fleet to cover the passage, it
employed small boats and a few borrowed triremes. The Mamertines
then drove the Carthaginian garrison out of the city and delivered the city
to the Romans. The government of King George II executed Admiral
Byng to "encourage the others," but the Carthaginians understood the
principle long before. After crucifying the general, who evacuated the
citadel of Messana, the Carthaginians sent a fleet and army to retake the
city, and Hiero joined his forces with the Carthaginians in the siege.
But the Roman Consul, Appius Claudius, defeated both the Syracusan
and the Carthaginian armies before Messana and then moved out against
the city of Syracuse.

In the meantime news of these events reached Rome and the new
Consuls for the year were dispatched with the usual double army, each
of two Roman and as many allied legions, in all, nearly 40,000 men.
Hiero now saw the error of his course and made a treaty with Rome by
which he was to pay a fine of 100 talents ($138,400). Thereafter, to the
end of his long life, Hiero was a faithful ally of Rome and afforded most

important aid to Roman military operations, as Syracuse became a principal base both for fleet and army.

After this success and alliance, the Romans withdrew one Consul and his army from Sicily, as they thought the other would be sufficient (Year 263); but the Carthaginians, being determined not to lose the island, recruited heavily in Spain, Liguria, and Gaul and re-enforced their Sicilian army, making Agrigentum (Acragas) their chief place of arms. The Romans advanced there and besieged the city for 7 months before they occupied it in 262 B.C. This success persuaded the Roman Senate that the Carthaginians would soon be driven out of Sicily, for the Consuls were prudent and successful, but it soon became apparent that, although many of the inland cities submitted readily to the Roman armies, yet those along the seacoast stood more in dread of the Punic fleets than of the Roman armies. Moreover, the hostile fleets were pillaging the coasts of Italy, bringing the war close to Rome. It became apparent to the Senate in 261 that it must provide a fleet, both to protect its own coasts and as a preliminary to developing military strength in Sicily.

CONSTRUCTION OF A FLEET

According to Polybius, who is the chief ancient authority for this war, the Senate now resolved to build 100 penteres (quinqueremes) and 20 trieres (triremes). The greatness of this effort whereby Rome extended her rule across the sea has been much admired, but there are not wanting those who say that its magnitude was exaggerated by the historian. Rome was not entirely without a navy, for we hear of her having had a small one as early as 282, and, after the subjection of South Italy, several of its cities became "naval allies," that is, they furnished ships instead of soldiers as their military contingents. But these ships were few in number and probably not large in size.

As a model of the penteres they were to build, the Romans are said to have taken a Carthaginian ship, which had run aground and been captured by them, and the 120 ships are said to have been completed in 60 days. It is Polybius' assertion that these penteres carried 300 rowers and 120 soldiers each, so that with seamen and officers they must have had nearly 500 men on board. It is clear that Polybius thought that quinqueremes of the Western Mediterranean were similar to penteres of the

Levant; but to many modern critics it seems too great a task for a country of no great riches and no more populous than Rome to build so fast. They believe that Polybius adopted his views from earlier and inaccurate writers who were acquainted only with the type of pentere as it had been developed in the Levant. A ship carrying 500 men can have been little smaller than the standard ships of Louis XIV, with 260 rowers, which displaced 300 tons. If we take it that the Roman ships averaged not over 120 tons and that, being built in haste of green timber, they were not so well built as they might be and that in consequence they only called for 80 days' labor per ton, in the forest as well as in the dockyards, it follows that about 165 woodcutters, carpenters, and metal workers must have been employed on each of these ships, in order to complete the task in 60 days, or 20,000 men in all.[2]

As these workers were in addition to the rowers who were being trained at the same time on shore, upon rowing frames similar in purpose to those now used in our colleges for boat-racing crews, the strain upon Roman man power must have been great, and consequently modern writers have sought explanations which might reduce Polybius' figures. Admiral Serre, in his *Marines de Guerre de l'Antiquité*, points out that the Carthaginian navy had not been developed for fleet actions like the Greek fleets and that, in spite of its battles with the fleets of Syracuse, it found its chief employment in raiding and in the suppression of piracy. It is not likely that this service would develop a class of large ships. Serre deems the type of pentere (quinquereme) to have been a comparatively small craft, which took its name from having 5 large oars on each side rather than from having 5 men on each oar as in the Greek penteres. Following out this idea he offers a sketch of a decked ship with superstructures at both ends, 60 ft. long and 14 ft. wide with 10 oars in all, manned by 4 men to each oar, facing each other in pairs. To the 40 rowers he adds 30 soldiers, making a crew of 70 men. But this hypothesis would reduce the greatest fleet of the war to a force of no more than 25,000 men, which seems small.

---

[2] In John Howell's *Galleys of the Ancients*, he quotes from a book of 1645 saying that piratical expeditions on the Black Sea were fitted out by Cossacks to cross to Asia Minor. For this purpose 60 men would build a 60-foot boat in a fortnight. These boats are described as needing a girdle of reeds for safety, so they cannot have been very seaworthy. They must have been of 30 or 35 tons' displacement, which would have called for 30 days' labor per ton. The Roman ships were no doubt more thoroughly built.

On the other hand, a number of statements (noted later) made by Polybius and Livy all indicate that a quinquereme had about 250 men.

SIZE OF FORCES

We have seen that in the wars of the Successors, with a population of over 40,000,000, the total numbers at Ipsus were about 175,000 and, in the greatest fleet action, that of Salamis (second), there were 260 ships with 50,000 to 60,000 men. As the population on which Rome and Carthage drew for men cannot have exceeded 20 per cent of Alexander's Empire, it seems probable that the ancient accounts must have exaggerated the numbers engaged in the Punic War. Further, we must remember that before the days of steam power and the telegraph it was much more difficult to handle and supply fleets and armies than at present. It was perhaps this difficulty as much as a lack of men that set a limit on the size of the eastern armies. Nevertheless, we may believe that in the First Punic War the aggregate of fleets and armies for both sides was little over 150,000 when greatest, including garrison troops. Although both Romans and Carthaginians seem to have had hexeres and even hepteres for their principal flagships, nevertheless, I assume that their penteres (quinqueremes) were small, not over 120 tons in displacement, with 15 long oars on each side and 150 rowers when full-manned, with a capacity of not over 250 men in all (see appendix to this chapter). In regard to the manning of these ancient ships, the statements of Pantero Pantera are suggestive. Writing at the opening of the seventeenth century, he tells us that it was then the custom to man the oars with 5 men each, if on scouting or raiding cruises when speed was essential; when expecting battle the same ships left port with 4 men to the oar to have more room for soldiers; but for local guard duty and for transport work they put only 3 men to the oar and filled up with soldiers. The same reasons for varying the number of men to each oar existed in ancient times. It is therefore reasonable to suppose that when the Romans built their new quinqueremes to carry crews of about 250 men, they manned many of them short on rowers and long on soldiers; i.e., with no more than 120 rowers (at 4 to the oar) and possibly 80 soldiers, besides 25 or 30 seamen and officers (230 in all).

The number of ships as given by Polybius seems very high for states of 3,000,000 to 5,000,000 population. I therefore follow the analysis of Polybius' account as given by W. W. Tarn in the *Journal of Hellenic Studies*, vol. 27, and take the numbers of ships as amended by him for the important events of the war. He shows that the data of various Carthaginian wars as given by Diodorus indicate that it was a tradition that Carthage could raise 200 warships when pressed and that her ordinary establishment was 130, and he believes it was difficulty in finding crews that placed this limit on the navy. Tarn also shows that after 311 B.C. the Romans maintained a small squadron of 10 ships under officers called "duovirs." Sometimes there was a double duoviral squadron. Later the towns of South Italy added small contingents, never more than 25 in all.

When Rome built the 100 quinqueremes and 20 triremes for a decision by sea, she scarcely would have started on a building project to challenge Carthage on an element to which Rome was so unaccustomed unless the program offered at least some superiority in numbers. Tarn assumes, therefore, that an excess of 25 per cent was the aim of Rome. It is therefore probable that the Roman fleet, as completed, included some of the duoviral ships, perhaps 15, and also the contingents of the naval allies, which may be placed at 25, bringing trieres to 60 in all, besides the 100 new penteres, and making a total available for the opening of the campaign in 260 B.C. of 160 ships. We may infer from Polybius that one consular army of two legions (and perhaps some allies) were embarked in the fleet, the other army was for operations by land. On the supposition that the lighter ships had full complements of rowers for reconnaissance, the entire fleet may have had 21,000 rowers, 11,000 soldiers, and 4,000 seamen and officers, with some non-combatant camp followers of both sexes.

As for the 130 ships of the Carthaginians, it is reasonable to believe that neither were they all quinqueremes and, since Polybius expressly states that the Roman ships were heavier and slower, we may further believe that the rowers and seamen were in a greater proportion than in the Roman fleet, and that the Punic fleet may have had 18,000 rowers, 6,500 soldiers, and 3,500 seamen. Of course, such figures are merely estimates, but some such proportions are suggested by the course of events. It may be further noted that the proportion of seamen, sailors, and soldiers is not very different from that of many ships of the Christian fleet at Lepanto, where, however, there was considerable difference in the ratios aboard the different ships.

EARLY ENGAGEMENTS OF THE FLEETS

Early in 260, the fleet having been completed while the rowers were exercising on shore, the ships put out from the various ports where they had been built and, after some further exercises at sea, they proceeded towards Sicily. The Consul Cornelius Scipio, who commanded the fleet, took 17 ships as an advance guard and went to Messana to make arrangements for the arrival of the others which he had told to follow on. (Among the principal matters was the usual one of providing a market, i.e., notifying farmers and merchants to bring provisions and other supplies to the selected market place, in this case the port of Messana.) After his arrival at Messana (see Map 10), the Consul heard that the town of Lipara in the island of the same name, about 30 miles away, might be readily taken and he went there and did so, remaining there at ease.[3] The entire Carthaginian fleet of 130 ships, under the command of Hannibal, was lying at Panormus (Palermo) and he sent 20 ships under Boodes to surprise the over-confident Romans. The Punic squadron arrived by night and lay off the harbor closing the entrance till daylight, when the Romans sighted it and the soldiers abandoned their ships in a panic and fled to the shore. Cornelius surrendered himself and Boodes returned in triumph to Panormus with the prizes and the Consul, who was thereafter known as Asina (ass).

Hannibal now felt encouraged to cross to Italy and advance to reconnoiter the main Roman fleet as it moved southwards along the coast. Taking only 50 ships with him, he ran unexpectedly into the entire hostile fleet ready for battle, but escaped after losing a few ships. Evidently, the country people had notified the Romans of Hannibal's movement. The Roman fleet continued its course to Sicily and, having there learned of the loss of Asina, the other Consul, Duilius, commanding the land forces, was notified and he assumed command of the fleet at Messana. At the same time it became known to the Romans that the hostile fleet was not far away on the north coast of Sicily.

---

[3] A glance at the map shows the importance of the Lipari Islands as an advance base for the Carthaginians from which to threaten the Italian coasts and the Roman communications with Sicily. These islands were similarly important to naval operations in Sicilian wars in the Middle Ages and even later, e.g., in 1293 and 1719.

The Corvus

The Roman captains were not satisfied with the performance of their ships. The enemy's vessels had been too nimble for them and could either choose their range for a missile action, in which their Balearic slingers excelled, or could back away with little penalty after a successful ram stroke or a side swipe on the enemy's oars. The result of the Roman deliberations was the invention of a contrivance for holding the hostile ships alongside whenever they attempted to ram. If the enemy could be prevented from getting away after a ramming collision, he would be obliged to accept a boarders' fight in which the disciplined Roman legionaries might be expected to prevail. Even though their own ships might be fatally damaged, the retention of the enemy alongside would allow the Romans to board the hostile ships and to save themselves by their valor. The new invention received from the soldiers the name of corvus, meaning a raven. Polybius' description has lent itself to many modern explanations. It consisted of a stout spar stepped as a derrick mast close to the bow. At the head of the mast was a tackle such as is now known as a topping lift, which hooked in a ring at the outer end of a boarding gangway about 18 ft. long and 4 ft. wide. The inner end, or heel, of the gangway rested on the deck and must have been firmly secured to a pivot built into the ship. Each side of the gangway had a parapet reaching knee-high and at its outer end and underneath it was a heavy iron spike. Although not mentioned by Polybius, there were undoubtedly side lines, now called guys, attached to the gangway, so that it could be held steady in any direction. When ready for battle, the gangway was held upright by its lift and, when the enemy came alongside, the topping lift was let go and the falling gangway, reaching beyond its own ship's side, drove the beak of the raven into the enemy's deck, holding him fast.[4] The soldiers then charged in double rank over the gangway, the leaders being well protected by their shields which they held in front of themselves, while those following rested the boss of their shields on the parapets and were even better protected until they issued on the deck of the enemy and had room to use their weapons.

---

[4] Dio Cassius mentions the practice of throwing grappling irons to catch the hostile ships, as was done as late as the Napoleonic wars and, as the corvus is not mentioned in the last battles of this Punic War, there are modern commentators who think it merely an exaggerated account of some form of throwing grapnel.

In short, the purpose of the corvus was to bring about by other means such a form of battle as the Syracusans had forced on the Athenians at the siege of their city 150 years before. On both occasions the desire was for a boarders' fight. The harbor of Syracuse restricted the movements of the Athenian ships as the corvus was meant to restrict the Carthaginians on the open sea.

BATTLE OF MYLAE, 260 B.C.

When all was ready in the Roman fleet, Duilius heard that the Carthaginian fleet had moved east from Panormus and was ravaging the fields of Mylae, on the north coast some 18 miles by road from Messana and 15 miles farther by sea. The original Roman fleet had been reduced by the losses at Lipara to something over 140, and Hannibal too had lost a few of his 130. A complete victory at sea would enable the victors to cut off the enemy's communications with the island of Sicily and isolate his army, as the American naval victory at Santiago in 1898 isolated the Spanish army in Cuba and decided the fate of the island. There can be little doubt that the Carthaginian foray upon Mylae was meant to draw the Roman fleet out of port and provoke a decisive battle in open waters where the Carthaginians would have best chance of profiting by their nautical skill. Anyway, such was the result.

The appearance of the Romans off Mylae was no surprise to Hannibal, who drew his ships from the shore with joy and, despising the enemy, bore down upon them without much order, himself leading in a heptere which had belonged to Pyrrhus when the latter was campaigning in Sicily. On getting close enough to observe the new construction on the bows of the Roman ships, the leading Carthaginians felt some surprise and checked their onset, but soon resumed their confidence and their advance without waiting for their rear to close with them. They found that contact with the Roman ships was fatal. The corvi plunged on their decks and the boarders charged safely over them. The Punic mercenaries could not sustain a hand-to-hand fight with the legionaries. The 30 ships in the leading group, including the great flagship, were captured with their crews, but Hannibal escaped in a small boat. The rear Carthaginian ships were now coming up, but having observed the fate of their comrades they kept their distance at first, perhaps using their missiles, but, after deliberation and realizing the superior handiness of their ships, they, too, resumed

INSCRIPTION COMMEMORATING THE VICTORY OF DUILIUS
OVER THE CARTHAGINIAN FLEET AT MYLAE IN 260 B.C.

Capitoline Museum, Rome

confidence and resolved to attack the sterns and broadsides of the enemy, hoping to avoid the corvi.

Polybius, who is our only authority for the battle, says that whenever a Carthaginian approached a Roman ship he found its corvus hanging over him. Of course, this is not literally true, for each corvus covered only the bow of its own ship. But the Romans were originally more numerous and had taken 30 ships in the first round of the battle, increasing their advantage in numbers. Consequently, although more sluggish than their opponents, yet when one of the latter had momentarily lost control of her movements through collision with an enemy, there must have been some disengaged Roman near by, available to creep up and spike her with the corvus, after which she was soon finished. The battle ended by the withdrawal of the Carthaginian fleet after the loss of 50 ships. It is apparent that the latter part of the action was fought with more reserve on the part of the Carthaginians than the early part, in which more than half the losses occurred.

This renowned battle was a victory of the individual soldier and his weapons rather than one of fleet maneuver, but to Duilius is due the great credit of finding the way to give his men their opportunity by the new invention, just as Themistocles gave his men their opportunity by choice of a narrow channel. The victory caused all Rome to rejoice. Duilius was awarded a triumph and a tablet (opposite) in somewhat pompous phrases has recently been discovered in Rome, recording that, first of Romans, he received the privilege of being escorted after dark with torch bearers and flute players in honor of his victory. To this day his memory is proudly commemorated by the Italian Navy in the name of its greatest battleship. Hannibal who had escaped from Mylae returned to Carthage where he seems to have rendered an acceptable explanation of his defeat, for shortly after, probably the next year, he went to Sardinia with re-enforcements to the garrisons there. The Roman fleet followed and caught his ships in harbor and captured many of them (Tarn suggests 60). Most of the crews escaped to the shore where they crucified their late Admiral Hannibal.

The Fleets Become Inactive

The season of 260 and the following years brought no decision in the army operations in Sicily, in spite of the naval successes of the Romans.

The reason seems to have been that Lilybaeum, the Carthaginian strong-hold in Sicily, was at the extreme western end of the island, and Carthage held also Panormus on the north side and as far as Heraclea on the western part of the south coast. Consequently, the Romans could not lie on the communications of the enemy nor, though superior, force a naval battle, because the ships of the time required an operating base very close to the area of operations. Thus the Carthaginians could supply their armies with men and stores, as could the Romans, yet neither army was strong enough to force a decision. But during these years of naval inactivity both sides were building ships.

The Roman Fleet Renews Activities

In 257 the Roman fleet became active. It raided Melita (Malta) and no doubt profited in its seamanship by the expedition. After returning to Sicily, while lying at Tyndaris on the north coast near Messana, the Romans saw the Carthaginian fleet passing in some disorder. Atilius Regulus, the Consul, chased immediately with 10 ships, telling the rest to follow as soon as they could. The Carthaginians turned on the Consul's small squadron and surrounding it sunk all but his own ship, which escaped by its handiness and its full crew of rowers. The rest of the Romans then arrived in close order and attacked so successfully that they sank 8 ships, took 10 more with their crews as prize, and drove the rest to the Lipari Islands.

This action determined both parties to increase their naval forces.

Battle off Mount Ecnomus

By 256 B.C. both sides had large fleets and Rome had determined to transfer the war to Africa where she might hope to disorganize the Punic Empire based upon a nexus of trade and tribute leading to the imperial city. In the summer of that year the Romans assembled their new fleet at Messana under the Consuls M. Atilius Regulus and L. Manlius Vulso and from there steered south to Cape Pachynum and then along the south-ern shore to Mount Ecnomus where the army lay, intending there to embark a selection of choice troops and take them to Africa. The Car-thaginians had no doubt been well informed of the preparations of their enemy and were aware of the weakness of their own coasts and the difficulty of defeating the Roman army after its landing in Africa. In consequence, the Council sent its fleet under Hamilcar to Sicily to break up the invasion before it crossed the sea. After touching at its main Sicilian base at Lilybaeum, the Punic fleet proceeded to Heraclea on the south coast, about 35 miles west of the Roman base and camp.

Polybius puts the Roman fleet at 330 ships and that of Carthage at 350, and the total number of men in both at 290,000. These figures are impossibly large. I therefore follow Tarn's estimate and place the Roman men-of-war at 250 and assume the rest of the 330 named by Polybius as being the cargo transport ships, with comparatively few soldiers or rowers. As for the 350 Carthaginian ships named by Polybius, it is probable that this number also includes many transports and merchantmen that availed themselves of the fleet's escort to cross to Sicily, but did not remain with it. Assuming the same average size of crews as suggested for the campaign of 260, the number of men in the entire Roman expedition, including transports, may have reached nearly 60,000 souls in 330 ships and the Carthaginians may have had 43,000 in 200 ships with no transports. Such was the military advantage of the less populous power based on the willing support of its people over a rich country relying on a mercenary force without real attachment to its employers.

The two fleets were now facing each other from their respective bases; each with its lines of communication by sea and land securely held behind it and each with a river near by to supply water for the ships. The battle soon to occur was one of the most skillful maneuver-battles in naval history. The account in Polybius clearly describes the strategic objectives of the campaign and the tactical story is so good that when an attempt is made to plot the movements on a chart, the result is consistent in all its parts. I shall therefore offer a description of the battle accepting every detail of maneuver by our only authority, Polybius, but supplementing him by making the inferences which his statements authorize and by what we know from other sources as to naval practice of the times.

To carry out the strategic object of the Roman campaign and land in Africa with a fair prospect of success, military supplies were no less necessary than the troops themselves. Both sides understood this and the Punic fleet under Hamilcar was at Heraclea for the express purpose of breaking up the Roman expedition before it could leave Sicily. As fleets of those

days avoided the open sea as far as possible, Hamilcar could count on the
Romans passing him on their way to the western point of Sicily before
taking departure for Africa. He could wait for the Romans to appear.
The tactical plan of the Romans had to provide for escorting the great
train of transports[5] past the hostile fleet to a safe landing in Africa. As
this could scarcely be done without a battle, the essential tactical point
was to cover the transports while fighting the battle. For Hamilcar also
the key of the problem lay in the transports. The progress of the war had
hitherto given him no reason to suppose that in a downright boarders'
battle he could overcome the Roman legionaries. He wanted an opportunity for free maneuver of his ships for ramming. It must have been
apparent to him that without their supplies the Consuls would not go to
Africa, and a successful attack on the more or less helpless transports
would stop the expedition. In any case it would make the heavy Roman
battleships maneuver under disadvantage and so give the Carthaginians an
opportunity to profit by the superior nautical skill of individual ship
captains. The general tactical situation recalls Homer's account of the
Greeks and Trojans fighting under the walls of Troy for the body of
Patroclus.

As the fleets lay awaiting the Roman advance, each must have had a
fairly good knowledge of the situation of the other. No doubt the Carthaginians had observers on the hill sides above the Roman camp and
fishermen off shore to report the enemy's preparations. At last the day
came. We may assume that the night before the engagement the Roman
ships lay close to the beach, riding to single anchors and with their sterns
aground. The army details to the ships had been made and the soldiers
spent the night near their own ships. Presumably the Romans got away at
earliest daylight, so that the fleet was formed and the advance begun no
later than sunrise. The course was somewhat north of west, hugging the
coast, which permitted close approach.

By riders and by fire signals afloat and ashore, the stir in the Roman
camp the night before must have been made known to Hamilcar in time
for him to embark his men and have his fleet under way only an hour or
two later than the Romans.

Although the Romans were assuming the strategic offensive, tactically

---

[5] Horse transports Polybius calls them, but no doubt they carried a full line of supplies also.

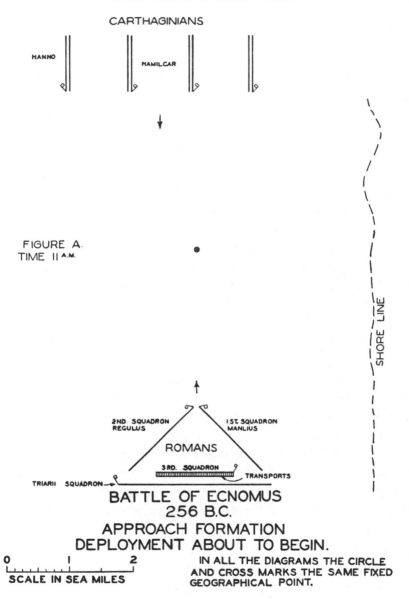

CARTHAGINIANS

HANNO

HAMILCAR

FIGURE A.
TIME II A.M.

SHORE LINE

2ND. SQUADRON
REGULUS

1 ST. SQUADRON
MANLIUS

ROMANS

3 RD. SQUADRON

TRIARII SQUADRON →

TRANSPORTS

BATTLE OF ECNOMUS
256 B.C.
APPROACH FORMATION
DEPLOYMENT ABOUT TO BEGIN.

0   1   2

SCALE IN SEA MILES

IN ALL THE DIAGRAMS THE CIRCLE
AND CROSS MARKS THE SAME FIXED
GEOGRAPHICAL POINT.

the presence of the transports threw them on the defensive with the penalty of handing tactical initiative to the enemy. Consequently, the Roman fleet took a formation to guard the transports, yet suitable for navigation and from which the fighting ships could readily deploy for battle as the enemy's movements might require. The fleet was divided into four squadrons and, as Polybius says, each battle squadron took a double name. The first three squadrons were called first, second, and third legions and the ships of the fourth squadron were called "triarii." We are not to suppose that the squadrons each carried a legion of men, including therein both Roman and allied troops. The two consular armies in Sicily amounted to some 40,000 men and half of them must have been left in Sicily as a garrison for the eastern half of the island. As the Carthaginian army was in Sicily and as it was a hired force, it would be difficult for Carthage to make an effective army in Africa on short notice, and the Romans may have felt justified in carrying the war to Africa with a part only of their field strength. A Consul was in command of each of the first two legions or squadrons, each having a hexere (6-banked ship) as his flagship. The two hexeres were together in the center of the van, each Consul having his own squadron extended in echelon on his quarter. Astern of the double echelon came the third squadron in line, forming the base of the triangle of which the other two were the sides. This third squadron had the transports in tow. The arrangement was probably not only to aid the transports on their way (for they had some oars, like all small ships), but also to keep them from straggling and so avoid confusion and delay. Astern of all came the "triarii," named after the rear division of the legion when in battle formation. The triarii were in line, like the third squadron, but with greater intervals between ships, so that the wings outreached the rear corners of the triangle. It is quite possible that this rear squadron had fewer ships than the other three. The entire Roman formation probably presented a front of about 2 miles (4,000 yards) and a depth of over 1 mile (say 2,500 yards) and was no doubt preceded by scouts several miles ahead, with what are now called "repeater" ships closer to the main body to pass signals, which were few and simple.

Polybius tells us, that on hearing the Romans were out, the Carthaginian admirals addressed their men as custom and the occasion required and put out of port full of hope and eager resolution, and headed eastward along the coast. All must have been told that the Roman ships were heavy and presumably would be embarrassed by their transports, and that the Carthaginians, having fighting ships only and those lighter and swifter than the Romans, would seek the opportunity to make their main attack on the cargo transports.

We may assume that the Carthaginians were in motion an hour later than the Romans, both fleets moving at a speed not over 2.5 knots an hour, in order to preserve the strength of the rowers for exertion in battle. By six o'clock, then, the two fleets were a little over 30 miles apart and closing at a combined speed of 5 knots.[6]

Polybius does not describe the Punic cruising formation, but from what he says incidentally and what we know from other sources as to usual ancient and medieval tactics, we may assume that the fleet was in a compound formation of four columns abreast of each other about a mile apart. For the sake of handiness in maneuvering, each column was perhaps a double one, so that 200 ships probably covered an area about 3 miles wide by 1 mile deep. As for the individual columns, it is a probability (which the result of the battle confirms) that, while the Roman fleet was stronger as a whole, the Carthaginian admiral strengthened the flank columns at the expense of the center ones in order to carry out his plan of encircling the enemy to get at the transports.

By nine o'clock the commanders in chief were beginning to learn something of each other from their respective reconnoitering ships. Not only were communications maintained by a few simple signals, but there were dispatch boats which carried aides up and down the battle line to pass orders and information by word of mouth. Such a rôle and such a ship is taken by the goddess in the famous statue of the winged Victory of Samothrace, now in the Louvre, which shows her embarked on a diere passing along the battle line and trumpeting good fortune to the fleet.

By eleven o'clock the two main bodies were 5 miles apart and "after seeing the enemy's dispositions" (this phrase of Polybius implies good reconnaissance), Hamilcar decided upon his battle plan and deployment (Fig. B). (In all the figures the asterisk indicates the geographical point which was halfway between the two commanders in chief when the Carthaginians began deployment.)[7] Hamilcar directed his left column along the shore, where at first it may have been more or less invisible against

---

[6] The times given hereafter are of course assumed, but they are such as to allow for each phase of the action and for the completion of victory before sundown of a summer day.

[7] At 5 miles off the hostile hulls were visible to each other even from the decks of these low ships and, of course, the admirals had the best eyes in the fleet by their sides to inform them. The present general use of telescopes makes us forget that in every large group of men there are some whose unaided vision is as far superior to normal good vision as a binocular is to the naked eye. The important part which such keen natural vision played in ancient navigation is recorded by the share Argus is alleged to have taken in the search for the Golden Fleece. In modern times Admiral Togo is said by the Japanese Navy to have had such a gift.

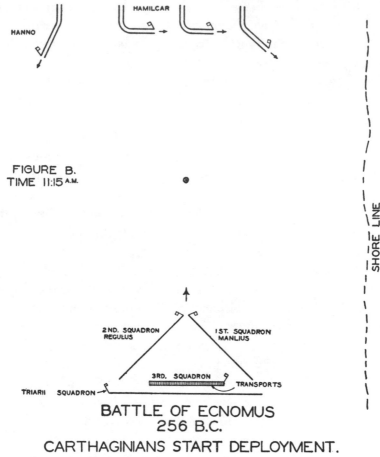

FIGURE B.
TIME 11:15 A.M.

BATTLE OF ECNOMUS
256 B.C.
CARTHAGINIANS START DEPLOYMENT.
ROMANS CONTINUE APPROACH.

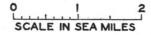

SCALE IN SEA MILES

the land, and the right column under Hanno, composed of the fastest ships, inclined to seaward with the intention of enveloping the enemy and getting at the transports. The two center squadrons under Hamilcar himself turned "head of column left" and when all ships had made the turn they executed "ships right," bringing all into one line, facing the enemy (See Fig. C). The lead of the flank columns over the center made the "forceps" mentioned by Polybius.

Naturally the Romans would slow as the enemy began his maneuver,

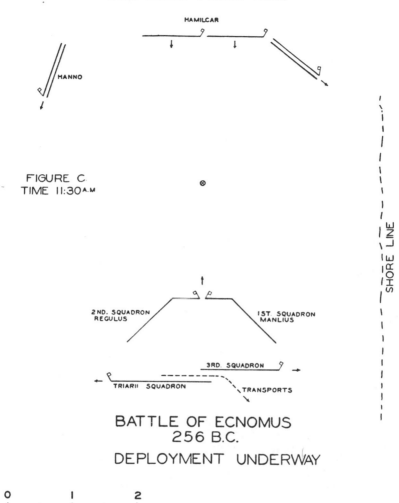

FIGURE C.
TIME 11:30 A.M

BATTLE OF ECNOMUS
256 B.C.

DEPLOYMENT UNDERWAY

0   1   2
SCALE IN SEA MILES

in order to give themselves more time to take their own formation before the enemy was upon them. Since Hamilcar naturally had the initiative, the Consuls had to grasp the objective of his movement before they could move to answer it. In a few moments the intention of the enemy must have become evident to the Consuls. They had to frustrate a general envelopment. The consular flagships continued to move slowly forward, while the flank ships of their own squadrons resumed speed and came forward, converting the double echelon into line, either straight or slightly

convex to the enemy. The third squadron turned towards the shore to
meet the hostile left wing under the land and the triarii moved seaward
somewhat and then followed the Consul Regulus on his seaward quarter

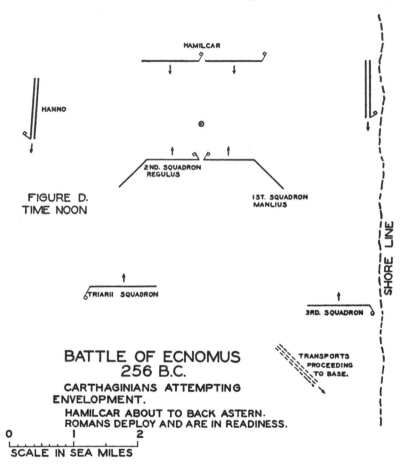

FIGURE D.
TIME NOON

BATTLE OF ECNOMUS
256 B.C.

CARTHAGINIANS ATTEMPTING
ENVELOPMENT.
HAMILCAR ABOUT TO BACK ASTERN.
ROMANS DEPLOY AND ARE IN READINESS.

until Hanno's intentions developed more fully. It was the business of the
triarii to support the Consuls, if Hanno should attack them in the rear, and
to interpose between Hanno and the transports, if the latter were the
objective. The triarii had chosen a commanding position from which by a
judicious choice of course they could force Hanno to fight them before he
could get at the transports (see Fig. D).

Polybius is not very clear about the transports. He says they were
towed by the third squadron, but at the close of the action he seems to
place them out at sea with the triarii. This does not appear a probable

location. The course of the battle indicates them as the original objective and, as they were not fighting ships, it seems that they must have fled from the enemy (as transports have always done) and scattered for the

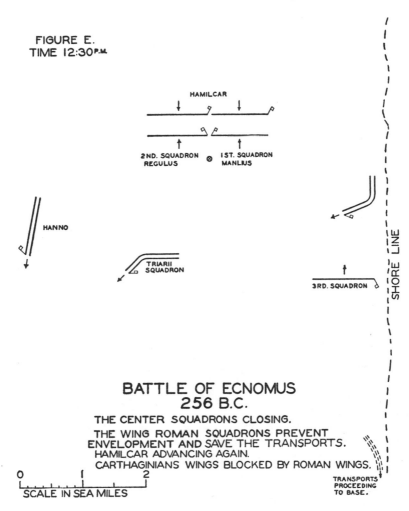

FIGURE E.
TIME 12:30 P.M.

HAMILCAR

2ND. SQUADRON
REGULUS

1ST. SQUADRON
MANLIUS

HANNO

TRIARII
SQUADRON

3RD. SQUADRON

SHORE LINE

BATTLE OF ECNOMUS
256 B.C.

THE CENTER SQUADRONS CLOSING.
THE WING ROMAN SQUADRONS PREVENT
ENVELOPMENT AND SAVE THE TRANSPORTS.
HAMILCAR ADVANCING AGAIN.
CARTHAGINIANS WINGS BLOCKED BY ROMAN WINGS.

TRANSPORTS
PROCEEDING
TO BASE.

0   1   2
SCALE IN SEA MILES

shore and the base, leaving the escort to do the fighting. Thus at least they could save the crews from capture and destroy the ships, if overtaken by the enemy. The Roman deployment prevented general envelopment and provided each Punic detachment with an opponent. Half an hour after noon the two Punic wing squadrons were passing the Roman center and, about the same time, the Punic center under Hamilcar, which had been closing with the Consuls, reversed its course (ships probably backing) and retreated, drawing the Consuls farther from the transports on which it was hoped to make the decisive blow. At nearly the same time the head of the third Roman squadron had reached the shore, cutting off the approach of the enemy left squadron to the transports and, after turning into line, it moved along the coast toward its opponent. The latter turned its head to seaward to get room to form line of battle and then it too swung into line and faced the Romans. Although the third Roman squadron had thus been able to interpose between the enemy and the transports (see Fig. E), in the action which followed it was hard pressed and skillfully and gradually backed its seaward (left) wing towards the shore, in which position the enemy could not get in the rear of the ships and the corvi kept him from decisive frontal attack.

A somewhat similar maneuver was going on out at sea where the triarii had also met and held Hanno's squadron of fast ships but were scarcely a match for it, as the slow moving Romans could not prevent attacks on their sterns in the open sea. In the meantime the Carthaginian center squadron having drawn the Consuls a couple of miles from the rest, Hamilcar again signaled to reverse course and attack, which was done with the greatest fury. By 1:30 P.M. the action was general and, as Polybius says, there were three different actions in three different places (Fig. F). In the center the Romans were decidedly stronger, but the light Punic ships were

much more nimble and skillfully handled, advancing to ram and withdrawing again, yet the Romans felt no less assurance of victory from the vigor and courage of their troops, the presence of the Consuls and the advantage of the corvi

which, when they fell on the enemy, enabled the legionaries to board in certainty of success. At last Hamilcar fled from the scene with his two squadrons, leaving his disabled ships. The Consul Manlius remained to secure the prizes and mop up.

Regulus with his squadron went to aid the triarii who were not faring well. He approached the enemy on their disengaged side opposite the triarii and, thus threatened between two enemies, Hanno retreated to seaward with such ships as could escape, and the second battle ended. While Regulus was engaged in his second battle, Manlius accomplished his task and moved towards the shore, where the third squadron was

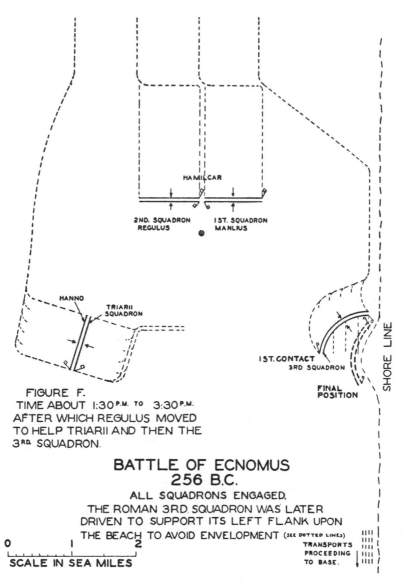

FIGURE F.
TIME ABOUT 1:30 P.M. TO 3:30 P.M.
AFTER WHICH REGULUS MOVED
TO HELP TRIARII AND THEN THE
3RD SQUADRON.

BATTLE OF ECNOMUS
256 B.C.

ALL SQUADRONS ENGAGED.
THE ROMAN 3RD SQUADRON WAS LATER
DRIVEN TO SUPPORT ITS LEFT FLANK UPON
THE BEACH TO AVOID ENVELOPMENT (SEE DOTTED LINES)

0   1   2
SCALE IN SEA MILES

fighting a drawn battle against the Punic left squadron. The Carthaginians could not get astern of the Romans and feared to close from ahead and be caught by the corvi, while the Romans dared not leave the shore. The approach of Manlius gathered the principal harvest of prizes. Between the third squadron and his own ships Manlius surrounded the enemy and Regulus also coming up, the Romans captured 50 ships with their crews from that squadron alone and few got away steering close along the shore. Thus the third battle closed, with the Romans victorious. The Carthaginians had 30 ships sunk and lost 64 prizes with their crews. The Ro-

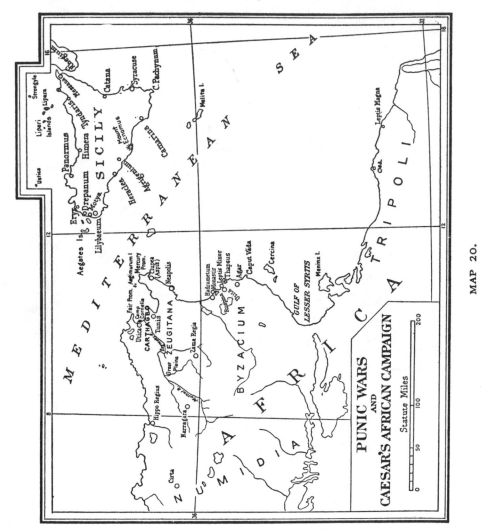

PUNIC WARS
AND
CAESAR'S AFRICAN CAMPAIGN

Statute Miles

MAP 20.

mans had 24 ships sunk, but none were captured and the transports were safe.

This battle is noteworthy in the history of naval tactics for several reasons. In the first place, the Carthaginian attempt to reach the transports compelled the Romans to separate their squadrons instead of holding them in the usual mass for a defensive battle. Secondly, the slow Roman ships were successful in meeting and holding each detachment of the enemy. Thirdly, each Consul took his own squadron into a second engagement after victory in the first. That the Consuls were successful in doing so much with their sluggish ships is the highest tribute to their leadership and tactical skill and to the Roman discipline which governed on the sea as on the land.

It is interesting to speculate on the probabilities of the campaign had Hamilcar allowed the Roman fleet to pass to the westward of his position before delivering the attack. In that case the Romans would have gone by Heraclea in the night and he might have missed them, but if he had overtaken them, as was more probable, the transports would have had a hostile shore and therefore the Consuls would have had to fight in a massed formation with the transports in the center.

Expedition to Africa

After the great success of Ecnomus, the Romans returned to port with their prizes, repaired damages, resupplied their ships, and (this time at ease about the enemy) started again for Africa. It is not necessary to believe that the Romans embodied all their prizes in their fleet, as some modern commentators suggest. The state would have had to replace the crews of the lost ships, besides finding additional men for the prizes; but, after the victory, the Roman need for ships of war was less than that for transports to carry the army and its supplies.

The expedition now made a safe passage to Africa and the first ships anchored off the Hermaean Promontory, now Cape Bon, and waited for the rest to arrive, showing by their confidence how complete was the defeat of the Punic navy. When all had come up, they coasted 10 or 15 miles south to Aspis where they disembarked their forces, drew the ships ashore, and threw up entrenchments around them and resolved to invest the city of Carthage about 75 miles away (by road), having first demanded its surrender (see Map 20).

Upon hearing of the disaster at Ecnomus, the leaders at Carthage were persuaded that the Romans would soon be off the city. They therefore made the necessary arrangements both by land and sea for securing the approaches to the coast; but when they heard that the enemy had already landed off Aspis and was besieging that city, they began to levy forces and devoted their efforts to fortifying Carthage and its environs. The Romans soon obliged Aspis to surrender. They now had a base for their communications with Italy and, having sent to Rome to tell the news and ask for further instructions, they raided in the neighborhood and returned to their ships, having taken many cattle and 20,000 slaves. Allowing 10 days more or less to get important dispatches to Rome (distant 300 nautical miles in a direct line, but 600 via Ecnomus, then across Sicily to Messana, and by sea along the coast of Italy to Rome), the reply would be back within the month. Winter was approaching. The senatorial instructions were to retain 15,000 foot and 500 horse with 40 ships under the Consul Regulus. The rest, say 5,000 men with the prisoners, were to return under Manlius to Rome. The return passage was safely accomplished, but the Carthaginians, seeing that the Romans intended to remain in their country, withdrew from Sicily 5,000 foot and 500 horse under Hamilcar.

The strategy of the Romans in thus carrying the war into Africa seemed justified. Regulus gained a very decided victory and occupied Tunis, 12 miles from Carthage, and wintered there while the Numidian tribes rose in revolt against Carthage. The city was in despair and Regulus invited the Carthaginians to discuss surrender. The offer was gladly accepted. Regulus wished to finish the matter before the arrival of the new Consuls of the year to assume the command and the credit, yet the terms he offered were so severe that the city rejected them and prepared to withstand his utmost efforts.

The over-confidence of Regulus was his undoing. About this time Xanthippus, a Spartan soldier of fortune, arrived at Carthage and offered his services to the city. They were accepted and, being an able soldier, he drilled and organized the army. By the spring of 255 he defeated Regulus with great slaughter and captured the Consul himself, only 2,000 Romans escaping to the base at Aspis where they were besieged. The new Consuls had been charged with the fitting out of a great fleet to push the attack, but Rome having heard of the destruction of the army in Africa the fleet was sent to bring away the troops in Aspis. And now the Carthaginians on learning of the new Roman fleet made every exertion of their own. Having repaired their old vessels and built some new ones, they sailed for the Hermaean Promontory and awaited the Roman fleet, which easily defeated them, taking 114 ships with their crews. The Romans then embarked the garrison of Aspis and returned with their prizes. Off the south coast of Sicily at Camarina, a heavy gale wrecked all but 80 of the fleet with great loss of life. The loss was attributed to the obstinacy of the Consuls who insisted on moving for military reasons, contrary to the advice of the pilots who thought the time unsuitable.

RENEWAL OF THE WAR IN SICILY

Both by their victory in front of their city and by the destruction of the Roman fleet in the gale, the Carthaginians were encouraged to think that they would now have the upper hand. They therefore sent Hasdrubal to Sicily with the troops that had been brought thence to defeat Regulus, and with them went 140 elephants which had much terrified the enemy in the battle before Carthage. They also got ready a fleet of 200 ships. The Romans were unshaken by the loss of ships and built 140 new ones, bringing the number in the fleet to 220. This new fleet was built in three months, not quite so much of an effort as the first fleet in two months, and joined the survivors of the gale at Messana. The new Consuls took the fleet and army by the north coast of Sicily to Panormus, which they besieged and captured without any great resistance, making slaves of 13,000 citizens and ransoming the rest at 200 drachmas ($46.00) each. Thereupon the Consuls left a sufficient garrison in the city and returned to Rome with all the army that was not needed. It was the custom, so far as possible, to dismiss the soldiers for the winter.

In 253 the Consuls sailed to Sicily with all the fleet and from there to Africa, where they made raiding descents of little importance. On one of these at the island of Meninx, through ignorance of the coast, the fleet was stranded at low water and in danger, but the tide coming in and the ships having been lightened, they got off and returned precipitately to Panormus. Thence on the way to Rome the fleet was again struck by a storm off Lucania and lost 27 ships.

The Romans now became less intent on war in Africa, and for 252 the Consuls confined their efforts to Sicily, with only 60 ships to convoy supplies for the army. On the other hand, as the Romans were not disputing the sea with them, the Carthaginians were encouraged and they thought they might be superior on shore on account of the terror of the Romans about the elephants. There was, indeed, great dread of these animals in battle. For two years, the war in Sicily was one of exhaustion, but then the Senate again began to rely on sea power for success. In 251 the Consuls built 50 ships and began to levy men for them. In 250 Hasdrubal took the offensive and advanced from Lilybaeum towards Panormus, relying on his elephants to overcome the enemy, but by this time the Romans had learned to parry the attack of elephants and the able former Consul Cecilius not only routed Hasdrubal, but captured several elephants and restored the confidence of the army and gave it new life and spirit.

Siege of Lilybaeum

The Senate was so encouraged by this great success, early in the summer, that it resolved to make a great effort that year, by land and sea in Sicily and, having made all preparations, the Consuls sailed for Sicily, with 240 ships and 4 legions besides allied troops, with the intention of besieging Lilybaeum (see Map 14), believing that, if they could take this great stronghold of the enemy in Sicily, they would have the most suitable base for the invasion of Africa. They felt the more secure in this opinion as Drepanum, the only other remaining important possession of Carthage in Sicily, would not be very serviceable as a point from which to operate against the Roman communications with Africa. The Carthaginians were fully alive to the situation and resolved to hold Lilybaeum as the best protection against invasion of their homeland. So began the Roman blockade that lasted to the end of the war in 241.

The city thus to be held was well defended by a ditch and wall of uncommon strength and depth and by lakes filled with sea water. The garrison numbered 10,000 mercenaries besides the inhabitants. The siege opened by vigorous attack and counter operations. The defense was desperate; nevertheless the besiegers made progress. During a long time no accounts were received at Carthage of the siege and, being persuaded that the city must need relief, 50 ships were sent with 10,000 men including some soldiers under Hannibal, son of Hamilcar, who had commanded at Ecnomus and was a friend of Adherbal who commanded in Sicily. Hannibal ran to Aegusa, an island about 6 miles from Lilybaeum, and awaited a suitable wind to force the blockade. It is an illuminative commentary on ancient naval practice that hostile fleets lay within such a short distance of each other without the great fleet of the Romans taking action, for it is scarcely to be supposed that news did not soon pass, whatever the weather. Fishing boats can brave severe gales and information soon leaks.

Hannibal's command was unequal to a battle and he was far from wishing one. His affair was to put men and supplies into the city. Accordingly, when the wind was fresh and favorable, he made sail (contrary to battle custom) and charged the harbor mouth. The Roman fleet was not only surprised by the sudden appearance of the enemy, but dreaded to oppose him to windward of the harbor, for it was difficult for long ships to head up to the sea under oars, and under sail they would drift to leeward. In any case, collision with the enemy would end in both ships drifting into the harbor while they struggled. As a result of these objections to action, the Romans watched the evolution without resisting it, while the citizens were filled with joy, which arose even more from the audacity and success of Hannibal than from the material aid which he brought. This bold operation under sail is almost the only one of classic times preserved for us. Another one under Cleopatra at Actium had wider renown. Such was the restoration of confidence at Lilybaeum by Hannibal's entrance that it was resolved to make a surprise sortie by 20,000 troops to set fire to the Roman camp and works. But after a very severe action the sortie was driven back with heavy loss without having accomplished its purpose. Hannibal then took his ships by night to Drepanum where Adherbal had the main Carthaginian fleet.

An interesting tale of ancient navigation is given by Polybius at this point of the siege. At Carthage the people were anxious to have information of the siege and a certain Hannibal, the Rhodian, who commanded a specially fast and seaworthy vessel, volunteered to break the blockade and return. He arrived near Lilybaeum and anchored off a nearby island. The next day, with a favorable wind and steering on a range known to him to lead him safely past all dangers, he passed through the blockading ships and was ready to go out the third day. The Consul, greatly irritated, stationed himself with 10 ships on both sides of the entrance, as near the harbor as the shoals permitted. But the Rhodian steered boldly past all and then, turning his bows towards the harbor mouth, he lay on his oars offering challenge to the enemy; but when none ventured to accept it he went on his way to Carthage. He came and went frequently, so that others also took up the feat and thus greatly encouraged as well as aided the general defense.

The Romans were so disconcerted that they endeavored to choke the harbor mouth, but the currents washed the obstructions away. At last, at one point they got something to remain in place and one of the finest Punic ships stranded on it. This the Romans manned with the best crew they could assemble and put it on station. It happened that soon after the Rhodian appeared coming out of port, which he had entered the previous night. He soon knew of the vessel pursuing him and endeavored to escape, but was obliged to turn and fight. The Romans were much superior to him in their crew and obtained an easy victory and now, with the two swift prizes, they effectually closed the entrance.

The Carthaginians now devoted themselves to the work of defense with little hope of success, but a strong gale arose by night, which they utilized to issue out and fire the Roman siege towers. The Romans suffered so much at this time that they made no further attempt to press the siege and contented themselves with a blockade by land until the end of the war, 8 years later.

Battle of Drepanum

It was now the year 249. The Roman fleet had lost most of its men in the siege operations for which they had been landed.

After hearing this, the Senate sent 10,000 new levies to render the fleet mobile[8] and upon their arrival the Consul Claudius resolved to attack the hostile fleet at Drepanum (see Map 14), only some 12 miles away, since he did not expect Adherbal to know that the fleet had been re-manned. Accordingly, he put on board his new levies with the survivors of the winter and filled up with volunteers from the legions who were attracted by the prospect of booty and the variety of a short operation at sea. Apparently the sight of the new levies made an unfavorable impression on the priests on the Consul's staff, for they reported their sacred chickens would not feed. This was bad, for Claudius expected the hostile fleet at Drepanum to be re-enforced soon. So it was now or never, and he lost his

---

[8] That the quinqueremes were not so large as Polybius formally alleges is shown by his statement that 10,000 men formed the majority of the crews of 123 ships with which Claudius set out. The rowers must have been well under 140 men per ship, since the re-enforcements included deck hands as well as rowers.

temper and drowned the sacred chickens, saying that if they would not eat they could drink, and proceeded. It was a bad commencement when he could not control his propaganda department.

The crews embarked at midnight and may be presumed to have formed their column and got away before two o'clock. Admiral Serre assumes the column to have been one of fours, with a distance of 80 meters between each four, making a column 2,500 meters long or less than 1.5 sea miles. Serre states that the column of fours was a usual one in ancient times, but, although very probable, I have not been able to verify it; double column, however, is mentioned occasionally by ancient authors and is probable on this occasion. A column less than 3,500 yards long would be too short to form single line. The movement of the fleet would be slow, between 2 and 2.5 knots, for the crews should not be exhausted before arrival. By five o'clock the fleet would be sighted from Drepanum and Adherbal notified. As soon as the news came Adherbal acted with extraordinary promptitude and good judgment. The general alarm was sounded, the seamen assembled on the beach by the ships, where the mercenary troops joined them, and Adherbal delivered the usual exhortation before battle and issued his battle order to the assembled crews, so that none could misunderstand, namely, that the ships in column should follow him as guide. With this simple order as directive he embarked (about seven o'clock) and led out by the northern side of the harbor as the enemy was approaching it on the south side. Thus, before meeting the enemy, Adherbal had an opportunity to establish regularity in the column and the consequent sense of security in the men. His people had reason to be pleased with themselves and with him—a great asset before battle.

On the other side all was confusion. The Consul had apparently issued his battle order as a command to enter the harbor and strike everything in sight, and had then placed himself at the rear of the column to hustle laggards, instead of at the van to guide and direct the battle. Consequently, he did not know that Adherbal was on the job until word could be passed to him from the van which kept on into the harbor according to plan, although the bird had flown. When Claudius was aware of the circumstances, he directed a reversal of course, but by this time every one knew that the Consul had miscarried and ships withdrew, those that had reached the harbor falling foul of each other, breaking their oars and in gloom.

The chickens had known their Consul. The odds were against the Roman before closing with the enemy, but nevertheless he did what he could to make ready for battle. Claudius was now at the head of the fleet in its reverse order and led it south along the shore, while the new rear was recovering itself and taking position. Then the Roman fleet turned ships right and faced to seaward in line and waited for the enemy.

In the meantime Adherbal, after passing beyond the rocky islets on the west side of the harbor and seeing that all was well with the rear, turned south parallel to the coast and to the enemy's line of ships. After he had gone far enough to outflank the Roman left with 5 ships, he turned towards the enemy and formed line-of-battle. Apparently his column had been straggling and his rear ships had to close distance more or less before turning into line. When line was established, Adherbal made the signal to advance against the enemy, who remained near the shore. Such a position had helped the Roman third squadron at Ecnomus, but now it was unavailing. At Ecnomus the Carthaginian frontal attack met the corvus and the shore protected the sterns, but here there is strangely no mention of the corvus and the frontal attack succeeded. As Polybius explains it,

> When the fleets were joined, the contest was for some time equal, being maintained by the choicest of the legionary troops. But by degrees the Carthaginians drew victory to them by the help of many favorable conditions. Their vessels were light and quick moving and their rowers skillful and experienced and they had much advantage from being to seaward. When one of them was closely pressed, it had both speed and room to retreat. If the enemy advanced too far in pursuit, they turned quickly on them and attacked on the side and sometimes on the stern and sunk many, for the Roman ships were both sluggish in themselves and manned by unskillful rowers. If one of their ships was getting the worst of it, others came up readily to assist it as the sea was open to them; but for the Romans conditions were otherwise. They had no room to withdraw under penalty of grounding, neither were they lively enough to break through the hostile line and turn again. Neither could they support a weak point in their line for there was no room for ships to pass along the line astern of the ships engaged. Many were thus stranded on the shoals or driven ashore. In the end the Consul escaped from the battle with 30 ships of his own left wing and the rest, 93 in number, were captured with their crews (20,000 missing) [9] except for a few crews who forced their ships upon the beach and escaped.

---

[9] As some crews escaped after landing, something less than 93 ships had 20,000 men, i.e., the crews of, say, 80 or 85 ships were not over 250 each, including soldiers.

Thus ended the battle, the only serious naval defeat for the Romans. The Carthaginian admiral reaped all the honor that was due him, but the Romans pursued the Consul with curses when he returned to Rome and, as the Senate was not beyond learning from an enemy, it inflicted a heavy fine on him (12,000 denarii, about the cost of a ship).[10]

The fault of Claudius was the very common one of unskillful leaders even to this day, of devoting himself to an administrative task in which he felt competent, instead of to tactics in which he was less skilled. The rear should have been in charge of some hard-boiled old seaman to curse the stragglers and keep the column closed. But the commander in chief went there himself for this purpose, instead of taking position at the head of the column to receive reports from the scouts and modify his plans as circumstances might require after looking into the harbor. Had Claudius been in the lead and an able seaman, it is conceivable that he might have retained the initiative by inclining the head of column to seaward and then falling on the enemy's rear as it left the harbor in haste and confusion. The essence of his plan was surprise, but owing to his predilections as a drill master and lack of orders for the van, the enemy was able to recover from the surprise and deliver battle on his own plan.

Minor Naval Operations

Notwithstanding this defeat, the Romans continued their efforts and dispatched the Consul Junius with 60 ships to escort provision ships to the army blockading Lilybaeum. At Messana he was re-enforced by additional ships from the camp at Lilybaeum and other points in Sicily and sailed to Syracuse where he assembled 120 ships of war and 800 transports. Probably most of the latter were of no more than 10 tons' burden. Here he sent forward his quaestor, with half the transports and a small escort, while he waited at Syracuse for the allies to send in their tribute of grain. About the same time Adherbal, after sending his prisoners and prizes to Carthage, gave 30 of his own ships to Carthalo who had arrived from Carthage with 70 more, and directed him to execute at Lilybaeum what had been Claudius' plan at Drepanum, i.e., he was to fall on the Roman fleet supporting the land blockade of Lilybaeum. Car-

---

[10] At this time a denarius was ⅛ ounce of silver, nearly the same as a drachma of 67 grains ($0.21).

thalo had better fortune. At daylight he drove into harbor and set fire to some ships and took the others, which were not many. While the Romans ran in confusion to save their ships, the garrison of the town made a successful sortie and the Romans suffered.

Carthalo was now encouraged to go to meet the fleet approaching under Junius' quaestor. The advance scouts of each fleet gave notice of the other's approach and, while Carthalo hastened on, the quaestor placed his ships, which must have been small, near a small town which had no port, but where certain small creeks permitted the ships to thrust themselves and take shelter. He borrowed some ballistae from the town and beat Carthalo off when he rashly attacked him. Carthalo thereupon anchored at the mouth of a nearby river and remained in observation. At this juncture the Consul Junius, having completed his stores at Syracuse, doubled Cape Pachynum with the rest of the fleet and in ignorance of events. Carthalo was warned of his approach by his outlying ships and hastened to meet him before the two Roman detachments could unite. Junius was unwilling to accept battle and anchored at a dangerous point of the coast, resolved to risk all there rather than deliver his ships to the enemy. The Carthaginians refused to attack him on such foul ground and anchored nearby between the two Roman squadrons.

Then it was seen that a heavy gale was approaching and by advice of his pilots Carthalo got under way and secured a safe anchorage in a lee under the other side of Cape Pachynum, while the Consul, less wisely advised, attempted to ride out the storm where he was and lost ships and men, arriving himself at Lilybaeum with only 2 ships, the rest being utterly destroyed. The Carthaginians now had complete mastery of the sea and their affairs on land in Sicily were by no means desperate. But the Roman resolution was unshaken and their armies in the field were still superior. Junius, indeed, succeeded in making more effectual the blockade of Drepanum, but was soon captured by a sally from Drepanum and, after his exchange, he committed suicide on arrival at Rome.

Both contestants were now exhausted, the Roman population was shown by the census of 247 to have lost nearly 20 per cent and Carthage was little better off. The war now ran heavily for some time, in consequence of exhaustion, yet the blockades of Lilybaeum and Drepanum, the only two Punic positions in Sicily, were resolutely maintained. Two reliable former Consuls were re-elected to hold on in 248. There was some cross raiding. A Roman squadron went to Hippo on the African coast and burnt much of the town and shipping. Nevertheless, the inhabitants got the harbor chains in place and confined the raiders within, who thereupon charged the chain with the soldiers well aft to raise the bows and, as each bow passed over the chain, the men ran forward and lifted the stern, and so the ships jumped the obstruction and got free. Of course, the point was that the chain was scarcely taut enough. The British ram *Polyphemus* jumped floating obstructions in somewhat the same way about 50 years ago at the annual maneuvers.

In 247 Hamilcar Barca, who had been put in charge in Sicily, began raiding the Italian coast, but Rome put garrisons in the cities and let them protect themselves, and established some new colonies without attempting a naval campaign. In 246 Hamilcar landed west of Panormus near Eryx and established a new harbor and fortified it and again raided the Italian coast. He now had an opening to the interior of Sicily, but no new Roman navy was in commission that year. There was little activity. In 244 Hamilcar attempted to isolate the Roman blockaders of Drepanum, but did not obtain entire success.

Battle of the Aegatian Islands, 242

Rome now turned resolutely to sea power as the way of ending the blockades of Lilybaeum and Drepanum, for it was evident that both could hold out so long as Carthage would send supplies. But Rome was too poor for the state to build ships and wealthy citizens came forward with loans enough for the purpose, to be reimbursed in case of success.[11] By the summer of 242 the loan ships were ready, bringing the fleet to 200. They sailed for Drepanum under the Consul Catulus, arriving there to find that the Carthaginian fleet was idle at home. The Consul invigorated the siege operations and got control of the entrances both to Lilybaeum and Drepanum, but he was careful not to expend his naval forces upon the siege. He knew the Carthaginian fleet was to be expected, and he exercised the crews and trained the fleet with the object of meeting the enemy at sea.

The Carthaginians heard with astonishment that the Romans were at

---

[11] It is said that the new fleets were built after a superior model captured from the enemy, but if this is true, it probably offered no great change in general design.

sea and prepared their fleet without soldiers, utilizing the ships to cross as transports and expecting Hamilcar to man them with soldiers for battle after they had discharged their supplies. The fleet (number of ships not stated by Polybius) sailed under the command of Hanno, who resolved to follow the example of Hannibal at the beginning of the siege and run to the harbor under Eryx on a favorable opportunity and get soldiers from Hamilcar. Accordingly he anchored at Hiera, the outer one of the Aegates Islands (see Map 10), nearly 20 miles from Lilybaeum, and 5 miles farther from Eryx, meaning to run the blockade, discharge stores, and complete his crews.

But Catulus was more alert than his predecessor and, hearing of the arrival of the Carthaginian fleet, he placed himself at Aegusa, nearer to Sicily than Hiera and only 8 or 10 miles from the two ports. He there made the usual harangue to his forces, both to stimulate them and to explain his purpose, and told the pilots he would offer battle the next day. But when the morning came there was fresh breeze from the west and some sea. The day was favorable to the enemy who could run before the wind under sail and enter port (he could not fight for lack of men), while the Romans could not well face the sea. Catulus deliberated on these points. It was dangerous to permit the hostile fleet to enter port and be inspired by the daring spirit of Hamilcar, and then to fight it after it had received its soldiers and ships had become light and handy by the discharge of supplies for the army. At the last he decided to venture battle, for the enemy had seized the occasion and was coming down under sail. He showed a resolution few admirals in history have equaled and now reaped the reward of his drill and preparation. The well-trained rowers had little difficulty in forming line of battle, facing both the unfavorable wind and the enemy. The Roman ships were light of stores and cleared for action. The Carthaginians were heavy with cargo, the rowers were untrained, and the few soldiers were recruits. It must have been with heavy hearts that they hauled down their sails and took to the oars to confront the Romans, whose highly trained soldiers now had the better ships under them. Under these conditions the story of the actual battle is short, the Romans took 70 ships with all the men and sank 50. But the wind continued to favor the Carthaginians, it shifted in the battle and Hanno brought the remainder of his fleet (Polybius does not say how many) back to Hiera, while the Consul was struggling to secure his prizes and get them safely to port against a head wind. The prisoners numbered nearly 10,000, which is another suggestion of small crews, i.e., 140 surviving prisoners per captured ship (few soldiers). This decisive victory was the conclusion of the war and Hanno was crucified on his return home for taking a sporting risk as circumstances and his orders required.

TERMS OF PEACE

Drepanum and Lilybaeum had been isolated from Sicily for years; now they were cut off from Carthage as well and the Punic Senate sent word to Hamilcar to make the best terms he could. Catulus and he agreed upon a treaty of peace to be approved by the Roman people, namely, Carthage to evacuate Sicily, not to war against Hiero of Syracuse, to release all Roman prisoners, and pay reparation of 2,200 talents ($2,239,200) in a term of 20 years.[12] The treaty was rejected at Rome, probably because the reparation money was not enough to repay the citizens who had built the fleet of 200 ships which closed the war, so commissioners were sent to Sicily to amend the terms, which they did by adding 1,000 talents ($1,018,000) to the reparation and cutting the time of payment to 10 years. Considering that the revenue of the Carthaginian state before the war was about 12,000 talents, the total reparations came to one-fourth of one year's income, or roughly equivalent to a sum for the United States in 1929 of about $100,000,000 a year for 10 years, a very moderate sum as reparations now go.

REVIEW OF THE WAR

In the course of this war of 23 years, during a large part of which the navies did not operate on a large scale, the losses by battle and recorded storms were about 500 for the Romans and about 450 for the Carthaginians. (See Tarn, *Journal Hellenic Studies*, 1907.) Taking the fleets at their highest as numbering 450 together, and busy years with slack years, this is a service expenditure of 9 per cent a year, and there must have been many additional casualties not due to great occasions. Taking the rowers

---

[12] At Rome, at that time, the ratio of gold to silver seems to have been 17:1.

and the seamen as averaging under 150 men per ship, we have for the full Roman fleet in this war about 35,000 men in the crews. The fighting men were withdrawn from the legions as occasion required at a rate probably under 80 men per ship, unless in the exceptional case of some huge consular flagship. Probably the whole fleet never had on board more than 20,000 soldiers.

The strategic feature of the war was the entire dependence of both sides on sea power for control of Sicily. Each had possession of half the island at the beginning. It was impossible for either to expel the other, unless the fleet of one could cut off sea communications of the other army. In the latter part of the war, when Rome had possession of the whole island except the two bases in the west and the region held by Hamilcar's army, she could not subdue them until she had a fleet there able to cut off supplies by sea. The tactical development of the war was the corvus which enabled the Roman soldiers to make victory turn on their valor and swordsmanship, instead of on the seaman-like skill of the Carthaginians in maneuver and the use of the ram.

In one way the First Punic War was the most important Rome ever fought, for it marked an entire change in her national policy regarding her extension of rule. In Italy, each victory brought her autonomous allies who paid her nothing but joined their efforts for the extension of good order and security under Roman leadership. But with the conquest of Sicily the Roman policy changed. The island became subject to Rome and paid tribute. Thenceforward, with the Italian peninsula as a base, Rome extended her authority over tribute paying subject allies; and from a community chiefly agricultural she became a commercial and financial power, ruling the basin of the Mediterranean under the shield of her legions and her navy. Her conquest of Sicily substituted in considerable measure the Greek forms of life and culture for the national ones and, with the defeat of Carthage, she assumed much of Carthage's methods of domination and exploitation of other peoples and used her navy to extend her rule through the Mediterranean basin.

PRINCIPAL AUTHORITIES CONSULTED FOR THIS CHAPTER

ANCIENT

Polybius.

MODERN

Cambridge Ancient History, vol. 7.
Delbrueck, H.: *Geschichte der Kriegskunst.*
Freeman, E. H.: *History of Sicily.*
Kromayer, J.: *Schlachten Atlas.*
Mommsen, Th.: *Roman History.*
Rostovtseff, M.: *History of Ancient World.*
Serre, P.: *Les Marines de Guerre de l'Antiquité et du Moyen Age.*
Tarn, W. W.: *Journal of Hellenic Studies*, vol. 27.

APPENDIX TO CHAPTER X

ROMAN QUINQUEREMES

Assuming that the Roman quinquereme of Duilius had 150 rowers, 75 soldiers, and 25 sailors and ship's officers, we have 250 in all. Making the high estimate of 8 days' allowance of food, water, and fire wood at 16 lbs. per day and, for the men themselves, of 220 lbs., including clothes, arms and armor, and sundries, we have a weight of 87,000 lbs. A single-decked hull would not exceed 50 per cent of the total load displacement even for the green wood and imperfect shipbuilding of the Romans. The ship's equipment and stores would not exceed 16.7 per cent. The whole displacement of the quinquereme would thus come to 116 tons. A rowing chamber 61 ft. long would be needed for 15 oars on a side and the whole length of the ship might be 100 ft. Oars for 5 men would be about 36 ft. long; with 12 ft. inboard and 2 ft. for passageway between them this would give 26 ft. beam between tholepins. A beam of 18 ft. at the water line would afford sufficient stiffness and that would require a draft of 4 ft. There would be two side rudders, an attached metal ram, raised ends, a single mast and sail, the former 47 ft. long from the keel, with a sail whose area would be about 1,400 ft. (rather small). With a wetted surface of 1,695 ft. the full speed under oars would be about 6.6 knots and 4 knots for 2 hours. Under sail with fresh winds without much sea (i.e., close in shore, with off-shore winds), she could make 9 or 9.25 knots. The deck space of about 2,000 sq. ft. would be enough sleeping room for 250 men, according to medieval practice.

The distinctive fitting of this craft was the corvus on the bow. As shown p. 307, it is a mast rising 14 ft. above the deck, with a gangway 4 ft. wide and 18 ft. long pivoted at the heel of the mast and its outer or upper end held nearly upright by a rope topping lift. Two guys, one each side, served to swing the gangway about. A heavy spike under the outer end of the gangway served to pierce and hold the deck of the enemy when the topping lift was let go.

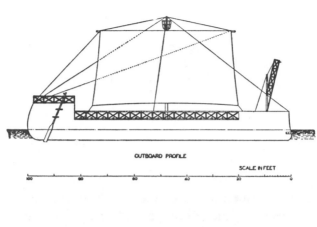

OUTBOARD PROFILE

SCALE IN FEET

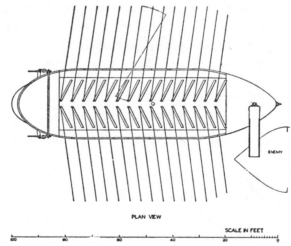

PLAN VIEW

ENEMY

SCALE IN FEET

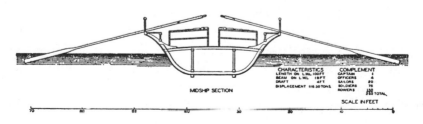

MIDSHIP SECTION

CHARACTERISTICS		COMPLEMENT	
LENGTH ON L.WL.	100 FT.	CAPTAIN	1
BEAM ON L.WL.	18 FT.	OFFICERS	4
DRAFT	4 FT.	SAILORS	20
DISPLACEMENT	116.30 TONS	SOLDIERS	75
		ROWERS	120
			220 TOTAL

SCALE IN FEET

ROMAN QUINQUEREME TIME OF PUNIC WARS

CHAPTER XI

THE SECOND PUNIC WAR

GENERAL SITUATION AFTER CLOSE OF FIRST PUNIC WAR

IN THE Second Punic War the ancient historians are chiefly occupied with the mighty deeds of Hannibal and the terror of Rome, and they pay little attention to the limitations which Roman sea power placed on Hannibal's resources and accomplishments and upon the efforts of his Macedonian ally, King Philip, to aid him. No great sea battle took place in the war, yet the preponderance of Roman sea power was an indispensable factor in the Roman endurance which wore down the Carthaginian strength. The development of Roman sea power under military and economic need we shall now follow, even though of naval tactics on the high seas we shall see little.

The First Punic War began the transformation of Rome from a chiefly agricultural community into one relying on tribute, commerce, and sea power for its prosperity, and the process was accomplished in the succeeding half century.

We cannot suppose that Rome was entirely without commercial relations with the outside world until her wars with Carthage, but until then it was commerce that sought her. She did not try to control commerce for the enhancement of her general prosperity. Of course, Rome herself had a market at her disposal arising from the foreign trade which passed along her coasts. It seems to have been the needs of the allies in South Italy, rather than the desire of Roman citizens to take up trade, that caused the Roman Republic to develop commerce and sea power.

Apparently other people saw the line of Roman progress long before it was realized in the city itself. When the Republic undertook the conquest of South Italy, after repulsing the invasion of Pyrrhus, the second Ptolemy sent an embassy to Rome in 273 B.C. Its purpose has not been recorded for us, but it is a plausible conjecture that Ptolemy saw that the great commercial interests of his kingdom extending to Italy and beyond were likely soon to come under the protection and control of the Roman Senate, and he probably desired to introduce himself and his commercial agents to its favorable notice.

After the peace of 241 with Carthage, the new national policy of peace and good order on the seas for the benefit of allied trade was grafted to the old policy of security for Roman and allied territories. At the same time the tribute from Sicily forcibly initiated Roman citizens and the Senate itself into the conduct of financial and mercantile affairs on a scale previously unknown to them, yet without any strong impulse from the body of citizens. The development of Roman finance in politics originally arose from the need of making contracts for supplying those armies which extended the area of the Roman peace in the interest of allied and provincial manufacturing and commerce.

Even the Senate does not seem to have realized the great change that had been accomplished, and it was consequently very slow to meet the situation by appropriate action. Unfortunately the great historians of the period, Polybius and Livy, do not dwell on the economic pressure developing the Roman policy. We are told of the political differences and the debates in the Senate and of the military events of the wars which were their outcome; but the economic and commercial situations, which gave rise to the political differences, did not seriously attract their attention and we must infer much from the slight allusions.

When the treaty of 241 was signed, Carthage was far more worn by the war than was Rome. Hostilities had been chiefly conducted in Sicily; but, in addition to the struggle with Rome, Carthage had lost her Spanish possessions, including the rich silver mines, through causes not well known, but which seem to have been owing to efforts of Massilia. Then, too, the mercenary army mutinied after coming home from Sicily, and a 4-years' war on the home territory was necessary for the Punic Senate to subdue the insurrection, under the leadership of Hamilcar Barca. During this time, the Carthaginian army of occupation in Sardinia also mutinied and applied to Rome for support against the authorities at home. After a refusal, Rome acceded to a second request and sent an army to occupy the island, and thenceforward Sardinia was her tributary province. By 237 the center of political responsibility for trade in the western Mediterranean had shifted from Carthage to Rome.

Carthaginian power and business were limited to Africa, except for some footholds on the Spanish south coast near Gibraltar. The Egyptian, Asian, Balkan, and Greek trade, which crossed the entrance of the Adriatic, came under Roman protection and profited the Roman people; at the same time the economic contact developed a Roman taste for Greek culture, which a generation later fostered the movement for political control beyond the Adriatic. Towards the west, Massilia was the ally of Rome; her trade connections reached in one direction to her sister Greek cities in South Italy (see Map 19) and in the other to her trading posts established on the eastern coast of Spain as far as Cape Palos. Through France, via the Garonne River and the Bay of Biscay, she seems to have had business as far as Britain. It is thus apparent that the Roman fleet, built up to conquer Sicily, became after the peace the chief guardian of commercial security and prosperity throughout the Tyrrhenian and Ligurian seas as far as Alicante, the outermost colony of Massilia. But the Spanish colonies of Massilia were far from the center of Roman power and almost beyond it.

CARTHAGE BEGINS TO RECOUP HER LOSSES

After the suppression of her military rebellion, Carthage set herself to retrieve her commercial prosperity which had rested so largely on Sicily and Spain.

In 237 Hamilcar Barca, having sworn eternal enmity to Rome, was made general of all the Carthaginian forces and crossed the Straits of Gibraltar with a strong army to undertake the reconquest of Spain as a necessary step towards reseizure of the commercial dominance which had existed previous to the war with Rome. Before his death nine years later, he not only had regained the former possessions of Carthage in Spain and established a great base seaport at Cartagena on the southeast coast, but had extended his authority as far as Cape Nao, to reach which he had occupied the country behind the Massiliot ports from which they drew their trade. In these operations, besides regaining a fertile country and securing the rich silver mines, he had also recruited and trained a mercenary army drawn from the conquered lands themselves.

With Carthage pressing aggressively forward in this way, Massilia could only expect to be entirely shut out from her Spanish commercial connections, and we can scarcely doubt that she strongly urged Rome to take up her quarrel. At any rate Rome did so, and in 231 sent an embassy to Hamilcar to remonstrate, who replied that his military operations were for the purpose of securing resources with which to pay the treaty indemnity to Rome. It was far from Rome to the area in dispute, and intermediate naval bases on the coast of Spain were lacking. In spite of her naval predominance as far as Corsica and the Riviera, Rome could take no effective action on behalf of her ally, and Hamilcar continued to consolidate Carthaginian power in Spain.

In 228 Hamilcar died in battle and was succeeded in authority by his son-in-law Hasdrubal, who pushed the Punic advance onward toward the Iberus River. The Massiliot overland line of trade with the Bay of Biscay and Britain was an inviting prize for the Carthaginians to seize and put out of competition with their own line through the Straits of Gibraltar. Again Rome was disturbed by the Punic encroachments on Massiliot reserved trade areas, and a treaty was made in 226 between Hasdrubal and Rome, by which the former agreed to make the Iberus the Carthaginian boundary. Polybius says that Rome could not push a quarrel with Hasdrubal at that time because the Celts in North Italy were threatening trouble. So the Roman recognition of the Iberus as the Punic boundary was itself a concession, because it recognized the loss of three Massiliot colonies south of the river.

The treaty left Hasdrubal free to consolidate his conquests south of the Iberus, while Rome was relieved from anxiety about his further advance in Spain and set herself to meet the Celtic hostilities in the basin of the Po. The Celtic war began in 225 and lasted till 222 when the Celts were defeated. It employed an army of 50,000 Romans and as many more in reserve, so that Rome was fully occupied, while the Carthaginians improved their base in Spain. Hasdrubal was assassinated in 221 and was succeeded in command by his brother-in-law Hannibal, son of Hamilcar, who thought himself ready to undertake the war with Rome which had been his father's impelling motive in the occupation of Spain.

Roman Sea Power on the Adriatic

Rome Feels Obliged to Protect Trade

During these years in which Rome had felt unable to prevent the reconstitution of Punic control in Spain, she had been obliged to extend her sea power across the Adriatic. As has been said previously, the Successors of Alexander warred for the control and profits of mercantile trade and ate up much of the profits in the cost of the wars. Nevertheless, the struggle continued through all the third century B.C., with Egypt and Macedon each endeavoring to hold for itself the bases offered by the Cyclades Islands. In the two great sea battles of Cos and Andros (see Map 2), about the middle of the third century (of whose details we know nothing), Antigonus Gonatas of Macedon, son of Demetrius, established control of the Cyclades and of business passing westward to Italy. He also controlled the line out of the Euxine to the ports of Macedonia and Greece.

Many of the cities of Greece were not satisfied with the somewhat burdensome rule of Macedon and united themselves into the two federations of Aetolia and Achaia, on opposite sides of the Gulf of Corinth. They hoped to manage their own affairs more to their own advantage than when under Macedon, but their hostility to her and to each other prevented their paying due attention to security on the seas for commerce in the Adriatic and across it to Italy and beyond. The result was that the Illyrians, a half-civilized group of tribes living on the coast of the present Yugoslavia (nearly corresponding to Dalmatia, Montenegro, and northern Albania), drew together under an able ruler, Agron, and their piratical operations which had always prevailed in the upper Adriatic began to extend more to the south and to interrupt commerce on the passage between Italy and Greece, while the coasts of Greece were raided with large forces.

The Romans were slow in interposing to protect Italian shipping, for they had difficulties to settle in Sardinia, and the Punic progress in Spain drew their attention. Still, in 230, they sent an embassy to Queen Teuta, who had succeeded her husband Agron on the throne of Illyria. To the Roman remonstrance against Illyrian depredations upon Italian trade, Teuta replied that it was "not the custom for Illyrian Kings to restrain their subjects from endeavoring to enrich themselves on the sea." The youngest of the ambassadors answered with some heat,

> Among the Romans, Oh Queen, it is one of the best and noblest customs to exact public reparation for private wrongs and at all times to redress the complaints of their subjects; and we shall endeavor shortly, with the assistance of the gods, to force you to reform the kingly customs of Illyria.

This undiplomatic reply cost the speaker his life, for the enraged lady had him followed and assassinated as the unsuccessful mission returned to the seacoast, but the threat is noteworthy as the embodiment of the whole foreign policy of Rome: the security of the citizens and allies and of their business as the affair of the state. It is the rule which is held to justify national expansion to this day.

In the spring of 229 the Illyrians began depredations early and drew a number of vessels together, with which they occupied Epidamnus (see Map 2) and laid siege to the city of Corcyra, whose inhabitants asked the Achaians and Aetolians for aid. A squadron of 10 Achaian ships was named by the joint efforts of the two federations and steered towards Corcyra to raise the siege. The Illyrians drove off the enemy in a battle which deserves notice if only for the method of fighting of the Illyrians. They lashed their small vessels side by side in groups of fours with plenty of men on board, and offered them, thus unmanageable, to the ram strokes of the enemy. As soon as the heavy Achaian ships crashed into one of the group and was held in the wreckage, all four crews leapt on the deck of the enemy and took him by boarding and force of numbers. Thus the Achaians lost four quadriremes captured and one sunk, while the rest took advantage of the wind and escaped under sail. The Corcyraeans thereupon surrendered the town and received an Illyrian garrison.

First Roman-Illyrian War

The Romans had not overlooked the murder of their envoy the previous year, and about this time both Consuls (Fulvius and Postumius) crossed the straits, one in command of the fleet of 200 ships and the other with a consular army of 20,000 men. The fleet went to Corcyra hoping to save the city. Although too late to do this, Demetrius of Pharos, to whom Teuta had committed it, seceded to Rome and delivered the city to the Romans. To this over-powering Roman force the Illyrian Queen could make no serious resistance.

By the treaty of 228 the Illyrians were obliged to relinquish all the Greek towns which they had seized and were forbidden to allow more than two ships in company, and those unarmed, to pass south of Lissus. Further to secure Italian commerce, the Romans held the Greek cities they had rescued from the Illyrians, but under a mild rule which gave complete satisfaction in the subsequent troubled times. In addition, Demetrius was established by them in his own island of Pharos and with greatly increased territories, in the belief that these would act as buffers between the other Illyrians and the line of trade across the Adriatic. One of the Consuls now paid a visit to the Aetolian and Achaian Federations and was admitted to the Isthmian games at Corinth, which was tantamount to recognition of Rome as a Greek power.

The Roman occupation of Corcyra and neighboring districts was not regarded favorably by Macedon which had the claim of former occupation. Nor were the other Greeks too much pleased by the Roman presence, which had accomplished a Greek task in relieving them all from the Illyrian menace as well as from Macedonian pressure. Nevertheless, the Roman expeditionary forces returned to Italy at the close of the campaigning season, leaving only a squadron of 40 ships for local coast patrol. With the Celtic Wars in Italy, the Romans now had much to occupy them for several years and were unable to give serious attention to Grecian affairs.

The new King of Macedon, Antigonus Doson, was thus able to devote himself to re-establishing Macedonian leadership in Greece, during the next 7 years. During that time Demetrius of Pharos ceased to fear the Romans and broke from them. He allied himself with Antigonus, invaded the territories on the west coast of the Balkans under Roman protection, and at last, in 221, went so far as to break the treaty of 228 by bringing his fleet south and ravaging about Malea and in the Aegean. He was driven out of the Aegean by the Rhodians who were always protectors of trade.

Since the Roman operations against the Celts in 225-222 did not require the use of the Roman fleet, it may be asked why it was not employed to put Demetrius in his place. The probable answer is that such ships as were in commission were needed not only for local coast service in the Celtic War, but also were themselves used to transport military supplies from Sicily and Lower Italy to the ports near the armies.

Second Roman-Illyrian War

But at the close of the Celtic War, it was necessary to restore security on the eastern side of the Adriatic as promptly as possible, for in Spain

Hasdrubal was succeeded by Hannibal, in 221, and his hostile intentions towards Rome could not be concealed. In the same year, Antigonus Doson died and was succeeded by the young and able King Philip. It was quite possible and even probable that the new King, jealous as he was of Roman authority in his neighborhood and friendly to Demetrius, might encourage the latter in his defiance of his obligations to Rome. With Hannibal threatening hostilities, it was highly necessary for Rome to cover her rear from an attack by a Carthaginian fleet operating with aid of and from a base supplied by Demetrius. Accordingly, in 219, while the Roman military strength was still disengaged and King Philip was occupied with war in Aetolia, Rome struck again at Illyria with a strong expeditionary force under both Consuls, L. Aemilius Paullus and M. Livius Salinator, and soon drove Demetrius from Pharos and into exile and restored the situation as it had been established by her in 229.

After this pacification in Greece and Illyria, the Consuls with their fleet and army promptly returned to Italy to await developments in Spain. Roman commerce was safe and Rome had put her house in order for the coming Punic War by securing her eastern line of supplies.

CIRCUMSTANCES AND CONDITIONS PREVIOUS TO OPENING OF SECOND PUNIC WAR

We now turn to Hannibal's invasion of Italy, which was the main movement in the great war, to which other operations were secondary, and which for 16 years threatened the existence of Rome. As he had been chosen by the army in Spain to succeed Hasdrubal as commander in chief, late in 221, the Senate in Carthage confirmed the choice of the soldiers and Hannibal was put in command of all the Punic forces by sea and land. The Barcide family policy of war against Rome was of course well known in Carthage, yet it was not entirely unopposed. There was a party in Carthage which perhaps preferred the continuance of peace and, in any case, doubted the possibility of destroying the Roman Republic by operations in Italy or even of diminishing its Empire. Consequently, Hannibal must have felt that a war in Italy directed from Africa would meet the same lack of support which his father, Hamilcar, had experienced in Sicily in the last years of the previous war. A war supported from the men and revenues of Spain entirely under the control of Hannibal and his family would at least have unity of direction. We may take it then that the Barcide policy was an aggressive commercial policy for the extension of Empire in the western Mediterranean, and the means for this extension was a campaign in Italy until Rome should be willing to relinquish her allies and protectorates to the rival power of Carthage.

The season of 220 was occupied by Hannibal in consolidation of his rule south of the Iberus (Ebro). In 219 he attacked the city of Saguntum lying south of the Iberus, but which not long previously had asked for and received the favor of an alliance with Rome. The grant of this alliance by Rome had been itself an infringement of the treaty of 226 with Hasdrubal, which recognized the overlordship of Carthage south of the Iberus. Now, when the time had come, Hannibal found in the alliance a plausible *casus belli*. Saguntum had engaged in quarrel with a neighboring tribe under the protection of Hannibal, and on the face of the matter the latter's attack and siege of Saguntum was a local punitive operation. Really, it was a defiance of Rome which noted Hannibal's challenge by sending an embassy to him remonstrating against his attack upon an ally. The embassy was refused an audience by Hannibal and went on to Africa to lodge its protest at Carthage, where the debate it was able to raise in the Council exposed the political reasons for Hannibal's preference of a war based on Spain. At the end of the discussion the Roman speaker dramatically said, "I hold for you the choice of war or peace in this fold of my garment." The Council replied, "The gift is yours," and the Roman shaking the fold from his hand answerd, "Take, then war." But instead of sending succor to the besieged city of Saguntum the Romans turned eastward, as has been said, and spent their efforts for the season of 219 in the restoration of order on the eastern shores of the Adriatic for the protection of their commercial connections with the Aegean Sea and beyond to Rhodes and so with Egypt. Upon the conclusion of the Roman campaign in the Adriatic, the siege of Saguntum was also drawing to a close and both sides were looking forward to operations in 218.

The line of Hannibal's action must have been more or less evident to the Romans, and they perceived that his attack on Saguntum ought not to be the means of luring their army into Spain. The military situation was that Rome had an almost inexhaustible supply of soldiers, the finest known, but led by generals chosen yearly as civil magistrates for political reasons of the forum, who occasionally were able generals but usually not so. Carthage, on the other hand, had a mercenary army, not so numerous, but led by professional military men, and at this time, although then unknown, the Carthaginian commander in chief was one of the greatest generals of all history. As for the available forces, we learn from Polybius that at the beginning of 218 Hannibal had an army which seems to have numbered over 130,000, but an analysis of Polybius' figures by Delbrueck in his *History of Warfare* gives us 82,000 as a more probable number. (The latter's figures as to army strength are chiefly followed hereafter.) In the fleet there were 50 quinqueremes in Spain and 55 were sent to sea from Africa at the outbreak of war. The Carthaginian fleet seems not to have had many more at any time during the war.

The Roman army was composed of an annual levy on the burgesses according to needs of the year and the allies of Rome sent contingents normally amounting to more than the Romans. For the year 218, the Romans proposed to raise two legions for North Italy with 11,000 allies in addition to the usual double army consisting of two legions each of 4,000 infantry and 300 cavalry, with about twice as many allies, for each Consul. As for the fleet, the Romans opened the war with 220 quinqueremes and 20 light craft in commission. Polybius (Bk. 6. Chap. 19) says the crews of the fleet were not included in the legions. There were in service that year ashore and afloat about 110,000 men.[1]

The overwhelming superiority in strength of the Roman fleet at the opening of the war gave the Romans control of the Tyrrhenian Sea and along the present Riviera as far as the territories of their ally Massilia. In Sicily Rome held the fortified ports of Panormus, Lilybaeum, and Messana (the latter was in alliance with King Hiero of Syracuse). From Sicily she commanded the coasts of South Italy and the passage across the Adriatic with an intermediate base at Brundisium. South of the line from northern Spain to Sicily, control of the sea lay with Carthage, although both sides occasionally cross-raided in the other's area. In the end, the outcome of the war turned on the superior ability of Rome to preserve lines of supply over-seas for her people and her fighting armies against the diplomatic and military efforts of Hannibal to break those lines and substitute his own. The situation was strategically much similar

---

[1] Ships' crews were taken from a poor class of citizens, but it is not altogether clear to me whether ship-soldiers were from the same class or from the legions. If not from the legions the whole force in service would be 125,000.

to that in the last war, when the allied blockade silently wore down the spectacular efforts of the Central Powers. It was the Roman sea power which, in addition to the political situation at Carthage, forbade Hannibal effectively to use Africa as the base of his effort against Rome. A war based on Africa would first have to conquer Sicily and then the Carthaginian army would still have to cross the straits to reach Rome.

Hannibal's movement from Spain by land was practicable and even advantageous. It is probable that Hannibal had a fairly clear idea of the strategic plans of his enemy, through the spies which we are told he maintained in Rome, for the intentions of a Senate cannot be kept entirely secret. Hannibal's preparation for the war had been to establish friendly diplomatic relations with the Celtic tribes in Gaul north of Massilia, and particularly with their kindred in the Po Valley, who had just been overcome by Rome. His plan of campaign was to pass quickly through Gaul, avoiding all entanglements with Massilia, and enter the Po Valley on the northwest side of the river. Here he proposed to make an advanced base, recruiting both men and supplies and then move on Rome.

Rome's plan also is not too indistinct. When Hannibal challenged her, early in 219 by the siege of Saguntum, her immediate response was to secure her commercial connections to the east, and she sacrificed a minor ally for ulterior advantage in the war. Although Hannibal's extraordinary ability was not yet in evidence, Carthaginian military strength in Spain was too great for Rome to seek war beyond the Iberus. But it was not impossible to put a consular army into Gaul, with the allied fortified seaport of Massilia as its advanced base, and from thence to hold the passes of the Pyrenees against the exit of the Punic army, and that this was the intention of the Roman Senate best explains the subsequent movements of the Roman army. Moreover, Rome intended to carry on an aggressive war of invasion, utilizing her powerful fleet to pass into Africa, as Regulus had done nearly 40 years before.

THE OPENING OF THE WAR

The season of 219 ended with the capture of Saguntum, after which Hannibal withdrew to New Carthage to prepare for the Italian campaign. In the same autumn, Rome elected the Consuls for the coming year,

Publius Cornelius Scipio and Tiberius Sempronius Longus. To the first, who was to meet Hannibal in the defensive effort, was assigned the northern army of 24,000 men with a squadron of 60 ships to accompany it to Gaul and to cover its communications with Italy. Sempronius was given the striking army of 26,000 men meant for Africa, which was directed to assemble in Sicily with a squadron of 160 ships; but apparently it was not meant to cross into Africa until Hannibal should come in contact with Scipio's army and so be held by it from returning to Africa to act against Sempronius.

As the campaigning season opened in 218, Hannibal was the first to get in motion. He sent 20,000 Spanish troops to strengthen the garrison of Africa, left 15,000 soldiers to his younger brother Hasdrubal to hold Spain south of the Iberus, and gave him 32 manned and 18 unmanned quinqueremes to keep communications with Africa. With less than 50,000 remaining he marched north from New Carthage early in May on his way to Italy. About the same time, he dispatched two raiding squadrons from Africa, one of 35 ships to the coasts of Sicily and the other of 20 ships to the Italian mainland. The obvious purpose of both was to disturb the flow of supplies to and from Sicily and check Sempronius from moving on Africa by giving him something to think about.

HANNIBAL STRIKES THE FIRST BLOW IN SICILY

It is convenient to deal with the naval operations first. The second Punic squadron bound for Italy got north of Sicily (see Map 19), when it was dispersed by a gale and three ships drifted before Messana, where they were promptly captured by the local squadron, and the Romans learned from the prisoners not only of the rest of their own squadron, but also that another larger one was coming over to make a landing at Lilybaeum. As often happens in war, this first stroke, coming unexpectedly as it did from Africa, altered the intentions of the recipients and threw them on the defensive. Roman ships and men were hurried to Lilybaeum, where they arrived in time to meet and repulse the first enemy squadron, which suffered a loss of 7 ships captured;[2] the remaining 28 ships withdrew. The Consul Sempronius, fearing the raid would raise an insurrection

[2] The 7 quinqueremes yielded only 1,700 prisoners and therefore were far inferior in size to those which Polybius asserts to have employed 300 rowers alone in the First Punic War.

in Sicily, was on his way to Lilybaeum to direct operations when he heard the Carthaginians had been driven off. In spite of the triple superiority of the Roman fleet, this slight attack had postponed a Roman invasion of Africa for 14 years. Sempronius altered his whole strategic plan and used his powerful fleet for counter-raiding instead of for invasion. He first captured Melita (Malta) which held a 'Carthaginian garrison and was a convenient base from which to raid the south side of Sicily, both for the purpose of supporting local uprisings against Rome and for the sake of booty. The Consul now heard that the Punic squadron driven away from Lilybaeum had gone to the Lipari Islands, where 17 ships of the other squadron had found refuge after the gale which dispersed them. On the arrival of the Roman fleet at the Liparis, it ascertained the enemy had gone on to the west coast of southern Italy where it was ravaging the shores.

These operations probably lasted until some time in July, when an insurrection in the Po Valley made the Senate disinclined to send the army to Africa. It was not long before Hannibal was in Italy (early part of October) and the Senate had called for the southern army to proceed north. Accordingly, Sempronius sent his army by sea to Ariminum and, after making suitable arrangements for the maritime defense of South Italy and Sicily, he followed his army. As Hannibal seems to have been commander in chief of all the Carthaginian forces, there is every reason to believe that he ordered this maritime raid in the south to divert Roman attention from the initiation of his own campaign and gain him a good start over his adversaries. Before going further, it seems advisable here to say that while Hannibal's invasion of Italy and his stay there of 15 years was the principal event of the war, nevertheless, Roman victory depended on success in five subordinate over-seas theaters of war, in which Roman sea power played a decisive part in cutting off Punic aid to Hannibal.

There was the 12-year war in Spain which prevented that country from being an effective base to Hannibal. Then there was the 9-year war against Macedon which prevented re-enforcements to Hannibal from crossing the Adriatic. A 4-year war in Sicily had the economic result of making Sicilian grain available to feed Rome and strategically, the conquest of Syracuse prevented that seaport from becoming an essential mid-way base on the direct line of communication from Carthage to Hannibal. After the conquest of Spain, Hannibal's brother Mago was able to take an army to the Po Valley, but his 3-year war there was ineffective because Roman sea power prevented adequate resources being sent him from home. Finally, the Roman war of two years in Africa, based on undisputed sea communication with Rome made Hannibal and Mago withdraw from Italy and closed the war. These six different wars were not very closely interlocked and the history of each is here given more or less independently, yet Roman victory in each was very essential to final success.

HANNIBAL'S INVASION OF ITALY AND THE ROMAN OPPOSITION

Taking up the main operation, Hannibal did not leave New Carthage (Cartagena) very early in the season of 218 and, even after crossing the Iberus (early in June), his first task was to subdue the present Catalonia before going farther. But he had so prepared matters in advance that, about May, the Boiian Celts in the Po Valley rose in insurrection at the news he was coming to Italy. The Roman levies for the year had not yet all been called from their homes. While they began to assemble it was necessary, under pressure of the news from Spain, to use the only two available legions against the rebellion, to secure the Po Valley and to see to the fortification and occupation of the new colonies for its defense. Scipio was therefore unable to carry out his plan of starting early to meet Hannibal north of the Pyrenees.

When the new levies were ready, he got off by sea from Pisa, and on the fifth day he reached Massilia (275 miles) with his army of about 25,000 men and landed at the eastern mouth of the Rhone. Here he learned that the disturbance in the Po Valley had cost him the opportunity of meeting the enemy at his debouchment from the Pyrenean passes. It was probably late in August. Hannibal had already overrun and pacified the present Catalonia and, after leaving a garrison of 10,000 there under Hanno, he had crossed the mountains and was marching towards the Rhone with a force of under 40,000 men. Scipio moved his army to oppose Hannibal at his crossing of the Rhone, but found the latter had already crossed (early September) and was marching up the river with the intention of reaching Italy from the northwest. He arrived in the Italian plain in the early part of October with 34,000 men. Although the crossing of the Alps was no doubt difficult, the losses were probably far less than Polybius states (see Delbrueck).

Being unable to overtake Hannibal on the Rhone, the Consul Scipio sent the army forward into Spain under the command of his brother Gnaeus, as the departure of Hannibal's army left there only a small force to hold the province for Carthage. It seemed probable, therefore, that Hannibal's base might be captured in his absence, and in fact the Romans made considerable gains in Spain in the next few years. The Consul himself, with a small escort and a part of the fleet, returned by sea to Genoa to organize the army of occupation already in the Po Valley to resist Hannibal on his exit from the Alpine passes. There was little reason to believe it would be unequal to its task.

Critics applaud the decision of Hannibal to refuse battle until safely in the Po Valley. A conclusive battle, even if a victory, would have cost him many men and it would have been difficult to renew supplies from Spain. By going on to Italy he found himself in the friendly country of the Celts in the Po Valley, willing to give him both recruits and supplies. It seems also that he expected to get ahead of the consular army in Gaul in the march down the Italian peninsula, thinking that it would try to follow. Instead, it entered Spain. Hannibal was much surprised on arriving in the Italian plan to find the Consul opposing him. But Scipio had returned alone from the Rhone and his army was the other one which had for the moment put down the insurrection in the Po Valley. In the following battle, about the end of October, on the banks of the Ticinus, Scipio was defeated and wounded, being saved from the enemy by the valor of his young son Publius who was afterward Hannibal's conqueror. The Roman army then fell back to a position on the River Trebia near the strong fortifications of Placentia and awaited the arrival of the other consular army which had been recalled from Sicily and was on its way. On his arrival, Sempronius took command of both armies, owing to the wound of Scipio, and rashly offered battle on the banks of the Trebia in early December. He, too, was defeated, the remains of his army being driven into Placentia near-by.

MAP 21.
NORTHERN ITALY

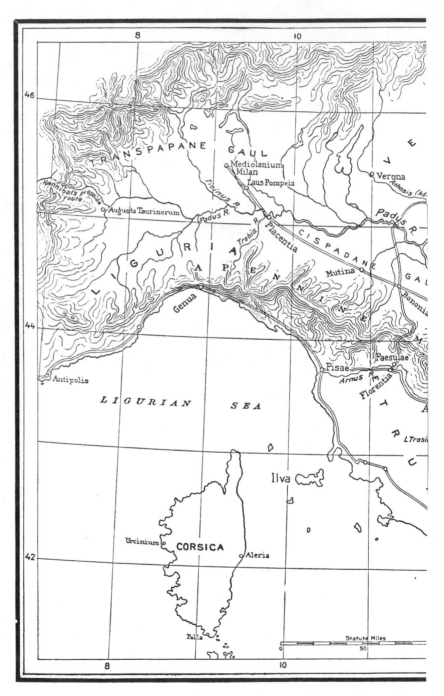

MAP 21. NORTH ITALY

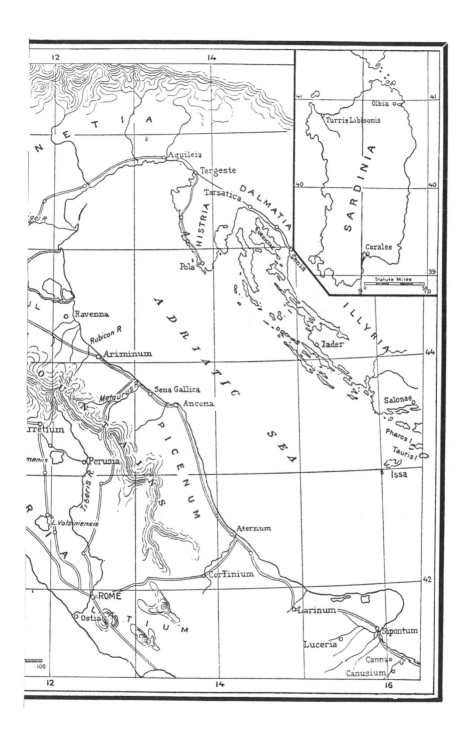

Hannibal's Advance through Italy

As my purpose is only to show how the Roman sea power enabled the Republic to withstand the terrible defeats by land that its great enemy inflicted on it, in discussing Hannibal's campaigns I shall not dwell on tactical details. The winter of 218-217 was spent by Hannibal in organizing the Celtic tribes of the Po Valley and strengthening himself with Celtic recruits for his advance into the south. The Roman Senate was not greatly disturbed by the loss of the army at the Trebia. It left the army in Spain under Scipio who had gone there as Proconsul after recovering from his wound, and in the spring of 217 it assembled only two consular armies of about 25,000 men each, to oppose Hannibal. One took position at Arretium (see Map 21) (Arezzo) and the other at Ariminum (Rimini) in order to guard the two main roads leading to the south. Hannibal made an early start and crossed the Apennines well to the west and then passed through Faesulae and towards Perusia (Perugia), passing about 15 miles southwest of the Roman army at Arretium. The Consul Flaminius followed incautiously from Arretium and was surprised by an ambush on the shores of Lake Trasimenus. His army was destroyed and he lost his life.

But Hannibal did not march on Rome. Instead, he crossed the mountains to the Adriatic and there was able to send news of his two great victories to Carthage. Rome elected Quintus Fabius Maximus as Dictator, and while it was gathering itself after the disaster, Hannibal improved his leisure by reorganizing his army and re-arming it with Roman weapons.

CARTHAGINIAN FLEET RAIDS ITALIAN COAST

About this time, apparently on hearing from Hannibal after the two battles, the city of Carthage sent out a fleet of 70 ships by way of Sardinia to harry the Italian coasts. The fleet struck in between Ilva (Elba) and Pisa and captured a number of supply ships bound to Spain to support the Roman army there. On hearing the news, the Dictator hastily manned 120 ships lying at Ostia, using men of the new levies then at Rome, and sent them under the surviving Consul Servilius to seek the enemy. The Carthaginians heard of the Roman fleet in good time and retired as they had come. Servilius followed them, making the round of Corsica and Sardinia, taking hostages as he passed along, and arrived at Lilybaeum (see Map 20). Here he seems to have made sure that the enemy had gone to Africa and, accordingly, as the Italian seas were free of enemies, he crossed himself to Africa and entered the Gulf of Syrtis Minor, where he landed in negligent fashion to pick up booty, and his people suffered severe losses. He thereupon returned to Lilybaeum and the fleet's work for the year 217 was over. Sudden operations by a weaker fleet had paralyzed Roman effort.

FABIUS, ROMAN DICTATOR, AVOIDS BATTLE

Some weeks after Hannibal's arrival on the shore of the Adriatic, Fabius cautiously followed him, resolutely declining battle, while keeping close to Hannibal to prevent him from sending out foraging parties. He hoped by this display of resolution to prevent defection of Roman allies to the enemy. Although the Dictator's caution saved Rome from another defeat, and checked Hannibal's ability to gather supplies for the winter, yet it did not make it impossible for the latter to pass the winter in Apulia (see Map 10) in comparative comfort. The one bright spot in the Roman outlook was that no Roman ally had yet seceded to the enemy.

During this campaign of 217, which gained for Fabius the title of "Delayer," popular opinion turned definitely against him and his policy. It was thus possible for the people to elect a political demagogue, Terrentius Varro, a man unskilled in war, to become Consul as Fabius laid down the Dictatorship about the end of the year. As colleague, Varro had the patrician Lucius Aemilius Paulus, conqueror of the Illyrians, whose duty, as Fabius told him, was to oppose not only Hannibal but also his colleague Varro. Great efforts were made in the winter of 217-216 to raise forces to meet the desperate situation of the Republic, and 13 legions were placed under arms for the campaign of 216, of which probably 6 had nearly full ranks and the rest, which were distributed through Italy and the islands as garrison troops, were probably much under normal strength. There were also soldiers in the fleet.[3]

---

[3] As has been said, when the war opened in 218 there were 6 legions with 70,800 men, all citizens or allies, and not over 55,000 men in 220 ships, making a total of about 125,000 men. In his *History of the Art of War*, Delbrueck estimates the Roman contingent of the Republican army at 66,000 men for the year 216. Usually the allied contingents were about double the Roman numbers but now, as Delbrueck suggests, were not so strong; but less is

BATTLE OF CANNAE

Since entering Italy Hannibal had received no re-enforcements from Africa, but he had recruited among the Celts when in the Po Valley, and his strength for the campaign of 216 seems to have been about 50,000, including 10,000 cavalry in which arm he was much superior to the Romans. He was, however, short of supplies, as he had made no allies among the cities of Italy. At the opening of the spring of 216, Hannibal moved south in search of supplies and captured the city of Cannae (see Maps 10 and 21), which was one of the principal army depots of Rome. The Roman field army, about 80,000 strong, under the two Consuls, each commanding on alternate days, followed Hannibal. In spite of the remonstrances of his more capable colleague, Varro accepted battle in front of Cannae and the army was destroyed on the field whose name has ever since remained the synonym for utter defeat. Aemilius Paulus, desperately wounded, refused rescue by a military tribune who offered his horse, but sent a public message to the Senate that he declined to be saved, either to be tried a second time on the conclusion of his consulship[4] or to bring charges against his colleague. As his last word he directed the Senate to fortify the city and provide it with a powerful garrison. Varro, on his part, was not ashamed to leave the field which his folly had lost.

---

known about them. In all there may have been almost 120,000 men with the army out of a free population of 2,500,000. The number of slaves supporting industry is not so well known, there may have been 500,000. (Beloch puts the population somewhat higher, at a little over 3,500,000, including 750,000 slaves.) From 212 to 207 the army was at its largest, varying from 25 to 21 legions. During these years the fleet seems to have run at about 230 ships—100 in Sicily, 50 in the Adriatic, and 80 in Spain. In 208 there were added 50 for the protection of the Roman coast. At this maximum, allowing for reduced crews, the fleet probably never exceeded 42,000 shipmen and rowers and 17,000 soldiers.

Kromayer estimates that in 207 the two consular armies of 2 legions each had almost full ranks, about 45,000 in all, and the other 11 legions in Italy, with few allies, numbered 40,000 to 45,000 men, making 85,000 to 90,000 in Italy. Spain had over 25,000 Italians and Sicily and Sardinia about 20,000. The whole 23 legions had about 130,000 soldiers, including allies. Adding the crews of 230 ships, the whole force of the Republic would be about 180,000 strong in 207. In 212 and 211 with 25 legions there may have been 10,000 more soldiers, making 190,000 in all. In this Italian force there were a few manumitted slaves in the army and many slaves as rowers in the fleet. After 207 the number of men in service was progressively reduced, and in the last year of the war there were only 16 legions and 160 ships, with probably about 125,000 men in both. To the Italian forces we must add a few local levies (say 10,000 to 15,000) recruited in Spain and Sicily during the latter part of the war.

[4] His first trial was after his Illyrian successful campaign when he was accused and acquitted of not dividing the booty equitably.

On his arrival at Rome with the tale of his defeat, the Senate came out to meet him and thank him that he had not despaired of the Republic, and marked by this vote of confidence the end of party struggles for the duration of the war.

The Destruction of the Roman Army at Cannae Is Inconclusive

Neither after the battle of Lake Trasimenus nor now after the overwhelming victory of Cannae did Hannibal attempt to end the war by the siege and conquest of Rome. The capital city remained the center of resistance; while the Consuls and other generals were thereafter chosen with regard to their proved ability in the field, rather than in the forum. The Romans changed their strategic plan of the war from one of overthrow of Hannibal in battle to one of exhausting him by Roman endurance. For his own plan, if Hannibal before leaving Spain contemplated the direct overthrow of the Roman state, he early renounced that hope. He seems to have regarded his tremendous tactical victories as political arguments for the detachment of the Roman allies and their transfer to his own side, and looked for final victory through slow exhaustion of Rome. It is probable that at best he expected to conclude a treaty of peace which would reduce, but not destroy, the strength of Rome and grant a great increase in power to Carthage. Hannibal got little assistance from overseas, while Rome sent her armies by sea to Spain, to Sicily, to Epirus, and finally to Carthage itself.

After Cannae, Hannibal's brilliant cavalry general, Maharbal, ventured to say to him that although he could win battles, in refusing to march on Rome he showed that he did not know how to use them. In this declaration, as Delbrueck says, Maharbal revealed himself as a mere swordsman. Had Hannibal invested the powerful fortifications of Rome, with the fidelity of Central Italy still unshaken, he could not have drawn supplies from the hostile countryside, for his detached parties would have been cut off, nor with them dispersed for forage could he have had the necessary men to hold the siege lines of Rome. Besides, his superiority lay chiefly in his cavalry and his own skill in maneuver, which found no field in a siege. The only way to take the city was first to take the port of Ostia and with that as a base of supplies from Africa he might concentrate all his efforts directly on a long siege; but this was impossible. In this war of endurance, which still had 14 years to run before its conclusion, it was Roman sea power which supported its military resistance. The neighboring seas belonged to Rome and it would be the task of her dominating fleet to hold communications with Ostia; if the port remained Roman, the siege of Rome would be impracticable.

So the war now settled into a new phase in which the Romans declined decisive battle and Hannibal relied on detaching Roman allied cities in South Italy by the plague of his presence if they did not become his own allies. At the same time he sought for aid from three different quarters outside Italy: from his brother Hasdrubal in Spain, from Carthage itself, and from Macedon in the East. It was the duty of the Roman fleet to sever Hannibal's communications with all these regions and maintain the nation's supplies from the great islands and from the East.

Nevertheless the Roman overthrow at Cannae brought local political results. Hannibal marched on Capua (see Map 10), the greatest city in Italy after Rome, and first of the Roman allies; it seceded to Hannibal before the Romans could place a garrison there. It was a great blow to Rome. Holding Capua, Hannibal hoped that he might succeed in seizing a Campanian seaport where he might receive the re-enforcements which his great victories entitled him to expect the opposition party in Carthage would now grant him. But the Romans were still able to assemble sufficient men from Rome and the wreckage of Cannae to garrison Neapolis (Naples) and the other Campanian ports before Hannibal could seize them. His thrust in that direction was foiled.

A few days after the battle, Hannibal sent his brother Mago to Carthage to ask for aid to finish the defeat of Rome; but Hanno, head of the opposition party, replied in the Council saying,

> Hannibal has overthrown Roman armies and asks for soldiers; he has taken two camps with booty and provisions and asks for money and supplies. His request would be the same had he been defeated.

Hanno then inquired if any of the 35 Roman tribes had revolted and, learning that they had not, he thereupon recommended that peace should be made with Rome. The Council was controlled by the war party and decided to support Hannibal and sent Mago into Spain to raise troops.

The war dragged slowly in Italy; after Capua, several cities in South Italy went over to Hannibal, and Rome made the most desperate effort to raise new armies, enlisting slaves and debtors. Hannibal, after Cannae (see Map 10), did not have a large enough force to form an army of occupation and have remaining a sufficiently large field army to face the Roman levies; but, on the other hand, the Romans had learned by sad experience that they could not win a great battle against the marvelous tactical skill of Hannibal. The war in Italy was thereafter one of exhaustion rather than of pitched battles. The Roman fleet prevented exhaustion from becoming fatal.

After his thrust at Naples failed, Hannibal sought to secure a seaport through which he could supply himself either from the East or from Africa. He would have been glad to have had Tarentum, but that was held by a Roman garrison.

In spite of continual maneuvering in South Italy during the year 215, the principal accomplishment there during the year was the capture of Locri and Petelia by a detachment of Hannibal's army which was sent to occupy Bruttium, and a small body of troops from Africa effected a landing there and joined Hannibal. Although the war in South Italy was not active in 215, the story of the Romans that the Punic army lost its morale during its luxurious winter of 216-215 in Capua is, of course, an absurd calumny. Nothing in the later course of the war shows that it was a less perfect instrument of battle in the hands of Hannibal.

The War Policy of the Punic Council Does Not Conform to That of Hannibal

The battle of Cannae brought to light a marked divergence between Hannibal and the Council of Carthage as to the policy of conducting the war. Thereafter it was Hannibal's desire to draw all possible forces into Italy—from Spain, from Africa, and from Macedon, through alliance with its King. His call this year to his brother Hasdrubal to join him out of Spain created much alarm in Rome. Yet when he demanded re-enforcements from Carthage, he got only a few thousand men the next year, although many more Africans were sent to Spain and to Sardinia. It is impossible to suppose that the refusal to give Hannibal full support arose merely from the wish to see his efforts fail. The Council must have desired victory over Rome. The probability is that the Council did not wish to attempt the utmost, and was content to strive for a more limited success than the great soldier. He wanted an army in Italy sufficiently large to win victory there. On the ground that Hannibal occupied, he was master, but he did not receive enough men from Africa to hold permanently what he gained by fighting. He needed garrison troops in addition to his field army, for the allies of Rome saw no reason to support Hannibal. The Carthaginian army did not come as a savior. The allies had not been oppressed by Rome's overlordship and Carthaginian rule had nothing to offer.

The rulers of Carthage tried to attain their purpose directly instead of by the overthrow of the hostile forces as Hannibal urged. They would have been satisfied to recover Spain with its silver mines, its mercantile bases, and its revenue from the trade of the back country. If Sicily and Sardinia could be added, so much the better. So the main levies in Africa were sent to Spain and the islands. Not only was there considerable risk at sea in sending a large expedition into Italy, but the Council must have believed that even with strong re-enforcements Hannibal would be unable to destroy the Roman Republic and dictate his own terms of peace under the walls of the city. Holding such an opinion, it seemed more advantageous to send the new levies to Sardinia and to Spain to drive out the Romans, or at least hold them north of the Iberus, so that when exhaustion should induce a negotiated peace, Rome would be unable to lay any claims to the productive provinces of Spain and Sardinia. Thus it was that the Council gave little assistance to Hannibal and regarded his marvelous successes and his superb army merely as means of keeping the Roman legions occupied, while the substantial gains of the war were to be made elsewhere. We must therefore reject the view that the faction opposed to the war policy of the Barcide family was actuated merely by jealousy. It had its own strategic views as to the conduct of the war. The immediate commercial objective of the government at Carthage, as indicated by its conduct, entailed the ruin of Hannibal.

The Roman Senate, however, took no such limited view of its objective as the Punic Council. Like Hannibal, the Senate had an unbounded resolution: The war was to be fought to a finish and what Rome held in Spain, in the islands, and in Italy she meant not to relinquish until it was inevitable. Such was Rome's simple plan, for in Italy Hannibal was far from having it all his own way, even in the regions his army occupied.

Even the seceding cities were not anxious to be ruled by Hannibal. They could not oppose him when he was at their gates and had to endure him, but did not welcome him and his army. On the other hand, the chain of Roman fortresses divided the land so that it was far from being under the control of the invader.

THE WAR IN SPAIN

We now may take up the war in Spain during the two years of Trasimenus and Cannae. Hannibal looked to that province for re-enforcements from his brother in command there and most earnestly did he wish them when his victories proved so unavailing to detach the Roman allies. While the Council in Carthage regarded that province as the prize of victory, Hannibal looked at its resources as the means of victory. Every incident either in Italy or Spain made itself felt in the other theater of war.

YEAR 218 B.C.

When the Consul Publius Cornelius Scipio, leading his army into Spain in 218, found that Hannibal had passed him and was already moving towards the Alps (see Map 19), it will be remembered that he turned back to organize the Roman forces available in North Italy to oppose Hannibal, while his brother Gnaeus entered Spain with the army of two legions, nearly 25,000 men, and some 35 or 40 quinqueremes. By the departure of troops to Africa and to Italy, the Carthaginian forces in Spain had been reduced to about 26,000, including 4,000 cavalry.

Gnaeus Scipio with his fleet and army zealously supported by the Massiliots and their shipping went on from the mouths of the Rhone and disembarked at Emporiae, a Massiliot colony which became a secondary Roman base. He then advanced along the coast as far as the Iberus, gaining the friendship of the local tribes. Tarraco (Tarragona) became the principal base of Rome, and Scipio greatly developed its port and defenses during the war. After securing Tarraco, Scipio turned into the back country where Hanno, commanding in that province, attempting to hold the deserting tribes by victory, was obliged to meet him with inferior numbers. Hanno was badly defeated and Scipio took much booty at the capture of the principal Carthaginian depot. On hearing of this disaster, Hasdrubal, commanding south of the Iberus, marched north and crossed the river. He surprised the crews of the ships at Tarraco, who were dispersed through the countryside, and drove them back to their ships with loss, and returned behind the Iberus upon the approach of Scipio.

There was some campaigning early in the winter of 218-217, after which Hasdrubal passed the rest of the winter at New Carthage and Scipio at Tarraco. At New Carthage Hasdrubal had good connections by sea with Africa, both directly and through Gades beyond Gibraltar, which Carthage held till near the end of the war. On the other hand the Roman army had free communication by sea with Rome, but as Italy became impoverished by the war and as difficulties increased in Rome, Scipio was at last told to rely on his own resources. Doubtless he depended greatly on the support of Massilia, which was the center of business for the Rhone Valley and the Riviera coast from the present Monaco to Emporiae.

YEAR 217 B.C.

Early in 217, Hasdrubal was the first to open the campaign. He started north from New Carthage, having added many local recruits to his forces, and marched along the coast, supported by 40 quinqueremes to cover his communications by water. Gnaeus Scipio intended at first to fight with his army, but hearing how large a force Hasdrubal had with him, he decided to use his fleet and attack the enemy's line of supplies. Accordingly, he increased the usual number of soldiers (about 50) on his ships and, with 35 quinqueremes, he left Tarraco and came to anchor about 8 miles north of the mouth of the Iberus, whence he sent forward two light Massiliot craft to reconnoiter. They returned, saying that the Punic fleet was anchored at the mouth of the river, with their sterns moored to the beach. The army camp was close by the ships. Scipio immediately got under way, hoping to surprise the enemy, before they could man the ships and form line of battle. He was only partly successful. Although his approach was concealed from the ships themselves by a tongue of land, the country had many watch towers for the purpose of observing the approach of pirates, and by some of these Hasdrubal learned that his fleet was in danger. The army heard the assembly call somewhat earlier than the shipmen, but soon dispatch riders summoned the latter also to the beach and they manned the ships which got under way hastily in some confusion. As they were forming their line, the Romans in good order of battle fell upon them and captured a couple by boarding and swept away the oars of four others.

The presence of Hasdrubal's army on the beach did not prove an encouragement to his crews to fight, but appeared to the surprised mariners as offering cover and a safe retreat. The ships fled towards the harbor mouth where, owing to the press of numbers, many took the beach outside and were there deserted by their crews. In spite of the presence of the hostile army on the beach, the Roman fleet succeeded in making fast to many of the stranded ships and towing them off. By this victory Scipio secured 25 out of the hostile fleet of 40 ships, and gained entire control of sea communications on the eastern coast of Spain. He at once advanced with the fleet to New Carthage, where he looted in the suburbs and returned to Tarraco by way of Aebusa (Iviza) with much good prize of war.

As a result of this complete victory at sea, many Spanish tribes went over to the Romans, so that Hasdrubal was obliged to fall back far into the interior. This general defection of the tribes was by no means because the Roman rule seemed desirable to them. It was rather because the Punic rule was offensive, whereas Scipio was considerate. Indeed, it was not until 80 years after this campaign that Rome was able to establish peace in the Spanish peninsula, and even then her authority did not extend over the northwest corner. Nevertheless, during all the war, in spite of the grievance which the tribes found in foreign domination, their young men found attraction in the well-paid and adventurous military service of both the foreign occupants of their country and served both gladly, subject to sudden defection from one side or the other, according to alteration of the relative situation of the contesting powers.

On hearing of the operations in Spain, the Roman Senate began to realize the great effect that Hasdrubal might exert on the war in Italy, if he should finally be able to drive the Roman army out of Spain and then devote his efforts to the support of his brother Hannibal in Italy, by forwarding supplies and men. Accordingly the Senate assigned 8,000 men, 30 ships, and large supplies to Publius Scipio, whose consulate had expired in the spring of 217, to go forward into Spain and assume personal charge of the government which his brother Gnaeus had been exercising for him so well during his consulship. After the arrival of Publius, his brother and himself continued to act always with the greatest harmony. Their first step was to advance against Saguntum where they secured all the hostages which the Spanish tribes had given to Hasdrubal and, when Scipio returned these hostages to their people, the tribes were ready to forsake the Carthaginian cause, but winter was approaching and put a close to all operations.

YEAR 216 B.C.

In spite of his naval defeat at the Iberus, Hasdrubal had not completely lost his communications with Africa since he always held Gades in the southwest, but that was a long way from the Roman operations on the eastern coasts, and therefore difficult to use. Nevertheless, ships could creep up the coast. Therefore, in reply to his solicitations for aid, the Punic Council was able to send him 4,500 men and he himself began to construct a fleet. Before he was ready to advance upon the Romans, some deserting officers of the fleet, who had been reprimanded for losing their ships at the Iberus, raised an insurrection in the country of the Tartessians (near Gibraltar) and it was necessary for Hasdrubal to subdue it previous to marching north.

By this time Hannibal was calling on Carthage for re-enforcements. The Council preferred to direct Himilco with what forces were available to Spain, at the same time, as is alleged, sending orders to Hasdrubal to follow his brother across the Alps into Italy. Evidently the Council was optimistic as to affairs in Spain. That the Council adopted this policy seems evidence that so long as King Hiero of Syracuse remained faithful to the Roman alliance, it was impracticable for any large military expedition to Italy to pass without a battle with the Roman fleet of 100 ships based on the fortified port of Lilybaeum. This fact did not altogether preclude raiding expeditions.

Hasdrubal refused to leave Spain or even to move north until Himilco arrived, as Livy says, with a powerful army and many ships. Livy does not give the strength of either, but as he says the ships were hauled on shore and were not brought into action, it is presumable that the addition did not bring the Carthaginian fleet to an equality with that of the Romans, which must have numbered nearly 90 after the captures of the previous year. As we hear no more of them, perhaps Himilco's ships were sent back to Africa after accomplishing their escort task. After Himilco had communicated with Hasdrubal, the latter moved out of Southern Spain, taking as he went heavy tribute to pay his way through Gaul, if indeed he meant to go to Italy. He was met by the two Scipios at the Iberus River and was badly defeated there with the loss of his camp about the time his brother conquered at Cannae. As we are told that his army at this time was mostly Spanish, it is far from likely that the re-enforcement brought to Spain by Himilco brought many soldiers as Livy asserts, but rather supplies and money. This victory on the Iberus in 216 caused much rejoicing in Rome, as it assured the city it would struggle with Hannibal alone, for in Spain Hasdrubal's position was much shaken politically, since the heavy tribute he had levied in his march caused great ill-feeling.

Operations in the Islands

Almost immediately after Cannae, while the Senate at Rome was taking measures of resistance, word came from the Propraetor in Sicily that a Carthaginian fleet was attacking the territories of Hiero, King of Syracuse, and that another fleet was lying at the Aegatian Islands (see Maps 10 and 19) off the west end of Sicily, ready to attack there should the Propraetor go to drive off the first fleet. The Senate could do nothing, yet apparently both Carthaginian fleets were driven off, for the next mention of the Roman Sicilian fleet is that it had returned from raiding the coasts of Africa without much success and that it needed money and supplies. Fortunately, these were furnished by King Hiero.

At Carthage, during the eventful year of 216 after the news of Cannae, the hopes of the Punic Council had been raised high and it proposed to follow its own war policy of securing economic advantage to be developed after the close of hostilities. It occupied itself in recruiting large forces in Africa to send to the front. It seems that at the close of the year it had something approaching 25,000 men available for foreign service.

Year 215 b.c.

Of these it was intending early in 215 to send 12,000 infantry, 1,500 cavalry, 20 elephants, and 1,000 talents of silver ($1,187,000), all escorted by 60 men-of-war under the command of Mago to join his brother Hannibal in Italy. But, hearing of Hasdrubal's reverse during 216, the Council diverted Mago's command to Spain to hold that province and, learning that it was a favorable time to stir up insurrection in Sardinia which provided grain for Rome, it sent there another fleet and army nearly as large under Hasdrubal the Bald. This expedition was blown off its course to the Balearic Islands, where it took a long time to refit.

The Romans had already learned that trouble was likely in Sardinia and had sent additional troops there to re-enforce the garrison. The new Roman commander in Sardinia, Titus Manlius Torquatus, drew his ships on shore upon arrival and with the legion he brought from Italy and the ships' crews, added to the men already there, he had a force of perhaps 20,000 men. With these he was overcoming the insurrection, when Hasdrubal appeared from the Balearic Islands and landed his army, sending his fleet back to Carthage. The insurrection revived at his presence, but he was entirely defeated in a battle soon afterward. The insurrection was pacified and Manlius was able to send money and grain to Italy.

About the time that Hasdrubal landed in Sardinia, the Propraetor Otacilius raided the coast of Africa from his base at Lilybaeum. As he was returning, he heard of Hasdrubal in Sardinia and was fortunate enough to meet his fleet at sea on its way home. After a slight encounter and the loss of 7 ships, the Punic fleet was dispersed and escaped. At this very time, Bomilcar, from Carthage, with 4,000 men and 40 elephants for Hannibal, landed at Locri (as already mentioned), and got away again with his ships in spite of the effort of the Roman squadron at Messana to intercept him. This was the only re-enforcement ever sent by the Carthaginian Council to Hannibal. It got through at the period when the great halfway seaport of Syracuse was not occupied as a base for the Roman fleet.

The conduct of the naval campaign was so unsatisfactory to the Roman Senate that it caused Otacilius to lose the nomination as Consul the next year but, nevertheless, he continued in the fleet in Sicily. The financial situation of Rome at this time was difficult. The usual supplies to Rome from Sicily and Sardinia were lacking in 215 and the Proconsuls there were told that they would be expected to support their armies by their own resources in the islands. In spite of successes in Spain during the past two years the Scipio brothers said that they also were short of money and supplies, and for them the Senate made every effort to contract for supplies on the credit of the state.

SIEGE OF SYRACUSE

In Sicily old King Hiero, of Syracuse, died in the summer of 215 after 48 years of loyal alliance with Rome, and was succeeded by his young grandson, Hieronymus. It was a blow to Rome, for it lost a fleet base. Already there was a party in the city unfavorable to Rome, and Hannibal sent two brothers, Epicydes and Hippocrates, as his emissaries to Syracuse. They were able to form an alliance and Hieronymus sent an expedition to seize cities with Roman garrisons. Hieronymus was assassinated in the summer of 214 and confusion again arose in Syracuse. Hippocrates and Epicydes were elected governors of the city but were not in complete control and negotiations were once more opened with Rome. There were already a Roman garrison of two legions and a naval squadron in the island, both under the command of Appius Claudius Pulcher. The Senate now sent the Consul Marcus Claudius Marcellus to Sicily with another legion to take general charge, and the fleet in Sicily was raised to 100 ships.

Marcellus was one of Rome's best generals. Some years before, during the war with the Celts, when Marcellus was Consul for the first time and commander in chief, he personally encountered a Celtic champion who challenged the Roman army, and cut him down in presence of both armies. Now he had to show ability as general rather than as champion.

During the winter of 214-213, while negotiations with Rome were proceeding, Epicydes and Hippocrates provoked disturbances and in the spring of 213, under their incitement, the city finally turned against Rome in great indignation. Marcellus marched to Syracuse (see Maps 10 and 11) and camped at Olympieum, closing the road to the south. As the city government would not listen to him, he moved most of his army to the other side of the city where he completely cut off communication with the interior. The fleet of Appius Claudius closed the water front.

The 2-year siege was now begun. The general strategic situation was that the Romans had a powerful army in Sicily and held the fortified ports of Lilybaeum, Panormus, and Messana, which, with the superior Roman fleet, gave the Romans entire control of the north coast and good communications with the homeland. At Syracuse the army covered the fleet base at Thapsus. But the southern coasts were always sympathetic with Carthage and much of the interior of the island had recently been offended and repelled by Roman cruelty at Leontini and elsewhere. The Roman army, strong as it was, could spare little strength away from Syracuse for field operations. As the Roman fleet had no secure base on the south coast, the Carthaginian fleet, although not so strong as the Roman squadrons in Sicily, could venture fearlessly to its south coast escorting Carthaginian armies.

Marcellus' first step at Syracuse was an immediate assault. Only five days after taking position he made a general attack with fleet and army. He had at his command all sorts of siege engines and the Romans had great hopes. They were opposed by the mechanical skill of the famous mathematician and engineer Archimedes, who already in Hiero's time had provided marvelous weapons of defense.

For the land attack, Marcellus selected a point on the north side of the Epipolae plateau opposite the harbor of Trogilus, where the wall was less formidable than elsewhere. The assault was covered by many catapults. Simultaneously with the attack by the army 60 ships in two lines charged the eastern front of Achradina. The front line carried the landing force of heavy-armed to storm the walls where they were closest to the sea and thrust in till the ships grounded. The second line kept a little behind the other and carried the covering force of archers, slingers, and spear throwers, whose duty was to keep the defenders below the parapets by their missiles.

Besides this infantry attack delivered by the fleet there were eight ships lashed in pairs alongside each other and rowed by the oars on the outer sides of each pair. These vessels carried scaling ladders, called from their shape *sambucae* or lyres. The *sambuca* lay fore and aft on the decks where the pair of ships was lashed together. Its side was protected by a screen. At the forward end of each was a cage which could hold four men. When the ship charged the shore, the *sambuca* was erected by tackles from the masthead and the cage approached the parapet. The men in the cage shot at the enemy on the parapet while other men climbed the ladder and, when they reached the top, a gangway from the cage was dropped on the parapet. Such was the purpose of the *sambuca*

But by land and sea the attack was repulsed by Archimedes' inventions.

On the land side the matter was not very difficult, for Archimedes had provided a number of engines of the usual type and the slope of the hill was enough to cause heavy stones launched from the wall to roll down and crush the Romans.

Archimedes' genius was most displayed in repelling the attack from the sea. Against the more distant ships his heavy catapults discharged large stones. More numerous and lighter artillery maintained a fire of smaller missiles. In order to offer better protection to his own men, many of these smaller weapons discharged through loopholes cut at various levels through the walls giving a great volume of discharge. When ships approached close to the wall, huge cranes appeared unexpectedly above the parapets. Some of them dropped great weights on the ships beneath them. Others had grapnels swinging from their ends suspended by long chains. After one had gripped the bow of a ship, the bow was lifted while the stern was depressed and then the grapnel was suddenly released. If the vessel did not capsize at least she shipped water and the crew was terrified.

In spite of the fury of the attack, the repulse of the Romans was so prompt and complete that Marcellus abandoned all further efforts at assault and confined himself thereafter to a blockade as already established. The navy anchored outside the harbor in good weather, but it was never able entirely to prevent the entrance of news and supplies.

Hannibal now urged Carthage to press the war in Sicily. If Syracuse could be saved and made available as a way port to Italy, throwing the Roman navy back to Messana, his own line of supplies would be cleared from Carthage through Locri and up to the Gulf of Tarentum and he might expect re-enforcements and success in Italy. This recommendation coincided with the Punic Council's idea of making territorial gains for the sake of business and it sent an army under Himilco of 25,000 infantry, 3,000 cavalry, and some elephants[5] to land at Heraclea Minoa.

A few days later Himilco took Agrigentum, the second city of the island, in spite of Marcellus' effort to forestall him there, with troops

---

[5] Elephants were used somewhat as tanks were used in the World War. They crushed and trampled down infantry by their weight. There were two ways of countering them. One was to open a path for them without breaking the battle formation through which they might pass doing no harm. The other way was to gall them until they became unmanageable and turned in fury to run through their own army.

drawn from the army besieging Syracuse, and the latter fell back on Syracuse with the force he had drawn thence.

The Roman Senate was disturbed by the great army which Carthage had thrown into Sicily and sent another legion to the island. Under the escort of 30 quinqueremes, the legion landed at Panormus with the intention of marching across the island to Syracuse. In order to intercept it, Himilco with his army came to the River Anapus about 8 miles from Syracuse and, at the same time, Bomilcar with 55 men-of-war entered the Great Harbor and lay under the city fortifications. No doubt Bomilcar's squadron escorted many supply ships, but this Polybius does not tell us. Himilco's hope of catching the legion marching from Panormus was disappointed, for it avoided him by moving along the north and east coasts, escorted and supplied by its squadron. As Bomilcar's squadron served only to consume the city's supplies, he soon took it back to Carthage. Himilco could do nothing against the Roman entrenched positions and he went off into the interior to strengthen the Carthaginian hold on the back country. So ended the year 213.

Early in 212 Marcellus was no longer hopeful of success at Syracuse, which seemed impregnable, as the Romans could neither push their way in nor starve it. The supply of provisions could not be stopped and Bomilcar with 90 ships again made his way into the Great Harbor. Yet searching for every means, Marcellus learned that the wall at a certain part of the north front of Epipolae was not as high as had been thought. A feast of Diana was soon to occur which would last three days and be the occasion of much drinking. Marcellus arranged to take this opportunity to storm the wall at night when the garrison would be in a drunken sleep. The attack was successful and the entire Roman army was soon on the heights of Epipolae.

The Romans were unable to pass the walls of Achradina but the commander of the important fortress of Euryalus, at the western end of Epipolae, feared he would get no help from Himilco, and unnecessarily surrendered his post. Thereafter, the Roman army had an excellent camp on the heights. During the confusion following the occupation of Epipolae, on a rough night when the Roman guard ships could not remain off the Great Harbor, Bomilcar ran out with 35 ships and returned to Carthage, leaving 55 at the disposal of the Syracusans.

Himilco and Hippocrates came up to the Great Harbor and encamped there with the Carthaginian army and Syracusan field forces which had slipped out from the city. Himilco and Hippocrates made an attack on the Roman post at the Olympieum while the Carthaginian fleet moved to the shore between the city and the Olympieum to prevent Marcellus from sending any assistance to that weak post. At the same time signals were made to the city and the garrison rushed out upon Marcellus. Both attacks were unsuccessful and the Roman position was even bettered.

Matters remained at a standstill until summer approached when a pestilence broke out which affected all the field armies. The Carthaginians, encamped in the low ground which had been fatal to the Athenian army two centuries before, were almost entirely destroyed. The Sicilians moved off to the interior and suffered less. The Roman troops on the high ground were least disturbed, but little more was accomplished during the rest of the year. Yet the destruction of the great Carthaginian army settled the fate of Syracuse, although the end did not come immediately.

In the spring of 211, Bomilcar came back to Sicily with 130 men-of-war and 700 cargo ships and lay windbound west of Cape Pachynum. The Roman fleet of 100 ships ran down to the Cape and lay on its other side, hoping to engage as soon as the weather was good. Epicydes went there from Syracuse to urge Bomilcar to fight. When the east wind moderated Bomilcar got under sail and stood off to weather the point. The Romans also got under way and were surprised to see Bomilcar, for a reason which was never understood, avoid them in the open sea. As was afterwards learned, he went along the coast of Sicily and then to Tarentum, having sent a dispatch boat to the cargo ships at anchor to return to Africa.[6]

The news of the disappearance of Bomilcar with his supplies reduced Syracuse to despair. An embassy was sent to Marcellus and, after a little minor fighting and some treachery, the city was entered and sacked by the Roman army. Archimedes was sought by the conqueror but was killed by a soldier as he was engaged in a mathematical problem.

[6] It is difficult to accept Livy's statement as a whole about Bomilcar. If he had 130 men-of-war, a battle with the Romans would not have been very unequal even if the fewer Roman ships were individually more formidable. Besides we do not hear of the arrival of a large fleet in Italy. On no other occasion did the Carthaginians assemble as many as 100 ships. It seems probable that Bomilcar had a smaller force than alleged and that only a few went on to Tarentum.

After the cessation of hostilities, the distress of the victorious army as well as of the long-beleaguered city was severe and it was fortunate that the Roman squadron of 80 ships based at Lilybaeum raided about Utica just at this time and returned with grain and booty after only three days out of port. These supplies the admiral at once sent to Syracuse for the relief of the army and the citizens.

Even after the fall of Syracuse there still remained a considerable Carthaginian army in Sicily with its stronghold at Agrigentum and in communication with Carthage by the ports of the south coast of the island. It was not until 210 that the Romans subdued the whole island, after which the banditti developed during the war were driven out. With the restoration of peace the crops of the island became available to support the Roman armies in Italy.

The strategic importance of the 2-year siege of Syracuse was twofold. The agricultural districts belonging to Syracuse were needed to supply Rome. The Roman fleet securely based at Lilybaeum, Panormus, and Messana covered the exportation of grain from such districts as Rome held. Besides this, if Syracuse were left to Carthage it would be comparatively easy for her to forward men and supplies to Hannibal in South Italy. Roman sea power prevented this and forced on the Punic Council the policy of seeking to hold Spain, Sardinia, and Corsica while Hannibal was left with insufficient armies in Italy. As long as the Roman fleet was firm on the eastern coast of Sicily, Carthage could not hope for complete victory but only for a negotiated peace.

HANNIBAL AND HIS MACEDONIAN ALLIANCE

Having carried the account of the important operations in Sicily to the close of the great siege, we now turn back to Hannibal and his policy after Cannae. During four years comparatively few really important engagements had taken place in Italy. The Roman historians tell of many great battles during this period, but they are scarcely credible. The total of the reported losses of Hannibal's army amount to much more than the greatest number that he ever had under arms at one time. These reports must have referred to skirmishes rather than great affairs and can be regarded as greatly exaggerated. When Hannibal found that he could not get aid from home to wear down South Italy, he was far from renouncing his effort, but turned to an alliance with Macedon as a means of increasing his forces.

The Romans fought with diplomacy as a weapon as well as by their own naval exertions, and were able to confine the war to the eastern side of the Adriatic. As no Macedonian troops ever entered Italy to affect the war there the whole account of the Macedonian episode to its close in 205 will be given at this point. Had Macedon ever been able to give important assistance to Hannibal, the outcome of the war might have been very different.

The King of Macedon Is Ill-Disposed to Rome

The young King of Macedon (see Map 2), Philip V, succeeded to the throne in 221, the same year that Hannibal became commander in chief of the Carthaginian army. The establishment of Roman power on the eastern shores of the Adriatic was offensive to him, as it had been to his predecessor, Antigonus Doson. It was apparent to him that war between Rome and Carthage would not be long deferred and he paid a visit to Rome immediately after his accession to learn how matters stood, for he did not want war in Greece. Nevertheless, he could not keep Greece quiet. Early in 220, Aetolians marauded in Achaia which was in league with Macedon. In consequence, Philip took up the cause of his allies and made desultory war against the Aetolians until 217 without any decision. In that year the commercial and naval states, Rhodes, Chios, Byzantium, and Egypt (see Map 1), intervened to end this inconclusive war. They pointed out that all the Greeks might soon be threatened from the west by the victor in Italy. While Philip was considering their proposal, news came of the battle of Lake Trasimenus. Philip's advisers therefore suggested that peace in Greece would enable him to take advantage of Roman difficulties and make good his ancestral claims in Epirus and Illyria. Later he might even hope to conquer in Italy itself. Accordingly, peace was made and it must have been agreeable to Rome. The results of the Illyrian War of 219, which had secured the crossings of the Adriatic for trade, had undoubtedly been impaired by Philip's war. As Rome's relations with South Peloponnese were friendly, her communications with the grain supply of Egypt were made fairly good by the general peace in Greece which seemed also to promise reductions in the price of neutral supplies, including grain from the Euxine.

But Philip had no intention of remaining at rest. On the contrary, he meant to regain Illyria as the former possession of his house. The seaports of Illyria would give him bases to cross to Italy and share the successes of Hannibal. He at once began operations against Illyria. After making some progress, he put his army into winter quarters (217-216) and during the winter he built 100 light ships, not so much for fighting as for transporting his army.

In the spring of 216 he embarked the army and, sailing round the Peloponnese, he steered to Apollonia where, upon arrival, he heard a rumor that a Roman squadron at Rhegium (see Map 19) was about to afford assistance to the Illyrians. It was true that Scerdilaidas of Illyria had requested assistance of the Romans, but they were sending only a nominal force of 10 ships. It was not enough to be a real aid, but Philip feared that the whole Roman fleet might be coming and withdrew in haste to Macedon, although without any loss. The overwhelming defeat of Cannae occurred about this time, but apparently Philip had already evacuated Ionian waters. He was much pleased, however, by the Punic success and the Romans thought it advisable to send a strong force to the east coast of Italy to meet any descent by the Macedonians; so the following year as a precaution a coast-guard squadron of 25 ships was based on Brundisium and Tarentum.

The King had long been wishful of seeing the Romans defeated and, after Hannibal's three great victories had failed to reduce Rome to submission, the King thought Carthage would welcome his alliance; so he sent ambassadors to Hannibal. These landed on the coast of Bruttium in 215, after avoiding the Roman cruisers, but were captured by Roman outposts. From these they made their escape to Hannibal's camp where they concluded a treaty of alliance. On their way back to Macedon, the ambassadors were captured by Roman cruisers and the treaty found on them.

When Philip learned that his ambassadors had been captured, he sent another embassy, as he was ignorant of what had been concluded. By the time of the final conclusion and acceptance of the treaty, the season of 215 was lost to him and the Romans profited accordingly. The treaty pledged the two parties to it to mutual friendship and aid, and no separate peace; further, that the Romans were to be turned out of their holdings on the east side of the Adriatic; that King Philip should supply help as requisite and in the manner stipulated; that all conquests in Italy should go to the Carthaginians and all the islands and mainland on the eastern side of the Adriatic to the Macedonians.

ROME'S FIRST MACEDONIAN WAR TO KEEP OPEN THE EASTERN SEAS

When the original captured treaty was brought to Rome, the Senate at once took steps to anticipate the new enemy (year 215). On the part of Rome, the purpose of the war was not only to occupy King Philip on his own side of the Adriatic, but also to keep open the trade routes to Egypt and the Aegean. The squadron already in Calabria was doubled by 25 ships sent from Ostia and the coast was garrisoned. The voluntary offerings recently made by King Hiero to the Senate, in money and rations, were now applied to the support of the Roman fleet in the war with Macedon. In view of the difficulty of recuperating after Cannae and the threatened revolution in Syracuse, it seems that in 215 the Roman fleet did not cross to Greece. It remained in readiness only, on the home coasts of southeast Italy.

The next year (214) the King attempted to regain the former possessions of his house on the eastern shores of the Adriatic. He appeared with his army embarked on 120 biremes and, after reconnoitering Apollonia (see Map 23), he captured Oricum. Marcus Valerius Laevinus, commanding in Calabria, left a guard there and placed on transports those soldiers that could not find room in the 50 ships of war (he is said to have taken a legion) and sailed from Brundisium for Oricum. He arrived there next day (75 sea miles) and retook the place from the weak Macedonian garrison with little difficulty. He then went on to Apollonia, to which the Macedonians had returned. Without the knowledge of the enemy, he threw a relief force of 2,000 men (allies) into the city, who routed the enemy the next day with great loss (3,000 men). The King was obliged to abandon his shipping and return into Macedon by land over the mountains and without his baggage. The Roman fleet wintered at Oricum.

The next year (213) Laevinus was assigned to command the province of Macedon and Greece with the fleet and the legion, a force probably numbering in all 16,000 to 18,000 souls. King Philip attacked the town of Lissus (see Maps 19 and 23) in Illyria and, as a sequence to his success there, almost all Illyria came into his power. In these operations in the interior of the land the Roman forces seem to have been unable effectively to oppose the King's movements; but the Roman strength at sea kept him from any opportunity of crossing the Adriatic.

It was not until very late in 212, or early in 211, that the Propraetor Laevinus played an active part by inducing the Aetolians to make war against Philip. The treaty which he made with them was to the effect that the Aetolians should attack Philip by land and that the Romans should assist them with not less than 20 quinqueremes, that all territories and buildings taken should belong to the Aetolians and all movable property to the Romans, and that the rulers of Thrace, Illyria, and Pergamum might become parties to the alliance as well as Elis and Lacedaemon. The treaty was referred to the Roman Senate for confirmation, but this did not delay action, for the Aetolians opened hostilities at once while Laevinus took possession of Zacynthus and some Acarnanian positions early in 211. Then, having turned these over to the Aetolians, Laevinus retired to Corcyra thinking he had done enough to keep Philip from making any attack on Italy (Livy: XXVI-24).

This clever diplomatic arrangement of the Roman Propraetor took advantage of the existing state of international policies in the eastern Mediterranean. The great commercial state of Egypt, together with Rhodes and Chios on the Aegean, and Byzantium and Cyzicus at the entrance to the Euxine, were all naval powers, all preferred peace on account of their commerce, and all were on excellent terms with Hiero, of Syracuse, until his death in 215. Aetolia was more or less their associate, as some cities in Thrace and the Bosphorus belonged to the League. Macedonia and the Seleucid monarch in Asia Minor on the contrary were each seeking for mastery in the Aegean for the sake of controlling the profits of trade rather than as meaning to promote trade. By his treaty, Laevinus had associated the naval and commercial interests of the Aegean with Rome in its difficulties. Thus the Macedonian enemy was distressed and thus the Roman trade lines to the east were improved through a line of allied ports from Corcyra along the Peloponnese and the Aegean to the Bosphorus. Philip, as will be remembered, had no combatant fleet. In this way the Romans made up in some measure for the loss of Sicilian crops.

When the navigational season of 210 was well open, Laevinus again set out from Corcyra and, after some success in Locris, he was recalled to Rome to assume the consulship for the current year. On his arrival home he informed the Senate that it might recall the legion in Greece, as the fleet there was sufficient to keep Philip from crossing the Adriatic. During the season of 210, the Romans left the war to the Aetolians, who were driven out of Acarnania and defeated at Lamia. The Punic squadron at Tarentum which came over to support King Philip the year before seems to have done nothing. The price of grain in Rome was three times normal and distress was great; but a Roman embassy was sent to Egypt where it was fortunate in getting large supplies of grain to relieve the city's needs. The bare mention of this fact by the ancient historians is an adequate explanation of the strategic reason for maintaining a Roman squadron across the Adriatic, namely, to protect supplies drawn from the East.

For the year 209, the Proconsul Sulpicius, who had succeeded Laevinus in 210, still held the command in Macedonia with the same fleet and legion which Laevinus had had (apparently the legion did not return home as Laevinus recommended until the following year). In 209, 4,000 pounds weight of gold (about $868,000) was drawn from the treasury emergency reserves, of which 500 was given to Sulpicius who may have supplied money to his allies, but he himself did little with his fleet, for Philip was occupied otherwise than in attacking Italy or the Roman fleet. We hear nothing of the Carthaginian squadron which came over in 211, except that in 208 it was still at King Philip's orders; but in 208 the Roman fleet again became active to keep Philip occupied near home. It raided the coast of Elis, acted in Thessaly with the Aetolians and later raided in the Gulf of Corinth.

In the meantime King Attalus of Pergamum had made himself a party to the war in alliance with the Romans and the Aetolians, and had appeared at the island of Aegina with a fleet. As King Philip had vacated the Peloponnese, Sulpicius, with half the Roman fleet, went round the peninsula to join Attalus at Aegina, and the two fleets wintered there. This junction, suggesting a threat of invading Macedon with the Pergamene army escorted by the allied fleet, gave Rome security from invasion from Macedon and at the same time it prevented any Macedonian privateering directed against the commerce of the Euxine passing around the Peloponnese.

In the spring of 207, the allied fleet, consisting of 23 Roman and 35 Pergamene ships, moved to Lemnos and then returned to attack Euboea (see Map 2). The Aetolians threatened their neighboring enemies, the Acarnanians, Boeotians, and Euboeans, while the allied fleet landed in Euboea. Philip came down to oppose them and the allies were driven off, as Philip's army was much larger. About this time Attalus learned that his own kingdom had been invaded by the King of Bithynia. He returned to Asia, and Sulpicius, with his ships, returned to Aegina, where he was safe from attack by land and could protect the Aegean commerce. The Carthaginian squadron now was summoned into the Gulf of Corinth by Philip, but it dreaded remaining there and avoided meeting the Roman guard ships left behind at Corcyra by Sulpicius.

After a stay in Peloponnese, Philip with only a few ships passed Sulpicius at Aegina on his return to Macedonia, and being convinced he needed more than army transports to accomplish his ends, he ordered 100 quinqueremes to be laid down.

During the next two years the Roman fleet in Greece was inactive, for Philip was fully occupied in getting the better of the Aetolians; but at last these two enemies accepted the mediation of Rhodes, Chios, Athens, and the other commercial cities, so that peace was made between them early in 205.

On hearing of the negotiations, Rome was not pleased by the prospect of desertion of her ally and, as conditions in Italy were much more favorable, she assembled a fleet of 35 ships of war and 11,000 soldiers to aid Aetolia, but Philip hastened to conclude the settlement and the Romans turned away to land at Dyrrhachium. Before any serious operations there were undertaken, the Proconsul Sempronius met Philip and terms were arranged which were inconclusive, but which established a general peace in the Grecian peninsula before the close of 205. However, this peace was really no more than a truce and was followed by war some years later after the close of the Hannibalic war.

This unspectacular and apparently inconclusive naval war in the east has been recounted at some length because the diplomacy of the Roman admirals and the activities of their fleets were the means of bringing indispensable supplies into Italy from neutral regions and kept Philip's army out of the peninsula.

HANNIBAL AND NAVAL WARFARE IN SOUTH ITALY
214-208 B.C.

Having now given an account of the war with Macedon to its conclusion, and the re-establishment of Rome's eastern line of supplies, we turn back to Italy and the year 214 to follow Hannibal's efforts to introduce Macedonian forces into Italy. In that year Hannibal moved towards Tarentum, hoping to get this port to serve his new ally, the King of Macedon, but he had no success and the King did not attempt to cross. The insurrection in Sicily caused a diversion of Roman effort in 214 to the siege of Syracuse and the control of the sea route between Africa and Hannibal, but in 213 the Romans were able to begin the siege of Capua which they maintained until its conquest in 211, in spite of Hannibal's efforts to relieve it. The turn of the tide had come in favor of Rome, yet Hannibal did not relax his effort to gain Tarentum (see Map 10), an important port to serve the Macedonian alliance, but which had held a Roman garrison for two generations. In 212 he made a successful effort and captured the city by treachery, but the citadel remained in the possession of the Roman garrison.

Owing to the peculiar geography of the place, the town was of little value without the citadel. Tarentum was at the head of the great Gulf of Tarentum at the end of a spit of land between the gulf and a land-locked bay several miles across. The channel leading to the harbor inside was narrow, although deep, and on the low rocky point making the west end of the spit was the citadel, which thus commanded the channel and the city also. The Tarentine men-of-war were inside the inner bay but, after taking the city, Hannibal caused them to be drawn overland through the city streets and launched on the other side, so that they were serviceable, and soon the fleet of Bomilcar came up from Sicily, as previously mentioned. He was able to cut off all supplies to the citadel which, however, had great stores within. The Carthaginian fleet was able to bring some supplies to the city from neighboring places, but not so much as it consumed itself; so it was sent away and withdrew to Corcyra to aid King Philip of Macedon. However, neither could the Roman fleet blockade the city closely, for it could not draw supplies from the neighboring interior where the Carthaginian army was master.

As the Romans were determined not to let Tarentum become a base for the Macedonian invasion, they maintained a small squadron on the Strait of Messana to guard provision ships on the way to the garrison of the citadel. The Tarentines had their vessels at hand to protect their own commercial visitors, and Livy gives a graphic account of a sea fight off Tarentum arising out of the effort to throw supplies into the citadel. The Roman convoy with its escorting squadron of 20 ships, most of them small but well manned and equipped, was drawing near the city and was about 15 miles off when the Tarentine ships in equal number appeared somewhat unexpectedly. The two squadrons joined battle in very close order, so that, as Livy says, the combatants could pass from one ship to another and scarcely any missile fell into the sea. The most determined efforts were between the two flagships, the Roman commander was struck through the body and fell overboard, the enemy boarded his ship and drove the Romans aft when another Tarentine ship came up on her quarter and by her aid the Roman was taken. Seeing this, the rest of the Roman fleet fled and most were captured. But the battle had given the provision ships an opportunity of escaping to the open sea and few were lost. At the same time a large foraging party sent out by the townsmen was cut off by the Roman garrison, so that neither side procured the much-desired supplies.

This battle deserves notice because it shows the Greek ships of Tarentum using the boarders' tactics of the Romans instead of the usual Carthaginian and Greek tactics of maneuvering. On both sides it was a soldiers' battle instead of a seamen's, and the Greeks won. However, the Roman ships were small and probably had few soldiers, although we are expressly told the oars were fully manned.

During the years 211 and 210 little of importance occurred in the war in Italy beyond the capitulation of Capua to the Roman armies. This great event showed definitely that Hannibal could not secure enough re-enforcements from home to occupy Italy and also overcome the Roman armies and so carry out the policy on which he had based his hopes for success. The policy of the Punic Council was forced upon it by the Roman fleet. The Council threw its major efforts into Spain and the islands, in order to have profitable provinces at the end of the war; and through lack of support Hannibal was undone as well as the Punic nation. The naval strength of Rome was sufficient to preserve Sicily from conquest, although not from serious attack, and greatly to check, although not to stop, the flow of sup-

plies to Hannibal both from Carthage and from the East. The situation
was very much like that in regard to smuggling between France and
England during the Napoleonic wars. The traders and the guard ships
then were all small craft, the opportunities of landing were very frequent,
and there was much illicit traffic, yet Napoleon could never find his long-
sought occasion for landing a great expedition in England.

The general superiority of the Roman fleets was such that early in 210
half the guard fleet of Sicily (50 ships) was thought available to send to
Africa, while the other 50 remained as a coast guard. After a successful
raid in the neighborhood of Utica, which secured much booty and many
prisoners, the expedition returned to Lilybaeum only 13 days after sailing.
This type of naval raid is one which persisted in the Mediterranean until
rowing men-of-war were replaced by sailing ships. It was favored by the
conditions of quiet and tideless waters in the Mediterranean and was very
suitable to small ships.

Through this expedition to Africa, Rome heard that Carthage was
gathering a force of 5,000 Numidians under Massinissa besides other
mercenary troops to re-enforce Hasdrubal in Spain, so that he might be
able to lead a large army to the aid of his brother in Italy. In addition, the
Senate was informed that a great fleet was fitting out for the recovery of
Sicily, but when it appeared late in the summer of 210 it was only 40
strong. It raided in Sardinia with some success, but withdrew on the
appearance of the Roman forces holding the island.

Although Livy tells us the news of these preparations in Africa made
a great impression on the Senate, yet all that the Senate did was to authorize the Consul, who had come to Rome to hold the annual elections, to
return to his province of Sicily without delay. It is evident that the Senate
felt that Carthage could not throw an army across the sea into Italy; and
that the Punic Council knew it to be so is shown by its sending re-enforcements to Hasdrubal in Spain.

At the beginning of the next consular year (March, 209), the Roman
admiral in Sicily was told to send 30 ships to aid the Consul Fabius Maximus in an attack on the city of Tarentum. In gaining the place Fabius
owed something to the Sicilian ships, although he chiefly relied on a
Roman Delilah within the walls who induced her Samson to admit the
Romans. The city yielded much booty and 30,000 inhabitants were sold

into slavery. The retaking of Tarentum immensely increased the prestige of Rome in South Italy and, in depriving Hannibal of his fortified port, it put an end to the prospect of seeing a Macedonian army coming to his aid in Italy.

From this date the power of Hannibal visibly if slowly declined, although he had several minor military successes. In 208 he was able by an ambush to kill both Consuls (Marcellus being one), who personally reconnoitered imprudently outside their own lines, and he cut to pieces a part of the garrison of Tarentum, but he did not get the necessary men and money from Africa.

It was now reported at Rome that Carthage was making ready a fleet of 200 sail to sweep the Roman coasts, and 50 ships were withdrawn from the squadron of 80 in Spain to form an Italian coast guard. With Italy thus made safe, the Roman fleet in Sicily was authorized to raid in Africa and effected a landing near Clupea (see Map 19). While the soldiers were gathering booty they were called hastily back to meet the Carthaginian fleet, which had put out to check their depredations. The Carthaginians proved to number only 83 ships and they were defeated with the loss of 18, and the Romans returned home with good prize. This year Rome had 280 ships in commission, probably employing nearly 60,000 men, even with short crews, of whom perhaps 17,000 to 18,000 must have been soldiers. The expedition to Africa was repeated the next year (207) with similar good fortune, 21 Punic ships being captured or destroyed, much booty taken, and abundance of provisions brought to Rome.

THE WAR IN SPAIN 215-208 B.C.
Roman Successes in Spain Followed by Disaster

We now return to affairs in Spain, which we dropped after the defeat of Hasdrubal on the Iberus in 216 and the arrival of his brother, Mago, in 215 with strong re-enforcements.

Although the Roman fleet preserved communications between Spain and Italy, the poverty of the latter was such that the Senate could send little aid either in men or in supplies to Spain. Nevertheless, the Scipios defeated the Punic army in two actions in 215 with such good results that most of the Spanish tribes came over to the Roman cause and the events of the war in Spain were that year more important than in Italy. In 214 and 213 little noteworthy occurred in the military operations in Spain except that in the latter year, owing to the lack of Italian recruits, Celtiberians were admitted to the Roman army as mercenary troops, this being the first occasion that any but citizens and Italian allies had followed the Roman standards.

In 212 the two Scipios put their new locally recruited troops to service and they failed. The Romans had not learned the conditions governing the employment of alien mercenaries. Hasdrubal bribed the Spanish troops to go home, and as a result the armies under both the Scipios were severely defeated and both lost their lives. The broken remnants of the Roman armies were assembled by a young subordinate officer, Lucius Marcius, who gathered a respectable force out of the garrison troops and reported with them to the commander of those who had escaped from Publius' battle. The soldiers elected Marcius as their general and he restored their courage by leading them in battles which Livy says were important victories but, nevertheless, the war long remained at a standstill. From what Livy says, it seems probable that the three Punic generals were on bad terms with each other and did not work well together, so that they contented themselves with drawing back and holding the country. Thus by the resolution of Marcius about 7,000 Italian troops continued to hold the Roman base at Tarraco and the line of the Iberus.

Roman Recovery of Spain

In the following year (211) after the siege of Capua had been successfully concluded, the Roman Senate was able to devote more effort to Spain and directed Caius Claudius Nero to choose from the Capuan legions 6,000 Roman infantry and 300 horse with as many allied infantry and 800 horse to restore the Roman predominance in Spain. This force marched to the nearest port, Puteoli, near Naples, and took ship for Tarraco, where it disembarked and joined the troops under Marcius on the Iberus, making a force of about 20,000 men.

Nero then advanced against Hasdrubal, who eluded him and retreated, refusing to be drawn into battle. But Nero did not conciliate the tribes sufficiently to recover those who had fallen away the previous year. As the Senate was now comparatively at ease about the situation in Italy, since the capture of Capua, but dreaded to see Hannibal re-enforced from Spain, it was decided to send additional soldiers to that province.

There was some difficulty about choosing a commander for the forces there who should unite the diplomatic skill of the Scipios with their military ability. Finally, Publius Cornelius Scipio, son of the late Proconsul in Spain, a young man of only 27, offered himself. Although he was too young to have held civil office entitling him to command an army, and his candidacy can scarcely have been pleasing to many of the sticklers for precedent in the Senate, he was already a distinguished officer with immense family influence and it was noteworthy that, in spite of the Senate's reluctance to see him go, there were no unfavorable auguries by the priesthood. The people elected him by acclamation and he went to Spain, the first Roman general chosen for military ability alone, the first Roman who did not owe his military command to his merits as political leader and as holder of civil office. Such was the effect of Hannibal's presence in Italy upon the Roman constitution.

With 10,000 infantry and 1,000 cavalry, Scipio embarked at Ostia early in 210 and, with an escort of 30 quinqueremes, he proceeded by sea to Emporiae to relieve Nero of the command. There he landed the soldiers and marched to Tarraco where the fleet joined him. The summer was spent by Scipio in diplomacy, in renewing the good relations of his father and uncle with the Spaniards, and in getting all possible information as to the enemy. He also won the affections of his army and, on the opening of the season of 209, he was ready to advance.

Scipio Conquers Cartagena

He launched the ships which, as usual, had been drawn on shore for the winter and appointed a rendezvous for fleet and army at the mouth of the Iberus. Of the three hostile armies, one was near the mouth of the Tagus, one near Gibraltar, and the third in the center of the peninsula. Scipio moved against neither army, for each could withdraw to the support of the others. He decided to seize New Carthage, which he had learned was held by a garrison of only 1,000 men. He explained to his men that New Carthage was the key to the possession of Spain and that in capturing it they would go far towards gaining the whole peninsula. It was, he said, the only harbor that could shelter a fleet between Gades and the Pyrenees, and from thence Africa spread its terrors over all Spain. There were the

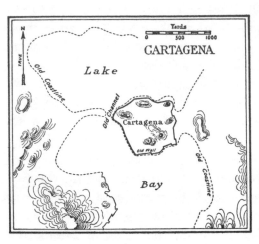

MAP 22.

hostages taken from all the Spanish peoples, there were vast stores of provisions and of weapons, and there was the repository of all the enemy's wealth. All being thus filled with confidence, he left a garrison of over 3,000 to hold the country north of the Iberus and, with 25,000 infantry and 2,500 cavalry, he set out on a forced march of 300 miles, which he is alleged to have done in 7 days. The fleet of 80 ships under his friend and confidant, Laelius, kept company with the army and they arrived together before New Carthage (see Map 22); so that all hostile re-enforcements of supplies and men were cut off at once by sea and land.

The attack upon the city differed from the long sieges which we have considered at Tyre and Rhodes. Here was a sudden and successful assault in which fleet and army worked together. The city occupied the eastern part of its present site. The modern fortifications follow much the same lines as the eastern remains of the early walls which were about 4,000 yards around. The city was at the end of a bay about a mile deep and nearly as wide, which reaches west and south of it. A narrow channel connected the bay with a shallow lake on the north of the city, whose depth was affected by the wind, a north wind depressing the water in the lake, a south wind raising it as much as 18 inches. On the eastern side the city was joined to the mainland by a low isthmus, about 400 yards wide. Within the walls were several hills, the highest 230 feet. The neighboring topography has changed somewhat with the passing of centuries, for the lake bottom has risen till it is now a mere swamp, and on the bay near the city the shores have gained on the sea so that on the east the narrow isthmus has become a wide stretch, and westward the naval dockyard occupies what was formerly a part of the bay.

As the fleet entered the bay the army arrived in front of the city and threw up an entrenched line across the isthmus, reaching from the bay to the lake, to defend itself against a hostile relieving army, and then camped between the city and the entrenchment without any second line to protect the camp from the city. In case of attack from outside Scipio would be supplied by sea.

The next day Scipio assembled the troops and explained his intentions. He pointed out the great importance of the city to the enemy, promised a golden crown to him who should first mount the walls, and finally said that Neptune had stood by his side during the night and had promised his aid at the proper time. Mago, commanding the city, placed half his troops in the citadel and the other 500 on a hill to the east. A body of 2,000 citizens whom he had armed were near the eastern gate ready to sally, and the rest of the citizens were manning the walls. About nine o'clock the fleet, heavily armed with missile weapons, approached the sea faces of the city threatening to land troops and drawing part of the garrison. Scipio directed 2,000 of his strongest men with ladders to assault the walls. As soon as the Roman trumpets sounded the advance, Mago led his sortie party against them. The Romans held back to induce the enemy to come out clear of the wall, and, after the first troops engaged, both sides fed the fight with additional men. As the struggle became more and more serious, the Carthaginians were driven back and the Romans placed their ladders against the walls and began to mount them under the eye of Scipio, who was everywhere to direct and encourage his men under cover of three shield bearers who took charge of his protection. The walls were high, the ladders broke, and about noon Scipio caused the trumpets to sound the retreat.

Scipio had been informed at Tarraco that the lake was fordable and had made his plan to take advantage of it. He then sent a body of 500 men with ladders to the far side of the lake and fresh troops to make a new attack on the land side. The defenders were dispirited by this new attack, although they resisted bravely. While this battle at the wall was at its height, the water was ebbing out of the lake aided by a north wind.

He now appealed to the superstition of his men, telling them that Neptune was coming to their aid as he had promised to do the night before and was driving the waters before him. Scipio had a remarkable gift of inspiring his followers and, under his personal leadership, the men forded the lake with no difficulty, believing that divinity was with them. They encountered little opposition as the garrison apprehended no danger from this side and was engaged elsewhere on the sea and land fronts. Having gained the top of the lake-side wall, this party ran along it and cleared the way for the others to enter by the northern gate. The Carthaginian forces fled; part to the eastern hill which was soon taken and the rest to the citadel with Mago, who capitulated when he found the city was in possession of the Romans.

The citizens to the number of 10,000 free males were restored to freedom with their property, and 2,000 mechanics were held as public slaves of the Roman people, being promised their freedom at the end of the war for faithful service; 300 Spanish hostages to Carthage were also taken, and immense amounts of military stores and weapons besides 18 quinqueremes and 113 merchant vessels, many with cargoes, were captured. The Romans also controlled the silver mines 2 miles from the city.

It will be remembered that Scipio had promised a golden crown to the first man to mount the walls and for this prize two candidates came forward, one from the fleet and one from the army. The cause of each was pressed with far more warmth by his own organization than by himself. Laelius commanding the fleet and Sempronius commanding the legionaries supported their own subordinates so that a riot seemed probable. Thereupon Scipio appointed a board of arbitration consisting of Laelius and Sempronius, with a third uninterested member to take evidence and decide. After hearing the testimony, the board reported to Scipio that the witnesses

> were ready to testify what they wished rather than what they knew to be true and to involve in the crime of perjury not only themselves in their own persons, but also the military standards and eagles and the sacred word of soldiers.

Scipio now summoned a general assembly and pronounced judgment, saying that he had evidence that both mounted at the same instant and thereupon he bestowed the mural crown on each. Although little is said by Livy of the services of the fleet in the assault, this little story shows that it bore an important part therein. No doubt the ships attacked the walls as Alexander's vessels did at Tyre.

Scipio spent a few days in the city restoring the walls, organizing labor and manufactures, and using his personal charm in diplomatic treatment of hostages and prisoners. At the same time the fleet was exercised in rowing and sham battles and the army had a 4-day schedule of exercise, the first day a 4-mile excursion under arms at fast speed, the second day cleaning of arms and inspection, the third day rest, and the fourth day fencing and javelin throwing with a button (at each other).

Further Operations in Spain in 209

During the year 209 the Carthaginian generals in Spain seem to have undertaken nothing. Such was the change in the situation, through the capture of New Carthage and the consequent defection of the tribes that the Carthaginians were thrown back to Gades as their base of communication with Africa.

Laelius was sent towards the end of the year with the principal prisoners by sea to Rome (taking 34 days, 850 sea miles), where he confirmed the report that Hasdrubal meant to march into Italy to the aid of his brother and was sent back with the ships which had accompanied him. Scipio returned from New Carthage to Tarraco, receiving on the way deputations from all parts of Spain and many important tribes, came over to the Roman cause during the winter of 209-208.

Scipio is a noteworthy character in Roman history and worthy of imitation by all aspirants to civil as well as to military success. While he had great strategic and tactical insight and the self-confidence and resolution necessary to make a great soldier, he owed much of his success to his high diplomatic qualities. Before beginning operations, he first took prisoner the minds of his own soldiers as well as of the Spanish tribes whose allegiance he needed. As he was first among Romans to receive military command for military ability alone, so was he first among them to work for the sympathy of his men. His youth, his manly beauty, his endearing manners, and his frank explanation of his purposes secured him the enthusiastic support of his followers. He employed the same policy in dealing with the Spaniards when he released the hostages the Carthaginians had immured in Cartagena. When a lovely maiden of high birth was presented to him as a slave at the capture of the city, he sent for her parents and her affianced husband and gave her a splendid wedding. By such means he secured the good will of the natives. In short, his method of command was the most approved method of today. He was one of the first of military leaders to be guided by the proverb that "one catches more flies by honey than by vinegar," preferring to lead by persuasion rather than by compulsion.

OPERATIONS IN SPAIN IN THE YEAR 208

Scipio felt that a Carthaginian naval force could not operate effectively beyond New Carthage while the Romans held that fortress and harbor. Consequently, as the army in Spain could look for little aid from home, he decided to reduce expense for 208 by drawing his ships on shore and using the best of their men in the army.[7] In accordance with the orders of the Senate, which Laelius had brought to him from Rome, Scipio opened the session of 208 by marching against Hasdrubal, who was nearly 200 miles west of New Carthage in southern Spain in the neighborhood of the silver mines in that district, which, of course, were of importance to him. A battle took place near Baecula, in which Hasdrubal had the worst of it, but faithful to his plan of joining his brother Mago he withdrew his army before he should suffer a decisive defeat and moved north towards the Tagus. Scipio decided not to follow Hasdrubal, fearing that the latter would be supported by the other Carthaginian armies. He therefore fell back to Tarraco and sent observation parties to watch the Pyrenean passes, while he occupied the remainder of the season in receiving submissions of the Spanish tribes. In Tarraco, he again passed the winter of 208-207.

HASDRUBAL GOES TO ITALY

Shortly after Scipio started on his march back to Tarraco, Hasdrubal met with the armies of his brother Mago and of Hasdrubal, son of Gisgo. They agreed that Scipio had established a firm hold on the allegiance of the Spanish tribes and it was advisable to take the Spaniards in the Carthaginian armies out of Spain. The policy of the Carthaginian Council to

---

[7] The Senate drew on him for 50 ships to use in Italy (see p. 351).

make sure of Spain had failed. The generals in Spain felt free to take up the alternative policy of winning the war in Italy.

They therefore resolved that Hasdrubal should go with the Spanish contingents to Italy where the final decision of the war now seemed to lie, that the son of Gisgo should retire into Lusitania, while a body of 3,000 cavalry should raid the Roman province (Catalonia), and that Mago, giving his army to his brother, should go to the Balearic Islands with a large sum of money and hire recruits.

The city of Rome was greatly pleased to hear of the Roman successes in Spain during 208, but soon it was learned through the Roman ally Massilia that Hasdrubal had crossed the western Pyrenees and was wintering in southern Gaul, intending to cross the Alps into Italy as soon as the passes were open in 207.

Thus, in spite of his great tactical and diplomatic successes in Spain, Scipio had failed in his principal objective. A great Carthaginian army had passed him and was on its way to re-enforce the army which had held Rome in terror for 10 years. It must have been a difficult, if not impossible, task for Scipio to close all the passes of the Pyrenees, for that would have taken his army far from the sea and his ports at Tarraco and New Carthage. He had to support the war with little help from Rome and did not harry the tribes as did the Carthaginians, and consequently he must have had less money to expend on army movements. Hasdrubal, on the other hand, had provided himself with a great treasure to buy his way through Gaul without driving the natives to armed resistance, and he took a precaution which he had neglected in 216. He moved on a western pass of the Pyrenees. Consequently, it is probable Scipio's ill success was unavoidable. If he had gone far west from Tarraco to meet Hasdrubal near the Bay of Biscay, a movement to the Iberus by the army of the son of Gisgo would have brought him back and Hasdrubal would have gone on.

SCIPIO IN SOUTHERN SPAIN

In 207, Scipio had a comparatively free hand in Spain. Although a new general, Hanno, with an army, was sent over from Africa to replace Hasdrubal Barca, and additional men were recruited in Spain, nevertheless the Romans advanced into Southern Spain. Hanno was defeated and made prisoner, and Scipio was prevented only by winter from making an attempt to capture Gades. He therefore dismissed the legions to winter quarters and he himself retired to Tarraco. Although Hasdrubal and his army had left Spain, the attention of the rulers of Carthage was still chiefly directed there, for they were most anxious to secure it, before the end of the war, and there the son of Gisgo was joined by Mago and was able to raise an army of over 50,000 in readiness for the year 206. Early in the year Scipio advanced against this new levy with a force of 40,000 men in which he was careful to avoid his father's error of having a dangerously large proportion of natives. A second battle occurred in the neighborhood of Baecula, which compelled the Carthaginians to withdraw from all the country except Gades.

Leaving a force in the south to take over the country, Scipio returned to Tarraco and then made an adventurous voyage with two quinqueremes to Africa to conciliate Syphax, King of Numidia. Here he entered the port in which Hasdrubal (son of Gisgo), fleeing from Spain, had just arrived with 7 triremes and was about to anchor. Scipio got into port and anchored before Hasdrubal could go outside to meet him and was thereafter protected by the neutrality of the port. The two enemies then proceeded to the King's residence and reclined on the same couch during the repast given by their host. After ratifying a league with Syphax, as an enemy of Carthage, Scipio returned to New Carthage after a prosperous but somewhat rough voyage of 3 days (110 miles).

At Gades, Mago had gathered a few ships, but the weakness of the Carthaginian garrison induced the inhabitants to offer to turn the city over to the Romans. Accordingly, Marcius was sent there with a light-armed force by land, and Laelius accompanied him by sea with 7 triremes and 1 quinquereme. In the meantime the plot in Gades had been discovered by Mago and the conspirators had been seized and placed on board a squadron under command of Adherbal for conveyance to Carthage. The prisoners, on board a slow quinquereme, were sent off somewhat in advance of the escort of 8 triremes and the two hostile divisions met in the Straits of Gibraltar where the current and eddies made ship control very difficult. Seeing the Romans coming out of Gibraltar and interposing between his triremes and the quinquereme ahead, Adherbal turned towards the enemy and the lighter ships found the current eddies very embarrassing; for when these caught the ships at the moment of contact, they might turn promising ram thrusts into exposure of the flank and vice versa. While the battle between the triremes was thus doubtful and irregular, the Roman quinquereme, being heavier and with more rowers, was under better control in the eddies and sank 2 triremes and swept the oars from another so that she was helpless. The other ships then escaped under sail to Africa. When Laelius learned from the prisoners that the plot in Gades had been discovered, he warned Marcius to go no farther.

The Carthaginian Council Shifts Its Effort to Liguria

While Mago at Gades was preparing to evacuate Spain, the Carthaginian Council seems to have perceived that it had no longer any chance of retaining Spain, for it sent money to Mago with an order to take the fleet he had at Gades and proceed to Liguria and, after enlisting there as many Gallic and Ligurian youth as possible, to go to his brother's aid in Bruttium. Too late the Council came over to Hannibal's policy. Mago then plundered Gades and its temples and treasuries and sailed up the coast where he attempted to surprise New Carthage by a night attack, but his ships had been seen in the offing during the day previous and the garrison was awaiting the attack in readiness, so he was repulsed with severe loss. He then went on to the Balearic Islands, where he made his winter stay for 206-205 and shipped 2,000 slingers to Carthage. (The islanders were renowned over all the Mediterranean for their skill with the sling shot.) After Mago left the coast of Spain, Gades capitulated to Scipio (late in 206) and thereafter the Romans were undisturbed by the Carthaginians, and Scipio became the idol of the Roman people.

The War in Italy after Hasdrubal Left Spain

Except for the dying war in the Adriatic, Italy became the sole theater of war after the settlement of Spain. At the time that Hasdrubal wintered with his army in southwestern Gaul, 208-207, Hannibal had been confined for some years to South Italy, where he was holding his own with difficulty. Now the approach of Hasdrubal and his aid might perhaps serve to bring Rome to terms, for at this moment Scipio was still strongly opposed in Spain. When the campaigning season of 207 opened, Hasdrubal was prompt to follow Hannibal's route across the Alps and appeared unexpectedly early in the Po Valley, where he picked up perhaps 10,000 recruits with the money he had provided from the tribute of Spain. The Romans had heard of his probable intentions and provided a force of 15 legions for the year in Italy. Two weak legions garrisoned Rome. The rest were divided into two army groups, each under a Consul. In the south, the Consul Caius Claudius Nero was opposed to Hannibal with a consular field army of two full legions with allies, numbering 20,000 to 25,000 men, and five other small legions as garrison and reserve troops, making in all a force of nearly 40,000 men.[8]

In the north, beyond the Apennines, the Consul Marcus Livius Salinator, who was to meet Hasdrubal, had a similar consular army and four other reserve and garrison legions. In all, there may have been almost 80,000 Romans and allies in the two Italian field armies. Both in Spain and in Sicily some troops were recruited locally. It is reported by Livy, apparently without entire confidence, that after Hasdrubal's departure from Spain Scipio sent 2,000 legionaries and nearly 10,000 Spaniards and Gauls to Livius Salinator by sea and that 4,000 light troops were drawn from Sicily. If true, Rome drew advantage from her sea power in the rapid movement of troops.

Hasdrubal seems to have had about 30,000 men and Hannibal scarcely as many.

On arrival in the Po Valley, Hasdrubal did not immediately march south to join his brother, but delayed to besiege Placentia—a grave error. In the south, Hannibal drew together all the troops which had been in winter quarters and which could be spared from garrison duty in Bruttium and started north. After an inconclusive battle at Grumentum, he arrived at Canusium, closely followed by the Roman army. There Hannibal waited, presumably to learn whether Hasdrubal would pass east or west of the mountains, on his way to the junction.

In the meantime Hasdrubal broke off the siege of Placentia, which had served only to delay him, and sent six riders in advance to tell Hannibal of his intentions. After going nearly the whole length of Italy, they took a wrong turn in the road and fell into the hands of the Romans. With their letter they were taken to Nero who, when he had read it, instantly made a selection of the best troops in his army to the number

---

[8] See Kromayer's *Antike Schlactfelder-Italien* for an analysis of the situation in Italy.

of 6,000 infantry and 1,000 horse, with which to go to the aid of his colleague while leaving Hannibal in ignorance.

This astonishingly bold plan proved successful. A forced march, aided by the good-will and transport facilities of all inhabitants on the line of march, brought Nero to the camp of Livius in the shortest possible time. The latter had united the garrison of the Po Valley to his own legions at a point where the eastern coast road crosses the Metaurus River, some 30 miles north of Ancona. Here the two Consuls, who must have had nearly 40,000 men, destroyed the Carthaginian army and killed Hasdrubal. Nero, marching back with equal speed, made the 250-mile trip in 6 days and announced to Hannibal that he had been away by casting his brother's head to the Punic outposts.

The battle of the Metaurus has been held to be one of the decisive battles of world history. Certainly its outcome ended Hannibal's hope of victory, but many have doubted whether the junction of the two brothers would have brought another finish to the war. The power of endurance of the Roman people and the fortitude and military worth of the Roman soldier were so great and had already so worn down the resources of the enemy, that another outcome on the Metaurus might only have deferred Rome's final victory. As it was, Hannibal was thrown farther back into Bruttium, where he was able to make some use of the ports of the province for supplies, yet in the next 4 years the area he controlled was gradually reduced by the defection of his Bruttian allies, and at last he held only the towns he garrisoned.

THE PUNIC COUNCIL CONTINUES WAR

Now that Spain seemed definitely lost to Carthage, the government determined to throw support to Hannibal, and Mago was directed, as has already been mentioned, to collect recruits for him in Liguria. After the Metaurus defeat, the Punic Council could scarcely have thought it possible to make any important gains which would compensate for prolonging the war. It was the visit of Scipio to Syphax which probably made the Council realize that there was an element in the Roman government anxious to push the war into Africa to annihilate Carthage, as Regulus had tried to do 50 years earlier. Should Hannibal be driven out of Italy, this party would be able to carry out its policy, whereas, it was known to all that

Rome was very exhausted and, if Rome found Hannibal could not be forced out of Italy, the Senate might be willing to make peace on the condition that Italy should be evacuated. So Carthage decided to re-enforce Hannibal from North Italy, hoping to obtain a negotiated peace before Africa should be invaded.

Rome was indeed very tired. The state and the citizens had been under great stress for the past 12 years and now for the first time since Hannibal crossed the Alps there was a lull. The fleet and the army were both reduced for 206. Farmers returned to their homesteads. Captured lands in Campania were sold to fill the treasury. There was a general setting to rights of the business of the community.

In this state of affairs at the close of 206, Scipio, the young hero, arrived from Spain to tell of his victories, to suggest rather than to urge the acknowledgment of his great services by the reward of a triumph, and to offer himself as a candidate for the consulship for the year 205, although far below the legal age, for, as he had said years before when running for the aedileship, "If the people elect me, I am old enough." It was no doubt clearly understood by all that Scipio stood for the policy of carrying the war into Africa. To this a large part of the Senate objected; nevertheless, when the election came off, there had never been so heavy a vote cast, and people had come to town not only to vote but to look at Scipio whose fine presence and endearing manners had won all hearts.

After his election, Scipio's plans were opposed in the Senate. The older Senators, led by Fabius, five times Consul, Dictator, and Censor, urged that Hannibal must first be overcome and that no expedition should go abroad till Italy was free. Scipio replied that he expected to draw Hannibal to Africa, and that it was by no means because he dreaded Hannibal that he urged the expedition to Carthage. It was rumored that, if the Senate were to refuse him the African campaign, he would appeal to the people. He refused to answer the Senate's question as to his intention in the matter, and at the last it allowed him to have his way as the people so much desired.

His colleague Crassus was given four legions to face Hannibal in Bruttium, while Scipio was assigned the province of Sicily with permission to pass into Africa if he should think it for the good of the state. Although not given authority to levy soldiers, he was permitted to enroll volunteers

MAP 23.

ROMAN WARS IN AFRICA AND THE AEGEAN

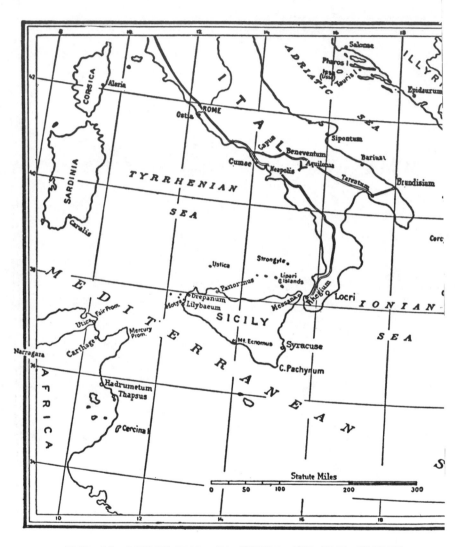

MAP 23. ROMAN WARS IN AFRICA AND THE AEGEAN

and to ask contributions for building the fleet to carry him to Africa. Evidently the Senate did not approve a campaign in Africa. Material for the ships and provisions poured in on him in such abundance that in 45 days after the timber was delivered the ships were ready for service, and the Consul proceeded to Sicily with 7,000 volunteers and 30 ships to add to the two legions and 30 ships already in the island.

During this consulate of Scipio (205), Mago enlisted a number of young men and left Minorca where he had wintered. With 30 ships of war and many transports, he conveyed 12,000 foot and 2,000 cavalry to Italy and made an unopposed landing at Genoa, where he proceeded to enlist more troops and rouse the tribes. The Roman Senate took precautions against Mago's invasion of Italy, and Marcus Livius, the conqueror of Hasdrubal, was sent to Ariminum with an army of volunteer slaves to meet him, while the city legions went to Arretium. It was the same distribution of force (in the north) that had been made in 217 when Hannibal was expected to enter. Nothing occurred that year in Bruttium for both armies were disabled by a pestilence.

THE WAR IN AFRICA

After his arrival in Sicily, Scipio organized and exercised the army and repaired the old ships in the island, while he hauled the new ones on shore to let their green wood season. The old ships he then sent under Laelius on a raiding expedition against the shores of Africa. Their arrival at Hippo Regius, 125 miles west of Carthage, created a panic, since the Carthaginians were not a military people and the neighboring tribes were unreliable. The two Kings of Numidia were also ill-disposed to Carthage. Syphax was under the influence of Scipio's visit to him and Massinissa was openly hostile. But when it was discovered that the main army had not come and that only a raiding party was at Hippo, the Council recovered itself and began to strengthen its alliances. An embassy was sent to Philip of Macedon, but he was already making peace with the Romans. Syphax was won to renounce his treaty with Scipio by a marriage to the very beautiful daughter of Hasdrubal (son of Gisgo), and orders were sent to both Hannibal and Mago to exert themselves to the utmost.

To Mago, also, the Council sent 25 ships of war and nearly 7,000 troops besides 7 elephants and large sums of money to pay auxiliary levies, so that he might advance on Rome. He thus had over 20,000 Spaniards and Africans, besides many local levies. It was evidently the hope of the Council that by such an advance the Senate might be induced to recall Scipio's army for the defense of Rome, just as Hannibal's invasion had withdrawn the Consul Sempronius from Sicily in 218. Although the reduction of the Roman fleet in 206 had enabled the Council to place these large forces in Liguria, that fleet was still far from negligible, for 80 transport ships which Mago sent south with provisions and plunder were taken on the coast of Sardinia by the Roman governor of the island. Carthage still found it dangerous to put large forces across the sea.

During the winter the hopes in Rome rose high that in the summer of the coming year (204) Scipio (who was now Proconsul) would pass over to Africa. Nevertheless, opposition to him in the Senate had not diminished during his consulate. His position with regard to the ancient system of government was unprecedented. The first of all Romans, he had arrived at the consulship by the military route. He was a professional soldier. His army, too, was of a new type, for the exigencies of the prolonged and desperate war had gone far to convert the citizen army into a professional one.

As a result of this change in the spirit of the army and its officers, there was an unfortunate abuse of the people of the town of Locri (see Map 10) by a garrison that was part of Scipio's army. The citizens sent an embassy to Rome where their complaints against the garrison and its officers gave an opportunity for the opposition to break out against Scipio's plan of campaign and against his personality and method of army discipline. It was proposed in the Senate to recall him for inefficiency which, of course, implied an abandonment of hope of a conclusive end to the war; but after discussion a compromise was arrived at whereby a committee of 10 was to visit Scipio at his headquarters, to investigate all charges on the spot, and to take such summary action as circumstances might require. On arrival at Locri, the committee found the charges of oppression brought by the citizens to be well founded and the offending governor was sent to Rome in chains, but the townspeople diplomatically avoided making any charge more serious than negligence against Scipio himself.

The political task of the committee was thus cleared; it did not have to investigate a scandalous charge against the favorite of the people and it went on to Sicily. There Scipio offered no verbal defense. He submitted his work during the previous year to inspection. The fleet and army were assembled at Syracuse, and the committee saw them both at exercise. It saw also the storehouses full of provisions and all other military supplies and was convincd that either the army under Scipio would vanquish the Carthaginians or no other army and general could do so. He was bidden to set out on his voyage with the blessing of the gods to fulfill the hopes of the Roman people.

On the other hand, Carthage was much disturbed by the prospect of the invasion of Africa, and after Hasdrubal had succeeded in seducing Syphax from the Roman alliance, he urged the latter to make his defection known to Scipio so that the loss of this ally might perhaps persuade Scipio to abandon his expedition and confine himself to operations in Italy. Scipio was undeterred by this news, but feared to tell the army of it. Yet since the arrival of the messengers was known throughout Syracuse, he gave out that they had come to hasten his departure.

The number of the expeditionary force was not known to Livy. He states that the highest figure named by previous writers was 35,000 horse and foot. This seems a small enough figure for a campaign to end a war which in previous years had employed as many as 130,000 soldiers besides those in the fleet. The shipping included 400 transports and an escort of 50 men-of-war. Accounts of other campaigns suggest that the average transport ship of those times was capable of carrying 100 infantrymen, or 15 to 20 horses. So that putting the cavalry strength of Scipio's force at the usual 10 per cent of the infantry, 400 ships would accommodate an army of nearly 30,000. The entire personnel may have been over 40,000 men.

Scipio ordered the fleet and army to assemble at Lilybaeum and all merchant ships on the seacoast were requisitioned for transport service. The mariners were first placed on board the ships by Laelius, who commanded the fleet. The military stores were then shipped by the Praetor Pomponius, including supplies and water[9] for 45 days.

When all the troops were embarked and the fleet was ready to depart, Scipio directed all masters and pilots with two soldiers from each ship

---

[9] The water allowance seems very excessive; alone it would require half the tonnage of the fleet.

to assemble in the forum, where he inquired of all whether their ships had full supplies on board. Then he announced to all the order of sailing, the distinguishing lights of the ships at night, and the point of rendezvous on the African coast (see Map 20). The transports were guarded by 20 ships on their right and another 20 on their left flank, and presumably the other 10 men-of-war were charged with rounding up stragglers among the 400 transports, always a necessary task. At daylight the fleet was ready to get under way when Scipio, having commanded silence by a trumpet, addressed all the gods by sea and land, asking them to watch over and aid the expedition and make it serviceable to the Roman people. He then cast the sacrifice into the sea and the trumpets gave the order for sailing.

A favorable wind was blowing and the expedition soon ran out of sight of land, but about noon it struck a fog which made care necessary to avoid collision, and the wind died down. The haziness continued till next sunrise, when it cleared off and the pilot told Scipio that land was visible and that they had made a good landfall at the Promontory of Mercury. Scipio prayed that his seeing Africa might be a happy omen for the state and for himself, and directed the fleet to head to the westward for another landing. A fog came up about nightfall and the fleet anchored for safety. Next morning it was clear and the pilots reported that the fleet was off the Fair Promontory (110 sea miles in 48 hours). Scipio replied, "I accept the omen" (of the name), and directed a landing. The spot was only about 20 miles from Carthage and less than that from Utica, a city second only to Carthage and an ally rather than a subject.

The city of Carthage was in great alarm, for it had neither a sufficient army nor a general who was a match for the Roman. Sending the fleet to the neighborhood of Utica, Scipio marched the army to high ground near it, fortified his camp, and was joined by Massinissa with a few hundred horsemen. His principal opponent was Hasdrubal (son of Gisgo), whom he had defeated and driven out of Spain. Apparently Hasdrubal had only about 15,000 men at his disposal. There were several cavalry actions in which the Romans were successful and on two occasions they sent to Sicily prisoners and booty which they had secured by their raiding expeditions from the camp near Utica. Scipio then turned all his energies to the siege of Utica, intending to make it his base for future operations. After 40 days Hasdrubal and Syphax came up with a relieving force and camped near. As winter was now approaching, Scipio broke off the siege and formed a camp for the winter on a neighboring promontory, hauling his ships on shore and including them in the circuit of the entrenchment, which was called Camp Cornelia. Great quantities of provisions and clothing were sent to the army in Africa from Italy, Sicily, and Sardinia.

During that year (204) of the invasion of Africa, one Consul with the southern armies held Hannibal down in Bruttium, and the other Consul maintained order in the Po Valley, in spite of its sympathy with Mago and his expected invasion. For the year 203 the Senate provided 20 legions and 160 men-of-war, divided into four squadrons for Africa, Sicily, Sardinia, and Italy. The soldiers on board each ship numbered 50 for the Sardinian squadron and 75 for the Italian.

The chief theater of the war was now in Africa, where Scipio lay near Utica, with Hasdrubal's army near by in one camp and Syphax and his army in another. The Punic fleet had also been manned and launched, and was ready to intercept the Roman shipping on the line of supply. When spring came Scipio again launched his ships and made as if he intended to attack Utica by sea and land. His real object was the two camps of Hasdrubal and Syphax. These he surprised by a night march and set on fire, and as the occupants poured out to extinguish the flames, the Romans fell upon them and both the African armies were driven back with great loss. The Punic Council debated whether it should ask for peace or summon Hannibal from Italy, or enlist more men in Africa and beseech Syphax not to abandon the cause. The war party prevailed. It was decided not to recall Hannibal, for of course his presence in Italy would enable Carthage to negotiate a favorable peace if Scipio should be defeated. As a result of this firmness, a considerable force was assembled about 30 days later at Great Plains under Syphax and Hasdrubal. Against this body Scipio moved with a strong force drawn from the lines about Utica and dispersed it.

Carthage Recalls Her Two Armies in Italy

Again consternation ruled in Carthage where it was expected that Scipio would immediately appear. Now the great decision was taken to recall Hannibal and Mago from Italy. It meant the abandonment of all idea of a successful war. Even if Scipio and his army were to be destroyed by Hannibal, Carthage could not expect to reconquer Spain or Sicily. Both sides were exhausted, whatever its outcome the war was approaching its end and the strategic objective of Hannibal's 15-year campaign was not to be obtained.

At the same time that the deputies left to fetch Hannibal from Bruttium and Mago from Liguria, the Carthaginian fleet was launched to attempt to surprise the Roman fleet blockading Utica, for it was understood that its naval camp was not well guarded. During these events in Carthage, Scipio was slowly returning to Utica from his field campaign and seized Tunis about 10 miles from Carthage. The city had been abandoned by its garrison and, while Scipio was encamping, the Carthaginian fleet was seen from the hills laying its course towards Utica. Carthage and Tunis were about equally distant from Utica and the army dropped the work of the camp and hurried to Utica, about 15 miles away. Scipio got there in time to direct the defense, for the Carthaginian ships made no haste and at sundown anchored at a halfway point called Ruscina to spend the night. It is permissible to believe that the Punic fleet, newly manned and unpracticed, was thrust out of port before its organization was well established, and that the delay at Ruscina was necessary to get it in hand.

The stop was fortunate for the Romans, as Scipio found his men-of-war loaded with siege machines and adapted to siege work rather than to sea battles. He therefore made what was later known as a "sea harbor," out of the storeships and other craft. The men-of-war were drawn close to land for safety and seaward of them he anchored a line of merchant ships at short distance from each other, which were lashed together by hawsers from ship to ship, and on the hawsers were laid planks so as to make bridges from ship to ship. Masts and spars were also used to improve the obstruction. Probably the spars were afloat in front of the line of ships to keep the enemy from coming between them. Livy says that there were four such lines of ships, one behind another to protect the men-of-war. About 1,000 men with a great supply of missiles were placed on board this floating fortress to defend it.

On the following morning about sunrise, the Carthaginian fleet formed line of battle opposite the Roman ships and, finding that the latter did not move, it closed with the enemy and a fight took place like the assault of a strong place on land. At first the Romans had some advantage from the greater height of their merchant ships, which enabled them to cast their weapons downward while the enemy cast upward. The smaller of the Roman ships pushed out under the hawsers binding the large ones together and engaged the enemy without much effect, for they were very light and besides they got in the way of the missiles of their own friends. At last the Carthaginians threw heavy grapnels with iron chains. When these had hooked an enemy they hauled back and were able to tear several ships adrift from the first line. At the end of the day they had taken six ships, which they towed back to Carthage, and were welcomed with more delight than the measure of success justified.

In the meantime, since the action at Great Plains, Massinissa and Laelius had followed up the retreating Syphax and Massinissa had taken Syphax prisoner and seized his kingdom. On the return of Laelius and Massinissa to the Roman headquarters, Scipio led back his troops to Tunis and completed the fortifications there while the Carthaginians, having learned of Syphax' reverse, sent ambassadors to Scipio to sue for peace. A truce was declared and Scipio offered as terms that Carthage should surrender all prisoners and deserters, abandon all pretensions to Spain, withdraw its armies from Gaul and Italy, retire from the islands between Italy and Africa, deliver up its ships-of-war, and pay a heavy indemnity in money and provisions. Massinissa went west to consolidate his rule in Numidia and to raise a cavalry force while Laelius was sent to Rome to report on affairs, taking Syphax with him, and ambassadors from Carthage went a few days later to take Scipio's terms to the Senate for confirmation.

During this summer of 203, the legions of North Italy met Mago's army in the neighborhood of Milan and inflicted a very severe defeat on it, seriously wounding Mago who made his way to the Ligurian seacoast and there met the Council's order to return to Carthage, as it was no longer possible for the state to maintain armies in Italy and Gaul. Accordingly, he sailed with his army, but died as he was passing Sardinia. Some of his ships were picked up by the Roman patrol squadron, the rest made port at Hadrumetum.

About the same time deputies reached Hannibal, who was thrown into violent agitation on being ordered to return to Africa. But as he had for some time anticipated the call, he had ships ready and, sending useless men to garrison several towns, with great rapidity he carried the rest of the army, perhaps 15,000 men, back to Africa and landed at Leptis Minor some 90 miles south of Carthage, late in 203. Probably his army was not included in the armistice. The exultation of the Roman people over the evacuation of Italy and Gaul was reduced by the anxiety felt for its single army in Africa, which was now to meet the whole remaining strength of Carthage under its ablest leader.

The Punic ambassadors now arrived at Rome to ask for peace and to place all the blame of the war on Hannibal. The Senate heard them and decided to leave terms to be arranged by Scipio and the ambassadors were dismissed. During the continuance of the truce and about the time Hannibal landed in Africa, 100 transports from Sardinia with supplies for the Roman army accompanied by 20 men-of-war arrived safely in Africa, but another fleet of 200 from Sicily, escorted by 30 men-of-war, had worse fortune. While struggling against a southwest gale, they came within sight of Carthage and took refuge at various points along the coast. A concourse of people took place in the city and in spite of having sued for peace and of the existing truce, it was resolved to send out Hasdrubal with a fleet of 50 ships and gather in the prizes which had so unexpectedly appeared and whose supplies the city needed. As might be expected, Scipio resented Hasdrubal's action and sent to Carthage for an explanation. The envoys were sent back without a reply, for Carthaginian hopes were so far raised by Hannibal's arrival as to wish the war to go on. The Roman ambassadors, who had come by sea, were even treacherously attacked on their return and, although they escaped personal injury, it was necessary to run their ship ashore to avoid its destruction.

Final Battle at Zama (Narragara)

The outrage induced Scipio to declare the truce at an end. He marched up the Bagradas Valley to ravage the country behind Carthage, while sending to Massinissa to hasten his return with cavalry in which the Roman army was deficient. The people of Carthage now besought Hannibal to save them and, after some delay, he moved out from Hadrumetum under pressure from the city before his preparations were entirely complete. It was early in 202. He had a force of about 40,000 men, including about 4,000 cavalry. Excluding the troops left to guard the expedition base at

Camp Cornelia, Scipio had only some 25,000, but expected Massinissa to join him with 10,000 including a strong cavalry division. Hannibal directed his march to Zama, about 80 miles southwest of Carthage, and then began to scout to find the Roman army. Scipio had cut loose from his base at Camp Cornelia because Massinissa's cavalry was essential to him before fighting Hannibal and he could not permit the latter to interpose between him and Massinissa. So Scipio was three or four marches farther west when Hannibal arrived at Zama. After Massinissa joined up, the two armies advanced towards each other for the battle.

Commentators dwell much on the extraordinary boldness of Scipio in thus sacrificing his communication with his base before fighting a battle in which defeat would be ruinous to his army. It is held that this decision alone puts him in the first rank of great captains. Undoubtedly it was a bold step, but it would have been ruinous also to let Hannibal fall on Massinissa alone.

Such critics give insufficient weight to the advantage afforded by the superior Roman fleet. Scipio could retreat to the sea at Hippo Regius, 50 miles in his rear. Although the Carthaginian fleet had got a slight advantage in its surprise attack the previous autumn, it was too small to profit by its success and now 50 additional Roman ships-of-war and 100 transports with stores were shortly expected at Utica. Thus in case of his defeat, Scipio was in a position to improvise a base on the coast and reopen his sea communications by falling back to a suitable point in the direction of Hippo and fortifying his camp on the shore. There the store ships from Camp Cornelia could join him with supplies while the fleet at Utica would cover them from any pursuit by the hostile fleet at Carthage. Scipio might even return to Camp Cornelia by sea. In short, Hannibal could not cut Scipio from his base at Utica by getting on the road to that point.

As it turned out, the point did not arise, for in the great battle known as Zama (although it took place at Narragara, 130 miles west northwest from Hadrumetum) Hannibal was overthrown with great loss and fled to Hadrumetum. After pursuing the defeated army for a little distance, Scipio plundered the enemy's camp. He then returned to his own camp near Utica with much booty, and found that Publius Lentulus had arrived with the expected naval re-enforcement and supplies. Scipio then got under way with his own ships and those of Lentulus and steered for the harbor of Carthage less than 16 miles away. He was met by a Carthaginian ship dressed with olive branches and carrying 10 ambassadors who ran under the stern of Scipio's ship, holding out the badges of suppliants, and asked his favor. He made no reply except to tell them he would see them at Tunis where the army was then marching. This meant that Carthage was to be blockaded. The ambassadors appeared again at Tunis and again asked compassion.

THE PEACE TERMS

Although Scipio's council, as well as himself, felt that Carthage deserved the severest measures, yet all appreciated the difficulties and delays in bringing the siege of such a great city to a fortunate conclusion, and Scipio was aware that a successor might soon be appointed in his place to claim the honors of the war. He called the ambassadors the next day and offered as terms for ending the war that Carthage was to live under her own laws and preserve her boundaries as before the war, and that he would that day cease devastation of her countryside; that the city should deliver up all prisoners and Roman deserters and all its ships of war except 10; that she was to make no war without the consent of Rome; that she was to make a treaty with Massinissa, and pay 10,000 talents of silver ($13,800,000) to Rome in 50 annual payments. If these terms were accepted, Scipio would grant a truce to refer all to Rome, provided that Carthage would immediately return all the ships and cargoes which had been wrongfully seized during the former truce. There were murmurings among the people at the terms offered, but Hannibal declared them to be not unreasonable.

Accordingly, ambassadors were sent to Rome and the captured merchant ships were restored and their crews were found, but the goods could not be traced. Scipio therefore ordered that the Roman quaestors should make a return from their books as to the amount of public stores on board and private owners also made their claims. As a result the 200 cargoes were assessed at 25,000 pounds of silver.[10]

---

[10] Assuming the cargoes to have been mainly wheat for the army and that it was worth 1 denarius a modius (an average price during the war) or 2.06 pounds of silver a ton of wheat, the individual ships average 61 tons burden each or, say, 150 tons load displacement.

As soon as the ambassadors arrived at Rome, the supplies of grain from Sicily and Sardinia became so cheap in Rome that the merchants often furnished grain to the mariners in payment for the freight of cargoes. The new Consuls for the year 201 had assumed office before the ambassadors met the Senate, and one of them, Cornelius Lentulus, who was anxious to be sent to Africa to take the credit of ending the war, endeavored, through a friend's speech, to have the treaty rejected, but the assembly voted in favor of peace and also forbade Lentulus to pass into Africa, so that Scipio was to conclude the peace and bring home the legions.

The Carthaginians having carried out the terms of the treaty, their fleet was taken to sea and burned and the Roman deserters were executed, the Latins being beheaded and the Romans crucified. After thus settling matters, Scipio went home to the most splendid triumph which had ever been beheld in Rome (year 201 B.C.) Thenceforward, he was known as "Africanus."

REVIEW OF THE WAR

Reviewing the struggle of 16 years which ended at Zama, it is apparent that Roman preponderance at sea obliged Hannibal to invade Italy through Gaul. It permitted Rome to maintain the struggle in Spain, until victory was reached. It forbade Philip of Macedon from coming to the aid of Carthage. It reduced the aid Carthage was able to send to Hannibal. Finally, it enabled Scipio to cross the Mediterranean and draw his supplies from Sicily for two years until the Roman legionaries could overcome the veterans of Hannibal. The whole naval side of the war is worthy of study, for it is singularly modern and may be compared with profit to that of the recent World War.

Without any overwhelming naval victory and without absolute and complete control of the seas at all times, nevertheless Roman sea power brought it victory in the end precisely as allied sea power brought final success to the armies in Flanders. The terms of peace prescribed by Scipio also resemble those of Versailles in the limitations placed on the Punic navy. In both wars the control of commerce was both a means of victory and the prize of the war.

PRINCIPAL AUTHORITIES CONSULTED FOR THIS CHAPTER

ANCIENT

Diodorus Siculus.
Livy.
Polybius.
Plutarch: *Fabius, Marcellus.*

MODERN

Beloch, J.: *Bevölkerung der Griechische-Römischen Welt.*
Cambridge Ancient History, vol. 7.
Delbrueck, H.: *Geschichte der Kriegskunst.*
Dodge, T. A.: *Hannibal.*
Hart, B. H. L.: *Scipio Africanus.*
Kromayer, J.: *Antike Schlachtfelder.*
　　　　　　 Schlachten Atlas.
Mommsen, Th.: *Roman History.*

CHAPTER XII

WAR OF RHODES AND PERGAMUM AGAINST MACEDON

Situation Leading to War

A T THE close of the war with Carthage, Rome and Macedon each found grievances against the other as to the conduct of the late war. King Philip of Macedon sent ambassadors to Rome to lodge his complaint, but the Senate replied coldly and made counter-charges. The ambassadors were dismissed and war with Macedon seemed probable as early as 201.

We must now turn to the origin of the war then existing in Greece and Asia Minor, into which the Romans were now being drawn. When Rome made peace with Philip, in 205, the Republic dreaded his restless ambition and had strengthened the ties binding it to the Greek states in opposition to him. The peace did not prevent him from permitting a division of Macedonians to take service in Africa under Hannibal, as just mentioned, but this alone was insufficient cause for war. Mercenary soldiers found service wherever they were well paid. The real cause of offense which the Romans found was in King Philip's wars with Roman allies and commercial friends. In the same year that Philip made his unstable peace with the Romans, Ptolemy IV of Egypt died (205) and was now succeeded by his infant son Ptolemy V. Ptolemy IV had overthrown King Antiochus of Syria at Raphia on the boundary of Egypt in 217, and the rule of a minor seemed a new opportunity to King Antiochus to seize the long-disputed cities of Coelo-Syria, which were valuable not only for the trade routes by sea and land, which terminated in them, but also for their own productive wealth. Antiochus accordingly made an agreement with Philip of Macedon that the two should share the spoils of the Egyptian Empire. Antiochus was to have Syria and Phoenicia and Philip claimed the Greek islands of the Aegean and the districts belonging to Egypt on its shores. Although Philip feared to make war directly on Rome, it was

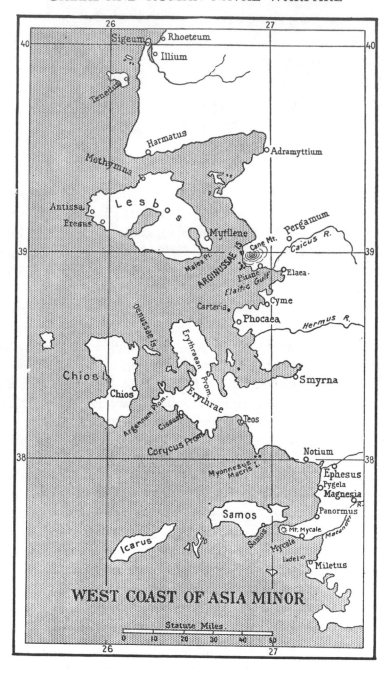

WEST COAST OF ASIA MINOR

Statute Miles

MAP 24.

doubtless his hope that while Rome was too much occupied with Carthage to send important aid to her friends, he could accomplish the seizure of these prosperous commercial centers and thus recoup himself to the east and southeast of Macedonia for the loss he incurred by the Roman protectorate over Greece.

The political situation was that the two Great Kings wished to turn into their own treasuries the profits of industry and commerce as the price of preserving order in the eastern Mediterranean. The commercial and manufacturing states, who preferred peace, were yet determined to stand together with Egypt in resistance to these attempts because they meant to hold the profits of business for their own benefit and maintain good order by their own armaments. In this group of commercial and peacefully inclined states the first places were held by Rhodes, Pergamum, and Egypt. Athens, Byzantium, and Chios were secondary in importance and even Aetolia had some interests in common with them, as she protected several Hellespontine cities. Behind all stood Rome in sympathy. Philip did not realize that he could not make conquests east and south without being made to feel Rome's displeasure. In the prosecution of the general plan of King Antiochus and himself, between 205 and 201, Philip gradually increased his enemies. He sent his general Heraclides to Rhodes under a false pretense and Heraclides took advantage of his friendly reception to burn the arsenal and disappear. He occupied the Cyclades, which were under the protection of Egypt, and the Hellespontine cities under Aetolia.

War between Macedon and Pergamum and Rhodes
Battle of Chios

In the year when Rome made peace with Carthage (201), Philip had acquired the fleet of large ships which he had lacked to oppose the Romans in 207. It was equipped by the cities subject to him. He opened hostilities by taking some cities in Thrace and then crossed into Asia. All the Greek commercial cities were disturbed at the prospect of exchanging the commercially minded rule of Egypt for the militarily minded rule of Macedon. In particular, Rhodes declared war and was joined by Attalus, King of Pergamum, and by Byzantium. While these allies were assembling on the Aetolian coast, Philip sent some of his ships to take Chios and Samos

and with the others he went to Elaea, the port of Pergamum, and sent
a force to besiege the city about 15 miles away (see Map 24). This incident occasioned an important naval battle between the fleets of Attalus
and the Rhodians on the one side and that of King Philip on the other.
A fragment of Polybius gives a most graphic account of the details of the
battle, but the general plan is somewhat obscure. It seems to have been
a general chase and "catch-as-catch can." Nevertheless, the details of
ancient naval warfare are so picturesquely described that it is well worth
while to study them.

The siege of Pergamum was proceeding without a high degree of
promise for the besiegers, part of whose fleet lay secure at Elaea, watched
at near-by points by the combined fleets of the Rhodians and of Attalus,
King of Pergamum, who commanded his fleet in person. Both were allies
of Rome which had just terminated the Hannibalic war and was free to
look about. They had in all 65 decked ships (cataphracts), 3 trieres, and
9 triemioli.[1] King Philip had 53 cataphracts and 150 open craft (lembi).
In due time Philip lost hope of a successful issue to the siege and he
resolved to abandon it suddenly and sail away to join his other ships
at Samos, but he did not wish a naval battle till he could assemble his
strength. As surprise was the essence of his plan, we may suppose that he
broke the siege soon after dark and marched to the shore where he embarked not long after midnight. His movement was unexpected and he
made a good start with his fleet. Nevertheless, he was overtaken.

If we search the chart for a commanding position in which to place
the watching enemy, the islands at the southwest point of Mt. Cane
control the northerly routes out of Elaea, and Phocaea controls the southern routes. But they are too far apart for mutual support. Philip's fleet
would be stronger than either part of the allies, if so divided. The northern
point of the Erythraean peninsula, which a south-bound fleet must pass,
is nearer to Mt. Cane than it is to Elaea. Consequently, with a good lookout on watch off Elaea, both allied fleets could lie off Mt. Cane and be
reasonably sure that the enemy could not get out without fighting. For
a chase, the fastest ships of the pursuer are very likely to be fast enough

---

[1] The etymology of the word suggests that it indicates a craft which is triere for only
half its length and diere for the other half. It is evidently a light craft which perhaps carried
a partial catastroma over the triere rowers only.

to overtake the most sluggish of the fugitives, and when these are attacked they will be supported by all their forces. A measurement of distances from Elaea and Mt. Cane to Erythrae shows that, unless Philip had more than a 2-hour start, he would have no advantage in distance to the entrance to the strait between Chios and the mainland, in which the battle must have taken place. With rowing ships, the strength of whose rowers had to be so carefully conserved before battle, it was a considerable advantage to the allies that they lay nearer the point of destination than their enemy, for when closing the Macedonian rowers would have put in almost 3 hours more of hard work.

After learning that King Philip was putting to sea, Attalus and Theophiliscus, the Rhodian admiral, pursued in haste and probably with little attempt to form in battle order, as when Philip should perceive that he could not get away, he would turn for battle and there would then be time for the allies to correct their formation. Still, although the pursuit was somewhat disorderly, as the occasion demanded, we may assume from the general tenor of Polybius' account that the allies were in two groups with Attalus leading on the port bows of the Rhodians, who had some disadvantage in their start, but were making it up by the fine nautical qualities of their ships. As commander in chief, King Philip led his right squadron which was now in the van. King Attalus seems to have passed the rear of the enemy and drawn ahead of it, threatening to turn and close with the van when the Rhodians should come within supporting distance. Philip saw that the enemy could force a battle when he pleased and preferred to accept it at his own moment.

Probably in the early afternoon, after passing west of the point of Erythrae, he made signal to his van to turn to port to engage the Pergamenes and left the immediate command to Democrates, while he himself continued on to the little islands in the middle of the strait of Chios (Oenussae) to await the outcome of the battle. Attalus, turning his ships simultaneously to starboard, placed them also in line heading towards the Macedonians. As battle was now certain, both opponents may have taken a little time to correct their alignments before advancing. Attalus' own ship was the first to encounter the enemy and the nearest ships on both sides soon joined also, without waiting for a signal. Attalus struck an octere below the water-tight deck and, in spite of the valiant battle of the soldiers on the catastroma, she sank. The decere of Philip, carrying the admiral's flag, was lost by a singular accident. This ship struck a triemiolus amidships below the wale strake under the upper oars. The pilot could not work the ram out of the hole with all the efforts of the crew and, while the ship was thus motionless, two penteres came up starboard and port and pierced her sides, so that she sank with all on board, including Democrates, Philip's admiral.

About the same time, Dionysidorus and Dinocrates, two brothers commanding Pergamene ships, had adventures equally singular. The first was attacked by a heptere, the second by an octere. Dinocrates had previously trimmed ship by the head, that is, he had shifted ballast forward so as to depress his ram. Consequently, the hostile ram, being higher, struck him a comparatively harmless blow above his water-tight deck, whereas his own blow (a little later) took effect below his enemy's deck and could not be withdrawn, although he tried to do so by rowing astern. In this situation the Macedonian soldiers fought with the greatest courage and Dinocrates was on the point of being overcome when Attalus came up and struck the Macedonian so hard that he freed the ship of Dinocrates. The Macedonians continued to fight until their ship was without defenders and fell into the hands of Attalus. Dionysidorus, charging his enemy at full speed,[2] missed his stroke and, passing on, he fouled her, sweeping away all his own oars on one side and his turret sponsons, crippling his own ship. Immediately he was surrounded by enemies with loud cries and the ship and crew were lost. Dionysidorus and two others alone were saved by swimming to a triemiolus, which picked them up. Here, the victory now seemed inclined to Attalus.

In the rear the Rhodians had at first been out of the action, owing to the unexpected start of the enemy, but, as the leaders drew alongside by superior speed and began to attack the rear ships, striking them on the quarter, the latter were obliged to turn and present their own rams. Thus the rest of the Rhodians got up to the line and the two squadrons fell on each other to the sound of the trumpets and the cries of the combatants. If

---

[2] Full speed was dangerous, as the ship was not under quick control to meet the enemy's maneuvers. This incident, as narrated by Polybius, partly explains why ram tactics have not developed with steam power.

the Macedonians in their line of battle had not mixed their lembi and cataphracts, the battle would have been shorter.[3]

As it was, the small craft were a great embarrassment to the Rhodians, for after the first charge when the ships were mingled in confusion, the lembi threw themselves on the big ships, sometimes ahead, sometimes astern, and prevented the play of the oars. The Rhodian pilots could not push the ships forward nor turn them, and the skill of the pilots and dexterity of the rowers were alike useless. Nevertheless, in this confusion, the Rhodians were able to use an expedient which was fatal to several. Having depressed the rams (by shifting ballast forward) the hostile blows were of little effect, being above the water-tight deck, while their own struck below the water-tight deck and were mortal. Still this maneuver was not that which they preferred. For when the ships lay alongside of each other, as sometimes happens in ramming, the Macedonian soldiers fought so desperately that the Rhodians chose rather to rely on their skill in ship handling and they passed through the hostile line, breaking the enemy's oars and rudders, and then turned to ram him astern or on the broadside. Thus they gained the advantage.

Three Rhodian penteres ran the greatest danger—the flagship of Theophiliscus, that commanded by Philostratus, and the one piloted by Autolycus and carrying Nicostratus. The last rammed an enemy and sank her, but the ram stuck in the sinking hull and was torn off, so that water entered forward by the wound. Autolycus and some of his soldiers fought bravely, surrounded by enemies, but at last he fell into the sea with his arms.[4] Theophiliscus now joined this encounter. He could not save the ship of Autolycus, but he damaged two enemy ships so that their crews had to abandon them. He was then surrounded by a crowd of lembi and several cataphracts. He lost most of his soldiers and himself received three

---

[3] It may be doubted if the words of Polybius mean that the lembi were in the same line of battle as the cataphracts. More probably the lembi moved freely in rear of, and between, the great ships in the line, thrusting themselves to the front at every opportunity to embarrass the enemy by missile action, as they were probably too low to board large ships.

[4] In mentioning that Autolycus fell overboard with his arms, Polybius thought it unnecessary to say that he was drowned. On the other hand, in saying that Dionysidorus swam to safety, it seemed equally unnecessary to add that he must have found a lull in the fighting in which to strip off his armor. It was more or less a point of honor to retain one's arms and armor.

wounds, but saved his ship by the aid of Philostratus, who came to his support. Theophiliscus soon joined the rest of his ships and again attacked the enemy. Although enfeebled by his wounds, his vigor of mind was unimpaired.

It thus happened that there were two distinct battles, for Attalus fought near the shore of Asia where Philip took the van and the rear Macedonians, which had turned about, fought near the island of Chios. As the squadron of Attalus pressed the leading division of Philip, the scene of battle moved towards the islands where the King had taken his station (probably owing to wind and current, for a ram fight does not change location like a modern one). Attalus had gained the advantage, when he saw 1 of his penteres in distress and about to be sunk by an enemy. He went to her aid with 2 tetreres, when the enemy took flight and ran ashore. Attalus pursued with more ardor than prudence and was seen by Philip to be separated from his comrades. Thereupon, gathering 4 penteres, 3 triemioli, and some near-by lembi, Philip pursued Attalus and drove him on shore, whence he escaped to Erythrae with all his crew, but Philip took the royal ship. The companions of Attalus facilitated his escape by displaying on deck his most precious possessions, so that the first vessels alongside delayed to pillage the rich garments and the precious vases.

Philip was completely defeated in this part of battle, but he turned the misfortune of Attalus to his profit. He towed off the royal prize and when enemy ships saw it they believed that Attalus must be dead. Dionysidorus, believing the worst, having succeeded to the command of the Pergamene fleet, assembled his own ships and anchored on the coast of Asia at the same time that those Macedonians engaged with the Rhodians began to withdraw one by one under pretext of aiding their companions (in the van division). The Rhodians took in tow some of their prizes and sank others and went to Chios, and the battle ceased.

Against Attalus, Philip lost a decere, hennere, heptere, and sextere, and 10 cataphracts, 3 triemioli, and 25 lembi with their crews. Against the Rhodians he lost 10 cataphracts and about 40 lembi. Two Macedonian tetreres and 7 lembi were taken with their crews. In all, the Macedonians lost nearly half their fleet. The squadron of Attalus lost 2 penteres and a triemiolus sunk, and the royal ship a prize. The Rhodians lost 2 penteres and a triere sunk and none taken. The allies lost 130 men and Philip about

9,000 killed and 2,000 prisoners.[5] Theophiliscus wrote an account of the battle to Rhodes, appointed Cleonaeus his successor in command, and died the day after the battle. It was he who merited the honor of deciding his people to declare war against Philip. As political leader, for his skill and valor in battle and for all his patriotic services, he received high posthumous honors from his city.

Philip claimed the victory because he had taken the royal ship and because he had picked up the wrecks which the wind blew to his anchorage by Cape Argennum, and had buried some of the floating bodies. But he did not believe his own claims, for the next day he would not accept battle when the two fleets under Dionysidorus and Cleonaeus came to his anchorage and offered battle. The fleets of Rhodes and Pergamum then separated and Philip obtained some advantage over the Rhodian fleet alone in an engagement off Cos. But the battle of Chios was important, as thereafter the Macedonian fleet was so weakened that it declined to engage the allied fleets during the rest of the war and the latter moved their supply ships as they wished.

ROME MAKES WAR IN SUPPORT OF HER ALLIES

In the same season as the battle of Chios (201), both the Rhodians and King Attalus sent ambassadors to Rome to complain that Philip was tampering in the affairs of Asia. The Senate replied that it would give the matter attention, and the determination as to making war was left to the Consuls. Accordingly, a fleet of 38 ships, drawn from Sicily where they were no longer needed, was sent across the Adriatic, under the Propraetor Laevinus. The Senate was advised that vigorous efforts would be needed to keep Philip from invading Italy as Pyrrhus had done 80 years before. In the meantime Philip attacked Athens, an ally of Rome. Early in 200 the new Consul Sulpicius brought the question of war before the Senate and after debate it was referred to the people who declared for war. Thus Rome joined the alliance of Pergamum and Rhodes (see Map 2) to deny to Philip the control of the trade of the Mediterranean.

---

[5] The allied loss in men seems extremely small in proportion to that of King Philip. Taking the figures for the latter as Polybius gives them, he lost half his ships and 11,000 men. So his crews must have numbered about 22,000. The 26 cataphracts taken or sunk must have averaged about 275-300 men each; the lembi, about 35 to 45; and the triemioli, 180.

A Roman army was landed at Apollonia and a Roman fleet was based on Corcyra. The war lasted until 197 when Philip was decisively defeated at the battle of Cynoscephalae by the Roman Consul Titus Quinctius Flamininus. Peace was then made with Philip, who surrendered his fleet, agreed to an army only enough to guard his frontiers, and paid an indemnity of 1,000 talents.

During the four seasons of the war, the Roman army had some re-enforcements from its Aetolian allies, but the possibility of its operations in the Balkan peninsula depended on the support afforded it by the allied fleets of Rome, Pergamum, and Rhodes. The fleet of Philip had been so weakened at Chios that it did not venture from its fortified base at Demetrias and the allied fleets went where they pleased, covered the allied trade, and brought supplies by sea to the nearest points where they could serve the army. Philip's operations against allied commerce were no more than piratical efforts from his fortified bases, like the sea raiders of Germany in the World War. The result of the war created a new political situation in the Balkans which enabled Rome, a few years later, to cross the Aegean without an enemy behind her.

PRINCIPAL AUTHORITIES CONSULTED FOR THIS CHAPTER

ANCIENT

Diodorus Siculus.
Livy.
Polybius.

MODERN

Delbrueck, H.: *Geschichte der Kriegskunst.*
Kromayer: *Antike Schlachtfelder.*
      Schlachten Atlas.
Mommsen, Th.: *History of Rome.*
Serre, P.: *Les Marines de Guerre de l'Antiquité et du Moyen Age.*

CHAPTER XIII

THE WAR OF ROME AND ANTIOCHUS

CONDITIONS LEADING TO WAR

AT THE close of the war with Macedon, Flamininus did not sufficiently consult the wishes of the Aetolian allies of Rome in arranging the terms of peace with King Philip and the cessation of hostilities did not end the political unrest in Greece. Consequently, the Roman army remained temporarily abroad in order to make the necessary adjustments. Rome did not wish permanently to occupy Greece, yet nevertheless, it became necessary.

The transformation of the early Roman agricultural community into one with large commercial interests, which was forecast when Rome first came into close contact with the Greek cities of South Italy and which began with the conquest of western Sicily in the First Punic War, was apparent in the Second when the Senate was helped out of its financial difficulties in prosecuting the war by the wealthy traders who took government contracts to supply the armies. At the close of this war the economic development of the state was accelerated by the possession of Spain, which was the greatest metalliferous country of the ancient world.

It was necessary to maintain and protect the trading connections of Spain and of the country back of Massilia, the Roman ally, with the rich manufacturing communities at the eastern end of the Mediterranean. Yet the Roman government was very slow to recognize the change in its political duties and was averse to acquiring new territory. The Senate did not want the responsibilities of local rule, although it felt its duty to establish good order and peaceful commerce outside of Italy and endeavored to establish both in Greece by preserving or setting up local authorities, who were expected to rule without too many abuses after the departure of the Romans, under penalty of seeing the legions again occupying the country.

Such was the policy which governed Flamininus for several years while the Roman army remained in Greece in spite of reports that Antiochus, King of Asia and Syria, seemed to be intending to extend his power into Europe and even to contemplate the conquest of Rome.

Objectives of King Antiochus

To understand the progress of the war, it is necessary briefly to review the previous history of King Antiochus and estimate his political objectives in entering into it. In 223 he had mounted the throne of an extensive and very much disorganized kingdom. Like the other partial heirs of Alexander's Empire, Antiochus desired sovereignty as a means of luxurious livelihood for himself and his principal supporters, offering the agricultural and industrial population of his dominions the advantages of a considerable measure of peace and security from invasion, by means of his army, in exchange for taxes to support the army and his court. Such bargains were not bad ones for the people as matters were in those times. The foundation of civilization, then as now, lay in the armed men who protected the fields, the workshops, and the homes, and if the ruler and his followers pushed tyranny too far they could be overthrown. Antiochus himself lost his life a few years later, at the hands of local residents, when he attempted to rob a temple treasury in order to pay his debts.

Although local security is now better throughout all occidental countries than it was 2,000 years ago, yet we get an idea of conditions then by looking at China which, for the last few years, has been ruled by warring military governors who oppress the people, yet not to such an extent as completely to ruin the country. There is still industry and commerce in China, in spite of the civil wars and misgovernment, and so it was on the shores of the Mediterranean in the past.

A little before his war with Rome, after a reign of nearly 30 years, Antiochus had succeeded in knitting his vast kingdom together, although not too firmly. It was his ambition to crown his life's task by rounding out his territories to include Thrace, which had fallen to his great ancestor Seleucus after the battle of Korupedion in 281. At that time Seleucus was ruler of substantially the whole of Alexander's Empire, except Egypt; but his Successors lost Thrace to the Antigonids of Macedon and much of the Greek coasts and islands of Asia Minor to Egypt. As has already been said, after the death of Ptolemy IV (Philopator) in

205, Philip and Antiochus undertook the conquest of the foreign possessions of Egypt, Philip attacking the cities of Asia Minor and Antiochus
falling on Coelo-Syria. When Rome checked the advance of Philip,
Antiochus did not go to help his ally withstand Rome, but thought to
profit by taking Philip's share of the spoil of Egypt. He overcame the
Egyptian army in a great battle at Panion in Syria in 198 and, when
Philip lost his war at Cynoscephalae, Antiochus sent a strong Syrian army
to Sardis to recover the Greeks of Asia Minor for his kingdom, and also a
fleet of 100 decked ships and 200 open boats to the Ptolemaic possessions
on the south coast of Asia Minor. At the same time he sent ambassadors
to Rome to justify his proceedings with regard to Egyptian possessions.
For the moment, Rome did nothing.

Antiochus Enters Europe to Regain the Lands of His Ancestors

In the early summer of 196 Antiochus occupied Thrace with fleet
and army and rebuilt Lysimachia on the Thracian Chersonese. This city
had recently been destroyed by Thracian barbarians and occupied a key
position in the Chersonese. By thus holding both sides of the Hellespont,
he controlled the trade of the Euxine with the Mediterranean regions,
in addition to that of Egypt and the Far and Middle East via the Syrian
and Cilician seas. He held the great manufacturing and industrial district of Syria and threatened the security of the Roman allies, Rhodes,
and Eumenes of Pergamum (who had recently succeeded his father
Attalus). It is hard to understand how Antiochus could have expected
to extend his rule farther west than Thrace. In many of his provinces
his authority was scarcely more than nominal and, such as it was, its
center was far east of the Aegean Sea. To push his armies beyond that
region weakened them at every step and the resistance of Rome, the
great adversary, would grow stronger as the line of resistance drew
nearer Rome.

Rome took the seizure of Thrace as a serious threat to its own stand
as the liberator of Greece from Macedonian tyranny. Although not the
local ruler, Rome regarded herself as the protector of peace and prosperity and good order in the Balkan peninsula. She over-estimated the
power of the Great King and gave more or less credence to the rumors

that were circulated that Antiochus intended to carry the war into Italy. That fancy led to Roman intrigue in Carthage, whereby Hannibal was driven from home in the Roman belief that he was ready to rouse Carthage whenever Antiochus should be ready to attack Rome. Immediately after Antiochus had entered Thrace the Roman commissioners, who had come out to the east to settle the peace with Philip, met the ambassadors of Antiochus at Corinth. The latter again attempted to justify the conduct of Antiochus relating to the allies of Rome in Asia Minor, but the situation was now very different from the year before. The war with Macedon was finished and the commissioners made a positive reply that the King was not to occupy any point in Europe nor to retain any possessions in Asia Minor, belonging to either Philip or Ptolemy or any Greek free city. The economic effect of this requirement is evident. He was not to have military control of Levantine and Aegean trade. The Roman commissioners went on to the Chersonese to interview Antiochus and tell him that all his proceedings since he had sailed with his fleet were displeasing to the Roman Senate. Antiochus replied that for what he did in Asia he was not responsible to Rome, and that as to Thrace he was only taking possession of the territories of his ancestor. No decision was reached. The commissioners reported in Rome that Antiochus had entered Europe, that the Aetolians were restless, and that Nabis, tyrant of Sparta, was ill-disposed to Rome and dangerous.

ROME MAKES WAR ON SPARTA TO PRESERVE ORDER IN GREECE

It was therefore not possible for Rome to evacuate Greece, and the Senate authorized Flamininus to act as he thought conducive to the public interests. In 195 Flamininus made war on Nabis with the aid of Grecian allies. A large fleet of Roman, Pergamene, and Rhodian ships attacked the piratical naval base of Nabis at Gythium, with a landing force supported by an army division sent by Flamininus, and the place surrendered. It had been a nuisance to the Romans during the war with Philip by its interference with military transports passing around Cape Malea. As Antiochus had already crossed into Europe with a large force and war was to be expected with him, Flamininus offered terms to Nabis which the latter refused, mainly because he was deprived of shipping and maritime towns which had been a source of great profit to him through their piratical business. Thereupon a great army moved against Sparta, the capital of Nabis, and after a few days Nabis agreed to the terms previously offered.

HAVING RESTORED ORDER IN GREECE, ROME WITHDRAWS HER ARMY OF OCCUPATION

The Roman Senate confirmed the treaty of Flamininus with Nabis and the next year (194), Greece being quiet, the Roman garrisons were withdrawn, including those at the fortified key points of Demetrias, Chalcis, and Corinth (see Map 4), to the great rejoicing of the Greek people, although they soon proved too unstable politically to govern themselves. It was an early example of granting "self-determination" to citizens who were incapable of exercising the privilege with discretion. Trouble followed, as has happened in similar circumstances in much more recent times.

NEGOTIATIONS WITH ANTIOCHUS

Although Rome had yet taken no action with regard to the presence of Antiochus in Europe, in the following year (193), he made a final effort to arrange matters with Rome and sent ambassadors to negotiate a treaty recognizing his pretensions and that he was only regaining the possessions of his ancestors. It was a diplomatic mistake to reawaken Rome's notice. She regarded the embassy as a challenge. The Senate committed its reply to Flamininus who had returned to Rome and he answered the ambassadors that the King must choose between evacuating Thrace or the Romans would maintain their alliances in Asia and contract new ones, for, he said, the Roman people, having delivered the Greeks from Macedon, would never suffer any other monarch to rule them. The two ambassadors then besought the Senate not to be hasty in a decision which would involve the peace of the whole world and to allow the King time for deliberation. So the Senate sent ambassadors to the King, but scarcely were they gone than reports arrived in the city, from Carthage, that Hannibal, who had been received by Antiochus when driven from home, was urging the King that the war should eventually be carried into Italy; that he should be given 100 quinqueremes with 10,000 infantry and 1,000 cavalry with which to proceed to Africa and prevail on the Carthaginians to revive the war with Rome; that the King himself should pass into Greece with all the rest of his forces and remain in readiness to cross over to Italy, impressing the Romans with a terrifying idea of the magnitude of the war.

The Aetolians by this time were much dissatisfied with the scanty recognition granted them by Rome for their aid in the war with Philip, and they now sent to Antiochus asking him to invade Greece while they sent also to Philip and Nabis asking them to take part in the war against Rome. In the meantime the Roman ambassadors on their way to Antiochus had arrived at Pergamum, where King Eumenes urged war, believing that Antiochus would not oppose a formidable resistance to the Romans and that Pergamum and its business would profit by the war as an ally of Rome. Nothing could be settled with Antiochus when the embassy met him at Ephesus, and it returned.

Antiochus Enters Greece

After the departure of the Romans, King Antiochus called a council at which it was considered that Aetolia, Sparta, and Macedon might be depended on to aid him. In consequence, having put aside the suggestion of war in Italy, Antiochus decided on an invasion of Greece, raising opposition to Rome in Europe as an answer to Rome's opposition to him in Asia Minor. In the meantime, at Rome, two legions with 15,000 allies were authorized for the expeditionary army to Greece; 30 new ships were ordered built and all the old ones were reconditioned and seamen for them were shipped. Altogether 130 ships were taken in hand. The ostensible purpose of these preparations was to subdue Nabis of Sparta, who had already renewed hostilities. The ambassadors now returned from Ephesus and, as they brought word only of Nabis' activities, no more than the fleet with 3,000 soldiers belonging to it were sent to Greece for the protection of the allies.

The season of 192 was now open and, as nothing seemed immediately threatening on the part of Antiochus, the Consuls marched with their armies into the north of Italy in order to reduce a Gaulish insurrection; but public discussion was more directed to the east and many rumors were in circulation.

Among others, one which attracted much attention was to the effect that Antiochus was about to invade Sicily from Aetolia. The Senate had already sent the fleet under the Praetor Atilius to the Ionian Sea, and now the two legions which had been assembled in readiness in Bruttium, under Baebius, were brought to Tarentum and Brundisium, ready to cross, and 30 ships were sent from Ostia to Sicily, where the local praetor raised 12,000 local troops for a coast guard. In the meantime the Achaian League made successful war on Nabis, and Roman ambassadors made the circuit of Greece, asking them to remain faithful to their pledges to Rome. The Aetolians alone seceded and Demetrias fell into their hands. They hoped its possession would be an inducement to Antiochus to invade Greece, for it was a good port for his army. An attempt on Chalcis was not so successful, and the Roman fleet arrived there and met Eumenes of Pergamum who put a garrison in the city.

Most of the year 192 passed away without any attempt on Europe by the King, who had been delayed by difficulties in Asia Minor, which he did not wish to leave unsettled behind him. But late in October, King Antiochus decided to cross, although it was rather late in the season for safe navigation. After going to Ilium to offer sacrifice, he made sail with 40 decked ships and 60 open ones, with 200 transports with provisions and stores. The expedition passed from the Hellespont into the Pagasean Gulf and after touching at Ptelium for information, it crossed the bay to Demetrias and landed 10,000 infantry, 500 horses, and 6 elephants near that city.

PLANS FOR THE WAR AGAINST ROME

On hearing of the arrival of the King, the Aetolian leaders sent to invite him into their country and he proceeded to Lamia where he met the Aetolian Council and said he was come to free Greece. His appearance with such a small force and in spite of the lateness of the season he alleged was to show his zeal in their cause, but he promised that in the spring he would cover Greece with his armies and its shores with his fleets. The King then withdrew from the Council and in the debate that followed two divergent views were offered. Phaeneas said that the King's army in Greece should be used for negotiation rather than for war, because, for the purpose of avoiding war, men would often remit pretensions which they would not yield after war had begun. On the other hand, Thoas urged that nothing could come of negotiation which had already long been tried and that the only hope of success for their policies was for the King to summon all his forces from Asia and appeal to arms.

It was voted that war was more advantageous than negotiation under menace of war, and the King was given the title of General of the Aetolians. The next day a council decided that Chalcis should be seized but the expedition for the purpose failed. Embassies were sent about the country and Amynander, King of the Athamanians, adhered to King Antiochus. The Achaians, under the advice of Flamininus, rejected the offers of the King and declared war both against him and against the Aetolians. The garrison of Chalcis was re-enforced by Achaians and at the same time Antiochus hurried a large force to anticipate their arrival. The arrival of the King's troops was sufficient to induce the city to surrender and the Achaian and Roman soldiers were allowed to withdraw (in December, 192). The King now occupied two great fortified seaports at Demetrias and Chalcis for his communication with Asia, and went into Boeotia where his presence led the people to declare in his favor, after which he returned to his main base at Demetrias. Here he held a general council (January, 191), at which Hannibal gave his weighty opinion on the course to be followed. It was substantially the advice of Phaeneas at the Aetolian Council. He remarked he would then say what he would have said, if he had been asked when the King first entered Greece. He pointed out that it was imperative to enlist King Philip of Macedon in the war against Rome. This would oblige Central Greece to be loyal to the cause, and with two Great Kings uniting the forces of Europe and Asia, it would be impossible for the Romans to win. But if Philip could not be brought into the war, then he should be given occupation. Seleucus, son of Antiochus, was then in Lysimachia with an army. He should pass through Thrace and his attack on eastern Macedon would prevent Philip from giving any aid to the Romans.

As for the main war, Hannibal said Antiochus' invasion of Greece had taken place with insufficient strength and that there were too many soldiers for the provisions available and too few for war. He thought, therefore, that Antiochus should withdraw from advanced positions and assemble all his land and sea forces. When his strength was concentrated, the King should send half the fleet to Corcyra, to guard the passage from Italy, and the other half to the coast of Italy opposite Africa. The whole army should then occupy the coast of Illyria (near Apollonia), in which position it would command all Greece and make the Romans think the King was meaning to pass into Italy.

If we believe that the possession of Thrace to round out the royal family's former dominions was the whole object and ground of the war and if we further believe that Antiochus expected that the never-ending difficulties of Rome in Spain and the Po Valley would make her pliant, the advice of Hannibal was sound for the attainment of Antiochus' objective, even if Hannibal himself wished and expected that the war might at last be carried into Italy. But Rome could not think that Antiochus wanted only a "limited" war. She knew that Hannibal was intriguing in Carthage and that she had hostilities on her hands in North Italy and in Spain. She could only believe that it was all part of a single plan of the Great King under the guidance of Hannibal.

After hearing Hannibal, Antiochus made a brief campaign to occupy part of Thessaly and then retired to Chalcis to wait in winter quarters until spring.

Unfortunately for himself, Antiochus attempted to appeal to Greek sentiment during his incursion into Thessaly, by burying the dead of Philip's army at Cynoscephalae, who had not received that honor from their own King, an unlucky attempt at propaganda which reacted against the practitioner, for Philip, furiously angry, turned heartily to Rome.

THE ROMAN ARMY CROSSES THE ADRIATIC

Antiochus had made a mistake in thinking that his menace in Greece would prove a negotiable point with reference to his occupation of Thrace. His main army was not at hand to execute Hannibal's plan at once and Rome acted too promptly. In her opinion, the time for words was past. She was not going to wait for Antiochus to assemble his main forces and bring them into Greece, nor for the intrigue in Carthage to come to a head.

In the late fall Attalus, brother of King Eumenes, arrived at Rome and said that Antiochus had crossed the Hellespont. The Roman army at Brundisium, under the Praetor Baebius, was put in movement and, as soon as the elections were over (end of 192), the city praetor was ordered to build 50 new quinqueremes and Baebius was ordered into

Epirus with nearly 25,000 men to stay near Apollonia for the winter. While Antiochus was in Thessaly (January, 191), Baebius and Philip had a meeting near the western borders of Macedonia and a detachment of the Roman army was hurried forward into Thessaly, where its appearance near Larissa caused Antiochus to renounce any attempt with his small army to push farther north. When the weather permitted, Philip and Baebius resumed operations and passed into Thessaly and, at the earliest favorable spring weather, the Consul Manius Acilius Glabrio crossed with strong re-enforcements to the army already at Apollonia and took command. He sent the legions to Larissa, while he, with the cavalry he had brought over, joined King Philip.

The two soon overran Athamania and restored it to King Philip, and in doing so they captured about 3,000 of Antiochus' men who were in garrison there. About the same time Antiochus moved into Acarnania, but, in view of the arrival of the Roman army in Athamania, the King did not venture to remain there and returned to Chalcis. He now regretted having come with so small an army and went into Aetolia with about 10,000 men (having received some replacement troops) and endeavored to raise the local levies but got very few, the reason probably being that a great part of the manhood of the nation preferred to remain in their own northern mountain passes to repel an advance of King Philip from Athamania, rather than to go east out of their own country to join King Antiochus. Being thus disappointed in the hope of getting Greeks to fight the Romans, Antiochus decided to fall back from Thessaly and stand at the pass of Thermopylae where Leonidas had fallen in the Xerxes campaign.

This position was the only pass by which an army could be led into Greece and, if it were held, the King would have ample territory behind him to disembark the great army he needed for the campaign. He would be able also to advance into Thessaly (see Map 5). He fortified the position a little east of the exact point where Leonidas had stood and sent the 4,000 Aetolians who had joined him to hold the towns of Hypata and Heraclea, near by. After a little he directed the Aetolians to secure the path through the mountains by which the Persian Immortals had gained the rear of the Spartans. In the meantime Glabrio was coming south from Larissa and near the end of April the battle took place. The

Romans could make little impression on the strong position of the King, but the Consul had taken the precaution of sending Marcus Cato with 1,000 men to thread the mountain path of Callidromus as the Persians had done. Cato found the Aetolians entirely unready. After killing most of them, he came out on the high road behind the enemy's position and, as soon as his 1,000 men were identified as Romans, the royal army fled in panic. Antiochus got to Chalcis and then embarked for Ephesus. The ships in the Malian Bay got away safely, but Atilius, commanding the Roman eastern squadron of 25 ships, intercepted a convoy of provisions and captured many ships which he took as prize into Athens. The Aetolians did not immediately yield and the Consul spent until August in subduing them.

THE NAVAL CAMPAIGN TO CONTROL THE HELLESPONT

At the same time, the Romans sent their main fleet into the Aegean, in order to prepare for crossing into Asia, while Antiochus, by the advice of Hannibal, was assembling and bringing forward his main army in Asia (see Map 24) for the decisive battle and organizing his fleet, for the passage of the Hellespont by either army would be controlled by its sea power. The King, therefore, with the ships that were ready, sailed for the Chersonese to garrison all the places there and left his admiral, Polyxenidas, at Ephesus to fit out the rest of the fleet and put to sea when complete. In the meantime, advice boats were sent to all the islands to procure intelligence.

Caius Livius, the newly elected Roman admiral, set out from Ostia with 50 quinqueremes early in 191, and picked up the allied naval contingents as he came by Naples, Messana, Rhegium, Locri, and other towns. At Messana he also found 6 Carthaginian ships, which later fought bravely under him. On arriving at Corcyra he learned that the Consul and the King were facing each other at Thermopylae (April). There he decided to move on to Piraeus as quickly as possible and, after ravaging in Cephallenia and Zacynthus because they favored the Aetolians, he arrived at the Piraeus in July while the Consul was subduing the Aetolians. With the local Roman squadron already there, Livius now had 81 decked ships (quinqueremes and triremes) and many lighter ones with which he crossed to Delos, as a central point for news and operations. There he was held for some days by bad weather (August), before going on to join the Pergamene fleet.

Battle of Cissus

Polyxenidas, who was mobilizing at Ephesus, quickly heard of the Roman fleet in the Aegean and sent word to Antiochus in the Hellespont that the King should retire with his ships to Ephesus before the Roman fleet should fall upon him. This he promptly did and, at a council which the King held immediately on his arrival, Polyxenidas advised a battle at once before the squadrons of Eumenes and the Rhodians should join the Romans. Ephesus, the advanced naval base of King Antiochus, lay between that of King Eumenes at Elaea on the north and Rhodes on the south, while the principal maritime districts of Antiochus lay in Syria and Cilicia. The grounds of Polyxenidas for seeking battle were that he was little inferior to the Romans alone, as far as ships went, and he had the advantage in the build and seaworthiness of his ships and the skill and local knowledge of crews and ship captains. Expecting the Romans to attempt a rendezvous with Eumenes, Polyxenidas proceeded towards Phocaea where he might interpose between them, and the King departed to Magnesia to assemble his army coming from the east. The force of Polyxenidas is differently given by Livy and by Appian. Accepting the latter's figures, it seems that he had a total of 200 ships, of which 70 were decked, comparable to those of the enemy, and the rest were open and smaller. Livius seems to have moved from Delos earlier than Polyxenidas from Ephesus, for he got to Chios, shipped provisions and went on to Phocaea, while Polyxenidas went no farther than Cissus on the south coast of the Erythraean peninsula, at which point he presumably heard that the Romans had preceded him. There he was still well placed between the Rhodians and the main enemy.

Eumenes had had an interview with Livius while the latter was approaching Athens, and now came out of Elaea with 24 decked ships and a somewhat greater number of open ones, and united with Livius at Phocaea, bringing the combined fleet to number 105 heavy ships and about 50 lighter ones. Now all prepared for battle, the two hostile fleets being less than 40 miles apart in an air line. Oral news of each other's movements could pass between daylight and dark, and signals faster. When the combined fleet sailed (September), Polyxenidas had warning in good time and rejoiced at the prospect of battle. Polyxenidas[1] probably had reports of the enemy from every headland on the way and at the proper time left port and drew out his ships in line of battle, heading northwesterly, his right flank covered by the shore, his left extending seaward. He advanced in the enemy's direction, yet did not pass beyond Point Argennum, for it was blowing a fresh breeze from the north and he wished to remain in quiet water, where he could maintain the fleet formation and better use his preponderance in light ships. Profiting by the breeze, the allied fleet came on under sail through the Strait of Chios, in column formation, as usual when cruising, but probably straggling a good deal owing to the breeze. Livius was in the van, leading the right squadron as commander in chief, and Eumenes in the left squadron bringing up the rear.[2] As Livius issued from the strait, he changed course to the eastward and headed for Corycus, the southern promontory of Erythrae. He lost some of the breeze under the lee of Point Argennum and, as he rounded the point and drew into smooth water, he sighted the enemy ahead of him in battle order. His own ship doused sail, struck the masts and slowed, clearing for action, and the ships following came rapidly up into line on his left, making ready for battle as they did so. When about 30 were in line, it seemed that there was not room for the whole fleet between Livius and the shore, so he made short sail again[3] for a few minutes (note the care to save the rowers' strength before battle) and stood off shore until enough sea room was gained for Eumenes to push the rear ships up as fast as possible and complete the battle line of the left wing. The two fleets were now properly extended facing each other and the battle was opened by 2 Carthaginian ships in advance of the general Roman line. These were met by 3 of the King's ships. Two of the latter fell on one of the Carthaginians, sweeping away her oars on

---

[1] In the following, Livy's account is somewhat expanded to take note of navigational and tactical points which he suggests but does not develop.

[2] The place of honor in battle being on the right, the squadron of the commander in chief is still the "right" even when it is actually the van in the order of sailing.

[3] He spread the "dolons," small sails forward for use in battle. See Cartault, *La Trière Athénienne*, p. 184, on this passage in Livy.

both sides as they ranged alongside so that she lay motionless. They then boarded and took her. The other Carthaginian withdrew from her antagonist when she saw her mate overcome and returned to the line of battle. Livius, fired by indignation, drove his single ship against the two victors as they advanced hopefully upon him and, as they came near, he checked his way with his oars and threw grapnels into them as they came up and drew them to him. The valor of his boarders soon overcame both. By this time the whole line was engaged and Livius soon had the advantage in his wing, and Eumenes was not long after him. When Polyxenidas saw his left wing was outmatched, he made sail and got away towards Ephesus, and was soon followed by the right wing also under "dolons." The Romans and Eumenes pursued under oars as long as the rowers could endure, but the enemy had faster ships, for the Romans were loaded with supplies, so that the enemy was not overtaken and the battle resulted in the loss to the King of 10 ships sunk and 13 taken with their crews. The allied loss was 1 Carthaginian.

Polyxenidas returned to Ephesus and the allies went into Cissus, which the enemy had just left. After spending a night there in refitting, they followed the enemy on to Ephesus and halfway there they met the Rhodian squadron, 27 strong, and all formed line-of-battle outside port with over 130 ships. Polyxenidas declined to come out with the 47 heavy ships left him. Having thus extorted the enemy's acknowledgment of defeat, Livius sent Eumenes and the Rhodians to their home ports, and with the Roman fleet he went to Chios and thence to Phocaea where he left four guard ships. As winter was then approaching, he hauled his ships out of water at Cane in Pergamum to pass the winter. For the moment the Roman fleet had accomplished its task. The Hellespont was clear of hostile ships and they now had to be kept away.

The battle had much resemblance to that of Philip with the Rhodians and the Pergamene King 10 years previously in the waters just to the north. In each case the fleet weaker in heavy ships had many light ones which proved less effective than had been hoped. In his account of the first battle, Polybius dwells most on the individual maneuvering of the ships. Of the second battle Livy tells us chiefly of the admirals' handling. We must therefore supplement Livy's account by picturing the light, open boats with only 30 to 80 men, each moving nimbly about the large ships, starting, stopping, and turning smartly to avoid the hostile rams and yet annoying the enemy by light missiles and by breaking his oars. The Romans, on the other hand, probably paid as little attention as practicable to the hostile small craft. They would be negligible if once the big ships of the enemy were defeated. Consequently, the fleet tactics of the admirals involved chiefly the quinqueremes. The flanks resting on the shore were protected from envelopment by the shore. Thus Livius had 35 ships available for enveloping the enemy's left or seaward flank after matching ship to ship with Polyxenidas. This surplus explains how it was that Polyxenidas' line began to crumple on the left. When resistance broke down here, the right and center could not long remain in action, nor the Levantine small ships continue in action without the support of the battle line.

CAMPAIGN OF 190

After the defeat off Cissus, Antiochus understood that he had to regain the command of the sea against 130 enemies who had appeared off Ephesus. For the next season, he directed Polyxenidas to repair and build as many ships as he could and sent Hannibal to Syria to bring up the Phoenician navy, out of reserve. Rumors of the King's action having reached Rome, the Senate ordered the city Praetor to build 30 quinqueremes and 20 triremes. Lucius Aemilius Regillus, Praetor for the year, was chosen as admiral for the year 190 and directed to take 20 ships from the squadron at home with 1,000 marines and 2,000 soldiers (the last probably replacement troops) and relieve Livius in the Aegean. It is evident that Antiochus now realized that his attempt to open negotiations for Thrace while his army had not yet come up had decided the Romans to vanquish him in Asia and that their passage into Asia must be resisted on the sea. On their part, the Romans also knew that they had to win at sea before they could win in Asia.

At the elections in November, Lucius Cornelius Scipio, brother of the conqueror of Hannibal, was elected one of the Consuls by his family influence. He was not a brilliant man, so in order that he might obtain the honor of defeating Antiochus, his brother Publius offered to go with him as his legate, i.e., as second in command and practically in control.

This was satisfactory to the Senate, which assigned Lucius the province of Greece and authorized him to pass thence into Asia. After arranging matters in Rome, the Consul gave orders for the replacement levies and the army in Bruttium to assemble at Brundisium at the middle of March, 190 (the beginning of good weather), and the transports were summoned for the same time. He took over 13,000 troops to add to the army of two legions (25,000 men) and the additional force brought by Glabrio already in Greece. Besides, Philip of Macedon had troops in the field as the Roman ally. Including the fleet of 100 ships, there were probably about 65,000 to 70,000 men in the Roman forces in Greece for the campaign of 190.

During the winter the Aetolian envoys returned from Rome with word that there was no prospect of peace and Acilius Glabrio renewed the war on Aetolia before the arrival of his successor Scipio, assaulting and taking Lamia, and then moving on to the formal siege of Amphissa. Here the new Consul took over the command from Glabrio and, under the advice of his brother, he was anxious to terminate the Aetolian war, to direct all his effort against Antiochus. He therefore agreed to a suspension of arms for 6 months to permit reference once more to Rome and the siege of Amphissa was raised.

Publius Scipio was unwilling to risk transferring the army directly from Greece across the whole width of the Aegean Sea and preferred to march through Macedon and Thrace to the Hellespont. But he wished first to ascertain if Philip would be loyal during the Roman march through his kingdom. It was necessary to surprise Philip's mind, and look into it. Scipio therefore called for a young nobleman, Tiberius Sempronius Gracchus, later himself to be Consul and husband of Scipio's daughter Cornelia, and father of the two great Tribunes of the people. Gracchus was of extraordinary activity of body beyond all the youth of his day, and was told to ride in haste to Pella and observe the demeanor of King Philip. By using relays of horses, he arrived at Pella, 200 miles from Amphissa, on the third day and found the King sitting at a banquet, drinking merrily and carefree without thought of deceit. The next day Gracchus saw the preparations which the King was making for the passage of the Roman army across Macedon and returned with the same speed, finding the army already on its way to the Hellespont. But some time had been consumed in the march from Apollonia into Greece and at Amphissa, so it was not until the first part of November that the army reached the Hellespont without incident.

THE NAVAL OPERATIONS OF 190

In the meantime the operations at sea for the control of the passage had fully occupied the opposing fleets. The main objective of the Roman fleet was to ferry the army over the Hellespont without interference and guard its supply ships. To accomplish this it had two subsidiary tasks, namely, to blockade the hostile fleet at Ephesus and to fend off the Phoenician reserve fleet coming to the Aegean under Hannibal. The blockade of Ephesus required the most ships. It will be remembered that the Roman fleet had wintered at Cane near the Pergamene squadron at Elaea. Seleucus, son of Antiochus, was wintering his army in the surrounding territory of Aeolia to keep the maritime cities in obedience, for they were solicited to revolt, both by the Romans and King Eumenes. The situation enabled Livius to find occupation for his men by raiding the back country with 5,000 soldiers belonging to his ships. There can have been only a small guard left on board in addition to the rowers.

For the season of 190 the Roman and allied ships numbered about 140 in the Aegean, with 20 more on the way from Ostia under the new commander in chief. In this combined fleet the Rhodians seem to have preferred to build the smaller types of decked ships, while the gross of the Roman fleet was of their own quinqueremes with a sprinkling of the larger ships of the Levant, hexeres and hepteres. Livius and King Eumenes had over 100 ships in all, with less than 90 ready for battle, since no doubt some of them were on detached duty here and there, holding important cities and supervising traffic. Antiochus had built many ships during the winter, including several heavier than quinqueremes, and now he also had nearly 90 in his principal battle fleet and nearly 40 far away in Syria, besides some in the Hellespont. It is evident that the battle of Cissus in 191 had demonstrated to Antiochus that large ships had their advantages, just as they have today. About the equinox (March 21), Livius opened the campaign by taking 30 ships of his own and 7 of Eumenes to the Hellespont to secure the passage. He appeared before Sestos, which made terms without resistance, and then crossed to Abydos, which it was necessary to besiege.

The Rhodian Fleet Is Defeated at Panormus

About the same time the Rhodian squadron of 36 ships under Pausistratus got under way to join the Romans and put in at Panormus about 15 miles south of Ephesus. While it was there, Polyxenidas, who was a Rhodian exile, heard that Pausistratus had publicly spoken against him and resolved on revenge. He sent an acquaintance of the other man to say that he was ready to betray the King's fleet, provided that Pausistratus in return would have the edict of exile revoked. After careful examination of the proposition, Pausistratus thought it sincere. Polyxenidas promised to neglect all preparation, to give his crews leave of absence, and to haul some of his ships on shore so that attack would find them more or less helpless. The unreadiness which he looked for in the other fleet Pausistratus then practiced himself. He sent some ships to Halicarnassus, 70 miles way, for provisions, and others to Samos, 15 miles away, while he waited with the rest for the word the the affair was ripe for execution. A soldier of Antiochus was brought to Pausistratus as a spy and, on being questioned, confessed that the King's ships were ready for sea with the rowers assembled within call at Magnesia, about 13 miles inland from Ephesus; but Pausistratus gave no credit to him.

Polyxenidas brought down his rowers and sailed after dark, but went only a few miles when contrary wind detained him and he put into Pygela before day. The next night he went a little farther and landed a force of soldiers under Nicander, a notable pirate, to march through the fields to the rear of Panormus, while the fleet proceeded to the sea front of the town and formed in a double line outside the harbor, so that the enemy ships would be obliged to issue from the narrow exit between the double lines of the King's ships. At first, Pausistratus was confounded by the surprise, but he recovered himself and thought he could repel the hostile fleet by placing his soldiers on the two promontories at the harbor mouth and using missiles. Of course, he could not control more than a couple of hundred yards' distance, but if he could hold the enemy that far away by missile action he would have room to push his ships out in

column and form some of them at least into line of battle before beginning the ship fight. But the sight of Nicander coming by land on his
rear obliged Pausistratus to recall his soldiers to their ships and get them
to sea at whatever cost, and he led out bravely in his own vessel. The
formation of Polyxenidas was overwhelming. As the Rhodian flagship
singly drew clear from the protection of the land, 3 quinqueremes fell
upon her. She was holed by the rams and her crew overcome. Pausistratus
was killed and, of the other ships, some were taken inside, some outside the harbor, and others were seized by Nicander before they had
shoved off from the beach. Only 7 ships broke through the hostile lines
and this they were able to do because they had a special weapon, which
Pausistratus had developed and trained his captains to use. A new device
is most effective when it is unfamiliar, for in the excitement of battle
reason is dormant to a great extent, and people cannot study how to parry
the novel attack. On this occasion the escaping ships carried blazing iron
pots suspended from two booms extending beyond their bows, and the
King's ships avoided contact with them for fear of the fire. Thus they
broke out. As 7 ships escaped and others were on detached service, we
may put the probable loss of the Rhodians on this occasion at less than
20 ships.

Strategic Concentration after Panormus
Blockade of Ephesus

The news of this serious misadventure arrived at the Hellespont
after Abydos had been pushed to ask for terms of capitulation and negotiations were then in progress. Livius was obliged to drop the siege and
hurry back to Cane, for, with the Rhodians out of the campaign and
Livius himself at the Hellespont with nearly 40 ships, the remaining
ones at Cane were quite unequal to the fleet of new and powerful vessels
which the King had built during the winter. For the Romans, the key
of the maritime situation lay in preventing the junction of the two royal
fleets, in order to fight the decisive battle against one only. The defeat
of either would throw preponderance at sea to the Romans.

The Rhodians rallied nobly from their losses at Panormus. They
at once sent 10 ships to sea and in a few days 10 more under Eudamas,
a more cautious man than Pausistratus, who now sought a rendezvous

with Livius. Anticipating that Livius would come south to join the Rhodians as he had done the year before, Polyxenidas took himself northward as before to intercept the enemy and lay at Macris, an island near
Myonnesus, a promontory 20 miles northwest of Ephesus, to pick up
stragglers or even attack the rear of the fleet itself. He did not want
a conclusive battle without the aid of the Phoenicians. As the habitual
order of cruising was in column, it will be seen that a well-timed attack,
delivered on the passing Roman rear from a concealed position behind
a neighboring point, might do considerable execution before the van
could return to join the fight. As to this point, the conception was an
early version of the battle of Trafalgar.

As foreseen, Livius and Eumenes came south from Elaea and the
second night out they spent at Corycus, some 15 miles from Myonnesus
and the enemy. In the morning the Romans got under way before daylight and before the weather had declared itself. A fresh northerly breeze
arose after getting outside and made it rough for the Romans who were
somewhat dispersed. Polyxenidas got under way to attack, but found the
seas too high for him also as he drew off shore. When the Romans found
the enemy was close by, they decided not to fight without the Rhodians
and returned safely to Corycus which they had left the day before.
Polyxenidas also returned to shelter and decided not to fight without
the Phoenician division, so he returned to Ephesus. On learning that
Polyxenidas had retired to his base and that the direct passage to Samos
was clear, Livius went to Samos and united there with the Rhodian fleet.
The entire force than made a demonstration in front of Ephesus for its
political effect on the coastal cities. As the enemy remained quiet, a part
of the fleet blockaded the harbor mouth so closely that it commanded
the entrance as Polyxenidas had recently commanded that of Panormus.
The other ships then landed soldiers and ravaged the countryside with
little advantage to either party. It was about the beginning of May.

The Praetor Livius, who was responsible for the whole of the eastern
waters, now detached 4 of his lighter craft to go to Cephallenia, 400 miles
away, to guard the route across the Adriatic from the pirates who were
annoying the trade with Italy. On the way, these ships met the new
Admiral Aemilius Regillus going out to take command with only 2 quinqueremes accompanying him. Hearing the news from the fleet, he turned

the detachment back and went on with them to Asia. Evidently, of the 20 quinqueremes which had left Rome with him, 18 had been dropped along the route to take care of local matters such as the piracy at Cephallenia. At Chios, Aemilius met an escort of 2 Rhodian ships to guard him from the hostile ships based in the Hellespont which raided frequently to pick up Roman supply vessels.

At Samos, Aemilius took over the command from Livius, offered sacrifice, and called a council, at which Livius who was about to go home recommended that the fleet should block the harbor of Ephesus by sinking ships in the channel. King Eumenes pointed out that if the fleet then went away, the enemy would soon clear the channel and, if it stayed, it would be more tied down than the enemy would be hindered. It was then proposed to attack Patara, a place on the mainland opposite the island of Rhodes and the capital of the province of Lycia. A success here and the establishment of peace with the city would enable Rhodes to turn all her strength to the war with Antiochus and particularly to the Phoenician fleet now expected. So Livius was sent with a small detachment to Rhodes where he was given a few more ships, making 11 in all, of which 2 quinqueremes were the largest. Livius had little success at Patara and the expedition returned to Rhodes in the latter part of May, while Livius went home, stopping with the Scipios in Thessaly to report on conditions.

It was not desirable for the army to arrive at the Hellespont before the sea battle, for as the army approached that region its supplies at sea were more and more vulnerable to the hostile ships cruising out of the Hellespont, of which we are told but without mention of their numbers. Aemilius was therefore anxious for battle and, while Livius cruised south, the former demonstrated without success off Ephesus, hoping to draw the enemy, but returned to Samos where he heard of the former's failure and was fired with somewhat hasty indignation which led him to start for Patara with the entire fleet. He stopped on the way for various trifling enterprises against the enemy and, on arriving on the coast opposite Rhodes, he was made aware of the comments of his lieutenants, who said he was forsaking the main fleet of the enemy and freeing it to do as it liked in the decisive theater of action about the Hellespont. Aemilius was induced to see his error and availed himself of a suitable pretext to return to Samos and watch Polyxenidas. He wished to destroy the enemy but had no strategic sense and was a handful for his staff to manage and direct.

In the meantime the King's son, Seleucus who was in Aeolia, took advantage of King Eumenes' absence from his kingdom to ravage the country and besiege Pergamum. About the same date King Antiochus assembled his main army and brought it to Sardis. When the news of this situation came to Eumenes at Samos, he took his fleet to Elaea and threw himself into the capital. The Roman and Rhodian fleets followed to Elaea, and Antiochus now learned that the Roman army had entered Macedonia without opposition. It seemed to him that it was advisable to negotiate a peace before the Romans should cross into Asia, but on the advice of Eumenes, Aemilius refused to listen to the King before the arrival of the Consul. The seat of war then drifted north of Pergamum and a large force of Achaians crossed to Asia and got into Pergamum, so that Seleucus soon discontinued the siege.

After some cruising about, the commanders of the allied fleets agreed that Eumenes should place himself at Pergamum and arrange for the passage of the Hellespont by the consular army, using his fleet as necessary in the northern Aegean, while the Romans and Rhodians should return to Samos and observe the fleet of Polyxenidas at Ephesus.

Battle of Side

It was now reported at Samos that the Phoenician fleet was on its way to Ephesus. Eudamas thereupon went to Rhodes with 13 Rhodian ships and 2 other quinqueremes of neighboring cities. There he found that 2 days before Pamphilidas with 13 other Rhodian ships had gone east to observe the enemy and had picked up 4 more ships on detached service (see Map 15). Eudamas followed him with 6 open ships additional and, making haste, he overtook Pamphilidas and lay in wait at Phaselis about 140 miles beyond Rhodes. It was now about July 1. This was a favorable observation point to detect west-bound ships, but unfortunately the heat of summer was causing a local pestilence which affected the crews before Eudamas could move farther east to the River Eurymedon, where Cimon of Athens had gained his great victory over the Persian fleet nearly three centuries before. It is interesting to note how on successive occasions enduring geographical conditions draw opposing forces to conflicts in the same neighborhood.

At the Eurymedon, Eudamas learned that the enemy, with Hannibal among its leaders, had been detained by the seasonal northwest wind and was now at Side, only 15 miles farther east. The coming battle would be between minor squadrons of the two belligerents, but a marked success for either would enable the victor to bring such a re-enforcement to his main fleet that it could scarcely fail to rule the sea and control the passage of the Hellespont, which was still in the hand of Antiochus. Eudamas now had 32 tetreres and 4 trieres beside 6 open craft. Besides some open ships, the Royal fleet had 47 decked ships including 3 hepteres, 4 hexeres, 30 penteres and tetreres, and 10 trieres. The relative strength was very unequal both in numbers and individual size of the ships. Both were drawing on the best classes of mariners for their crews. As the Rhodians were equipped with flame throwers of some sort in the earlier and the subsequent battles of this year, presumably they used them here also.

We have seen that in the battle by Cissus of the previous year, where the battle was decided by the infantry excellence of the Romans, in the boarders' struggle, the heavy ships had the advantage over the numerous open ships. Taught by experience Antiochus had built his new ships to meet the Romans, and probably had many soldiers on board to fight in Roman style, but they were not of Roman quality. The Syrian squadron was now about to face an enemy which likewise had no Roman infantry and was not going to make a kind of fight suitable to develop the peculiar virtues of the legionaries. The style of fight would fall to the choice of the Rhodians, because they had ships whose speed and handiness enabled them to accept or refuse combat as they pleased.

Each fleet was aware of the presence of the other and they moved out at dawn the day after the Rhodians reached the river. The two anchorage grounds were separated by a promontory near Side, which concealed the two fleets from each other until the Rhodians passed beyond it. The King's ships were already in battle line; presumably they had been notified of the approach of the enemy by scout ships at the point or by signal from the promontory. Hannibal commanded the left wing of the King's fleet which was Phoenician, and one Apollonius commanded the right which probably had Cilician ships. As Apollonius had the post of honor on the right, we may therefore suppose that Hannibal was only second in command and that he had not won the full confidence of the King.

The Rhodians were still in column, in their cruising formation, with Eudamas leading and Pamphilidas and Chariclitus commanding the center and rear, respectively. Were the Rhodian line to be formed before closing, the enemy would have an overlap of 11 ships on the seaward flank. Haste was necessary. Eudamas turned his ship's head to seaward, signaling to form line and, as he was followed by the others, the column began to draw out parallel to the enemy's front; but before Eudamas had gained enough sea room for all his ships to interpose between himself and the shore, he faced the enemy with the 5 ships next him and charged. This occasioned some confusion among the ships in rear that found no place for themselves opposite an enemy, but they had expert captains who worked to seaward until they found opponents. Instead of the Roman type of naval battle, depending on the maneuvering ability (if any) of the admiral but chiefly on the bravery of the individual soldier, this one depended on the maneuvering skill of the individual captains and the handiness of the Rhodian ships. It was a reversion towards the tactics of the Athenian navy in its great days, with diekplous, anastrophe, and periplous —the pass-through, and turn-about-and-ram, and the pass-around.

One of the King's hepteres was sunk at the very first by a single ram stroke and its neighbors were much discouraged. On the landward flank the Rhodians soon established their superiority. On the seaward flank Hannibal had the decisive advantage of numbers, although the Rhodians were superior in all other respects, and Eudamas would soon have been defeated, if Apollonius on the right had not made the signal for the Syrian squadron to rally to his aid. This ill-timed signal drew so many ships from Hannibal that he could no longer sustain the action and victory fell to Rhodes.

But the pestilence caught a few days before at Phaselis had so weakened the Rhodian rowers that they were unequal to pursuit. The ships lay to, while the crews went to dinner. Eudamas saw the enemy towing off several crippled ships by the small craft accompanied by the uninjured vessels. He cried out at this mortifying sight and organized a chase under Pamphilidas and Chariclitus, as his own vessel was crippled. Hannibal made close in to shore and the chasers were afraid of being wind bound on a hostile coast; so their chief prize was a heptere which they took into Phaselis.

Livy tells us that more than 20 King's ships were uninjured, but as for direct losses he names only the 2 hepteres. As the Syrians saved several damaged ships, we cannot suppose more than 10 or 12 ships were destroyed, but the blow to the fleet morale must have been very severe, for Hannibal did not venture to pursue his voyage to join the main fleet. After the Rhodian fleet had returned home regretting that it had done no more, rather than rejoicing in its victory, the city thought it sufficient to send Chariclitus with 20 ships to Megiste in Lycia to prevent Hannibal from going farther west. It seems that Apollonius must have been killed or taken in the battle, as the responsibility for the fleet after the battle is assigned to Hannibal. Eudamas, with the 7 best ships, was sent to Samos to ask the Romans to besiege Patara, near which, at the islands of Megiste, Chariclitus was lying with most of the Rhodian ships. The capture of Patara would be a permanent acquisition for Rhodes besides being a more convenient base for the squadron watching Hannibal.

The news of the victory at Eurymedon occasioned great rejoicing among the Romans at Samos, and when Eudamas arrived a few days later to ask for aid against Patara, Aemilius realized that if the Rhodians could establish thorough control in that district, navigation would be reasonably secure in all those seas. However, Aemilius was unable to release enough ships for that purpose, because Antiochus had already started his army on its march north from Sardis and the Roman fleet was needed to protect the maritime cities of Ionia and Aeolia from any attack on them. Nevertheless, Pamphilidas, with 4 decked ships, was dispatched from Samos to increase the force at Megiste. The Pergamene squadron under its King, which had left Samos some weeks before to go to the Hellespont "to prepare for the Consul and his army," was probably engaged in patrol and escort service for the supply ships as the Roman army marched along the Thracian coasts. Although Livy expressly says the Pergamene ships went to the Hellespont, there was little they could do inside the stream; but outside, based on Tenedos, Lemnos, or Samothrace, they could render real help against the commerce raiders working out of the Hellespont. During the leisurely march of the Roman army to the

Chersonese, Antiochus made a last attempt to induce Prusias, King of Bithynia, to join him against the Romans and his neighbor Eumenes, but Caius Livius, the late admiral of the Roman fleet, appeared as Roman ambassador and secured the benevolent neutrality of Prusias. It was an important accomplishment, for Antiochus already had a far larger army than the Romans, and a new enemy operating on their flank as they moved against Antiochus would have been embarrassing.

Final Naval Battle at Myonnesus

Upon this diplomatic failure, the King turned again to his fleet, which had been idle at Ephesus for some months, for a last effort to keep the Romans out of Asia. He could not do otherwise. If the main fleet at Ephesus did not fight now, its maintenance was useless, for, if the fleet remained inactive, Eumenes was ready to enter the Hellespont and aid the Consul to seize the Chersonese and Abydos as soon as the latter should arrive. Apparently the King now expected no more from his Phoenician squadron under Hannibal. It must have been more punished than the Rhodians thought, or else the pestilence which only touched the Rhodians had smitten their opponents more severely.

Upon consultation with Polyxenidas, after the King's arrival at Ephesus, it was decided that the latter should attack Notium, a town attached to the Roman interest, standing on the shore about 5 or 6 miles north of Ephesus. It was the assumption that Aemilius could not suffer an ally to be attacked without leaving port to assist it and thus Polyxenidas would have an opportunity of bringing the Roman fleet to action.

The news of this movement was a delight to Aemilius. He seems to have been a fine fellow who understood little of war and was anxious to distinguish himself. His father had been nominated for Consul at the height of the war with Hannibal and lost the election because Fabius Maximus opposed him on the ground that the times required a good general. Aemilius now wanted to redeem the family reputation. The Rhodians had beaten Hannibal and Eumenes was actively assisting the army while Aemilius seemed to himself to be lying useless at Samos. He was not in the picture, was eating his heart out about it, and yet knew not what to do. At Patara, his staff had had trouble enough to get him back to Samos and all summer Eudamas had had difficulty in preventing him from abandoning the blockade and going off in search of adventure; so now Eudamas felt free to give him his head and advise him to aid Notium. It was October.

Although Samos was the Roman supply base, for the moment it was short of provisions and before meeting the enemy it was necessary for the fleet to complete its stores. In the search for supplies the fleet was already out of port when the Praetor heard that a squadron of Roman supply ships was wind bound at Chios. He was about to direct his course there, when he heard that the people of Teos, a place on the way to Chios, had furnished supplies to the King and were going to give more. As he was looking for an occasion to distinguish himself, it seemed better to him to take supplies from Teos by force rather than use what the government was sending him from Italy. As he drew near the land off Myonnesus on the way to Teos, he saw a number of ships which he mistook for some of Polyxenidas' fleet, so he chased them as a visible objective. They proved to be pirates who had been looting on Chios with good success. He is really very amusing. His pilots should not be held responsible for such an unseamanlike error as to mistake light craft for cataphracts. Their swift ships took the pirates quickly to safety on the promontory of Myonnesus. They did so the easier since the unfamiliar waters caused the Roman pilots to be cautious. The pirates manned the face of the vertical cliffs which formed the promontory and defied the approach of the Praetor.

At nightfall he withdrew and the next morning in a rage he went to Teos and, after occupying the harbor at the back of the city, he sent his soldiers out to ravage the countryside. That his object in leaving Samos had been to save his allies at Notium from destruction seems entirely to have disappeared from his head. The nearest fight was the only one he could contemplate with pleasure. The inhabitants of Teos sent representatives as suppliants to ask for leniency. They retired from the Praetor's presence with harsh terms for the city to consider.

In the meantime Polyxenidas had learned of the Praetor's movements and came to Myonnesus in pursuit hoping to find a favorable opportunity for battle. He anchored in concealment behind the island of Macris, as he had done in the previous spring to surprise Livius, and formed the plan of catching the Roman fleet as he had caught the Rhodians at Panormus. The harbor of Geraesticum behind Teos, where the Romans had entered, was completely surrounded by two promontories whose points were so close that no more than 2 ships could come out abreast, and it was the intention of Polyxenidas to put 10 ships at each of the promontories by night to attack the issuing Romans from both sides and to land all the soldiers from the other ships (probably 5,000 men) to attack from the shore.

Unfortunately for the plan, 2 Roman ships had fouled each other in the narrow entrance and broken their oars, showing the danger; besides, the King was not very far away with his army and Eudamas had persuaded Aemilius to take the ships into the second harbor on the other side of the city as a safer point as well as more convenient for shipping the supplies which the townspeople had now promised. While the crews were dispersed about the town, bringing down stores and sampling the wine which formed a large part of the delivery, a peasant was brought before the Praetor and reported that the enemy had been lying at Macris, only 10 miles away, for 2 days and showed some signs of getting under way a short time previously. Great was the confusion. The trumpets sounded the recall to the stragglers in the country and the military tribunes ran through the city to hasten all to the shore. As might be expected from his personal character and in entire propriety with his office as commander in chief, the praetor was in the first ship to sally from the harbor, leaving Eudamas to struggle with the confusion on shore and get the ships manned and away and come out last himself. Finally, all was in order before the enemy appeared and the line formed heading south.

Although the Roman fleet in eastern waters numbered over 100 ships, so many were engaged on special service that only 58 were available on "the day." Eudamas with 22 Rhodian ships brought the total number to 80 (with perhaps 20,000 men), and belonged, himself, on the left wing. Polyxenidas had 89 ships and among them 3 hexeres and 2 hepteres (with perhaps 24,000 men). On sighting the enemy he still had his ships in cruising order in double column, and hastened to form line to face his opponents. As Appian says that Polyxenidas was on the left when the fleets closed, we must believe that he led the van and turned his head of column to the left to bring his formation parallel to the allies. It was his intention to take advantage of his excess of numbers to outflank and envelop the Roman right, where the fiery but somewhat dull commander in chief was showing the formal emblems of his presence. What Aemilius did to meet this maneuver of Polyxenidas, neither Appian nor Livy tells us. Presumably he made a gallant gesture like King George II at the battle of Dettingen and then charged the nearest enemy, setting in himself, as battle instructions of navies have always run, "a good example of valor and patriotism." We see him in history forever in an anti-climax, rushing bravely out of port on his great "day" and then, in spite of his anxiety for battle renown, we know nothing more of him until he is mentioned a fortnight later as supervising a secondary task. However, he claimed and received a triumph on his return to Rome.

It fell to the Rhodian most skillfully to direct the course of the allied battle. As the intention of Polyxenidas to envelop the Roman right flank became apparent to Eudamas, it is not clear from our two ancient authorities whether the Rhodian ships which were last out of port had already all formed themselves on the left of the battle line, or whether some of them were still "chasing their positions" as the French say. However that may be, Eudamas hurriedly led some of his own best and fastest ships from the rear or left, as the case may have been, to parry the threatened envelopment of the Roman right flank and left reduced numbers to guard the left flank near the shore.[4]

After the Asiatic column had swung into line to face the allies, the tactical situation was peculiar. The heavy Roman ships, 58 in number, faced the right of a similar line of 89 similar ships. There was neither occasion nor opportunity for the Romans to display much nautical skill. Each ship had only to head for his opposite and cling to him till he was finished and follow the valiant example which Aemilius no doubt offered to all. The task of the 30 Levantines who overlapped the right of the Roman line was obvious. It was to envelop the Roman flank and attack the sterns of as many occupied enemies. It fell to the 22 light and skillfully piloted Rhodians under their brilliant admiral to see that envelopment was not accomplished and in this they were completely successful. Eudamas himself faced the hostile admiral. Fighting according to their

---

[4] It may be that Eudamas thought the Roman left needed no flank guard and took all his ships to the Roman right.

own traditions, under the disadvantage of inferior numbers, the Rhodians had to paralyze the effort of adversaries with the same maritime traditions as themselves who had abandoned them to follow the practice of their enemy. For as long as was necessary the Rhodians fought an elusive action. Using their superior skill, speed, and handiness for the various forms of the ram stroke and the get-away and with archery fire and, above all, the dreaded threat of Pausistratus' fire baskets overhanging their bows to make the enemy reluctant to close with them, the Rhodians induced their opponents to turn their ships unfavorably to the seas to avoid the fire devices which nevertheless took effect in some cases. While Polyxenidas and his would-be enveloping wing were thus held to futility, the downright Romans had time and opportunity to do their share. The ships at the center of the Asiatic line (i.e., at the Roman right) were the first to yield and the victors breaking through turned upon Polyxenidas and the Levantine left wing which Eudamas and the elusive but terrifying Rhodians had been teasing with such happy effect. Soon Polyxenidas with the Levantine left wing was in flight. When the right wing, which had been holding its own very well, saw itself deserted by the others, it declined to stay longer and, hoisting sail, it ran with a fair wind to Ephesus.

The Romans lost 2 ships so shattered that they sank and several more were badly damaged. The Rhodian loss was 1 ship captured. It rammed a ship of Sidon (a stray from Hannibal's division?) and was caught by the latter's anchor in such a way that in backing off the anchor cable tore out the Rhodian's oars and, while lying helpless, the Sidonian that it had holed was able to carry it by boarding, and Polyxenidas brought the Rhodian into port, his only trophy, to set against his loss of 13 ships sunk and 29 taken prize.

While this victory merely confirmed the result of the defeat of the Phoenician division, it is more interesting tactically to the historical student, on account of the brilliant use by Eudamas of two types of ships in tactical support of each other. The Levantine fleet was of one type, much more numerous than the entire enemy force but with crews of inferior quality to the Romans, yet attempting to fight after the Roman style. It was Eudamas' great distinction that by an instantaneous decision he placed his fast Rhodians on the Roman flank to prevent, by skillful ship handling, a disastrous overlap of the hard working Roman squadron to which victory was certain if each ship met only one adversary at a time. It was like a typical land battle of the period in which a heavy phalanx meets a smaller force of better infantry with flanks thoroughly protected by cavalry.

After the battle, the Roman fleet proceeded to Ephesus to claim by its uncontested presence that it was victorious and then it went to Chios to complete its stores. After necessary repairs, the Praetor sent 30 ships to the Hellespont to transport the army and then, decorating the Rhodian ships with naval trophies and giving them their share of the prize, they were authorized to go home. Instead, Eudamas resolved with spirit that his ships would see the war through and they also went to the Hellespont to ferry the army over before returning to Rhodes for the winter.

The Effect of the Naval Victory on the Operations Ashore

The loss of the naval battle brought immediate results in Europe. The King concluded that he could not hold his outposts; it was obligatory to concentrate for battle and, in particular, he felt that it was necessary to abandon Lysimachia with its great magazines. The Roman historian says Antiochus lost his judgment with the news of Myonnesus and that he should have held Lysimachia and suffered a siege to delay the Roman advance till the next spring. Most modern critics follow the opinion offered by Livy, but it is doubtful if it is sound. The King had no expectation of taking his great army into Thrace after Myonnesus, nor could delay enable him materially to increase his army which he had been assembling for a year. Nor was it imperative for the Romans to delay before a hostile Lysimachia, even if it was at the neck of the Chersonese. The army did not have to pass within range of its walls to get to Sestos. It was not even necessary to go to Sestos to embark, nor did it do so, for the overwhelming naval strength available gave the Consul entire freedom in bringing his supplies to any point of the neighboring shores and also enabled him to transport the army with the utmost speed over the short passage of 3 or 4 miles of water at the utmost. With 80 men-of-war and numerous supply ships and open boats, the transfer of the whole army (train excepted) was possible in 24 to 36 hours. It was therefore very justifiable for Antiochus to abandon Lysimachia and due neither to Scipio's proverbial luck nor to Antiochus' deception by the gods, as Livy suggests.

Scipio heard both of the battle of Myonnesus and the consequent evacuation of Lysimachia at the same time, when he was a week's march or less from the city. He rejoiced greatly at having the town at his disposal with its abundant supplies when the army was anticipating difficulty there, and he waited in it for some days for the sick and stragglers to come up before going to Sestos where he seems to have arrived not later than the middle of November. After crossing at several points with no trouble, the army lay on the Hellespont for several days for the observance of certain religious rites. As the fleet had executed its primary task at Myonnesus and had nothing pressing to accomplish before going to a winter base, Aemilius, its busy admiral, was able to gain an additional line in history during this leisure period, by laying siege to Phocaea in order to take up his winter quarters in a hostile city on the mainland, instead of in the friendly island of Samos. Phocaea provided also an additional point of support and supply on the expected route of the army.

The Roman Army in Asia

For this study of naval history there is little more to say of the campaign. Publius Scipio was taken ill and could not go with the army. His son was taken prisoner and Antiochus attempted to use the son as a means of extorting favorable terms from the Romans, but Publius declined to offer anything but gratitude for his son's ransom, and he was returned after the kindest treatment by the King. Publius then advised the King not to fight before he, Publius, should have rejoined the army. By the time the sacred season was over and the army was free to march from the Hellespont, it was December. Frequently the climate there does not become definitely unfavorable to campaigning until January.

Antiochus had mobilized about Sardis. He advanced to Thyatira (see Map 2) with some 60,000 infantry and 12,000 riders of many types and nationalities, while the Romans, with 22,000 Italian legionaries and 6,000 light troops from the Balkans and Asia and 2,800 riders, marched south, keeping near the coast within easy communication with the seaports. Domitius acted under the Consul to replace Publius Scipio as chief of staff. As the Romans drew near, Antiochus fell back to an open position near Magnesia, where his cavalry and his excess in numbers would have room for maneuver.

The battle took place about the new year, probably before the middle of January, 189, and, in spite of their numbers, the eastern army was defeated and Antiochus fled to Sardis and asked for peace. He was offered the same terms as before the battle, namely, to resign all pretensions in Europe and cede the western part of Asia Minor and pay 15,000 talents ($17,800,000) indemnity, part cash down, a second payment on ratification of the treaty, and the rest in 12 annuities. Besides, Antiochus had to surrender all but 10 of his men-of-war and none of them was to pass west of the center of Cilicia. Most of the Greek cities of Asia Minor received their freedom. Rhodes received Lycia and much of Caria and Antiochus guaranteed the financial claims of the Rhodians within his kingdom. The rest of Western Asia Minor fell to Eumenes, whose father Attalus, like himself, had been a faithful and zealous ally of the Roman people. The treaty required Antiochus to pay to Eumenes the debt he owed to Attalus, and Eumenes was the recipient of the elephants of Antiochus but not of his ships, which were burned. Rome intended to be mistress of the eastern sea. For herself, after subduing Aetolia, she took only the islands of Zacynthus and Cephallenia which, with Corcyra, gave her a substantial hold on the maritime communications of the Adriatic.

The political result of the war was in the establishment of an economic situation. The commercial states, which protected their own business, had put down the sovereign whose policy was to draw the profits of business from his subject states, in order to support the expenses of the protectorate and of his own court. Rome became responsible for the security of Mediterranean commerce and in another century she had learned to abuse her strength.

REVIEW OF SHIP DESIGN AND BATTLE TACTICS

We turn back to review the naval tactical development of the war as a whole, for some of its changes convey lessons of permanent service. At Cissus in 191 the adversaries each had the types of ship which were suited to the character and the style of fighting of the men who stood on their decks. The Levantines had faster ships and they averaged much smaller. The Romans gained the day chiefly by their soldiers' personal courage and skill, although the valor of the men was rendered more effective through the superior size and the equipment of the ships. Many of the Levantine ships were too small, but the failure was not wholly due to them. After Cissus the souls of Antiochus and his seamen were somewhat dominated by the stubborn Romans; although not yet ready to relinquish the contest, they had perhaps, as we say today, acquired an "inferiority complex." They took the winter to think about the matter and they made the not unusual mistake of attributing their ill-success to the instruments of the victors rather than to their personality. As a result of their deliberations, both the Ionian and the Phoenician new ships which were ordered for the next season were heavier than their immediate predecessors, as is shown by the special mention of hexeres and hepteres in both squadrons. The increase in size was necessarily accompanied by an increase in soldiers and artillery, for otherwise they would have had no counter valency for their loss of handiness.

The first engagement of the new type was that between the Phoenicians under Apollonius and Hannibal and the Rhodians under Eudamas. In regard to this battle Mommsen says, "the excellence of the Rhodian ships and naval officers carried the victory over Hannibal's tactics and his numerical superiority"; but it does not seem that "Hannibal's tactics" (he was second in command) had anything to do with the matter. The Roman tactics depended on the nautical feature of grappling the enemy when he came within reach, and ships were heavily built with a view to a boarders' fight. Antiochus had adopted the Roman type of ship, yet when the Rhodians came in contact with the Phoenicians, the latter did not grapple. They could not win unless they did.

In the final battle at Myonnesus it was unnecessary for the Levantines to seek to grapple the Roman ships. The latter attended to that maneuver and the Levantine center was defeated because the King had not matched Roman soldiers with others equally good. On the flanks, as at Side, the Levantine fleet could accomplish nothing because it could not seize an elusive enemy who threatened, apparently, without accomplishing a great deal. This is shown by the Rhodian loss of one rash ship only. Yet the Rhodians were entirely correct in declining decisive battle, and fully performed their part in keeping the hostile wings from enveloping the Romans while the latter destroyed the ships in front of them. The course of this naval war shows how dangerous it is to change the traditional style of warfare which is suited to the people, unless the new style is capable of adoption in all its essential points. Antiochus did not have soldiers who could utilize his new ships in the way the Romans meant such ships to be used, and did use them.

The tactical development of this last war marks a point in the history of naval tactics at which it is convenient to review the changes of 300 years as to which we have formal history.

First, we have seen the progress of fire as a weapon, from its early tentative employment to an important tactical feature. At Marathon, after the Greeks had broken the Persian ranks, they pursued the enemy to the beach and seized the ships, endeavoring to detain them as the men embarked. Here Callimachus, the Athenian general, and Cynaegirus, the brother of Aeschylus, were killed as they cried aloud to "bring fire"; but the fire did not come. The idea was not yet in the practical stage. Then, on various later occasions, fire makes a modest appearance, until in the Syrian War the blazing fire baskets were developed into an important technical and tactical resource which was on the way to reach its highest development 2,000 years later.

Second, in those 300 years we see alterations of the perennial contest at sea which still endures, in which superior worth and valor of individual fighters on one side are matched against the superior skill of ship captains in handling better ships. Is the man or the ship going to win? At Artemisium and Salamis, opposing tactical policies are in evidence. Themistocles wanted to let his heavy-armed men fight equal numbers of personally inferior, although not less brave, opponents. The Persians sought unsuccessfully to reach victory through superiority in number of men and number of ships. In the Peloponnesian War, the individual combatants were of the same race and style of armament. In the early part of the war Phormio pitted skillfully handled ships against big crews of soldiers and he made the ships win against the infantrymen. Polyanthes at Erineus was the first to put the ram in its subordinate place and at Syracuse Nicias could not restore the superiority of the ram and the Syracusan soldiers got the upper hand.

Then came the invention of mechanical artillery and, with the increase of weights on board, the dependence on handiness and individual ship handling seems to have been reduced and the admiral's tactical effort was devoted to enveloping the hostile flank after the fashion of land battles.

With the wars of Rome and Carthage we get back to the early form of tactical plan, the mobile ship of Carthage against the Roman soldier. The soldier won because of the grappling device in its various forms. The Roman did not have the initiative in any individual ship contest of the general battle, but the handy Punic ship could not withdraw to attack anew with the ram, and so the Romans won.

Finally, in the war with Antiochus we see the highest form of tactics, in which two types of armament are used in mutual support against an enemy who is not prepared to deal particularly well with either, and numbers are overcome by adaptability.

The tendency to depend upon well-handled ships as the chief tactical reliance and the opposing tendency to regard high quality of men as able to overbalance skill and weapons are evident today. Neither good point should be neglected. When Britain and Germany, 25 years ago, were preparing their fleets for war, the former relied on numbers and the assumed superiority of the British seamen, on the "Hearts of Oak" of Nelson. To oppose greater numbers with some prospect of success, the Germans relied on skillful handling, better ship protection, and better ammunition. When the "show down" came, it proved that the Germans also had not forgotten to bring their "hearts of oak." Thus the outcome was that superiority in the size of the fleet was only able to achieve a "draw" in the greatest naval battle in three centuries.

As we look forward to possible war, it is difficult to see how we Americans can rely surely on the tactical point of superiority in the individual fighters as Themistocles and the Romans did. America renounced by treaty a few years ago the right to exercise the privilege of its wealth to win by numbers of its ships. Our only recourse is to win by excellence at all points—by ship construction and skill in ship and fleet management, as well as by high standards of the personnel.

PRINCIPAL AUTHORITIES CONSULTED FOR THIS CHAPTER

ANCIENT

Appian.
Livy.

MODERN

Cambridge Ancient History, vol. 6.
Delbrueck, H.: *Geschichte der Kriegskunst.*
Kromayer: *Antike Schlachtfelder.*
          Schlachten Atlas.
Mommsen, Th.: *History of Rome.*

CHAPTER XIV

NAVAL WARFARE IN THE FIRST CENTURY, B.C.

Maritime Quiet after the Conquest of Asia

AFTER the close of the war with Antiochus in 190, naval affairs attracted comparatively little attention for nearly a century and a half. The Romans were in virtual control of the Mediterranean area, and as they moved their armies about they needed shipping for transport and supply, but encountered little opposition from hostile fleets such as Antiochus had controlled. No great naval battles occurred. Under these conditions of supremacy the government of Rome had no need to replace the great fleets of powerful ships which had enabled her to win the war against Hannibal and which had covered the passage of Scipio into Asia. Rome depended more and more on the local squadrons maintained by her maritime clients such as Rhodes for the defense of traffic against piracy which existed everywhere. The great Greek ships of the early part of the third century, the 16-ers, are not later heard of. The deceres are the largest mentioned in the second century and afterwards, but they do not seem to have been numerous, and apparently even they were never the fashion in the western Mediterranean. But even with the acknowledged supremacy of Rome she found as time went on that it was dangerous to be without sea power.

Pontic Wars

When Mithradates of Pontus went to war with Rome, in 88 B.C., he had prepared for it through many years and had a large fleet. With his naval preponderance he was able first to seize control of the Aegean and then to raise an insurrection in Athens. When the internal situation at Rome enabled the Senate to send Sulla with his legions across the Adriatic to repulse the King, the former found during his siege of Piraeus in 87-86 B.C. that Mithradates by his mastery of sea communications was able to throw supplies into the besieged city at pleasure and, later, when the siege works had so far progressed that Sulla was on the point of victory, the Pontic garrison withdrew by sea without loss. After Sulla had cleared up the Balkan peninsula, he was unable to cross into Asia and bring the war into the base of opposition until he had sent Lucullus on a dangerous voyage through the enemy's fleets to Syria and Egypt to collect vessels from the client states with which to cover the army's passage of the Hellespont. Two naval victories by Lucullus enabled Sulla to threaten Mithradates at home and negotiate a not too satisfactory peace. Such was the necessity for a navy to protect the Roman sea communications, and such it is today to maritime nations.

Again, in the Second Mithradatic War, beginning in 74 B.C., in which Lucullus was now commander in chief, the Romans found their lack of a fleet at the opening of the war was a very serious handicap. However, Lucullus called on the Roman client states and built ships himself until he finally got control of sea communications. We have no good surviving tactical account of the naval events of these two wars, but the most noteworthy incident of which we are told is one in which Lucullus himself took part. It showed how the distinguishing characteristic of naval campaigns of those days differed from the present. The difference was in the lack of specialization in maritime training and weapons. Lucullus was pursuing a smaller Pontic squadron escaping from the Hellespont which took refuge on a little island near Lemnos. There the Pontic vessels rested on the shore and refused to come out and accept battle. Neither did Lucullus venture to drive in on them and attack, but the Roman squadron had numbers to spare. After some difficulties in landing, a part of the Roman crews were established on the back of the island and crossed to where the hostile ships were moored. These now found themselves between two lines and unable to withstand the double attack, one from the shore and the other from the sea.

PIRACY IN THE MEDITERRANEAN

Even before the second war with Pontus, the lack of a Roman fleet had opened a fine field for piracy. In the northern Adriatic where the small client states had no commerce-protecting squadrons, it had been necessary to fit out a Roman expedition of five legions against the Dalmatian pirates, for they were destroying the business of the Empire and merchants feared the winter storms less than the pirates. When the war opened, Mithradates enlarged the scope of his naval operations by encouraging the pirates of Cilicia to operate against Roman commerce. The line between piracy and privateering was not well marked in those days and as the Roman sea power was weak at the outbreak and increased only as necessity required, the pirates found their share in the war most profitable and increased their numbers and improved their organization until they infested the entire Mediterranean. Even within a few miles of Rome noble ladies were seized for ransom and it became apparent that most vigorous measures must be taken against this far-reaching ally of the principal enemy, the King of Pontus. In the year 67, while the war languished in Asia under Lucullus, Gnaeus Pompey was granted a special commission giving him almost unlimited authority over the whole Mediterranean and for 50 miles inland from its coasts to enable him to suppress piracy. He took office for 3 years with 25 lieutenants of senatorial rank, and was given a huge sum of money and power to raise 125,000 men and employ 500 ships. By good administration his great task was thoroughly accomplished in 3 months without any serious battle. Pompey divided the Mediterranean coasts into 13 districts and assigned a lieutenant to each with men and ships, for local patrol, while he himself swept Sardinian, Sicilian, and African shores with a view to re-establishing the grain supply of Rome. That being accomplished, he moved on with a squadron of 60 ships to the piratical headquarters in Cilicia where little serious resistance was made.

In settling affairs after his success Pompey was aided by his moderation. He recognized that the war and hard times had made his opponents pirates, so he rendered it easy for them to return to honest lives by finding suitable places for them as colonists.

CAESAR'S NAVY IN GAUL

Towards the end of the long period with which we are now dealing, there was a naval battle with some tactical interest which took place in 56 B.C., as an incident of Caesar's conquest of Gaul. It was the first venture of the Romans on the ocean and was remarkable for the use of a mechanical device whose tactical object was similar to that of the corvus of Duilius 200 years before, namely, to allow the valor and soldierly skill of the Roman legionaries to overcome the nautical aptitude and local knowledge of the Gauls by matching sword play successfully against ship handling.

Our authority for the battle is no less than Caesar himself, equally great as general and as writer, who witnessed the battle from a neighboring hill as Xerxes saw Salamis from Mount Aegaleos. Caesar undertook the conquest of Gaul in 58 B.C. and in 2 years had subdued all but the southwest corner. He placed the northwestern region under the command of

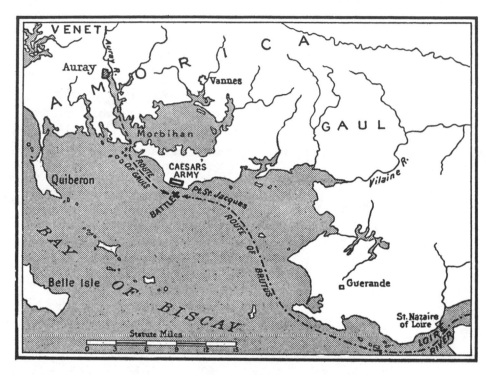

MAP 25. CAESAR'S FIGHT WITH VENETI

his legate Publius Crassus, who during the winter of 57-56 sent out his quartermasters to obtain grain.

Those who were sent among the Veneti, a tribe occupying a district now forming the department of Morbihan in Brittany, were seized and detained. Neighboring tribes followed this example, arresting the Romans who came to them. The following is Caesar's account of the naval campaign.

These Veneti exercise by far the most extensive authority over all the sea coasts in the neighborhood. They have numerous ships which it is their custom to sail to Britain, and they excel the rest in the theory and practice of navigation. As the sea is very boisterous and open with only a few harbors which they hold themselves, they have as tributaries almost all those whose custom is to sail those seas. They urge the remaining states to choose rather to abide in the liberty received from their ancestors than to endure Roman slavery.

It may be here interjected that it seems probable that Caesar gives neither his own true reasons nor those of the Veneti for making the war of this year. Another ancient writer suggests that the Veneti knew that Caesar was contemplating an expedition into Britain, of which island they controlled the commerce by means of their shipping. That profitable business they were unwilling to see transferred to Rome, and on the other hand Caesar knew that he could not enter Britain until he ruled the sea. Rome pressed, 200 years before, her conquests for the political object of extending good order. Now it seems she is prosecuting war for the commercial object of gaining the profits of international trade.

The whole sea coast was rapidly won to the Venetian opinion and all dispatched a deputation in common, bidding Crassus restore the (Gaulish) hostages if he wanted back his own men. Caesar was informed by Crassus concerning these matters and as he was at some distance, he ordered long ships to be built on the Loire which flows into the ocean, rowers to be assembled in the Province (now Provence) and seamen and pilots to be assembled. These requirements were rapidly executed and as soon as the season allowed Caesar hastened to join the army. The Veneti and likewise the rest of the states were informed of Caesar's coming and began to realize the magnitude of their offense. * * * Therefore, as the danger was great, they began to prepare for war on a corresponding scale, and particularly, they fitted out their fleet. This they did the more hopefully because they relied on the nature of the country. The roads are intersected by estuaries and they knew our ships would be hampered by want of local knowledge and by the scarcity of harbors. They trusted also that the Roman army would be unable to remain long in the neighborhood for lack of grain.

Moreover, they felt that even if things turned out contrary to expectation, nevertheless they were preponderant on the sea, for the Romans had few ships, no knowledge of shoals, harbors, or islands in the region of the war and they realized the Romans would find the difference between war in the landlocked Mediterranean and on the great open ocean. Therefore, having adopted this plan, the Veneti fortified their towns, gathered into them their grain, and assembled as many ships as possible in Venetia, where it was known Caesar would begin the campaign. For allies they took . . . [Here follows a list of neighboring tribes both on the Bay of Biscay and along the Channel as far as the Straits of

Dover.] and sent to fetch allies from Britain which lies opposite those regions.[1]

Although Caesar realized the many difficulties of the campaign, he had to undertake it for many reasons: above all, to prevent revolts elsewhere. He knew that almost all the Gauls were bent on rising and could be quickly aroused. Caesar knew also that all men naturally desire liberty and therefore he dispersed his army to check insurrection.[2]

Decimus Brutus was put in command of the Roman fleet and of the Gallic ships ordered to assemble from the pacified tribes between the Loire and the Garonne, and he was directed to proceed as soon as possible to the country of the Veneti, where Caesar himself hastened with the land force. The position of the strongholds were generally of one kind. They were set at the ends of promontories and tongues of land, so as to allow of no approach on foot when the tide was high as happens every 12 hours; nor by ships because at ebb tide the ships would be damaged by the shoals. By either way assault was impracticable. When in fact, the natives were overcome by huge siege works, that is to say, when great moles had been built out to the walls so as to exclude the waters and the defenders began to despair of their fortune, they would bring close in shore a large number of ships of which they had plenty, and take off all their goods and move to the nearest stronghold there to defend themselves with the same advantage.

For the greater part of the summer, the Veneti pursued this course the more easily because our own ships were detained by foul weather and because of the great difficulty of navigation on an open sea with strong tides and scarcely any harbors. The Gallic ships were built and equipped in the following manner. Their bottoms were considerably flatter than ours so that they could sit on the shoals more easily when the tide went out. Their bows were very high as well as the sterns to meet the force of winds and waves. The ships were built entirely of oak to endure violence and buffeting. The cross beams were secured with iron spikes as thick as the thumb to wales [longitudinal planks on the side] a foot wide. The anchor cables were of iron chain instead of rope. The sails were made of skins and thin leather instead of canvas, either because the natives had no supply of flax or because they thought the mighty ocean storms and the great size of their ships forbade its use. When our fleet encountered these ships it proved superior only in speed under oars. In other respects, having regard to the locality and the heavy weather, the others were more suitable and adaptable.

---

[1] The area occupied by the allies was some 24,000 sq. miles and the population of Gaul as estimated by various authorities was 18 to 30 per sq. mile, a total of 500,000 more or less in the revolted area.

[2] Caesar had a garrison of 8 legions, say 40,000 heavy infantry. He sent his cavalry towards the Rhine, and 3 legions into the present Normandy and Brittany. More than a legion with cavalry went into Aquitania. Of the remaining force we may assume that about a legion went aboard the fleet, and nearly 3 legions formed the field army of invasion.

For they were so stoutly built that our ships could not damage them with the ram nor by reason of their height was it easy to hurl a pilum [throwing spear] effectively.[3] And for the same reason grapnels did not easily fasten on them. Moreover in bad weather they could run before the wind more easily, and rest on the shoals without danger where stranded by low tide, whereas our ships dreaded these possibilities. After taking several towns by assault Caesar perceived that all his labor was going for nothing since the flight of the enemy could not be checked by the capture of towns, nor could damage thus be inflicted on them. Accordingly, he decided to wait the arrival of the fleet. When it had come and was first seen by the enemy, about 220 of their ships fully prepared and equipped sailed out of port and took station opposite ours. It was not clear to Brutus, who commanded the fleet, nor to his tribunes and centurions in charge of single ships what they should do, nor what plan they were to follow, for our commanders knew that the enemy could not be damaged by the ram; and although towers were erected on deck, the high poops of the enemy commanded even these so that from the lower level the pila [heavy short range throwing spears] could not be properly thrown, while those of the Gauls had the more force. One device prepared by our men was of great service. Sharp and pointed hooks were secured to the ends of long poles, after the fashion of siege hooks. When these contrivances had caught the halyards supporting the yards, the [Roman] ship was driven away by the oars and the halyards were cut in consequence, so the yards fell to the deck. [The operation would not be difficult if the halyards belayed at the ship's side, as is now common.] As the Gallic ships relied wholly on their sails, they thus lost all mobility at once.

From this moment the outcome of the battle lay in valor, in which our men excelled, and the more so because the engagement took place in sight of Caesar and all the army, so that no specially gallant deed was unseen, for all the neighboring hills having a view of the sea were held by the army. When the yards came down as we have mentioned, and two or three of our ships were able to surround a single enemy, our soldiers made the greatest efforts to board their foes and after several ships had been taken in this manner and no remedy was seen they took to flight. And as they turned to leeward, the breeze suddenly fell to so great a calm that none could move. This was a most opportune circumstance, for as our men reached each ship they boarded her so that very few were able to take advantage of the night to reach the shore. The battle had lasted from the middle of the forenoon until sunset.

This battle finished the campaign against the Veneti and all the seacoast. For all the fighting men with their chief leaders and all their ships had been assembled for this occasion and after such losses they had no place to go to, nor

---

[3] Another version of this last clause is "they could approach the rocks with less fear and so avoid our missiles."

means of defence. Accordingly, they surrendered themselves and all their property to Caesar, who decided that their punishment must be severe that the natives might observe the privileges of envoys more carefully.

Such is the account which Caesar[4] gives of his campaign of 56.

ROMAN TACTICS

During the 200 years of Roman naval warfare, of which we have examined the most striking campaigns, we have seen the Roman fighting foreigners and the tactical effort of Roman admirals was always to make the contest of battle take such a form that the outcome would be decided by the valor of the legionary soldier. This has been the decisive factor. The corvi, the grappling irons of the Mediterranean, and the scythes of the Bay of Biscay were all used to prevent the enemy from running away, so that the more skillful, seamanlike adversary might never have a second attempt to ram if he ventured within reach of the more sluggish Roman.

PRINCIPAL AUTHORITIES CONSULTED FOR THIS CHAPTER

ANCIENT

Appian.
Caesar, Julius.
Dio Cassius.
Plutarch: *Lucullus*.

MODERN

Mommsen, Th.: *History of Rome*.

---

[4] Napoleon's *Life of Caesar* points out that the Veneti must have had their ships in the northern part of Quiberon Bay and that they came out of the River Auray by the Morbihan entrance to the gulf instead of waiting for Brutus inside. At the end of the summer the winds are usually east and northeast and must have been so on this occasion to let the Veneti get out while Brutus was approaching from the Loire. If, as Napoleon supposes, there was a legion embarked in the fleet, we may take the average number of soldiers to each ship to have been about 75 as in the Punic Wars, which would give 70 or 80 Roman ships besides the Gallic allies. The Roman ships may have had a draft of 5 ft., and with a beam of 16 ft., and length of 85 ft., they may have displaced 100 tons and carried a crew of 200 souls in all. Since they were much lower than the Gallic ships, they can scarcely have had a deck over the rowers who must have worn armor for protection. The Gallic ships were of lighter draft, say 3.5 ft., and since they were high-sided sailing ships and probably built to carry cargo, must have been wide and short so that probable dimensions would be 3.5 x 18 x 55 ft. with a displacement of 50 to 60 tons. Since they had no rowers their crews would not be over 80 to 100 men. The ship dimensions here suggested are in general accord with the data given by Caesar for the ships he built for his second expedition to Britain, which seem to have been intermediate in size between his own first ships and the Gallic type.

CHAPTER XV

NAVAL WARS OF CAESAR 49-45 B.C.

Preceding Political Conditions

THE long political and military contest of 19 years in which the Roman Republic was transformed into an Empire took the form of struggle between the eastern and western halves of the state in which sea power was a most important factor during the entire period. It was not until the beginning of the last year of the war that the great naval battle of Actium took place, deciding its outcome and resulting in the establishment of the Empire with a form of government which was little changed in principle for three centuries and the influence of which is felt throughout the European world to this day.

Before undertaking the examination of the purely maritime features of these wars, we must glance at the political and economic situation which led to hostilities and which controlled the military operations ashore and afloat.

We have already seen that when Rome's political expansion beyond Italy began, she seems to have been actuated chiefly by a political motive for the good of her allies. Under the slow growth of the Roman hegemony since the Punic Wars, the city of Rome and the Roman people had been depending less and less on national industry and more and more on conquest and the profits of trade and high finance for the economic support of the peninsula.

From the subject states came tribute money and gifts exacted by the military governors. Roman citizens obtained favored positions in provincial trade and the wars provided slaves with which to work the farms of Italy. The whole Mediterranean area slowly became one great market in which the special products of each province could be freely exchanged. The Italian legions, directed by the senators and financiers of Rome, maintained a fair degree of order throughout the state, and soldiers and ruling classes lived off the increased profits of the industry and commerce which their rule promoted. In spite of wars and many administrative abuses, the unification of government, on the whole, was generally advantageous.

But these changes in economic life entailed political corruption. Gradually the Senate usurped authority, because the assembly of the people was unequal to the conduct of foreign affairs. The small farmers were dispossessed by slave labor and discharged soldiers poured into Rome to form an idle proletariat whose votes were at the disposal of any politician who would buy them. At the beginning of the first century the army became a hired service and soldiers took an oath to each commander in chief, whoever he might be. That oath conferred practically monarchical authority within his province on any political leader who could obtain military command; for soldiers cared little for politics, although they were available as political instruments of their respective generals. Those changes in the economic life of the Roman people injured their moral standards and required corresponding changes in the system of government. A progressive party appeared which wished to reform the government, and was opposed by a conservative party upholding the old abuses. Under party pressure the Senate's rule became nominal. It was no longer a governing class but was a crowd of greedy individuals in high places controlled by political leaders. Early in the first century B.C. Italy was torn by civil war and peace was restored by the dictator Sulla who reestablished the Senate in authority. Again the Senate showed its incapacity to govern under the old system.

Between 70 and 60 B.C. Gaius Julius Caesar became the head of the Liberal party, but he had no army to support his policy. At that time Gnaeus Pompeius Magnus returned with an army from great victories in Asia Minor and he and Caesar, with Marcus Crassus representing the moneyed classes, formed a triumvirate to control the Senate and rule the state. Under that arrangement, Caesar was made Consul and in 58 was given the governorship of Italy north of the Po and an army with which in the next 8 years he conquered Gaul. During those years the Triumvirate dissolved.

As time passed Pompey was worked on by the Senatorial party and he became jealous of Caesar. In order to have a leader, the Conservative party in the Senate made Pompey governor of Spain, with the command of several legions. By the end of 50 B.C. the Conservatives felt they could rely on Pompey to support them in quarreling with Caesar who was soon due to lay down his governorship and army command in order to run again for the consulship as the law authorized him to do. The Senate set conditions upon Caesar's candidacy which he refused to accept and civil war seemed imminent.

CHARACTER OF THE COMING WAR

The contest differed much in type from the ordinary foreign wars of which Rome had waged so many. It differed even from the ordinary type of civil war in which a region attempts a revolt or secession, and one geographical group of men is arrayed against another on account of racial or economic oppression. The question at issue was what type of government was to extend over the entire state. It was the retention or transformation of the republican system. Both parties drew their soldiers from the same people and promised them rewards of land from the same districts. Both parties were anxious to retain or gain the good will and financial and political support of the same body of citizens and of client nations. On both sides the purpose of the war was to control the resources of the state in the interests of the successful party and its supporters. The resources were unequally distributed throughout the state. Manufactures and wealth were chiefly to be found in the East; metals, in the West. All those products of industry were brought together by the great banking facilities of Rome and the senatorial aristocracy and the capitalists lived by the control of trade and the management of finances. Political unity was essential to confer the maximum advantage on the rulers and wealthy classes of the state.

OPENING OF THE WAR

The Senate's objections to Caesar's claims rose high and on January 7, 49 B.C., it declared the country in danger, calling the people to arms. Thereupon, 5 days later, with only a single legion, Caesar crossed the boundary of his province at the River Rubicon, with the nominal purpose of sustaining the constitution, but really to establish a strong government and put an end to old abuses in senatorial government. The entry into Italy with troops was an act of war against the existing senatorial government of which Pompey was the nominal head and effective army leader. Of the two opponents, Caesar had the more solid though less considerable position. His military power rested on his 11 legions of faithful veterans of nearly 50,000 men, trained by him and drawn chiefly from his province of Cisalpine Gaul, or Upper Italy, to which he had given burgess rights and which was politically of his party. His political strength came from the same province. The Roman colonists in the newly conquered Further Gaul were devoted to him, but on the whole the province was scarcely an aid and in Narbonese Gaul there were many adherents of the other party. In Italy proper Caesar's influence was comparatively slight, for there the burgesses saw Pompey as the defender of legitimacy and feared Caesar would cancel debts and repeat the political massacres of the previous generation. In the rest of the Republic Caesar had little influence. Caesar's strength lay in his unlimited authority within his own party. He decided both political and military matters, for he was without colleagues, having only aides who had almost all risen from the army and obeyed without question. Although he was without brilliant subordinates, he gained much from the consequent unity of his action, and he was a great leader of men, both as a politician and as a soldier.

Pompey began the war as chief of the Roman commonwealth but, although he controlled a far vaster region, his leadership was not so unquestioned as that of his opponent. The unity of command which Caesar enjoyed was not Pompey's because it was incompatible with his position as the Senate's man. He knew as a soldier that it was necessary for him to be sole and absolute generalissimo and he had himself so nominated, but in policy the Senate could not be set aside and exercised a preponderating influence. Both the Senate and Pompey realized that their first victory over their common enemy would be the signal for a rupture between themselves; but material power now was with the Senate and Pompey. The two Spains were ruled by his administrators, the provinces were filled by his appointees, and even Massilia in Caesar's own province was indebted to Pompey for extension of territory. In the east where Pompey had conquered and ruled, the client states stood by him. His 7 Spanish legions made his principal army; elsewhere he had only weak and scattered forces. In Italy he had only 2 legions recently transferred to him by Caesar, and stationed in the south. But everywhere at home and abroad Pompey could call Roman citizens to the colors and in Italy all the available men had already taken the military oath to him. A little time only was necessary to assemble a great army. Then Pompey and the Senatorial party would be able to attack Caesar in his province of Gaul from two sides, Spain and Italy. Although Pompey was an able soldier, he was always a cautious one and desired preponderance before committing himself.

Besides all this Pompey commanded the sea. The merchant fleets and navies of Egypt, Phoenicia, and Asia Minor were at his disposal as soon as they could be summoned. He had the seaports and the means of equipping ships. With them he could be sure of army supplies from the East and have the means of transporting his own troops quickly while putting corresponding pressure on Caesar and his troops and civil supporters. A few months later Cicero in a letter to Atticus, which has come down to us, gives Pompey's views as to seapower at a moment when his affairs were not prosperous, and he had left Italy (Atticus: X-8).

> Pompey will not lay down arms for the loss of Spain. He holds with Themistocles that those who are masters of the sea will be the victors in the end. He has neglected Spain. He has given all to his ships. When the time comes, he will return to Italy with an overwhelming fleet.

As for Caesar, he had to find resources in himself to oppose Pompey. He was distinguished beyond other men for rapidity of resolution and of action, and that was his resource against Pompey whose present strength was capable of greater growth than he could expect for his own forces.

Already in December, as it became apparent that the Senate intended no compromise with Caesar, Pompey had left Rome to make arrangements for summoning an army to the standards. Seeing this, Caesar started also to mobilize. Of his 11 legions, only 1 was south of the Alps, and that was called to Ravenna near the border of his province, while those beyond the Alps were brought nearer Italy. On January 10 or 11, Caesar heard of the senatorial action declaring him a public enemy, whereby it assumed the onus of terminating the negotiations in favor of hostilities.

Caesar Invades Italy

Caesar instantly took the initiative with his single legion, crossed the Rubicon River bounding his province, and seized the slightly fortified town of Ariminum (Rimini) on January 12, 49 B.C., or by the later reformed calendar, November 24, 50 B.C.[1] He had only about 5,000 infantry and 300 cavalry at hand (see Map 21). Long before the rest of Caesar's troops could appear from the River Loire and from Belgica, the 2 weak legions which Pompey had at Luceria could be increased by the reserves which were pouring in to him at the various senatorial rendezvous. As Pompey said, he had only to stamp with his foot to summon soldiers, and, indeed, he expected soon to have 10 legions. Still, a little time was necessary, and this Caesar would not allow him.

As Caesar marched along the Adriatic coast road he encountered no resistance; the gathering bands of recruits were not yet organized and the inhabitants wanted no hostilities. When Caesar had gone so far that he had to make choice between going to Rome or advancing against Pompey's 7,000 men at Luceria, consisting of 2 weak and untrustworthy legions which had recently formed part of Caesar's Gallic army, he decided to attack Pompey who was unaccustomed to improvisations (see Map 10). Had Caesar gone to the city, he would have permitted Pompey to organize an overwhelming army while his own main body was coming from Gaul.

In Rome, at the news of Caesar's rapid advance into Italy, all was thrown into confusion. Pompey had returned there, but he now abandoned the city with most of the Senators, and went to Apulia to organize the levies. As Caesar moved south, many of Pompey's gathering recruits who had been overtaken by the former's rapid movement, joined Caesar's army, as did also many volunteers, so that by the latter half of December, after 2 more legions from Gaul arrived, Caesar had a force of about 40,000 men before Corfinium in Samnium where the Pompeians had assembled about 15,000 recruits. Instead of evacuating Corfinium as Caesar approached, the occupants held on, hoping for relief by Pompey. When he failed to appear, they surrendered and most joined Caesar's army.

By that time Pompey had recognized that Italy was lost to him, at least temporarily, and he retired with his army to the fortified port

---

[1] The calendar had been allowed to fall into error by those in charge, and the error was now 7 weeks, and increasing. As the military operations must be considered with regard to the season of the year, subsequent dates are corrected to conform to the Julian calendar adopted in 46 B.C.

of Brundisium, there to meet the shipping which he had already summoned from the East, in order to cross to Epirus and assemble all his strength under the protection of his sea power. Of the 10 legions which he had expected to oppose to Caesar, about 30,000 men had gone over to Caesar during his southward march and Pompey had been able to add only about 18,000 men to the original 2 small legions at Luceria.

POMPEY ABANDONS ITALY

The embarkation began at once, but as the shipping was insufficient to take all, it was necessary to divide the army, sending only the Consuls with the larger part on January 12, while Pompey himself remained with 10,000 men.

While Pompey waited for his transports to return, Caesar arrived before Brundisium with his army. As Caesar tells us in the Commentaries, he did not know whether Pompey was detained for lack of ships, or was intending to stay in Brundisium to hold it as a base for the Consuls to return with the whole eastern army. Whichever was the case, it was necessary to deprive Pompey of the opportunity of following the Consuls to Epirus, and Caesar at once began operations.

Where the harbor entrance was narrowest, he threw out two moles on each side of the harbor, where the shoals favored them. Farther out, as the water became too deep for an earth fill, he put two rafts 30 feet from the moles and moored them at the four corners. To the two he added others like them, building out the obstruction. He covered all with earth and fascines so that they were protected from fire and men could walk on them. Ramparts were built on all and towers two stories high on every fourth one to protect them from ship attack. Against them Pompey opposed large transport ships with towers three stories high and filled those ships with engines and missiles to break up Caesar's rafts, and each day there was battle.

After 9 days, when Caesar had half finished his obstruction, Pompey's transport ships returned from Epirus and Pompey made arrangements to evacuate. He walled up the city gates, barricaded the town plazas, and dug ditches across the streets. As for the two roads leading from the city to the port, he closed them by heavy beams. He then embarked the garrison by night without noise, leaving a few veterans and archers on the walls. When all the others were shipped, these last ran to a safe place where there were some light ships and Pompey was off before daylight of January 29. Although Caesar was notified of his escape by citizens and his soldiers quickly climbed the walls, they were delayed by the obstacles in the streets, and were able to capture only 2 ships which had stranded on Caesar's dyke.

Caesar was without ships to pursue Pompey, who was at liberty to assemble and organize the great resources of the East in men, shipping, and money. Caesar now garrisoned the towns and ports of South Italy against the return of Pompey and went to Rome where, in the course of a fortnight, he did much to regularize his political position and seized the great sums in the treasury.

CAESAR'S SETTLEMENT OF AFFAIRS IN ITALY

In accordance with his cautious temperament, Pompey preferred to undertake no major offensive operations until he had his whole strength in hand. Not so with Caesar, whose most marked characteristic was rapidity of thought and action. He placed Lepidus in charge of the city and Mark Antony in command of Italy, while deputies went out to rule the provinces Caesar controlled. Recruiting was pushed and two fleets were ordered to be built, by Hortensius and Dolabella, one in the Tyrrhene Sea and one in the Adriatic. Italy had long been unable to supply Rome with grain and nothing could now be procured from the eastern Mediterranean, as Pompey controlled that region and its commerce. It was therefore imperative to seize the grain provinces of Sicily, Sardinia, and Africa before Pompey could mobilize his squadrons in Messana, Utica, and Gades to hold them. That was immediately undertaken. A legion went to Sardinia and two under Curio to Sicily, in April. On his way to Sicily, Curio acknowledged to Cicero that were Pompey to act with his fleet, Sicily would become untenable for him, but Pompey did not move. Both expeditions were successful, with little opposition, and Rome was free from immediate danger of starvation.

CURIO'S CAMPAIGN IN SICILY AND AFRICA

Curio was soon re-enforced in Sicily by two more legions and it is convenient to trace his operations to their conclusion in advance of the main campaign. After establishing his authority in the island, he felt able to move into Africa and, leaving 2 legions in Sicily as garrison, he embarked the other 2 in transports and, under the escort of 12 men-of-war, he crossed to Africa in the last part of June, 49 B.C. The Pompeians in Africa had had time to organize a small field army of 2 legions from the Roman settlers there (another Roman legion was also in Africa). They had a small squadron of 10 men-of-war, besides a considerable African army belonging to Juba, King of Numidia. The Pompeian squadron failed to check Curio's passage or his disembarkation, but after several initial successes he was killed in battle a few days after landing, and few of his expedition got back to Italy. Caesar was deprived of the harvests of Africa and the Pompeian party had an uninterrupted period of over 2 years to secure itself in Africa, before Caesar could get around to attend personally to its affairs.

General Strategic Situation in Spring of 49

We may now return to the general strategic situation as it existed at the beginning of April while Caesar was in Rome organizing his political and military resources. Although the eastern and western halves of the Republic were in opposition to each other, as they were destined to find themselves from time to time in the future, there was no question of a permanent division of the state.

The preservation of the Empire was secured by the Roman garrisons throughout the provinces and by the Roman colonies established everywhere as centers of Roman influence and, if need be, of Roman force. All Roman citizens wanted to preserve economic unity. Division of opinion was about the form of government; and an early settlement with the least possible disturbance was desired by all.

Caesar had assumed the responsibility of government and had to answer for the political unrest and financial distress of the Republic, and had to hasten the course of events. It was therefore pleasing to public opinion as well as advantageous to his own party and his cause that Caesar did not delay the main campaign as Pompey was doing. Caesar had the choice of two principal theaters of war. In Spain was a Pompeian army of 7 legions of experienced troops. East of the Adriatic a much larger army was in process of formation, and with it decision would finally lie.

Were Caesar to march into Epirus and Greece by the route around the Adriatic, the enemy could rest on the fortified ports of the Aegean and be supplied indefinitely from over seas, while Pompey himself and the Spanish army would reoccupy Italy and Rome.

The War in Spain

Caesar could not afford to sacrifice the advantage of prestige he had already acquired and he decided to follow the sound military rule, to strike the most threatening enemy of the moment, wherever it may be. He moved against the Spanish legions while Pompey was mobilizing the eastern army; but, as he told Curio, he was looking forward to attack Pompey afterwards, wherever he might be (see Map 19). Caesar had already called 3 legions out of Gaul since crossing the Rubicon and he now threw 3 more towards the Pyrenees to seize the passes and contain the Pompeian armies in Spain.

As for Pompey's course, it has been alleged that after he realized that he could not remain in Italy, he should not have crossed the Adriatic as he did, but should rather have gone to Spain with such troops as he could embark from Campanian ports and make active war from Spain, while waiting for the eastern troops to become available. Pompey had delayed his movement southward in the hope his recruits in Corfinium might get away and so lost the chance of occupying the seaport of Naples before Caesar could get there; but, even had he secured Naples, it is scarcely likely in any case that he could have got his army out of Italy with his troops by that route, as most of his shipping came from the east. In getting them only to Brundisium he could not assemble enough transports to evacuate Italy before Caesar was upon him.

However Pompey's habitual caution as to undertaking an offensive campaign did not prevent him from doing what he could to check Caesar in the west. He sent a distinguished soldier, Vibullius Rufus, to take instructions and advice to the three provincial armies of Spain and sent Domitius Ahenobarbus to Massilia with a small squadron to induce the city to withstand Caesar. He also sent a group of Massilian noblemen to tell their fellow-citizens that for previous favors they owed it to him to close the city against Caesar.

The enmity of Massilia was a very weighty factor in Caesar's Spanish campaign. It will be recollected that Massilia had been a most important ally of Rome in the Second Punic War when the two Scipios first invaded Spain. To have her turn against him would be very embarrassing to Caesar. In ancient times, the principal lines of supply for far-flung military operations were preferably by sea and the local squadron of Massilia, if hostile to Caesar, would oblige him to supply his army in Spain exclusively from Gaul and by the passes of the Pyrenees, across which some years before Pompey had built a good, although a long, road.

About the middle of February Caesar left Rome for the Spanish campaign and, on arriving at Massilia 10 or 15 days later, he found that Pompey's emissaries had been partially successful and that Massilia had announced her neutrality and would defend it by arms. She had called the Albices, a tribe of neighboring mountaineers, into town, for a garrison, and was making arms and rebuilding the walls and repairing her ships. Consequently, to Caesar's demand that the city should follow the sentiment of Italy, its rulers replied that it owed much both to Caesar and to Pompey and would therefore admit neither. When this news became known in Rome early in March, it raised the hopes of Pompey's partisans that he would march immediately through Illyria upon Caesar in Gaul.

Domitius now arrived at Massilia with 7 men-of-war which he had picked up from private owners on the coast of Etruria. He had manned the ships with his personal slaves, freedmen, and tenants. His presence brought the city completely over to Pompey's cause and he took command. He sent out the Massilian squadron in all directions to secure shipping and to bring it to Massilia. Thus Domitius raised a very serious obstacle on Caesar's line of communication with Spain. A mere blockade of the city on the land side would not serve to keep it open. Caesar had to confine a hostile fleet in port, yet he had no ships of his own. For all that, he did not renounce his Spanish campaign. He called on his legions in Gaul and dispatched 3 under Fabius across the Pyrenees. He detailed 3 others to the siege of Massilia. He built 12 galleys on the Rhone at Arles in 30 days after cutting the timber and assigned the naval command to Decimus Brutus who had commanded the fleet in the campaign against the Veneti. Trebonius took charge of the siege by land in March.

When Vibullius arrived in Spain with Pompey's instructions, it was arranged that of the 7 Pompeian legions, 2 should remain in the south under Varro and the other 5 under Afranius and Petreius in the north should hold the province against the army from Gaul. They did not occupy the passes of the Pyrenees. Perhaps they were not quick enough or they may have wanted to draw Fabius far from Rome. If they were not sure of overcoming him completely, it was wisdom for them to delay decision in order that Pompey might come either to Spain or to Italy with his eastern army while Caesar was still engaged in the west. It was delay that Afranius and Petreius chose. Perhaps their soldiers were not well trained, nor the ranks full.

Early in April the two forces faced each other on the banks of the Sicoris River about 35 miles north of the Iberus, near Ilerda. There the Pompeians refused to offer battle, and Fabius began to suffer for lack of supplies. The siege of Massilia dragged, and towards the end of April Caesar left there to go to Spain where his personal presence was needed to force a battle before his army suffered too much from scarcity of food. Two more legions and 6,000 cavalry had arrived from Gaul when Caesar came to Ilerda, making 5 legions[2] in all to oppose 5. Caesar could not force an action and his people suffered the more from hunger on account of their increased numbers until relieved by naval events at Massilia.

While Trebonius pressed Massilia by land, both sides were making great efforts on the sea. The Massilians built 17 ships of war of which 11 were decked, and also equipped many lighter ones to alarm the Caesarians by their number and manned them with crews of Albices (men of a neighboring tribe). Domitius got some additional ships for himself and manned them with herdsmen from his estates in the Rhone Valley.

Naval Battle at Marseilles

When the Massilians had completed their naval preparations they came out and offered battle to Brutus who had placed his naval base on an island close to the city. The Massilian squadron was much more numerous than that of Brutus, but he had on board the best men in the army, commanded by centurions who had volunteered for the fleet. Brutus had

---

[2] See Ferrero, Vol. II, p. 255. *Greatness and Decline of Rome*.

provided his ships with many iron hands (apparently, grapnels with chain cables attached), harpoons, javelins, and other weapons. As the Commentaries say,

> as the enemy approached our ships came out and attacked them. The fight was well sustained on both sides; the Albices were as good as our men. The Massilians trusted to the speed of their ships and the skill of their pilots. Avoiding our rams, they extended their wings and tried to envelop us so far as the space permitted. They put several vessels against one and tried to break our oars. When the ships were in contact the valor of the mountaineers replaced the skill of the pilots. Our ships were heavy and had poor oarsmen with pilots taken at random from the transport ships. But when they could close, they seized their enemy with an iron hand and took him by boarding. After a severe action we sank some and took others. The rest were driven back to port after a loss of 9 ships.

CAESAR AT ILERDA

The effect of this naval victory about the end of May, upon Caesar's situation at Ilerda, seems to have been greater than is acknowledged in Caesar's Commentaries. According to Dio Cassius, Caesar spread exaggerated accounts of the victory among the Spaniards but, in any case, the result was that the tribes on the coast between the Pyrenees and the Iberus came over to Caesar and thereafter the famine in Caesar's camp disappeared; food became plentiful for him and the enemy became distressed. It is therefore evident that the coastal tribes were no longer impressed by the Pompeian squadron at Massilia and thought that Caesar's fleet and army at Massilia would soon be upon them and accordingly went over to the winning side, precisely as their forefathers had done in the Punic War. Thus they simplified Caesar's method of supply by enabling him to draw freely on the resources of the Rhone Valley by the convenient sea route. The mountain road across the Pyrenees was so long as to be almost prohibitive.

Shortly after this change in conditions, brought about by Brutus' naval victory far away, the Pompeian army attempted to withdraw from Ilerda and cross the Iberus, but in a series of brilliant maneuvers Caesar headed it from the river and, after a campaign of 40 days, while refusing battle, he forced it to surrender on June 9, without having fought a major battle, an operation of war which stands almost alone in history. Caesar then went on to Southern Spain where a legion of Varro's army mutinied and Varro himself made terms. The soldiers joined Caesar who then organized the province and went back to Massilia where he arrived early in August, taking Varro's squadron of 10 ships with him.

While Caesar was in the south of Spain, Trebonius and Brutus had pressed the siege of Massilia. The advance was slow and there were many sorties. Pompey sent L. Nasidius from the East with 16 ships to aid the city. On his way he got into Messana, where Curio had been negligent in establishing his garrison, and took a galley prize. He then went on towards Massilia, sending a dispatch boat ahead to encourage the defense. After their defeat by Brutus, the Massilians replaced their lost ships by old ones drawn from their arsenal, found men for them, and added fishing boats which they decked over to protect the rowers. Backed by adjurations of the crowds, the fleet put out from the city to make a junction with Nasidius who had put in at Tauroenta (either Ciotat 35 miles or Toulon 50 miles east of Massilia) and did not venture to force his way to the city. There the squadrons were reorganized, and Nasidius took command of the left wing of the whole force.

Having added to his squadron the 6 prizes he had taken (making 18 in all), Brutus addressed his men as usual before battle and went out to meet the enemy, probably a little after Caesar's victory at Ilerda. The soldiers and camp followers of Trebonius on the hills saw the people of the city thronging to see the departure of the hostile fleet and pray for the success of their own. In the battle off Tauroenta the Massilians showed the greatest valor. The Caesarians gradually extended their intervals and gave the enemy a chance to use the skill of their pilots. If by chance the Romans seized a ship with the iron hand, the others rushed to save it, and the rain of arrows was very effective. Two of the Massilians who recognized Brutus' ship charged on him at the same moment from opposite sides, but his pilot was adroit enough to back out quickly so that they struck each other and both were much injured, one losing her ram. The ships of Nasidius did nothing and soon withdrew, so that the Massilians alone sustained the action. In spite of their gallant conduct, they were badly defeated. Five ships were sunk and 4 were taken; 1 escaped with those of Nasidius to Hither Spain. Although 1 of the captured ships was sent into Massilia to convince the citizens of the defeat, nevertheless they continued to fight for some weeks. Finally, when the breach in the wall was nearly ready for the besiegers to enter it, the city asked and received an armistice until the return of Caesar to decide the terms of surrender. Although the city treacherously violated the armistice before Caesar's arrival, he did not destroy it, but gave it easy terms and left it to be a center of Hellenic culture in the great province he had conquered.

Caesar returned to Rome in September where he had been nominated as Dictator by Lepidus who was his representative in the city.

The Illyrian Campaign

While Caesar had been completely successful in Spain and had secured the great islands, his generals in the Illyrian district had failed entirely, during the summer, and cramped his means very considerably for the next year. In the spring of 49, Caesar had desired to establish a position in Illyria to check Pompey's entering Italy by that route and depriving Caesar of the Po (Padus) Valley (see Map 21), the inhabitants of which were devoted to him and furnished him a great part of his army.

Accordingly, during the Spanish campaign, Caesar sent two new legions under C. Antony to hold the roads around the northern end of the Adriatic and supported him by the squadron of 40 ships which Dolabella had built. We can scarcely suppose that Caesar expected Antony to be able to prevent Pompey from coming through Illyria if he chose to take his whole force by that route, for he had the whole eastern fleet to supply him as he marched; but 2 legions could hold the country and garrison strong points for Caesar and at least cause some delay to any invasion. Antony and Dolabella took positions near each other; but, unwisely, Antony selected for his main camp a strong position on an island, Curicta (Gulf of Quarnero). His mobility and his military usefulness depended, therefore, on the dominance of Dolabella's squadron in the neighboring waters to secure his line of supply and escort his soldiers to points where there were needed. Pompey, however, had assembled four strong squadrons on the Epirotic coast and found no difficulty in sending two under Octavius and Libo against Dolabella. The outcome of the naval battle was that Dolabella was thrown out of those waters with very heavy losses and Antony was isolated on the island. Octavius now landed and Antony's position was closely invested on land by Octavius' soldiers. A relief force of two more Caesarian legions under Sallust and Basileus came from Italy and took position on the mainland opposite to Curicta and endeavored to withdarw the besieged. It was difficult to effect a relief in presence of the superior fleet of the enemy.

Some rafts were made to embark the fugitives, and 3 tried to get away on a dark night; 2 only succeeded while the other was held by some under-water obstructions. The crew held out for a day and then killed themselves sooner than surrender. The remaining 15 cohorts, after starving for some time, mutinied and surrendered and were incorporated in Pompey's forces. As Illyria and Dalmatia were now without Caesarian troops, Octavius completed the subjugation of that coast with the exception of Salonae which was garrisoned, and Caesar lost, for the time being, a province which had been ill-disposed to him since it had been assigned to him during his consulate of 59.

CAMPAIGN OF PHARSALUS 48 B.C.

We now return to Rome in the fall of 49 after Caesar arrived from Spain. Even before Caesar's return he was arranging for attacking Pompey in Macedonia, and was sending available troops and ships to Brundisium, besides building up great depots of supplies there. To the 11 legions with which Caesar had begun the war, he had now added perhaps 17 more, most of them built up from men who had gone over to him from Pompey; but 4 of those had been lost in Africa and Illyria. Of the entire force remaining, a full half was needed to garrison Spain, Italy, and Gaul. Twelve legions were detailed for the field army, including many veteran troops of the Spanish and Massilian campaigns. Owing to the long march of the latter into Italy, the bad weather thinned the ranks very much and there was even a mutiny at Placentia which was overcome by Caesar's personal authority.

But the serious difficulty was in water transportation. Of the men-of-war which Caesar had ordered built early in the year, one squadron had been wiped out at Curicta and the other was either not completed or otherwise unavailable. Only 12 ships were at Brundisium to escort the army and only enough transports to take half the force, for Pompey had swept the ports of Southern Italy to get ships to take his army overseas.

The question has been debated why Caesar did not move against Pompey by the land route through Illyria. Although this province had been under Caesar's government since 58, he had never been favorably regarded by the inhabitants and his legions had been driven out during the summer. Were he now to attempt to pass through, he would have a long march through a difficult country with scant supplies and unfriendly people. Had predominant sea power been his, it might well have been tried, since he could have established bases of supply at successive seaports. Such a transfer had been accomplished by Flamininus in the campaign of 198 against Philip of Macedon when he transferred his army supply base from Apollonia to the Gulf of Ambracia as he marched southeastwards. But there was an additional reason for making the entry into Epirus by sea, risky as that was. Caesar was preparing for the campaign with all the activity that was his and he was doubtless desirous of working upon Pompey's natural temperament which delayed action until fully ready. Had he started his troops from Massilia towards Illyria, his move might have suggested to Pompey the idea of seizing Rome by using his sea power to make a junction in Italy of his own army of Epirus with that of Africa. The latter could have spared some part of its numbers from the duty of holding the province and watching its ally King Juba.

By assembling his field army in Southern Italy, Caesar encouraged Pompey to believe that he would use the oncoming winter to build his fleet and material and complete his preparations. In short, Caesar preserved his initiative by going to Brundisium. At Rome, Caesar spent only 11 days before setting out for the campaign against Pompey. He held the consular elections which made him Consul and took various measures to overcome political enmity against himself.

POMPEY'S SITUATION AND RESOURCES

As for Pompey, his position during the past year had been more difficult politically than militarily. He had been accompanied to Epirus by the "die hards" of the constitutional government, who formed themselves into a pseudo-senate which looked with jealousy on everything that Pompey did. As such bodies are accustomed to do, they offered worthless military advice, they were jealous of Pompey's position and their hopes rather than their knowledge led them to believe that Caesar's position was weak and that Pompey should hasten his action. Pompey therefore was far from having the supreme position as party leader and as general that Caesar had. Pompey had crossed to Epirus during March with 2 legions and about 18,000 recruits. With the latter and levies of veterans and Roman citizens in Crete, Greece, Macedonia, and Asia Minor, and the Caesarian soldiers taken at Currictae, Pompey organized 6 new legions, summoned a veteran legion from the garrison of Cilicia and 2 from Syria composed of the remains of Crassus' army, making 11 legions in all, of perhaps 50,000 men. To this nucleus he had added a large body of local light-armed troops and of cavalry, mostly from the eastern client and subject states of Rome.

The headquarters of the army had been at Berrhoea in the southeast part of Macedon, where it was easily supplied from the resources of the East (see Map 2). There the army was trained during the summer of 49 for the expected campaign of the next year, but the 2 Syrian legions were marching slowly and were to winter in Asia Minor. The principal sources of the public revenue were in the East where Pompey's name had been formidable a few years before, and every means had been taken to accumulate treasure. Dyrrhachium was selected as the main army base for the campaign of 48 and great depots of every kind of supplies were established there. To put all the vast forces to service, Pompey had drawn a great fleet to the Ionian Sea. There were the Roman vessels which had brought the Italian contingent across the Adriatic in January to which had been added the men-of-war of Egypt, Colchis, Tyre, Rhodes, Athens, Corcyra, and other Asiatic and Greek maritime states, so that in all there were nearly 500 ships. Pompey meant to assemble the entire fleet and army on the coast of Epirus during the winter of 49-48 ready for a spring campaign. Before the end of the year, Bibulus, the naval commander in chief, was at Corcyra with 110 men-of-war and 18 more at Oricum, and was able to control all the ports of Epirus by the help of their own defenses and the local levies. Although the main army had not arrived from Berrhoea where it had mobilized, the season was so far advanced that Pompey and his associates expected no activity of the enemy until spring.

Caesar Crosses the Adriatic

On arriving at Brundisium, Caesar found 12 legions and 10,000 cavalry, but very little shipping. Caesar declined to wait until spring for more ships, when Pompey would be ready, but embarked 7 small legions of only 15,000 men with 600 cavalry, and supplies reduced to a minimum. With an escort of only 12 men-of-war, Caesar took advantage of a promising wind, November 5, 49, and hoped to make a fortunate landing near Dyrrhachium. After a run of about 90 miles, having been driven by the wind to the east southeast, he arrived the next day at a convenient anchorage at the present Paleassa, about 20 miles north of Corcyra, but unfortunately 80 miles south of Dyrrhachium. The landing had to be made. The fleet of transports was seen by the hostile lookouts both at Oricum and Corcyra, but the squadron at Oricum felt itself too weak to attack and at headquarters ships were not ready for service. Thus Caesar landed without difficulty and sent his transports back the same night for the other half of his army. Unfortunately, after leaving port the ships were becalmed. By that time Bibulus at Corcyra had got his ships out of port and captured 30 transports (perhaps a quarter to a fifth of the whole number). Bibulus caused them to be burned with all on board. The cruelty with which the Pompeians habitually acted contrasted with Caesar's clemency and did nothing to gain the good will of the mass of citizens who asked only to live in security.

The risk which Caesar took was considerable, but it was not foolhardy nor nearly so great as would be the case now. There were not any scout ships on the Italian side, for their maintenance there would have been most difficult and, if there had been, they could not expect to outsail the hostile main body as scout ships do now. On the other hand, Caesar would have been glad to have landed 60 miles farther north, nearer Dyrrhachium. From such a landfall, the return of the transports would have been less perilous. Such were the uncertainties of navigation under sail and without a compass.

Upon landing Caesar moved north the same day, and took Oricum and Apollonia and then pushed for Dyrrhachium to seize the great stores which Pompey had accumulated there. Pompey himself was on the Egnatian highway with the army, and he hastened his march towards Dyrrhachium and was ahead of Caesar in arriving at the cross road about 20 miles south of Dyrrhachium. The southerly drift of the ships on the passage across the Adriatic lost Dyrrhachium and its stores for Caesar. He took position on the Apsus River and there the two armies remained facing each other for at least 3 months without undertaking active operations. Pompey delayed on account of the winter season and to complete the army's training, while Caesar's veterans were too few. He could only urge Mark Antony at Brundisium to hasten with the rest of the army.

In the meantime, Bibulus, commanding Pompey's fleet, was extremely mortified that Caesar who was his personal enemy of many years should have been able to cross. In spite of the winter weather, Bibulus now kept a close watch on all the coast to prevent supplies as well as re-enforcements from reaching Caesar. His main base was at Corcyra and his principal anchorage in the great Bay of Oricum, although he could not land there on account of the measures taken by Caesar. Although the whole of Epirus yielded allegiance to Caesar, yet the province could with difficulty support Caesar's army, which had crossed without adequate supplies. It was therefore essential for Caesar to make the enemy's blockade as ineffective as possible, so he placed patrols along the shore to prevent the blockading ships from obtaining water and firewood. Thus they were obliged to provide themselves with those necessaries from Corcyra and some ships were even reduced to collecting the dew that fell on the deck for drinking water. Bibulus sent ashore to ask to communicate with Caesar and a truce was established, during which the ships got some water, but when Caesar came from the interior to the coast, he told Bibulus that he must have free passage for his ships if Bibulus wished to supply himself with water, so the truce was broken off. In his zeal, Bibulus slept every night on board ship and soon died of exposure to the winter. Pompey did not appoint any successor to him as naval commander in chief and thereafter the four principal squadrons acted independently under general instructions from Pompey. It is reasonable to assume, although the Commentaries do not say so, that blockade runners were able to supplement local supplies for the use of Caesar's army, through Oricum and Apollonia.

At Brundisium every effort was made to get the army across. Calenus who had brought the transports back from Paleassa actually was under way with the second convoy when he received a letter from Caesar telling him not to attempt the passage as the blockade was effective.

Soon Libo with his division of 50 ships crossed from Oricum Gulf to Brundisium to blockade the expedition in its port of departure. By surprise, he seized a small island just outside the port and caught some supply ships which he burned. He landed some soldiers and wrote back to Pompey, somewhat prematurely, that he could haul the rest of the fleet ashore and clean their bottoms, a frequent measure in former times when foul bottoms made hard work for rowers.

But Antony took counter-measures. On 60 boats belonging to large ships, he mounted osier parapets, manned them with good crews, and placed them along the shore. He then sent 2 triremes to show themselves outside the port. Libo sent 5 quadriremes against them, which followed them so far in that the launches had their chance to jump at the quadriremes; 1 was taken and the others driven off. The island base which Libo had seized was without water and Antony imitated Caesar's measure of putting cavalry posts along the shore so that Libo could not obtain water and had to abandon his station on the Italian side.

Antony Crosses; Operations Begin

Brundisium was now an open port, yet Caesar found the matter of supplies in Illyria very trying and sent to hasten the departure of the second division in order to begin operations. Particularly, he was anxious to have the sailing transports attempt the passage before the advancing spring should make it easy for the rowing men-of-war to get at them. At last, "before the winter was gone" (at the end of February), Antony sailed with a good southerly breeze, having 4 legions numbering 20,000 men and 800 cavalry. The next morning the wind carried him too far north, past both Apollonia and Dyrrhachium, and 16 Rhodian ships pursued out of the latter port. The wind fell enough to permit the Rhodians to approach within range of archery, but then sprang up again and Antony's

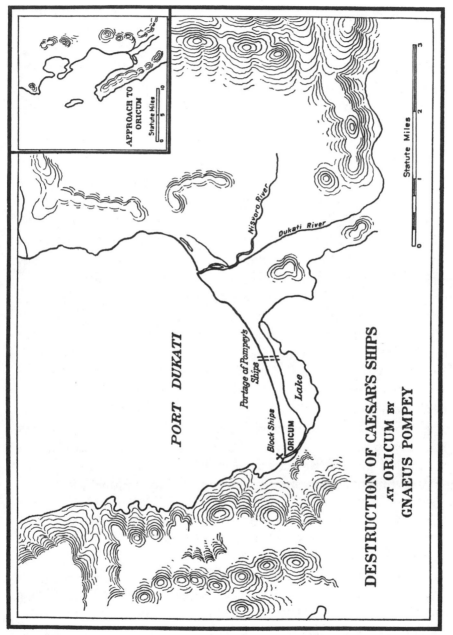

APPROACH TO ORICUM

Statute Miles

PORT DUKATI

Nisvoro River

Dukati River

Portage of Pompey's Ships

Block Ships

ORICUM

Lake

Statute Miles

DESTRUCTION OF CAESAR'S SHIPS
AT ORICUM BY
GNAEUS POMPEY

MAP 26.

entire force drew away and landed at Nymphae, 3 miles north of Lissus, while the wind increasing to a gale threw all the Rhodian ships on the coast and wrecked them. Both Caesar and Pompey put their armies in motion towards Antony who avoided the enemy and made a junction with Caesar, whose supplies were even scantier after this addition.

Caesar sent 3½ legions to the interior, 2 to oppose the Syrian legions which were now approaching under Scipio, and the others to Greece to forage.

Siege of Dyrrhachium

With the rest of his smaller army, Caesar threw himself between Pompey and Dyrrhachium, but Pompey retired to the shore at Petra, 5 or 6 miles southeast of Dyrrhachium, where he had a fairly sheltered anchorage. There Caesar attempted to throw siege works entirely around Pompey's position. The purpose was no doubt twofold. It prevented Pompey from interfering with Caesar's forage parties and kept the strong Pompeian cavalry from adequate pasture; and besides it was a challenge to Pompey to fight before his army training was complete. In addition, Caesar diverted Pompey's best water supply. Pompey merely shipped the greater part of his cavalry to Dyrrhachium and supplied his army readily by sea from Dyrrhachium, while the Caesarians were reduced to roots which they ate without losing heart.

Caesar extended his fortifications in a line of contravallation reaching around Pompey 16 miles from shore to shore. Of Caesar's long drawn-out and hazardous position, Pompey said that he would forfeit all claim to military skill if he suffered Caesar to withdraw without great disaster. Pompey's fortifications were impregnable and delay of action was favorable to him.

A minor mischance soon occurred to Caesar. After Antony joined him, Caesar called his coastal garrisons to him for which he had little further use, but left three cohorts at Oricum, apparently to protect the transports which were lying there. Acilius who commanded at Oricum put the ships in the harbor behind the city. One transport he sank in the narrow harbor entrance to block it. On another he built a tower, manned it with many soldiers, and placed it beside the sunken obstacle to keep the enemy from removing it.

Attack on Oricum

The withdrawal of Caesar's garrisons from the seacoast made it comparatively easy for the Pompeian squadrons to lie in the sheltered Gulf of Oricum, and get water. Young Gnaeus Pompey, commanding the Egyptian squadron, now attempted to destroy Caesar's ships. He assaulted the town by sea and land as a diversion and made his main attack on the guard ship which he assailed with others having still higher towers and fed those ships continually with fresh men while he sent divers to empty the sunken ship of the stones which filled her. In the end he towed her away. Overcome by showers of arrows, the men in the guard ship had at last to take to their boats and their ship was captured. Yet the Pompeians did not enter the port by the channel. During the fighting Pompey got possession of a hill which enabled him to drag some triremes across the tongue of land joining the city to the mainland and he succeeded in burning the unmanned ships which had been put in shelter. He then withdrew with some loss and went to Lissus where he had equal success in destroying a part of Antony's transport ships which had not been sent back to Brundisium. Thus Caesar's scanty means of communicating with Italy were still further reduced.

As the spring advanced, Caesar's situation improved relatively to that of Pompey. The detachments sent out to Macedon and Greece were well received and the approach of the new harvest season assured the Caesarians of an early increase in the food supply. On the other hand, Pompey's large cavalry force was greatly suffering from insufficient forage, owing to Caesar's blockade on land, and the ships could not secure enough from other ports, so action was forced on Pompey to preserve his superiority in cavalry, on which he greatly relied.

Pompey now ventured an attack, making use of his shipping. The plan of the attack was suggested by two Gallic noblemen of Caesar's army, whose men had complained to Caesar that their chiefs were embezzling their troop supplies. The offenders deserted to Pompey and told him in detail of the condition of Caesar's works. The line of contravallation rested on the sea and Caesar feared that Pompey might send a party by boat to land and attack from the rear. Consequently, he had built a line of circumvallation parallel to the main works and about 1,000 yards south. This second line was not finished and Caesar was extending it as he could. He meant also to build a rampart along the beach between the ends of the two main lines to make all safe; but nothing had been done on it. After learning the situation from the deserters, Pompey prepared for an attack at dawn on the southern sea end of Caesar's works. The northern line had a 10-foot rampart and a 15-foot ditch. Against it Pompey assembled 60 cohorts. The southern line was similar but not quite so strong. To attack it Pompey used his light troops, who depended on missile weapons, and were provided with fascines to fill up the ditch. They went by boat and landed south of the lines to attack simultaneously with the legions. The Caesarians had only stones to reply to the enemy's missiles and against them Pompey had prepared his men by mounting osier buffers on their helmets. After a little, an assaulting party in boats appeared and landed along the beach between the two lines and moved up, taking all the Caesarians in flank, and driving them back. That was decisive. The Caesarians lost much ground, but Antony came down from a central position with 12 cohorts. Pompey now was satisfied and merely secured his gains, having now an open road to the interior for forage and good communication with his ships. The day was early and Caesar, having been summoned by smoke signal, decided on an immediate counter-attack. It went wrong and Caesar was very seriously defeated with heavy loss, but Pompey did not push pursuit.

Caesar Retreats from Dyrrhachium

Caesar felt that his army was not able immediately to fight again and withdrew to the interior, although his soldiers implored him to let them show their worth. It was early in May. It is worth noting that Caesar's lack of sea power made it necessary for him to send large detachments into the interior to collect supplies which he could not draw from Italy in the face of Pompey's fleet. Those detachments might have turned the scale in his favor at Dyrrhachium.

By skillful logistics Caesar lost touch with Pompey's army on the fourth day of his retreat and Pompey had to decide on his plans for utilizing his great success. He had three possibilities as Caesar himself says: (1) direct pursuit of Caesar; (2) an abandonment of Caesar and his army in order to cross to Italy and occupy the seat of the military and political power of both parties; (3) he could hold his present position and, utilizing

fleet and army, he could cut off all Caesar's ports of supply and deprive
him of communication with Italy. As for Caesar's corresponding action,
he would be glad to have an action in the open country. If Pompey were
to go to Italy, Caesar could go there by land and fight at Rome or in
North Italy. Finally, if Pompey were to remain on the Adriatic coast,
Caesar would pursue Scipio who was now approaching Pompey along the
Egnatian high road.

Although some of Pompey's ablest generals urged him to leave Caesar
and cross to Italy and seize the center of political strength, yet Pompey
cut adrift from his fleet and its ready supplies and followed Caesar. There
were several reasons for preferring that course. In the first place, he was
not the undisputed master of his political party as was Caesar. The pseudo-
senate which accompanied Pompey was very anxious to punish Caesar and
finish the war by his destruction. The army also was greatly intoxicated by
its victory and wanted battle. Although Pompey's inaction during the winter season had good grounds when Caesar had scanty rations, it had not
brought success and its continuance would be unjustifiable during the
harvest season when Caesar had supplies. The postponement of a conclusion
by crossing to Italy was also rejected. The decision was doubly wise because, as Pompey knew and said, a great part of his military strength lay
in his mobility based on sea power which he drew chiefly from the East,
and anywhere in the Balkan peninsula he would not be far from sea-borne
supplies. The experience of previous campaigns, notably that of Alexander, showed that the fleets of client states fell away when their home
ports were taken by the enemy. If Pompey were to cross to Italy, Caesar
would be in a position to profit by the wealth of the East and by its fleet.
Like Hamlet and Laertes in a later duel, Caesar and Pompey would
exchange weapons and Caesar would seize the decisive blade of sea power
with which Pompey had not struck.

Battle of Pharsalus

Caesar moved by Apollonia to place his wounded in safety and get
the treasure held there to pay his soldiers. He then struck into Thessaly
whose fertile plains promised him food, there to join with Domitius Calvinus and his 2 legions which came south from Macedon to meet him (see
Map 2). Pompey marched directly towards Macedon and met his father-

in-law, Scipio, at Larissa, and thus each army united its forces, before coming into contact at Pharsalus. Pompey was now easily supplied from the sea via Larissa or Pherae. There the armies remained facing each other in their entrenchments for about a month while Pompey again applied his plan of delay. This he was to do more effectively than at Dyrrhachium for his overwhelming cavalry superiority enabled him to restrict Caesar's foraging parties, and Pompey himself was only some 30 miles in an airline from the great port of Demetrias. Although Pompey offered battle frequently, it was only under very advantageous circumstances of ground.

Caesar was on the point of moving to cut Pompey's road to Larissa and supply his army from an unexhausted neighborhood, when Pompey again threw away the advantage he held in the matter of over-seas supply and offered battle on more equal conditions of ground. The group of politicians unskilled with war who surrounded Pompey wanted immediate battle. Already they were deciding on the successor to Caesar as Pontifex Maximus (a life office) and were saying that Pompey desired to prolong his command over so many consulars and play the part of Agamemnon.

So, just as Pompey's plan began to distress Caesar, he yielded, as was said at the time, to the pressure of the nobles, and advanced across a little stream which had withheld Caesar from battle. Yet it is probable that Pompey could gain little by further delay, although he told his soldiers he was fighting to please them rather than because he thought it wise. He had no further re-enforcements to expect after Scipio joined and as Caesar had managed to keep his army in shape through the winter season, he would surely be able to do so now that the harvest was coming in, and it was possible that re-enforcements from Italy might arrive for him. Delay was unprofitable to both opponents. On the other hand, Dio tells us that, although Pompey usually made every preparation for battle and did not discount his success, in this his last battle, he thought himself superior and made no thorough preparations, counting on his money and his control of the sea which he ruled even after the battle. Pompey had 45,000 infantry, 7,000 cavalry, and 4,600 light-armed troops. Although Caesar had brought 35,000 men across the Adriatic, he had on the battle field only 22,000 infantry and 1,000 cavalry. It was now a question of superior numbers on Pompey's side against veterans whose morale had been restored

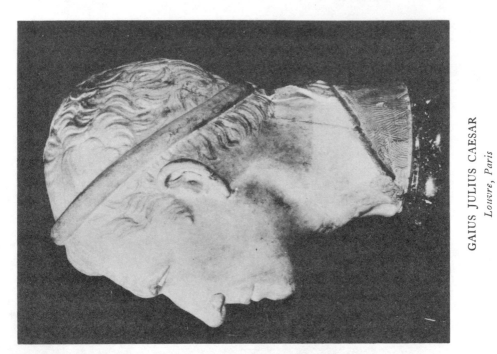

GAIUS JULIUS CAESAR
Louvre, Paris

GNAEUS POMPEIUS MAGNUS
Palazzo Spada

by Caesar's careful handling since the defeat at Dyrrhachium a month before.

The tactics of the battle are not germane to the object of this study. It is enough to say that on June 6, 48, by skillful arrangements Caesar drove his enemy from the field and then took his entrenched camp. When Pompey saw his line broken, he withdrew to the camp; when that too was stormed, he fled in disguise to the seacoast and thence to Egypt where he hoped to get continued support from that kingdom. According to Caesar's account of the battle, the enemy lost 15,000 killed and 24,000 surrendered. Many fugitives escaped to Corcyra and Dyrrhachium where Cato commanded and where 300 ships of war were ready for service.

The Pompeian Fleet in the Pharsalus Campaign

In one particular Caesar's victory at Pharsalus resembled that of Gettysburg in our Civil War. It marked the turn of the tide in the course of the war, but that it did so was not at once fully realized. There was another great army growing up in Africa which Caesar had yet to subdue, but he was now without the shipping to reach it. He made it his immediate task to organize Greece and the eastern provinces and pursue Pompey, and so cause the hostile sea power to melt away or come over to him as he overran the East and took possession of its seaports.

Let us first follow the fate of the Pompeian fleet and fragments of the defeated army which, for the moment, Caesar was neglecting owing to lack of shipping. Previous to the last battle at Dyrrhachium, one of Pompey's four principal squadrons, that of Marcus Octavius, had been operating north on the Dalmatian coast. After his failure to take Salonae in 49, Octavius had returned to Dyrrhachium for the winter. In the spring or early summer of 48, after Caesar had sent Q. Cornificius to reoccupy Illyria with two legions as successor to C. Antony, Octavius again took his squadron north to encourage the inhabitants in their resistance to Cornificius, and did not finally abandon the coast till the following year, as will be told later. The other three squadrons had been blockading the coast of Epirus early in 48 against Caesar's efforts to obtain supplies from Italy.

The success of Dyrrhachium and the retreat of Caesar brought immediate change in the distribution of the blockading squadrons. The expectations of the Pompeians were greatly raised. While the assembly of leaders was debating whether to go to Italy or pursue Caesar, Pompey directed two squadrons, under Laelius and Cassius to proceed to Italy and destroy the hostile ships building there, and open the route to Italy. The third or Egyptian squadron, under his son Gnaeus, Pompey retained for local service and the fourth under Octavius was already on the Dalmatian coast where it remained.

Laelius went to Brundisium and occupied the island opposite the entrance as Libo had done in the previous winter, and Vatinius at Brundisium replied, as Antony had done, by patrols along the coast to keep the blockaders from getting water. Laelius lost a ship or two by rashness, but could not be driven off because it was now the good season and he had little difficulty in having water sent to him from Corcyra. Neither his losses nor the lack of necessaries caused him to renounce his stand and return to base until after the news of Pharsalus.

Cassius went to Sicily and, in attacking the ships which Caesar was gathering at Messana and at Vibo, Cassius was more enterprising than Laelius (see Map 10). He arrived at Messana unexpectedly and immediately sent in fire ships under sail. As the Caesarian ships were unready, 35 were burned, of which 20 were decked. The alarm in the city was great and, with a little time, Cassius would have taken it; but the news of Pompey's great defeat arrived opportunely for the city. Cassius sailed for Vibo where he again made use of fire ships with a favoring wind but with less success. He sent in 40 fire ships and 5 ships caught from them, but as the flames extended, the convalescent soldiers who were acting as ship guards went on board the others and got them under way and took 4 of Cassius' ships. Shortly afterward Cassius' soldiers heard of Pompey's defeat and would no longer fight, so Cassius, like Laelius, sailed back to base. Pompey's powerful squadrons were now mere marauders without army support.

The base, however, was no longer at Dyrrhachium. When news came there that the army had been captured or dispersed on June 6 and that Pompey was missing, Cato transferred the base to Corcyra which was secure, for it was an island and Caesar's fleet was negligible. But the transfer was made with great loss. The soldiers at Dyrrhachium became unmanageable and, as Cicero who was present, wrote to a friend; the soldiers looted the store houses, spilled the grain on the roads, and burned the ships which were not ready to go. At Corcyra fugitives began to come in and the squadrons reassembled, but the fleet began to break up, for the Asiatic and Egyptian contingents went home as Caesar approached their own countries.

The Roman ships were the chief remnant of Pompey's great maritime force. As Cato shifted his headquarters and the ships farther south to Patras in Greece, it was not difficult for Caesar to send Antony with a large part of the victorious army back to Italy to rule there in Caesar's name and make his hold there doubly sure. Cato did not stay long at Patras. Caesar's lieutenant in Greece approached him and, as the bad season drew near, Cato transferred his entire force to Africa to add to the republican army there, but lost a great part of his ships in bad weather on the southern coasts. Africa was now the main center of republican military strength.

Caesar's Pursuit of Pompey

Turning now to Caesar's movement—after a day or two at Pharsalus, he took up the pursuit of Pompey and the restoration of Roman authority over the districts in Asia Minor, Syria, and Egypt which had looked to Pompey as the embodiment of that authority. Pompey himself had taken passage on a chance ship which he found on the coast of Thessaly. After a brief delay at Amphipolis to pick up a little money from his friends, he sailed for Lesbos where he took his wife and younger son Sextus on board and continued his flight to the south. Urging a squadron of cavalry to a forced march, Caesar arrived at Amphipolis, 180 miles distant, 8 days after the battle and found that Pompey had escaped.

Pompey proceeded to the shore of Pamphylia where he met a number of refugees and there was much discussion as to the proper course. He heard of Cato's removal to Africa and might have gone there to take charge once more of the republican forces, had he not lost his wits at Pharsalus in the first lost battle of his life, and left the camp in disguise when the victorious army attacked its entrenchments. He had thereby lost prestige and probably was unwilling to meet the reproaches of the Senators whom he had deserted. He went on to Cyprus, collected money from rich Romans there, enrolled some slaves as soldiers, and decided to go on to Egypt, of which kingdom the Senate had long before appointed him guardian and where there were still many of his former soldiers. In Egypt he thought he might rely on his prestige in the East and on his escort to secure hospitality, and there he arrived July 24.

Having found that Pompey had left Europe, Caesar's pursuit necessarily became slower, for he had to have troops and also ships to transport them. He could no longer expect to take republican soldiers into his ranks as he advanced, for Pompey had stripped the East of its garrisons to fight in Thessaly and all were now in Caesar's rear. He had to wait for a legion from Pharsalus to come up, and from Achaia he ordered another to Rhodes, which island sent its submission and placed its ships at his disposal. Caesar himself went to Sestos, the usual ferry point to Asia, and there a certain Cassius submitted to him with 10 ships. The story is that Cassius met Caesar crossing the Hellespont in a skiff and that the news of Pharsalus was such a shock to all the fleet that they hastened to surrender without resistance. Yet as Pompey and other fugitives were telling the coasts of Asia of their defeat and as the presence of Caesar and his escort confirmed the news along the shores of Thrace, it is clear that any squadron passing, as ships then did, from port to port must have learned of the event before arriving in the Hellespont. Cassius' surrender to Caesar in person must therefore have been a prearranged matter [3] Caesar did not wait to accumulate a large force before following Pompey. With 2 weak legions, numbering together only 3,200 men and 800 cavalry, escorted by 10 Rhodian ships and 25 others, he set out for Egypt where he arrived July 28, only to find that Pompey, 4 days previously, had been killed on the beach as he landed to ask for hospitality, while his wife looked on from the ship. The murder was owing to the civil war which had recently broken out between the partisans of the two co-heirs of the kingdom of Egypt, Cleopatra and her younger brother, Ptolemy.

CAMPAIGN OF EGYPT

Caesar remained in Egypt to settle the dispute. It has been much discussed why he remained and, indeed, why he did not return to Italy immediately after Pharsalus instead of sending Antony to represent him at Rome. Great political questions were awaiting him at Rome, the cancellation of debts among other matters, for Italy was very poor owing to the

---

[3] To leave Vibo after the battle of Pharsalus and arrive at the Hellespont before Caesar crossed about June 20 or 25 was a very fast voyage. The Cassius at Vibo was not the same man as the one at the Hellespont.

disturbances of the civil war. Besides, the republicans were organizing in Africa. The answer is that the money necessary to restore prosperity to the Italians and the fleets necessary to take an army to Africa both had to be found in the East and Egypt was the richest country with the greatest fleet in all the East. The network of Roman trade and finance which brought profit to Rome and the tribute which did away with taxes depended on the Roman legions and of many of them the country had been stripped. Already Pharnaces, King of Pontus, was trespassing on Roman provinces. Whatever might be the political party questions in Rome, the maintenance of Roman prosperity depended upon the restoration of Roman authority in the East and the consequent renewal of tribute to Rome for the settlement of the economic difficulties of government.

Both Romans and Egyptians expected that Caesar would proceed west to the province of Africa to attack the Pompeian army there, but in accordance with his practice of settling each difficulty as he met it, he stayed in Alexandria, where he expected that his prestige as Consul and as victor would cause the people to accept him as the arbitrator in the dispute between Cleopatra and her brother. As Consul he had the right to require Egypt to arrange for the payment of the debts which the late King Ptolemy had contracted at Rome, and Caesar much needed the money. Accordingly, he occupied the royal palace in the northeast part of the city. The appearance of the consular forces roused an outbreak in the city and on successive days many soldiers were killed. Caesar, who was held in port by the northern winds, sent to Asia to summon the legions which he had organized from Pompey's soldiers. Without waiting for them to arrive, he asked the two young sovereigns to submit their dispute to him. Ptolemy came in and was held practically as a hostage, but Cleopatra was kept away by the ministers of her brother. She found means to pass to Caesar's presence rolled up in a carpet and carried on a slave's back. Her arguments, offered in privacy, persuaded Caesar to adjudge the kingdom of Egypt in accordance with the late King's will to Cleopatra and her husband-brother. Her liaison with Caesar was a most important political event. Thereupon the ministers of Ptolemy called up the Egyptian army of some 20,000 men, which included a number of the old Roman army of occupation, men who had married Egyptians and had lost their loyalty to Rome (see Map 27).

The city of Alexandria, numbering over 250,000 free inhabitants, besides slaves, lay on the sea shore west of the western or Canopic mouth of the Nile. It was walled and extended along the shore for 3 miles and reached about a mile back from the coast beyond which there was a marshy district and still farther a lake. Abreast the city and 0.75 mile away, a narrow island (Pharos) about 2 miles long lay parallel to the shore. Towards the southwest the axis of the island was prolonged under water for some miles by shoals which had several navigable passages through them. Pharos was an important suburb, the inhabitants of which were in the habit of pillaging all the ships driven ashore on the outside. The sheltered anchorage space between the island and the city was divided into two harbors by a causeway joining the middle of the island to the city, through which were two waterways, each with its overspanning bridge, permitting ship movements between the two harbors. The northeast, the New, or Great, Harbor, was protected by a breakwater 1,500 yards long, running from the mainland nearly to the end of the island and enclosing an anchorage area of perhaps 900 acres. The only opening in the breakwater adjoined the island and was indicated and protected by the great fortified lighthouse which took its name from the island and became the word for all later lighthouses in languages derived from Latin. The old harbor on the other side of the causeway had the principal Alexandrian naval dockyard.

Achillas, the Egyptian general, full of confidence in his army and feeling contempt for Caesar's scanty numbers which could not occupy all the city, seized the parts which were not held by the Romans and even attacked the palace in which Caesar was living. Caesar resisted the attack by street fighting and at the same time had to defend himself against attacks from the harbor side, and prevent the enemy from seizing the Egyptian fleet, which lay at the palace dockyard in the Great Harbor and included 50 ships which had just returned from Corcyra. Besides, there were 22 ships belonging to the local station. If the seizure had been accomplished, the fleet of Caesar would have been captured and the Egyptians would have been masters of the port and of the sea, and the Roman army could have had neither supplies nor re-enforcements. The battle on one side was for a decisive victory and on the other for salvation. At last Caesar was successful and, knowing that with his small force he could not guard everything, he burned all the Egyptian ships. While fighting at other points, Caesar also sent to capture Pharos (the fortified lighthouse) and put a garrison there, for afterwards, while holding the lighthouse point, he could receive supplies and men from outside, whereas elsewhere the fighting was without decisive importance.

Now that Caesar was master of the more important points, he fortified them during the night so that he held a strong position within the town.

Hostilities having begun, Caesar sent to Rhodes, Cilicia, and Syria for all his fleet (that is, for the squadrons whose states had gone over to him since Pharsalus), and also he sent elsewhere for men and engines of war. He leveled much of the city and took the ruins within his lines, so that he would occupy a part of the city where it came nearest to the marshy plain which offered water and forage. On their side the Alexandrians showed the greatest activity and their industrial city gave them every kind of munitions. The leading citizens headed the defense, saying that Caesar proposed to reduce their kingdom to a Roman province.

Achillas was murdered by the effort of Arsinoe, the younger sister of King Ptolemy, and her governor, the eunuch Ganymede, took charge of the army. He cut off the conduits giving water to the city and Caesar's men were greatly disturbed by it, but he reassured them by telling them that water could always be brought by ship either from the East or West, for the wind would always be good for one route. He then caused wells to be dug which gave a good supply, after a single night's labor.

Two days afterward a squadron carrying the XXXVIIth legion, formed out of Pompey's soldiers, and supplies of arms, ballistae, and arrows arrived on the coast a few miles west of the city. There the ships lay for some days as the wind was contrary. The anchorage was excellent, but the ships began to suffer for water and sent a boat to tell Caesar of their arrival. He ran down himself to see what was necessary, taking all his ships with him. As he was to be gone for some hours he did not venture to strip the defenses of their garrison in order to complete his crews with their complement of soldiers.

It seems evident that Caesar must have left Alexandria because he thought it important to meet those late soldiers of the other party and to establish his personal ascendancy over them before he sent them into battle. On reaching a point known as Chersonese, Caesar sent his rowers on shore to water the ships (it cannot have been so plentiful in town), and some of them, going off to pillage, were captured by a cavalry patrol and the enemy learned Caesar was there in person with no combatants on board. It was a chance not to be neglected and Ganymede filled with soldiers all the ships that were ready to move, and went out to meet Caesar who was returning with his squadron.

Naval Battle West of Alexandria

The Consul wished to avoid an action as he had few soldiers, besides it was late in the afternoon, so that the approaching darkness would be favorable to the enemy who knew the locality, and also in the dark his own voice and presence would be without effect in stimulating his men. So Caesar hugged the shore, hoping the enemy would not close. A Rhodian galley got too far ahead and was noticed by the enemy who fell upon her with 4 decked ships and several lighter ones. Caesar felt that her misfortune was the proper reward of her fault, but still he could not permit the shame of seeing her taken without aid. The other Rhodians attacked vigorously to rescue her. Always in the lead, both in skill and courage, they endeavored to make good the fault of their comrade by assuming the weight of the battle. The outcome was fortunate; an Egyptian tetrere was taken, a second was sunk, and 2 others lost their soldiers. Night fell before all the fleet could be taken. The contrary wind moderated, and Caesar returned to port with his victorious galleys towing the transports.

The Alexandrians were dismayed because they were not overcome by soldierly courage but by nautical skill on which they prided themselves, so they hauled their remaining ships on shore where they could be defended from the tops of the houses and they laid obstructions along the shore. Nevertheless, when Ganymede pledged himself in the Council to replace the lost ships and find others, the people recovered and with great diligence began to repair the ships. Although they had already lost in the port and at the arsenal over 110 ships, they began to rebuild, for they knew that if they were stronger on the water they could cut off provisions and help for the Romans. At all the mouths of the Nile there were customs ships on station and in the arsenal there were many old ships; these were all made to serve. Oars were lacking. The people stripped the roofs off public buildings and made oars of the rafters. The resources of a great

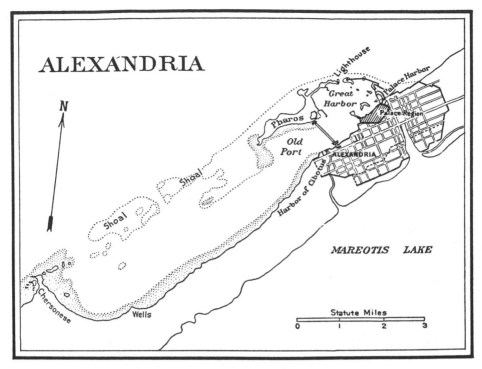

ALEXANDRIA

N

Lighthouse

Palace Harbor

Great
Harbor

Palace Region

Pharos

Old
Port

ALEXANDRIA

Harbor of Cibotus

Shoal

Shoal

Chersonese

Wells

MAREOTIS   LAKE

Statute Miles

0   1   2   3

MAP 27.

city sufficed for all. To be sure, it was not necessary to equip for distant service, since the fighting was in the harbor.

SECOND NAVAL BATTLE

After having tried their oars and exercised in the old port, they embarked their best soldiers and were ready with 22 tetreres and 5 penteres besides a good number of lighter ships and open boats. In the New Harbor Caesar had 9 Rhodian ships (1 had been lost), 8 from Pontus, 5 from Lycia, and 12 from Asia. Among them were 5 penteres and 10 tetreres, the others were smaller and most were undecked.

Caesar relied on the bravery of his soldiers and decided to attack.[4] He took his fleet around the Pharos and formed outside the western line of shoals in two groups 2,000 feet from each other, corresponding to two

---

[4] The chief authority is *Alexandrian War.*

channels through, which was a proper distance for deployment. (As there were 17 ships in each group, the distance from ship to ship after deployment into line would be 40 yards.) The Rhodians were on the right, the Pontics on the left, and the smaller ships were in the rear as reserve. The Alexandrians promptly got under way and faced the Romans on the other side of the shoals with 22 ships in the line and the rest in reserve as a second line. Besides these ships a great number of small craft put out with torches and reeds filled with sulphur, hoping to alarm the Romans by their number and cries and the sight of the incendiary devices.

Each of the two opponents hesitated long about entering the passages through the shoals, for the exit and subsequent deployment would be disadvantageous, as well as the retreat if that became necessary. Euphranor commanded the galleys of Rhodes. As the Roman account says, he was Greek with the courage and greatness of soul of a Roman. His skill and courage made him the choice of his countrymen. Seeing the doubt of the Consul he said,

> Caesar, you fear that the leaders going through will have to fight before the others can come to their support. Let the Rhodians take this risk; we will meet the onset of the enemy and show ourselves worthy of your confidence until the others can get through. As for those fellows there we cannot permit them to dare us longer.

Caesar praised him and gave the signal for battle. Four Rhodians passed through. Surrounded and charged by the enemy as they issued from the passage, they made good and, by a skillful maneuver, they deployed and were so well handled that none lost her oars or exposed her broadside in spite of their scanty number, and all kept their rams towards the enemy. During that encounter the rest got through also and then the space was narrow for the water was not everywhere deep enough aand there was no room for maneuver.

The outcome lay in the valor of the soldiers, as the Romans always wished. By that time there was not a man of either side in the city who did not forget the siege and run to the highest place to see the fight and pray for victory. If the battle were to go against the Romans, it would be total destruction, but a defeat of the Egyptians might be remedied. The handful of Romans were fighting for their comrades as well as for themselves. To impress that on them all Caesar had been addressing them for several days previous. So neither the maritime skill nor the valor of the Egyptians could overcome the fury of the Romans. An Alexandrian pentere and diere were taken by the Romans with all on board and 3 were sunk without any Roman loss. The rest of the Egyptian fleet fled to the city which was only a short distance away and was there protected by the soldiers on the moles and the buildings which commanded the shore.

Capture of Pharos Island

Caesar could not again risk such a battle and he resolved at any cost to seize the whole island of Pharos and the causeway connecting it to the city. His defenses on the side of the mainland were nearly finished, and he thought he could attack both the city and the island. He embarked 10 cohorts of his best light infantry and some Gaulish cavalry on a number of small craft to land on the island from the harbor side. At the same time he sent several large ships to attack the outside of the island, promising great rewards to those who were first ashore. At first the islanders did well. They fought from the roofs of the houses and the high points of the shore where climbing was difficult and at the same time 5 Egyptian galleys and some boats were skillfully handled among the shoals which were an assistance to the defense. But when the Roman pilots had sounded out the passageways, some were able to land their soldiers, others followed, and soon they charged the defenders on top of the bluff, who ran to their houses while the Egyptians on ship board deserted to look out for their own houses. Although the houses resembled those of the city itself on a smaller scale, and had a line of towers, and although the Romans had no ladders nor other material for assault, the inhabitants were too frightened for serious resistance. Those who had attempted to resist the Romans on equal terms now abandoned walls 30 feet high and threw themselves into the sea to swim to the city 0.75 mile away. Caesar allowed the soldiers to pillage and then threw down the houses near the causeway and used the material to strengthen the tower commanding the northwestern bridge in the causeway. That tower had been abandoned by the fleeing Alexandrians, but they held the other and stronger one at the bridge nearer to the city.

The Fight on the Mole

The next day, in pursuance of his plan, Caesar attacked the second bridge from his ships in the Great Harbor because, if he were master of both, the enemy could no longer pass from port to port and commit damage. Already the crews of the Roman galleys had driven the defenders of the bridge into the city by missile weapons. Caesar then landed 3 cohorts on the mole (a larger number would have had no room) and the rest stayed on board. That done, he sent to make a bridge head on the end of the causeway towards the enemy and dropped stones into the archway through which the ships passed. Enough were dropped to prevent even the smallest ships from passing, but the bridge head was still unfinished when the Alexandrians with all their troops came out of town and faced the Roman works. At the same time, they sent boats all along the length of the mole to set fire to the Roman ships which had landed the soldiers. The Romans fought to hold the bridge and the causeway, which the enemy attacked from the bridge-head tower and from the ships alongside the causeway.

While Caesar was giving all his attention to that double engagement, a great number of Roman rowers and sailors left their ships to land on the causeway, some for curiosity and others for pillage. Once there, they began to drive off the hostile ships with stones and slings and they seemed to be doing good work but, when some Alexandrians ventured to land on the causeway beyond the point where the Romans were fighting, the seamen, being unorganized and without any standards for rallying points, and having entered the struggle without any good reason, fled to their ships with too much precipitation. The Alexandrians pursued with vigor. The men who had stayed on board ship started to haul on board their landing gangways and push off from the causeway.

The soldiers of the 3 cohorts with Caesar, hearing the noise behind them and seeing the fugitives and having a hard struggle where they were, began to be afraid for their rear and left their positions to get aboard the ships. Some of the legionaries got on board vessels which sank under their weight and others were killed by the enemy. Some got aboard the more distant ships and others swam to boats, after throwing away their shields. Caesar, doing what he could to hold the people to the defense was at last obliged to go to his galley. A crowd followed him and as he could not make them take orderly positions nor push away from the causeway, he saw what was about to happen and jumped overboard and swam to the ships anchored at some distance. From there he sent boats to help and saved a few, but his own galley sank under the weight of men who ran on board. In the fight 400 legionaries and more than 400 rowers and sailors lost their lives. On the spot that the Romans lost, the Alexandrians threw up great works to complete the defense of the tower already there, and equipped it with many ballistas. They swept the boat passage which the Romans had blocked up and thereafter could pass their boats through at pleasure.

There seems now to have been a pause for some weeks, during which a division of transports with the XXXVIIIth legion was decoyed on shore at the Canopic (western) mouth of the Nile by false lights and seemingly it was in trouble. Caesar sent a detachment of the fleet under Tiberius Nero, father of the Emperor Tiberius, to meet it and this was driven off. Seemingly, on this occasion the fight was left to Euphranor, who alone engaged the Alexandrians and was lost with his ship. However, the legion arrived at Alexandria.

In the meantime a relief army made up of Asiatic contingents came through Syria under the leadership of Prince Mithridates, and after assembly at Ascalon, it moved along the coast accompanied by a fleet (see Map 17). After taking Pelusium, the fortress which guarded the eastern mouth of the Nile, the army ascended the eastern branch, crossed the Nile at the head of the Delta, and moved down the western branch towards Alexandria. The Egyptian army left Alexandria to take position near Mithridates who called to Caesar for help. The latter was already in motion. He put a detachment of his army on shipboard and sailed eastward as if he were going to follow Mithridates from Pelusium, but at dark he turned back and, sailing without lights, he landed on the peninsula known as Chersonese just west of Alexandria, and joined Mithridates on the west branch of the Nile. There was then a hard-fought battle in which the Egyptians were defeated. Many fled to the river boats and were drowned through overcrowding. The city of Alexandria then surrendered on January 15, 47.

It was expected at Rome that Caesar would immediately return there, for there had been much unrest in the city, but Caesar meant to settle the affairs of Asia before going to Italy and it was not yet suitable campaigning weather. Accordingly, he made a trip up the Nile with Cleopatra and their son was born before he set out in March for his war with Pharnaces, King of Pontus, who had decided to make something for himself out of the disorders of Rome. While Caesar was in Egypt, Pharnaces had had the advantage over Caesar's lieutenant in Asia Minor, who attempted to make head against him. With one very small legion Caesar left Alexandria. With troops he picked up on the way, he marched through Asia Minor and defeated Pharnaces at Zela in Pontus on May 20, 47, in 5 days after meeting the enemy, and announced his victory in the famous message, "I came, I saw, I conquered." He now had secured money and returned to Rome in July, 47.

NAVAL OPERATIONS IN THE ADRIATIC

After Cato transferred the remains of Pompey's army to Africa, where it was reorganizing during the Alexandrian campaign, the only activity of the senatorial opposition was in the fleet, for the Pompeian fleet had not altogether dissolved and a squadron remained on the Dalmatian coast under M. Octavius to maintain the insurrection in Illyria and cut off the communications of Italy with the East. In the spring of 47, Octavius' vessels were a serious threat to Caesar's government in Rome.

Early in the campaign of 48, Caesar directed his legate, Cornificius, to go into Illyria with 2 legions from Italy and reduce it. By ability and diligence, Cornificius did well and took some towns. When Octavius came up with his fleet, Cornificius got some ships from a city friendly to Caesar and seized some scattered ships of Octavius and was thereafter able to maintain himself through the summer. After Pharsalus, Caesar, far away in Egypt, heard that the remains of the Pompeian army were assembling to attack Cornificius and he sent Gabinius from Italy with 2 legions to aid him. It was essential not to let the opposition secure a good position between Italy and the East. It was late in the season of 48 when Gabinius crossed to Salonae (see Map 19). As it was the time of rough weather, his sailing transports had an advantage over the rowing ships of Octavius and the hostile fleet was not so strong as when Caesar had crossed the previous winter. Gabinius found the country ruined and the people indisposed to aid the new rule; so it was hard to get supplies and Gabinius raided the interior and was driven back with heavy loss of men, and soon died.

Hearing of this misadventure Octavius put to sea and besieged Salonae. He was driven off, as is alleged, by the women of the town who made a sortie by night, dressed in black and carrying torches with their hair flying. Before those furies, the besiegers fled in terror to their ships and the siege was broken, but Octavius remained still in control of Illyrian waters throughout 48.

As the year 47 began, there was great distress in Rome, for Italy was not self-supporting and it was imperative for the government of the city to free the transit of the Adriatic. Africa had furnished nothing for 2 years and the East was a principal source of food, although it, too, was pinched by the war. Octavius was attacking the Caesarian ports of the Adriatic by sea and, sometimes, with the help of the natives, by land. Accordingly, at the opening of navigation in 47, Vatinius at Brundisium, decided to attack him in order to clear the route to Rome.

Although Vatinius was ill, he overcame the difficulties of the season and of his own health. He had few ships but sent to Achaia to get some. As time was pressing, he put rams on his transport ships of which he had many, though small. These he joined to his own men-of-war and manned all by the best of the veterans who had remained at Brundisium through illness when the army crossed the year before. He crossed to Illyria and, passing by the towns which declined to yield immediately, he hastened to reach Octavius who was blockading Epidaurum (Ragusa Vecchia), by land and sea. Octavius withdrew on his approach, and having heard that the enemy's ships were small transports, he stopped at Tauris, a small island opposite Lesina, and lay in wait.

Vatinius arrived there in pursuit, not knowing the enemy's presence. Owing to bad weather, his ships were scattered, when Vatinius, leading his squadron, saw through the haze a vessel full of soldiers charging him. At this he doused sail, cleared for action, and hoisted the battle signal. Although surprised, the Caesarians were quickly ready, the enemy were already prepared. Vatinius realized the inferiority of his ships in numbers and size and resolved to attack first. His quinquereme fell on the quadrireme of Octavius and the latter lost its ram and was held by the wreckage.

The battle grew general in a very small area around the leaders as each hastened to help his friends. Vatinius' men were better soldiers and with admirable courage they quickly boarded and soon won. Octavius' ship sank and others were captured or water logged, and the soldiers were killed or driven overboard. Octavius, wounded, got in a boat which sank under its crowd, but he reached an escort ship which escaped in the rough weather. Vatinius entered the port which Octavius had just left, having taken 1 quinquereme, 2 triremes, 8 biremes, and many rowers. The next day he repaired damages and then pursued to Issa (Lissa) whose townspeople were much attached to Octavius. On his arrival they came out to surrender and said Octavius was off for Greece and Africa. Thus Vatinius cleared away the last of the hostile fleet and pacified Illyria which he turned over to Cornificius. That victory opened the way for free communication of Rome with Asia and its grain supply, and gave to Caesar the control of the sea, necessary for him to pass into Africa the next year and destroy the senatorial army there.

CAESAR'S AFRICAN CAMPAIGN

On Caesar's return to Rome in the first half of July, 47, he found much political unrest. Antony, who had been governing Italy since the battle of Pharsalus, had made enemies; a strong republican army had gathered in Africa; and Spain was unquiet owing to the excesses committed there by Caesar's governor, Cassius Longinus, after the battle of Ilerda, and the legions in Spain, which had originally been Pompey's, were negotiating with Scipio in Africa. Caesar decided to strike at the republican army in Africa without delay. He could not permit public opinion in Rome to develop against him while he remained inactive.

It will be recollected that at the outbreak of the civil war, there had been 3 legions there under Varus, which had taken up the republican cause and defeated Curio. After Pharsalus, the remains of Pompey's fleets and armies drifted there, accessions were drawn from Spain, and senatorial sympathizers joined from Italy, so that while Caesar was in the East, the Roman troops in Africa were increased to 10 legions, of perhaps 35,000 men, besides light infantry and 10,000 cavalry. The fleet of 500 ships which had been Pompey's in 49 had much shrunken. The number in Africa is not clear from the ancient sources, but was certainly not less than 55 and perhaps may have been 60. Besides the Roman army, Juba, King of Numidia, had an army of 4 legions armed after the Roman fashion, and he also had a strong force of cavalry, in all perhaps 30,000 men. On the other hand, the two brothers, Bogud and Bocchus, chiefs of Mauritania west of Numidia, were ready to take Caesar's part and attack Juba's territories, making a useful diversion, and they were much aided by Sitius, a Roman adventurer in those parts, who raised a force of his own and looked to Caesar for reward. The Republican party in Africa had attempted nothing beyond some naval raids on Sicily and Sardinia.

It may be asked why that powerful army had not taken advantage of Caesar's absence in the East to cross to Italy before his return and attempt to seize the capital and political center. In the first place the Republicans had no brilliant military leaders who were in a position to make the political decision to move on Rome. Labienus, who had been trained in Caesar's campaigns in Gaul and was an excellent soldier, was not prominent politically. There was no one in the camp capable of taking a great resolution. All were jealous of each other and they preferred to continue training and wait on developments in Rome and in Spain. Besides, they could not count on Juba, who, although an irreconcilable enemy of Caesar, yet might not prove a trustworthy friend of the Republicans should their army leave Africa. The advance into Italy might entail the loss of their present base. It probably seemed better to the Republicans to let Caesar cross the water, which he promptly decided to do. He remained little over 2 months in Rome, during which time he arranged civil affairs and put down an insurrection of the legions, among them his favorite 10th legion which demanded discharge with land grants. He met the 10th legion and granted the soldiers all their demands, but addressed them as "quirites" (citizens). To those veterans, proud of their service, the term was mortifying and they returned at once to duty. The mutiny was then ended.

Late in September 6 legions, of which 5 were recruits, had assembled at Lilybaeum ready for the African campaign. Although Caesar expected to take 4 more veteran legions, they had not yet arrived at the port of embarkation and Caesar determined to sail, on October 8, 47, with the men he had, rather than let the enemy get news of his preparations before his arrival in Africa (see Map 20). By his early departure, he would get into Africa with little risk of winter storms on the passage.

It may be noticed that, although ocean traffic habitually ceased in the winter months, yet Caesar was always ready to force the season and to profit thereby. Now again, Caesar gained by his extraordinary celerity. The hostile fleet had already been laid up for the coming winter and was not ready for immediate service, and Caesar was off before the enemy expected him. He departed from Lilybaeum with 6 legions of about 25,000 men and 2,000 cavalry embarked in the transports. He had also 7 cohorts of veterans on board the escort of men-of-war, which may therefore have amounted to some 40 to 60 ships. What Caesar's entire fleet may have numbered we are not told by the ancient historians, but it was certainly much stronger than that of the enemy, for the latter never ventured on a formal battle. Sea power had definitely and decisively passed to Caesar, who now added Gallic ships to those of the East and of Italy, and Caesar must have had over 100 men-of-war in that campaign, besides the local squadrons everywhere which remained in home waters to protect commerce against pirates.

P. Scipio Nasica, the hostile commander in chief, lay at Utica with 8 legions and the fleet. Two legions under Considius garrisoned the strongly fortified port of Hadrumetum where Hannibal had landed his army in the campaign of 203. There was a small garrison at Thapsus. Juba, with his 4 legions, was still in his own country, somewhat sulky that he was not given a more prominent place in the Roman counsels. The Mauritanian princes, already mentioned, were anxious to get an advantage over Juba and their activities obliged him to use his army to protect his territories.[5]

Caesar's plan of operations is not specifically given in the Commentaries, but apparently he meant to fall on the 2 legions at Hadrumetum by surprise from the sea and overpower them before assistance could reach them from headquarters at Utica.

For a reason inadequately explained in the Commentaries, Caesar sailed with his fleet of perhaps 300 ships without announcing an assembly point in case of separation, and although Caesar himself arrived off Hadrumetum (140 miles from Lilybaeum) on October 11, after 3 days at sea, unfortunately, most of his ships were astray with no assigned destination. He had with him only 3,000 legionaries and 150 cavalry. Nevertheless,

---

[5] The following account generally follows that of Kromayer in *Antike Schlachtfelder, Afrika.*

he landed and demanded surrender of Considius. This was refused and, as hostile cavalry now came up, it was impossible for Caesar to effect anything against the fortified city and he had to secure a base promptly, now that his presence was known. Eleven miles east of Hadrumetum was an elevated point of land on which stands the present town of Monastir, and on the far side of the point was a small harbor. Still farther, about 6 miles off, was the city of Leptis Minor with a good harbor. Guarding against the hostile cavalry, Caesar pushed on from Hadrumetum the next morning and seized the Monastir point, making himself temporarily secure at the small town of Ruspina 3 miles inland, which has given its name to his position. There Caesar waited in some anxiety for his missing ships.

On the following day, Caesar moved to Leptis which surrendered. He now had a satisfactory harbor and some stragglers came in from sea, bringing cavalry. He sent 10 ships to look for the missing ones, and also an expedition to the island of Cercina, about 60 miles southward, to seize a store of republican supplies. The squadron returned after some days with large prize. He sent back to Sardinia to hasten the dispatch of men and stores and, leaving a garrison at Leptis, he returned to the strong position of Ruspina. There his uneasiness increased; he did not disembark his cavalry, fearing he might not be able to remain, and he went on board ship with the intention of personally looking up the missing ships in the morning. Fortunately, they all came into port on the morning of the fourteenth before Caesar got away, in spite of the fact that, after making their landfall at the promontory of Mercury (Cape Bon), some of them had turned west towards Utica, instead of south.

Caesar was now able to hold his strong position at Ruspina until all his army should cross, and his superior fleet was security that the hostile fleet at Utica could not seriously interfere with the transports. He landed everybody and on the fourteenth and fifteenth threw a strong line of entrenchments from both sides of Ruspina to the sea to form a permanent base. On the sixteenth Caesar went out at the head of nearly half his command to forage and was surprised by a large cavalry force under Labienus, which had come from Utica, about 90 miles distant in an airline. Probably the fleet had been sighted going south when passing the promontory and word went by sea or land to Utica. Caesar was able to fall back to Ruspina, after hard fighting, for his cavalry was too weak to protect his infantry.

It was now clear to the Republicans that Caesar was committed to his present position, and on the twenty-fourth Scipio arrived with his whole army and offered battle, which Caesar refused. He could only wait for his later divisions to arrive, and few of the supply ships passing singly seem to have encountered an enemy at sea, so good was the escort and patrol system which was now established. In order to counter the diversion raised by Caesar in Mauritania against Juba, Scipio now sent young Gnaeus Pompey with 30 ships, few of them men-of-war, and 2,000 men, but Pompey was repulsed in Mauritania and went on to the Balearic Islands to foment disturbance in Spain.

Caesar was completely penned, and as there was little available space within his lines to pasture the horses, the soldiers daily washed seaweed in fresh water to provide forage. There was delay in the arrival of supply ships, for the season was turning bad. Juba now came up with his troops, but immediately the Mauritanians invaded his lands and took Cirta, his capital, whereupon Juba withdrew all his troops except an elephant corps of 30 animals. On November 1, the second division of 2 veteran legions with cavalry and light-armed infantry arrived after a good passage of 4 days, and Caesar now felt strong enough to leave his base at Ruspina, on November 7, for a campaign of maneuver. He was still dependent for success on the activity of the fleet in covering his sea communications. The enemy had made only few captures, yet about this time a transport ship of the second division was taken by local forces when blown ashore near Thapsus and Caesar punished the commanders of the ships stationed in the neighborhood for negligence in not rescuing her.

While Caesar and Scipio were observing each other for an opportunity of attack, Juba returned to Scipio with 3 legions and at last Caesar's third division of 2 more legions with ample supplies arrived from Sicily about January 1, 46, having had a misadventure. It saw the blockading squadron off Thapsus and mistook it for the enemy and fled to sea so that it did not get back for some days, very much exhausted. Caesar now had his entire force in Africa, about 40,000 legionary troops, 4,000 cavalry, and a number of light-armed troops. His men had been trained to meet elephants, using some brought from Italy for the purpose.

As Caesar was insisting on a winter campaign for the fleet and was maintaining constant communication with Sicily and Sardinia, Varus at last concluded to make some general effort against him by sea even though winter cruising was entirely irregular. Accordingly, he came with 55 ships from Utica to Aegimurum, an island off Mercury promontory and, having filled his ships with rowers and sailors from local levies, he went to Hadrumetum. Just at that moment Caesar sent 27 ships under Cispius from Leptis eastward to patrol off Thapsus and 13 others under Aquila to the north and west to observe Hadrumetum. Cispius reached his station without difficulty, but Aquila could not weather the point of Ruspina (Monastir) and accordingly anchored for the night under its lee, but out of range from the shore, to wait for a change of wind.

Having heard from deserters that the rest of Caesar's fleet was relying on the outlying squadrons for patrol (as indeed was necessary since rowing ships could not always be maintained in immediate readiness), Varus selected that night for a raid on the merchant ships anchored off Leptis. Of course, Varus expected to overpower the patrol squadron on his way but, as it happened, he passed outside of its temporary anchorage on his way to Leptis where he arrived unexpectedly at dawn and burned the supply ships lying at anchor, and took 2 triremes which had no soldiers on board.

Although Varus' adventure was a hit-and-run affair, yet all this took an hour or two during which the crews of the fleet were recalled to their ships. Caesar was notified and galloped in from his camp with the army 6 miles away, and organized the pursuit of the enemy. Caesar, indeed, was so quick in following that Varus was unable to delay on his way back to gather in Aquila's squadron which joined in the chase. Caesar followed for 4 miles and retook one of the captured ships with its own crew and a prize crew of 130 men. By hard work Varus got safely around the point of Ruspina, but the head wind held Caesar, so he anchored for the night. It may be noted that once Varus had got by the point he would have had a great tactical advantage had Caesar persisted in going on and meeting him, while heading to windward. South of Ruspina both were probably in a fairly good lee.

The next morning Caesar proceeded to Hadrumetum about 12 miles farther on, where Varus refused to come out and protect his supply ships which Caesar burned. We are not told how many ships Caesar had at Leptis, but it is reasonable to suppose that the two patrol squadrons of 40 ships could not have included more than half the ships there and probably were much fewer, so that his squadron of pursuit was probably larger than the whole force of Varus.

In January Caesar began a campaign of maneuver. He left a garrison and marched 25 miles south and east from Ruspina to get supplies at Agar near the coast south of Thapsus. Cispius and Aquila remained at Leptis to cruise and keep the seas free for the last re-enforcement of 4,000 replacement troops to fill the ranks of the legions; they soon arrived. The enemy followed Caesar and kept in touch. From Agar Caesar made the concluding movement of the campaign. Early in February he marched on the fortified seacoast town of Thapsus to besiege it and Scipio was obliged to protect it.

Battle of Thapsus

The city stood on a point looking to the northeast, so that the coast ran westward from the town in one direction and south in the other. Behind the town was a pond about 5 miles across, so that approach to it was by two isthmuses each less than 2 miles wide. Caesar fortified himself close to the city, blockading it, and could easily move out on either side of the pond. The enemy attempted to confine Caesar by holding both necks of land, with divided forces 7 or 8 miles apart. Scipio personally commanded the northern detachment which reached its position by a long night march from Agar around the pond and began the usual entrenched camp on the morning of February 6, 46 B.C.

Before Scipio could extend his entrenchments from pond to sea to enclose Caesar, the latter advanced against him by sea and land. Two legions remained in camp before the city, the patrol squadron moved along the shore, threatening to land its soldiers and attack Scipio from the rear, and Caesar with 6 legions formed the main line of battle. Before the rear troops could reach position on the left of the line, and before Caesar intended, the trumpeters of the 10th legion on the right sounded the charge. Caesar gave the word "Good Fortune," and leaped on his horse. The whole line went forward, the right leading. Scipio's elephants on his left wing were met with a hail of missiles from the 5th legion and turned against their own men. In a few minutes the whole of Scipio's command was on the run before Caesar's ships could beach and disembark, but no doubt their presence hastened the enemy's retreat.

Caesar directed only a part of his force to follow the chase, and with the rest and the 2 legions from the camp, he moved by the short way against the other two camps, those of Afranius and Juba. They did not wait for his arrival but fled in disorder and never came together again, while Caesar occupied the abandoned camp of King Juba. There the fugitives from Scipio's army arrived in the afternoon by the long way around the pond and, to their surprise, saw the ensigns of the enemy. They occupied a hill near the sea and offered to surrender, and Caesar was willing to accept, but his soldiers were tired of his clemency and wanted to end the war. They were entirely out of hand and massacred all there, about 10,000. Most of the leaders escaped from the field, but only Labienus and Varus got out of Africa.

Caesar returned to Thapsus, the garrison of which had attempted to break out after Caesar marched south, but it was repulsed by Caesar's camp followers. The town surrendered and, after a sacrificial service, the 5th legion was awarded the privilege of bearing an elephant on its standard in commemoration of its success of the previous day against the elephants. Caesar next marched on the base and headquarters at Utica, accepting the surrender of Hadrumetum and Uzita, on the way. He arrived at Utica on February 15 and received the keys of the city but the republican fleet had escaped.

About the same time Juba's army in the west under Saburra was wiped out by Sitius, and the republican detachments of Scipio's army were destroyed piecemeal by the local inhabitants, or surrendered to Caesar. The campaign established Caesar as master of the Roman state. After settling the affairs of the province and levying tribute, he departed with the fleet for Rome via Sardinia on April 14. In Sardinia he arrived in 3 days, staying some 10 days to raise some money, but being delayed by contrary winds, he did not arrive in Rome until near the end of May.

Remarks on African Campaign

The African campaign is remarkable for Caesar's use of his sea power in winter. It was the custom to suspend important maritime affairs in winter, although, of course, fishing and local business never entirely ceased. As an instance of cessation of movement it will be remembered that on his voyage to Rome, the great ship in which St. Paul sailed from Lycia meant to lie up for three winter months in Crete, when halfway, but was caught in a gale and was wrecked before she reached port.

Caesar depended on men and supplies from Europe and yet he did not hesitate to force his ships to sea in winter, contrary to all maritime tradition. The reason was that his ultimate enemy was public opinion in Rome. If that had been wholly favorable to his cause, he could well have afforded to wait until the spring of the following year, for the army in Africa would have been little more dangerous in the interval. But with sentiment in Rome as it was, with hard times, financial distress, and lack of the usual African supplies for the proletariat, Caesar's immediate movement across the Mediterranean arrested the development of overt political opposition in Rome until the outcome in Africa should be seen. Besides, from the purely military point of view, the unexpected initiation of a winter campaign over-seas was as advantageous as that against Pompey had been 2 years before. The hostile fleet was making itself snug for the winter, and there was no opposition to the passage. After the first detachment crossed to Hadrumetum, however, the situation was quite different from the situation before Dyrrhachium, for now Caesar had the more powerful fleet and he only had to overcome the habitual reluctance of seamen to venture to sea in winter. Yet this seems to have been considerable, for he had to send repeated orders, and moreover he had to requisition supplies from the neighborhood to supplement those sent from Sicily, although losses by peril of the sea are not mentioned in the contemporary accounts.

It has been urged that Scipio should have fallen back into the interior to make it more difficult for Caesar, who wanted a quick decision. But Scipio may have felt that he also would lose by retreating. He could not afford to let Caesar overrun territory and capture local supplies. As for the naval campaign, as such, the noteworthy point is that the superior fleet of Caesar was so well placed that it controlled the sea, and his maritime traffic suffered only trifling losses by the hostile fleet.

Second Spanish Campaign 46-45 b.c.

On his return home to Rome, Caesar set about political reforms and paid off the army with the treasure he had secured in Asia and in Africa. But in spite of what he did to restore the finances, to form new colonies, and to raise the status of the poorer classes in Rome and of the provincials, he could not get the warm adhesion of the aristocracy. Besides, the disaffection in Spain, which had been smouldering since Caesar left there in 49, was growing worse, even after the arrival of Caesarian forces from the African expedition.

The naval part of Caesar's second Spanish campaign is very slightly sketched in Dio Cassius and in the *Commentaries on the Spanish War*, but fortunately each complements the other, so that it is possible to see how Caesar used sea power when it was available as well as how he evaded its weight when he was without it, as in the Macedonian War.

The misgovernment of the province by Cassius Longinus, after the victory of Ilerda, had produced a mutiny of the soldiers which Lepidus had overcome in Caesar's name during the Macedonian campaign, but the culpable legions were afraid that Caesar's punishment was only delayed and they entered into negotiations with Scipio in Africa (see Map 19). Early during the campaign of Thapsus, Scipio detached young Gnaeus Pompey, with a few ships, who, after a misadventure in Mauritania, took the Balearic Islands where he fell ill and remained for some time with his forces. In the meantime the unfaithful legions in Spain heard of the end of the African campaign before the end of February, 46, and broke into open revolt, driving out Trebonius, Caesar's governor, and Baetica too revolted. By that time, Pompey was able to take the field and secured several towns, but Cartagena would not yield and Pompey besieged it. Then the remains of the republican forces in Africa began to drift into Spain and among others came Varus with what was left of the fleet.

The representatives of Caesar did not feel able to maintain themselves, and sent to Caesar for aid. Their request reached him in April during his stay in Sardinia on his way home with fleet and army. Caesar did not think his own presence was necessary in Spain, but sent C. Didius about the end of April, 46, with the fleet and certain elderly troops which he did not care to have in Rome.

As Dio puts it, "the sea now became hostile to Pompey" and he withdrew to Baetica as Caesar's re-enforcements began to arrive. What we are to understand by this terse phrase is that Pompey's strength was in Baetica and that the arrival of the powerful fleet under Didius caused the coastal towns to shift their allegiance once more, so that it was possible for the Caesarians to throw an army ashore at any point, to cut off any advanced force of the Republicans from their base in Baetica. Varus retired before Didius until he was defeated near Carteia (Gibraltar) and driven into that port whose entrance he defended by making a submarine *chevaux-de-frise* by a line of anchors which caught some of the leading enemy ships and deterred the others from entering. There the republican fleet remained until the close of the war, and wherever the Caesarian army was, it could be supplied without interference, from the nearest seaport. Pompey, on the other hand, now found little use for his fleet, for it was neither equal to interrupting the enemy's communications, nor in its own waters did it have any important lines of its own to cover, since Caesar controlled the rest of the known world and by embargo could hinder aid for Pompey, although he could not check it entirely

The war dragged through the year with little done until Caesar arrived very unexpectedly from Rome early in December, 46, and proceeded to the seat of war near Corduba. He had 8 legions against 13 of the Republicans, but only 4 of the latter were reliable and probably most were far from full. It is probable that Caesar's communications with Gaul and Italy were through Malaga and thence by sea, but the ancient authorities give no information. Nevertheless, Caesar's supplies were not on a good footing. He pushed the fighting, as always, while Pompey wanted a war of endurance. In the end, Caesar got his battle and won complete victory at Munda about 70 miles north of Malaga on March 17, 45. Caesar said that for the first time he fought for life rather than for victory. He now spent some months in Spain and Gaul before returning to Rome. Most of the republican leaders lost their lives, but Gnaeus Pompey escaped to Carteia and rejoined his fleet there.

There was a riot at Carteia between the citizens who wanted to deliver Pompey to Caesar and those who supported him. Pompey was wounded and took flight with 30 ships which he did not have time to complete with water. Didius was at Gades where he was able to watch the Baetis River, navigable as far as Corduba at the center of military operations. On hearing that Pompey was off, Didius pursued him with the fleet and sent both cavalry and infantry to watch the shores. On the fourth day the fugitive was obliged to water his ships and Didius came up and took some and burned others of his ships. Pompey himself escaped to a castle with a few men and was there overtaken and killed. Didius now landed to rejoice

in comfort and was surrounded in his villa by a party of fugitive Lusitani-
ans, who killed him as he tried to break through them to board his ships.
A few of his party got on board the ships at anchor which then got under
way and placed themselves in safety. So ended the naval part of the war,
in which the fleet maintained Caesar's line of supplies and made victory
possible.

PRINCIPAL AUTHORITIES CONSULTED FOR THIS CHAPTER

ANCIENT

Caesar's Commentaries and Their Continuations.
Appian.
Dio Cassius.
Plutarch: *Caesar, Cicero, Pompey.*

MODERN

Delbrueck, H.: *Geschichte der Kriegskunst.*
Ferrero, G.: *Greatness and Decline of Rome.*
Kromayer, J.: *Antike Schlachtfelder.*
        Schlachten Atlas.
Merivale, C.: *History of the Romans.*
Serre, P.: *Les Marines de Guerre de l'Antiquité et du Moyen Age.*

CHAPTER XVI

CAMPAIGN OF PHILIPPI, 42 B.C.

SECOND MACEDONIAN CAMPAIGN IN 42 B.C.
Affairs in Italy after Caesar's Death

AFTER Caesar had returned from his second Spanish campaign in September, 45, as he continued his measures of reform and of change and as it became apparent that he was monarch and had no intention of restoring the Senate and its aristocratic members to their previous pre-eminence in the affairs of the state, he disappointed many even of his own friends and political supporters. In consequence a wide conspiracy formed in the Senate and Caesar was murdered in the Senate House on March 15, 44 B.C. It was the belief of the conspirators that upon the death of Caesar the system of government would automatically revert to the old republican form. They had made no plans for enforcing this outcome and, to their great surprise, vested interest of many kinds were deeply offended. The mass of the people did not ask for the change, nor did the Senate become the heir of Caesar's authority. In the panic which overcame the Senate and the people at the sight of the murder, Antony, the surviving Consul, assumed authority in opposition to the senatorial majority and was supported by Lepidus, who commanded the only legion in the city.

As to the contest between Antony and the conspirators to assume control of the state, this study of the maritime side of the war may say only enough to explain the political background of the military situation. With the consent of the Senate, the conspirators went forth from Rome to take charge of the provinces and the armies to which Caesar had appointed them. Antony and Lepidus remained in the city with executive authority and military strength. Antony drew several legions from the Balkan region to overawe the Senate.

Gaius Octavius, the young great-nephew and adopted son of Caesar and his principal heir, left his studies in Apollonia and appeared in Rome to take up his inheritance under the name of Caesar Octavianus. Antony, who was Caesar's executor, refused to recognize the young man's claim to inherit, for Antony needed Caesar's treasure to meet the Senate's opposition. In consequence, the Senate patronized Octavian (Caesar Octavianus) who raised an army among Caesar's veterans. There were now three parties in Italy, the Senate, Antony, and Octavian, all seeking to inherit Caesar's authority.

After over a year of confused and changing alliances between the parties and several battles in Italy, a new revolutionary government was formed in October, 43, under a second triumvirate composed of Antony, Lepidus, and Octavian. Neither then nor afterwards were the triumvirs ever cordial friends. Other generals joined them and they became masters of 43 legions. Rome and Italy they governed jointly and the western provinces and the islands they divided among themselves for individual rule. Octavian now formally took the name of Caesar.

Opposition in Asia

While the triangular contest was being fought out in Italy, the chiefs of the conspirators, in the name of the Senate, were establishing the power of the reactionary Republican party east of the Adriatic in a manner similar to that of Pompey in his struggle with Caesar. Again the wealth and sea power of the East were mobilizing to oppose the unconstitutional supremacy in Italy of the successors of Caesar. When it became apparent after Caesar's death that the Senate could not regain its authority without war, the two chief conspirators, Gaius Cassius and Marcus Brutus, crossed the sea in October, 44, to rule in Syria and Macedonia, respectively. After much political maneuvering and some fighting, by June, 43, the two had overcome all of the Caesarians in the East and there they ruled in the name of the Senate. This great accession of strength in the East to the reactionary party led the Senate to summon Cassius and Brutus to Italy to overcome the Caesarians who were still in divergence among themselves. It was the prospect of interference by the eastern armies which led Antony, Lepidus, and young Caesar to sink their differences and form the triumvirate as already mentioned.

Cassius and Brutus worked in greatest harmony and well knew how much the Senate needed them, but delay could not be avoided, for no fleet was available. Cassius was an able soldier who understood that an army must eat before it can fight, and fully realized that in the distressed condition of Italy it would be necessary for his army to appear there assured of continuous supplies from the richer East through a powerful fleet. To secure the ships, he was therefore thinking of marching on Egypt to secure one which Cleopatra had earlier refused him, but at the call of Brutus, he went to Smyrna to meet the latter, who had withdrawn from Macedon with his 8 legions, probably to subsist off a richer country than Macedon. They now agreed on their plan of operations against the newly formed triumvirate, in which the first step was the procurement of ships. Time was passing and it was now the beginning of the year 42. Not only in the East, but nearer to Italy in the great islands of which Octavian had assumed the nominal control, was the Senate hoping to find a fleet to put pressure on the triumvirate government.

Sicily Turns against the Triumvirate

After Caesar's victory at Munda early in 45, Pompey's younger son, Sextus, escaped to the wilder parts of Northern Spain where, with the help of the native tribes who still remembered his father, he continued to defy Roman authority. His strength increased, he gathered a squadron and several legions, and he was master of Spain by the time of Caesar's death. In the subsequent turmoil, as he naturally sympathized with the Republicans, the Senate rescinded his exile, whereupon he came to Massilia to observe events. Although he was thinking far more of his own advantage than that of the state, the Senate took him up to play against Antony and still more against Octavian.

In June, 43, the Senate made Sextus commander of all its fleets, directing all squadron commanders to obey him. With the Senate supporting him, he continued to grow in power and a few months later, when the triumvirate was established, Pompey took the Massilian squadron, together with his own Spanish ships, and sailed for Sicily, of which he soon made himself master and thus had a fleet, a base, and an army composed of those opposing the new government, who fled from Rome. Besides, many seafaring men came to Pompey from Africa and Spain.

As the life of any government in Rome depended not only on its military strength, but also on its ability to keep the seas open to supply the city, Pompey's seizure of the grain province of Sicily was a serious threat to the new government by the end of the year 43. Upon its establishment the triumvirate found itself in a very trying position both with regard to the people and the army. What between Brutus and Cassius in the East and Sextus Pompey in Sicily, it was very difficult to secure the imports which are necessary to every country at war and doubly so to Italy which was not self-supporting. There were 43 legions to pay and the country was exhausted.

Largely to get money, the triumvirs set on foot a great proscription in which their political opponents were put to death and their property confiscated; but real estate prices fell with the glut in the market and the distress of the triumvirs remained great. The only hope for the existence of the triumvirate was immediate military action to open the way for imports for the army and the population.

Campaign in Macedon

Accordingly, Antony sent his legions to Brundisium for the passage across the Adriatic, and in the spring of 42 he sent over an advance force of 8 legions while Brutus and Cassius were far away in Asia. That relieved the burden on Italy and was an evidence of action to the people of Italy. More troops in Macedon might find difficulty in finding supplies.

Sicily was the immediate danger, for early in 42 Pompey had complete mastery there and was devastating the Italian coast and cutting off the grain for Rome. Unless Pompey's fleet could be overcome or deprived of its Sicilian base, Rome was subject to want and operations beyond the Adriatic would be very hazardous.

Accordingly, it fell to Octavian to make an effort to assume actual control of the island which he nominally governed (see Map 10). With that purpose, he sent Rufus Salvidienus with such ships as could be found in Italy to protect the passage to Messana of the army with which Octavian himself marched to Rhegium. But Pompey met Rufus in the current off Scylla where his lighter and better-handled ships had an advantage. The two squadrons separated after a drawn battle and Rufus withdrew to a point on the strait where he could watch the enemy at Messana. Such was the situation when Octavian arrived at Rhegium. But events had been moving too fast in Asia for Octavian to continue with his effort against Sicily and Antony called him to Brundisium. The risk of famine and revolution in Rome had to be faced in order to overcome the military danger in the East.

It will be remembered that at the opening of 42 Brutus and Cassius had decided on their plan of operations in support of the Republic. This was to neglect for the moment the force which Antony had sent into Macedon, while making their rear thoroughly secure and acquiring an adequate fleet. Brutus had already called out the squadrons of the Euxine and he now undertook operations in Lycia to get the ships belonging there. Cassius demanded the ships of Rhodes, where he had formerly been a student. Relying on old acquaintanceship, Rhodes answered, appealing to him to respect old treaties and forego his requisition for ships. As he persisted, 33 Rhodian ships issuing from Cnidus attacked his larger Syrian squadron at Myndus. The Rhodian ships were lighter and maneuvered better, but with his superior numbers Cassius was able to envelop their formation and deprive them of maneuvering space. In the end, the Rhodians lost 2 ships sunk and 3 captured with their crews and the rest fled. Cassius repaired damages at Myndus and then assembled his army opposite Rhodes and crossed the strait on merchant ships. With the army and 80 men-of-war he then blockaded Rhodes which was unready for a siege. Again the Rhodians attacked at sea and were defeated.

Cassius then appeared in the city by treachery and took possession of the public treasure. He now had a considerable fleet and Brutus had conquered Lycia whose squadron he ordered to the Hellespont to combine with the ships already there to cover the crossing into Europe.

All was now ready for the campaign against the triumvirate (see Map 2). There were garrisons by the sea and land throughout the East, but Egypt remained autonomous. Cassius learned that Cleopatra was about to aid the triumvirs (she had known Antony in Rome) by sending her fleet to escort the army across the Adriatic. To avoid Cassius' navy, the Egyptian fleet was proceeding via Libya and Crete. Cassius countered that attempt by sending Murcus with 60 ships carrying a legion of the best soldiers to lie at Taenarum (southern point of Peloponnese) to intercept the Egyptians, and he himself went to Sardis to meet Brutus and proceed with their joint movement upon Italy. At Taenarum, Murcus heard that the Egyptian fleet had been greatly damaged by gales on the Libyan coast and had returned to Egypt, whereupon he moved forward to Brundisium where he established a blockade with an advanced base on the island in front of the town whence Libo had watched Antony in the spring of 48.

The appearance of Murcus and the knowledge that Brutus and Cassius had begun their march towards Europe caused Antony to realize that it was necessary at all risks to cross the Adriatic and support the advance guard already over the water. At his urgent demand Octavian abandoned his unprofitable campaign against Sicily and joined his colleague at Brundisium. As Appian tells us, the arrival of Octavian caused Murcus to withdraw somewhat from Brundisium. Apparently it is to be understood that as Antony had sent the greater part of his own army into Macedon the strong fleet of Murcus was able to hold a suitable entrenchment close to the city from which it supported an active sea patrol based on the little island. When Octavian arrived with several additional legions, Murcus had to move his position on the mainland farther off and give greater opportunity for his enemy to get to sea with sailing ships when the breeze was good. Under such circumstances the rowing ships of the blockaders were unable to overtake the transports. Consequently, the transports watched their time and crossed on each favorable wind and returning crossed again "with full sails" until both triumvirs and 12 more legions had joined the 8 legions in the advance guard. Murcus, however, still maintained station on the Italian coast to intercept supplies. That was an easier task with most of the hostile army on the other side and soon Domitius Ahenobarbus joined him with 50 more ships and another legion. Before the end of the campaign, 130 big ships and other smaller ones lay across the triumviral line of supply from Italy and greatly influenced its strategy.

While the triumvirs were transferring their legions across the Adriatic, Antony ordered the advance guard forward to delay the approach of the enemy. The Via Egnatia was the principal highway for Rome's communication with her Asiatic provinces. It ran from Dyrrhachium to Thessalonica and Amphipolis and then near the sea as far as Byzantium. On that road, Norbanus and Decidius, commanders of the advanced guard, moved to a strong pass about 30 miles west of the Hebrus River. There they awaited the approach of the enemy's 19 legions (ranks not full) and 20,000 cavalry which was supported by an adequate fleet. The two forces of Brutus and Cassius remained separate organizations.

How strong the republican fleet in the Aegean was we do not know, but a small combatant force to guard supplies against pirates would be enough, since no serious attack could be made on the eastern army's over-seas supplies while Murcus attended to his task in the Adriatic. When the republican army arrived opposite the enemy, it was not necessary to force the mountain pass. Cassius merely sent his fleet with a landing force to the rear of Norbanus to threaten the seizure of the Via Egnatia and the Caesarians hastily retired to an even stronger defile about 70 miles in the rear near the port of Neapolis (now Kavala). There the republican advance was checked. Apparently Amphipolis, not far to the west, must have been garrisoned by the Caesarians, for the Republicans did not attempt to repeat their threat against communications by seizing Amphipolis.

After some delay, a difficult route was opened through the mountains by which the Republicans could move around the hostile left flank and interpose between Norbanus and the main body which was hurrying from Italy along the Via Egnatia. Norbanus was informed of the matter before the road was fully practicable for the eastern army and retreated in great haste to Amphipolis, expecting the enemy to follow him. Antony soon arrived with the main army and Octavian, personally, a few days later (the date uncertain, about the end of September). Instead of advancing on Amphipolis, Cassius and Brutus had remained at Philippi where they had prepared a strong position covering the road to Neapolis, whence their two armies, each in its own camp, drew their supplies which arrived by sea from all Asia. The fleet lay there also and the island of Thasos, about 15 miles away, was made the base and depot. Antony left 1 legion at Amphipolis and with 19 full legions, 114,000 men and 13,000 cavalry, advanced opposite the enemy and entrenched in one great camp.

The stage was now set for the decision. Both sides had 19 legions, but the triumvirs had more men and better soldiers in their ranks. On the other hand, the Republicans had the great advantage of wealth and sea power. Their garrisons in Asia Minor enabled them to draw munitions from districts as far as the Euphrates, and their fleet not only protected their own line of supply, but in the Adriatic it was astride that of the enemy, so that the triumvirs were forced to rely on the scanty resources of the Balkan peninsula, which could not last long. Antony was obliged to fight early or the army would starve; the Republicans had only to avoid action. Antony therefore attempted to extend his right by a series of field works, so that he would get across the road to the port of Neapolis, which, of course, was impossible for Cassius to permit.

After ten days of trench work it came to a battle. Antony boldly attacked Cassius and Brutus attacked Octavian's legions. The latter was momentarily absent; his troops were undirected and were dispersed and Brutus' troops plundered his camp. Antony, however, was entirely successful and took Cassius' camp. Thereafter both victorious forces began pillaging, and in the end returned to their respective camps. Having been driven out of sight of the camps which were hidden by dust clouds, Cassius was unaware of his colleague's success and committed suicide, thus putting Brutus, a much less able man, in command.

The political and economic situation was now of great weight in the military strategy. Asia was accustomed to the Roman rule, whereby the garrisons afforded local order and the people paid their local taxes to the de facto government. Resting on his sea communications, Brutus was thus sure of his resources. As before the battle, he had only to wait for the enemy to exhaust the neighboring country's supplies and he wished to do so. But, politically, his own leaders and even the Roman soldiers were anxious to get back to Italy; the Asiatic auxiliaries wanted to go home. In spite of superior numbers the enemy's losses in the battle had been much the greater. So the republican army wanted battle, although it was unwise.

In the triumviral army, distress was beginning to be felt, and a legion was sent into Achaia, 300 miles away, to beat up food. For the triumvirs, battle was necessary; first, for the army, to end the want of supplies, also because revolt in Italy could only be staved off by early success. Sextus Pompey, the Senate's naval commander in chief, was occupying Octavian's small fleet and was threatening Italy. Rome might not wait: final victory would be found in the acquiescence of the ruling classes in Italy, whence both sides were drawing the strength of their armies.

Antony continued to push his line of works by the right flank and in the meantime both armies learned that on the very day of the battle a reenforcement for the triumvirs of more than 2 legions and some cavalry under Calvinus had been destroyed or turned back while crossing the Adriatic. Calvinus had started his expedition in sailing transports with a small escort of triremes and had been under sail, like the preceding divisions. They had been sighted by the powerful fleet of Murcus and Aheno-barbus and, owing to the failure of the wind, only a few transports had been able to escape. The weak escort was ineffective for their protection. The transports lashed themselves together to make better defense (more men were thus available for defending a given length of exposed side), but the enemy shot flaming arrows, which endangered all in each group and consequently the ships separated again and were attacked individually by the quickly moving rowing ships. Many of the immobile transports were burned and their soldiers jumped overboard, but most surrendered and their crews took the oath to their captors; 17 triremes were also surrendered. Calvinus himself escaped and got back to Brundisium after five days. There can be little doubt the expedition was bringing much needed supplies also, and the loss must have been the more serious.[1]

The tension in the opposing camps increased. The triumvirs pushed their works towards the sea to cut off the enemy from his base at Neapolis, and Brutus kept pace with counter-works. The usual appeals to the armies were made on both sides. Brutus pointed out that they were sure of victory if they could avoid a general battle, for as he told his men, the enemy had exhausted Macedonia and was now foraging in Thessaly. Antony and Octavian admitted the danger of famine and encouraged their soldiers to look on battle as a means of relief. As Appian says, Brutus' generals preferred a quick decision to slow certainty of victory. The republican soldiers became very unmanageable; they felt sure of victory and probably the slow advance of the enemy towards the road to Neapolis allowed Brutus only the choice between battle and retreat to his supply ships.

The temper of his soldiers forced Brutus to offer battle and 20 days after the first battle he led out his army and engaged in the afternoon. The battle immediately became close. Octavian's men on the left wing were the first to push back their opponents but, when the break came, Octavian held the camp and Antony pursued. With a force of 4 legions, Brutus was able to withdraw to the hills, leaving his camp still intact. In the morning, he asked advice and was counseled to surrender. Instead he killed himself and his army then surrendered (about November 1). The triumvirs took

---

[1] The battle is noteworthy for an early use of flaming projectiles. Previously, we have heard of pots of fire being dropped on the enemy, but this was work at longer range.

possession of the stores and treasure of the enemy and the legions took service with the triumvirs.

PRINCIPAL AUTHORITIES CONSULTED FOR THIS CHAPTER

ANCIENT

Appian.
Dio Cassius.
Plutarch: *Antony, Brutus.*

MODERN

Ferrero, G.: *Greatness and Decline of Rome.*
Merivale, C.: *History of the Romans.*
Kromayer, J.: *Schlachten Atlas.*

CHAPTER XVII

SICILIAN WAR 38-36 B.C.

THE NEW GOVERNMENT

THERE was now a new division of the provinces between the triumvirs after Philippi. Antony proceeded into Asia and from there went to Egypt, nominally to pacify the country, but really to get money. Octavian returned to Italy to attempt to settle the confusion. Lepidus retired to the government of Africa. Philippi had killed many of the leaders of the Republican party and ended the senatorial government, yet when Antony arrived in the East the status of his government with regard to the local peoples was not greatly different from what it had been under republican rule. He was able to rule, as long as he had adequate garrisons, and he had to find money in the East to pay the troops who had won victory. In Italy Octavian found very different conditions. Italy had very little money and was dependent for prosperity on the treasures and products of other regions and Octavian had to maintain order among the distressed population from which he drew the army which was the instrument of order. At the same time he had to reward the discharged soldiers with confiscated lands.

CONFUSION IN ITALY

A great difficulty arose out of the attitude of Sextus Pompey and the strength he drew from the remnants of the republican forces in the East. During the campaign of Philippi, Sextus Pompey had been acting against the triumvirs as the Senate's commander in chief, but he thought more of his own interests than of those of the Senate. After Philippi he received considerable accessions. A certain Cassius who had commanded the republican squadron in the Aegean came to Pompey with 30 ships and some men and Murcus also came to Sicily with 80 ships and 2 legions. The squadron of Ahenobarbus (70 ships) and 2 legions remained in the Adriatic and devastated the coast of Italy.

In the spring of 41 Sextus added to the distress in Italy by cutting off

496

the corn supply and Antony's friends, led by his wife Fulvia and his brother Lucius, raised an insurrection against Octavian without the knowledge of Antony. The insurrection was defeated early in 40.

During the 18 months after Philippi, Antony accomplished little in the East. Queen Cleopatra met him in Cilicia and they went to Egypt where they spent the winter of 41-40. The liaison of the two was a matter of first-class political importance. Thence forward Antony relied on the riches of Egypt as the basis of his system of finance.[1] Early in 40 the news from Italy obliged Antony to go to Greece in spite of the beginning of a war with Parthia. He arrived in Greece with a great fleet; many of his ships were Egyptian. By that time Pompey had seized Corsica and Sardinia in addition to Sicily and Antony was urged to join with him to overthrow Octavian, but the proposal Antony declined. Soon afterward Antony crossed to Brundisium with many ships but few troops. There were some hostilities between him and Octavian (the last in Italy for 350 years) yet without formal war. The troops wanted peace and the triumvirs were the slaves of their own legions.

In consequence, a new treaty was concluded at Brundisium in the middle of 40. Octavian took all the West, including Dalmatia and Illyria. Antony took the other provinces except Africa which went to Lepidus. For the better preservation of the treaty, Antony married Octavia, his colleague's sister. As for troops, Antony took 19 legions, Octavian 16, and Lepidus only 6.[2]

In the three great islands Pompey had 9 legions besides his fleet but he was abandoned by Antony, and Octavian could make war on him, if he interfered too much with commerce.

The Treaty of Brundisium shows the Empire threatened with anarchy and poverty through the antagonism between East and West. For the moment Antony seemed to be ready to desert Europe and retain for himself only the wealthy East. In this we may see the influence of his winter of 41-40 spent with Cleopatra. Antony would take the East with Egypt as his main source of wealth and complete the conquest of Parthia with Italian troops. If eastern revenues were to be spent by Antony in the East,

---

[1] There is no clear evidence that Cleopatra had any illicit relations except with the two greatest political and military leaders of the time, who were the fathers of her children.

[2] Apparently there were already 4 legions in Africa.

it would be the ruin of the Roman state by breaking the old system of spending them in Italy. The Treaty of Brundisium had no element of permanence.

OCTAVIAN'S SICILIAN CAMPAIGNS

After the treaty Antony arranged to transfer his legions in Europe to the East. He showed that he was becoming an Asiatic by his dress and manners. Neither Antony nor Octavian could pay their soldiers, and a revolt (military) broke out. Italy was in great distress. In the summer of 40 the two triumvirs returned to Rome for the marriage, which was to confirm the treaty. It was necessary to recover Sardinia where Octavian's general, Helenus, had been defeated. In spite of the starvation which Pompey was inflicting on the city of Rome, the public sympathized with him politically. Octavian undertook to raise additional taxes and there was a people's revolt. There was a great famine in Rome in November, 40, but the people acclaimed Pompey, while Antony and Octavian had trouble to restore order, and early in 39 were obliged to seek terms with Pompey.

By that time the latter had established a despotic sea power on the three islands, with three of his father's freedmen as principal lieutenants— Menodorus, Menecrates, and Apollophanes. Many of the Roman nobility who had taken refuge with him chafed at this preference of Greeks. Sextus believed that the triumvirs needed peace more than he did and that the continuance of the famine would increase the political dangers of his opponents in Rome. The Romans with him, including his mother, urged that Italy would turn against him and counseled peace. At last terms were arranged. It was agreed that Pompey should retain the islands and also be given the Peloponnese; that he should be given indemnity for his father's confiscated property; that he would raise the blockade, receive no more fugitive slaves, put down piracy, and for this his soldiers were to receive the same rewards as those of the triumvirs. In the course of the summer of 39, the two triumvirs went to Misenum with an army, and Sextus met them there with a fleet and ratified a peace. The fleet of Sextus, with its accessions under Cassius and Murcus, can scarcely have been less than 200 ships.

In September, Antony left Rome for Athens whence he ruled the East.

Money was lacking everywhere in the West and a revolt broke out in Gaul, which was crushed by Agrippa.

After the peace of Misenum, Octavian seems to have begun ship-building in both the Adriatic and Tyrrhene Sea. He soon alleged that Pompey was not carrying out the terms of peace, that he was sheltering slaves, building ships, and permitting piracy. At the same time Meno-dorus, ruling Sardinia and Corsica, went over to Octavian with both islands, 3 legions, and 60 ships.

First Sicilian Campaign

When Sextus heard of Menodorus' desertion, he considered it an act of war by Octavian, and ravaged the coast of Italy. Octavian asked Antony to come to Brundisium to give advice and called on Lepidus for help. He ordered his fleet at Ravenna to go to Brundisium and that of Menodorus to join the other ships on the Etrurian coast. New ships were laid down at Ravenna and Rome. Lastly, Octavian recalled troops from Gaul and Illyria. His plan was (with the approval of Antony) to attack Sextus from two bases, Naples and Brundisium.

Antony did not approve of hostilities and the two quarreled. Octavian felt he had to act, in spite of Antony's disapproval. He arranged for an expedition late in July, 38, to seize Sicily. Cornificius was to go to Tarentum with the Adriatic fleet, and thence to Rhegium. The Etrurian fleet under Calvisius and Menodorus was to move from Naples and cover the passage of the army which Octavian himself was leading to Rhegium to throw across the strait when the fleet of Pompey should be defeated. Could Octavian once control the sea passage from Rhegium to Messana, his powerful army would soon make an end of Pompey's rule.

Pompey put another Greek, Menecrates, in command of his fleet and it sailed north to attack Calvisius, leaving only 40 ships before Rhegium under Pompey himself. Menecrates may have had 100 ships (see Map 10). Calvisius sighted Menecrates off the bay of Naples and retreated into the bight of Cumae while Menecrates went to Ischia for the night (10 miles off). At daybreak the Roman fleet (which may have been the smaller) formed close to the shore to prevent a break-through. The Pompeian fleet came up, with Menecrates leading in the right wing, and attacked. The northern and southern wings of the fleets had different fortunes. On the south the Roman ships backed under pressure to the beach, where they grounded, and thereafter Menecrates was able to take as much of the fight as he liked and could replace wearied crews by fresh ships. Menodorus, commanding the Roman left (southern) wing, was opposite Menecrates. They recognized each other's ships and, inspired by personal hatred, they both charged and both ships were damaged, Menodorus having the advantage of the higher ship. Menodorus lost his ram and Menecrates had his oars swept away. Grappling irons and boarding bridges were thrown by both, Menodorus was wounded in the arm by a missile which was withdrawn, but Menecrates got a barbed javelin in the leg which could not easily be extracted. He remained on deck and when his ship was taken, he jumped overboard to his death and Menodorus towed the prize ashore.

On the right or northern wing, where Calvisius was present in person, his vessels pushed off shore and cut off some of the enemy from their main body. These he pursued to sea. Then Demochares, Menecrates' vice admiral, fell on the remainder of the Roman right wing and put several ships to flight while others were forced on the rocks or burned. Finally Calvisius, returning from pursuit, checked further loss. The Pompeian fleet had suffered less material damage, but the death of Menecrates outweighed that advantage.

Calvisius remained in position off Cumae till he heard that Demochares had retired to Sicily. He then repaired his damaged ships and followed to the point of rendezvous at Rhegium. In the meantime Octavian had arrived at Rhegium with a large fleet and army. His friends urged him to attack Pompey who had only 40 ships, but he said it was bad policy to attack when re-enforcements were expected; but, instead of Calvisius, it was Demochares who returned to Messana with the main body of Pompey's fleet.

The two squadrons of Octavian now were widely separated, with Pompey's whole force lying opposite to one of them (Pompey's total amounted to perhaps 130 vessels). Having refused to fight when he was superior, Octavian was still more unwilling after Pompey assembled his fleet. Accordingly, he remained quietly at Rhegium until he heard that Calvisius was about to arrive and then he slipped out of port to join

him, passing in front of Messana, less than 4 miles away. Pompey promptly pursued him, seeking a battle before the two hostile divisions could assemble, and was able to force an action.

When Octavian saw battle was unavoidable, he anchored his ships
along the beach with their bows to seaward, near Scylla. It was a variation on Calvisius' arrangement at Cumae, from which it is a fair inference
that the Roman ships were heavy and slow and unequal to a battle of
maneuver. No doubt the Roman fleet was outnumbered, and Demochares
took full advantage of his superiority. As at Cumae, this action also had
different results in the two wings. Demochares put two ships against
every enemy in Octavian's wing and threw them into confusion. They
dashed against the rocks and each other and bilged. Octavian leaped
ashore himself, and rescued others.

Cornificius with his part of the fleet in the other wing cut the anchor
cables and attacked the enemy. He captured Demochares' ship, and then
at the height of the conflict but late in the day, Calvisius and Menodorus
came up and the Pompeians withdrew without waiting for the new arrivals to get in action. Octavian's fleet suffered severely during the night.
The people who had escaped to shore also suffered a good deal, but a
legion came up over the mountains to help them and in the morning Octavian put the squadron of Calvisius off shore as a guard while he repaired
damages. The enemy remained quiet.

A south wind came up which much damaged Octavian's ships as they
were on a lee shore and not fully manned, but Menodorus anchored his
squadron in deep water and rowed up to his anchors and suffered little.
Although Octavian much feared Pompey would take advantage of the
storm, since his ships were safe in Messana, yet the latter did nothing
and Octavian moved his fleet to Vibo and closed the year's work. Pompey
was still secure.

RENEWAL OF THE TRIUMVIRATE

The effort to clear the sea to protect Rome from hunger had failed.
It was now late in 38 and Octavian sent to Antony for aid. The latter
had been having great success in Parthia, whereby his prestige in Rome
was raised in contrast with that of Octavian. The triumvirate was to end
the next year and its renewal was called for. The political need was the

basis for military adjustments. A tentative agreement was made at Athens whereby Antony was to help Octavian by giving him a strong squadron and in return the former was to get soldiers, not mere recruits, but good legions from his colleague's army. As Antony was short of money and going into Parthia where a fleet was of no service, he thought ships for soldiers would be a good exchange. Immediately (end of 38) Octavian set out to build a new fleet, in order that he might drive a better bargain at the final negotiation. He put Calvisius aside, as the latter had allowed Menodorus to desert back to Pompey, taking 7 ships with him.

Marcus Vipsanius Agrippa assumed charge of the fleet, which may have numbered over 100, after the disasters of the summer.[3] He had greatly distinguished himself in the campaign of 41-40 against Lucius Antonius and more recently in Gaul and was now about to enter on his naval career in which he showed himself the greatest of Roman admirals, although now only 27 years of age. Agrippa began his work as Minister of Marine, with the construction of a great naval base near Puteoli (Pozzuoli) (see Map 10) where he cut a canal from the sea through Lake Lucrinus to Lake Avernus, making the Portus Julius. The building of ships went on with that of the dockyard and the assembly of equipment. And as the rowers mustered, he trained them on wooden benches as had been done in the First Punic War. The work of shipbuilding was continued through the year 37, but Octavian could not renew the war with Sextus until he had a positive agreement with Antony as to the triumvirate.

In May, 37, Antony reached Tarentum with 300 ships to carry out the proposed exchange, but he did not find Octavian there to meet him. After some delay Octavian sent word he had all the ships he needed. Antony could not carry out his plans for the eastern expedition until he had more troops, and he sent his wife Octavia to be an intermediary with her brother. At length, in August, Octavian appeared at Tarentum, for he and his advisers, Maecenas and Agrippa, understood that they must make some concession or drive Antony to unite either with Pompey or Lepidus and overthrow the balance of power. It was pretty diplomacy. In the end, the triumvirate was renewed for five years from the preceding January. Antony gave Octavian 130 ships and received 21,000 men in

---

[3] This is only an estimate.

exchange. Besides, the Treaty of Misenum with Pompey was canceled, so that Octavian could make war on him without offense to Antony and the latter immediately departed for Syria, with his new troops.

SECOND SICILIAN CAMPAIGN 36 B.C.

For Octavian there was delay. The confiscation of property and the land grants to soldiers were transforming Italy, yet there was very little money available, for there was no tribute from Asia. It was not until the summer of 36 that Octavian completed preparations for his final effort to free Roman commerce from the great burden which Pompey laid on it. For the campaign against Sextus, Octavian had provided an overwhelming force. He had secured the co-operation of Lepidus, which had been lacking in 38. The plan was to throw Lepidus' army of Africa into southwestern Sicily while the armies of Italy were to cross the Strait of Messina.

The main task fell to the navy, for as soon as the entrance into Sicily should be effected, the army would be irresistible. To secure the army's passage, the navy was first to clear the way, and Octavian's fleet was greatly stronger than in 38. Lying at Tarentum under Taurus was the fleet of 130 ships which Antony had provided the year before, but pestilence had reduced the crews so that only 102 could be manned. In the new Julian Harbor which Agrippa had created west of Naples, there was a large fleet whose size is not given by the ancient histories; but, as will be seen hereafter, we may think there must have been as many as 150 ships there, perhaps more. The army of Octavian had 21 legions, but probably they were very much under the normal strength of 6,000 men (say, 3,000-3,500) for it was desirable for political reasons for the government to provide as many offices as possible both civil and military, and small legions employed many officers per 1,000 men. Lepidus had 70 ships and 12 legions,[4] which he embarked on 1,000 (?) merchant ships together with great supplies. He was not on very good terms with Octavian, as he resented his subordinate position in the triumvirate, and he did not cordially support his colleague during the campaign.

---

[4] When Lepidus assumed rule in Africa, he had only 10 legions and the province had been quiet. It is hard to understand how he now drew 12 legions and later 4 more from this quiet region.

Pompey had only 8 legions to oppose to 33 of the enemy, and they were composed in great part of slaves and fugitives. His hope lay in the active use of his fleet to prevent a landing. We do not know how many ships he had, but from such figures as are mentioned we may conclude that he had between 175 and 200.[5]

To meet the overwhelming forces arrayed against him, Sextus put one legion and a few ships at Lilybaeum to hold that important fortress and seaport and, after garrisoning a number of the more important landing places, especially in the northeast of the island, he concentrated the greater part of his fleet and army at Messana. This disposition suggests the probability that, politically, Sextus had more to dread from Octavian than from Lepidus and that, if he could keep the former out of the island, he might be able to negotiate with the other.

In memory of his adopted father, Julius, Octavian selected July 1 as an auspicious day on which a simultaneous movement to the island should be made by the three fleets at Puteoli, Tarentum, and Carthage. A southerly gale on the third day upset the plan. Lepidus alone reached his destination on that day (distance 113 sea miles), with the loss of a few ships. He landed without difficulty but could not take Lilybaeum, although he took several small towns in the neighborhood. He then waited for developments elsewhere.

Agrippa's squadron, sailing from the Julian Port, suffered most from the gale. The van, which Octavian accompanied, made the little port of Elea with the loss of only one ship, but during the night the wind shifted and many more were lost. The rear of the squadron also suffered heavily off the promontory at the south side of the Bay of Naples. Altogether, Agrippa lost 6 heavy ships and 26 lighter ones, besides some liburnicas,[6] leaving him perhaps about 110 to 115 ships. Apparently, Taurus with the squadron from Tarentum was able to ride out the gale without damage but, when he heard of the disaster to Agrippa, he returned to Tarentum.

---

[5] The total number of men employed on both sides during the campaign may have come near to 200,000, supposing small legions and under-manned ships, Pompey had about 50,000. The above assumes that Lepidus brought no more than about 20,000 soldiers and 10,000 seamen, and that the legions furnished soldiers for the ships.

[6] Liburnicas were the small light craft of which Agrippa had built a number for this war.

Sextus flattered himself that Octavian would be forced to postpone the campaign till the following year and showed his elation by putting on a dark blue mantle to indicate that he was a son of Neptune who had favored him by the gale.[7] But the political situation at Rome was too serious for Octavian to delay. The city was too poverty stricken and too hungry to remain quiet if it saw operations deferred for a year, so immediate success was necessary for him. Thirty days were necessary to repair the damaged ships. Maecenas was sent hastily to Rome, to prevent disorder at the capital at the news of the mishap, and while repairs were expedited, the crews of the wrecked ships were marched overland to Tarentum to man the vessels which Taurus had been obliged to leave in port for lack of men. The interval was used by Octavian in making a round of South Italy to encourage the colonies and to inspect the squadron at Tarentum.

During this suspension of effort, although Pompey was not strong enough to attack Octavian in Italy, he did not confine his exertions to the display of his blue mantle as Appian states, for the same writer goes on to tell that he took advantage of the absence of any enemy on the Italian side of Sicily to send a squadron under Papias to lie on the line from Africa to Lilybaeum, where it fell by stratagem upon a transport squadron bearing 4 more legions from Africa to Lepidus. The transports were dispersed and 2 legions with much stores were destroyed. The other 2 legions got back to Africa and eventually reached Sicily, so that Lepidus had 14 legions in the island before the close of the campaign.

Besides that successful operation, Pompey sent Menodorus, with the 7 ships which had deserted from Octavian with him to reconnoiter the enemy at the Julian Port. Menodorus realized that Sextus no longer trusted him and determined to desert a third time but, before doing so, he thought it would be desirable by a deed of valor to show Octavian how valuable he was to Sextus. Accordingly, he made the passage from Messana to the Bay of Naples in the very quick time of 3 days (65 miles a day), apparently under oars, and by surprise captured some small guard ships off the dockyard, besides destroying several merchant ships. He then communicated with Octavian through some friends in the latter's

---

[7] It is also said that the campaign of 38 was the occasion for the mantle.

camp and said he was willing to serve under Agrippa, who had done him no wrong as had Calvisius. The offer was accepted, and Menodorus again joined Octavian's fleet, but was given no duty and was secretly watched.

About August 2,[8] Octavian left Naples to renew the campaign and arrived at Vibo about the fifth, where he directed Messala with 2 legions to "cross to Sicily, join Lepidus, and pass through to the bay under Tauromenium and wait there" for the other operations to develop. At the same time, Taurus started from Tarentum, moving his fleet and army side by side, with cavalry and liburnicas reconnoitering ahead by sea and land. When Taurus was as far as the Gulf of Scylletium, Octavian crossed the peninsula to inspect his division of the army and approve his conduct while Agrippa sent a reconnoitering squadron to examine the Lipari Islands and the northeast coast of Sicily.

Sextus was holding the northeastern tip of the island in force with all his fleet and most of his army. There were detachments at the principal landing places. Pompey was not seeking the initiative, but was on the strict defensive. He hoped to use his fleet to keep the enemy from landing. Apparently, Octavian had expected Lepidus to be present with his troops at Tauromenium to aid him, but nothing was heard of him and the operation had to be done without his help. Messala with 3 legions was ordered to Stylis at the entrance to the Strait of Messana and at Leucopetra on the tip of Italy he was to join Taurus, who was coming from the Gulf of Scylletium. Together they were then to cross to Tauromenium when ordered.

About August 8, Octavian sailed from Vibo with Agrippa and all the squadron belonging to the Julian Port to seize the Lipari Islands and threaten the northern coast of Sicily. While the landing there was in hand, Octavian went on to examine the northern coast of Sicily only some 10 or 15 miles away. He saw naval forces under Demochares ready to repel him and troops extending from Tyndaris to the point of the strait and jumped to the conclusion that Pompey must be there. Octavian returned to the mainland, determined to bring Messala and Taurus together at Leucopetra and ferry the army to Tauromenium under cover of the squadron from Brundisium.

---

[8] We know that the original campaign began July 1, and on the third day the gale caused a suspension of 30 days and the end came on September 3. The intermediate dates are estimates.

GAIUS JULIUS CAESAR OCTAVIANUS AUGUSTUS

Vatican Museum

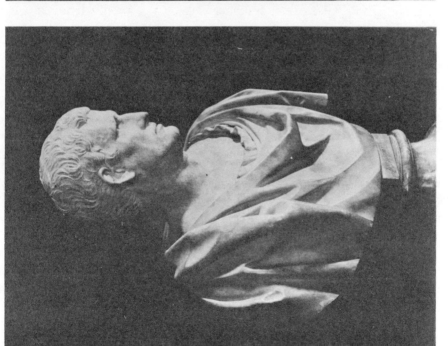

MARCUS VIPSANIUS AGRIPPA

Uffizi Palace, Florence

Battle at Mylae

Agrippa undertook the attack in diversion on the north coast and first spent a day or two establishing himself securely at Hiera and in reconnoitering the hostile squadron on the shores of Sicily. Agrippa saw only 40 ships of Demochares and on the morning of the twelfth he set out for Mylae with his fleet. He was surprised to find a much larger force, for during the night Apollophanes had arrived from Messana with 45 ships and Pompey himself with 70, making a total of 155 men-of-war.[9] Since the losses the previous month, Agrippa probably had no more than 115 to 120 ships, and apparently he had left some of them behind at Hiera. Although Agrippa probably had less than 100 ships with him, he realized that he had to fight immediately without waiting for the vessels at Hiera. Pompey's main fleet was in front of him and the sea was clear between Leucopetra and Tauromenium for Octavian to cross with the army. If Agrippa could hold Sextus' fleet for a day or two until the army should cross to Sicily, Pompey would lose the war even if Agrippa lost his ships. So Agrippa sent a dispatch boat to Octavian at Leucopetra, 40 miles away, to tell him of the opportunity and another to Hiera to call out his reserves there. Then he placed his heaviest ships in the center of his line and did not hesitate to engage.

After the usual exhortations on both sides, the fleets closed. The ships of Sextus were generally smaller and lighter than those of Agrippa, which the latter had built for this occasion, with towers fore and aft for the bowmen and javelin men. They were meant to give and take heavy blows. Pompey had the better seamen, and his pilots tried to break their opponents' oars and rudders. Agrippa's ships tried to ram or break through the hostile line. At close quarters they had an advantage in discharging missiles and in hurling the grappling irons for as a special feature the decks were built higher and the men cast downward. When a Pompeian ship was overcome, its sailors threw themselves into the sea and were picked up by small boats which hung about the fight.

Agrippa and Demochares singled each other out for personal encounter and Agrippa struck Demochares on the bow, bilging him, and shaking men out of his towers. "The rowers on the lower deck were cut off by the rising water, but those at the upper oars got on deck and swam

---

[9] A port guard must have been left at Messana, which could scarcely be under 25 ships.

away."[10] Demochares himself escaped to another ship and remained in action. Pompey was observing the action from a neighboring hill and, when he saw his ships were having little success and that the re-enforcements from Hiera were coming up, he gave the signal to retire, which was done in good order and his vessels took refuge on the shoals caused by the river silt.

Agrippa's pilot kept him from running the fleet on the shoals and he anchored, intending to renew the fight at night, but his friends urged him to consider the exhausted state of the crews and not to fatigue them more, so he withdrew to the islands at dark.

Pompey praised his crews and rewarded them as for victory, promising them to make his vessels' decks higher to meet the enemy on more equal terms.

The Army Crosses the Straits

The army from Vibo and the squadron from Scylletium were near Leucopetra ready to enter Sicily at the first opportunity, which now seemed at hand with Pompey's fleet engaged at Mylae. Pompey suspected, however, that Octavian had left Mylae for the sake of crossing the strait from the tip of Italy, so he returned to Messana with the fleet during the very night of the battle, leaving only a few ships at Mylae.

Towards the close of the day of the naval battle, Octavian must have received word that most of Pompey's fleet was engaged there and, as at next daylight no enemy was visible, Octavian thought his chance had come. He crossed from Leucopetra to Tauromenium with as many troops as he could embark, under the escort of the fleet of Taurus. The expedition met with no incident, probably arriving in the afternoon. The city refused to surrender and Octavian anchored a little south of it and disembarked the army. While laying out the camp hostile cavalry and infantry appeared and the former made an attack.

At the same time Pompey's fleet arrived from Mylae[11] probably hav-

---

[10] This statement is hard to understand. It may mean that the lower rowers had trouble to work their way through the rowers' scaffolding to get to the hatches.

[11] Although the ancient historian says that Pompey left Mylae the very night of the battle, yet after the exhaustion of fighting at Mylae, it is not likely that Pompey's oarsmen could have brought their ships to Tauromenium without an interval of at least two nights; so it is possible and even probable that Octavian lost a day at Leucopetra and crossed on August 14, the second day after the battle.

ing been increased by ships from Messana. Pompey may have had more vessels present than Octavian, although the latter's individual ships were larger. Octavian had not heard from Agrippa after the close of the battle, and had landed only three legions with a few thousand cavalry and light-armed troops. Appian says, if he had then been attacked simultaneously by sea and land, he would have had much difficulty to maintain himself; but the enemy fleet and army both went off to camp.

Naval Battle off Tauromenium

For the action of the next day (August 15) Octavian put Cornificius in command of the legions and himself went aboard the fleet. He took the ships somewhat off shore to get freedom of maneuver (he twice had been in difficulty through being too close to the shore). After making the complete round of his ships in exhortation, he hauled down his admiral's flag, as was customary, as Appian says, in time of great danger. Of the tactics of the battle Appian says nothing. There were two great encounters with Pompey's fleet during the day and the night ended the battle. Some of Octavian's ships were captured, some were burned, and others made sail, contrary to orders, and reached the Italian shore. Some of the crews swam ashore and were killed by Pompey's men after landing. It seems that 60 ships were lost, for Octavian only returned 70 to Antony and paid for the others. Pompey's losses are not known.

The Army Crosses Via Hiera

Octavian spent most of the night with his small boats, doubtful whether to join Cornificius or Messala. He finally decided to cross the strait and landed in Italy, greatly exhausted, early on the sixteenth with only a single armor bearer for escort. Maecenas was sent back in haste to Rome to keep the city quiet in view of the disaster. Octavian sent to Cornificius to say he would send aid, and that night when somewhat recovered he went with Messala to Stylis where there were three legions ready to embark, which he sent to Lipara, saying he would follow (August 17).

In the meantime, as soon as Agrippa's fleet was rested, it seized Tyndaris and other towns, although not Mylae, and began to land troops, whose first task was to rescue Cornificius who was in difficulty at Tauromenium. Cornificius was easily able to defend his camp, but lacked supplies to remain there and wait for rescue. He offered battle, but Pompey refused, as famine was working for him. Two or three days after the naval defeat off Tauromenium, Cornificius was obliged to undertake the difficult march across the mountains to the north shore. The road was difficult, the weather hot, and on the fourth day they could not get any water, as the fountain at the end of their march was held by the enemy in force. Just as they were in despair, the relief party of three legions from Tyndaris appeared on the other side of the spring and they were saved. We are told that Cornificius was so proud of the march to Mylae that thereafter whenever he went out to dine in Rome he assumed the honor of returning home riding on an elephant. Later the honor was restricted to the Emperor.

Troops were now pouring into Tyndaris by sea, and by August 22 Octavian had 21 legions with much cavalry and 5,000 light-armed in its neighborhood. Pompey's garrison still held Mylae and all the north shore as far as the strait, besides the passes through the mountains by which the roads led into Messana. About that time Lepidus came up from Lilybaeum by the north shore route and joined Octavian near Tyndaris, making 35 legions in the island and, if Lepidus brought his squadron too, about 200 or more ships. Those escaping from Tauromenium are not mentioned thereafter; perhaps they, too, joined Agrippa.

Sextus had summoned his legion from Lilybaeum, which easily got into Messana a little later by the east coast road, as the enemy was on the northern ones. Pompey was led to believe that Agrippa was about to land troops in his rear between Mylae and the city. As his lines were very greatly extended, he thought it necessary to abandon Mylae and the coast as far as the strait and the mountain passes also. When he found that Agrippa had not moved his fleet, he much regretted his sacrifice, for Agrippa was quick to occupy all the abandoned positions, which he did about the twenty-sixth or twenty-seventh; and Taurus, on the east coast, being now unopposed, moved to cut off the towns which were supplying Messana.

Pompey realized that he could not resist successfully with his army, but if he could destroy Agrippa's fleet the great hostile army would soon lack supplies, and might be then willing to grant him favorable terms. Appian says that Pompey sent to arrange for a naval battle which Octavian accepted with some misgivings, thinking it base to decline, and a day was fixed in which "300 ships" fought on each side. If Octavian had misgivings, it must have been because Lepidus' ships were not present, in which case Agrippa would have had no superiority in numbers, perhaps 130 against 150 to 160 weaker ships. No doubt Sextus fought at sea because the odds were better. The ships and their crews were much as before the battle of Mylae.

Perhaps Pompey had done something since that action to raise his fighting men to the same height as the enemy, for Appian says both sides now had towers on deck, but Agrippa had added an invention which was effective because it was new and the enemy was not prepared with a device to meet it. The novelty was a "harpago" (harpax). This was a piece of timber about 7 or 8 feet long, protected from axe blows by iron strips nailed to it and with a ring at each end. To one ring was fastened an iron claw and to the other a long rope. The harpago was hurled upon the enemy by a catapult and, when its hook caught hold, the end of the rope retained on board was brought to a winch and the two vessels were drawn together so as to permit a boarders' fight, in which the veterans of Octavian had the advantage over the escaped slaves in Pompey's army. The defense against the harpago would have been a long pole with a knife at the end to reach the rope of the harpago, such as Caesar had used against the Veneti, but this had not been foreseen by Pompey.

Battle of Naulochus

The battle took place near Naulochus on the north shore about 10 miles from the strait about August 29 or 30. It seems to have been a stand-up fight in full sight of the shore where the soldiers of Octavian watched in doubt. As the fleets lined up missiles were thrown, then the ships closed, and the harpago had great success, as it could be thrown a long distance and checked maneuvering by Pompey's skilled pilots. As the ships drew together, every kind of fighting was used and there was difficulty in knowing friend from foe, for all had the same weapons and almost all spoke the same tongue. Soon each side knew the other's watchwords and many frauds were practiced on that point. Fire was not used by either side because each dreaded it when locked together by the harpago. Agrippa was able to judge of the progress of the flight by the color of the towers, which was different in the two fleets, and saw the enemy was getting the worse. He cheered on the ships close to him and the nearest enemies yielded sea. They then destroyed their towers (to increase speed) and turned in flight. Seventeen ships escaped to Messana with Pompey; others were cut off and driven ashore; then those still fighting surrendered. Demochares killed himself; Apollophanes went over to the victor. Agrippa lost 3 ships destroyed in the battle and Pompey 28. All the rest except the 17 fugitives were captured or run on shore or burned. At Messana Pompey turned the command of the city over to Plennius, who was just outside with the legion on its way from Lilybaeum, and fled with his 17 ships, to Asia.

Agrippa's two victories at Mylae and Naulochus were boarders' battles. He had the better soldiers and won by their superiority. Naulochus was the more complete victory because the harpagoes prevented any maneuvering by the enemy. The ancient historians give no explanation of Octavian's defeat at Tauromenium. As far as we know, his fleet was not inferior to that of Pompey. We may believe either that he landed too many troops and had not enough on board when the enemy appeared, or else he was surprised and did not get all his vessels into battle at one time. In either case the fleet was badly handled. Pompey's quick shift from Mylae to Tauromenium showed praiseworthy perception. The strategy of Octavian and Agrippa was complicated and well carried out. The assembly of the two fleets and armies at the tip of Italy was well done. First there was the feint of landing at Mylae, followed by a real attempt to make the main crossing to Tauromenium and, when that miscarried, the transfer of the main effort to the north shore of Sicily was bold and successful. Pompey's strategy was a waiting one only.

THE SURRENDER OF MESSANA

Octavian remained at Naulochus and sent Agrippa to accompany Lepidus to the siege of Messana. Lepidus was on bad terms with Octavian and negotiated secretly with the enemy. Plennius asked for terms. Agrippa wished to postpone decision until Octavian could be consulted, but Lepidus accepted Plennius' proposal and, in accordance with it, after the eight legions had surrendered to him on September 3, he allowed them, in conjunction with his own army, to pillage the city. In consequence, the legions of Plennius saluted Lepidus as Imperator and the latter thought to dispute jurisdiction with Octavian who now came up and reproached him for pillaging the city. Lepidus answered, claiming equal authority as triumvir and ordering the Pompeian fortresses of the island to be closed against Octavian. The latter soon found that the armies did not want to fight each other and with great courage he entered Lepidus' camp and appealed directly to his soldiers. After something of a riot he withdrew, unharmed, although his cloak was pierced by a javelin. Cohorts and legions rapidly came over to him, so that Lepidus came to him as a suppliant and was allowed to retire to private life. Octavian added the African provinces to his own.

The great accomplishment of the campaign was that the seas were now peaceful and freedom of trade was restored to the Italian peninsula. But the eastern provinces were still divided from the western, and economic prosperity of the Empire could not be achieved until they were politically united.

PRINCIPAL AUTHORITIES CONSULTED FOR THIS CHAPTER

ANCIENT

Appian.
Dio Cassius.
Plutarch: *Antony*.

MODERN

Ferrero, G.: *Greatness and Decline of Rome*.
Merivale: *History of the Romans*.

APPENDIX TO CHAPTER XVIɪ

AGRIPPA'S SHIPS

The ships built by Agrippa before the Sicilian campaign of 36 B.C. were designed to overcome those of Sextus Pompey, which themselves were mostly built to prey on Roman commerce rather than for hard fighting. It is therefore probable that many of Agrippa's ships were of a rather small type.

The relief of Palestrina now in the Vatican (opposite) is generally believed to represent one of those ships. We see only the bow and most of the rowing chamber. The rest of the sculpture is lost. The drafting is conventional, the vertical scale being about 2.5 or 3 times the longitudinal one. The rowers are placed below the main deck on two levels, with 12 oars visible in each rank. There is a raised platform forward and Appian says that there was also one aft, both being occupied by javelin men or slingers who cast over the legionaries below. A peculiarity of the ship is that the outrigger frame for the oars supports a gangway above it, but lower than the deck on which are soldiers. Thus there were two ranks on each side and those in the upper rank standing on deck could hurl their pila over the heads of those on the outrigger platform.

In attempting to reconstruct such a ship, I think we may assume more oars than shown in the relief, let us say 18 on each side in each rank, and place 2 men on the upper and 1 on the lower oars, giving 108 rowers in all. The mariners would be about 25 and, allowing soldiers every 6 ft. along the deck and outrigger and a few for the towers, we have 80 soldiers in all, making a crew of 213. Providing 6 days' food and water at 15 lbs. per day, and an average weight of 200 lbs. for men and clothes, with arms and armor for those on deck, we have a weight of cargo of 61,770 lbs. Allowing 46 per cent of the displacement for the weight of hull; 5 per cent for the ram and towers; 15 per cent for masts, sails, anchors, and equipment, and 34 per cent for cargo, we have a displacement of 81 tons. Allowing 70 per cent of the water-line length for the

RELIEF BELIEVED TO REPRESENT ONE OF AGRIPPA'S LIGHTER SHIPS AT ACTIUM (PROBABLY SERVED AT NAULOCHUS), FOUND AT PRAENESTE, NOW IN THE VATICAN

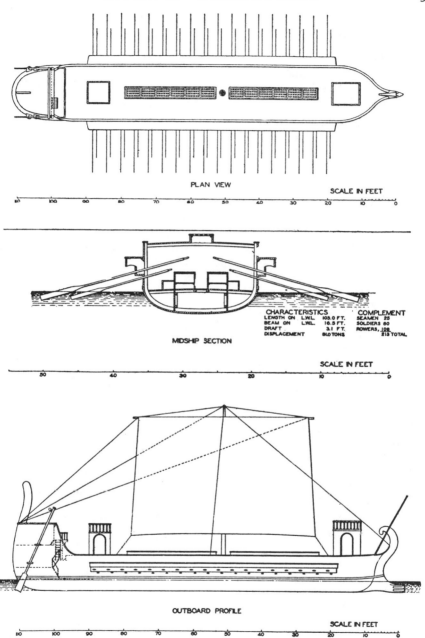

PLAN VIEW

SCALE IN FEET

MIDSHIP SECTION

CHARACTERISTICS		COMPLEMENT	
LENGTH ON L.WL.	103.0 FT.	SEAMEN	25
BEAM ON L.WL.	16.5 FT.	SOLDIERS	80
DRAFT	3.1 FT.	ROWERS,	108
DISPLACEMENT	810 TONS		213 TOTAL.

SCALE IN FEET

OUTBOARD PROFILE

SCALE IN FEET

RECONSTRUCTION OF A BIREME OF THE PERIOD OF AUGUSTUS
From Relief in the Vatican Found at Praeneste

rowing chamber (at 4 ft. per oar), the length will be 103 ft.[1] A beam of 17 ft. will give sufficient stability and the draft will be 3.1 ft.; meta-centric height about 2.5 ft.; wetted surface 1,460 sq. ft. Thirty-six 2-man oars and thirty-six 1-man oars would give an e.hp. of 14.0 and a speed of about 7.3 knots for a short spurt and 4.8 knots for 2 hours with all the rowers.

---

[1] The drawing is entitled "Bireme" because only 2 oars are visible in each rowing space in the bas-relief. The reconstruction would make her a trireme.

CHAPTER XVIII

CAMPAIGN OF ACTIUM, 31 B.C.

ECONOMIC SITUATION

THE removal of Lepidus from the triumvirate at the close of the Sicilian campaign of 36 left the Roman world divided into eastern and western halves, each under a military ruler who based his authority on an army not thoroughly reliable. The two halves of the Republic still had need of each other as in 49. Economic prosperity was to be reached by political union and reduction of armaments. The new dual government of Antony and Octavian suspended the commercial unity of the state and each half absorbed its revenues in military expenses for overcoming the opposing party. The public, as well as the supporters of both leaders, wanted reconciliation and the veteran soldiers wanted discharge with a bonus, but no compromise could be effected.

POLITICAL SITUATION OF OCTAVIAN

The political situation of the party supporting Octavian is comparatively easy to understand. After Philippi Octavian returned to Rome where Antony's retention of the tribute from Asia had created distress. Octavian's followers of all ranks expected rewards and riches, but the sources of wealth were chiefly in the East. After the destruction of the power of Sextus Pompey and the opening of the sea for the importation of African and Sicilian grain to feed Rome, Octavian could only continue to please the people of Rome and satisfy his soldiers and political supporters by securing the unity of the state, once more bringing the wealth of the East to Rome. This might have been accomplished by some arrangement with Antony, and for four years after Naulochus politics turned on this objective. In 32, the solution of the problem of the economic unity of the state was sought by war instead of diplomacy.

POLITICAL SITUATION OF ANTONY

To understand how the development of Antony's authority in the East resulted in war, we must go back a little. When after Philippi the

GREEK AND ROMAN NAVAL WARFARE

triumvirate needed money, Antony assumed the control of Syria and Asia with the intention of conquering Parthia to provide much-needed funds. As he proceeded east with this purpose in 41 he met Queen Cleopatra of Egypt at Tarsus.

It has been the general assumption that the association of Antony and Cleopatra was mainly one of dalliance, but there is strong reason to believe that it was chiefly political on Cleopatra's part, although no doubt she made the most of her personal charms in her diplomacy. She had already attempted to aid the triumvirate before Philippi; she was not very secure on her throne and she was desirous of having her son Caesarion accepted as her heir. She felt she had a valid claim to Antony's support as he was Caesar's political heir and she obtained a promise from him to spend the winter of 41-40 in Alexandria. This stay had far-reaching effect on Antony's policies and laid the origin of the war. To maintain his position with his army on which his authority rested, he needed money and Egypt was the richest country in the world. On the other hand, Cleopatra needed the support of military force to retain her throne. The liaison of the two during that winter was therefore a political incident of primary importance. Antony had gone east to seize the wealth of Parthia; Cleopatra urged him to forego the war and instead take her and the wealth of Egypt as the financial basis of his rule. He did not accept the idea at once and in the spring of 40 he left Alexandria with the intention of repelling a Parthian invasion into Syria. Instead, he went west and renewed his alliance with Octavian.

It is unnecessary to recount in detail Antony's variations in policy and in military objectives for the next few years. He tried to keep a hold on Italian affairs where he recruited his best soldiers. His lieutenant Ventidius gained a great victory over the Parthians in 38 but not much money, and in 37 Antony was in Italy and renewed the triumvirate and gave aid to Octavian for the destruction of Pompey's piratical government. He then left for Syria to carry on the war against Parthia with 16 legions, several of which had been given him by Octavian. Hitherto the colleagues were serviceable to each other. At Antioch, on his way east, Antony met Cleopatra, whom he had not seen for three years, and early in 36 he married her without divorcing his Roman wife, Octavia.

Thus he secured for himself and his supporters the resources of the richest country known for beginning the Parthian war, while Cleopatra seemed to ensure her throne and her dynasty. In spite of Cleopatra's aid, the war in Parthia was not fortunate and Antony lost prestige throughout the East as well as in Rome. Cleopatra now besought Antony to appear publicly as her husband and King of Egypt and rule the eastern half of the Roman state from Egypt instead of Rome. The winter of 35-34 Antony spent with Cleopatra, having refused to let Octavia join him.

This was the decisive period as between the opposing policies of the Egyptian Queen and the Roman Senators in the East struggling to control the conduct of Antony who still held the affection of the eastern legions. The Romans who were following Antony had left all that they most valued in Italy. They were in the East to make their fortunes and they did not wish Antony to break with Octavian by divorcing his sister and thus raise the probability of the sacrifice of their ties with Italy. Cleopatra used every means of seduction as Queen and as woman to subdue Antony. The time in Alexandria was filled by feasting and dissipation; the Queen spent money freely to keep Antony's principal supporters favorable to her and from abandoning him for Octavian, for upon them he depended as intermediaries to control his Italian soldiers and govern the provinces. Thus Cleopatra was able to sow dissension among Antony's Roman friends and in the spring of 34 it became apparent that she had won. In the summer of that year a successful raid into Armenia provided much treasure and Antony returned to Alexandria and entered the city with a triumphal procession modeled upon the imposing ceremony which no city but Rome had yet seen. Soon afterwards he transferred several Roman provinces to his children by Cleopatra and announced his act to Rome and to Octavian by a document known as the "Donations of Alexandria."

When the news reached Rome, it seemed that Antony intended to cut himself off from Italy and base his rule on the wealth of the Ptolemies whose dynasty he assured. The public resented the prospect of losing its richest provinces and their tribute. Not only did Antony thereby forfeit the regard of Italy and of many of his immediate prominent associates who hoped to return in honor to Rome, but the great host of Italians and other foreigners who were engaged in small business in the East under the protection of the legions now feared that their possessions might be sacrified. It seemed quite possible, moreover, that after a successful eastern campaign Antony might attempt to rule Rome with Cleopatra, and on this supposition Octavian started a nationalistic movement against him.

In the spring of 33, when Antony was concentrating a great army in Armenia for a new Parthian war, he learned that the news of the Donations had been ill-received at Rome and reproached Octavian for it. The latter did not reply directly to the accusations of Antony, but instead blamed Cleopatra as the seductress of a noble Roman and directed the wrath of the people upon her. Late in the summer Antony decided it would be better to postpone his Parthian campaign and settle his political dispute with Octavian. He directed his army of 16 legions and many auxiliaries upon Ephesus and summoned Cleopatra to meet him there. She joined him with munitions, 200 ships of war, and 20,000 talents from her own treasury. It is not clear whether at this time Antony contemplated war, or whether he marched his army westward merely as a diplomatic measure to influence Octavian's resolution.

Antony does not seem to have meant to renounce his connection with Rome and probably Cleopatra did not wish him to do so either, provided that he would continue to support her as Queen of Egypt, but she feared to be sacrificed if she should not be present to influence his diplomacy and his war. The Queen bought the support of Canidius, Antony's chief adviser and commander of the army, but the Senators about Antony divided into an Egyptian party seeking to gain all by the overthrow of Octavian and a Roman party seeking to share power with him by negotiation and reconciliation. In April, 32, Antony moved to Samos and the Queen urged the divorce of Octavia to make a complete breach with Rome. Octavian was in a difficult position in Rome, for he was without money and the term of the triumvirate had expired three months before. The Senate could not be relied upon to re-elect him to office. But he sent through Italy to get the cities to take the oath to support him. About May Antony sent his letter of divorce to Octavia and ejected her from his house in Rome. It was a political as well as a personal act, and in reply every means was employed to work up feeling against Cleopatra who was bringing a war into Italy.

Under the good government which Octavian had given Italy since 36, there was beginning some revival from the disorders of the previous warfare. Rome was looking forward to recovering control of the business of the eastern provinces and the tribute which Antony had spent in his wars beyond Syria. Now when Octavian made it appear that Antony was desirous of seceding from Rome, or at least of making Alexandria the capital instead of Rome, public opinion began to turn against the latter. But Octavian declined to make formal war on Antony. He induced the Senate to declare war on Cleopatra only. Antony was merely deprived of his command and his dignities. Octavian was unprepared for immediate war and feared that Antony would take advantage of his unreadiness by an immediate invasion of Italy, but Antony also had difficulties. Although Cleopatra and her supporters were willing enough to go forward, many Romans about Antony were still inclined to diplomacy rather than war and, as he had both money and supplies, he decided to remain with the army in Greece for the winter of 32-31 and send his emissaries into Italy to buy political support, raise riots, and corrupt the legions.

MOBILIZATION

As the year 32 drew to a close Antony distributed his forces in readiness for a campaign in 31, intending to carry the war into Italy. His resources were drawn by sea from Asia Minor, Syria, and Egypt, but, as these provinces were not undertaking a national war, they yielded their supplies only so long as they could not refuse. Consequently, Antony left strong forces of occupation behind him—4 legions in Cyrene, 4 in Egypt, and 3 in Syria. The main army of 19 legions, with many light infantry and cavalry; numbering 112,000 men in all,[1] was distributed in Greece. Antony and Cleopatra fixed their headquarters at Patras. Of Antony's

---

[1] Plutarch gives Anthony 112,000 men in all, but W. W. Tarn in the *Classical Quarterly* for April, 1932, gives good reason for thinking that he had no more than 65,000 legionaries. In light infantry and cavalry the two forces were nearly equal, about 10,000 to 12,000 of each on each side. Possibly Octavian's cavalry was somewhat stronger, as it was successful in a most important cavalry battle.

800 ships, 500 were in forward positions; the majority in the Gulf of Ambracia without soldiers on board. A squadron held Corcyra as the reconnaissance point and advanced base for the invasion of Italy and other ships were placed at intermediate posts.

To make sure of his line of supply, Antony placed garrisons at important halfway points; Cape Taenarum, Methone, and Corinth are particularly mentioned. While the long line of sea communications was open to raiding attack, it was impossible for Octavian to throw himself upon it in any great force, for by so doing he would open the passage into Italy, the prize of the war. Nevertheless, although it proved that Antony's line of supply was his "heel of Achilles," it seemed impossible for him to place a stronger force than he did along that line while contemplating an aggressive campaign calling for his best exertions.

During the winter of 32-31 Octavian assembled his army at Brundisium (see Map 10) and his fleet at Tarentum and Brundisium. Agrippa commanded the fleet and probably the army also. He had legionary troops and auxiliaries, amounting in all to 80,000 infantry and 12,000 cavalry. The great majority of Agrippa's combatant ships were triremes and quadriremes; none was larger than sexiremes and many were of the fast Liburnian type[2] which Agrippa had learned to prize since he had been made Minister of the Navy and Admiral of the Fleet at the end of 38. Orosius says Agrippa had 230 beaked ships and 30 unbeaked ones "as fast as liburni."

During the winter Antony's crews suffered from disease and a third of his rowers were lost. He was obliged to recruit ass-drivers, vagrants, and boys, but he said he would not permit himself to want rowers as long as there was a population in Greece. In consequence, he was somewhat slow in mobilizing his fleet upon the opening of navigation in the spring of 31. Agrippa was more prompt. The outcome of the war hung upon the skillful use which Agrippa made of his speedy ships. As he brought to success one minor naval operation after another he reduced his opponent's military freedom of action and thereby forced upon him an entire change in his political objective.

---

[2] Modern writers sometimes say that Agrippa's fleet was exclusively of this type, which was apparently the case with later Roman fleets when small ships as coast guards were adequate for the duties which usually fell to them.

AGRIPPA RAIDS ANTONY'S COMMUNICATIONS

Very early in March Agrippa got under way from Italy and struck at Antony's line of supplies. He seized Methone (see Map 2), an important intermediate port on the west coast of Peloponnese, and raided several other points. When he returned to Italy Agrippa left a squadron at Methone, in order to intercept Antony's supply ships coming from the East. Moving singly, the latter would easily be captured when making the usual call at Methone. That they were caught in considerable numbers is shown by the distress which developed in the camp which they should have supplied. Having created an alarm in the south, Agrippa returned to ferry the army across to Epirus.

THE WESTERN ARMY CROSSES THE ADRIATIC

To guard against political disturbances in Rome during his absence, Octavian brought the Senate with him and soon after the middle of March the fleet escorted the army from Brundisium. Apparently the objective was to seize the large division of Antony's fleet lying in the Gulf of Ambracia before the army in winter quarters in the Peloponnese could get north to man the ships and garrison the base. Agrippa put his cavalry ashore at the foot of the Acroceraunian Mountains, probably at Panormus which is a good port, and it marched south to attack the fleet base.

The ships went on some 30 miles to Corcyra, which the enemy had deserted and there the main advanced base of the expedition was established, as was the case so often before and since in wars between Italy and Greece. It does not appear where the legions were landed, but Antony first heard of them as being at Toryne. He promptly brought his army up to the Gulf of Ambracia to cover the fleet, which in the meantime, without its soldiers, had been in great danger by Agrippa's naval reconnaissance. The peril was obviated by the admiral (Antony or another) who armed some of the rowers and put them on deck while the others slowly worked the oars. The bluff was effective; the enemy withdrew without attacking and Antony's ships made themselves secure within the strait.

The narrow entrance, whose navigable water was only 400 or 500 yards wide, was 5 or 6 miles long and opened into the Gulf which was nearly 20 miles long and 3 to 6 miles wide (see Map 28). The channel ran between

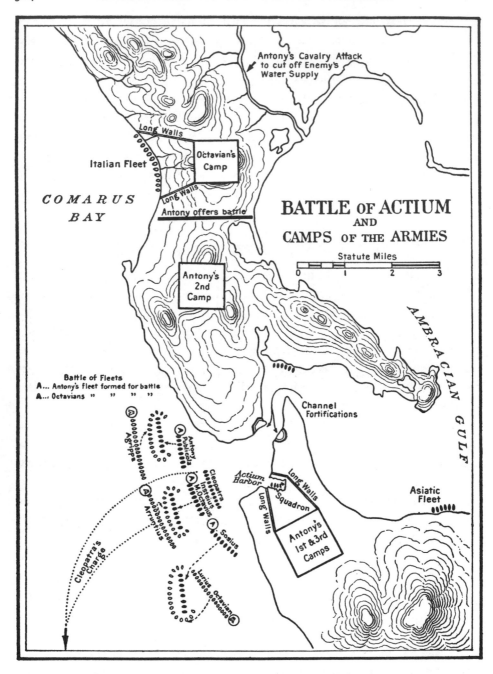

Antony's Cavalry Attack to cut off Enemy's Water Supply

Long Walls

Italian Fleet

Octavian's Camp

COMARUS BAY

Long Walls

Antony offers battle

BATTLE OF ACTIUM
AND
CAMPS OF THE ARMIES

Statute Miles

0   1   2   3

Antony's 2nd Camp

AMBRACIAN GULF

Battle of Fleets
A... Antony's fleet formed for battle
A... Octavians "   "   "   "

Agrippa

Antony
Publicola

Cleopatra
Insteius
M.Octavius

Arruntius

Channel Fortifications

Actium Harbor

Long Walls

Squadron

Long Walls

Asiatic Fleet

Cleopatra's Charge

Sosius

Lurius Octavian

Antony's 1st & 3rd Camps

MAP 28. SHIPS ARE NOT REPRESENTED INDIVIDUALLY ON THE MAP

two peninsulas, both of which were secured by Antony's advance-guard garrisons, and the passage was commanded by mechanical artillery. Under the ancient conditions of warfare the garrisons in their prepared positions could not be readily attacked.

Octavian's army soon approached and occupied a healthy piece of high ground on the north side of the entrance, about 10,000 yards from the point. This camp was fortified and from it connecting walls were run to a strip of beach which the ships occupied as base and landing station. Octavian offered battle, but Antony's weak garrison very wisely refused. A blockade was established and supply ships were intercepted as they tried to enter.

The Fleets and Armies Face Each Other at Actium

Antony soon arrived with his main army, marching into a blockaded port (see Map 28). He established his camp on the plain south of the entrance, in a position which proved very unhealthy as the summer drew on, and thus reduced his combatant strength. The main fleet Antony kept inside the strait, but a squadron was maintained outside and walls connected its beach with the main camp. With his whole army up Antony naturally desired battle, for he could not wait.

He crossed his army to the north side of the strait and offered battle on the broad plain between his entrenchments and those of the enemy. But Agrippa wanted no battle. Conditions had changed since the previous fall. Then Antony had been willing to delay and let distress affect the morale of Italy. Now distress in Antony's camp was reason for Agrippa's refusal to fight. Tentative measures by Antony who sought to force a fight now ensued for about three weeks or a month. He sent his cavalry around the bay to cut off Octavian's water supply but the effort failed. To both sides defeat might come either by general battle or by interruption of supplies coming over-seas to both armies. On each side fleet and army were on the watch to strike at the supplies of the other. The precise sequence of events as told by Dio Cassius is not very clear, but the spring passed into summer and the latter wore away, yet Antony's army had not secured a battle nor had his fleet broken the blockade.

The Naval Attack on Antony's Communications

About May it became evident to Agrippa that he held effective superiority on the sea over the enemy, who did not issue from port. Accordingly, to break the deadlock, Agrippa began to venture with a detached squadron. He ran down to Leucas and took possession of the island. He now had a convenient harbor at its north end, from which he could better intercept shipping bound to the enemy. Since his capture of Methone, the ships from Asia, which previously had been making a direct passage to the west coast of Greece, had to go to Corinth and transship their cargoes for a voyage via the Gulf of Corinth and around Acarnania. The capture of Leucas forced the ships from Corinth to discharge at the most convenient port of Acarnania, and then the supplies had a difficult portage over the mountains to the Gulf of Ambracia.

A little later Agrippa's flying squadron captured Patras, Antony's former headquaters, and threw the disembarkation point for Antony's supplies somewhere within the Gulf of Corinth. Soon after Corinth itself was taken, so that Antony's main line of supply could only pass from the Aegean through Thessaly, and this route was difficult and costly.

While the communications of Antony by sea were thus gradually impaired, they were further restricted through cavalry. Octavian sent expeditions into Greece and Macedonia to arouse the inhabitants, whom Antony had oppressed by heavy taxation. Antony likewise found it necessary to send into Macedonia to secure supplies, but disaffection was already sapping the loyalty of his followers and he followed his expedition himself and brought it back, as he feared its leaders might not return to him. Desertions of some of the eastern monarchs occurred and after Antony returned from Macedon his cavalry was defeated in a most important engagement, seemingly east of the Gulf of Ambracia. This action completed the blockade by the fleet and was conclusive as to communications. No longer could Antony gather the provincial crops or escort his food convoys across the mountains from the ports of the Aegean. All supplies became scanty.

Only one attempt seems to have been made to break the blockade at sea. Sosius went out one misty, late summer morning with a squadron to attack the blockading patrol and drove it back, inflicting some loss, but Agrippa put out with his whole fleet and severely defeated Sosius, and the eastern fleet lost morale. The latter part of August was now at hand and Antony's army on low ground was suffering from illness, while the enemy several miles away on the 500-foot heights was doing well. Octavian was winning now by mere inaction. The desertions to him were reassuring and he had only to wait until the enemy should choose some course of action. Antony could not venture to attack Octavian's entrenched camp and he could no longer remain passive without starving. He had the choice of breaking out by sea or by land.

A Change in Political Situation in Antony's Camp

In making his choice Antony was no doubt influenced by the entire change in the political outlook both of the Romans with him and of Cleopatra, which had come about owing to the misfortunes of the summer. Antony's movement on Italy was originally supported by the Roman party, because its members wanted to go back to Rome and resume their life as Roman aristocrats with Rome as the center of the Mediterranean world. They were never warmly in favor of a desperate battle and now negotiation was their best hope. Cleopatra's original desire for overcoming Octavian was because victory would make her dynasty secure in Egypt through Antony's gratitude for her assistance with the wealth and the fleet of Egypt. She wished no negotiation in which she felt her own position at home might be a principal point at issue. But the gradual impairment of the situation of the eastern army by hunger entailed changes in the political objectives which it was possible to reach by its military efforts. As the Romans became doubtful of the outcome of battle, they began to go over to the opposite camp and make their personal terms with Octavian while it was yet time. It must be remembered that by the Roman practice the great military commands were occupied by holders of the principal civil offices, and the seceders probably felt that leaving Antony was a political act, and not so much a military desertion as it would now be.

To the last Cleopatra continued to hold her original objective, but she now realized that it was no longer probable that it could be reached through defeating Octavian. She felt that she could make herself and her family secure in Egypt only by persuading Antony to renounce his designs upon Italy and against Octavian and retire to the provinces he had ruled since the battle of Philippi, continuing to govern them by her help and riches as Queen of Egypt. Antony's soldiers still retained their confidence in the great leader they had followed so long and the generals and officers who remained faithful no doubt thought that it was better to hold the greatest positions in the East rather than secondary ones at Rome. Should Antony effect a retirement, it appeared unlikely that Octavian would follow him to the East to restore the unity of the Roman state, for Octavian was not liked in Italy and had difficulty in maintaining his authority there.

CHANGE IN ANTONY'S STRATEGY

Accordingly, about the end of August, Antony resolved to retire from Actium and hold only Asia, Syria, and Egypt, and possibly Greece. It was not advisable to make the primary move by the army, for on its leaving the gulf the fleet would be unprotected and lost. As Macedon alone could not supply the army, it would still need supplies from Asia, but after the destruction of the fleet these could not be secured, for Agrippa would be able to send part of his own fleet to blockade the Aegean seaports while keeping enough at Corcyra to guard the passage to Italy. Therefore, if Antony should move the army into Greece or Macedon, Agrippa, still supplied from Italy, would follow him and refuse to fight by land as Fabius did with Hannibal, and Antony would be reduced by lack of supplies.

So Antony resolved to take his fleet to sea. If, contrary to his expectation, he should defeat Agrippa, he might hope to gain Italy, but if otherwise he would withdraw into Syria and Egypt with his fleet and all the soldiers on board and have the army follow as it could.

It was the best that could be done short of surrender, but the discussion and decision caused great controversy in the camp. The Romans accused Cleopatra of every villainy and even of attempting to poison her husband. Antony began to suspect her and insisted on her tasting the dishes served to him. To show the futility of such precautions, at the next banquet she put a chaplet on his head and later invited him to cast the flowers in his goblet and drink her health. As he was about to raise his glass, she stopped him and, calling a condemned slave, she told him to drink the cup. As he did so he fell dead. The Queen turned to Antony and said "you see how easy it would be for me to poison you, but I cannot do without you," and so she persuaded him that his suspicions were false and that she was loyal. Under such circumstances did Antony make up his mind to retreat and make a new start, determined to rule in the East at least, if not in Rome. The date of departure was set for August 29.

PREPARATIONS FOR THE NAVAL BATTLE

In preparation for battle, Antony's advanced camp on the north shore was abandoned. The ships lacked rowers and Antony is alleged to have destroyed many[3] so that the rest might have less inadequate complements, and among these he retained 60 Egyptian ships upon which he placed his treasure, i.e., the army funds, of which most must have been Cleopatra's gift. Contrary to custom before battle, Antony placed the ships' sails on board for use on the long voyage to Egypt, but under the pretext that they would serve to pursue the enemy. As for the total number of ships which went out to battle, we have varying accounts. We may believe that Antony had under 200 vessels, among which the 60 Egyptians made a single squadron under Cleopatra.[4] Antony embarked 20,000 legionaries and 2,000 archers. The number of men embarked corresponds well to about 170 to 180 large ships. The seamen and rowers may have numbered 40,000 to 45,000 men (very few).

The vessels were high and large compared to their adversaries, for Antony attributed Agrippa's victory at Naulochus to his bigger ships and therefore had prepared to meet him by building the old type Levantine vessels. A few were tetreres (4-ers) and a few were deceres (10-ers). The others were intermediate in size. They carried high towers of several stories bearing heavy mechanical artillery and the archers. They relied on grappling irons and a boarders' fight.

The knowledge that Antony had little hope of seizing Italy encouraged desertions of noble Romans and others. Amyntas, King of Galatia, and Dellius, a typical Roman turncoat, now went over to Octavian and brought positive news of Antony's change of policy and his intention of fighting at sea. On hearing of it Octavian was at first inclined to let him go and then chase him, but Agrippa convinced him this should not happen. Dio says

---

[3] After either victory or defeat Antony would have no use for these superfluous ships.

[4] Orosius gives Antony 80 ships, Plutarch says the Egyptians were 60. A number less than 200 in all is indicated by the large size of Antony's vessels and the total number of soldiers. Plutarch says they were well manned and, as they were large, they must each have had perhaps 125 soldiers or more.

Agrippa used the tactical argument that the enemy was taking his sails and could not be overtaken, but the political argument is far stronger that the long civil war called for immediate settlement and that Octavian could not seem to wish to postpone it. So both sides prepared for a naval battle.

Many of Agrippa's smaller ships had probably fought at Naulochus, where they had won against still smaller ships. Now they had to win against ships bigger than themselves and Agrippa prepared to turn the scale by the provision of new devices for throwing fire. I do not mean to say that fire-throwing was previously unknown, for we have seen how it was used to defeat Calvinus in the campaign of Philippi, but Romans had been accustomed to win at sea against inferior soldiers by the exertions of hard-fighting legionaries on the ships' decks. Here would be legionaries on both sides and Agrippa was preparing a tactical surprise. Contrary to Roman practice, he was going to make a principal effort against ship structure instead of relying chiefly on infantry.

On his fleet of 260 or more ships Agrippa embarked, according to Orosius, 8.5 legions, probably about 30,000 men, for the legions habitually ran much below their nominal strength of 6,000. In addition there were probably a few archers and slingers, perhaps as many as 2,000 or 3,000. Roughly, we may believe that Agrippa had about one-half more soldiers on shipboard than Antony and perhaps over a half more ships, with 50,000 to 55,000 rowers and seamen. The big ships of Antony were handicapped not only by a shortage of rowers, but also by their heavy loading, for they were equipped for a cruise while those of Agrippa were stripped light for battle. On the other hand, the greater height of Antony's ships and heavy structure was an advantage should Agrippa's ships close with them.

When Antony's arrangements were complete, he took his principal supporters with him in the fleet so that they might not raise any political disturbance among the soldiers. Canidius retained the command of the army with orders to retire to the fortified points of Greece which Antony already held. Eventually, no doubt, Antony meant to transfer it to Asia, if possible. The interposition of the Gulf of Ambracia gave Canidius the opportunity of a long start in any march to the southeast, but the country had been denuded of supplies, by its long occupation by the army. If he failed to conquer at sea, Antony could have had little hope of retaining any soldiers left with Canidius.

Previous to battle the usual allocutions were made on both sides, on this occasion with many political appeals. Antony praised his men and himself and abused Octavian, who had, he said, behaved badly towards him and would ill-treat the soldiers after victory. He admitted the superiority of the western army (his own had deteriorated during the summer), but magnified the strength of his ships and dwelt on their great size and the thickness of their sides to resist ramming by their light opponents. He showed that victory at sea would turn the tables and ruin the enemy through loss of his line of supply. Octavian also talked politics and made the point of Antony's subjection to the Egyptian siren who hoped to rule Romans. He went on to say that no ship ever hurt anybody by itself and that the size and thick timbers of the enemy would not avail against his soldiers' valor. The hostile ships, he said, could neither attack frontally nor by envelopment. If they were to remain motionless they would be subject to the ram and the fire-throwing engines and, if they moved, they were slow, either for attack or pursuit.

BATTLE OF ACTIUM

Antony was ready to go out on the appointed day, August 29, but the weather was unfavorable until the morning of September 2, when it was calm and both fleets embarked their crews and shoved off from the shore.

As Octavian with his staff was going down to the beach before dawn he met an ass-driver who saluted him. Octavian fell into conversation and asked his name. He answered "my name is Eutychus (Good Fortune) and that of my ass is Nicon (Victory)." Whereupon all went on their way rejoicing at the omen, which was doubtless communicated to the whole fleet. After the battle, Octavian put up a bronze statue of the ass and his driver on the spot where he had met them. The story is illustrative of the thought of the time, but moreover it is militarily important if we take the meeting as prearranged and as an effective bit of propaganda by an efficient staff to increase the battle ardor of the combatants.

Although Antony contemplated a withdrawal under sail from Actium, if unsuccessful, the customary sea breeze was not due until the afternoon and it was preferable to issue from the narrow strait under oars. Probably both sides moved about dawn. The western fleet would easily be the first in position. It drew up opposite the entrance where it waited, divided into three squadrons. Although Agrippa was in command, Octavian put himself in the place of honor with the right squadron under M. Lurius. Arruntius took the center and Agrippa chose the left squadron in which he might expect to face Antony, the hostile commander in chief. The leading friends of Octavian took station in dispatch boats to move along the line carrying orders and information and encouraging the fight. After issuing from the strait, the eastern fleet formed in four squadrons parallel to the shore and rather close to it. Antony went with the right which was under Publicola. Sosius had the left, and M. Insteius and M. Octavius, who had commanded one of Pompey's squadrons in 48, were in the center, all three making the front line. The fourth squadron was the Egyptian of 60 ships under Cleopatra which took position in the rear as reserve, and to hold position without effort, it seems to have dropped anchors under foot. Antony moved about in a dispatch boat and ordered his vessels to hold their stations and receive the attack. Agrippa formed line opposite and remained inactive at a distance of about 1,600 yards. We may suppose the average interval from ship to ship to have been from 40 to 45 yards.[5] Antony's line of about 110 to 120 larger ships would then have been about 5,000 yards long. Agrippa, with not less than 260 smaller ships would have had a longer line even if each division kept some vessels in a rear line as a reserve. His front must have been at least 8,000 yards long. The fleets remained motionless for a time after they had faced each other.

About noon Antony's left wing opened the battle by advancing, as Agrippa's inaction required him to do, both to fight and to get sea room

---

[5] At the close of his reign Octavian inscribed on bronze tablets at Rome a summary of the events of his long rule. A copy has survived which is known as the "Monumentum Ancyranum." In this inscription he tells of an artificial lake which he dug at Rome long after Actium, in order to give the people of Rome the spectacle of a sea fight. The lake was 1,800 by 1,200 feet in size and on it 30 beaked ships, biremes and triremes, besides smaller ones found room to fight. With 15 ships in line on each side they had not less than 80 nor more than 120 feet per ship. These ships were small. A somewhat larger interval would have been needed by Agrippa's ships and a still larger one by Antony's. I am inclined to think that the lines of battle may have been parallel to the long sides of the lake and that the interval between ships was less than the maximum of 120 feet, in order to have room for some opportunity to maneuver and envelopment of the opposing flanks. Three thousand soldiers fought in addition to the rowers; less than 100 soldiers per ship.

to weather Leucas in case of defeat. As Sosius approached him, Lurius withdrew in order that the former's advance might afford ample space towards shore for maneuver in his rear. About the same time Agrippa extended his left wing to the northward to envelop the enemy on that flank. To frustrate this maneuver Publicola moved north also, drawing away from his own center squadron which was simultaneously attacked by Arruntius.

The battle was now on, and Antony's ships had increased their intervals from one another to avoid envelopment, but in so doing they fell into another difficulty. Owing to their superior mobility, the western ships were now able to combine three or four at once against single adversaries. Owing to the sluggishness of Antony's vessels and the comparatively short range of missile weapons, many of them lacked enemies within effective range.

Soon after the fight opened, say at one o'clock, the usual fresh afternoon sea breeze sprang up and a little later, while the outcome was not yet decided, Cleopatra's squadron in the rear made sail, charged through the center of both lines and made off. Antony put himself in a light craft and followed her while the action still continued. His departure had no immediate effect; a few ships only were able to follow him as they should have done. These threw overboard towers and equipments to lighten ship and made sail.

For the remainder, the battle increased in intensity. Antony's ships were higher and used their artillery and hand missiles. By a quick advance, the ships of Agrippa attacked with the ram and swept away oars and rudders. If a vessel sank an opponent, good. But if not, she backed off. Agrippa's ships avoided delay at long range, nor did they remain in contact for a boarders' fight after they had made their ram stroke. The efforts of the eastern ships to grapple seem to have met little success.

At first, Agrippa was anxious to make prizes to secure any money on board, but in the end, to decide the event, he brought into use the incendiary weapons which he had previously held in reserve. Many of Agrippa's ships must by now have worked in rear of the hostile line. As Dio Cassius says,

the assailants coming from many sides shot blazing missiles and with engines threw pots of flaming charcoal and pitch. The defendants tried to ward off these fiery projectiles and when one lodged it was quenched with drinking water. When that was gone, they dipped up sea water, but as their buckets were small and few and half-filled they were not always successful. Then they smothered the fires with their mantles and even with corpses. They hacked off burning parts of the ships and tried to grapple hostile ships to escape into them. Many were burned alive or jumped overboard or killed each other to avoid the flames.

With soldiers of the same nation, accustomed to the same method of fighting and with the same fleet organization, it was the unexpected weapon, the flames, which decided the victory in Agrippa's favor. By four in the afternoon the battle was finished and the remains of Antony's fleet escaped and entered the harbor before a fresh breeze. [6]

Plutarch alleges that Agrippa captured 300 ships, but it may be this number refers to the losses of the entire campaign. The "Monumentum Ancyranum" tells us that in all his campaigns Augustus took or destroyed 600 triremes or larger ships. It may well be that Antony lost 300 ships, including those burned before the battle and those in port when the army surrendered. That many ships re-entered port is shown by the fact that Agrippa and his fleet anchored for the night on the scene of the battle to close the exit.

Cleopatra's Part in the Battle

The world has always been attracted by the romance of the two lovers as it affected world history in this memorable battle which secured the unity of the Roman state for over three centuries. We need not believe contemporary gossip nor the assertion of the ancient historian (Dio Cassius) as to Cleopatra that "true to her nature as a woman and an Egyptian, tortured by suspense and fearful of either outcome, she turned to flight herself and raised the signal for others." The same authorities who condemn her conduct in the battle tell us that as a sovereign she was as capable as a man. It is certain that it was politically important to Octavian both before and after the battle to vilify her as the wicked foreigner who had

---

[6] The usual afternoon winds of Actium in September are west southwest, west, and northwest. Probably it was from the latter direction during the battle or Antony could not have weathered Leucas.

That these escaping vessels treacherously deserted Antony without fighting, as alleged in the *Cambridge Ancient History*, vol. 10, seems to the present writer a somewhat fanciful view.

MARK ANTONY
Vatican Museum

CLEOPATRA
Capitoline Museum

misled and betrayed the noble Antony. After the war the abuse of Cleopatra was something in which the survivors on both sides could cheerfully agree. A modern historian (Merivale) speaking of Horace, who sums up the tone of Roman gossip, says

> the same writer who sneers at the effeminacy of her habits and the frivolousness of her vanity does justice to her manly courage, her philosophic fortitude, and her kingly pride.

He adds as his own opinion

> as a queen her ambition was bold and her bearing magnanimous: she contended gallantly for the throne of her ancestors with the weapons which nature had given her. Her noblest epitaph is written, not in the language of amatory rhapsodies or of sickly compassion, but in the ferocious sarcasms of her exulting conquerors.

Let us believe then that she and her chief pilot used her squadron as Antony planned to use it, accepting Admiral Jurien de la Graviere's opinion (*La Marine des Ptolémées*) that her charge through the fighting centers was a last bid for victory. Under oars, her heavy ships could not move fast enough to ram their lively opponents, but charging under sail with a free wind every Egyptian had one chance to sink an enemy. The charge did not turn the scale of battle and once down to leeward the squadron could not re-engage. For it, the battle was over and Cleopatra went on to Egypt according to plan. Unfortunately, for her and Antony, it did not prove possible for the ships in the main line of battle, violently attacked by fire and missiles, to break off the action and follow Antony as they should have done.

I cannot believe with Kromayer (*Schlachten Atlas*) that the battle was purely a measure for escape. Like every good commander, Antony was ready for the worst while hoping for the best. If, contrary to his expectations, his fleet should get the better of the enemy, the relative position of the two opponents as it had existed all summer would be reversed, and he would enter Rome, as he told his soldiers. But to provide for failure, he gave orders that in that case ships were not to return to port where starvation awaited them. He preferred to escape with as many soldiers as he could and make a new stand in Egypt with the eleven legions he had there and in Africa and Syria, for the political indications in Rome were such it was very possible that Octavian would not dare to attempt to disturb him in the East.

The Pursuit and Subsequent Outcome

The pursuit of the escaping Egyptians was slight and short, for Agrippa's ships were without sails. After leaving the battle in his light craft, Antony was taken up in Cleopatra's ship, but he did not meet her. Instead, he went to the bow of the ship where he sat in despair for three days (for his fleet had not followed him), until they reached Taenarum (200 miles), in spite of the messages Cleopatra sent him by her women. There some ships and friends joined him from Actium and he resumed relations with his wife. He learned there, also, that his fleet was lost, but that Canidius still held the army intact. He sent orders to lead it through Macedonia into Asia.

In the meantime, the day after the battle, Octavian summoned Canidius to surrender. The latter refused, but when it became apparent that Antony had gone off, desertions of Roman leaders and eastern princes began again. Canidius himself slipped away by night to join Antony in Egypt, and a week after the battle the army broke up. A part surrendered to Octavian and some escaped to their homes.

The news of the battle at sea and of Antony's flight with the Egyptian woman and the surrender of the army completely destroyed Antony's prestige both in Rome and elsewhere, turning public opinion strongly and seemingly most unexpectedly in Octavian's favor, so making it possible for him to pursue the fugitives to the center of their power in Egypt. Octavian easily occupied Greece and found Asia Minor free of troops. These provinces fell to him without difficulty, and after returning to Italy to settle some disturbances during the winter of 31-30, his departure for Asia in the spring of 30 met with general approval, since the financial basis of eastern opposition to the rule of Rome lay in Egypt and its conquest would end the civil war.

Antony and Cleopatra in Egypt

As for Antony and Cleopatra, they landed in Egypt and the Queen made the most gallant efforts to meet the coming attack. As Octavian drew near from Syria, she opened negotiations with him, apparently in the hope that before hostilities were renewed she might be able to arrange terms permitting her to hold her throne as a client of Rome, but she met with no success. At last Octavian arrived before Alexandria. Antony led his cavalry in a successful skirmish and then as he was about to draw up his infantry for a general battle he saw his ships and cavalry go over to the enemy (August 1, 30 B.C.). He committed suicide under conditions which should be read in Plutarch or in Shakespeare.

After his death and Octavian's occupation of Alexandria, the Queen still attempted to preserve her inheritance for her family. When she saw that was impossible and that she was destined to be shown as a prize in Octavian's triumph in Rome, where she had lived as the guest of Caesar, she too committed suicide as bravely as she had lived. Octavian succeeded to the sovereignty of Egypt, where his name still appears on its monuments in the royal cartouches. The wealth of Egypt was a foundation stone of the reconstructed Roman state, which existed in comparative peace and prosperity for many generations afterwards.

The tactics of the battle of Actium were contrary to the whole development of Roman naval history. From the First Punic War onward, Roman admirals trusted for success to the disciplined valor and skill of their legionaries. Their own efforts were confined to seeking a way to insure the soldier a chance to show his personal qualities. This was the object of the "corvus" and all its modifications. Even Agrippa himself at the battle of Naulochus, only five years before, thought his soldiers so superior to the vagabonds and former slaves of Sextus Pompey's army that he too trusted everything to his infantry and his own contribution to victory was the use of the "harpax" which obliged the hostile ships to stay and take their beating.

It was the mark of pre-eminent ability that at Actium he found a new way to victory, renouncing Roman tradition and his own experience. His veterans, drawn from campaigns in Gaul, at Perusia, in Illyria, and in Sicily were matched by their equals who had fought in Parthia and Armenia. Antony trusted wholly to his private soldiers in close fight, as all previous Roman admirals had done, and gambled on the result. Agrippa had the high merit of perceiving that he should give active aid to his men to overcome enemies of equal worth, and he loaded his dice. A completely thought-out system of "surprise" tactics overcame the traditional methods of Antony.

It was the fire-throwing devices of Agrippa, following his short attacks against the hostile oars, that won him success, for when the sluggish great ships of Antony were further slowed by loss of oars, concentration of numbers against individual ships became easy.

In his two great battles of Naulochus and Actium, Agrippa appears as the greatest of Roman admirals. He is even more, for, like Themistocles, he first built and administered his navy before he fought with it. Both were statesmen as well as warriors, and both maintained occidental civilization against the encroachment of the alien East. Their deeds, together, with their nautical and political ability, place them at the head of admirals of all time.

In these civil wars it is worth noting that in the three principal campaigns of Pharsalus, Philippi, and Actium, the influence of sea power was the same in all. All were Balkan campaigns of the East against the West. In each, the possessor of sea power was able to wait for its slow and silent influence to take effect, and in each the opponent was obliged to press for a decision by battle to avoid starvation. The business of a navy is to throttle the enemy's supplies. In two cases, at Pharsalus and Philippi, the hand of the eastern commander in chief, holding preponderance at sea, was forced by politics to accept a land battle which he did not desire and on each occasion he lost the encounter which it would have been better to refuse. In the third campaign, at Actium, Agrippa, holding sea power, declined to the last the land battle which Antony constantly sought. Finally, when Antony could endure no longer, as a last resort and to avoid starvation, he accepted naval battle and the result fell short of his hopes.

In the whole course of Roman expansion, from the First Punic War to Actium, her fleet was indispensable to Rome's conquests. She frequently neglected her navy, but to advance again she had to restore it.

After many centuries of naval warfare, the battle of Actium established the economic unity of the Mediterranean basin and thereafter, for over three centuries, the peace of Rome prevailed over those waters, during which period the Roman navy shrank to a mere coast guard for the protection of the public against pirates.

PRINCIPAL AUTHORITIES CONSULTED FOR THIS CHAPTER

ANCIENT

Appian.
Plutarch: *Antony*.

MODERN

Cambridge Ancient History, vol. 10.
Ferrero, G.: *Greatness and Decline of Rome*.
Gravière, Jurien de la: *La Marine des Ptolémées*.
Kromayer, J.: *Schlachten Atlas*.
      Hermes, 34 for year 1899.
Merivale, C.: *History of the Romans*.
Tarn, W. W.: *Journal of Roman Studies*, vol. 21 for year 1931.
      Classical Quarterly for April 1932.

INDEX

Abydos in Hellespont, Battle of, 181; Pharnabazus aids fleet with army, 181; Alcibiades joins in battle, 181

Achaemenes, Brother to Xerxes, 77; Commanding Egyptian squadron, 77; Advises against dividing fleet, 77

Achillas, Egyptian general, heads Alexandrian revolt, 464

Acilius commands at Oricum and loses his fleet, 454

Actium, Campaign of, 517; Mobilization, 521; Strength of forces, 521; Western army crosses Adriatic, 523; Description of locality, 523; Fleets and armies face each other, 525; Battle, 531; Pursuit after battle, 536; Roman peace follows battle, 538

Adherbal, Carthaginian admiral, 294; Overcomes Roman fleet at Drepanum, 297; Battle off Carteia, 360

Adeimantus, Corinthian admiral, Always in opposition to Themistocles, 82; Assails Themistocles, 83

Aegatian Islands off Sicily, Battle of, 301

Aegina, Greek fleet mobilizes, in 479 B.C., 97

Aemilius Paullus, Lucius, Consul, Commands in Illyrian war, 315; Defeated and killed at Cannae, 325

Aemilius Regillus, Lucius, Praetor, Commands Roman fleet, 401; Fleet operations in 190 B.C., 403; Arrives in Aegean, 406; Hasty action, 407; Battle of Myonnesus, 412; At Teos, 413; His conduct at Myonnesus, 415; Gains a triumph, 415; Besieges Phocaea, 418

Aeschylus' account of Salamis, 106

Aetolia, Asks Antiochus to enter Greece, 392; Aetolia secedes to Antiochus, 393; Decides on war with Rome, 394

African campaign of Caesar, 474; Republican forces there, 474; Caesar sails from Sicily, 475; Battle of Thapsus, 480; Review of campaign, 481

Agrippa, Marcus Vipsanius, Crushes revolt in Gaul, 499; Builds naval port at Puteoli, 502; His fleet injured in gale, 504; Naval battle at Mylae, 507; Strength in battle, 507; Lands army on Sicily's north shore, 509; Naval battle of Naulochus, 511; Raids Antony's communications, 523; Again raids, 526; Fleet's strength at Actium, 530; Commands left squadron personally, 532; His tactics at Actium, 537; His pre-eminent position as admiral, 538

Agron, King of Illyria, 312

Alcibiades, General in expedition to Syracuse, 146; Does not wish decisive action at once but should sieze Messana, 149; Recalled to Athens and deserts to Sparta, 150; His recommendation to Sparta, 152; Goes over to Tissaphernes, 174; Gains confidence of Athenian army at Samos, 175; In battle at Abydos, 181; Brings Athenian fleet to relieve Cyzicus, 182; Battle off Cyzicus, 182; Takes Athenian fleet to Notium, 184; His fleet is defeated in his absence, 184; Deprived of his command, 184; Warns Athenian fleet at Aegospotamos, 191

Alexander, the Great, Campaigns, 218; Becomes king of Macedonia, 219; Reduces Thrace, 219; Subdues Thebes, 219; His army on leaving Europe, 219; His navy, 219; Battle of Granicus, 221; His economic problem, 221; Battle of Issus, 222; Siege of Tyre, 222; Enlarges fleet at Tyre, 223; Leads assault on Tyre, 225; Founds Alexandria, 226; Re-establishes commercial business, 226

Alexandria, Occupied by Caesar, 463; Description, 464; Rebels against Caesar, 464; First naval battle, 466; Second naval battle, 467; Battle at Pharos, 469; Battle on the Mole, 470; Surrenders, 471

Amynander, King of Athamanians, adheres to Antiochus, 394

Amyntas, King of Galatia, deserts Antony, 529

Anastrophe, ship maneuver, 10

Antalcides, Spartan admiral, Method of chase of Athenian ships, 215

Amorgos, Naval battle at, 232

Amphipolis, Athenian loss of, 143

Antigonus, Ruler of Phrygia, etc., 231; Wishes to break Alexander's Empire, 233; His fleet destroys the Macedonian fleet in the Bosphorus, 234; Defeats Eumenes, 234; Attempts to dominate the Empire, 235; His policy, 235; Raises insurrection in Greece, 235; Fails to enter Europe and peace with Lysimachus and Cassander, 237; Raises Greece against Cassander, 239; Fails to invade Egypt, 243; Siege of Rhodes, 245; Ends the siege, 250; Sends army into Europe, 251; Defeated and killed at Ipsus, 252

Antiochus, King of Syria, He and Philip of Macedon wish to divide Egypt, 377; War with Rome, 387; His objectives, 388; His aggressions, 389; He enters Europe, 389; His strategic situation, 389; Sends Embassy to Rome, 391; Lands army at Demetrias, 393; Plans with Aetolians, 393; Seizes Chalcis, 394; His unlucky attempt at propaganda, 395; His advance is checked, 396; Defeated at Thermopylae, 396; Enlarges fleet, 401; His fleet in 190 B.C., 403; His army at Magnesia, 419; Defeat, 419; Terms of peace, 419

Antipater, Regent of Macedonia, 230; Becomes joint regent, 231; Checks revolt in Greece, 232; Breaks with Perdiccas, 233; Becomes sole regent, 233; Reverses Alexander's Policy, 233; Dies in 319 B.C., 233

Antonius, Lucius, brother of Mark Antony, raises insurrection, 497

Antony, C. Antonius, Campaign in Illyria, 446

Antony, Marcus Antonius, Commands Caesar's army at Brundisium, 451; Crosses Adriatic with army, 452; Forms 2d triumvirate, 487; Crosses advance guard to Epirus, 489; Army crosses and moves east, 491; Battle of Philippi, 493; Redivision of provinces, 497; Marries Octavia, 497; Renews triumvirate, 501; Situation in 35 B.C., 517; Marries Cleopatra, 518; Brings his army to Ephesus, 520; Divorces Octavia, 520; Mobilizes forces, 521; Camps at Actium, 525; Change in political situation, 527; Change in his strategy, 528; Suspects Cleopatra, 528; Prepares for naval battle, 529; His fleet's strength, 529; Takes position on the right at Actium, 532; Deserts the battle, 533; His reasons therefor, 535; In Egypt, 536; His death, 537

Apollonius, Syrian admiral, commander in chief at Side, 409

Apollophanes, Pompey's admiral, 498; At Mylae, 507; At Naulochus, 512; Goes over to Octavian, 512

Appius Claudius Pulcher, Commands army in Sicily, 336; His fleet blockades Syracuse, 336

Archimedes, engineer, His weapons at Syracuse, 337; Killed, 340

Arginussae Islands, Battle of, 185; Tactics of battle, 187; Failure of Athenians to save wrecks, 189; Victorious Athenian admirals executed, 190

Argo, Jason's ship, 38

Aristides, Athenian leader, Arrives at Salamis with news and is reconciled to Themistocles, 88; His action on Psyttalia, 93; Commands Athenian army, 98

Arruntius, Lucius, Commands center squadron at Actium, 532

Artabazus, Held command in Macedonia and Thrace in 480-479 B.C., 96; Takes command of fugitives from Plataea, 101

Artayntes, Persian admiral in 479 B.C., 96

Artemisia, Queen of Halicarnassus, Advice to Xerxes before battle, 84; Advice to Xerxes after battle, 94

Artemisium, Greek naval base at, 61; Greek fleet at, 62; First battle, 68; Storm, 69; Second battle, 69; Third battle, 70; Munro's critique on the three battles, 70; Tactical lessons, 71; Comparison with army tactics at Thermopylae, 75; Persian fleet at, 79

Artillery, mechanical, Developed by Dionysius, 197

Astyochus, Spartan admiral, 175

Athenian navy, Training, 120, Battle at Sybota Islands, 121; New system of tactics, 123; Battle off Patras, 131; Battle of Naupactus, 133; Second battle off Sybota Islands, 137; Battle of Bay of Pylos, 137; Athenian fleet at Syracuse, 153; Squadron under Diphilus defeated, 162; Naval battles before Syracuse, 159, 163, 164, 166, 168; Naval battle off Eretria, 176; Battle of Kynossema, 179; Battle of Abydos, 181; Battle of Cyzicus, 181; Battle of Notium, 184; Battle of Arginussae, 185; Battle of Aegospotami, 191

Athenian Empire, Developed by the fleet, 119;

Strength of, 126

Athens, Dispute with Sparta and appeal to Persia, 14; Campaign of 490 B.C., 14-25; Political situation in 490-480 B.C., 54; Ownership of silver mines, 54; Persian siege of, 81; Persian fleet at, 81; Recalls squadron from Delos, 98; Is destroyed by Mardonius, 99; Economic position in 5th century, 118; Commercial rival of Corinth, 118; War against Corinth, 119; Long walls, 127; Strategy in the war, 128; Her seaport bases, 128; Battle of Corcyra, 128; Her desire to maintain her power in the west, 128; Need for seaports there, 128; Maintains a fleet at Sicily, 129; Peloponnesians attempt to get a hold in Acarnania, 129; Captures Messana in 427 B.C., 139; Has to withdraw ships from Sicily, 143; Defeat of her army at Delium, 143; Expedition against Syracuse, 144; Previous relations with, 144; Reasons for war in 416 B.C., 145; Siege of Syracuse, 146; Loss of prestige after Syracuse, 171; Persian satraps aid Sparta, 172; Her recovery in 412, B.C. 173; Efforts to control Euxine trade, 175; Army at Samos does not support home govevrnment, 175; Controls Euxine commerce after capture of Cyzicus, 183; Athens ruined by defeat at Aegospotami, 191; Its capitulation 192; Political reasons for failure, 192; Attempts to re-establish commercial connections, 232; Fleet at the Hellespont, 232; Fleet defeated at Amorgos, 232; Seized by Demetrius, 239

Athos, Canal at, 57

Attalus of Pergamum, Envoy to Rome, 395

Attalus, King of Pergamum, Allied with Rome, 346; Battle of Chios, 379, Fleet at Mt. Cane, 380

Autolycus, Rhodian ship captain, 383

Baebius, M. Baebius Tamphilus, Praetor, 395; Crosses to Epirus with army, 396

Bibulus, Marcus, Pompey's admiral at Corcyra, 449; Burns Caesar's transports, 450; Stops Caesar's supplies, 451; Dies, 451

Bireme, boat with 2 men per oar, 36; Dispatch boat, description, 49

Bocchus, chief of Mauritania, partisan of Caesar, 475

Bogud, chief of Mauritania, partisan of Caesar, 475

Bomilcar, Takes troops to Hannibal, 335; Enters Syracuse harbor with fleet, 339; Second entry, 339; Returns to Carthage, 339; Third appearance in Sicily without consequence, 340; Takes squadron to Tarentum, 348

Brasidas, Spartan, Commands a ship at Pylos, 140; Takes Amphipolis, 143

Bridges at Hellespont, 58

Brutus, Decimus Brutus Albinus, 429; Commands Caesar's fleet in Brittany, 429; Builds and commands Caesar's fleet, Siege of Massilia, 442; First battle, 443; Second battle, 445

Brutus, Marcus Junius, Forms republican army in East, 487; Suicide at Philippi, 494

Brundisium, Siege of, 438; Treaty of, 497

Caesar, Gaius Julius, His navy in Gaul, 426; Its strength, 431; His navy's "scythes," 430; His naval tactics follow the Roman tradition, 431; His naval wars, 432; Political conditions, 432; Head of liberal party, 433; Forms triumvirate with Pompey and Crassus, 433; Type of approaching civil war, 434; Crosses Rubicon, 434; His army, 435; Invades Italy, 436; His strength grows, 437; Besieges Brundisium, 438; Settles affairs in Italy, 439; Strategic situation early in 49 B.C., 440; Makes war in Spain, 441, Besieges Massilia, 442; In Spain, 443; Naval victory at Marseilles improves his situation in Spain, 444; Victory at Ilerda, 444; Returns to Rome, 446; Campaign in Illyria, 446; Campaign of Pharsalus, 447; Crosses Adriatic, 450; Siege of Dyrrhachium, 454; Battle of Pharsalus, 457; His forces, 458; Pursuit of Pompey, 461; Arrives in Egypt, 462; Hostilities at Alexandria, 464; Defeats Egyptian army, 471; Conquers Pharnaces at Zela, 472; Gains control of sea, 474; African campaign, 474; Sails from Sicily, 475; Lands in Africa with small force, 476; Seizes Monastir, 477; Takes position at Ruspina, 477; His transports arrive, 477; Battle of Thapsus, 480; Fleet at Thapsus, 480; Second Spanish campaign, 482; Sends fleet to Spain, 483; Sea is hostile to Pompey, 483; Conquers at Munda, 484; Roman affairs after his death, 486

Callimachus, Greek commander in chief at Marathon, 21; His death at the Persian ships, 25

Callicratidas, Spartan admiral, Commands Peloponnesian fleet, 185; Takes his fleet to Lesbos, 185; Defeats Conon, 185; Loses life when defeated at Arginussae, 189

Calvinus, Cneius Domitius, triumviral general, His army destroyed on the sea, 493

Cambyses, King of Persia, 13

Calvisius, C. Sabinus, Octavian's admiral, 499; Naval battle at Cumae, 499; Battle near Scylla, 501

Canal at Athos, 57

Canidius, P., Antony's general, Commands Antony's army, 520; His orders at Actium, 530; Deserts his army and it surrenders, 536

Cannae, Battle of, 325

Capua, Secedes to Hannibal, 327; Taken by Rome, 348

Cartagena (New Carthage), Carthaginian base in Spain, 310; Conquered by Scipio, 354

Carthage, Establishes herself in western part of Sicily, 196; Defends Motya, 199; Population in First Punic War, 266; Economic condition, 266; Revenue, 267; Size of fleet, 273; Naval battle at Lipara, 274; Condition after First Punic War, 309; Power limited to Africa, 309; Recoups her losses, 310; Her fleet raids Italy, 323; Council's policy not in accord with Hannibal's, 328; Shifts efforts to Liguria, 361; Decides to aid Hannibal, 363; Recalls Hannibal, 369; Breaks truce, 372; Peace terms, 374

Carthalo, Carthaginian admiral, defeated off Sicily, 300

Cassander, son of Antipater, opposes Polyperchon, 234; Seizes Athens and Macedon, 234; Struggle with Antigonus, 236-37; Besieges Athens, 250; Opposes Demetrius in Thessaly, 251; Alliance with Lysimachus and Seleucus, 251; Sends troops to Lysimachus, 252; Remains King of Macedon, 252

Cassius brings a squadron to Pompey, 496

Cassius, Gaius Longinus, Takes Pompeian squadron to Sicily, 460; To Libo, 460; Returns to Corcyra, 460; Forms republican army in East, 487; Gains Rhodian fleet, 490; Suicide at Philippi, 493

Cassius, Longinus, Misgovernment in Spain, 483

Catana, Seized as fleet base by Athenian expedition, 150; Naval battle off, 202

Cataphract, Successive meanings of, 210

Catastroma, Deck over rowers, 45

Cato, Marcus Porcius, at Thermopylae, 397

Catulus, C. Lutatius, Consul, Defeats Carthaginian fleet in 242 B.C. and ends war, 302

Chariclitus, Rhodian admiral, Battle at Side, 410

Cimon, Son of Miltiades, Victory at Eurymedon, 119; His development of Athenian fleet, 119; Forms naval school of maneuver, 120; Alters Themistocles' system of tactics, 121

Cissus, Naval battle, 398

Claudius, Publius C. Pulcher, Consul in 249 B.C., Defeated in naval battle off Drepanum, 296; His tactical error, 299

Cleitus, Commands Macedonian fleet, 232; Defeats Euetion, 232; Loses his fleet in the Bosphorus, 234

Cleonaeus, Rhodian admiral, succeeds to command of Rhodian fleet, 385

Cleopatra, Queen of Egypt, submits to Caesar, 463; Bears son to Caesar, 472; Sends her fleet to aid Antony, 490; Gales drive it back, 490; Meets Antony, 497; Her political relation with Antony, 518; Marries Antony, 518; She brings Antony to her policy, 519; Accused by Octavian, 520; Her political stand at Actium, 527; Antony suspects her of treachery, 528; Her squadron at Actium, 532; Leaves the battle, 533; Her own part, 534; In Egypt, 536; Her death, 537

Clupea, Africa, Naval battle off, 351

Cnemus, Peloponnesian admiral, Operations in Gulf of Corinth, 130; His mistake in strategy, 133; Battle at Naupactus, 133

Conon, Athenian admiral, Takes Athenian fleet to Lesbos and is defeated in chance encounter, 185

Considius, C. Longus, of the army in Africa, commands at Hadrumetum, 476

Corcyra, War with Corinth, 121; Battle with Peloponnesian allies, 137; Naval battle off, 313

Corinth, Economic position in 5th century, 118; Commercial rival of and war against Athens, 119; War with Corcyra, 121; Sends a fleet to fight Athenians at Naupactus, 158; Fights a fleet battle at Erineus, 161; Captured by Agrippa, 526

Corinth, Gulf of, Naval operations to control, 131; Battle at Erineus, 161

Cornificius, L., Octavian's general, 499; Naval battle near Scylla, 501; Lands army at Tauromenium, 509; Marches across island, 510

Cornificius, Quintus, Caesar's legate in Illyria, 472

Corvus, Description of, 275

Crassus, Marcus Licinius, forms triumvirate, 433

Crassus, Publius Licinius, Consul, opposes Hannibal in Bruttium, 364

Craterus leads army into Greece, 232

Cumae, Naval battle at, 499

Curio, Takes army to Sicily, 439; Loses army and life in Africa, 440

Cynoscephalae, Battle of, 386

Cyrus, King of Persia, 13

Cyzicus, Siege of, 182; Naval battle at, 182

Dyrrhachium, Siege of, 454; Pompey counter attacks from the sea, 455; Caesar retreats from, 456

Darius I, King of Persia, Invades Thrace, 13; Campaign in Europe in 492 B.C., a failure, 14; Campaign of 490 B.C., Marathon, 14

Darius III, King of Persia, Overcome by Alexander at Issus, 222

Datis, Persian commander in chief, 15

Decidius, Saxa, Antony's general, 491

Delian League, Its fleet, 118; Athenian policy, 119

Dellius, Q., Deserts Antony, 529

Delos, Greek fleet base in 479 B.C., 97

Demaratus, Exiled King of Sparta with Xerxes, 71; Advises Xerxes to send 300 ships to Cythera, 76

Demetrius, of Pharos, 313-15

Demetrius, son of Antigonus, Commands army at Gaza, 236; Defeated by Ptolemy, 237; Campaign of Cyprian Salamis, 239; Fails to get fleet into Nile, 243; Siege of Rhodes, 245; His forces at Rhodes, 246; His siege engines, 246-48; Failure at Rhodes, 250;

Takes fleet to Greece, 251; Fails to guard Hellespont, 251; Defeated at Ipsus, 252; Remains a sea king, 252; As ship builder, 254

Demochares, Pompey's admiral, Naval battle of Cumae, 500; Naval battle near Scylla, 500; Naval battle at Mylae, 507; Kills himself at Naulochus, 512

Democrates, Commands Macedonian fleet, 381; Killed, 382

Demosthenes, Athenian admiral, Occupies Pylos, 139; Appointed to take re-enforcements to Syracuse, 158; Arrives at Syracuse, 165; His attack fails, 166; He wishes to raise the siege, 166; Commands fleet in final battle, 168; Executed after surrender, 171

Didius, C., Commands Caesarian fleet in Spain, 483; Defeats Varus, 484; Defeats Pompey, 484; Killed, 485

Diekplous, Ship maneuver, 10; At Artemisium, 68

Diere, Boat with 2 men per oar or 2 oars per bench, 36; Dispatch boat, 49

Dinocrates, Pergamene ship captain, 382

Dionysidorus, Pergamene ship captain, 382; Succeeds to command of Pergamene fleet, 384

Dionysius, Tyrant of Syracuse, Establishes himself in power, 196; Reorganizes fleet and army, 197; Develops mechanical artillery, 197; Size of army, 199; Besieges Motya, 199; Tells Leptines to fight Carthaginian fleet, 202; Defeats Himilco at Syracuse, 204; Seems to have used fire as a tactical weapon, 204

Diphilus, Athenian admiral, Defeated at Erineus, 162

Dolabella, Gnaeus Cornelius, Builds a squadron, 439; Takes squadron to Illyria, 446

Dolphin, Falling weight as weapon, 7

Domitius, Ahenobarbus Lucius, Takes command of Massilia, 441; Takes squadron to blockade Brundisium, 491; Interrupts Triumviral supplies, 491; Takes fleet to Pompey, 496

Drepanum, in Sicily, Battle of, 296; Blockade endures, 301

Duilius, C., Consul, Commands Roman fleet

in 260 B.C., 274; At Mylae, 276; His triumph, 277

Ecnomus, Battle of, 278-91; Plan of, 281
Egypt, Caesar's campaign in, 462
Elephants, Tactical use of, in battle, 338
Ephesus, Peloponnesian naval base, 184; Blockade of, 403
Ephialtes betrays pass to Persians at Thermopylae, 72
Epicydes induces Syracuse to follow Carthage, 336
Eretria, Campaign of 490 B.C., 19; Battle off, 176
Erineus, Naval battle at, 161
Eteonicus saves squadron at Mytilene, 189
Eudamas, Rhodian admiral, 405; Battle of Side, 408; Battle of Myonnesus, 412; His great tactical skill, 415-16
Euetion commands Greek fleet at Hellespont and is defeated at Abydos, 232
Eumenes, Ruler of Cappadocia, 231; Raises army, 233; Defeated and killed, 234
Eumenes, King of Pergamum, 389; Battle of Cissus, 398, 400; Unites with Livius, 405; Takes his squadron to Hellespont, 411
Euphranor, Commands Rhodian squadron at Alexandria, 468; Lost in battle, 471
Eurybiades, Spartan commander in chief of allied fleets, 61; His authority as commander in chief, 81; He consents to fight at Salamis, 82; Awarded prize for valor, 96
Eurymedon, Cimon's victory at, 119
Eurymedon, Made a colleague of Nicias, 158; Defeated and killed at Syracuse, 167

Fabius, Quintus, Maximus, Dictator, Elected dictator, 323; Avoids battle, 324; Captures Tarentum, 350
Flaminius, Gaius, Consul, Defeated at Lake Trasimenus, 323
Flamininus, Titus Quinctius, Consul, Defeats King Philip, 386; His policy in Greece, 387; Makes war on Nabis, 390
Fleet, Roman, in First Punic War, 270; Naval battle at Lipara, 274; Raids Melita, 278; Battle off Ecnomus, 278; Defeats Carthaginian fleet on African coast, 292; Ruined by gale, 293; Fleet is rebuilt, 293; Destroyed at Drepanum, 296; Another lost in gale, 300

Fulvia, Antony's wife, raises insurrection, 497

Gabinius, Aulus, Caesar's general in Illyria, 472; Opposes Octavius, dies, 473
Ganymede, Commands Alexandrian army, 465-66
Glabrio, Manius Acilius, Consul, Restores Athamania to Philip, 396; Defeats Antiochus at Thermopylae, 397
Gorgopas, Spartan admiral, surprises Athenian squadron, 214
Gracchus, Tiberius Sempronius, visits Philip V, 402
Granicus, Battle of, 221
Greco-Persian Wars, Fleet tactics, 11; Relations between Greece and Persia, 13
Greece, Revolts after Alexander's death, 232; Subdued at Crannon, 232; Commerce controlled by Macedonia, 232
Greek Army, Strength at Thermopylae, 62; Strength at Plataea, 100, 116
Greek Fleet, Style of fighting, 58; At Artemisium, 62; Uninjured by gale, 66; First attack at Artemisium, 68; Arrives at Salamis, 80; Deployment for battle, 90; Assembles at Aegina in 479 B.C., 97; Attic contingent recalled, 98; Attic contingent returns to Delos, 101; Fleet invited to Samos, 101; Finds Persian fleet drawn on shore, 102; Destroys it, 103; Goes to Hellespont, 103; Seizes Sestos and ends the war, 103; Fleet at Mycale, 116; Exercises and stratagems, 213-17
Greek preparations for war with Xerxes, 59
Greek soldier, 17
Greek hoplite, 17
Greek peltast, 17
Greek strategy, War against Xerxes, 59; Attempt to hold Thessaly, 60; Line at Thermopylae-Artemisium, 60
Gylippus, Sent by Sparta to Syracuse as general, 153; Reaches Sicily with Corinthian ships, 155; Arrives at Syracuse in time to prevent surrender, 155; His early operations, 155; Makes Syracuse secure for winter, 156; Recommends a sea battle, 159; Captures naval base at Plemmyrium, 159; Aids in fourth naval battle, 167; Pursues retreating Athenians, 171

Hamilcar, Carthaginian admiral, commands fleet at Ecnomus, 279

Hamilcar Barca, Carthaginian general, Commands in Sicily, 301; Subdues insurrection, 309; Reconquers Spain, 310; Death, 311

Hannibal (No. 1), Commands Carthaginian fleet in 260 B.C. and defeats Scipio, 274; Raids Italian coast, 274; At Mylae, 276

Hannibal (No. 2), Son of Hamilcar, Takes fleet through blockade of Lilybaeum, 295

Hannibal (No. 3), Son of Hamilcar, 308; Succeeds Hasdrubal, 311; His policy in Second Punic War, 315; Attacks Saguntum, 316; His army in 218 B.C., 317; Opens campaign, 319; Sends squadron against Sicily, 319; Invades Italy, 321; Crosses Alps, 322; Fights at Ticinus, 322; Battle at Trebia River, 322; Defeats Roman army at Lake Trasimenus, 323; Captures Cannae, 325; Cannot win Italy, 326; Urges Council to press war in Sicily, 338; Turns to alliance with Macedon, 342; Treaty, 343; Captures Tarentum, 348; His situation is poor, 351; Recalled to Africa, 369; Lands at Leptis Minor, 372; Defeat at Zama, 373; Exiled from Carthage, 390; Received by Antiochus, 391; His opinion on war with Rome, 394; Commands Phoenician squadron at Side, 409; Apparently later commander in chief, 411

Hannibal, the Rhodian, Blockade runner at Lilybaeum, 295

Hanno (No. 1), Carthaginian admiral, at Ecnomus, 284

Hanno (No. 2), Defeated in battle of Aegatian Islands, 302; Crucified, 303

Hanno (No. 3), Carthaginian general, replaces Hasdrubal in Spain, 359

Harpago (harpax), Agrippa's new weapon, 511

Hasdrubal, son-in-law of Hamilcar, Succeeds him, 311; Treaty with Rome, 311; Death, 311

Hasdrubal (the Bald), Takes fleet to Sardinia, 335; Defeated, 335

Hasdrubal, son of Gisgo, Carthaginian general, Defeated in Spain by Scipio, 360; Defeated in Africa by Scipio, 368-69

Hasdrubal, brother of Hannibal, Commands in Spain, 319; Attacks at Tarraco, 331; Scipio attacks his fleet, 331; Receives aid from Carthage, 333; Defeated by two Scipios, 334; Defeated at Baecula, 358; Goes to Italy, 358; His army, 362; Defeated at Metaurus, 363; Killed, 363

Hecatonter, Description, 41

Helenus, Octavian's general, defeated in Sardinia, 498

Hellespont, Bridges at, 57; Greeks controlled it after Mycale, 103; Naval campaign to control, 397

Hermocrates, Syracusan leader, Urges general peace in Sicily, 145; Recommends meeting Athenian fleet in Italy, 147; Induces Syracuse to arm and fortify, 152; Checks Athenian retreat, 170

Hiero, King of Syracuse, Besieges Messana, 269; Dies in 215 B.C., 336

Hieronymus, King of Syracuse, Turns against Rome, 336; Killed, 336

Himilco, Carthaginian admiral, Attacks Syracuse shipping, 200; Invades Sicily, 201; Marches army supported by fleet against Syracuse, 202; Besieges Syracuse, 203; Defeated by pestilence and by Dionysius, 204

Himilco (No. 2), Brings aid to Hasdrubal, 333; Takes an army to relieve Syracuse, 338; Encamps opposite Syracuse, 340; Army destroyed by pestilence, 340

Hippias, Greek renegade, with Persian army, 19

Hippocrates induces Syracuse to follow Carthage, 336

Hortensius, Quintus, builds fleet for Caesar, 439

Hydarnes, Leads immortals through Asopus gorge, 73; Commands "Immortal" myriad, 109

Illyria, Caesar's campaign in, 446; Finally subdued, 474

Illyrian War, First Roman, 313; Treaty, 313

Illyrian War, Second Roman, 314; Makes Rome ready for Punic War, 315

Insteius, M., commands Antony's center squadron, 532

Ionian Revolt 499-494 B.C., 14

Iphicrates, Athenian admiral, method of training Athenian fleet, 216

Ipsus, Battle of, 252
Issus, Battle of, 222

Juba, King of Numidia, Aids Republicans, 475; His army, 475; Joins Scipio, 478
Junius, L. Pullus, Consul, His fleet off Cape Pachynum is lost in gale, 300; Commits suicide, 300

Kynossema in Hellespont, Battle at, 179

Labienus, republican general, Attacks Caesar at Ruspina, 477; Escapes from Africa, 481
Lamachus, Athenian general, 146; Urges decisive action at Syracuse, 149; Killed at Syracuse, 154
Laelius, C., Commands fleet in Spain, 354; Leads naval attack on Cartagena, 355; Raiding squadron in Africa, 365
Laelius, Decimus, Takes Pompeian squadron to Brundisium, 460; Returns to Corcyra, 460
Laevinus, Marcus Valerius, Commands in Calabria, 344; Takes force across Adriatic, 344; Commands in Macedon, 344; Keeps Philip from crossing to Italy, 344; Induces Aetolians to fight Philip, 345; Becomes Consul, 346
Laevinus, Marcus Valerius, Propraetor, crosses Adriatic with fleet, 385
Lepidus, Marcus Aemilius, Forms triumvirate, 487; Redivision of provinces, 497; Renews triumvirate, 502; Brings army to Sicily, 503; Its strength, 503; Pillages Messana, 512; Breaks with Octavian, 513; Retires to private life, 513
Leptines, brother to Dionysius, Attacks Carthaginian fleet of transports, 201; Attacks Carthaginian fleet off Catana and is defeated, 202; Probable cause of defeat, 202
Leonidas, King of Sparta, Takes an army detachment to Thermopylae, 62; Makes successful effort to keep his force there, 71; Herodotus' version of his last stand a political legend, 73; Herodotus' account of the battle, 74
Leonnatus becomes ruler of Phrygia, 231
Leotychides, a Spartan, Commands Greek fleet in 479 B.C., 97; Goes home with his squadron after Mycale, 103

Libo, Lucius Scribonius, Commands Pompey's squadron against Dolabella, 446; Blockades Brundisium, 452
Liburnicas, Definition of, 504
Lilybaeum, City in Sicily, Siege of, 294; Blockade endures, 301
Livius, Caius, Roman admiral, Leaves Ostia with 50 ships, 397; Has 81 ships in Aegean, 397; Battle of Cissus, 398; Winters at Cane, 400; Opens campaign in 190 B.C., 403; Drops blockade of Hellespont and unites with Eumenes, 405
Livius, M. Livius Salinator, Consul, in Second Illyrian War, 315; Defeats Hasdrubal, 362
Lucullus, Naval victories against Mithradates, 425
Lurius, M., commands right squadron at Actium, 532
Lysander, Spartan admiral, Commands allied forces in Asia Minor, 184; Defeats Athenian fleet at Notium, 184; Reappointed to command, 190; Destroys Athenian fleet at Aegospotami, 191; Blockade and capitulation of Athens, 192
Lysimachus, Ruler of Thrace, 231, Opposes Antigonus, 235; Prevents Antigonus from entering Europe, 237; Peace with Antigonus, 237; Alliance with Cassander and Seleucus, 251; Battle of Ipsus, 252
Macedon, King Philip II, 218; King Alexander, 219; Conquers Greece, 219; Army enters Asia Minor, 219; Controls Grecian commerce, 232; Control of Euxine commerce, 312; War with Rome, 342, 344; Peace with Rome, 347; War with Rhodes and Pergamum, 377; Rome and Macedon, 377; Rome protects commercial cities of Aegean, 379; Battle of Chios, 379; War against Rome, 385
Macedonia throws off Persian dominion, 14
Maecenas, Caius Silnius, Octavian's supporter, Concessions to Antony, 502; Sent to Rome, 505
Magnesia, Roman army at, 418; Its strength, 418; Antiochus' army, 418; Terms of peace, 419
Mago, Carthaginian admiral, defeats Leptines off Catana, 202

Mago, Hannibal's brother, Asks re-enforcements from Carthage, 327; Takes army to Spain, 335; Defends Cartagena, 355; Defeated by Scipio, 360; At Gades, 360; In Minorca and to Genoa, 365; Recalled from Italy, 369; Defeated near Milan, 371; Dies at sea, 371

Maharbal, Carthaginian general, at Cannae, 326

Mamertines in Messana, 268

Manlius, L. M. Vulso, Consul, At battle of Ecnomus, 278; Takes army to Africa, 291; Returns home, 292

Manlius, Titus Torquatus, Defeats Hasdrubal, the Bald, in Sardinia, 335

Marathon, Campaign of, 13; Comparison of land tactics with naval tactics, 13; Persian plan of campaign, 14; Persian forces, 15; Account of, 19-23; Description of ground, 19; Greek forces, 21; Position of camps, 22; Review of campaign, 26; Established a norm for naval tactics, 27; Campaign was inconclusive, 28

Marcellus, Marcus Claudius, Consul, Commands in Sicily, 336; Begins siege of Syracuse, 336; Assault by land and by sea, 337; Despairs of success then gains Epipolae, 339; Syracuse taken, 340; Continues war in Sicily, 341; Killed, 351

Marcius, Lucius, maintains defense in Spain, 352

Mardonius, cousin and son-in-law of Darius, Commands abortive expedition of 492 B.C., 14; Left in command in Greece, 480-479 B.C., 94; No fleet to aid him in 479 B.C., 95; Plan of campaign in 479 B.C., 97; Moves against Athens, 98; Destroys Athens, 99; Moves north into Boeotia, 99; Fights at Plataea, 100; Killed, 101

Mardontes, Persian admiral in 479 B.C., 96

Massilia, Relations to Carthage, 309; Ally of Rome, 310; Urges Rome to protect her, 311; Opposes Caesar in 49 B.C., 441; Siege 442; Builds fleet, 443; First battle, 444; Its effect on Spanish campaign, 444; Second battle, 445; Capitulates, 446

Massinissa, King of Numidia, 365; Joins Scipio, 368; Conquers kingdom from Syphax, 371; Raises large cavalry force, 371

Memnon, Persian general, At the Granicus, 221; Commands fleet in Aegean, 222; Death ends Persian naval effort, 222

Megara, Seizure by Athens, 119; Refuses to submit to decree of Athens, 125

Menecrates, Pompey's admiral, 498; Commands Pompey's fleet, 499; Attacks Calvisius at Cumae, 499; Killed, 500

Menelaus, brother of Ptolemy, commands at Cyprian Salamis, 239

Meninx, Island on African coast, Roman fleet gets ashore there, 293

Menodorus, Pompey's admiral, 498; Deserts to Octavian, 499; At battle of Cumae, 500; At Scylla, 501; Deserts back to Pompey, 502; Deserts to Octavian, 505

Messala, Octavian's general, Directed to cross to Sicily, 506; Camped on Sicilian Strait, 509

Messana, Captured by Athens in 427 B.C., 139; Alcibiades proposes seizing it, 149; Governed by mercenaries, 268; Appeals to Rome in 265 B.C., 269; Surrender of, 512; Pillaged by Lepidus, 512

Metaurus, Battle of, 363

Methone captured by Agrippa, 523

Miletus, Principal Peloponnesian base in Asia Minor, 173; Abandoned as base, 177

Miltiades, Greek soldier, 20; Commands at Marathon, 22; Management of battle, 27

Mindarus, Spartan admiral, Takes fleet from Miletus to Hellespont itinerary, 177; Commands in battle of Kynossema, 179, 181; Besieges Cyzicus, 182; Naval battle of Cyzicus, 182; Defeated and killed, 182

Mithradates, King of Pontus, war with Rome, 424

Mithridates, Prince of Pergamum, Brings relief army to Alexandria, 471; With Caesar defeats Egyptians, 471

Mnasippus, Spartan admiral, Bad method of administration, 216

Motya, Siege of, 199

Murcus, L. Statius, Commands republican fleet, 490; Blockades Brundisium, 491; Takes his fleet to Pompey, 496

Mycale, Naval campaign of, 101; Persian fleet goes to Mycale, 102; Phoenician ships sent home, 102; Account of battle, 102;

Formation of League of Greek allies after battle, 103
Mylae, Battle of, 276, 507
Myonnesus. Naval battle at, 412; Forces at, 414; Tactics, 415; The battle's results for the army, 417

Nabis, tyrant of Sparta, 390; War with Rome, 390; Subdued by Achaian League, 393
Nasidius, L., Takes Pompey's squadron to Massilia, 445; Battle at Tauroenta, 445
Naulochus, Naval battle of, 511
Naupactus, Athenian naval base at 129; Battle off, 133
Naval operations in 428-427 B.C., 136
Naval tactics based on interplay of attack on person and attack on ship structure, 6
Naval warfare, Objectives of, 3; Organization of, at time of Graeco-Persian War, 4; Particularity of, 5; Attack on ship structure and on personnel, 6; Naval weapons, 6
Naxos, Burnt in campaign of 490 B.C., 19; Athenian expedition welcome at, 150
Nero, Caius Claudius, Takes an army to Spain, 352; Relieved of command, 353; Opposes Hannibal and victory over Hasdrubal, 362-63
Nero, Tiberius Claudius, Caesarian general, 471
Nicander, pirate, at battle of Panormus, 404
Nicias, General in expedition to Syracuse, 146; His force increased, 146; Wishes to avoid decisive action, 149; Becomes sole general and is ill, 154; Transfers fleet base to Plemmyrium, 155; Asks for help from Athens, 157; Refuses to raise the siege, 166; At last consents to withdrawal, 170; Executed after surrender, 171
Norbanus, C. Flaccus, Antony's general, 491; Takes position at Amphipolis, 492

Oars, As motive power, discussion, 30; Scaloccio system of rowing, 34; Zenzile system of rowing, 35-36; Ancient system of rowing, 37; Ancient system of rowing for trieres, 42; Thalamite, 42; Thranite, 42; Zugite, 42; In 17th century, 206
Octavia, Octavian's sister, Marries Mark Antony, 497; Not divorced when Antony married Cleopatra, 518; Divorced, 520
Octavius, Gaius (Caesar Augustus Octavianus), 486; Formed second triumvirate,

487; Attempts to seize Sicily, 489; Takes army to Brundisium, 490; Crosses Adriatic, 491; Battle of Philippi, 493; Redivision of provinces, 497; Treaty of Brundisium, 497; Naval battle near Scylla, 501; Renews triumvirate, 501; Second Sicilian war, 503; His army's strength, 503; Assembles forces to invade Sicily, 506; Decides to invade at Tauromenium, 506; Crosses straits, 508; Fleet defeated at Tauromenium, 509; Dispute with Lepidus and enters his camp, 513; Political situation in 35 B.C., 517; Makes war on Cleopatra, 521; Mobilizes forces, 522; Propaganda at Actium, 531; With right squadron, 532; Follows Antony to Egypt, 536; Roman peace, 538.
Octavius, Marcus, Commands Pompey's squadron against Dolabella, 446; Completes subjugation of Illyrian coast, 447; Opposes Cornificius, 472; Checks supplies to Italy, 473; Overcome by Vatinius, 473; Commands Antony's center squadron, 532
Octere, Reconstruction of, diagram, 255; Description of, 256
Oricum, Caesar's fleet at, destroyed, 454-55
Otacilius, Crassus, T., Praetor, raids African coast, 335

Pamphilidas, Rhodian admiral, at battle of Side, 408
Panormus (Palermo), city in Sicily, captured by Roman fleet and army, 293
Panormus in Asia Minor, Battle at, 404
Parmenio, Macedonian general, leads army into Asia Minor, 219
Patara, Naval attack on, 407
Patras, Battle at, 131; Captured by Agrippa, 526
Paullus, L. Aemilius Paullus, Consul, commands in Second Illyrian War, 315
Pausanius, Regent for son of Leonidas, commands Greek army at Plataea, 99
Pausistratus, Rhodian admiral, Fleet defeated at Panormus, 404; His fire-baskets, 405
Peloponnesian War, Economic causes, 117; Outbreak, 125; Relative strength of opponents, 126; Strategy of the war, 127; End of the first part of the war in 421 B.C., 142; Review of first phase, 143; Interval in hostilities, 144; Athenian expedition to Syracuse, 146; War in the Aegean, 171; Review of the war, 192

Pentekonter, 8, 9; Early type, 37

Penteres, Developed by Dionysius, 197; Penteres carry mechanical artillery, 197; At Catana, 202, Their crew and tactics, 202; Knowledge of penteres (or quinqueremes) of 17th century, 206; Oars of in 17th century, 206; Speed trial, 207; Horsepower per oar and speed, 208; Dionysius' penteres, 209; Admiral Serre's view as to Dionysius' penteres, 209; Probable dimensions, 210; Diagram of Dionysius' pentere, 211; Advantage in increase of size, 212

Perdiccas, Receives Alexander's signet ring, 230; Is made joint regent, 231; Distributes Satrapies, 231; Breaks with Antipater and with Ptolemy, 233; Marches on Egypt and is killed, 233

Pericles, Athenian statesman, Follows Cimon's naval tradition, 120; Issues Megarian Decree, 125; Builds long walls of Athens, 127; Raids in Peloponnese, 128; Death in 429 B.C., 129

Periplous, ship maneuver, 10

Persian army, Force at Marathon, 15; Organization, 16, Armament, 16; Preparation for campaign, in 480 B.C., 57; Size of, 57; Movement into Europe, 57; Strength at Thermopylae, 108; Strength at Plataea, 100; Most of Mardonius' army never got home, 101; Strength of, at Thermopylae, 108, 115

Persian Empire, 13

Persian fleet, Organization, 58; Style of fighting, 58; Strength at Therma, 58; Sends scouts from Therma, 64; Gale and loss, 65; Detachment sent around Euboea, 67; Battles at Artemisium, 68; Destroyed by gale, 69; Hypothesis as to Cilician squadron, 70; Strength after Artemisium, 86; Takes position before battle of Salamis, 86; Deployment of, 88; Battle of Salamis, 91; Returns to Asia, 94; Placed under command of Mardontes and Artayntes, 96; Assembles at Samos, 96; Strength in 479 B.C., 96; Retires from Samos to Mycale, 102; At Mycale, 102; Phoenician squadron goes home, 102; Remaining ships at Mycale destroyed, 103; Strength of, in 480 B.C., 113

Phaeneas, Aetolian leader, 393

Pharnabazus, Persian satrap, Aids Peloponnesian allies, 173; Draws Peloponnesian fleet to Hellespont, 177; Puts cavalry into water at battle of Abydos, 181; Aids at siege of Cyzicus, 182; Gives Persian money to rebuild Peloponnesian fleet, 183

Pharnaces, King of Pontus, 463; Defeated at Zela, 472

Pharos, Island at Alexandria, Battle at, 469

Pharsalus, Campaign of, 447; Caesar's difficulties of transport, 447; Battle of, 459

Philippi, Campaign of, 486, 489; Army movements, 491; Strategic situation, 492; Part played by the fleet, 492; Strength of armies, 491-92; First battle, 493; Second battle, 494

Philip II of Macedon, Becomes master of Greece, 218; Sends an advance guard into Asia Minor, 219; Murdered, 219

Philip V, King of Macedon, Ill-disposed to Rome, 342; Operations in Illyria, 343; Sends ambassadors to Hannibal, 343; Terms of treaty, 343; Captures Lissus, 344; Commercial cities of Aegean against him, 345; Opposes Romans and Aetolians, 346; Peace with Rome, 347; Battle of Chios, 379; Ships in battle, 380; Defeated at Cynosephalae, 386; Turns against Antiochus, 395; Operates with Baebius, 396; Scipio finds him faithful, 402

Philostratus, Rhodian ship captain, 383

Phocians at Thermopylae, 72-73

Phormio, Athenian admiral, 129; Battle at Patras, 131; Battle at Naupactus, 133; Address before battle, 134; His memory revived in early days of steam naval tactics, 143; Review of his tactics, 193

Pikes, Use of, on shipboard, 7

Piracy, In the Mediterranean, 425; Put down by Pompey, 426

Plataea, Peloponnesians mobilize at isthmus of Corinth in 479 B.C., 97; They advance and are joined by Athenians, 99; Numbers of Greek army, 100, 116; Account of battle, 100; Tactics at, 104

Pleistarchus, Cassander's brother, 252

Plennius, Pompey's general, Brings legion to Messana, 512; Agrees with Lepidus, 512

Polyanthes, Corinthian admiral, Defeats Athenian squadron at Erineus, 161; His structural arrangements of his ships, 162; His tactics, 162, 193

Polyperchon, Succeeds Antipater as regent, 234; Opposed by Cassander who drove him from Macedon, 234; His disappearance marks the break up of Alexander's Empire, 234

Polyxenidas, Syrian admiral, 397; Battle of Cissus, 398; Increases fleet, 401; Defeats Rhodians at Panormus, 404; Battle of Myonnesus, 412

Pompey, Gnaeus Pompeius Magnus, Subdues pirates, 426; Commands in Spain, 433; Forms triumvirate with Caesar and Crassus, 433; His army and his military situation, 435; His naval strength, 436; Retires to Brundisium, 437; Abandons Italy, 438; Strategic situation early in 49 B.C., 440; His course in 49 B.C., 441; Campaign of Pharsalus, 447; His resources, 448; Siege of Dyrrhachium, 454; Counter attacks, 455; Battle of Pharsalus, 457; His forces, 458; His fleet after Pharsalus, 459; His flight to Egypt, 461; Death, 462

Pompey, Gnaeus, son of Triumvir, Commands Egyptian squadron at Oricum, 455; Destroys part of hostile transport fleet, 455; Takes squadron from Africa to Spain, 478; In Balearic Islands, 483; Successes in Spain, 483; "Sea is hostile" to him, 483; Battle of Munda, 484; Escapes to fleet at Carteia, 484; Fights Didius and is killed, 484

Pompey, Sextus, Masters Spain, 488; Made admiral of Senate's fleet, 488; His base in Sicily, 488; Cuts off Italy's corn, 489; Seizes Corsica and Sardinia, 497; Size of his fleet, 498; Ravages coast of Italy, 499; Arrangements for defense of Sicily, 504, 506; Strength of his forces, 504; Battle at Mylae, 507; Transfers fleet to Tauromenium, 508; Battle at Tauromenium, 509; Abandons Mylae, 510; Defeated at Naulochus, 512; Flees to Asia, 512

Pomponius, M. Pomponius Matho, Praetor in Sicily, 367

Pontic Wars, 424

Potidaea, Tributary of Athens, opposes Athenian policy, 125

Ptolemy I, Brigade commander, Seizes Egypt, 230-31; Allies himself with Antipater, 233; Invades Syria and controls oriental trade, 233; Opposes Antigonus, 235; Defeats Demetrius, 237; Peace with Antigonus, 237; Extends his sea power, 238; Campaign of Salamis, 239; Loses bases in Asia Minor, 242; Defeats Antigonus' attempt on Egypt, 243; Aids Rhodes, 248

Ptolemy II, King of Egypt, Embassy to Rome, 308

Ptolemy XII, King of Egypt, submits to Caesar, 463

Publicola commands right squadron at Actium, 532

Punic War, First, 266; Terms of peace, 303; Review of the war, 303

Punic War, Second, 308; Development of Roman sea power, 308; Transformation of Roman industry, 308-9; Conditions leading to, 315; Opening of the war, 318

Pylos, Operations at, 139; Spartan attack on, 140; Naval battle in harbor, 140

Quinqueremes, Roman, Crews of, 272, 296, 298, 319; Discussion of character, 306

Ram, Its tactics, 10; Secondary weapon at Salamis, 123; Phormio's use of ram, 143; Primary under Phormio, 193; Made secondary by Polyanthes, 193

Regulus, M. Atilius, Consul, At battle of Ecnomus, 278; Takes army to Africa, 291; Defeated and captured, 292

Rhodes, Neutral in war between Antigonus and Ptolemy, 239; Siege of, 245; Battle of Chios, 379; Fleet at, 381; Its fleet defeated at Panormus, 404; Naval battle at Side, 408; Naval battle at Myonnesus, 412

Rome, In First Punic War, 266; Policy, 267; Commerce, 267; Population 268; Interferes in Messana, 269; Builds a fleet, 270; Size of army and navy, 272; Terms of peace, 303; Protects Mediterranean commerce, 310; Takes up Massilia's quarrel, 311; Treaty with Hasdrubal, 311, Celtic War, 311; Protects trade on Adriatic, 312; Sends Embassy to Illyria, 312; Bad relations with Macedon, 314; Fleet in Celtic War, 314; Allied with Saguntum, 316; Embassy to Carthage, 316; Military strength, 317; Rome's plan of war, 318; Altered by Hannibal's attack on Sicily, 320; Fights five wars subordinate to Hannibal's invasion, 320; Strength of army and navy at various times, 324; Senate's view of the war, 329;

War with Macedon, 342; Rome's relations with eastern states, 342; Peace with Macedon, 347; Its fleet in Sicily establishes policy of Carthage, 349; Roman fleet raids Africa, 350-51; Fleet numbers 280 ships in 208 B.C., 351; Army and fleet in 203 B.C., 369; Peace with Carthage, 375; Sends fleet across Adriatic, 385; Allies herself with Pergamum and Rhodes, 385; Peace with Macedon, 386; War with Antiochus, 387; Conditions leading to war with Antiochus, 387; Takes offense at Antiochus, 389; Refuses to agree with Antiochus, 390; Makes war on Sparta, 390; Withdraws army from Greece, 391; Hears Hannibal is urging war, 391; Builds ships, 392; Sends fleet to Greece, 392; Terms of peace, 419

Rufus Salvidienus, Roman admiral, fails to subdue Pompey, 489

Salamis, Campaign of, 54; Greek preparations for, 59; Themistocles dominates the preparation, 59; Stand at Thermopylae-Artemisium, 60; Opening of campaign, 62; Greek fleet retires to Salamis, 78; Situation there, 80; Number of Greek ships, 80; Council at Salamis, 81; Tactical situation, 86; Greek dispute before battle, 88; Corinthian Squadron sent into Bay of Eleusis, 88; The battle, 90; Greek pursuit after battle, 95; Tactics at battle, 104; Aeschylus' account of, 106

Salamis, in Cypress, Siege and battle, 239-42

Sallust takes legions to Illyria, 447

Salonae, the women of, drive off Octavius, 473

Samos, Athenian base in Asia Minor, 174

Sardinia, Conquered by Rome, 309; Re-enforcements to, 335

Scipio, Gnaeus Cornelius, Consul, Commands Roman fleet in 260 B.C., 274

Scipio, Gnaeus Cornelius (No. 2), Leads Roman army into Spain, 322; Defeats Hanno, 330; Attacks Hasdrubal's fleet, 331; Receives men and supplies, 332; Successes, 351; Killed, 352

Scipio, Lucius Cornelius, Consul, Commands against Antiochus, 401; His army, 402

Scipio, Publius Cornelius, Consul, Commands army opposing Hannibal, 319; Takes army into Gaul, 321; Returns to Italy, 322; Defeated by Hannibal, 322; Goes to Spain, 333; Defeats Hasdrubal, 334; Successes in Spain, 351; Killed, 352

Scipio, P. Cornelius Africanus, Consul, Commands army in Spain, 353; Conquers Cartagena, 353; His management of troops, 356; His character, 357; His campaign in 208 B.C., 358; Goes to Africa to meet Syphax, 360; Fails to retain Hasdrubal in Spain, 359; Becomes Consul, 364; Raises army in Sicily, 365; Senate investigates his conduct, 366; His expeditionary force assembles at Lilybaeum, 367; Order of sailing, 368; Camp near Utica, 368; Naval battle off Carthage, 370; Final battle at Zama, 373; Peace, 375; Legate to his brother, 401; Marches army to Hellespont, 402

Scipio, Publius Cornelius Nasica, Brings legions to Pompey, 458; Commander in chief in Africa, 476; Appears with army at Ruspina, 478; Defeated at Thapsus, 480

Seleucus, Receives a command of cavalry corps, 231; Is driven from Babylon, 235; Establishes dynasty in Babylon, 237; Alliance with Lysimachus and Cassander, 251; Battle of Ipsus, 252; Takes most of Antigonus' kingdom, 252

Seleucus, Son of Antiochus, besieges Pergamum, 408

Segesta appeals to Athens in dispute with Selinus, 145

Selinus in dispute with Segesta, 145

Sempronius, Tiberius Sempronius Longus, Consul, Commands army to invade Africa, 319; Counter raids on African coast, 320; Withdraws army from Sicily, 320; Is defeated by Hannibal, 322

Servilius, Gnaeus Geminus, Consul, drives off fleet raiders, 324

Serre, Paul, Admiral, Student of ancient ships, Views as to, 29; Description of Jason's *Argo*, 38; Opinion as to penteres, 209

Sestos, Greek seizure of, after Mycale, 103

Sicily in First Punic War, 268; Roman occupation of, 269; Hiero, King of Sicily, 268; Submits to Rome, 269; In 262 B.C., war confined to Sicily, 270

Sicilian War, 496; Opening of war situation, 498; Second Sicilian campaign, Its plan, 503; Termination, 513

Ships of Agrippa, 514; Relief of Palestrina, 514

Ships, Rowing, size and speed, 7; Sailing, size, 8; Types of ancient, present knowledge based on ancient history and on medieval practice, 29; Discussion of small types of rowing vessels, 30; Horsepower needed, 32; Two ways of increasing rowing horsepower in middle ages, 33; Telaro, an outrigger frame, 49; Sails, 51; Speed under sail, 52; Speed under oars, 53; Method of installing oars, 254

Side, Naval battle of, 408-11

Sikinnos, Carries a message from Themistocles to Xerxes, 84

Sixteener (16-er), Ship with 16 banks of oars, Diagram reconstruction, 257; Description, 258

Sosius, Caius, Antony's admiral at Actium, Attacks Agrippa's fleet, 526; Commands Antony's left squadron, 532

Spain, War in, 330, 351; Scipio loses Spain, 352; Recovered, 352

Sparta, An ally of Athens, 20; Wished to defend Greece at isthmus of Corinth, 59; Maneuvers to get command of both army and navy, 61; Fears Athens will desert Greek cause, 97; Army passes north to Plataea, 99; Forsakes Greek League after Mycale, 103; Refuses arbitration before Peloponnesian War, 126; Her professional soldiers, 126; Cannot make her allies keep the peace of 421 B.C., 144; Defeats Athens at Mantineia, 144; Sends troops to Syracuse, 158; Invades Attica, 158; Vigorous war in 412 B.C., 172; Asks peace in 410 B.C., 183; Asks peace in 406 B.C., 190; Carries on with Persian money, 190; Athens capitulates to Spartan King, 192

Sphacteria (see Pylos), Spartan troops land on, 140; Blockade of, 141; Athenian assault of, 141; Tactics at, 142

Stratagems, Naval, Practiced by Timotheus, 217; Another stratagem used several times, 217

Successors of Alexander, Their wars, 227; Economic situation after death of Alexander, 227

Sulla, His war against Mithradates, 424; Needs sea power, 425

Sulpicius, Publius, Proconsul, Commands in Macedon in 209 B.C., 346; Acts with Attalus, 346

Sybota Islands, First battle at, 121; Corcyraeans saved by the Athenian squadron, 124; Second battle off Sybota Islands, 137

Syphax, King of Numidia, Scipio visits him, 360; Hostile to Scipio, 365; Defeated by Massinissa, 371; Sent to Rome, 371

Syracuse, Athenian expedition against, Causes for, 144; Athenian fleet departs for, 146; Debate on war at, 147; Strength of Athenian expedition, 148; It arrives in Italy, 149; First landing at, 152; City arms and fortifies, 152; City seeks allies, 152; Beginning of siege, 153; Athenian fleet enters Syracuse Harbor, 154; Nicias transfers local fleet base to Plemmyrium, 155; First naval battle at, 159; Obstructions in the harbor, 160; Second naval battle, 163; Third naval battle, 164; Demosthenes arrives with Athenian re-enforcements, 165; Is defeated in assault, 166; Fourth naval battle, 166; Last naval battle, 168; The expedition retreats by land and is destroyed, 170; Review of campaign, 193; Ruled by Dionysius, 196; Fortifications, 197; Size of fleet and army, 199; Himilco attacks Syracuse, 200; Siege of, by Carthage, 203; Siege of, in Punic War, 336

Tactics, Fleet, 11; In war of Rome and Antiochus, 419; Development of tactics during 300 years, 421; Lessons for the present day, 422

Tarentum, Hannibal desires it, 348; Its situation, 348; Hannibal captures it, 348; Roman squadron to stop supplies, has battle, 349; Taken by Fabius, 350

Tarraco, Principal Roman naval base in Spain, 330

Tauris, Naval battle at, 473

Tauromenium, Naval battle at, 509

Taurus, Statilius, Octavian's general, 503; Escorts Octavian to Tauromenium, 508

Teleutias, Spartan admiral, Management of men, 213; Captures Athenian squadron, 214

Tempe, Xerxes examines pass at, 59; Greeks renounce effort to hold defensive line at, 60

Tesserakonter, Ship with 40 banks of oars, Diagram reconstruction, 259; Description from Athenaeus and reconstruction, 260

Teuta, Queen of Illyria, Received Roman Embassy, 312; Cannot resist Roman attack, 313; Treaty, 313

Thebes, ally of Mardonius, urges bribery of Grecian cities, 98

Themistocles, Attains leadership in Greece, 54; His plan adopted for war with Xerxes, 59; Plan for taking Ionian Greeks from hostile fleet, 78; His personality retains fleet at Salamis, 82; He gains Eurybiades' consent to fight at Salamis, 82; His character, 82; His public speech, 83; His message to Xerxes, 84; Awarded prize of wisdom, 96; Not in office in 479 B.C., 97; His tactics altered by Cimon, 121; His policy for defending Athens extended by Pericles, 127

Theophiliscus, Rhodian admiral, Battle of Chios, 381; Killed, 385

Thermopylae, Selected as battle ground, 60; Dispute as to its selection leads to choice of Spartan naval commander in chief, 61; March on, 62; Hero legend about, 63; Battles at, 71; First Persian attack, 72; Second Persian attack, 72; Persian detachment marches around Thermopylae, 73; Final battle, 74; Comparison of, with naval tactics at Artemisium, 75; Neither side deem tactical conclusion, 104

Thessaly, Greeks cannot hold it, 60; Submits to Xerxes, 60; Persian army winters in, 95

Thoas, Aetolian leader, 393

Thrace, Conquered by Darius, 13; Throws off Persian dominion, 14

Thrasylus, Athenian admiral, Takes fleet from Samos to Hellespont, 177; Battle at Kynossema, 179

Thrasybulus, Athenian admiral, Joins Thrasylus at Lesbos, 177; Battle at Kynossema, 179

Trebonius, Caius, Commands Caesar's army, Siege of Massilia, 442; Governor in Spain, 483

Tissaphernes, Persian satrap, Aids Peloponnesian allies, 173; Balances Athenians against Peloponnesians, 174

Triemiolus, type of ship, 380

Triere, 42; Description of, 42; Speed, 43; Size of, 44-45; Sketch of early triere, 45-47; Sketch of Peloponnesian war triere, 46-47; Busley's reconstruction, 48; Trieres of Themistocles, size and cost, 55; Peloponnesian War, size of, 55

Troops, Light-armed, become prominent in Greek warfare, 142

Troy, Siege of, and early naval warfare, 4; Persian army arrives at, 58

Tyre, Siege of, 222; Mole at, 223; Tyrian naval counter attack, 224; Conquest of, by Alexander, 225; Siege by Antigonus, 235

Varro, G. Terrentius, Consul, defeated at Cannae, 324-26

Varus, Commanding in Africa in 49 B.C., 474; Commands fleet in 46 B.C., 478; Attacks Caesar's squadron, 479; Escapes from Africa, 481; Fleet is defeated at Carteia, 484

Vatinius, Publius, Defeats Octavius at sea and opens commerce to Italy, 473; Pacifies Illyria, 474

Veneti, Caesar conquers, 427; Reasons for war, 428; Population, 429; Comparison of ships of Veneti and Caesar, 429; Caesar's new weapon, 430

Ventidius, P. Bassus, Antony's general, Victory over Parthians, 518

Vibullius, Rufus, Lucius, sent to Spain, 441

Wars, Cost of, in 4th century B.C., 262; Cost of armies, 262; Cost of navies, 263; Cost relative to population, 264; Cost of civil government, 265

Xanthippus, Commands Athenian squadron in 479 B.C., Succeeds to command Greek allied fleet after Mycale, 103

Xanthippus, Commands Carthaginian army, defeats Regulus, 292

Xerxes, Decides on war with Greece, 54; Plan of campaign, 57; Demands submission of Greece, 57, Reviews and numbers army, organizes fleet, 58; At Thermopylae, 71; Deliberates as to method of advance, 76; Announces fall of Athens, 82; Council on shore resolves to fight, 84; Watches battle from Mt. Aegaleos, 92; Returns to Asia with fleet, 94; Reasons for his return, 95; Reasons for attacking at Salamis, 104